SOUTH-WESTERN

THE OFFICE

3D EDITION

PROCEDURES AND TECHNOLOGY

ANNOTATED TEACHER'S EDITION

Mary Ellen Oliverio
Graduate Program
Lubin School of Business
Pace University
New York, New York

William R. Pasewark
Professor Emeritus
Texas Tech University
Office Management Consultant
Lubbock, Texas

Bonnie R. White
College of Education
Auburn University
Auburn, Alabama

Contributing Authors:

Connie Morrison, Instructional Technology Consultant, Fenton, Michigan

Carol Young Mull, Chairperson, Computer Technologies
Asheville-Buncombe Technical Community College, Asheville, North Carolina

JOIN US ON THE INTERNET
WWW: http://www.thomson.com
EMAIL: findit@kiosk.thomson.com A service of I(T)P®

South-Western Educational Publishing

an International Thomson Publishing company I(T)P®

Cincinnati • Albany, NY • Belmont, CA • Bonn • Boston • Detroit • Johannesburg • London • Madrid
Melbourne • Mexico City • New York • Paris • Singapore • Tokyo • Toronto • Washington

ISBN: 0-538-66739-7

1 2 3 4 5 6 7 8 9 0 VH 03 02 01 00 99 98 97

Printed in the United States of America

I(T)P®

International Thomson Publishing

South-Western Educational Publishing is an International Thomson Publishing Company.

The ITP logo is a registered trademark used herein under license.

Contents

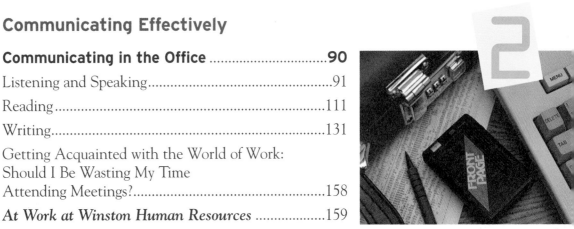

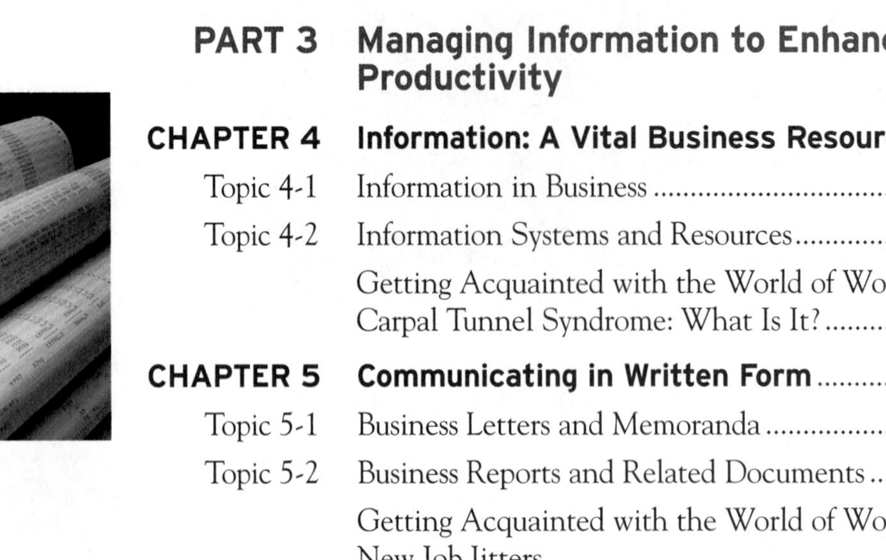

PART 3 Managing Information to Enhance Productivity

PART 4 Managing Time, Tasks, and Records

5

Preface

To the Student

You will enter a world of work that is being transformed. It will be a challenging and demanding world because of the rate and nature of change. Many of the changes taking place in the workplace relate to the technological innovations that have resulted in an information revolution. The workplace is not necessarily at a specific location. For example, four individuals in four different countries may be employed by the same multinational corporation with each working from a home office. Yet the four have virtually instant communication—via telecommunications—to develop plans and make decisions.

More and more, executives, managers, engineers, accountants, and administrative assistants—among others—are accessing databases, preparing electronic spreadsheets, and creating presentations. No longer are information processing tasks primarily the responsibility of secretaries and administrative assistants. All workers are expected to communicate effectively; access, analyze, and share information; make decisions; and use technology to improve productivity.

THE OFFICE: Procedures and Technology, Third Edition, is designed to help you develop skills that will be important in your career in a professional or business position. The content you study will help prepare you to enter the workforce now and to face the inevitable changes you will encounter in the future.

Objectives for the Course

The critical concern for productivity throughout the workforce imposes on *all* workers the need to handle information management, problem solving, and communication tasks both effectively and efficiently. These tasks must be performed skillfully for employees to achieve high

vii

productivity levels. As a student, you face a twofold challenge: to prepare for the initial demands of full-time employment and to acquire the skills to learn on the job and adapt to new procedures and technologies. This challenge is reflected in this comprehensive instructional package. THE OFFICE: *Procedures and Technology, Third Edition*, has been designed to:

- develop information management, technology, and communication skills that are valuable for all types of workers.
- develop an awareness of how to learn as new technology and new processes and procedures are introduced in an organization.
- develop a comprehensive view of time management and productivity.
- reinforce and extend basic skills involving math, language, decision making, critical thinking, and teamwork.
- develop understanding of basic qualities and attitudes that are critical in the work environment.
- develop awareness of one's own interests, strengths and weaknesses related to the demands of a technologically driven work environment.

Features of the Textbook

THE OFFICE: Procedures and Technology, Third Edition, is organized into six general subject areas and 16 chapters. Each chapter is subdivided into two or three segments called topics. The text contains features designed to facilitate comprehensive learning.

Part and Topic Objectives	Part and topic objectives focus on key concepts that serve as guides in becoming familiar with the content.
Vocabulary Reinforcement	General vocabulary terms that may be unfamiliar to some students are defined in the margin of the page on which the term is first introduced.
Activities	Activities to reinforce the major concepts and procedures and to provide realistic experience in working independently and in groups are included in each topic and at the end of each chapter.

viii

Getting Acquainted with the World of Work	The final part of each chapter is a letter and response in advice-column format that deals with a problem typically of concern to beginning workers in a wide range of occupations.
Glossary	Selected terms introduced in the text are listed and defined in the glossary.

Student Activities and Projects Workbook

The *Student Activities and Projects* workbook includes review activities for each chapter and documents needed for completing selected activities found in the text. In addition, five workplace simulations, complete with company descriptions, instructions, documents and other materials, are provided. A Reference Section provides commonly needed information for completing the textbook and workbook activities.

Template Disk

A template disk containing the files required to complete selected chapter and simulation activities is available.

Tests

A printed set of tests (16 chapter tests, two comprehensive tests, and an application test) is available. The tests are also available on a *MicroExam II* disk.

Teacher's Resource Guide

The *Teacher's Resource Guide* is available to teachers who adopt the textbook for class use. This *Guide* is a comprehensive and invaluable source for practical ideas in course planning and enrichment. It includes teaching and grading suggestions; solutions for chapter activities, workbook review activities, and simulations; transparency masters; and test solutions.

Acknowledgments

The authors acknowledge the contributions of previous users, thoughtful reviewers, the editorial staff, content developers Joseph Powell III and Donna Everett, and contributing authors Connie Morrison and

ix

Carol Mull. Business executives, technical and professional personnel, administrative office managers, and other office workers were generous in answering questions and reflecting on the needs of workers in the future. To all these persons, the authors express thanks and appreciation.

Reviewers:

Mrs. Terry C. Barton, Vocational Business Education Instructor/Chairperson, Hillsboro High School, Hillsboro, MO

Ms. Candie Hurley, Management Consultant, Lucent Technologies, Basking Ridge, NJ

Dr. Linda Mallinson, Business Instructor, OTEC • Orlando Tech, Orlando, FL

Mrs. Christine Marshall, Business Education Instructor, Emily Griffith Opportunity School, Denver, CO

Mrs. Michele Parent, Business Education Chairperson, Mt. Healthy High School, Cincinnati, OH

Ms. Gwen Wright, CRM, Director of Education Services, Association of Records Managers and Administrators, Prairie Village, KS

A Commitment by the Authors

THE OFFICE: Procedures and Technology, Third Edition, continues a long tradition of providing training for marketable skills for many types of workers who function, at least in part, in an office environment. It has been a challenge to assess the transformation of work driven by technological change. The projections to the new century are clear about the universal need for the information, technology, and teamwork skills that are emphasized in this text. We believe that students with a wide range of occupational goals can profitably study together. Our perceived outcome is a student with highly portable skills and understandings.

Mary Ellen Oliverio William R. Pasewark Bonnie Roe White

x

The Office:
Procedures and Technology

2nd Edition

wins

The Office: Procedures and Technology, *Second Edition* was honored by the Textbook and Academic Authors Association with two prestigious awards.

TEXTY AWARD

The Texty Award is presented each year to recognize excellent textbooks for various grade levels and categories. ***The Office*** was chosen as the best high school textbook in 1994 in the Business and Economics category.

MCGUFFEY AWARD

The McGuffey Award is presented each year to one elementary/high school textbook and one college textbook with a tradition of excellence for at least 15 years. ***The Office***, providing instruction in current office procedures for 67 years and 13 editions, won the McGuffey Award for 1994.

THE OFFICE
Procedures and Technology
2d Edition
OLIVERIO
PASEWARK
WHITE
SOUTH-WESTERN PUBLISHING CO.

TEXTY

and

McGUFFEY

Awards!

Continuing the Tradition of Excellence...

The first edition of the ***The Office*** was first published in 1931 as Fundamentals of Office Practice. Nine other editions in this successful series followed. Because of the enormous impact of computers and other technology on the office, a new series was launched in 1988 with the first edition of ***The Office: Procedures and Technology***.

The authors and publisher are proud to present this Third Edition of ***The Office: Procedures and Technology***, continuing an award-winning tradition.

The Textbook and Academic Authors Association is a national, professional organization of textbook writers in nine academic disciplines. The association promotes and recognizes quality in learning materials.

The Office in the Business World

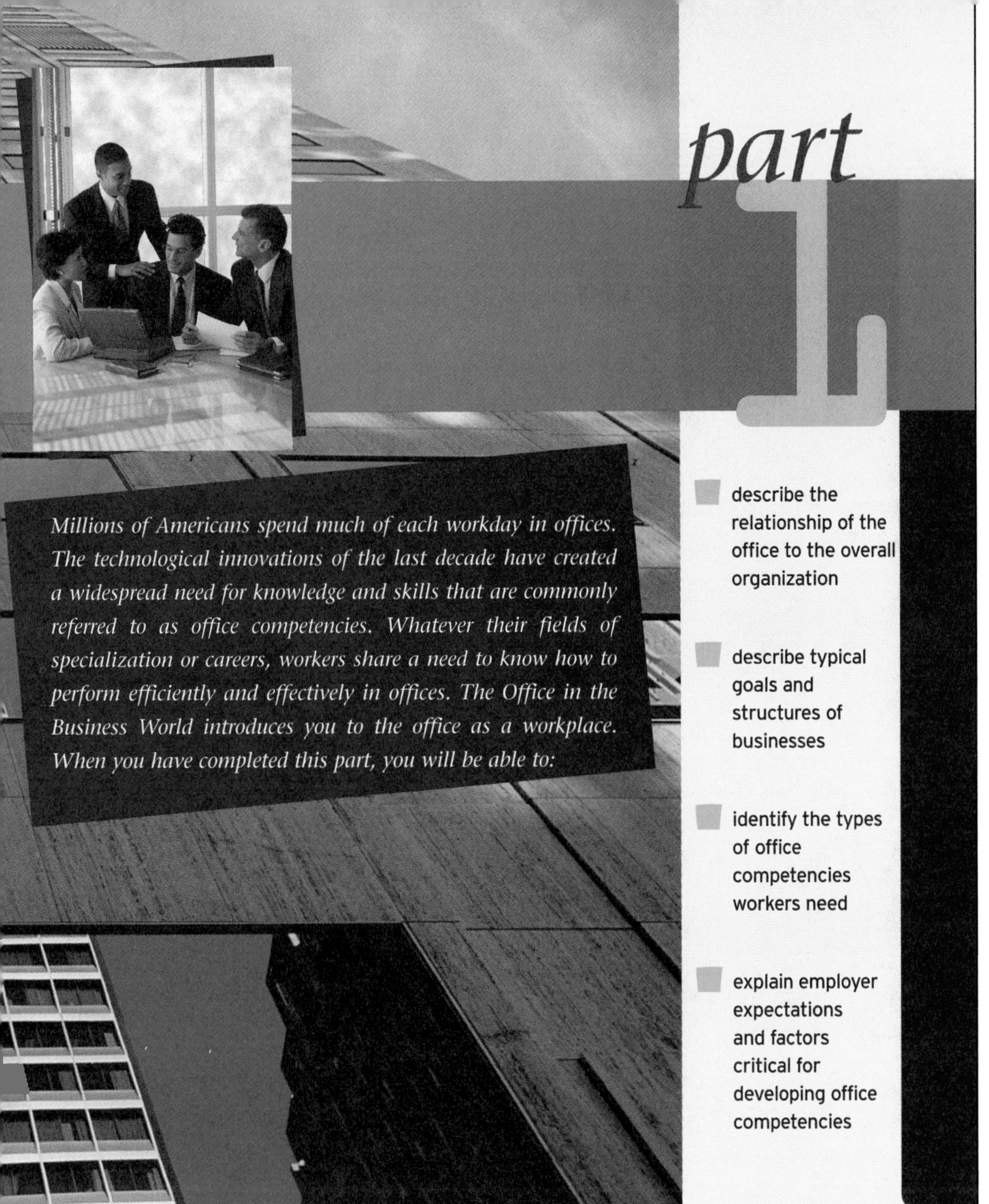

part 1

Millions of Americans spend much of each workday in offices. The technological innovations of the last decade have created a widespread need for knowledge and skills that are commonly referred to as office competencies. Whatever their fields of specialization or careers, workers share a need to know how to perform efficiently and effectively in offices. The Office in the Business World introduces you to the office as a workplace. When you have completed this part, you will be able to:

- describe the relationship of the office to the overall organization
- describe typical goals and structures of businesses
- identify the types of office competencies workers need
- explain employer expectations and factors critical for developing office competencies

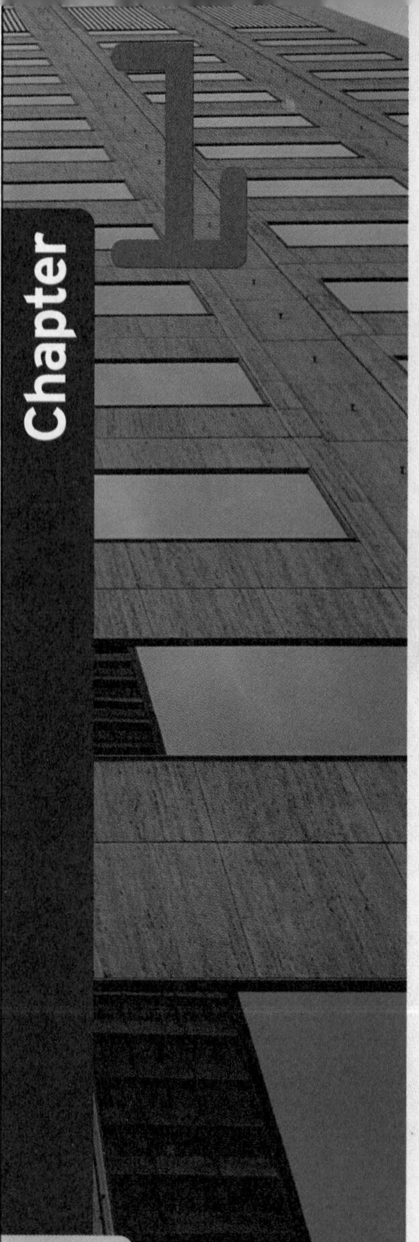

The Office in a Changing Business World

The office is changing. Many workers now must be able to handle office tasks. The recruiter in a human resources department, the technician in a chemical laboratory, the curator in a museum, the buyer in a department store, and the CPA in a public accounting firm all perform a range of office tasks during a typical workweek. All office workers, regardless of their responsibilities, must understand the significance of office functions in relation to their work and to the total organization.

In Chapter 1, you will learn about various types of offices and office workers. You will also gain an understanding of typical goals and structures of businesses, not-for-profit entities, and governmental units.

Chapter 1

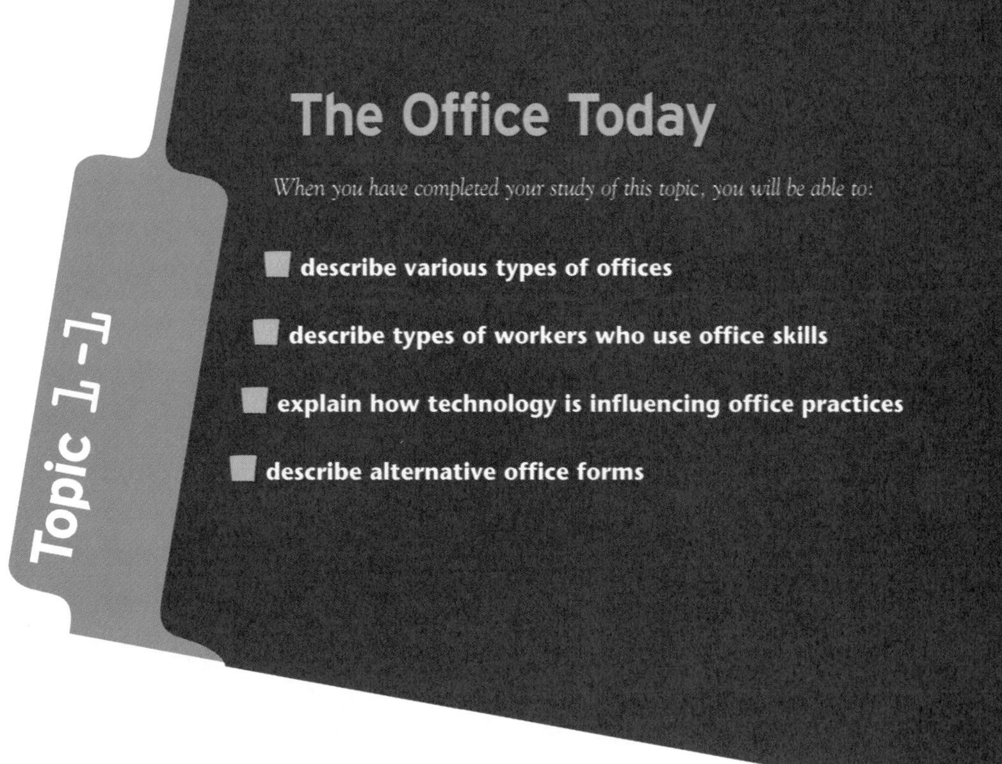

Topic 1-1

The Office Today

When you have completed your study of this topic, you will be able to:

- **describe various types of offices**
- **describe types of workers who use office skills**
- **explain how technology is influencing office practices**
- **describe alternative office forms**

The term *office* is used in a variety of ways. For example, you may have heard a lawyer say, "I will be out of the office during the afternoon," or a teacher say, "Come by my office." The office is a place of work for many **categories** of workers. Accountants, marketing managers, systems analysts, human resource directors, as well as secretaries, records clerks, administrative assistants, and many others work in offices. While each of these employees will assume varying responsibilities, all of them must be knowledgeable about many office practices.

categories: classifications, types

The office as discussed in this textbook reflects a **focus** on the many workers who need to understand office practices and use a variety of office skills. Regardless of what you plan for your life's work, you will benefit from studying the topics in this book and from the competencies you will develop.

focus: put attention on

getting started

The local community is a realistic context for introducing students to what happens in offices and how offices relate to the total organization. Students' experiences with people who work in offices can be used as the basis for an initial discussion.

getting started

An overview of the usefulness of office skills and knowledge—in everything from managing one's personal life to handling tasks related to many different types of jobs—can highlight the range of topics that will be included in this book.

points to emphasize

Office tasks are performed by many types of workers. While students may not have made a commitment to a particular field of specialization, their skills in performing office tasks are likely to have considerable value regardless of the career ultimately chosen.

Topic 1-1

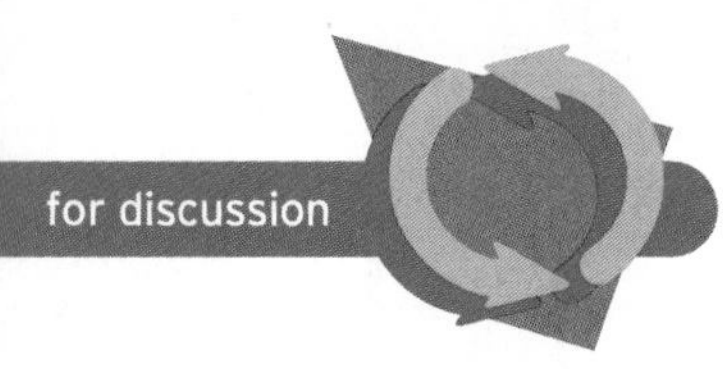

Describe the word processing skills Carole must have.

What office tasks have you observed being handled by a manager in a grocery store, a nurse in a dental office, or the principal in your school office?

Carole Federman is an internal auditor for an international bank with headquarters in Philadelphia. Her work requires traveling to branches throughout the United States as well as to such cities as Paris, Milan, and Tokyo. She must write many reports about what she did, including her conclusions and recommendations. Before she had a notebook computer, Carole wrote reports in longhand on yellow legal pads and sent the copy back to her home office for keying by a secretary. Now, she composes her report at her computer, often completing it herself with no assistance from office support staff.

Illustration 1-1:1
This executive prepares her own report.

Offices Are Information Driven

Information is at the core of all office activities. Consider the ways in which information is critical to tasks. Some illustrations include:

- Creating information: A manager writing the policy for sales returns
- Searching for information: A securities broker accessing a database for current price of a company's stock
- Processing information: A sales clerk entering details of a customer's order at a computer
- Communicating information: A customer service representative responding by telephone to an inquiry about procedures for installing a new piece of electronic equipment

Workers need to understand thoroughly the organization in which they are employed. Each task is related to the organization's purposes and goals. For example, a purchasing agent or a purchasing clerk often makes telephone calls to place an order for materials or supplies. To answer questions that the **vendor** may ask, the employee needs to know the specifications for what is being ordered, when it is needed, what the company believes the cost to be, and similar details.

vendor: a seller of goods or services

What tasks do you think you could do now based on what you have learned in school, observed in organizations, and developed from experience?

Office Functions Are Varied

In some offices, every employee does a wide variety of tasks; in others, there may be **specialization.** Even within the field of administrative support services, there may be some employees doing a limited number of tasks while others have varied tasks. Note some common information-related office tasks performed in the workplace in Illustration 1-1:2. Can you identify two activities that might be completed by a manager? Can you identify two that might be performed by an office assistant? Think of an office career that interests you. Identify two activities that might be performed by someone in that career.

specialization: concentration in a particular field

What ways of searching for information have you used as students that might be helpful at work?

> *Helen Serreno works as an office assistant to the director of a relatively new art gallery in Santa Fe, New Mexico. Helen talked about her job in these words: "I never know what a day will be like—I really handle all the office tasks for the director, the art assistant, and the manager of exhibits. There are, of course, some tasks I do every day such as open and organize the mail and write notes about the correspondence to assist the director in responding as quickly as possible. I have a* ***state-of-the-art*** *personal computer, a photocopier, a fax machine, and a wide range of software programs that I use daily. I'm responsible for maintaining all the equipment, too."*

state-of-the-art: using the latest technology

Engage students in imagining what Helen has learned about the gallery that helps her perform her daily tasks.

OFFICES HAVE VARYING RESPONSIBILITIES

If you were to visit a number of offices in a large company, you would note very different responsibilities. Even in a small company, there may be different types of business offices. You are more likely, of course, to find more specialized offices in large companies and general business offices in smaller companies.

Students have had experience in visiting offices. Ask them to identify those that seemed to be general and those that seemed to be specialized.

Illustration 1-1:2

Could you handle some of these tasks now?

KEY OFFICE ACTIVITIES

Creating/Analyzing Information

Composing memorandums, letters, and reports
Organizing, summarizing, and interpreting data
Creating presentations
Making decisions and recommendations based on information studied

Searching for Information

Accessing databases and the Internet
Inquiring of persons within the company
Inquiring of persons outside the company
Using reference manuals/ books

Processing Information

Editing and proofreading
Keyboarding
Opening and reviewing incoming communications
Photocopying
Preparing outgoing communications
Preparing checks, orders, invoices
Preparing spreadsheets

Communicating Information

Answering telephones
Greeting callers
Responding to persons within and outside the organization
Providing instruction to colleagues
Making oral presentations before small and large groups

Managing Information

Maintaining calendars
Maintaining databases and files
Maintaining financial records

You might ask: "Why are some offices specialized while others are not?" Offices tend to be specialized where there are large volumes of the same type of transaction. For example, a large manufacturing company that buys 500 different raw materials is likely to have specialized buying offices, while a company that uses only a dozen raw materials may have a single buying office. In a single buying office, all buyers may participate in purchasing the same materials.

There is likely to be a specialized accounts payable office if a company buys from 5,000 suppliers. This office will process invoices from suppliers and prepare checks. On the other hand, in a small company, there may be only fifteen to twenty suppliers. The volume of activity

Illustration 1-1:3
The assistant manager in a small company is instructing a new staff member.

with suppliers is limited and a general accounting office handles a variety of financial tasks, including accounts payable.

OFFICES PROVIDE SUPPORT SERVICES

Even though many employees in today's organization handle many office tasks, there are individuals, as well as entire departments, that devote full time to *administrative support services*, sometimes referred to as *office support services*. Some organizations, for example, have a word processing center where reports, letters, and other documents are prepared. Specialized office functions are often seen as a vital link between the **aspirations** and accomplishments of the company. The president of a midsize bank in Columbia, South Carolina talked about the role of administrative support services in these words:

> *From the communication of our* **mission** *statement, which provides the overall inspiration for all our employees, to the timely payment of wages and salaries, we are completely dependent on the large staff of dedicated office employees. There would be chaos throughout this company without our efficient and effective office personnel. We value them and provide them with state-of-the-art technology.*

aspirations: strong desires to achieve something

mission: an overall goal

What does "support services" imply? Illustrate.

What must the president of the bank mean when he states: ". . . we are completely dependent on . . . office employees"?

Some students may have had work experience where they were able to observe office activity. Ask them to describe the equipment in use where they worked.

Technology in Modern Offices

Technological innovations are common in today's offices. The architect in a company that designs and constructs commercial buildings is working at a computer instead of at a drafting table. A secretary is accessing a site on the World Wide Web to determine a schedule for an executive who must travel to London and Madrid rather than referring to a copy of an airline's schedule. Sales representatives from several states communicate with the regional manager at headquarters in Philadelphia through an **intranet** rather than sending weekly reports via postal services.

intranet:
a communication network within an organization

Many companies have made a decision to maintain up-to-date technology throughout their offices to help employees be highly productive. **Emerging** technologies relate to increased computer power and speed, wider instant distribution of communications, and more user-to-user interactive communications.

emerging:
being developed

TECHNOLOGY IS CHANGING AT A RAPID RATE

With the rapid growth of computer technology and the rate of **upgrading** software programs, many offices seem to be continuously changing. Marie Ann describes what she is doing today that she was not doing just three years earlier:

upgrading:
improving by introducing changes

> *Three years ago, we were a domestic company. Today we do business in 60 countries. I regularly send e-mail messages to China, Singapore, Hong Kong, Prague, and Moscow—to name a few places. I used to prepare letters at a typewriter, put copies of correspondence in a file drawer, and communicate by telephone. Now I compose letters at a computer, manage database files in memory, and access the Internet to find and communicate information.*

Periodicals related to technology in the office discuss new developments. Such publications identify what are considered **"hot"** technologies. In many companies, one person or group has full-time responsibility for **monitoring** developments and making recommendations for changes in the organization's use of technology. In the United States, there is great interest in technology that increases efficiency and effectiveness of global information transfer and communication.

"hot":
brand new and getting much attention

monitoring:
keeping track of

Illustration 1-1:4

Some periodicals that deal with emerging technologies.

IMPLICATIONS OF TECHNOLOGICAL INNOVATIONS

Since the technology available is changing, the way work is accomplished is being **reengineered.** Workers may expect their responsibilities, as well as the way they work, to change markedly from time to time. The pressure for high productivity and quality performance means that all workers must maintain an attitude of willingness to participate in change. Furthermore, office workers must be skillful learners—on their own and in more formal training and educational settings.

reengineered: organized in a new way

Alternative Offices

Where is the office? It may be at headquarters, in a carrying bag, or at home. It may be a temporarily assigned workspace. No longer is the office clearly a specified space used for the same purpose day after day.

The typical office from earlier days—permanent and located where the business of the organization takes place—is referred to as the **traditional** office. In such an office, employees traveled daily to a central location, spent the working day at the same desk or in the same workspace, and generally reported directly to a supervisor or manager. While there are still many traditional offices, there are also other types of offices.

traditional: that which has been in vogue for a long time

Two vice presidents are competent in keying copy at their computers. However, while one prepares reports, the other asks an office assistant to handle this task. Is there any justification for this difference?

Why are there still traditional offices in organizations?

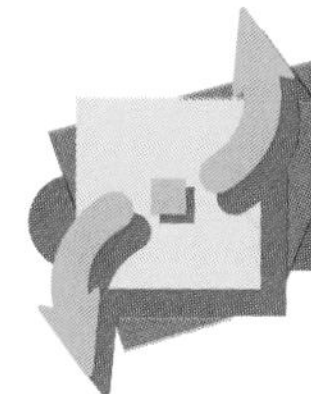

Students may volunteer to get statistics from the local chamber of commerce, or other association, dealing with employment of office employees during the past year.

Technology has aided in expansion of business to the global community. Ask students to describe why it is easier to engage in worldwide business activity now than it was a decade ago?

How does a computer add to efficiency and effectiveness in the preparation of reports?

Illustration 1-1:5

This office worker is reviewing a manual for a new software program.

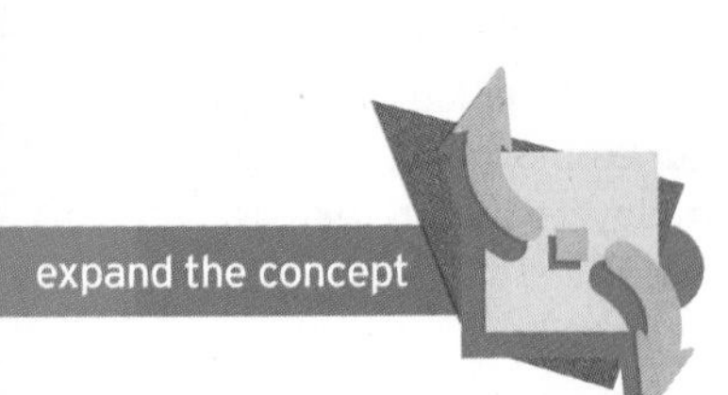

Ask students to identify problems that might develop when workers telecommute.

Today you will find references to virtual offices, mobile offices, and home offices. Persons who work at other than the traditional office are considered to be *telecommuting*. The telecommuting worker does not travel to the office or to meet with clients or customers daily, but receives information via a variety of telecommunications methods, greatly decreasing the need to travel. Many workers can perform their tasks at a variety of locations and maintain communication with others.

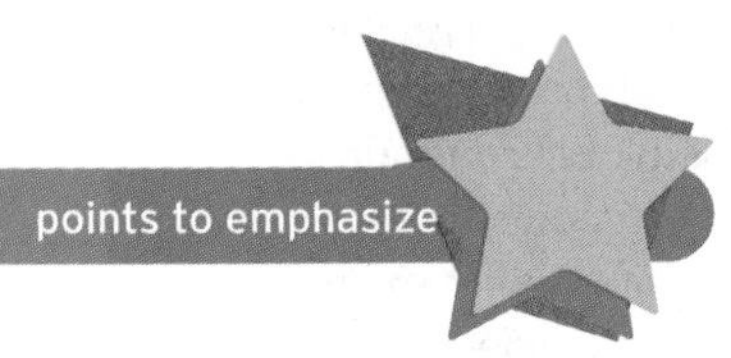

Technology makes virtual offices a possibility.

VIRTUAL OFFICE

nonconventional: not according to how things were done in the past

Advances in technology are the inspiration for the new concept of *virtual*. Virtual means providing the same resources in a **nonconventional** environment as would be provided in a conventional environment. You are acquainted with your local library, which contains shelves of books that you can use to get information. A virtual library, though, would be merely a computer station capable of providing you access to many libraries from your school or home. So, the virtual library is accessibility to databases—and real libraries—through computers. The contents of the famous Library of Congress in Washington, DC, for example, can be browsed via modem by many people throughout the world 24 hours a day without leaving their own homes.

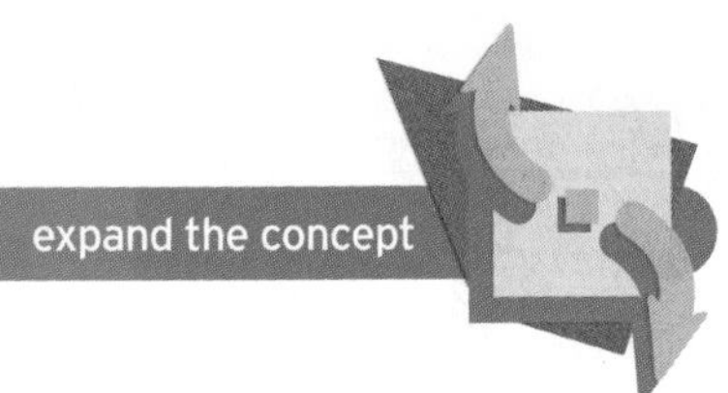

Ask students to identify the technology critical for effective and efficient telecommuting.

The virtual office is, therefore, the capability to perform work activities away from the traditional office setting. Although Susan Gray refers to her office as the *portable office*, it is really a virtual office and at the same time, a mobile office.

> *Susan is a successful interior designer in St. Louis. Susan visits prospective clients as well as clients for whom projects are underway. In her bag she can carry a cellular phone, a very lightweight computer with fax and e-mail capabilities, and a portable copier/printer. Susan can provide plans for a room, cost estimates, and a contract right in the client's living room.*

Illustration 1-1:6
Portable equipment is easily carried between office and home.

MOBILE OFFICE

In some instances, the mobile office is a virtual office, as in the case of traveling company representatives who may maintain in their cars all the equipment they need to handle their own office tasks. In other instances, mobile offices are very much like traditional offices but they are temporary. Offices set up at construction sites and manned by office staff are one type of mobile office.

Another type of mobile office is the **nonterritorial** workspace. Nonterritorial workspaces are available on an assignment basis. They are not assigned to anyone permanently. This type of workspace, which is

nonterritorial: not assigned to a specific person or task

Why would a company choose to have nonterritorial workplaces?

found in professional organizations, is another kind of mobile office. An organization such as an accounting firm, management advisory firm, or law firm may have many staff members who work away from the company a great deal of the time. Since such personnel do not need a permanent office, they may function in an environment where they can request an office on their arrival at headquarters. In some places, using this style of office is referred to as *hoteling,* since the assignment process is similar to that of a hotel determining a room to be assigned to a guest. Computer software makes maintaining information and assigning space prompt and effective. A database can be accessed easily to learn the current location of a staff member. Employees who generally work from a home office, for example, may also be assigned an office on those infrequent occasions when they do work at the company.

Engage students in a discussion of the attitudes a person who works at home should possess.

HOME OFFICE

A space within a person's home that is organized for the efficient performance of office tasks on a full- or part-time basis is referred to as a home office. In many home offices, electronic capabilities make it possible to communicate easily with others. Some people who work at home are able to participate, for example, in teleconferencing with persons at headquarters as well as at other locations in any part of the world.

Some people who work at home are self-employed. Such persons are often called freelancers. There may be occasions when they meet with customers or clients. However, they may communicate primarily by e-mail, telephone, and mail.

> *Ingrid Thomason owns and manages an accounting service business as a freelancer, working from her home. Having worked in the accounting department of a large company, she was knowledgeable about accounting systems. She decided that she would prefer to live in a small rural town and believed there were many small businesses that would find her service appealing. She was successful in lining up as many clients as she could handle. Her state-of-the-art computer and software programs allow clients to transmit financial information to her for processing and organizing. Her clients have online access to their financial statements on a timely basis. Ingrid noted that she had a number of clients that she has never seen in person!*

Illustration 1-1:7
Home offices are increasing in popularity.

Predictions Are for Further Change

The current era is considered one of rapid change. However, all organizations do not implement change at the same rate or in the same way. Some monitor what is happening to technology and introduce the newest equipment and software related to their work as quickly as possible. Such organizations see value in the technological **transformation** of their operations. At the same time, there are companies that decide no changes are needed.

transformation: a major change in character or condition

A company with the latest ideas and technology, though, may not necessarily be as effective and efficient as a company that continues to uses more traditional ideas and technology. While new technology may be an aid to high productivity, it does not assure that high productivity will take place. For example, highly competent workers may be able to complete more work with older equipment than indifferent workers are able to complete with the latest equipment. However, over time, highly successful technology tends to be accepted by most organizations.

What offices have you seen that continue to use technology of an earlier period, such as typewriters?

Why might the latest technology not lead to improved productivity?

topic 1-1 review

Reviewing the Topic

1. What are some technological developments that have changed the way office tasks are performed?
2. What kind of employees need to have office competencies?
3. As you consider the office functions in Illustration 1-1:2, identify at least three that you believe would require skill in using equipment.
4. As you consider the office functions in Illustration 1-1:2, identify at least two that you believe at this point you could handle. Explain why.
5. Why might an organization have a number of specialized offices? Give an illustration of such an office.
6. Why does reengineering take place in offices?
7. How does a traditional office differ from a virtual office?
8. What makes telecommuting a feasible way of handling office work?
9. The offices in Company A are state-of-the art, while those in Company B are traditional. Explain the difficulty of determining which offices are most effective.

MAKING DECISIONS

Assume that you have completed your studies and are seeking your first full-time position. You have been interviewed by a personnel recruiter in two companies. Each has offered you a position. You like both companies as far as the nature of the work, the salary, and the employee benefits. But there is a difference in *where* you will work.

In Company A, you would be expected to come to headquarters each day. The company has excellent computer facilities and the supervisor seems very helpful and friendly. In Company B, you would be telecommuting. Company B would provide you with all the equipment and furniture for your workstation at home. You would have access to the supervisor via telecommunications. From time to time—possibly no more than once in three weeks—you would be expected to attend a training session or a team meeting at headquarters.

topic 1-1 review

The Office Today

Which position would you accept?

What you are to do:

(a) Make a list of the factors you would consider in making a decision.

(b) Write a brief paragraph in which you discuss your decision and the basis for it.

REINFORCING ENGLISH SKILLS

For a group of words to be a complete sentence, they must contain both a subject and a verb. In this exercise, you will identify complete and incomplete sentences. You are to change incomplete sentences into complete sentences, choosing words that make sense to you.

What you are to do:

Open the template file *Sentence*. Read the paragraphs, noting which sentences are complete and which are incomplete. For all incomplete sentences, add a word or words to make complete sentences. Save and print your edited sentences.

Filename: Sentence

APPLICATION ACTIVITIES

ACTIVITY 1 Getting Acquainted with Local Offices

In this activity, you will become familiar with the types of offices in your own community.

What you are to do:

The class as a whole:

Develop a list of the major employers in your area.

Each student or team:

For the company you selected or were assigned, learn what types of offices are provided. Find answers to the following questions through inquiry or observation:

1. What is the primary product(s) or service(s) of the business or organization?
2. What percentage of the employees work in offices at this location?

17

3. How many workers telecommute? If there are workers who telecommute, how many of them are considered office workers?
4. What technology is being used in preparing letters and memorandums? for telecommunications? for records management?
5. In general, determine if the technology in use is state of the art, somewhat up to date, or primarily noncomputerized type.

topic 1-1 review

What you are to communicate:

Prepare a written report of three or four paragraphs in which you provide the information you gathered in response to the questions.

The class:

Participate in a discussion that summarizes what offices are like in your community.

ACTIVITY 2 Assessing Skills and Knowledge

In this activity, you will identify your present skills and knowledge of office activities.

What you are to do:

See Workbook page 5.

Refer to your *Student Activities and Projects* workbook for a checklist to complete. (If you are not using the workbook, create the list of key office activities shown in Illustration 1-1:2). Make an assessment based on these factors:

Have Observed/Performed Activity in an Office
Yes No

Level of Skill or Knowledge
Some Little None

18

Topic 1-2

The Office in Relation to the Total Organization

When you have completed your study of this topic, you will be able to:

- **explain how employees develop understanding of organizations in which they work**
- **describe common types of organizations**
- **identify goals for different types of organizations**
- **explain a common structure for personnel**
- **describe the role of office employees within an organization**

Workers do not perform office tasks in **isolation.** Office tasks are related to the work of others in the organization. Completing tasks often requires **judgment** and making decisions. Understanding the organization will help you make sound decisions in completing your work.

isolation:
being apart from others

judgment:
using one's own thinking for coming to a conclusion

Understanding the Organization

Office activities are basically related to information. Through creating, processing, communicating, and maintaining information, you learn much about your organization. Such learning, however, is not automatic. A **deliberate** effort on your part is needed. Tasks become more interesting and employees become more valuable when they give attention to understanding their organizations.

deliberate:
carefully thought out

Is there an office all students know, such as that of the counselor, principal, or superintendent? If there is, such an office may be the focus for a discussion of what employees in the office need to know to do their jobs competently.

Further discussion of how the office employees become acquainted with the organization would be helpful.

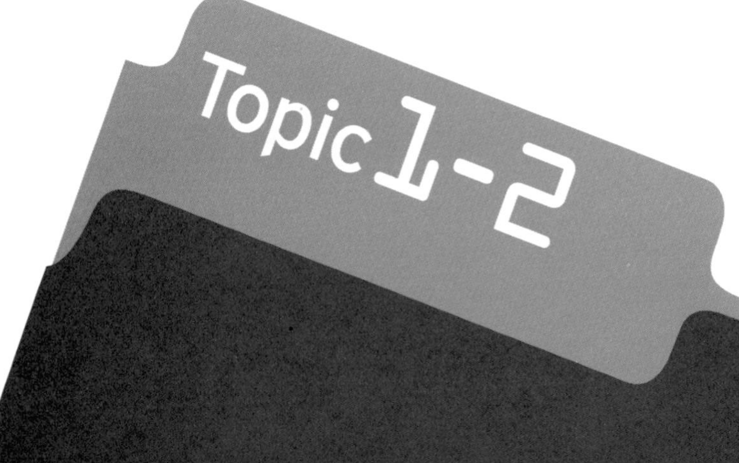

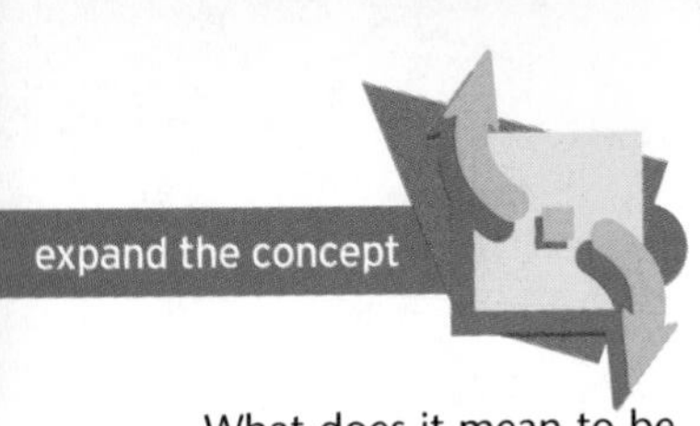

What does it mean to be alert to opportunities to learn? Explain.

LEARNING FROM YOUR WORK

The information you handle is related to your organization. Workers should be alert to opportunities to learn from the content of their work. Of course, workers must realize at all times the potential **confidentiality** of some information they encounter.

confidentiality: private or secret nature

Linda Jansen works for a senior vice president who is responsible for buying small advertising agencies. The company is intent on rapidly expanding its services throughout the global community. Although she knows that much information about possible **acquisitions** *is confidential, she notes for her own use what the reports state. She finds that her understanding of the specific deadlines, for example, can help her prioritize her work.*

acquisitions: that which is purchased

Why must Linda keep details of pending acquisitions confidential?

LEARNING FROM RESOURCES AVAILABLE

Many organizations encourage employees to become well acquainted with the total company's work. Annual reports, which contain much valuable information about the company's achievements, are sometimes provided to all employees. Employees find such reports **enlightening,** for example, in explaining the company's mission as well as its goals for the forthcoming fiscal year. Company newsletters and other communications are also valuable sources of knowledge for employees.

enlightening informative

Noting articles in local newspapers or periodicals about your organization is a worthwhile practice. Employees frequently have access to

Why do managers subscribe to periodicals that deal with the industry in which their company operates?

Illustration 1-2:1
Reading trade magazines is a good way to learn about trends in your field.

publications that deal with the industry in which the company operates. These are another source of information for increasing understanding of the company's business. Workers who understand the company know whom to call when they need information related to their work or to answer an inquiry from someone else.

Types of Organizations

In the United States, organizations are categorized as:

- businesses
- not-for-profit entities (but not governmental)
- governmental units

Use the local business community to illustrate the three types of organizations. Introduce students to the yellow and blue pages of the telephone directory and to some World Wide Web sites of local organizations.

BUSINESSES

Businesses are profit-seeking entities. For the most part, businesses in the United States are organized as single proprietorships, partnerships, or corporations. Additionally, there are some variations within the type of organization. Single proprietorships and partnerships can be organized without approval by any governmental body. Corporations, on the other hand, are required to secure **charters** from the states in which they incorporate. All businesses, regardless of form, must adhere to the laws and regulations governing business activity.

charters: written grants from authorities

Single proprietorship. A business owned by one individual is a single proprietorship. Such a business may or may not also be managed by the owner. Single proprietorships may be of any size, but the great majority are small.

> *Welsh Internal Access is owned by Jennifer W. Hayes. This small company with about 1,000 customers provides Internet access for companies as well as consulting services for those who want to build intranets.*

Partnership. A business that is not incorporated and has two or more owners is known as a partnership. Different types of partners may participate in a partnership. Some partners may provide funds for the business but not participate in managing it. Other partners may actively lead and manage the business. Partnerships, too, may be of any size; many are small, however.

Illustration 1-2:2

This small store on Prospect Street is a single proprietorship.

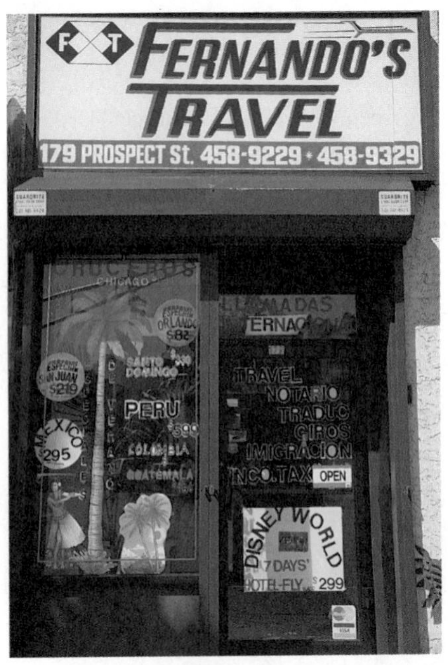

Ramos & Saunders Graphics is a partnership owned and operated by Bill Ramos and Sally Saunders. The business provides a wide range of artistic services to a variety of clients.

Illustration 1-2:3

These two attorneys have formed a partnership.

Corporation. A business organized under the laws of a particular state for which a charter was secured is a corporation. Corporations may be privately or publicly owned. Owners have shares of ownership, which are represented by stock certificates. Owners are called *stockholders* or *shareholders*. The corporation is considered a legal unit, separate from its shareholders. Most **giant** companies in the United States are corporations. Publicly owned corporations are required to report to shareholders on a timely basis. Such reports become available to many others besides the stockholders.

giant: among the largest

> *S. C. Johnson and Son, Inc., is a privately owned corporation. The company develops and sells software systems to individuals, companies, and government agencies.*

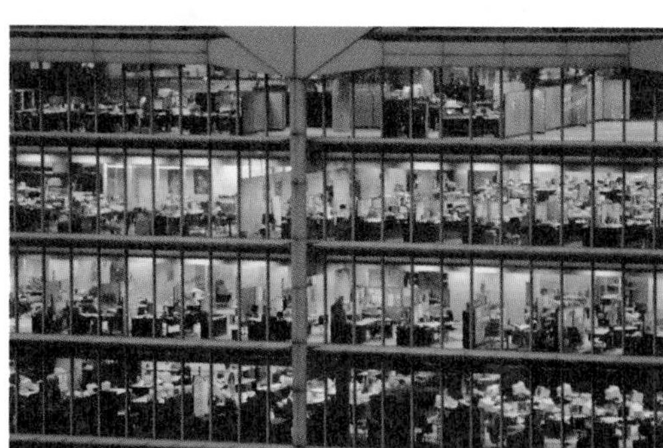

Illustration 1-2:4

A range of activities is evident in the headquarters of a computer company.

Professional service organizations are considered businesses, too. Lawyers, physicians, dentists, and accountants operate as single proprietorships, partnerships, or corporations. However, the laws and regulations governing a corporation of professional persons, such as physicians, are different from those that apply to a business corporation. The basic difference is that the participants in a professional corporation continue to have personal responsibility for their behavior. Shareholders in a corporation, on the other hand, are not held responsible for the behavior of managers of the business. However, in a professional corporation of doctors, for example, the doctors who have incorporated their practice continue to have personal responsibility for their behavior and that of their coworkers.

Use local not-for-profit entities as a basis to discuss the office tasks that are important. (Some recent activity of a major organization, such as a fund-raising drive or special program, might be the focus of a discussion of key office skills.)

NOT-FOR-PROFIT ENTITIES

Many organizations in the United States provide services without the intent of making profits. Among these organizations are associations that sponsor developmental programs for young people, such as 4-H clubs, Girl Scouts, Boy Scouts, and the Future Business Leaders of America. Other common not-for-profit groups include centers for performing arts, museums, libraries, hospitals, and private colleges and universities. However, there are hospitals and schools that operate as businesses and do seek to be profitable.

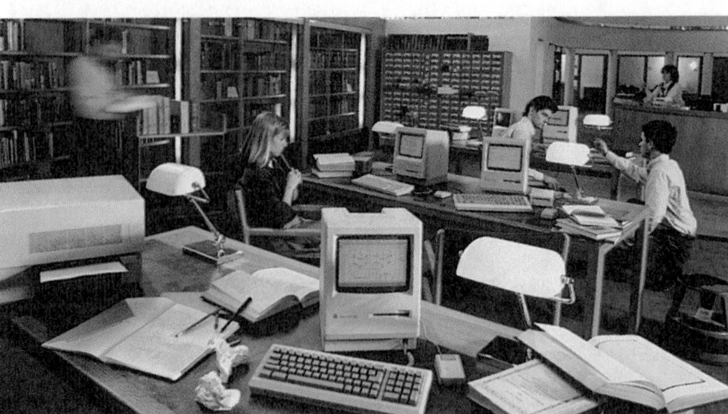

Illustration 1-2:5
The public library provides many services.

Not-for-profit organizations secure funds from a variety of sources. Many depend on contributions from individuals and groups. They also obtain financing from dues and fees paid by participants. In some instances, funds are provided to not-for-profit entities by governmental agencies at the local, state, or federal level. For example, the Metropolitan Museum of Art in New York City is a not-for-profit institution that gets some funding from the local government. Increasingly, not-for-profit entities function in what is referred to as a businesslike manner. This means that resources are carefully budgeted as though the entity were a profit-making business.

GOVERNMENTAL UNITS

Governmental units at the local, state, and national levels play a critical role in society. They are called by different names, including *agency*,

Illustration 1-2:6

The Internal Revenue Service plays a critical role in society.

commission, *bureau*, *department*, and *board*. Each unit has specific responsibilities for services considered important for the citizens served. Examples include:

National	*Department of the Treasury, Bureau of Labor Statistics, Environmental Protection Agency*
State or Province	*Department of Commerce, Occupational Safety & Health Division*
Local	*Marriage License Bureau, Board of Education*

Goals of Organizations

Each of the three major types of organizations has different overall goals. These general goals influence the tasks performed within the company by all employees. As you learned, businesses, including professional organizations, seek to make a profit. On the other hand, not-for-profit entities and governmental units, while not seeking to earn profits, have overall goals that relate to the services they provide.

GOALS OF BUSINESSES

You may have heard a comment such as, "It's the bottom line that counts." This is a reference to profit. Prior to the comment, there may

Determine from the pages of the telephone book all the local offices of federal and state agencies. Discuss services provided and the role of office employees.

In identifying its commitment to values, one major company noted that it believes in the highest standards of integrity. Discuss how that value relates to an overall goal of profit making.

have been a discussion of what a business should choose to do. The alternatives under consideration were reviewed in the light of the **potential** profit of each plan. In general, plans that are projected to provide the most profit—increase the bottom line—are selected. There are times, however, when businesses choose to follow a plan that is likely to be most profitable in the long run rather than immediately.

potential: capable of development

When a company sells goods or provides services, it earns revenues. The money spent to earn the revenues are referred to as *expense*. A company seeks to have revenues greater than expenses. Only then is a profit realized. Profits allow a business to expand through investment of profits in new facilities and new equipment. They also provide the means to reward shareholders in a corporation, for example, through the payment of **dividends.**

dividends: payments made to stockholders

Many tasks that workers perform relate to helping to meet the profit goals of the business. Closely tied to such goals is all the activity required to obtain and maintain information about how profitable the business actually is.

> *Hans Welenz works in customer services for a large personal computer manufacturing company. The company sells computers through a nationwide network of dealerships. Hans's main task is to understand exactly a complaint or request from a dealer. He communicates the information to the person in the company who can resolve the matter. Customer service functions with what is called a 24-hour* **turnaround,** *which means that the staff strives to resolve the matter within 24 hours of receipt of the call. Hans knows that his work is critical if the company is to meet its targeted profit level. A dissatisfied dealer is likely to seek another source for computers.*

turnaround: processing time

GOALS OF NOT-FOR-PROFIT ENTITIES

Not-for-profit organizations, as the title states, do not seek to make a profit. The chief goal of such organizations is to provide valuable services to those who can benefit from them. Museums strive to provide interesting exhibitions of various types of art. Social agencies providing food and cleaning services for the elderly who are **infirm** try to make sure all who need their services actually receive them.

infirm: in poor health

Workers in not-for-profit entities perform many office tasks. Here is just one example:

> *Elvira Sidney works as a counselor in a not-for-profit outreach program in Apopka, Florida. Much of her time is spent helping those who come to enroll in literacy and job skills programs. Elvira realizes that many of them are shy and unfamiliar with offices. She is friendly, helpful, and sensitive to the need for encouragement. The outreach organization is aware of the numbers of people in the community who could benefit from the programs offered. They strive each year to increase the enrollment in their programs, which are free.*

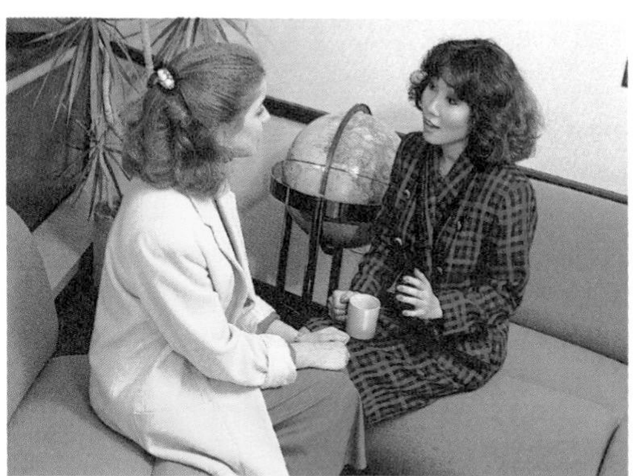

Illustration 1-2:7
Not-for-profit agencies offer many services, including counseling.

GOALS OF GOVERNMENTAL UNITS

Governmental units, like not-for-profit entities, do not seek to make a profit. These units are supported primarily by tax receipts. The overall goals of governmental units are related to providing services that citizens desire or need. For example, the government maintains a federal highway system, which assures ease of travel throughout the country. Such a system is an aid to commerce and to the quality of life that citizens enjoy. Each local unit of government has a board of education to oversee the nature and quality of the public schools under its **jurisdiction.**

jurisdiction: extent of authority

multiple: consisting of more than one part

Many workers are required throughout governmental units to take care of the **multiple** tasks required to meet the needs of citizens. There are

In a follow-up to identifying local governmental units, ask students to describe the overall goal of the governmental agencies noted.

What must Judy be doing when she is giving attention to details?

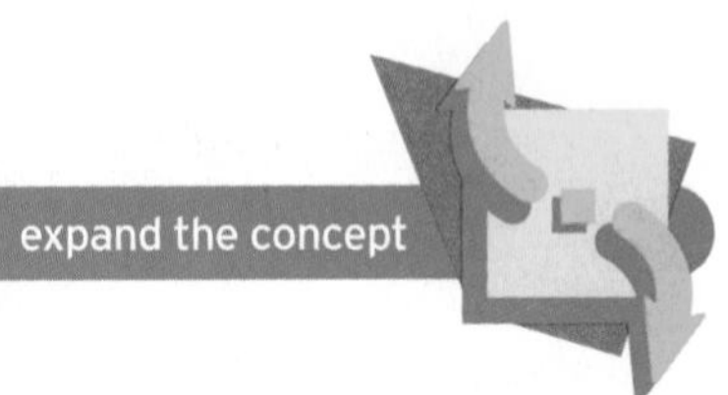

The size of a company generally refers to the total number of employees. However, sometimes it refers to the amount of revenues earned during a year. Explain how employees' responsibilities will differ if they work in a very small organization rather than a giant one.

What attitudes are critical for a single proprietor who is also managing his/her business?

many types of jobs available. The brief description of the duties of one worker in a federal office will provide an idea of what is done in one governmental office.

> *Judy Chen works as an assistant at the Federal Deposit Insurance Corporation, which is the primary federal agency regulating most insured banks in the United States. Judy's office is responsible for assigning staff to examine banks throughout the country and receiving reports. Attention to details and to prompt updating of all records is critical in Judy's position. She finds her work challenging as well as interesting. She feels she is learning much about the total banking system in the United States through her interaction with examiners and their reports.*

Types of Employees Required

Organizations require many different types of employees. There is much interaction among workers with varying responsibilities in the organization. Therefore, it is important that they have an awareness of the overall nature of the work of other employees. Office workers, especially, find it helpful to understand the responsibilities and authority of those with whom they work.

The size of a company influences the types of workers needed. In a small company, a single person may, as is commonly stated, wear many hats. For example, a single proprietor may determine how the funds will be spent, authorize all expenditures, sign all payments for goods and services, and be present to manage the business on a daily basis. You can imagine that an office assistant in such a company would be likely to do tasks related to communications, records management, and purchasing, for example, in the course of a single day.

In a large corporation, one person would not have the range of responsibility and authority that is common in a single proprietorship. Many companies require the services of several types of managers as well as specialized technical and administrative workers. Governmental units and not-for-profit entities have the same general needs as businesses. That is, there must be policy-making leaders, top management, and

Illustration 1-2:8
An assistant aids the proprietor of a small business.

possibly several layers of middle management as well as technical and support staffs.

BOARD OF DIRECTORS DETERMINES POLICIES

Many large corporations have boards of directors. Publicly owned corporations must have such boards. Owners elect members of the board of directors. The board establishes the policies that guide senior management in directing the company. Generally, some senior managers of the company are members of the board. The board has a number of committees that may meet more frequently than does the full board. Members of boards of directors who are not in senior management are not employees of the company. They are considered **independent** outsiders who are expected to bring a high level of **objectivity** to decision making. Such outside directors receive a payment for their participation, which is limited to a number of meetings each year. Generally, the full board of directors may meet no more than four to five times each year.

independent: acting on one's own

objectivity: state or quality of considering the facts

Not-for-profit entities also have a board of directors (sometimes called a *board of trustees*) whose responsibilities parallel those of a corporation's board.

SENIOR MANAGEMENT IMPLEMENTS POLICIES

Those persons who provide direction in carrying out the policies of the board of directors are identified as senior management, or top

What kind of policies would a board of directors of a business likely make? What kind of policies would a board of directors of a not-for-profit entity make?

Illustration 1-2:9

The board of a not-for-profit organization discusses a policy matter.

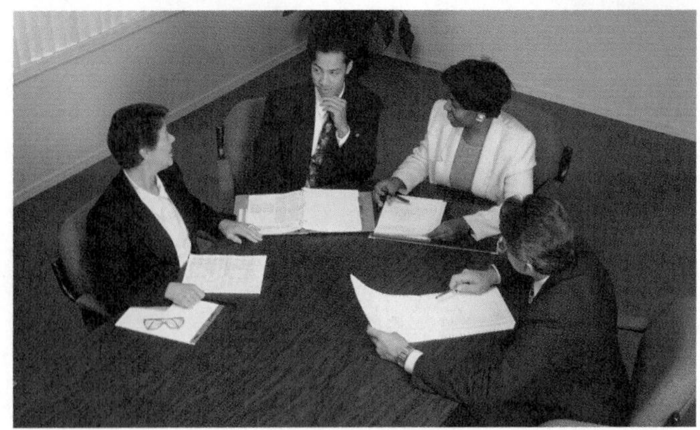

management, in both businesses and not-for-profit entities. The chief executive officer (often called the CEO), the president, the chief operating officer, and the chief financial officer are generally included in this group.

The CEO and president have overall responsibility for everything that happens in the company. In some companies, one person holds both of these positions, and even additional ones. For example, in a large chemical manufacturing company, one person is the CEO, the president, and the chief operating officer (COO). Senior management personnel often devote far more hours to the company each week than are considered standard for the average work week.

DIVISION MANAGEMENT OVERSEES SPECIFIC UNITS

Companies and not-for-profit entities are subdivided into units in some manner that is appropriate for the work of the company. Often the units are called *divisions* or *departments*, and they are managed by vice presidents. Persons who direct division or department operations are called *division management*. Those at this level have responsibility for working with managers who actually carry through policies and plans initiated by the board of directors. You are likely to find a wide variety of vice presidents at this level, including vice presidents for sales, manufacturing, product development, and communications.

MIDDLE-MANAGEMENT SUPERVISES

Companies and not-for-profit entities may have several levels of managers and supervisors who direct day-to-day activities. The employees who function at this level are referred to as middle management. Increasingly, there are fewer middle managers in American companies. You may have heard references to a flatter organization. This means that there are fewer layers of employees. Workers are given authority to make decisions without review by one or more higher-level managers. Computers have helped in processing and managing information in new ways that enable companies to reduce the ranks of middle management.

expand the concept

Discuss in what ways technology makes it possible to have a flatter organization.

TECHNICAL PERSONNEL PROVIDE CRITICAL KNOW-HOW

Many different types of specialization are represented among the employees of a company. The nature of a company's activities determines the types of **technical** specialists that will be employed. In many organizations, you will find specialists in areas such as computer programming, systems analysis, accounting, marketing, communications, law, and administrative support. The value of programmers, for example, in a software development corporation was noted by the president who said:

> *Our products are intellectual in nature, and people are our most important asset. Programmers are at the heart of our innovations—and they are called developers, code sizzlers, and code cowboys! Their creativity and commitment are critical to our growth.*

technical: having to do with special facts or knowledge

challenge option

What technical positions that are found in local businesses require the ability to perform office tasks?

Structure of Organizations

The types of employees briefly introduced have specific responsibilities that, added together, are expected to meet the goals of the organization. There must be a definite understanding of who is responsible for each activity and what authority each person has. To be sure it is clear how responsibility and authority are **delegated,** most organizations prepare a **formal** organization chart. Such a chart shows positions in

delegated: assigned to another person

formal: according to established rules

thinking critically

Have students consider what factors make products of a software company intellectual. The task of developing software might be contrasted with that of sewing garments in a dress manufacturing company, for example.

What does a hierarchical structure for an organization imply about responsibility?

Discuss with students how a company that manufactures a wide range of toys might find it difficult to have all decisions made at a central office. Ask students, for example, to consider what a manager of computerized toys for children six to eight years old would need to know about potential users in contrast with what a manager of toys for children under six would find useful.

Illustration 1-2:10

Programmers help develop new software programs.

hierarchical: in order of rank or authority

hierarchical order. As you can imagine, the organization chart for a company with a large number of employees will have many pages. Illustration 1-2:11 is a partial organization chart for a relatively small publicly owned company. Note the several levels of responsibility indicated and the differences in titles at the different levels.

Office Workers Help Meet Goals

As you have learned in this chapter, office workers are found in all types of businesses. Indeed, in every organization, office workers assist in carrying through the plans and policies originally established by the board of directors or other policy-making personnel.

This illustration introduces the concept of an organization chart. Knowing how an organization is structured will help you understand more clearly the duties of a particular position.

You must remember, though, that companies do not maintain the same structure indefinitely. From time to time, there is a review of how well the company is functioning. Frequently, such a review leads to a restructuring of the company. It is not uncommon, for example, for a company to determine that the operations would be more effective if the units were organized differently from their present form.

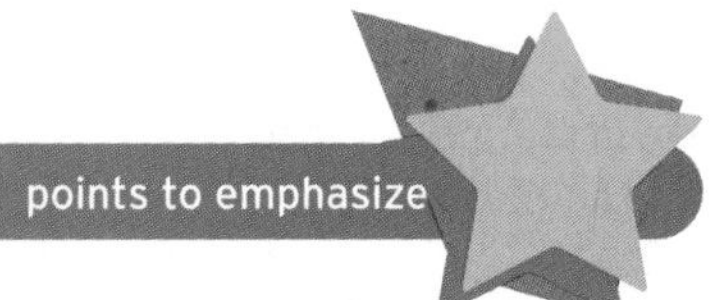

Tasks done by various office workers overlap those office tasks done by office support staff.

Technology makes it possible for many office workers to handle their own office tasks. However, office support staff continue to be employed in many organizations.

Companies have varying policies about responsibilities of executives and managers. In many companies, office support staff workers are provided to extend the productivity of managers and other office workers.

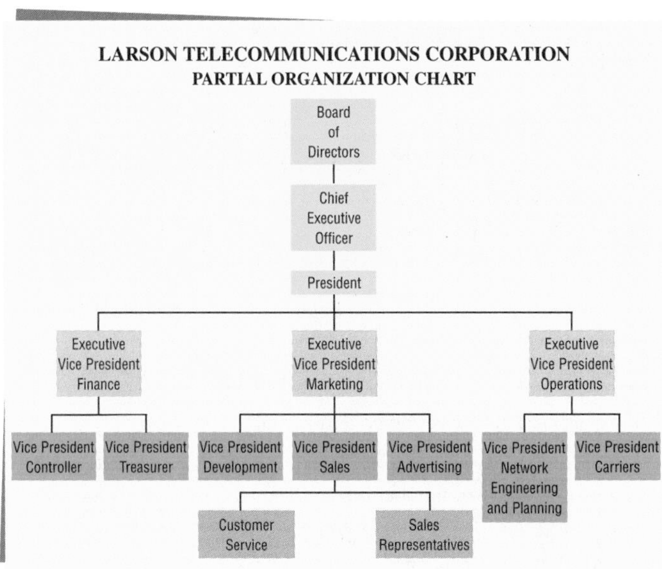

Illustration 1-2:11

The board of directors sets policies.

A toy manufacturing company had been organized with functions centralized. For example, all advertising for all types of toys was handled in a single office. Over the years, with the growth of the company, this structure caused problems. A careful review resulted in a restructuring by divisions, with each division head given authority for all functions that were formerly centralized.

As you have just learned, employees in an organization work at specified levels of responsibility and authority. Some companies have a limited number of levels, while others may have several levels. With few exceptions, you will find office workers at all levels of an organization.

topic 1-2 review

Reviewing the Topic

1. Why is it valuable for a worker to understand the business of the organization in which he or she is employed?
2. In what ways can workers learn about the organizations in which they are employed?
3. What are common forms of businesses?
4. How does a corporation, in general, differ from a single proprietorship or a partnership?
5. What do not-for-profit entities provide?
6. What kind of services do governmental units provide?
7. Contrast the overall goal of businesses with that of not-for-profit entities and governmental units.
8. What are common titles for persons who are in top management, and what is the general nature of their responsibilities?
9. How does an organization chart aid in understanding a company?
10. At which levels in a large organization are you likely to find office workers?

INTERACTING WITH OTHERS

You were standing at a desk of a coworker when her telephone rang. This is what you heard her say:

> *Who do you want?*
>
> *A Mr. Ted Wells? Are you sure he works for this company?*
>
> *Gee, I really don't know who the executives are. I don't work for any of them. I work for the director of catering services.*
>
> *Oh, you work for Johnson Corporation. Well, you know how hard it is to know your own job, let alone know what is going on in the company.*
>
> *You say our operator gave you this extension? Possibly, the operator doesn't know much more about the company than I do.*

topic 1-2 review

The Office in Relation to the Total Organization

34

If I knew the extension for the president's office, I'd transfer you because I'd guess the president's secretary knows where everyone is — but, I don't know the number offhand and I could never find my directory on this messy desk. . . Let me transfer you back to the operator. Is that okay? I so wish I could be helpful.

Just hold on. But, first where are you calling from? Why don't you call when you aren't busy, and we can have a chat. Do you have my number? It's 513-555-0192, extension 344.

Hold on. Good luck in finding Mr. Wells. Goodbye.

What you are to do:

1. Describe the impression you think the caller has of your coworker's knowledge of the company and of her way of working.
2. Identify what you believe the coworker said that reflects positive attitudes toward others.
3. If your coworker maintained an orderly desk, what would she have done as soon as it was clear that the caller had the wrong extension? What might she have said instead of the comments shown here?

REINFORCING MATH SKILLS

As you learned in this chapter, the goal of a business is to make a profit. In order to know the extent to which the profit goal is being met, businesses analyze their sales on a regular basis. Assume that you are working for a technology development company. The director has given you sales figures related to a new style of wireless communications. You have actual figures for four years and projections for three.

What you are to do:

Create a table and use formulas to analyze the sales as follows:

1. Determine the percentage increase for U.S. sales and international sales each year, using sales for 1994 as a base year for all calculations. Note that the figures for the final three years are projections.

35

ACTUAL AND PROJECTED SALES
($ In Millions)

	United States			*International*			*Combined*
Year	*Yearly Sales*	*% Increase Over 1994*	*% of Total Yearly Sales*	*Sales*	*% Increase Over 1994*	*% of Total Yearly Sales*	*% Increase Over 1994*
1994	70		70%	30		30%	
1995	100	43%		40	33%		140%
1996	150			50			
1997	200			50			
1998	240			80			
1999	300			100			
2000	350			170			

2. Determine the percentage increase for the combined U.S. and international sales, using sales for 1994 as the base year for all calculations.
3. Determine the percent of total sales for each year that will be U.S. sales and the percent that will be international sales.
4. Format the information attractively and add a comment below the table giving your impression of the rate of growth for this technology.

APPLICATION ACTIVITIES

ACTIVITY 1 Organization Chart

An organization chart is often used to show the structure of an organization. Creating an organization chart will help you understand the relationship of the personnel listed below from the World Wide Sales and Service Division of a multinational company.

What you are to do:

Prepare an organization chart showing the management team for the World Wide Sales and Service Division. Refer to Illustration 1-2:11 on page 33 for a sample chart.

1. Begin with the company name, GLOBAL MANUFACTURING, followed by the division name, centered at the top as the chart title.

36

2. Place Thomas McEwen's name and title, Chief Executive Officer, in the top block of the chart.

3. Insert a block for Paul B. Kalis, Senior Vice President, World Wide Sales and Service, who is head of the division and reports to Thomas McEwen.

4. Insert blocks for the following vice presidents who report to Paul B. Kalis:
   Marco Ortiz, Vice President, Latin America
   Akira Komuro, Vice President, Asia, Pacific
   Rachel J. Kohnstamm, Vice President, Europe, Middle East, and Africa

5. Insert a block for James E. Phelps, Assistant Vice President, Europe, who reports to Rachel J. Kohnstamm.

6. Insert blocks for Jean L. Lucent, Manager, France, and Howard A. Toole, Manager, Denmark, who report to James E. Phelps.

ACTIVITY 2 Agenda

As you learned, the board of directors has responsibility for setting policy for the company. In this activity, you will prepare an agenda to communicate with board members about a forthcoming meeting.

What you are to do:

1. Key the agenda using the information provided below. Refer to Reference Section H, Sample Documents, for a sample agenda format.

2. Compose a brief memorandum addressed to Board of Directors, using a date two weeks earlier than the scheduled date for the Board of Directors meeting. In the memo indicate that the enclosure is the agenda for the next meeting. Invite members to call Gail T. Storey, Secretary, if they have additional matters for the agenda.

See Workbook page 235.

37

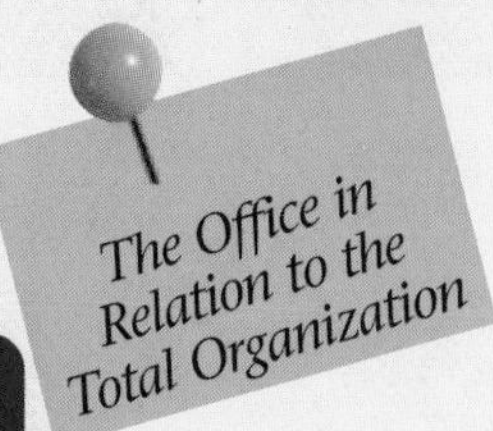

topic 1-2
review

Information for the agenda:

Company name: Rollines Manufacturing Corporation
Group meeting: Board of Directors
Date of meeting: October 12, 19xx at 2:30 p.m.
The person calling the meeting is: L. W. Wootsen,
Chairman of the Board

Items to be covered:

- Roll call and reading of the minutes of September 14 meeting by the secretary
- Committee Reports
  - Search Committee for Executive Vice President: Update of progress
  - Report of the Restructuring Committee, Chairperson Tony Ramez
- Unfinished Business
  - Opening of our learning center
- New Business
  - Consideration of a new information system, presented by Roberta Rogers
- Date of the next meeting and adjournment

38

Chapter Summary

During your study of Chapter 1, you learned about the role of the office in today's organization, types of organizations and their goals, as well as their structure. Also, you have become acquainted with the varied personnel required by organizations. Consider the points listed below as you reinforce your understanding of the topics in this chapter:

- Offices are found in almost all types of organizations, and many workers in today's workplace must perform office tasks.
- Offices are information driven.
- Modern offices are subject to rapid change as new technology is introduced.
- The office is not necessarily a place at the organization's official location, since technology makes the virtual office an appealing alternative.
- An understanding of the total organization increases an employee's ability to handle office activities effectively.
- Organizations are categorized as businesses, not-for-profit entities, or governmental units.
- Organizations, beyond the very small, require varying types of employees to be assured of meeting the goals established by those who lead the organization.
- While many employees perform office activities, there are administrative support services employees whose responsibilities are related fully to office activities.

chapter 1 summary

The Office in a Changing Business World

KEY CONCEPTS AND TERMS

administrative support services
annual report
board of directors
chief executive officer (CEO)
corporation
division management
governmental unit
"hot" technologies
information driven
intranet
middle management
mission
not-for-profit entity
office
organization chart
partnership
profit
reengineered
senior management
shareholders
single proprietorship
specialized office
state-of-the-art
technical personnel
telecommuting
traditional office
upgrading
virtual office

INTEGRATED CHAPTER ACTIVITIES

ACTIVITY 1 Organizations in Your Community

Learn more about the organizations in your community by working with classmates to develop a comprehensive listing or database of the organizations. Arrange the data by type of entity: business, not-for-profit entity, or governmental unit.

What you are to do:

1. You and the other classmates assigned to your group are to develop the list of local organizations in the category assigned to your group (business, not-for-profit entity, or governmental unit). From the list, each of you is to select at least two organizations.
2. For each organization selected, obtain the information listed below.
3. Meet with other group members after obtaining the information requested. As a group, discuss the most

40

appropriate way to present your information to the class. Work as a group to complete the database, report, or presentation.

Information to learn about each organization:

- Complete name and address of the main office
- General telephone number
- World Wide Web site address(es), if any
- Brief description of the main activity, product, or service of the organization

  For businesses, include the form of organization
  For not-for-profit entities, include the major sources of funds
  For governmental units, include the level—local, state, or national
- Brief description of types of workers employed

ACTIVITY 2 Considering a Place of Employment

In this chapter, and perhaps in Activity 1, you have learned about the three types of organizations found in most communities. Now consider what you think would be appealing about working in each type of entity.

What you are to do:

1. Select the type or organization (business, not-for-profit entity, or governmental unit) that you would like to consider as a place of employment.
2. Discuss the advantages and disadvantages of this type of organization with classmates.
3. Prepare a brief essay in which you identify your choice. Give reasons why you think you would like to work at this type of organization.

41

Getting Acquainted with the World of Work

Leslie Norwood
Director of Human Relations

Empowering Employees—What Does that Mean?

Dear Ms. Norwood

We had a speaker in our school—a manager in a software development company. The speaker made many interesting comments. Among them was: "In our firm people are empowered."

There really wasn't much time for questions—and I hesitated to ask, but I would like to understand what she meant by empowered.

What do you have to know to be empowered?

Heidi in Seattle

Dear Heidi

You are raising a good question. Only in recent years has the idea of empowerment *been given attention. Technological innovations have made it far easier than was the case in past years to process, store, and access information. The timely availability of information has meant that companies do not need as many levels of workers. Through giving individuals authority to make decisions, employees have been* empowered. *Let me give you an example:*

A large telecommunications company maintains a 24-hour customer service office. Customers who question their monthly statements are common callers. At one time, calls that a customer claimed were improperly charged would require a review by a supervisor. The supervisor was the only person who had all the details of a customer's record. The customer service representative would have to talk with a supervisor before responding to the customer.

Now, the customer service representative has access to a complete computer record of the customer. The representative also has had training in assessing the nature of calls that are fraudulent and is authorized to resolve the issue with a customer. So, when a customer called to say that the $1,450 of calls to China, Senegal, and the Republic of Yemen, which were listed as Convenience Calls, had not been made by an authorized party, the representative said: "These are fraudulent calls. Stay on the line. I will call your local carrier and authorize the carrier to drop all these charges from your account."

You see, Heidi, the customer representative was able to resolve the problem immediately. It wasn't necessary to record the details, promise to call back, and engage in a discussion with a supervisor. Empowerment extends the range of job responsibility of the person who is at the point where a decision is needed. It implies an understanding of the company's policies as well as an understanding of the problems encountered. Empowerment is appreciated by both customers and employees. Where it is properly introduced, it has added to both efficiency and effectiveness of operations.

Leslie Norwood
Director of Human Relations

42

Office Competencies

As you learned in Chapter 1, office competencies are a requirement for many workers in performing their jobs. Whether or not you know what you want to do as a worker, you will find the content of this textbook valuable. You will develop skills and understandings that have application to all types of careers and will be useful preparation for work of any kind.

In the first topic of this chapter, you will find a brief overview of overall occupational projections to the year 2005. Next, you will be introduced to basic office competencies. These competencies are discussed in relation to basic skills and job opportunities. The second topic of the chapter focuses on overall goals of organizations and the contribution expected of employees. A discussion of how you can plan your strategy for developing office competencies follows.

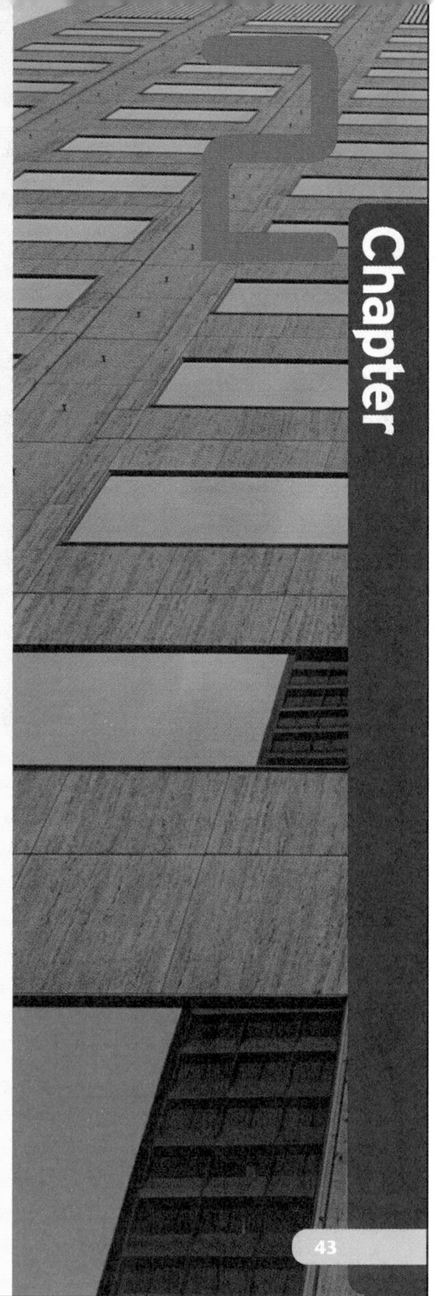

43

Chapter 2

Office Competencies Needed for Employment

Topic 2-1

When you have completed your study of this topic, you will be able to:

- **discuss the need for workers through the year 2005**
- **identify office competencies**
- **explain future prospects for employment where office competencies are valuable**

getting started GO

Increasingly, the secondary school is assuming the responsibility for developing basic work skills that are important in all types of jobs and careers. The focus continues to be on the universal nature of office competencies for most jobs.

The business office has changed a great deal. Before the personal computer became common in business offices, companies often employed two office workers to support each executive or manager. Today, newly employed executives and managers are not likely to have the services of office support staff as full-time assistants. **Projections** to 2005 show a high level of demand for executives, managers, professionals, and technicians. Yet that demand is not matched by equal demand for office support services personnel.

projections: guesses about the future

Most persons entering the workforce are expected to have basic office competencies. **Proficiency** can be acquired through your studies while you are still a student gaining your basic education.

proficiency: ability to perform

There is much information available about types of jobs in the United States. The Federal Government, through the Department of Labor,

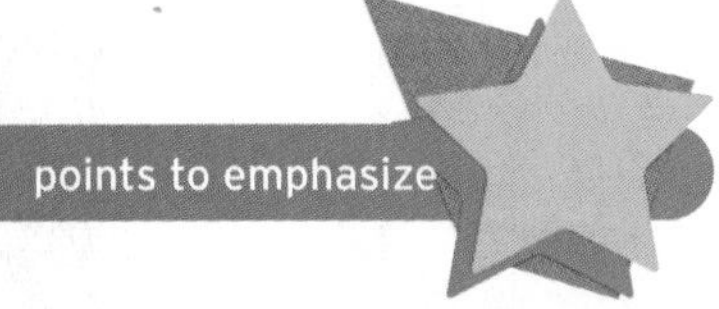

The capability of the computer leads to its widespread use throughout the workforce.

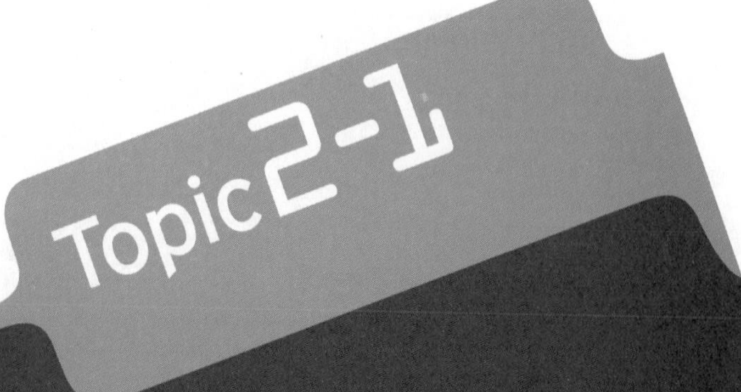

Illustration 2-1:1

A purchasing manager of a large chemical company uses office skills daily.

monitors the total workforce and provides analyses of the current employment situation. Also, the Department of Labor undertakes research to predict the need for workers in the future. Such information is valuable to individuals as they plan for their future careers. Schools and universities, too, use such predictions to plan courses that prepare students for jobs.

monitors: observes, checks

You do not have to have made decisions about your future job to benefit from studying the topics in this book.

National Overview of Employment

The U.S. Department of Labor publishes *The Occupational Outlook Handbook*, which discusses the major occupations in the country. From this book you can learn about job prospects in a wide range of fields. The projections are for ten years. The 1996–97 issue has projections to 2005. The monthly magazine *Monthly Labor Review* updates projections and provides additional information about job opportunities.

In projecting employment to 2005, the government's economists judged rate of increase. They made three projections: low, moderate, and high. The one used for most projections was the moderate alternative, which is considered the most realistic of the three. The overall rate projected was 14 percent. Professional specialty occupations are expected to increase by 29 percent from 1994 to 2005. Administrative

Consider the range of types of workers in the local workforce. Surveys of local chambers of commerce will help students gain an overview of the local job market.

Illustration 2-1:2

Occupations projected to grow the fastest, 1994–2005.

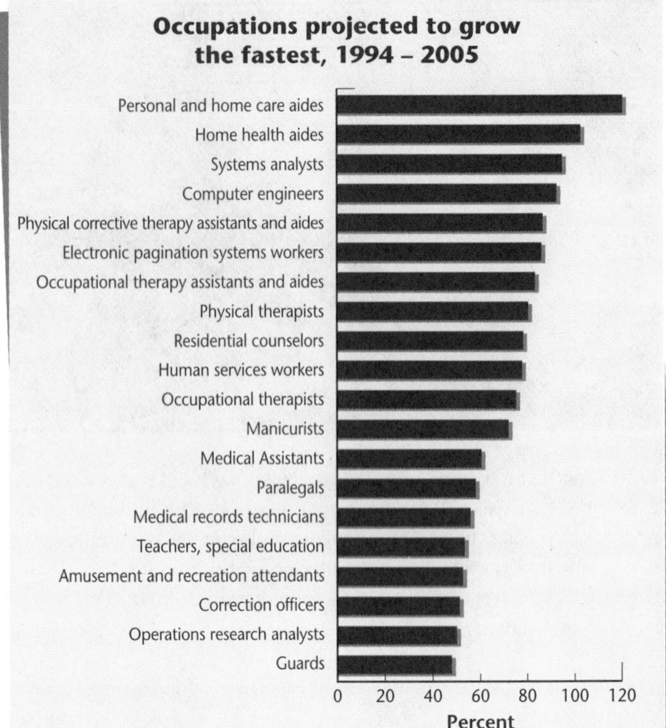

From United States Department of Labor, Bureau of Labor Statistics, *Occupational Outlook Handbook,* 1996–97 Edition, p. 3.

support occupations, which are also referred to as office support services, are expected to increase by 4.3 percent during the same period. Note the occupations projected to have the largest numerical increase in employment during the 1994–2005 period in Illustration 2-1:3.

OUTLOOK FOR EMPLOYMENT OF OFFICE WORKERS

The Handbook noted that automation will have a great effect on many administrative and clerical support occupations. This effect is shown in the low rate of growth projected to 2005. However, there

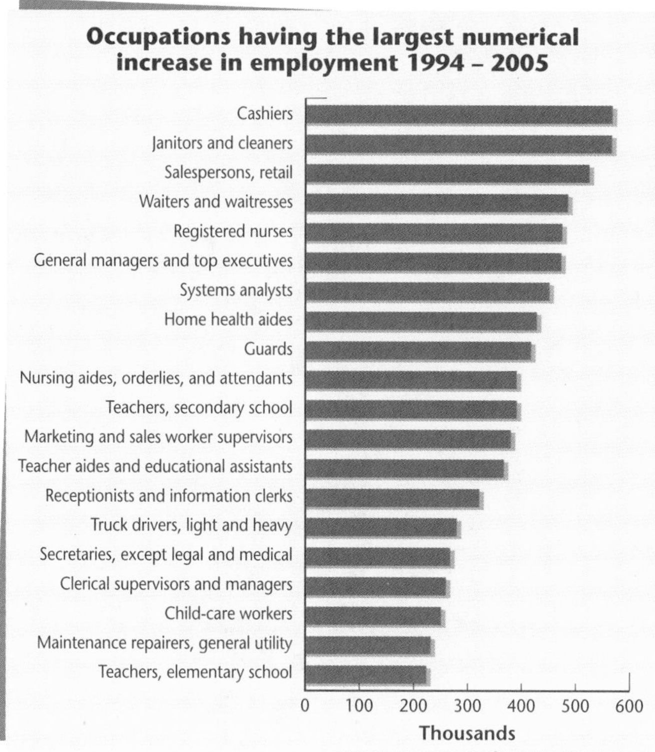

From United States Department of Labor, Bureau of Labor Statistics, *Occupational Outlook Handbook*, 1996–97 Edition, p. 3.

Illustration 2-1:3

Occupations projected to have largest numerical increase in employment, 1994–2005.

will be jobs in this area because many persons in this group will need to be replaced. Note the figures in Illustration 2-1:4. Some workers will leave the field to enter new jobs or to retire. For example, over 3.3 million persons work as secretaries and 1.4 million work as information clerks. These are among the largest of all the job groups in the U. S. workforce.

Toula Ahara was hired nine months ago as a receptionist in a large travel agency in Boston. She acquired office skills while in high school. She completed a liberal arts program at a local community college

expand the concept

What is the value of information about the workforce and occupations to an individual citizen, such as students in this class?

points to emphasize

There continue to be opportunities in office support services.

What attitudes do you believe may have aided Toula in gaining a promotion?

before she accepted the job. Toula loves travel. She had taken many trips while a student. Soon after her job began, the manager asked her to assist clients. Toula enjoyed this part of her job. Just a short while ago, Toula was promoted to travel agent. She said this about her new job: "My love of travel is one key to my promotion. The other key is my skill with the personal computer—from word processing to database management."

Illustration 2-1:4

Employment in administrative and clerical support jobs to arise from replacement for persons leaving jobs.

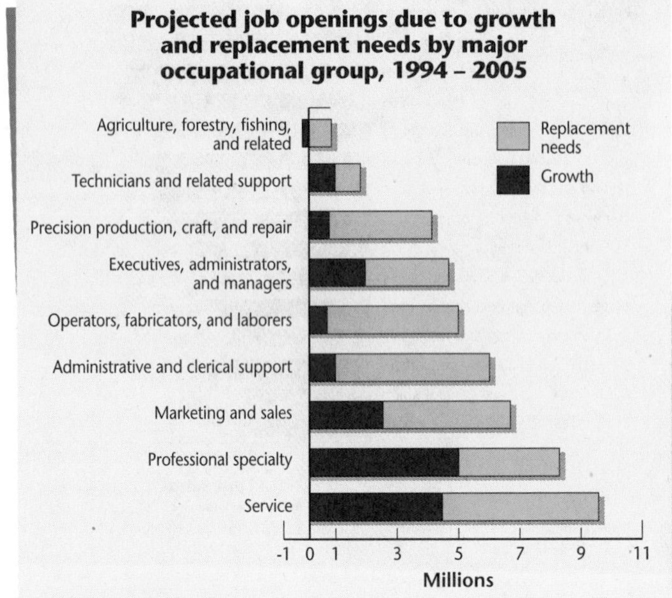

From United States Department of Labor, Bureau of Labor Statistics, *Occupational Outlook Handbook,* 1996–97 Edition, p. 2.

WORKERS FACE EXPANDED JOB RESPONSIBILITIES

expansion: increase

A low rate of increase in office support jobs does not indicate a reduction in office activity. Actually, there is an increase in office activity because of the **expansion** of business throughout the global community. What has happened is a marked shift in who handles such tasks. Far more workers are performing office tasks than in the past. Modern technology is responsible for the shift. All types of workers can handle office tasks because of the technology on their desks. Also, technology makes it possible for many workers to do office tasks on their own. Remember, though, that there continue to be many office support workers.

Consider today's level of office activity. If there were no **innovations** during the last 20 years, there would have to be about six times as many office employees as are now employed to handle the volume of activity! Here is just one manager who now does most of her own office work:

innovations: new methods, ideas

> *Donna Komari is a product manager in the international division of a home appliance company. She spends much time traveling. Donna works for hours during a flight from Newark to London. With her notebook computer she corresponds, accesses databases, sets up a spreadsheet, and talks with colleagues. When she reaches London, she has done a day's work! Her comment about her way of working was: "Before we had today's technology, I would have needed two full-time secretaries to do what I did alone while on the flight from Newark to London."*

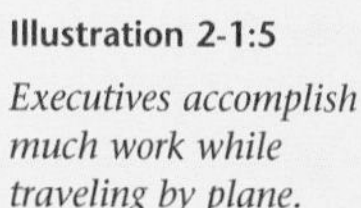

Illustration 2-1:5

Executives accomplish much work while traveling by plane.

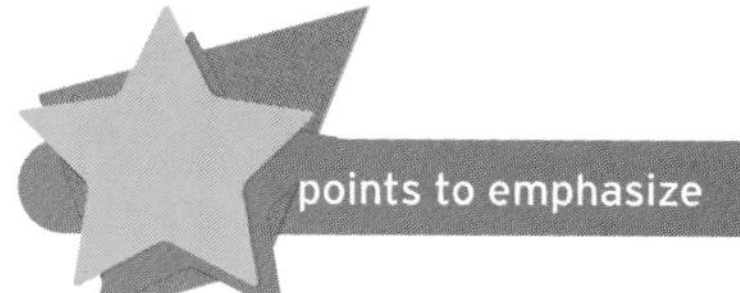

Electronic capabilities have made it feasible for all workers to assume many office tasks. Ask students to observe the extent to which workers they encounter—delivery personnel, utilities meter readers, waiters and waitresses—must perform some office skills to do their jobs effectively.

Why would one company provide office support staff for employees while another company does not?

Innovations have markedly changed the way tasks are done. Compare preparing a letter at a typewriter and at a computer keyboard. Consider what happens when an error is noted in your copy if you are at a typewriter or at a computer keyboard.

There is considerable overlap in the requirements for the four categories of office skills.

Which of the basic skills for word processing have you been developing through your experiences in school?

An Overview of Office Competencies

A wide range of activities make up office competencies. However, four major groups based on primary skills reflect the overall nature of office work. These are:

- word processing
- data processing
- information management and transmission
- general managing and interacting with customers

You will now become acquainted with each of these categories. Pay attention to the basic skills needed for doing tasks effectively and efficiently.

WORD PROCESSING

Information is of critical value in all types of organizations. Word processing is the producing of communications by using software programs at personal computers.

Basic Competencies. The proper and efficient use of a personal computer in composing, revising, and preparing all types of documents is the goal of skill development in this category.

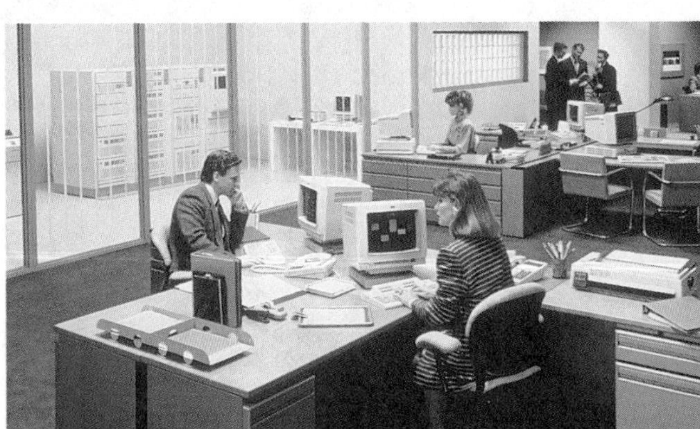

Illustration 2-1:6
Word processing is a basic competency for office workers.

The essential skills include:

- keyboarding with speed and accuracy
- knowledge and skill in use of software programs
- skill in formatting and proofreading documents
- a large vocabulary
- command of grammar, punctuation, and spelling
- ability to learn special vocabularies
- ability to follow instructions
- skill in preparing copy from audio recordings, if employed as a transcriptionist

Illustration 2-1:7

These software packages are useful in handling word processing tasks.

Workers Who Need These Competencies. Word processing skills are needed by many workers. Executives and managers, both general and technical, spend much time composing written communications. Technical personnel, such as engineers, advertising designers, architects, and public relations specialists, are employees likely to use word processing skills in their work.

Opportunities in Office Support Services. There are office support staff who provide full-time assistance handling word processing activities. Among the positions observed in organizations in this category are: typist, word processor, and transcriptionist.

Why would a newspaper reporter find word processing skills valuable? Are such skills valuable for the assistant in a public relations office that prepares and transmits many press releases?

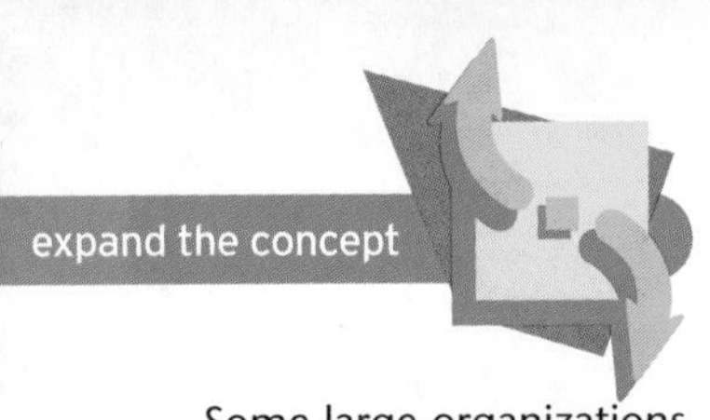

Some large organizations, such as law firms, investment banking companies, and brokerage houses, have centralized word processing centers. Why would such organizations centralize such services?

How would you describe "good writing skills"?

How do data processing skills differ from word processing skills?

Bob Wells is a transcriptionist in a company that provides recording and transcribing services to all types of organizations. At the moment, Bob is transcribing from a tape a speech given to a group of executives in a large financial services company. After Bob keys the speech, the supervisor will review the draft. There are times when the draft is sent to the speaker to be sure that the copy is as the speaker wants it. When the draft is considered complete, Bob will prepare multiple copies.

Such workers prepare drafts as well as final copies of letters, memorandums, and reports. They may assist one other worker or several. Some word processing workers assist an entire department.

adept: able to function well

Such office support workers are considered for promotions to jobs in the same category that require more advanced skills. For example, workers who are **adept** at learning all aspects of software programs and at explaining the details to new employees may be promoted to a supervisory or training job. Workers with good writing skills may become administrative assistants.

DATA PROCESSING

Data processing is the collecting, organizing, analyzing, and summarizing of data, generally in numeric form. Many positions require competency in such skills. Increasingly, this type of activity is done at a computer, using spreadsheet and statistical software programs. Though we think of data processing as primarily dealing with numerical data and word processing as dealing with text, the two processes often blend with one another. This blending process is made easier by the integration capabilities of today's software programs. Data processing and word processing are often collectively referred to as *information processing*. Many workers do this type of office activity.

Basic Competencies: Among the skills important for workers who handle data processing activities are the following:

- excellent command of spreadsheet and related software programs
- command of arithmetic processes and statistical methods
- ability to be consistently accurate
- knowledge of methods of organizing and analyzing data

- ability to interpret data
- ability to prepare reports that communicate numerical information in a meaningful fashion
- ability to maintain an organized workstation

Workers Who Need These Competencies. Accountants, budget analysts, brokers, insurance salespersons, and many other types of personnel found in all kinds of organizations deal with data and prepare reports.

Illustration 2-1:8
An accountant is preparing a plan for a client.

Cathy Leitman is a budget analyst in a large company. She is at her computer much of the time accessing information from various units of the company in relation to matters under review, such as the extent of defects from manufacturing processes in some of the company's factories. She then does analyses and prepares tables to present to the executives who must make decisions using her information. Cathy studied economics in college. When asked what prepared her for her job, Cathy said: "My college studies were of great value for what I do; however, the basic skills I learned in my high school office procedures class are critical to my work every day!"

Opportunities in Office Support Services. There continue to be many workers employed in the data processing category. They

What workers have you observed performing data processing skills?

A budget analyst works with figures that are a part of the company's financial system. Companies monitor what actually happens in the company in comparison with what was planned, or budgeted, for the period.

Illustration 2-1:9
An accounts payable department is a vital part of the organization.

include specialized clerks, such as accounts payable clerk, billing clerk, order clerk, payroll clerk, and shipping clerk. Such clerks prepare and process sales, purchases, invoices, payrolls, and other types of transactions. Their work is vital to the whole organization.

thinking critically

An accounts payable department is responsible for handling vendor invoices and assuring that payments are made on a timely basis. What traits should clerks in such a department possess?

Office support employees in this category have offers for promotion. Companies need workers who can oversee increasingly more automated systems for processing data. Consequently, beginners who have an **aptitude** for understanding the total operation and have learned their jobs thoroughly are good candidates for promotions. The experience of one beginner reflects this type of opportunity:

aptitude: ability

> *Gail began working as an order clerk in a large manufacturing company in Illinois when she graduated from high school. After six months, she was* **temporarily** *transferred to the controller's office to help with analyses of manufacturing operations. The controller noted that she learned quickly, and talked with Gail about her future plans. He suggested that Gail consider enrolling in a college program to study accounting. Gail liked the idea. She began night studies at a local college. She realizes that she will not complete her college studies in four years. She likes working full-time and studying part-time. She plans to keep her goal to complete a college program and become an accountant.*

temporarily: briefly

What do you think the controller observed that led him to conclude that Gail could learn quickly?

INFORMATION MANAGEMENT AND TRANSMISSION

Information management and transmission refers to the organizing, maintaining, and accessing of records and to the communicating of information both within and outside the organization.

Basic Competencies. There is considerable variety in the skills considered basic in this category:

- identification of information needed in the situation
- skill in determining the factors needed to develop an information system
- ability to give attention to details
- ability to use established procedures
- command of basic filing principles and rules
- good keyboarding skills
- basic knowledge of accessing databases
- ability to meet deadlines and solve problems

Workers Who Need These Skills. A wide range of workers is likely to need the skills for information management and transmission. Personnel such as buyers, real estate brokers, and property managers

Illustration 2-1:10
A buyer maintains an organized information system.

Why are established procedures important in maintaining information?

Note that workers who communicate with customers must know how to use information, but they may not be involved in developing such systems or updating them.

A major direct mail order company has a knowledgeable staff responding to customer telephone calls. What must such staff know to do the job well?

What should beginning employees learn about their companies? (Hint: Think about the topics discussed in Chapter 1.)

must have well-organized information systems. The details they need to make decisions often require them to design their own systems. Often their information must be available to others, too. Following a well-designed system is the key to easy use of information.

Opportunities in Office Support Services. Those who find it interesting to gather and organize data will enjoy work in this category, which consists of updating information on a timely basis and transmitting information promptly. Among common jobs in this category are: **dispatcher,** hotel and motel desk clerk, mailroom clerk, records clerk, reprographics clerk, travel clerk, and communications center operator. Alert beginning employees in this category learn much about the organization. Such knowledge is a key to gaining promotions.

dispatcher: person who directs the movement of goods or services

GENERAL MANAGING AND COMMUNICATING WITH CUSTOMERS

General managing and communicating with customers is a general category that includes guiding tasks and interacting with customers. As you have learned, the office is information driven. Yet office activities require good managing skills. Setting up schedules, adhering to deadlines, and monitoring the progress of tasks are components of general managing. Communicating with customers is a common activity for many types of workers in a company.

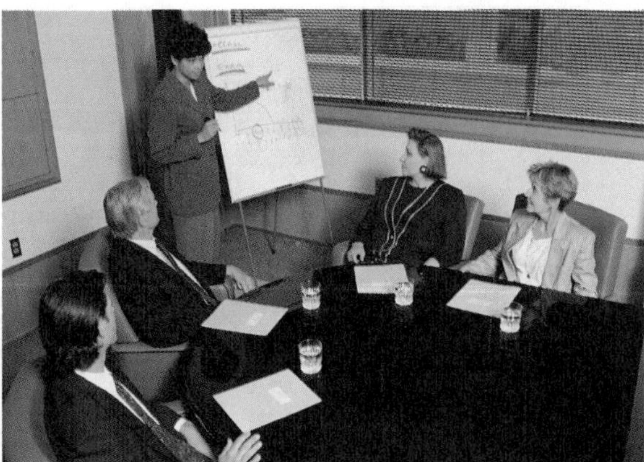

Illustration 2-1:11
A department manager holds regular staff meetings.

Basic Competencies. The skills and knowledge needed to handle the activities that arise in this category are **diversified.** In general, they include the ability to:

diversified: varied

priorities: a listing in order of importance

- establish **priorities**
- adhere to schedules and deadlines
- motivate others to adhere to work responsibilities
- use a personal computer
- handle telephone calls
- give attention to several tasks **simultaneously**
- determine time required for completion of tasks
- communicate effectively both orally and in writing
- interact with many types of people at all levels of an organization

simultaneously: at the same time

Workers Who Need These Competencies. General managing and communicating with customer skills are critical for a wide range of employees, from executives to office support staff. Many employees must be good managers of their own time. In addition, they must be skillful in guiding the work of those who report to them. They must be able to establish priorities and adhere to schedules for the completion of tasks. The marketing manager of a packaged goods company commented about his work in these words:

> *"Our staff of ten is hardworking. I set the pace. We have just developed a database to* **capture** *far more information about product sales. We have achieved our goal: the supermarket's bar code reader and our PCs are connected. We have staff members working on various ways to connect with our customers in an* **interactive** *fashion. As I think of our progress, I realize that basic managing skills, including establishing priorities, communicating clearly what has to be done, and keeping aware of what is happening are critical.*

capture: obtain

interactive: mutually active

Opportunities in Office Support Services. Many office support staff provide the services of this category. The most common jobs include administrative assistant, secretary, customer service clerk, receptionist, and general office assistant.

What would you observe if a person was a good manager?

What topics might be discussed at a staff meeting that relate to general management?

Some positions in this category require specialized skills. The position of secretary, for example, may require high-level information processing skills. Receptionists must be at ease in meeting and talking with all types of people, both inside and outside the company. General assistants learn the special responsibilities of the offices in which they work. Then they take the **initiative** in completing tasks in the proper manner. For example, office assistants in travel agencies answer questions about advance payments required for tours, penalties for canceling tours, and documents required for travel to other countries. Office assistants in a governmental office, such as immigration services, understand the rules and procedures for processing an application for admission to the country.

initiative: introducing action

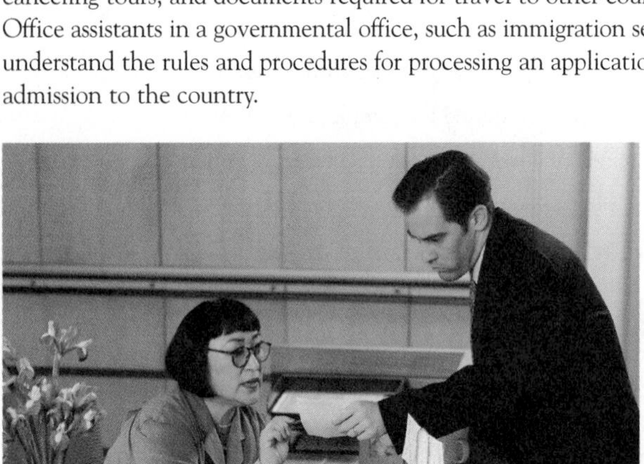

Illustration 2-1:12
A receptionist should give full attention to a visitor.

Higher-level jobs are available to those who perform their initial tasks with success. There are many jobs in companies for those who have the ability to:

- follow through on tasks with little or no supervision
- use **exceptional** oral and written communication skills
- meet deadlines
- organize tasks, be **self-starters**
- evaluate their own performance **objectively**

exceptional: superior

self-starters: those able to work independently

objectively: realistically and free of bias

What attitudes are valuable if you are to be a self-starter?

YOUR FUTURE PROSPECTS

Your education, including your study of business subjects, provides you with a background of value in many occupations. You can enter some jobs after your high school graduation. Others require further education.

Illustration 2-1:13
High school graduates need to plan for their futures.

There continue to be openings for high school graduates. However, increasingly, jobs require skills and knowledge beyond those acquired through high school studies. Many organizations have on-the-job training and formal courses to prepare employees for new tasks or new ways of performing their jobs. Additionally, post-secondary schools that provide specialized training, such as business schools, community colleges, four-year colleges, and universities, have degree programs and continuing education programs. Continuing your education will add to your competencies for jobs that interest you.

Further education can be gained on a part-time basis.

What are the local institutions that provide evening part-time study to people who work full time?

Many companies reimburse employees who study at the college level.

On-the-job experience can help you determine career goals that match your abilities and interests.

Reviewing the Topic

topic 2-1 review

1. In what way has the computer changed the nature of employment in companies?
2. What information is provided in *The Occupational Outlook Handbook?*
3. At what rate is the entire workforce expected to increase by 2005?
4. Explain why job responsibilities are expanding because of technological innovations.
5. Identify skills needed to handle word processing tasks.
6. What kind of workers need data processing competencies?
7. What are the critical skills and understandings needed to effectively perform information management and transmission tasks?
8. What are examples of good managing skills?
9. What qualifications do office support workers in entry-level positions need in order to be promoted?
10. What types of educational opportunities are available after graduation from secondary school?

MAKING DECISIONS

Craig is soon to be a high school senior. He needs very few courses in order to graduate at the end of the forthcoming school year. He has asked you and a couple of other friends to give him your opinions about what he should do about his school program. He has listed on a sheet of paper what he believes are his options. His list has these options, which are not in order of preference:

1. Take only the courses required in the mornings. Relax in the afternoon until my friends are free.
2. Take some extra courses, such as accounting, business law, or office procedures. Since I think I want to work in the business world or become a lawyer after college, these courses might be helpful.

topic 2-1 review

Office Competencies Needed for Employment

60

3. Get a part-time job at one of the local fast-food places.

4. Really learn all about the new computer at home.

What you are to do:

With a group of three or four students, discuss the alternatives Craig has outlined. Select the alternative your group believes is best for Craig. Support your choice with reasons. Write a brief group report and be prepared to share your ideas with the class.

REINFORCING ENGLISH SKILLS

The following description of the nature of work of general office clerks is taken from *The Occupational Outlook Handbook*. There were no spelling errors in the original copy. However, misspelled words have been introduced in this version.

What you are to do:

Read the copy, noting on a separate sheet of paper all misspelled words. If you are not sure about a word, check a dictionary. Key a correct copy of the paragraph.

Nature of Work

The dutties of general office clerks are to varied and divirse for them to be clasified in any specific administrative suport occupation. General office clerks do not perform a single specialized task. They may spend some days filing or keying, others intering data at a computer terminal. They also may operate photocopers, fax machines, or other office euipment; prepare mailings; proofreed copy; and answer telphones and deliver messages.

61

topic 2-1
review

APPLICATION ACTIVITIES

ACTIVITY 1 Jobs in Your Community

In this activity, you will become acquainted with jobs in the community that are among those projected to grow the fastest during the period 1994–2005, as shown in Illustration 2-1:2.

What you are to do:

Each student in class will be assigned to a group of three or four. In your initial meeting with your group, do the following:

1. Make a decision about which occupations you would like to investigate in your own community. Someone in the group should make a list of occupations named. There should be twice as many occupations as there are members of the group.
2. Determine in a group discussion who will investigate each of the occupations listed. You may choose to work in groups of two investigating the same four occupations, or each member of the group may select two occupations to investigate. The group should explore twice as many occupations as there are members of the group.
3. Through group discussion, determine the places in the community where you are most likely to get information about the occupation. (There may be a local association of persons in an occupational field, for example.) Your investigation should result in answers to these questions:
    - In what local organizations do you find workers in this occupation?
    - What are the basic educational qualifications for these workers?
    - What are the key duties of persons in this occupation?
    - To what extent are workers responsible for office tasks?
    - What promotional opportunities exist for persons in this occupation?

62

4. Review the information gathered by all group members and prepare a report that presents the information in table form. (Hint: Vertical headings can be the occupations. Each row will deal with the response to a question.)
5. Participate in a class discussion of job opportunities in the community from among the fastest growing occupations.

ACTIVITY 2 Study an Occupational Field

For this activity, choose an occupational field that interests you. It may be an occupation you explored in Activity 1 above, one listed in Illustration 2-1:3, or any other occupation. Do some research to become acquainted with this field.

What you are to do:

For the occupation you chose, do the following:

1. Use the resources of your school or local community library to get information about your occupation. A reference that is likely to be helpful is *The Occupational Outlook Handbook,* which was described briefly in this chapter. The information you want includes:
   - educational requirements
   - general responsibilities
   - employment opportunities
   - promotional opportunities
2. Interview a person working in this occupational field. In your interview, seek answers to these questions:
   - What are the primary duties of a beginner in this occupation?
   - What do you consider your primary duties?
   - For each primary duty, would you consider education, on-the-job experience, or training the best source of preparation?
   - To what extent do you use a personal computer in completing your job tasks?

63

- What office skills do you find most valuable in your work?
- What advice would you give a student who is thinking of preparing for your field?

3. Key a report that summarizes the information you gathered. The final paragraph of your report should be your current opinion about the appeal of the occupational field as a career for you.

topic 2-1
review

64

Topic 2-2

Developing Office Competencies

When you have completed your study of this topic, you will be able to:

- **describe the goals to which employees are expected to contribute**
- **explain the general expectations for workers**
- **prepare a strategy for developing office competencies**

Organizations in the United States give attention to wise selection of personnel in order to achieve a high level of productivity. In this topic, common goals of organizations to which all personnel are to contribute will be introduced. Then the general expectations for employees will be described. Finally, a strategy for you to consider as you develop office competencies commonly needed at work will be presented.

Contemporary goals of companies as discussed in the business press of local newspapers can be identified for discussion.

Goals Influence Expectations for All Employees

If you were to read a dozen annual reports of **Fortune 500 Companies,** you would find information about company achievements during the past year. You would also read about goals for the future. In some instances, goals are simply expressed as a long-term vision

Fortune 500 Companies: largest companies listed in *Fortune* magazine

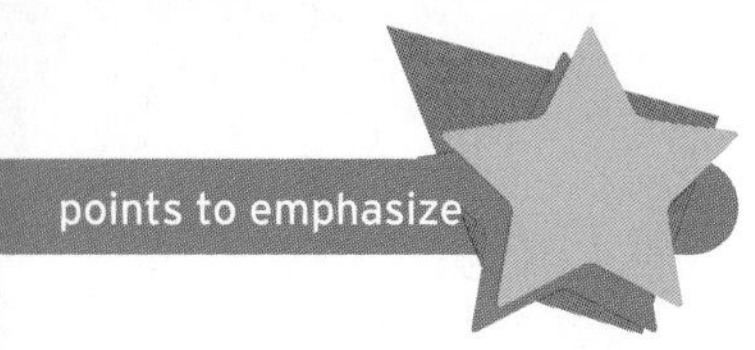

All employees have a stake in an organization's achievement of goals.

Annual reports of companies are of interest to students in learning what CEOs say about goals and plans for reaching goals.

What does TQM mean to you when you shop at a supermarket? at a specialty store?

statement. For example, the head of one software company declared that the company's vision was "to have a computer on every desk and in every home." Others make predictions about level of earnings, new markets, new products, or improved customer service. To continue to make progress, businesses give attention to the matters discussed in this topic. These matters are not **independent** of each other; there is considerable overlap. These topics represent key concerns in today's workplace.

independent: not requiring or relying on others

Illustration 2-2:1
The goals of one company.

Goals for the Next Five Years

- Sharpening our competitive edge
- Forging new strategic partnerships
- Investing in power technologies
- Increasing revenues
- Winning customer loyalty by exceeding customer expectations
- Expanding our base of customers
- Expanding high-growth businesses
- Achieving growth in new parts of our industry
- Adding spectacular product options

TOTAL QUALITY MANAGEMENT

A concept that has high **visibility** in business is total quality management, commonly referred to as TQM. TQM means establishing and maintaining high standards in how work is done and in the output of goods and services.

visibility: recognition

All personnel, from the president to staff in the mailroom, are asked to view their responsibilities with awareness of TQM. Chief executive officers talk about "shifting from **apathy** to enthusiasm and energy" throughout the organization. One CEO discussed what was happening in these words:

apathy: lack of interest or attention

> *In factory by factory, higher manufacturing yields more on-time shipments, new orders, fewer workplace accidents, reduced pollution... in the office, there is consideration and courtesy reflected in encounters among colleagues and outsiders.*

The thrust of TQM is that it is everyone's business. Quality standards apply throughout the company. For example, in one company, all office support workers were asked to keep track of the errors in their work. Two common errors were omitting an attachment with a letter and failing to answer questions of callers. After recording such errors, each employee was to review them. The next step was to establish a new way of working so the error would not recur. One employee's comment in regard to the two types of errors noted above was:

> *It is amazing how you can maintain quality standards without feeling unreasonable pressure. I realized, for example, that I was not as careful as I should be in checking that attachments accompany letters and memoranda. The care required takes a few seconds, but saves many minutes. You can imagine that a memorandum without the attachment is worthless. The recipient had to call me. Then I had to find the copy and forward it. We can't measure the inefficiency caused by my carelessness. Keeping track of questions I can't answer has been an eye-opener. Some questions were outside our department and outside my range of responsibility. Many, though, were proper for someone in my position. I began to learn as I worked so I understood what we do. I am so much happier than I was earlier. I confess that TQM has made my job more interesting and me far more competent.*

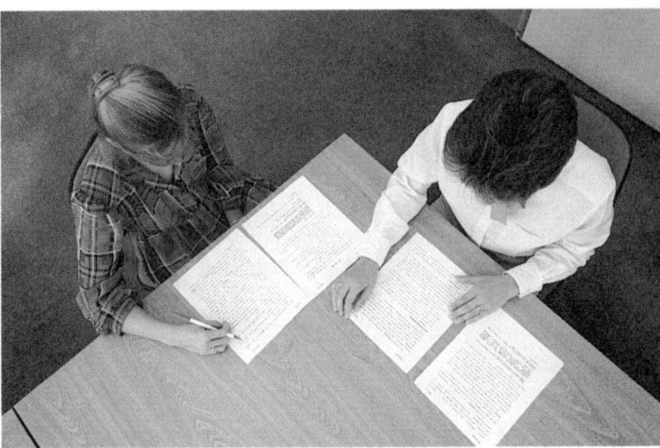

Illustration 2-2:2
How does proofreading by two employees contribute to total quality standards?

Does TQM have any relevance for you as students?

for discussion

What is likely to be the attitude of an employee who believes that maintaining quality standards is not stressful?

What do you think of this employee's response to failures?

In some companies, there is a director of corporate quality. This executive works with groups of employees to find out what will improve quality performance. Many companies have developed slogans such as "Quality is everybody's business" or "We want to be **premier** in all we do" to highlight their quality goal.

premier: of first quality

In what ways is the concept of continuous improvement related to TQM?

CONTINUOUS IMPROVEMENT

As noted earlier, there is overlap among the concerns that are getting attention in today's organizations. Such is the case between TQM and continuous improvement. Being alert at all times to ways of working more productively is the essence of continuous improvement. All employees are encouraged to participate in continuous improvement efforts.

Continuous improvement begins with an attitude of critically assessing what is done and how it is being done. Improvements are often possible. In many instances, tasks are done just as they have always been done. No one gives any thought to new ways of doing the tasks. Companies are finding many inefficient policies and procedures in many parts of the organization.

Give illustrations of how curiosity is important in continuous improvement.

The attitude reflected in the question "Could this be done in a better way?" helps workers realize new ways may be promising. One office assistant found a strategy that pleases her.

> *I must telephone many people to get specific information. Oh, so frequently the person I needed was out and I would leave a message, which stated: "Please call Sally at . . . ." Often when the person called back I was out. I would find a message on my voice mail. When I thought about how I handled such calls, I thought: Why not leave a message asking for the information I need? Then the caller could leave an answer at my voice mail if I were away from my desk. This is a time-saving way of handling my calls. When I get to my office after lunch or after a meeting, I now find answers to my questions. There is no need for a follow-up call.*

In what way is the attitude of "let me do just what is needed to get by" contrary to continuous improvement?

Because of new technology, companies are finding that many aspects of their work require changes. Many employees find what they do challenging as they think **creatively** about improvements.

creatively: with an open, exploring attitude

Can we apply continuous improvement to the way we are studying this subject?

CUSTOMER SATISFACTION

"We are here to serve customers" is a message that the leadership in all kinds of organizations is communicating to employees. Thinking through what you do in relation to what it will mean to customers is a key focus in many organizations. Many people believe that attention to customers is a key to achieving long-term success.

Companies undertake surveys to determine if they are consistently delivering the value demanded by customers. They study the results of such surveys and then attempt to eliminate the **barriers** to customer satisfaction.

barriers:
obstacles to the accomplishment of some goal

What are ways you have observed that a company is responding to their responsibility to serve customers?

ABC CUSTOMER SATISFACTION SURVEY

Please consider only our handling of your most recent problem or complaint when answering the following questions.

1. How long did it take from the time you FIRST contacted us with your most recent problem or complaint until FINAL action was taken to resolve your problem or complaint? **(CHECK ONE.)**
   _____ 1–3 days
   _____ 4–7 days
   _____ 8–14 days
   _____ 15 days–less than one month
   _____ more than one month
2. How satisfied are you with the LAST WRITTEN RESPONSE you received from us in each of the following areas? (Circle one number between 1 and 10 for each item or X if it doesn't apply.)
   NOTE: 1 means extremely dissatisfied; 10 means extremely satisfied.

Answered your questions and addressed your concerns in a simple, straightforward way	1 2 3 4 5 6 7 8 9 10 X
Treated you as a valued customer.	1 2 3 4 5 6 7 8 9 10 X
Its believability/honesty	1 2 3 4 5 6 7 8 9 10 X
Showed that the company is looking out for your best interests	1 2 3 4 5 6 7 8 9 10 X
Provided a clear explanation of why the problem occurred	1 2 3 4 5 6 7 8 9 10 X
Clearly described what follow-up action, if any, you could expect	1 2 3 4 5 6 7 8 9 10 X

Illustration 2-2:3
Questions in a survey sent to customers.

Have you encountered office personnel that you feel do not have the proper attitude toward customers?

The staff of an organization is involved in a variety of ways in meeting the goal of customer satisfaction. One beginning worker, for example, described his experiences in these words:

fluent: flowing smoothly or easily

> *I serve as an assistant in our Customer Hotline office, which is open seven days a week, 24 hours a day. Among the team are members* **fluent** *in English, Spanish, French, Chinese, and Japanese. Together, they are able to provide customers around the world with information about our products. They can quickly put a customer in touch with a technical person, if additional assistance is needed.*

Companies think about what their present and prospective customers will want in the future. One CEO commented that . . "we build lasting relationships by understanding and serving our customers' needs. We serve them better the second time than we did the first time."

Why does a company strive to have honest employees?

ETHICAL STANDARDS

Ethical standards require honesty, fairness, and justice in all business dealings. These qualities provide the foundation of trust. Leaders of organizations are responsible for making clear their attitude toward standards of ethical behavior. Companies strive to be **perceived** as trustworthy by both their own employees, their customers, and others with whom they interact.

perceived: viewed, thought of

Companies have developed standards of conduct for their employees, called codes of ethics or codes of conduct. Such codes are communicated to all workers. Companies also have procedures for handling violations of ethical standards.

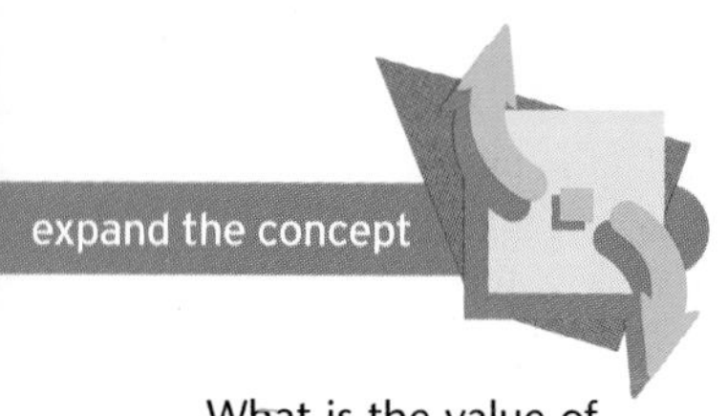

What is the value of being "perceived as trustworthy"?

Employees are generally informed about the code of ethics when they first join the organization. From time to time, employees are called together for discussion of the code of conduct. Attention is given to what the code means in relation to specific behavior and actions taken by employees in their work.

> *All staff involved with purchasing—from directors to office staff—attended a session dealing with a new conflict of interest statement. This staff interacts with many vendors who are eager to sell their products. The new statement makes clear that no employee is to accept gifts of any value, including trips to attractive vacation spots, from any vendor.*

Statement of Policy Internal Management

All employees are expected to be truthful in regard to all matters relating to operational or financial information. No employee shall knowingly furnish false or misleading operational or financial information to anyone in the Company, to its outside auditors, or to any person dealing with with Company.

Each employee is to be responsible in assuring that (a) all company assets are safeguarded against loss from unauthorized use or disposition; (b) the Company's financial reports and records are reliable and reflect transactions completed for the Company, and (c) a climate of adherence to internal management controls is maintained throughout the Company.

Illustration 2-2:4

A page from a company's code of ethics.

Why is it important for new employees to understand the company's code of ethics?

RESPONSIBLE TEAMWORK

Some people work alone at the company offices or at home. However, most workers interact with others to some extent. Frequently, employees must work cooperatively to complete a task. This teamwork may not be confined to a single department.

Customer collections were a problem in a relatively small shoe manufacturing company. The controller realized that those involved worked in order entry, shipping, and billing. A team composed of several members of these departments was assigned the task of reviewing the policies and procedures involved. Through teamwork, the group recommended a new policy and related procedures. Soon thereafter, the problem was resolved to everyone's satisfaction.

Teamwork demands a high degree of responsibility. Fairness requires that each member contributes appropriately.

GLOBAL OUTREACH

Companies throughout the United States have extended the marketplace in which they provide their goods and services. The demands for U. S. products and services throughout the world are appealing to United States businesses. The shift from a domestic company to a global company has changed the nature and type of activity in companies.

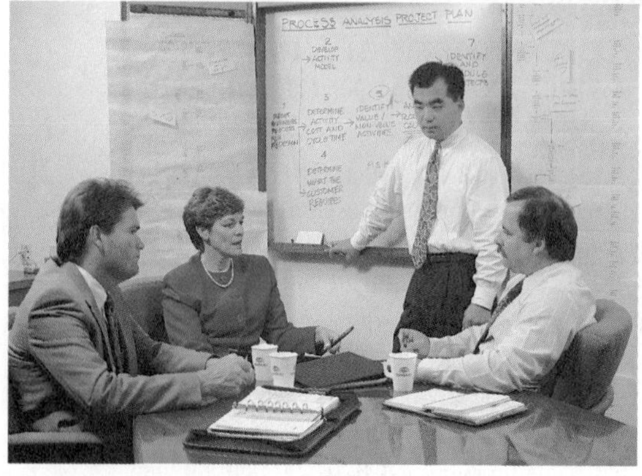

Illustration 2-2:5
A team reviews a plan for a new project.

Executives must travel beyond the United States to other countries. Company officials who live in other countries visit headquarters in the United States. Communications, too, must be international. All personnel must be sensitive to variations in culture as they communicate with people of other nations. Employees must be acquainted with varying time zones, sources for information about travel, accommodations, and facilities in other countries.

In what ways does modern technology encourage global business?

ATTENTION TO DIVERSITY

Diversity, in the context of organizations, means a workforce that has personnel from a wide range of **ethnic** and cultural backgrounds. For example, one company president stated:

ethnic: related to races and cultural characteristics of people

> *Our employees are diverse at all levels of our organization. We demand that our people respect diversity. We are moving closer to a truly global economy. We need people with different backgrounds and new perspectives to help us meet the needs of our diverse customers. Diversity among our employees will inspire improved approaches to our business.*

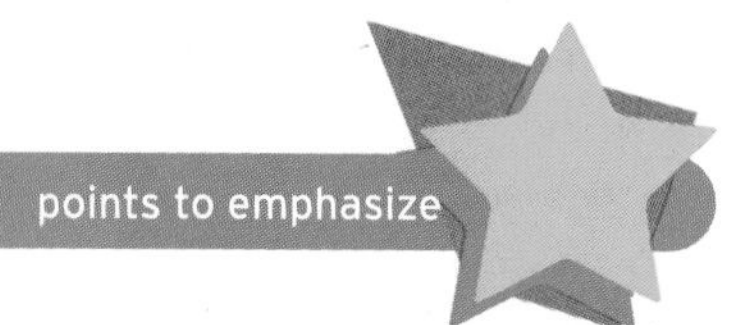

In the United States, there is a strong belief that all persons, regardless of gender, race, religion, or ethnic background, should have equal opportunities for employment commensurate with their job-related qualifications.

Companies believe that they must have the best talent available among their personnel. They cannot limit their search to a few sources. To be sure that they get the best talent, they identify potential employees from diverse population groups. In some companies, there is a diversity coordinator who collects data about the company's hiring and promotion policies. This person also assesses the progress of the company in achieving its diversity goals, and may plan diversity training programs and advise management about the next steps in the company's program.

> *Meg works in the human resources department where diversity is getting attention. She is one of the staff members planning diversity seminars. She was especially interested in comments from the managers who participated in the seminars. They described how their evaluations of employees are now influenced by what was learned in the seminar. Her company has an awards program honoring individuals who demonstrate a* **dedication** *to the principles of diversity in their work.*

dedication: giving earnest attention to some purpose

What kinds of attitudes about people may lead to unfair evaluation of ability and talent?

General Expectations for Employees

A company expects the same basic work qualities in all employees. However, the way these qualities are manifested will vary depending on the nature of the employee's position. Qualities most highly regarded are discussed in the following paragraphs.

RELIABILITY

Getting work done according to instructions and on schedule are important for the proper functioning of an organization. Companies

Illustration 2-2:6
Imagine what these managers from different countries are discussing.

do not have supervisors to watch closely what a worker does. One director of administrative services in a large bank stated:

> *Employees who have to be watched every minute in order to keep them doing what they should do are worthless in our bank. We must have reliable employees. One of the most common reasons for dismissal in our bank is unreliability. For example, one new employee failed to be at the office at 8:00 on the mornings she was scheduled to open the office, so the office was unattended. She didn't call to explain her lateness; she just arrived two hours later. This pattern persisted for a month. At that point, we had to dismiss her. We cannot function with such indifference to schedules.*

What motivates a reliable person to meet the requirements of a job without minute-by-minute supervision?

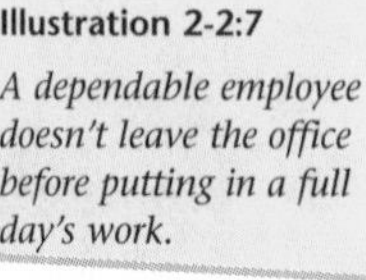

Illustration 2-2:7

A dependable employee doesn't leave the office before putting in a full day's work.

Why do you think a measurement such as number of pages keyed a day may not be a good basis for determining the productivity of a word processor?

PRODUCTIVITY

Organizations are cost conscious, meaning that they are aware of how they are spending their funds. Personnel payroll is one of the major expenses in many organizations. Employers expect employees to produce a reasonable amount of work and contribute toward achieving company goals. Often it is not possible to have specific, measurable standards for a day's work. Supervisors and managers have some level of output that they believe is reasonable for an employee. Following a schedule that assures you will complete the amount of work expected of you during a day is important.

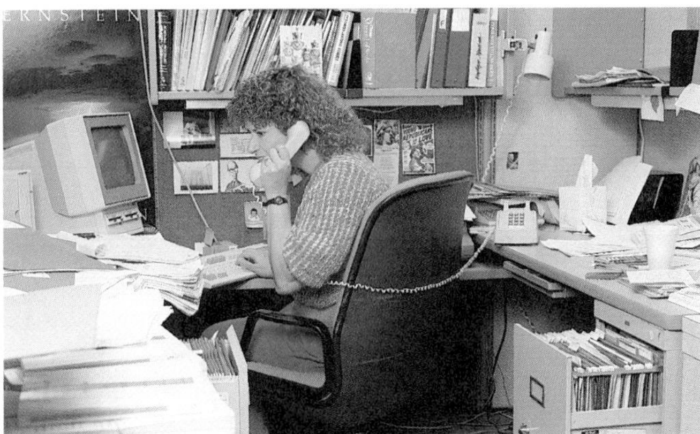

Illustration 2-2:8

A cluttered desk limits the productivity of an office worker.

Valuable workers are those who are aware of what they are accomplishing each day. They are able to evaluate their own work and make changes as needed. Some managers discuss productivity with their workers in **informal** ways from time to time. Other managers expect workers to decide on their own what changes are needed to improve productivity.

informal:
without a predetermined, fixed plan

Managers and executives identify the following barriers to high productivity among employees:

- *talking with friends by telephone*
- *chatting with coworkers for long periods of time*
- *failing to maintain an organized workstation*
- *failing to determine priorities*
- *moving from task to task before any one is completed*

COOPERATIVENESS

Office workers seldom work without interaction with others. Information must be shared, and tasks often require more than a single worker. Being cooperative is a critical quality for most employees. Most office workers have job descriptions, but seldom do such descriptions fully describe the nature of cooperation that is expected of an employee.

How would you determine if you had done sufficient work during the day to be considered a good employee?

Illustration 2-2:9

Is chatting on the phone with a friend proper during the workday?

On what basis might an employee determine whether or not to be cooperative?

Employees who believe they need to do only what is outlined in their job descriptions are not effective workers.

Employees must be prepared to modify what was specified as their responsibilities as circumstances change. One manager described an employee who did not respond cooperatively in these words:

> *As long as Betty was not interrupted, she was a good worker. However, when I asked her to spend the next day at a conference center at midtown, she said she didn't understand that she would have to work in another location. She said she was hired to work in the office. Even though nothing explicit was stated about where she would work, she was right in assuming that she would be located at headquarters. However, from her own observations, she should have realized that employees traveled out of town and many workers did work at conference sites. After this encounter, I became more aware of Betty's attitude, which was reflected in small ways as she worked with others. At the end of the year, Betty's performance was assessed. Her level of cooperativeness was listed as an area for improvement. She was not added to the list of persons to be considered for promotion.*

INDEPENDENCE IN LEARNING

As you undoubtedly realize, all you need to know to be an employee—in any field—will not be learned while you are a student. One of the characteristics of modern life is that learning must be a lifelong activity. Professional workers, such as lawyers, doctors, and accountants, for example, must have continuing education experiences each year in order to maintain their professional credentials. While some continuing education can be in formal programs, much of it is self-directed. Workers are in an environment where they can learn much from what they do and what they observe. Furthermore, organizations have resources such as databases and libraries that are available to employees.

Why is it important that each person be an independent learner?

> *Jackie, after three weeks in her position at an advertising agency, commented: "I was happy I knew the basic word processing program that is on my computer. However, I soon realized that I should know the advanced features. I see I can complete assignments more efficiently. So, last week I began a plan to learn the advanced features. All the materials I need are available. Our offices are open late every night. So, I just stay after work. I am happy with what I have been able to learn on my own.*

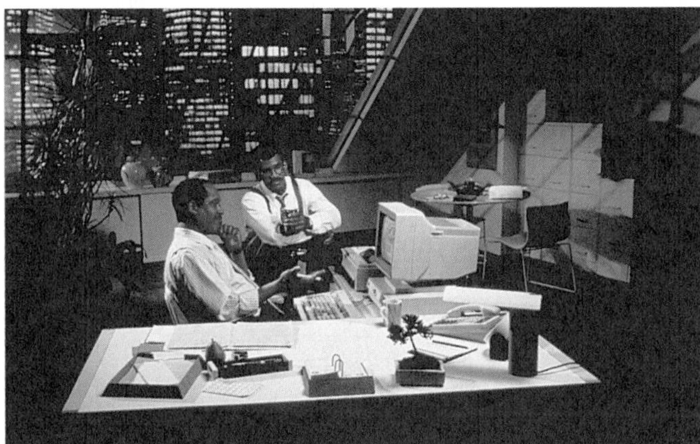

Illustration 2-2:10
These office workers are studying after the end of the workday.

Strategy for Developing Office Competencies

You are a student. What you have experienced as a student is of great value to whatever you choose as your career. You are evaluated when you submit assignments, complete quizzes, and take examinations. You

Why is it worthwhile to develop office competencies if you are not going to be an office worker, but will likely be a sales representative, a teacher, a firefighter, a lawyer, or an automobile mechanic?

have some idea of what you are able to do, what you would like to learn, and, possibly, how you can learn.

You will develop many competencies as you study and participate in the activities provided in this textbook. You can develop general and specific competencies for becoming an effective worker. These competencies will be valuable in a wide variety of jobs and careers.

TAKE A LOOK AT YOUR KEY COMPETENCIES

What skills and understandings do you have today that would be of value to an employer? You may have work experience, either paid or volunteer. This gives you an introduction to what work is like. Think about what those experiences required and the extent to which you were comfortable in doing the work.

Your education has been focused on developing basic competencies that are critical for gaining the most value from your life. Those basics included reading, writing, arithmetic, speaking, and listening. You have also studied math, literature, history, social studies, physical sciences, languages, and other subjects. Think of your educational experience. Identify your key competencies that you believe will have value at work. Competencies commonly developed in elementary and secondary school are valuable competencies for the office. Note those listed in Illustration 2-2:11.

Illustration 2-2:11
Which of these competencies do you think you can improve during this course?

COMPETENCIES FOR THE OFFICE

- Formatting memorandums, letters, reports
- Keeping my workstation clear of clutter
- Keyboarding
- Listening and following instructions
- Maintaining records in good order
- Managing time wisely
- Meeting all deadlines
- Organizing tasks in order of dates due
- Proofreading
- Skill in learning software programs
- Speaking appropriately by telephone
- Using references such as a dictionary
- Writing memos and letters in good form
- Working with others effectively

As she thought about her school years, Geri realized that from her middle school years, she has tried to remember her teachers' insistence on orderliness and neatness in every task done in class or at home for submission to the teacher. She realized that she now has a highly developed skill in organizing what is to be done, keeping track of her work, and completing a task in an orderly manner.

ASSESS YOUR COMPETENCIES

You have undoubtedly heard that it is important to be honest with yourself. Honest appraisal of your own competencies will be a rewarding task. Don't be afraid to acknowledge the truth, even if it is rather harsh, about how well you did a particular task.

SET GOALS FOR MAKING PROGRESS

What do you want to accomplish this year? What skills do you want to improve? What new skills do you want to learn? Only you can make such plans. Only you can make a commitment to seriously follow the plan you devise. Be realistic in your plan. Shape it in relation to what you truly wish for yourself at this point in your life. Listen to what others might suggest for you. Understand, though, that in the end you must feel comfortable with your goals.

Why is it sometimes difficult to candidly evaluate your own progress?

Reviewing the Topic

topic 2-2 review

1. What information are you likely to find in a company's annual report?
2. What does a company hope to achieve with a total quality management program?
3. Who is expected to participate in a program for continuous improvement?
4. Why do companies value customer satisfaction?
5. To what do ethical standards relate?
6. Why is teamwork considered important in today's world of work?
7. What changes are likely to made in a company that shifts from being a domestic company to being a global one?
8. Why is a company interested in diversity?
9. Describe what you might observe to conclude that a worker is reliable.
10. "If it isn't in my job description, I will not do it." What does this comment imply about cooperativeness?

PARTICIPATING IN A TEAM PROJECT

Tanya, a manager in an advertising agency, called a meeting for three members of the staff, Jill, Dave, and Donna. Tanya explained that she had just received a telephone call about an exciting offer to submit a proposal for a new account. Tanya told them the project will require an intensive period of work, since a proposal must be submitted within two weeks.

The project is complex. Tanya believes, though, that the three of them can do the task successfully. They will be given some assistance from the departmental secretary. They must research the types of advertising campaigns used in the industry. They must also gain information about what the company seeking proposals has as its goals and what its present

topic 2-2 review

Developing Office Competencies

80

image is in the marketplace. After they have gathered the information, the three are to develop what they believe are promising campaigns. Tanya told them that they can determine among themselves how to subdivide the tasks to be done.

When Jill, Dave, and Donna met immediately after leaving the supervisor's desk, Jill said: "Look, I feel rather tired and I just don't want to immediately begin intensive work. Could I just beg off the research? Then I'll be happy to help you develop some plans for a campaign. I think I'm better in the creative part of such a project. I know that there will have to be many overtime hours during this first week of work. I just do not want to change my plans."

What you are to do:

1. In groups of three or four students, discuss what you would say to Jill if you were Dave or Donna.
2. Prepare notes on your response for use for a class discussion.

REINFORCING MATH SKILLS

As a first step for considering what next year's budget should be for the accounts payable department, you have been asked to do some calculations based on last year's expenditures. Those expenditures were:

- *Salaries (one supervisor and four clerks)* $133,000
- *Supplies* 4,000
- *Repairs and Maintenance* 5,000
- *Depreciation* 3,000
- *Telephone* 3,500

A study was done of how the work of the department could be improved and costs reduced. The conclusion was that the office could function with a supervisor and two clerks, rather than four clerks. State-of-the-art equipment was purchased to facilitate the work of the remaining staff. (This new equipment will increase the depreciation charge.) The proposed budget under the cost-cutting plan is:

- *Salaries* $96,000
- *Supplies* 3,800

81

- *Repairs and Maintenance* 2,500
- *Depreciation* 6,000
- *Telephone* 3,900

What you are to do:

1. Calculate the total expenditures for the department using last year's figures.
2. Using last year's figures, calculate the percentage of total expenses each of the following represents:
   - salaries
   - supplies
   - repairs and maintenance
   - depreciation
   - telephone
3. Using last year's figures, calculate the departmental cost per invoice processed if there were 144,500 invoices handled during the year.
4. Determine the difference in total costs between last year's figures and what is being considered as a cost-cutting effort.
5. Calculate the percentage decrease in costs if the cost-cutting is realized using the proposed budget.

topic 2-2 review

APPLICATION ACTIVITIES

ACTIVITY 1 Checklist for Evaluating Team Projects

For this activity, work in a group of three or four to develop a checklist for evaluating team project participation.

What you are to do:

1. Prepare a list of factors to be included on an evaluation checklist. For example, one factor might be:

   Completed work on time.

2. Determine what you believe is an appropriate basis for rating how well a student meets the established expectations. (Hint: Should there be A, B, C grading? or 1, 2, 3, 4, 5? or Excellent, Good, Poor?

82

3. Prepare a final copy of the checklist with the rating factors and rating scale for the basis of class discussion.

ACTIVITY 2 Expectations of Employers

Become acquainted with workers' opinions regarding basic expectations employers have for employees.

What you are to do:

1. Either alone or with one other student, interview someone about his or her work. The purpose of the interview is to learn opinions about the importance of basic expectations in specific situations. Collect the following information:
   - Name and current position of the interviewee
   - The interviewee's opinion of how important each of the following qualities is to his/her employer.

     Reliability

     Productivity

     Cooperativeness

     Independence in learning

     Ask the interviewee to respond using these evaluation ratings:

     Very Important, Somewhat Important,
     Of Limited Importance, Of Little or No Importance
   - A specific example used in making a judgment about the importance of each of the qualities listed above
2. Key a report of your findings.
3. Discuss findings in class, noting similarities and differences in responses.

83

Chapter Summary

Chapter 2 gave you an overview of the workforce as provided by the United States Department of Labor in *The Occupational Outlook Handbook*. You also learned about four key categories of office competencies needed by many workers in today's workforce, employer expectations, and a strategy for developing office competencies.

Consider the points listed below as you reinforce your understanding of the topics in this chapter:

- The information provided by the United States Department of Labor is useful in learning about occupations. Projections for workers are given through the year 2005.
- While there will continue to be job opportunities in office occupations, the rate of increase is lower than that for other occupational groups.
- In many occupations, workers are expected to have office competencies. Therefore, your study of this subject is valuable for your future, regardless of your career interests.
- Office competencies are considered in four categories: word processing, data processing, information management and transmission, and general managing and communicating with customers.
- Goals of companies influence their expectations for all employees.
- Organizations focus attention on concerns including total quality management, continuous improvement, customer satisfaction, ethical standards, responsible teamwork, global outreach, and diversity.
- Qualities considered important for employees are reliability, productivity, cooperativeness, and independence in learning.
- Planning a strategy for developing office competencies will be valuable to you no matter what you choose for your life's work.

chapter 2 summary

KEY CONCEPTS AND TERMS

continuous improvement
cooperativeness
customer satisfaction
data processing
diversified job
diversity
ethical standards
general managing and communicating with customers
global outreach
goal
independence in learning
information management and transmission
occupational outlook
productivity
projected growth of labor force
reliability
replacement workers
responsible teamwork
total quality management (TQM)
word processing

INTEGRATED CHAPTER ACTIVITY

ACTIVITY Employer Expectations and Class Activities

In this activity, you will explore the relevance of employer expectations for developing office competencies to your classroom activities. You will be assigned to a group to study one of the following skill categories:

- word processing
- data processing
- information management and transmission
- general managing and communicating with customers

As a member of your group, consider your skill category in relation to each of the following concepts:

- total quality management (TQM)
- continuous improvement
- ethical standards
- responsible teamwork and cooperativeness

85

Assume that the goal of all students in your class is to achieve high skill levels in all four areas of office competencies. The outcome of all the groups will be some specific suggestions for incorporating employer expectations in your individual and class activities.

What you are to do:

1. Review the basic competencies that are included in the textbook for your assigned skill category.
2. Determine who will be responsible for each basic competency expectation.
3. For the expectation(s) assigned to you, to do the following:
   - Search a database in your school or community library using as a key word(s) the expectation assigned to you. Identify two or three references that seem related to your interest. Read the references identified.
   - Consider what you have learned about the skill category and the concepts listed.
   - Prepare a report that includes what you have learned. Give suggestions for incorporating employer expectations and the related concepts listed during your class activities.
4. Discuss your suggestions with your group. Together, prepare the list of suggestions in chart form.
5. Make a group presentation of your combined suggestions to another group or the entire class.
6. Participate in a group to evaluate another group's listing and make suggestions for revisions.
7. Participate in your original group to consider the comments made in the reviewing stage. Make changes to your list of suggestions as appropriate based on the class or group review. Prepare a final listing for posting on the classroom bulletin board.

86

Garth Howells
Vice President of Finance

Getting Acquainted with the World of Work

A Code of Ethics Violation—What Should Be Done?

Dear Mr. Howells

I had lunch with a friend who works in a large bank here in Chicago. My friend was upset about what had happened to her that morning. A manager in her department asked her to sign a travel report indicating that she had incurred expenses during a business trip to Paris. She only had to sign the form; she did not have to fill in the figures. Her manager had done that for her. My friend had not been to Paris. It was the manager's girlfriend who had accompanied him. My friend said to me: "I was absolutely stunned at what I was asked to do; and my mind just froze. I just signed. I said nothing. He thanked me and made no further comment. Now, I don't know where to turn. I lied. Do I follow the procedures published about how to report violations?"

I could not be helpful since I am a relatively new employee myself. I am thinking of my friend, though. There is a code of ethics in our company. Could you help me understand what a person should do in a situation such as my friend faces?

Olga in Chicago

Dear Olga

I can imagine how your friend feels and how you feel, too. Maintaining high ethical standards in organizations is difficult. Many companies issue a code of ethics. For a code to be effective, there must be procedures for considering violations. In many companies, there is a vice president responsible for seeing that the code functions effectively. I have such a position in our company. I monitor our code of ethics. We have established a procedure that assures total confidentiality to any worker who reports a violation. I would suggest that your friend carefully read the code of ethics for her company. Then she should schedule a meeting with her manager. She should tell the manager that she did not think through what he asked her to do. She signed the form, now she realizes, too quickly. She would like to undo what she did. She knows that a travel expense form should be signed by the person who actually traveled for the company and is entitled to reimbursement. If the manager responds that it is too late to make a change, your friend should tell the manager she will report the violation.

Olga, you will want to establish firmly in your mind what ethical behavior is as implied in your company's code of ethics. Then you are not likely to respond as your friend did. An employee tends to think a manager's request is to be honored. However, you must maintain your independent thinking, especially where ethics are concerned.

Garth Howells

Vice President of Finance

87

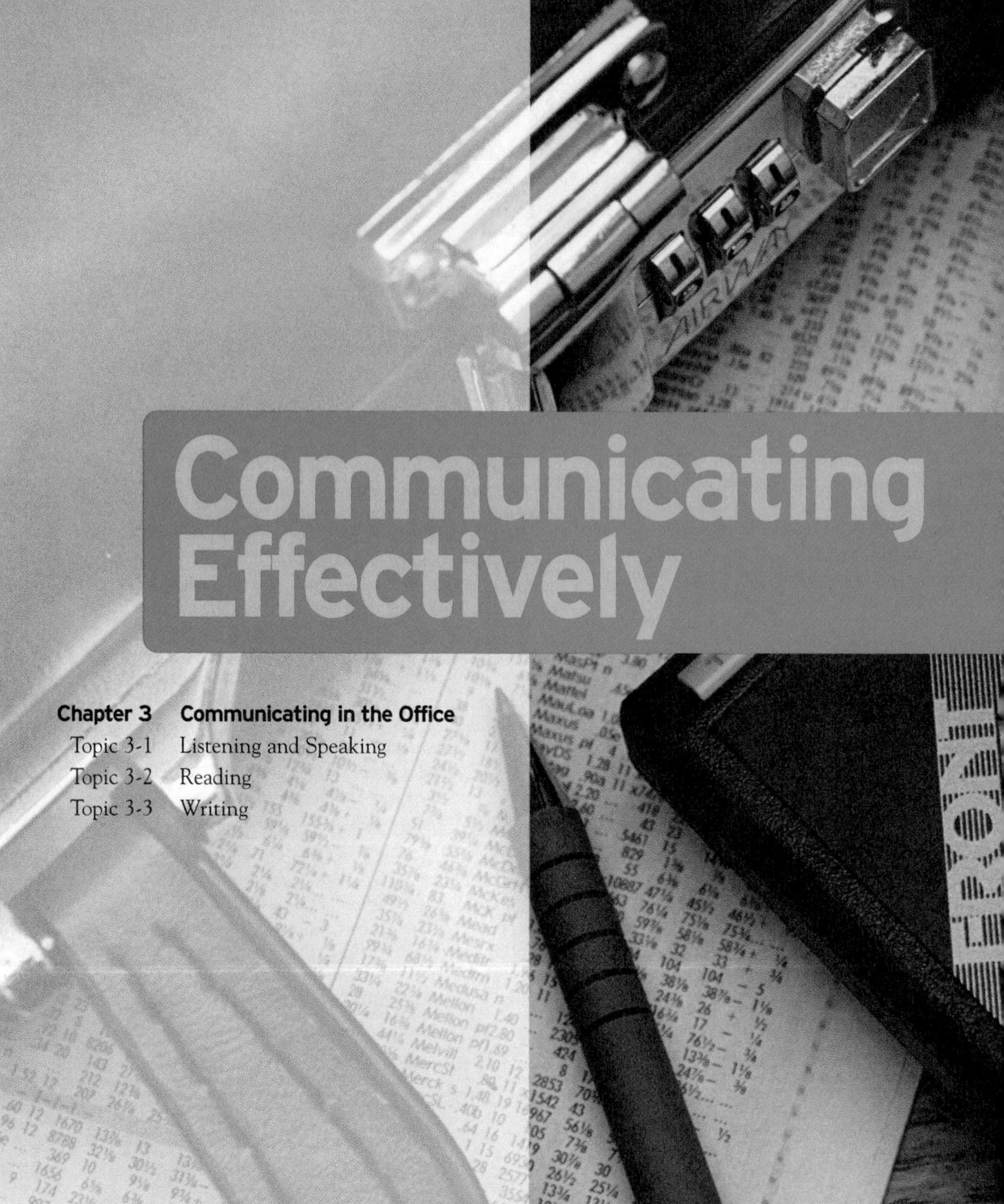

Communicating Effectively

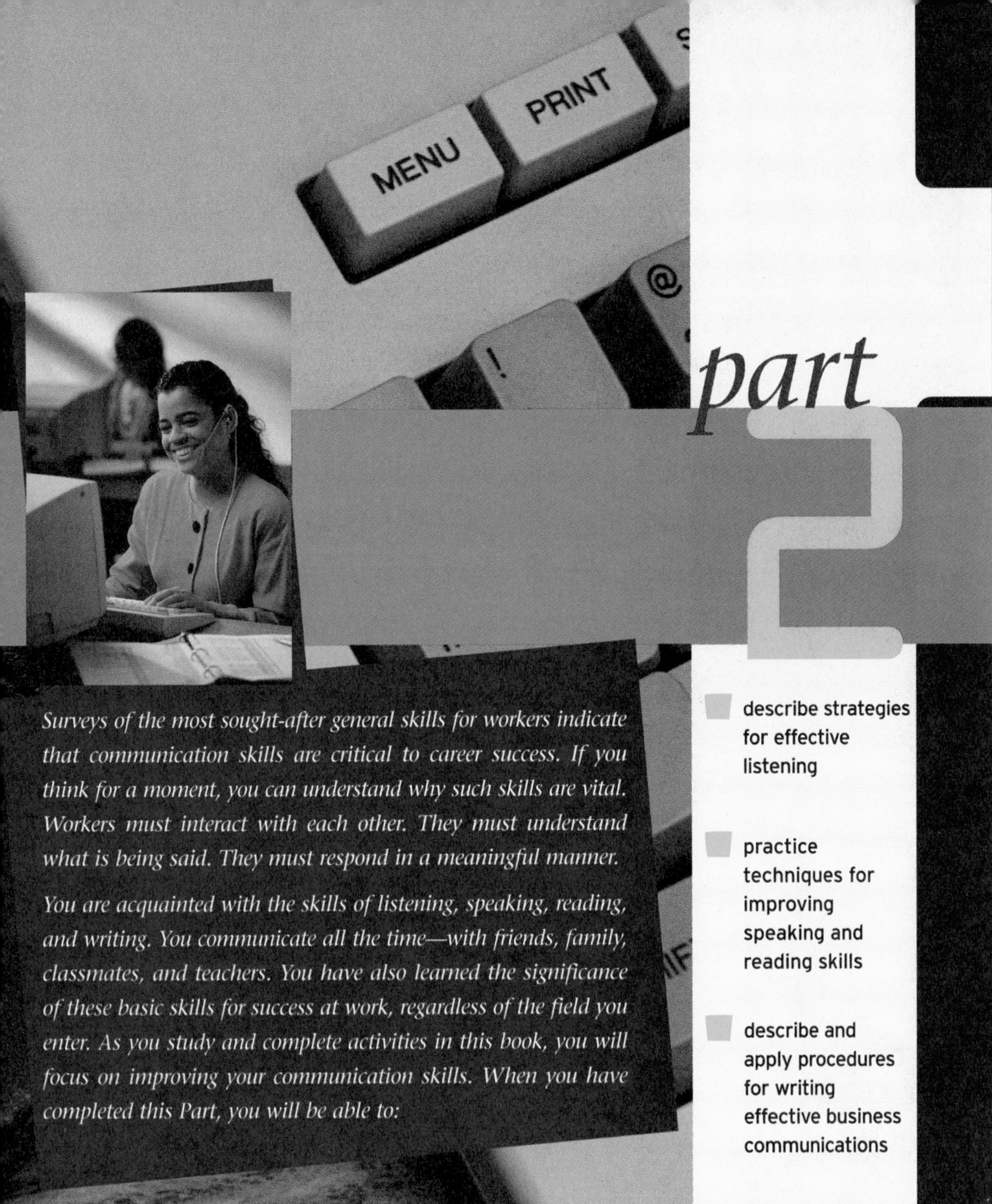

part 2

Surveys of the most sought-after general skills for workers indicate that communication skills are critical to career success. If you think for a moment, you can understand why such skills are vital. Workers must interact with each other. They must understand what is being said. They must respond in a meaningful manner.

You are acquainted with the skills of listening, speaking, reading, and writing. You communicate all the time—with friends, family, classmates, and teachers. You have also learned the significance of these basic skills for success at work, regardless of the field you enter. As you study and complete activities in this book, you will focus on improving your communication skills. When you have completed this Part, you will be able to:

- describe strategies for effective listening
- practice techniques for improving speaking and reading skills
- describe and apply procedures for writing effective business communications

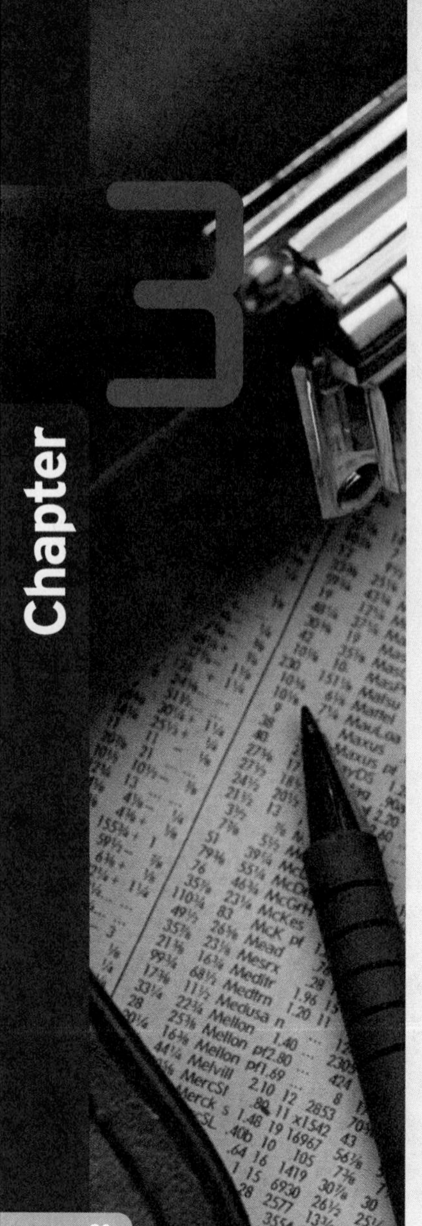

Communicating in the Office

This chapter focuses on communication skills and their importance to your success at work. Considering the skills in this context will help you clearly understand appropriate applications of each skill to key office tasks and give you an opportunity to improve your basic skills. Make a candid assessment of your communication skills as you begin your study of the topics in this chapter. Then target what you would like to improve. As you complete related tasks, focus on the extent to which you are actually adding to your skill.

Consider what one student who emigrated from the Ukraine at the age of 14 accomplished. During her senior year, her teacher complimented her on her communication skills. She responded:

> *Thank you, but I must say I struggled with your language. Yes, I had studied English beginning in grade 5, but our teachers were not native speakers of English. In the United States, I saw quickly that reading, speaking, and listening to English required far more skills than I had. I sought out new American friends so I would be forced to improve my English. I listened to the radio. I recorded myself speaking. I listened to myself, which was not an easy thing to do. . . .*

You, too, can make remarkable improvements as you strive to develop skill in listening, speaking, reading, and writing.

Chapter 3

Topic 3-1

Listening and Speaking

When you have completed your study of this topic, you will be able to:

- **describe the importance of listening**
- **explain techniques that aid in active listening**
- **describe what an effective speaker achieves**
- **explain the factors considered in speaking**

Regardless of the career you choose, you will want to be confident about your listening and speaking skills. These oral communication skills are basic to all aspects of your responsibilities.

The Importance of Listening

Imagine you are walking along a hall in a high-rise office building downtown. You notice that many conversations are underway. You cannot hear what is being said because voices are **modulated** so that only persons nearby hear the actual words. You would undoubtedly observe persons talking by telephone and others in conference with one or more other persons. In every instance, there are listeners. Listeners are important to the progress of activity in any organization.

modulated: toned down

getting started

Students have studied communications skills since they entered school. They bring to a revisiting of the topic a wide range of attitudes and levels of competencies. The persistent criticism of inadequacies in communications in the work environment justifies continued attention. Alerting students to becoming aware of effective communications skills will reinforce what you are endeavoring to include in the study of this subject.

You may choose to assess students' abilities in the basic skills through brief exercises. For example, you may use a listening exercise related to the next week's assignment. Ask students to listen to the information. Then ask them to write down the essential points of what you presented. Brief reading and writing exercises can be designed based on the content of the sections.

Businesses are increasingly operating in the global community where communication is difficult.

Topic 3-1

How do you evaluate a person who is speaking loudly to another person in the corridor at school or in a business office?

How does listening aid productivity?

Fellow workers expect to have the attention of others when matters must be discussed, instructions understood, or decisions made.

Illustration 3-1:1
Effective listening skills are vital to every office worker.

There are countless times when you listen to others. When you listen effectively, you will be able to:

- follow through on oral instructions correctly
- consider the additional information as you continue your work and make decisions
- use time productively

Helena, an assistant manager, wasn't sure what the manager told her about a task she was about to begin. She had not taken notes. When she got back to her desk, she realized she did not understand when the information was needed from the Hong Kong and Tokyo offices. Did she have enough time to send messages via e-mail or should she call and talk with them directly? She decided that she would not bother the manager, but would just send e-mail messages and trust that the information would be forwarded in time for the manager's schedule. Unfortunately, the manager called early the next morning wanting the information. Can you imagine what happened in the conversation at this point?

Later, as Helena thought about this incident, she realized what had happened. She realized her mind was elsewhere when the manager turned to her after a telephone call, which had interrupted their discussion. However, Helena's mind did not return to the matter at hand; she continued thinking about something else. Helena made a promise to herself to be a more attentive listener.

Illustration 3-1:2

This worker is not listening effectively.

What Is Listening?

Listening is a mental process. While it has physical aspects, they do not provide absolute assurance that a person is listening. For example, many believe that a listener should look directly at the person talking. This is perceived to indicate "listening." There are times, when a person seems attentive because there is **eye contact.** When you raise a question, though, you realize that while physically listening, the person was not mentally listening! The mental participation is the critical part of this skill. The mind must be engaged with the content of what is being discussed. The mind processes the information through reshaping what is already known about the matter and storing the information for future use.

eye contact: looking directly into the eyes of another person

For what reasons do persons fail to establish eye contact?

Listening is required if you are to gain an understanding of what is being said. Conversations, meetings, lectures, answering machines, and voice mail will be meaningless if you fail to listen.

Illustration 3-1:3

Meeting participants listen attentively to the speaker.

Effective Listening Strategy

receptive: willing to receive ideas

feedback: return of information

Effective listening begins with a **receptive** attitude toward learning and ends with a mental **feedback** procedure that gives you assurance that you have listened.

BE WILLING TO LEARN

An attitude of openness to wanting to know—to learn—is critical if you are to be an effective listener. Hearing, which is a physical sensation, is not the same as listening. You can hear without listening. However, you can listen only while hearing. To be sure you are listening, and not merely hearing, you must assess your attitude. An open, confident, positive attitude will help you to listen effectively.

There are a number of reasons for ineffective listening. Some common reasons are

- a feeling of insecurity in the presence of the person who is attempting to explain something; the listener is so fearful that it is difficult to pay attention to what is being said
- an attitude on the part of the listener that what is being said is something already known
- an immediate judgment that there is no value to what is about to be said

What attitudes keep you from being willing to learn?

Ask students to observe how well their friends listen to them and others in their presence.

In what situations do you find that it is difficult to listen? Why?

Carefully assess your immediate mental response when someone begins to talk with you. Notice what **prejudgments** or attitudes are influencing your own listening.

prejudgments: coming to conclusions before having full information

Illustration 3-1:4
What attitudes or prejudgments influence this worker's listening ability?

FOCUS ATTENTION

Have you ever heard someone—a parent, a good friend, or a teacher—say: "Please pay attention!" If you have, you may recall that the person was encouraging you to listen. Possibly, during a conversation you were asking again and again, "What did you say?" In such a situation it is clear that you were not really listening to what was being said. And, after the plea to pay attention, you may have sharpened your focus and put aside mental **distractions.** Your willingness to respond aided your listening. A **deliberate** effort to think about what is being said can be successful.

distractions: things that draw away attention

deliberate: made or done on purpose

> *Harold worked in a busy office as an industrial engineer. There were times when he had to be on the factory floor. Often he would return from the factory to find a number of messages in his voice mailbox. He would retrieve the messages, but he found that even though he heard the messages, he wasn't listening. He had to replay the messages two or three times. He realized he was wasting valuable time because of his failure to listen effectively. He made a promise to himself: "I will listen carefully the first time, so I do not need to repeat messages." He listened to his own promise. He was surprised at his success.*

teaching tips

Ask students to develop a list of distractions they have encountered when they are supposed to be listening.

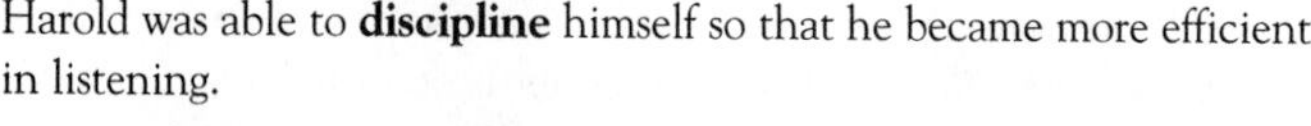

discipline:
exercise control over

Harold was able to **discipline** himself so that he became more efficient in listening.

Illustration 3-1:5

The activity in the background does not distract a good listener.

Ask the students to develop a mental outline for what you are going to present to them about how they are to handle Application Activity 1, for example.

MENTALLY SUMMARIZE

If possible, anticipate what you are to hear and prepare for listening by mentally structuring an outline. For example, if you know that the manager often gives you assignments, you should set up a mental outline with the following sections: What is to be done? Why must it be done? What is the deadline? With such a mental outline, you can listen to your supervisor and put what is said in its proper place. A quick review of your mental outline will assure you that you have all the information you need or help you identify what is missing.

constructed:
developed

Jerry listened attentively to each sentence as his manager spoke with him. He placed each comment in proper order in his mental outline. He had **constructed** *the outline in his mind as soon as he realized that Ms. Willens wanted to give him instructions for the statistical data that needed to be collected and reported. His mental outline included the following questions:*

- *What is the purpose of this activity?*
- *What data are needed?*
- *Where do I get the data?*

Listening Mental Outline

- ❖ Purpose?
- ❖ Data needed?
- ❖ Where are data?
- ❖ Data presentation?
- ❖ What is needed for review?
- ❖ Time allowed?
- ❖ Reporting required?

Illustration 3-1:6
Use a good mental outline for listening.

- *How should the data be presented?*
- *How much time do I have for the job?*
- *At what points does Ms. Willens want to know about my progress or review the data?*

TAKE NOTES

Frequently, there are details involved in talking with someone in person or by phone. Dates, figures, telephone numbers, and **complex** scheduling requirements are likely to require written notes to supplement your careful listening. The process of writing notes can sometimes strengthen your listening power.

complex: made up of a number of parts

Kimberly maintained a notepad at her desk so that she could easily record the details of instructions when the manager called from one of the district offices. She also took notes as she listened to her voice mail so that she would not need to repeat messages.

ASK QUESTIONS

The person talking with you is interested in your understanding clearly what is being discussed. In most cases, he or she will welcome your questions. By listening carefully and raising questions, you can confirm that you understand the message. Your questions can also focus on points that were not clearly specified.

Ask the students to raise questions about asking questions.

Jerry: "Ms. Willens, do you want me to organize the data I get in a format that makes sense to me or do you want to give me the details of the format?"

Ms. Willens: "Thank you, Jerry, that's a good question. At this point, why don't you just get the data and set up a table that makes sense to you. Then let's look at it together before a final draft is prepared."

REVIEW WHAT YOU HEARD

Pause, even if momentarily, to recall what you have heard. Assess whether you have clearly understood what you heard. Does it make sense? Do you have all the information you need? This review acts as a reinforcement of your new information. It assures you that you have gained what you needed to move ahead with your work or undertake a new assignment.

What attitude changes are necessary for you to listen more effectively?

ASSESSING YOUR ABILITY TO LISTEN

Listening skills can be improved. You might ask, "Why improve them?" The answer is, "To reap some marked advantages in how you interact with others and accomplish what you wish to accomplish." Here are some questions for you to consider about your experience in listening during this week. You should answer merely "yes" or "no":

1. Did you have to replay messages on your answering machine in order to know what was said?
2. Was there an instance when a teacher or fellow student said to you: "Oh, you weren't listening to me!"
3. Did you have to redo something because you had not heard the instructions correctly?
4. Was there a time when you realized that you were not listening to someone to whom you should have been giving your attention? (for example, a teacher, a fellow student with whom you are completing a group assignment, etc.)

If you answered all four questions "yes," you will want to give intense attention to how you listen. You should strive to answer all four

Illustration 3-1:7

This student is redoing his homework because he did not listen to the instructions.

questions with "no" within two weeks. During this period, seriously assess the extent to which you follow the strategy presented in this section.

Speaking Effectively

The companion skill of listening is speaking. When both are effective, there is little wasted time. Furthermore, the management and progress of the related activity are being done effectively.

Much speaking is informal. You speak with colleagues, superiors, and strangers, often without any forethought. You are, for the most part, responding to an interaction that was not planned in detail, if at all.

Speaking at work is much the same as speaking with friends and family members. You will have many occasions when you must speak to coworkers about your work and what is to be done. On such occasions, you will want to speak with ease and confidence.

There are some basic points to keep in mind whether you are speaking to one person or to a group in a conference room. You will have opportunities throughout your study of office procedures to **implement** what you learn about effective speaking.

implement: carry out

teaching tips

Have students describe speaking experiences they enjoyed and some they thought were unsuccessful.

teaching tips

Identify some speeches that will be available on local television channels. Ask students to watch a speaker and take notes of behavior they found appealing and unappealing.

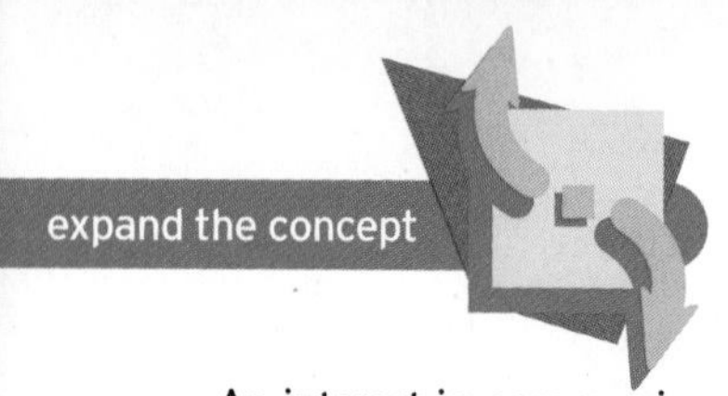

An interest in communicating is helpful for effective communications. What do you do when you must discuss something in which you have virtually no interest?

TAKE AN INTEREST IN COMMUNICATING

Being indifferent, or not caring to communicate makes effective communications difficult. Have you ever listened to a speaker who seemed to be reading a speech with no understanding of the words? In such an instance, the speaker seemed to have no involvement with the content. The words were **mechanical** expressions, without meaning to the listeners. If you have heard such a speaker, do you recall whether you enjoyed what you heard? You probably did not. Did you learn much? Probably not.

mechanical: without thought, like a machine

On the other hand, you may have heard someone who was very much involved in what was being communicated. Your attention was captured mainly because of the interest reflected in the speaker's manner. The interest of the speaker in communicating with the listeners **enhanced** the effectiveness of the experience for those present.

enhanced: made greater, improved

What should a speaker who has a prepared manuscript do to present the material with interest?

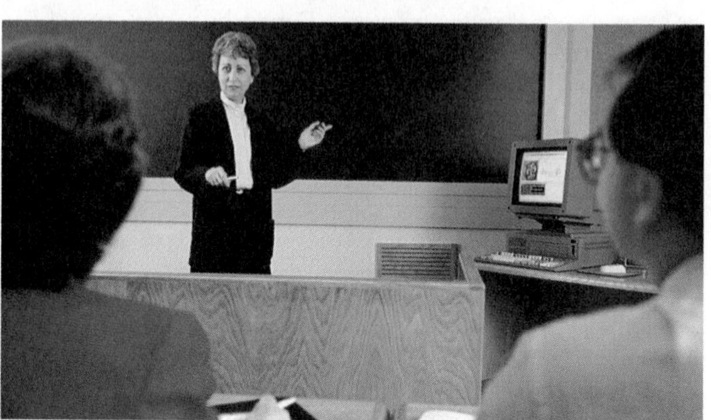

Illustration 3-1:8
A speaker who is interested in her topic will capture the audience's attention.

Why do you enjoy hearing a speaker who seems very interested in the information being communicated?

Karen was the manager of special events and reported to the director of food services in a large manufacturing company's headquarters offices. The director praised Karen for her skill in working with so many different people who came to the office to arrange luncheons, dinners, and other special events in the company dining rooms. As the director noted: "Karen is happy to explain the alternative menus that are available and she clearly conveys her interest in being helpful and giving them all the information needed to make choices."

Someone observing Karen might say she is very patient. Why do you think she is patient in her explanations?

Leon was asked to instruct a new employee, Abby, in the use of a spreadsheet software program. Leon sat at the computer with Abby, beginning the explanation as though she knew nothing about the computer.

Leon did not inquire about Abby's experience at the computer and with spreadsheets. If he had, he would have learned that Abby had considerable experience with spreadsheets, even though she didn't know the one Leon was explaining.

In what way might Leon learn how much Abby knew?

Leon should have asked some **preliminary** questions. He then would have realized that Abby was not a beginner. He could have quickly moved to the explanation specific to the spreadsheet program that Abby needed to learn. Also, Abby would have a more positive impression of Leon if he had been considerate of what she already knew. Both of them would have saved valuable time if the explanation was focused on what needed to be learned.

preliminary: coming before the main consideration

What are the problems, as you see them, in speaking clearly?

SPEAK CLEARLY

Your oral communication is virtually worthless if the listener is unable to hear your words exactly. Generally, you can improve the quality of your voice by deliberately speaking in a modulated tone. Then, if you think of the listener, you are likely to focus on your words in such a manner that they will be understandable by the listener.

Gigi has had problems with a colleague. The two send messages via voice mail. They must make joint decisions, even though they are in offices 300 miles apart. Gigi's colleague, Matthew, mumbles his words. She listens carefully to his voice mail messages. Far too often, she feels, she must call Matthew to ask what he was really saying. Matthew's excuse is that he is too busy to speak more slowly. As Gigi says: "Matthew is a nice fellow. I really like how he makes decisions. If I could only get him to speak clearly when leaving messages, I would be very happy."

Isn't stating each word carefully boring to the listener?

Speaking clearly requires that you say each word carefully. This is referred to as proper **enunciation.** When you enunciate words properly, your listener hears them correctly. You will find it interesting to listen for examples of poor enunciation. Two common problems for listeners occur when speakers run words together and when syllables are not sounded. Note the examples in Illustration 3-1:9.

enunciation: pronouncing words clearly

Illustration 3-1:9
Do any of these enunciations sound familiar?

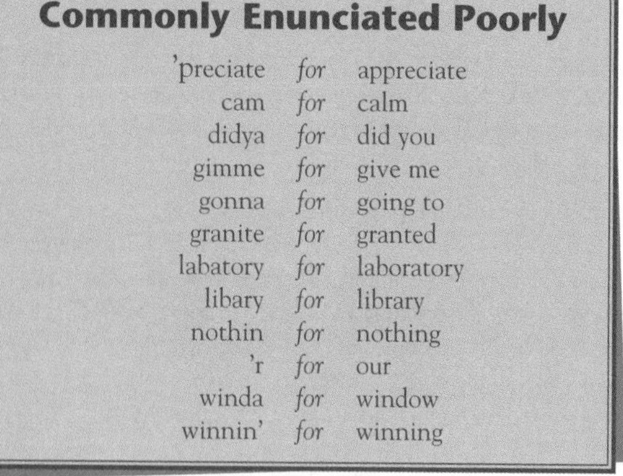

Words and Phrases Commonly Enunciated Poorly

'preciate	*for*	appreciate
cam	*for*	calm
didya	*for*	did you
gimme	*for*	give me
gonna	*for*	going to
granite	*for*	granted
labatory	*for*	laboratory
libary	*for*	library
nothin	*for*	nothing
'r	*for*	our
winda	*for*	window
winnin'	*for*	winning

expand the concept

Why does interaction with people from all parts of the world make the use of standard language important?

USE STANDARD LANGUAGE

Standard language is that language taught in English courses in elementary and secondary schools. It is the language explained in current dictionaries. However, most dictionaries acknowledge common terms that are not standard language. Such terms are identified as being other than standard.

Communications at work should be in standard English for the most part. Using such language assures understanding. Global communications are increasingly important. Many persons in the global community have learned English as a second language. Their knowledge and skill are likely to be primarily related to standard language. They use the English language in an environment that may be very different from the environment in which you speak English as your native language or as a second language you learned in the United States. You can imagine the difficulty persons from other countries are likely to have when talking with persons in the United States who use colloquialisms and slang in their conversations.

Colloquialisms are informal words and phrases used among persons who know each other well or among persons from a specific geographic

Illustration 3-1:10

Those who learned English as a second language can communicate easily with people who speak standard English.

area. You will find some colloquialisms commonly used at work among employees who know each other well and tend to speak informally. A few of these are

- finish off for *complete*
- get out of line for *fail to conform*
- head up for *serve as chairperson*
- touch bases for *discuss a matter*
- walk the talk for *carry through what you say*

Slang expressions tend to be inappropriate most of the time when you are at work and communicating with others. Slang is informal language and has hard-to-discover meaning to those outside the group in which such language is popular. Slang expressions are often short-lived.

EXPRESS YOUR IDEAS CONCISELY

Thinking must precede speaking, if only **momentarily** so. Try asking a mental question such as: "What is it that I really need to say to communicate my meaning?" You are not likely to be misunderstood if you think about what you want to say before speaking.

momentarily: briefly

The supervisor asked an assistant: "What do you still have to complete for the Thompson report I gave you on Monday?" Without a pause for thought, the assistant responded: "Not much."

Why have colloquialisms developed? Why are they useful in environments where everyone knows those in use?

Why do you use slang? Where are you most likely to use it?

How does thinking ahead of time help you to speak concisely?

For what reason did the supervisor need more information than that provided by "not much."

If the assistant had given thought to the question, the response might have been: "I have to key the conclusions, the three short appendices, and the bibliography. Then I will print the entire document."

Which of the two responses do you believe the supervisor would consider more satisfactory?

CONSIDER YOUR AUDIENCE

Whether you are talking with one person, several people in a small conference room, or with a large group in an auditorium, you will want to consider the interests and needs of your listeners. Talking with a single person or a small group usually permits you to be more informal than when you are speaking with a large group.

You want to consider: (a) what your listeners want to know; (b) what they might already know: and (c) how what you are saying can be related to their experiences to date. You also want to be sensitive to how listeners are reacting to what you are saying. Are they looking away with lack of interest? Do they seem impatient with the length of your comments? Are they **perplexed** by lack of understanding? Do they seem eager and attentive while you are talking? Do they seem ready to move on to another topic?

perplexed: troubled

BE AWARE OF NONVERBAL COMMUNICATION

When you are talking with coworkers in person, more than your actual words are a part of your communications. Facial expressions, gestures of hands and arms, posture, and various other movements of the total body also communicate to your listeners.

Two managers are talking together in the office. The one in whose office the meeting is taking place is glancing at the clock frequently. The other appears to be unaware of this behavior, and continues to talk in great detail. What do you think the constant looking at the clock could mean?

An assistant goes to the workstation of another employee who immediately stops working and makes eye contact with the office assistant. What do you think this immediate attention means?

You can never be sure that you are interpreting nonverbal behavior accurately. For example, some are likely to say that glancing at a clock

How can you know your audience when you have been asked by the Human Resource Department head to make a presentation to new employees?

Ask students to make a list of key nonverbal cues that they have noted in their interactions with classmates and friends.

What facial expressions do you find most informative when you are talking with others?

How can you be sure your nonverbal cues are matching the words you use? Can you give illustrations?

is considered evidence that a person is eager to get away as quickly as possible. However, it might mean that the person wants to remain there to the last possible minute before going to a scheduled appointment elsewhere in the building. Making immediate eye contact with someone who comes to the workstation may indicate a **genuine** interest in being helpful, or it might merely reveal pleasure in having an excuse to interrupt some intensive work underway!

genuine: real

A facial expression, such as a smile, can convey understanding or support for what is being said. A frown, on the other hand, may indicate lack of understanding or disagreement.

Many studies have been done on nonverbal communications. Interpretations vary, so that such communications are not generally as clear as words. However, your sensitivity to the possible meaning of nonverbal cues can aid you in determining their appropriateness as you speak with others. For example, if you are talking with a colleague while you are tapping your fingers on the desk or bending a paper clip, you may be distracting your listener from the meaning of the words you are using. Constantly glancing out at the corridor while speaking with a colleague can convey disinterest and may reduce the effectiveness of what you are saying. Divided attention may lead to an incomplete presentation of key points, for example.

Be aware of the nonverbal behavior that accompanies what you say. Make sure it agrees with the **intent** of the words you are using. You want your nonverbal behavior to reinforce what you are saying, not distract from its meaning. You do not want to confuse your listener or listeners by saying one thing and having your nonverbal behavior communicate something else.

intent: purpose

BE INTERESTED IN THE LISTENER'S RESPONSE

When you speak, if possible, allow time for interaction. You will be communicating effectively if you give your listeners a chance to respond. One of the major advantages of oral communication is that there can be immediate feedback. When you talk with others, you should be interested in getting questions, comments, and reactions to what you are saying. Actually, a skillful communicator is a good

Why should questions from an audience be of interest to a speaker?

listener. Future speaking can be improved by allowing your listeners to comment or raise questions.

implied: suggested

Unfortunate Situation: The manager of customer services called a meeting of the staff members. Without any introductory comments, the manager stated that everyone must work faster and be more productive. There had been an increase in customer requests, but the company was not employing any additional workers. The manager **implied** that employees were deliberately working too slowly and were not interested in working as rapidly as they could. When the announcement was completed, the manager said that everyone could go back to work. There was no request for questions or comments.

For what reasons might a manager or executive not seek feedback? What attitudes are being conveyed to those who heard a presentation where there was no time for questions?

What Might Have Been Done: The manager should have made some introductory remarks about the purpose of the meeting and the considerations that resulted in the decision to be presented. Furthermore, the basis for believing that higher productivity could be realized might have been communicated to the staff members. There should have been time for questions, comments, and reactions as to the reasonableness of the request.

Complementary Skills—Listening and Speaking

The skills of listening and speaking are closely related. When both are well developed, few of the problems often seen with oral communications at work will arise.

There are frequent occasions at work when you must speak with others and when you must listen to what is being said. Speed in accomplishing tasks and making changes in tasks or plans is dependent on many person-to-person interactions as well as communications by voice mail and telephone. Being responsive and attentive to the basic skills critical for such communications will be invaluable in your overall effectiveness in handling responsibilities.

Reviewing the Topic

topic 3-1 review

1. What are possible outcomes of listening effectively?
2. In what way is listening a mental process?
3. Why is listening necessary at work?
4. What are some reasons for ineffective listening?
5. How do you mentally summarize?
6. What does it mean to have an interest in communicating?
7. What is required to speak clearly?
8. What is standard language?
9. Why should you avoid the use of slang at work?
10. What factors should a speaker consider about the audience before preparing a speech?

THINKING CRITICALLY

Three classmates were talking together after school one afternoon. One of them, Jack, said to the other two: "Listen, can I talk with you about my problem? I will confess to you that I don't want to give a talk in class next week. I'll just pretend that I am sick and not come to school for a few days. It is fine sitting here and talking with you. But I can't get up before the class. I have figured out a way to get out of doing this all through high school. I'll be honest with you. I remember having to stand before the class in the seventh grade to recite part of a poem. I was so scared that after the first two lines I couldn't remember a word. Oh, was I embarrassed. Aren't these assignments ridiculous? I'm not going to have to stand up before anyone and talk when I am out of school and earning a living. Do you agree with my scheme for next week?" What would you say to Jack? What decision do you think would be best for him?

What you are to do:

Write or key a response to the questions raised.

topic 3-1 review

Listening and Speaking

107

topic 3-1 review

REINFORCING ENGLISH SKILLS

You overhear the following conversation at the photocopying machine between two colleagues. Both of your colleagues have made a number of errors in their use of pronouns.

> *Melissa: "Do you plan to take the continuing education class for we staff people that Ms. Galson discussed at the meeting yesterday? Do you think she means for us to attend?"*
>
> *Steve: "I don't know if I'll go. Both me and Earl wonder if we would be better off taking a course later in the year. The topics are interesting though, aren't it?"*
>
> *Melissa: Well, between you and I, I think there are likely to be some good courses later; but Betsy and me have pretty much decided we will go. We believe Ms. Galson would like we to go."*
>
> *Steve: Melissa, if you go, will you tell us what them said at the meeting?"*
>
> *Melissa: Of course; the instructor will be good, I guess. I won't be as good as her, but I'll do my best."*

What you are to do:

Key a copy of the conversation between Melissa and Steve, changing all pronouns used incorrectly. Underscore all the pronouns you substituted for those in error.

APPLICATION ACTIVITIES

ACTIVITY 1 Preparing and Presenting a Speech

Assume that you are employed in the Human Resources Department of a large company. (You may choose the business of the company in which you are employed.) You have been asked to make a presentation to a group of approximately 20 new employees from a variety of departments. All these employees are beginning their first jobs. They have had no full-time experience in the business world. You are to choose one of the following topics for your presentation:

- How listening attentively is an aid to productivity throughout our company
- Understanding the importance of continuous improvement in our company

108

- The importance of integrity at work
- Why the customer is important in our company

What you are to do:

1. For the topic you have chosen, find appropriate sources through accessing databases in your school library or your local public library.
2. Read articles that you have selected as related to your topic, and prepare a three-minute presentation.
3. Outline your presentation in sufficient detail that you will have confidence in talking before the group.
4. Make your presentation to a small group in your class or to the entire class.
5. Write an evaluation of your presentation based on your own thinking about what you did. Note especially what you would do differently if you were to use the same topic for another presentation.
6. Review the comments of your classmates about the presentation to see how they differ from your self-evaluation.

ACTIVITY 2 Listening to Presentations

Filename: Evaluate

You will be listening to your classmates make presentations in small groups or to the entire class as described in Activity 1. Presentations are to be evaluated on the factors listed below on a scale of 1 to 5, with 5 being the highest rating and 1 the lowest.

- Content of presentation
- Speaker conveys interest in the topic
- Speaker speaks clearly
- Speaker uses standard language
- Speaker expresses ideas concisely
- Speaker considers the audience

109

topic 3-1 review

What you are to do:

1. Open the template file *Evaluate* and print a presentation evaluation form for each presentation you will evaluate.
2. Listen carefully to each presentation, making notes to aid you in evaluating each one.
3. Give your evaluation form to the presenter.
4. After you have heard all presentations, key a brief report in which you assume that you are a new employee. Identify what you found most worthwhile in the presentations.

110

Topic 3-2

Reading

When you have completed your study of this topic, you will be able to:

- **explain the attitudes that enhance development of reading skills**
- **describe the kinds of reading common at work**
- **identify critical components of reading skills**
- **explain common techniques for improving reading skills**

You have been reading for many years. You continue to use your reading skills in your studies. Yet it is likely that your reading skills could be improved. Few people have reached the skill level where no further improvement is possible.

Be objective in thinking of each aspect of your reading skills as you study the content of this topic. Attempt to maintain a willingness to reconsider your attitude toward reading as well as the way in which you read.

Attitude Toward Reading

A positive attitude toward reading is likely to be rewarding both in your personal life and your work life. Regardless of what job you

What is the level of reading skill in your class? What is the attitude toward reading? You may want to determine answers to these two questions in as informal a manner as a general discussion. Or you may choose to use the chapter itself to determine level of reading skill by developing a quick exercise. A brief excerpt for which you allow no more than 10 minutes of class time might be selected. A follow-up may be a frank discussion of attitudes reflected as students were reading.

choose, you will find that reading skills are critical to carrying out your responsibilities effectively.

Describe a person you know who likes to read. Why do you think he or she likes reading? What attitudes about reading do you believe the person has?

Illustration 3-2:1
Reading skills are critical to career success.

As you think of classmates you have known during your school experience, why do you believe some have a negative attitude toward reading?

If at this point you don't have a positive attitude toward reading, think of the reasons why. Consider what would help you change your attitude. Plan to give particular attention to what these skills involve and where you might make changes in how you read. Read this topic with an open mind. Improving your reading skills may be a critical step in succeeding at school or work.

Illustration 3-2:2
Do you believe this student is intent on reading his class assignment?

Kevin realized that he wasn't a good reader. He had encountered problems in reading all through his school years. As he began to study about reading skills in his office procedures class, he thought: "Oh, here I face my limitations again!" However, when the teacher said that earlier problems could be overcome, Kevin began to listen attentively. He thought: "Maybe if I try again in relation to being a worker, I can more clearly understand what I have been doing wrong." And then he thought: "I don't have anything to lose and maybe I can make up for past lack of interest and involvement."

The Value of Reading Skills

Regardless of your career choice, you will find that you will spend a considerable amount of time reading. A major study entitled, "What Work Requires of Schools: A SCANS Report for America 2000," includes the following comment:

> . . . First, all employees will have to read well enough to understand and interpret diagrams, directories, correspondence, manuals, records, charts, graphs, tables and specifications. Without the ability to read a diverse set of materials, workers cannot locate the descriptive and quantitative information needed to make decisions or to recommend courses of action. What do these reading requirements mean on the job? They might involve
>
> - dealing with letters and written policy on complaints
> - reading the text of technical manuals from equipment vendors[1]

[1]U.S. Government, Department of Labor, The Secretary's Commission on Achieving Necessary Skills, WHAT WORK REQUIRES OF SCHOOLS: A SCANS REPORT FOR AMERICA 2000 (June 1991). Washington, D.C.: U.S. Government Printing Office, xvi

Present Reading Skill

reinforce:
strengthen understanding

Although you may not have high-level reading skills at this time, you are able to read. You spend some of your time reading. How much you read is undoubtedly related to what you must accomplish and also how much enjoyment you get from reading. You read to learn for subjects you are studying in school. You read to **reinforce** what a teacher presented in a class lecture/discussion. You read what you have accessed at a computer. You read instructions for new equipment you have purchased, and you may read for pleasure from newspapers, magazines, and books.

Illustration 3-2:3
The student in the school library is giving full attention to her reading assignment.

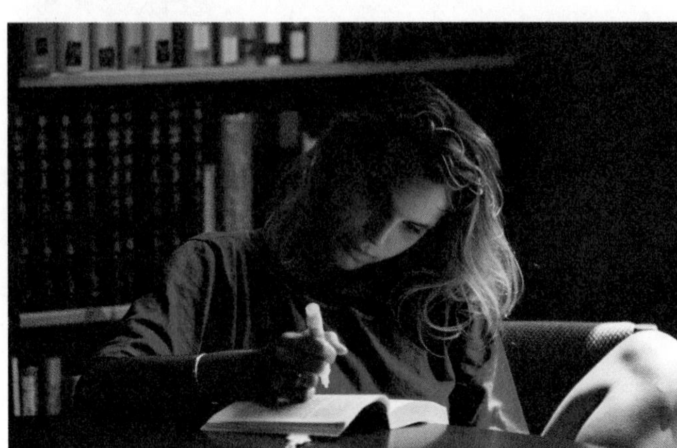

Regardless of the level of your skill, there is likely to be considerable opportunity for improvement if you find such improvement a worthy goal. As you learned in Chapter 2, one of the key strategies in today's business world is continuous improvement. This idea for continuous improvement is credited to Japanese companies. It is now a common feature of the goals of American-owned companies and alert employees. Each problem is seen as an opportunity for improvement. This choice of seeing a problem as an opportunity is one you will want to consider as you strive to read more effectively and efficiently.

Ask students to talk with parents or adult acquaintances about the reading that is required for their jobs. Students might inquire about the extent to which such reading is done at home.

The Reading Process

Reading is actually simple when viewed in a general sense. It is the process of **translating** written information into useful mental impressions that inform, **clarify,** or extend your understanding of the material. What you have read becomes knowledge that influences how you think and act from that point forward.

translating: changing from one form to another

clarify: explain further

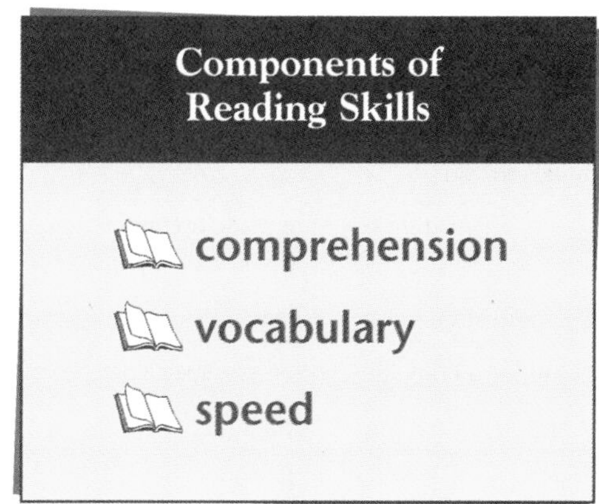

Illustration 3-2:4
High-level reading skills require all three components.

Assume that you are an assistant to a senior executive who is responsible for technology use in your company. This executive asks you to find some information on interactive voice-response systems. These systems are in use in many companies. There may be justification for considering them for the company in which you work. You search for **relevant** articles and you find one with some information. You read the following on your screen. Then you print it:

relevant: related

> *Interactive voice response is appropriate in many business applications, especially as a resource for answering frequently asked questions and sending out current product information. Its automation of tasks minimizes* **overhead** *and can increase caller satisfaction. Are these common situations in your organization?*
>
> ▸ *Personnel frequently answer the same questions or provide the same information to calls.*

overhead: business expenses not related to a particular product or service

In what ways do you believe you and your classmates could improve your reading skills?

Under what circumstances do you find it relatively easy to remember what you have read?

Reading requires attention and thinking. What does this statement mean in a practical sense?

How much interest do you have in learning about interactive voice response?

- *Clients request information after regular office hours.*
- *Operators continually forward calls to certain key departments.*
- *Field service personnel wait on hold while managers look up their next call assignment.*

If these situations sound familiar, consider interactive voice recognition. An interactive voice recognition system expands services without adding additional manpower. Your office is literally open around the clock without anyone having to be there.

How much interest do you have in interactive voice response after reading the excerpt given in our textbook?

What do you know now about interactive voice recognition that you did not know before you read these paragraphs? What terms are unfamiliar to you?

Adequate reading skills are made up of several factors. As you have learned in your English courses, good reading means that you read with:

- attention to *what*, not *how*
- understanding and reasonable speed
- few pauses because of unfamiliar words

How would you describe reading naturally in contrast to reading unnaturally?

naturally: without deliberate thought

Some say that reading with attention to *what*—the meaning—and not *how* you read is reading **naturally.** A good reader has developed the process to the point where it seems automatic. Attention is, therefore, on meaning.

What do you think is necessary in order to read with understanding? What type of prior experience is necessary?

You need to understand what you read in order to learn something you can use—either at the time of completing the reading or later. For example, when you conclude the reading of instructions for formatting a report, you want to be able to actually format the report.

excessive: more than seems proper

Reasonable speed means that you are not spending an **excessive** amount of time reading. If you have to complete a report quickly but must read the instructions for the format, you will be grateful for having the skill to read quickly.

Why is speed in reading important for a professional person who is in a field that is changing at a rapid pace?

extensive: broad

It is difficult to understand the meaning of a passage when you do not know the exact meaning of every word. You are more likely to understand the message if every word is familiar to you. Command of an **extensive** vocabulary is helpful.

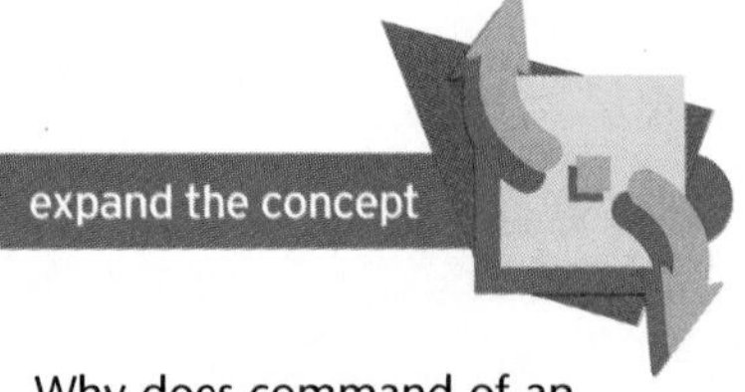

Why does command of an extensive vocabulary aid in reading with speed?

Begin now to assess your own reading skills in relation to the three points mentioned above. Do you have an opinion about each point?

Improving Reading Skills

High-level reading skills aid productivity in your work. A positive attitude is important for improvement. You want to strive for reading skills that are so natural you need not give detailed, deliberate attention to the reading task itself. Instead, you can focus on the content of what you are reading. The critical skills for high-level reading are comprehension, vocabulary, and speed.

COMPREHENSION

Comprehension is the ability to understand what you have read. To comprehend is "to know." It implies a transfer of information from the printed page or the computer screen to your mental storage (your memory). A simple example of comprehending is keeping in mind a number that you have just found in the telephone directory. A more complex example is reading about a supplier's new product and being able to determine whether the product appears superior to the brand your company is currently using. Some techniques you may find helpful as you strive to increase reading comprehension are listed below.

1. *Focus:* Put aside anything else on your mind when you begin to read.
2. *Identify Purpose:* Before you begin, ask: "What do I want to know when I have completed this reading?"
3. *Scan:* Get an overview of the page, the chapter, or the entire article or book so you can anticipate what you will encounter as you read carefully.
4. *Summarize:* Mentally summarize as you move from one paragraph to another, particularly if you are reading to gain information for handling a task.
5. *Sequence:* After reading several paragraphs, try to think of the ideas in an appropriate order.

In what ways can deliberate attention be given to the textbook we use in this course?

Think of the reading you have done in the last month. Identify the reading that was easiest as far as your comprehension was concerned. Why do you think the material was easy to comprehend?

You often hear about focusing your attention in many of your classes. What are the barriers you face as you attempt to focus on a specific matter related to your studies?

Exactly what do you do when you scan a page? Will two or three of you give us a detailed demonstration?

What did you learn from the demonstrations of scanning?

Exactly how should a person reread material? In what way will a second reading be useful?

Ask students to make a list for a week of words they encounter that are unfamiliar to them. Suggest that they listen for new words in all their classes, in their reading of newspapers and magazines, in listening to programs on television, or in searching World Wide Web sites.

Illustration 3-2:5
Which of these techniques have you used?

Techniques for Developing Comprehension

- focus
- identify purpose
- scan
- summarize
- sequence
- draw mental picture
- checkup
- reread

6. *Draw Mental Picture:* Attempt to imagine what it is that is being discussed, especially if your reading is about a matter that is unfamiliar to you.
7. *Checkup:* Determine, through a fast review process of recalling key points, whether you have learned what you believe you should have learned.
8. *Reread:* Begin anew to read what you have just read if you are not satisfied with your checkup process.

VOCABULARY

A vocabulary is a stock of words. Having an extensive vocabulary means that you know the definitions of a large number of words. Words that are unfamiliar to you are a **barrier** to your reading. There are techniques that can expand your vocabulary and help you to be an effective reader. Consider using some of these as you study the content of this book:

barrier: something that stands in the way

1. When you encounter an unfamiliar word, try to determine its meaning from the way it is used in the sentence. After you have a meaning you think is correct, check the dictionary. If you were right, you will now be more confident as you consider what unfamiliar words might mean.
2. When you encounter an unfamiliar word, try separating the word into parts to see if you can guess a meaning for one or more of the

parts. You read, for example, the word *rearrange*. You know from earlier experience that *rekey* means that you must key again. You know the meaning of *arrange*. You then guess that *rearrange* means to put in a new or different order. You check the dictionary and find that your guess is right.

3. While reading, have at hand a notepad and pencil to record words you don't know. Write down your best guess of what the word might mean. Also, record the page on which the uncertain word appears.

When you pause to reflect on what you have read, check the words on your list in a dictionary. As you read a definition, compare what you thought the meaning was with the dictionary's definition. You may want to refer back to the place where the word occurred. Reread the passage and assure yourself that you understand what is being said. If there is more than one definition provided, be sure to select the definition that is appropriate in the context in which the word appeared. Context refers to the parts of a sentence or paragraph around a word that can help you with meaning. You may find it useful to collect new words and review your list from time to time. Try using new words in your conversations as a way of reinforcing your new knowledge.

Unfamiliar Words
From an article on the hottest technologies in telecommunications:

unprecedented
ubiquitous
prerequisites
configured
digital speech interpolation
deployed
throughput
infrastructure
compatibility
data mining

Illustration 3-2:6
A student's list of unfamiliar words

Why might a person need to be aware of unfamiliar words on the job?

Ask students to discuss with acquaintances who work if they have the need for a specialized vocabulary and how they developed their knowledge of it.

specialized: related to a specific matter

You may find a **specialized** vocabulary required in your work. You will want to be alert to such terms so that your understanding of your own work is comprehensive. You may have available a specialized dictionary or other reference that will help you master new words.

SPEED

Another reading skill relates to the time required for reading a passage. Problems with comprehension and/or vocabulary can slow the rate at which you read. However, some people have good comprehension and extensive vocabulary but read slowly. The rate at which you read can merely be a habit. You have the capability to read more quickly. Some techniques that have been useful in increasing reading speed include the following strategies.

1. Focus your attention on a whole paragraph at one time. Tell yourself, "I want to read this paragraph as a single thought and I want to know what it says." By doing so, you are forcing yourself to break a common habit of deliberately pausing at each word or each sentence as you read. When you have finished reading the paragraph, try to summarize it in a sentence or two. If you realize that you have not grasped the meaning, read it once again as quickly as possible. Again, attempt to summarize it. You are likely to make much improvement on your second attempt.

How much time is required to check the meaning of a word in a dictionary?

Illustration 3-2:7
Several techniques may be used to increase reading speed.

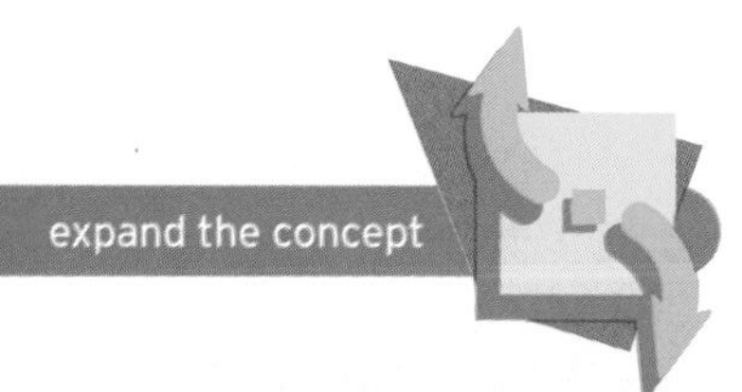

How can you read with speed and still comprehend what you read?

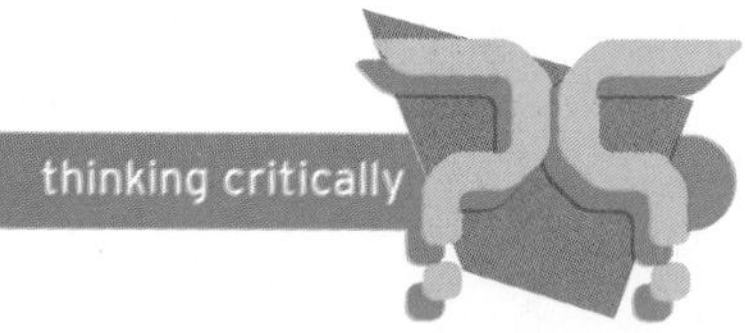

How can you read a page at a time? Do we have some students willing to describe exactly how they might follow such a procedure?

You might choose a page from a later chapter of this textbook and ask the class to read the page in a half-minute.

2. Time your reading. Set a goal such as: "I will read this page, which has approximately 350 words, in three minutes." Check to see if you reached your goal. If you did, try the same passage with a reduced time allowance.
3. Deliberately force yourself ahead as you read. Do not set a specific time goal. Note the extent to which you return to your slower way of reading. Determine why you do not continue reading quickly.

What did you do exactly to read the page in a half-minute? What did you really read? What do you know?

Reading at Work

There are many occasions when you must read on the job. You will find that reading is vital to understanding the total company in which you are employed. Furthermore, there are many occasions when employees must read in order to complete tasks assigned to them or for which they have responsibility.

You may want to develop some speed-reading exercises using excerpts from this chapter or others. Begin with two-minute readings.

LEARNING ABOUT YOUR COMPANY

Employees who want to understand how their work relates to the total company will do much **voluntary** reading of information about the company that is available in memoranda, internal newsletters, and other documents. Here is how one worker, a new receptionist, described what she chose to do:

voluntary: by personal choice

> *I had never heard of this company when I came here to work six months ago as a receptionist/clerk. How could I be able to answer questions of callers if I was completely uninformed about the company? We were introduced to the company and received some* **brochures** *about our products during the initial orientation day. That was helpful, but I wanted to know more. So I asked for copies of the last three annual reports and for any historical information available. I learned we have a small library with a part-time librarian who manages the services. When there are lulls in my work or when I am having coffee in the snack bar alone, I generally find something to read—and for several weeks it was something related to the company. I also read every announcement that is sent from the office of the president and other bulletins from our Department of Public Affairs.*

brochures: brief written materials

How do you react to pressure to read faster?

What attitudes are reflected in this employee's reading?

Have students identify attitudes toward work that would be necessary if workers read voluntarily about their company and their jobs.

Why would this employee have the attitudes reflected here?

Another receptionist reflected a very different point of view:

> *A visitor called at a major telecommunications company in Philadelphia. The visitor had just read in the morning's paper that the company had named a new chief executive officer. In the brief conversation with the receptionist, the visitor said: "I just read that you have a new chief executive." The receptionist responded: "Oh, ya? I really don't know . . . I guess that memo that was distributed late yesterday afternoon reported that, but I never waste my time with such matters that don't interest me."*

Consider the difference in attitude toward reading held by these two receptionists. Which one is likely to find her work more enjoyable?

Employees who understand thoroughly the information related to their job are invaluable.

Illustration 3-2:8
An informed employee works more effectively.

Many policies and procedures related to your job will be available in written form. A manager may explain how a particular task is to be done or what policies are to be implemented. You will find it helpful, though, to read the written version of what was presented. You read to have a thorough understanding of what you are to do. From time to time, memoranda related to ways of doing tasks or changes in policies are sent to employees. Such correspondence should be read and filed in an appropriate manner for easy reference later.

David works as an assistant manager in the Order Department of a major professional organization that publishes a wide variety of materials—books, videotapes, CD-ROMS—for a membership of almost 500,000. When David received a memorandum detailing the new procedures for handling orders from outside the United States, he read it carefully. Then he filed it appropriately so that he could refer to it later.

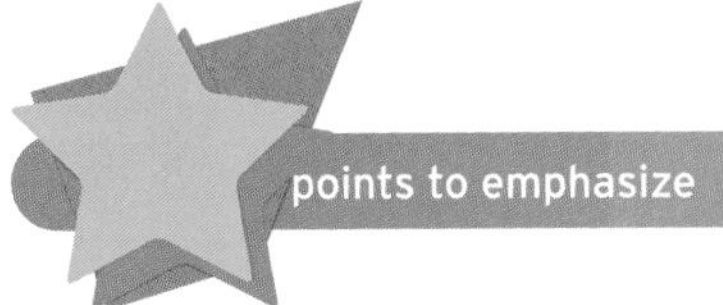

Demonstrations of new equipment are helpful. However, you can reinforce your understanding of the capabilities of such equipment by becoming familiar with the written manuals available.

UNDERSTANDING INSTRUCTIONS FOR EQUIPMENT

Employees are frequently provided new equipment that requires them to learn new methods of work. Sometimes demonstrations of the equipment are provided. However, workers generally find that they must read and understand the instruction manual in order to use the equipment properly.

Sheila works for a company that does sociological surveys. She was to accompany one of the researchers in the field and needed to use a portable tape recorder to which an external microphone was attached. She carefully read the information provided, shown in Illustration 3-2:9.

Recording from Various Sound Sources

Recording with an External Microphone

Connect a microphone to the MIC jack. There is a small projection to show the position of the MIC jack near the jack. Use a microphone of low impedance (less than 3 kilohms) such as ECM-T10 (not supplied).
When using a plug-in power system microphone, the power to the microphone is supplied from this unit.

Note

- When recording with an external microhone, the VOR system may not work properly because of the difference in sensitivity.

Recording from Another Equipment

Connect another equipment to the MIC jack using the RK-G64HG connecting cord (not supplied).

Illustration 3-2:9

Excerpt from instructions that Sheila read

Why should a worker read instructions before filling in forms?

You may suggest that students become familiar with some World Wide Web sites that are related to topics that will be discussed during this course.

FOLLOWING INSTRUCTIONS ON FORMS

Businesses develop forms to simplify the task of getting appropriate and complete information. You will find forms that facilitate such tasks as recording telephone messages, requesting supplies and equipment, ordering goods, reporting travel expenses, and submitting time reports. It is very important that you read all instructions on forms and fill in all information requested. If some item of information is not needed in a particular instance or is not available, some comment should be added. Note Illustration 3-2:10, which shows a telephone message recorded on a form. What information did the person who recorded the message fail to add?

Illustration 3-2:10

A message should include all information necessary to respond to the call.

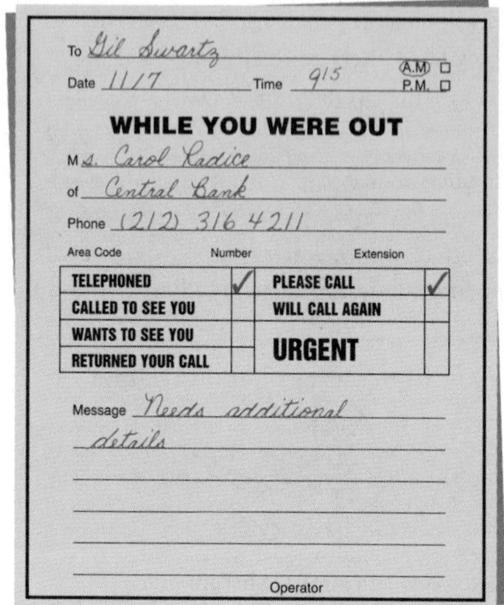

To Gil Swartz

Date 11/7 Time 9:15 A.M. ☐ P.M. ☐

WHILE YOU WERE OUT

Ms. Carol Radice

of Central Bank

Phone (212) 316 4211

Area Code Number Extension

TELEPHONED	✓	PLEASE CALL	✓
CALLED TO SEE YOU		WILL CALL AGAIN	
WANTS TO SEE YOU		URGENT	
RETURNED YOUR CALL			

Message Needs additional details

Operator

Harold works as a counselor in a youth services organization. He interviews adolescents who are referred to the agency for help. In the initial interview, Harold must get certain details that are to be recorded on a form. This form is valuable as others on the staff need it to determine the best service for the particular adolescent. Harold is careful to review the form before the client leaves his office so that he will have all the information needed.

RESPONDING TO INQUIRIES

Many employees must respond to inquiries from other departments and from customers or clients. The subject of inquiries **varies** considerably. Employees are not expected to know every requested detail from memory. Knowing the sources of information in company-developed databases is critical to responding promptly. Once the appropriate source is accessed, the worker needs to read quickly and accurately the information sought by the caller or visitor.

varies:
having differences

Linda works in customer services for a mail-order company that sells a variety of items related to books, such as bookcases, lamps, and reading tables. It is not uncommon for Linda to get specific questions, such as: "I have a bookcase that is not the exact size as the one you advertise. I need a bookcase to place on top of the one I have, so I need to know what your bookcase's exact dimensions are. Can you help me?" Linda is able to access her database quickly and provide the caller with the correct information.

USING WRITTEN REFERENCES/DATABASES

At work you will frequently need to use a variety of references. References commonly found in many offices are dictionaries, atlases, telephone directories, and policy and procedures manuals. There are also likely to be databases subscribed or maintained by your organization. You will be expected to become familiar with all sources available, so that you will know where to search when requests are made. You will also want to develop references to aid you in your specific responsibilities.

How would you evaluate Melissa's attitude toward her job?

Melissa, an assistant to the director of the Pacific Basin Division of an international utilities company, needs to know about the currencies of a number of countries since she helps executives prepare for overseas trips. She has designed her own list of the currencies of the several countries where the executives regularly travel. Note her listing in Illustration 3-2:11.

READING AS A SINGLE PROCESS

The critical areas of comprehension, vocabulary, and reading speed have been highlighted separately. However, when you are actually

Illustration 3-2:11

Melissa's list of currencies of countries to which executives travel regularly

PACIFIC RIM CURRENCIES
Example Exchange Rates

Country	Currency	U. S. $ Equivalent
Australia	dollar	.8108
China	yuan	.1200
Hong Kong	dollar	.1293
Japan	yen	.00889
Malaysia	ringgit	.3961
New Zealand	dollar	.7082
Philippines	peso	.03807
Singapore	dollar	.7138
South Korea	won	.001206
Taiwan	dollar	.03638
Thailand	baht	.03927

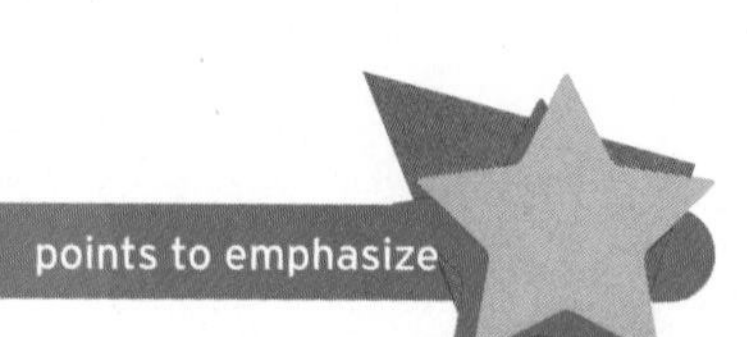

Plan to implement what you have learned about improving reading skills as you read instructions for activities and the chapters in this textbook.

compensated: made up for

encounter: see; come into contact with

reading, these areas interact. In some cases, a weakness in one area may be **compensated** for by strength in another. For example, you may comprehend well what you read. If you **encounter** an unfamiliar word, you figure out its meaning from your understanding of the rest of the sentence or paragraph. Or, you may read rapidly, but your comprehension is limited. By reading rapidly, you have time to reread the material to improve your comprehension. Ultimately, you want high skill levels in all three components.

As you consider the variety of reading tasks you may handle at work, you realize how much good skills are worth. As you complete the varied assignments in your study of office procedures, regularly assess your reading skills and think of ways to improve them.

Reviewing the Topic

topic 3-2 review

1. What kind of attitude should you have toward reading?
2. What is the reading process?
3. List three appropriate business uses for an interactive voice-response system?
4. What does it mean to read with attention?
5. How can you determine the meaning of an unfamiliar word that you encounter while you are reading?
6. What are the key components of reading skill?
7. Describe a procedure to increase your comprehension of what you read?
8. What might you do to build your vocabulary through reading?
9. In what ways might the speed of reading be increased?
10. Identify several situations that require reading at work.

INTERACTING WITH OTHERS

Brad works as an assistant manager in the office of a warehouse facility where he interacts with a number of employees. The office is a busy place since an inventory of over 11,000 items is maintained.

On several occasions, Charles, a part-time employee, asked Brad to help him with instructions for incoming merchandise. Brad began to realize that Charles, who was still in high school, did not understand instructions. Then Brad began to wonder if Charles was having problems with reading. One evening after work, Brad and Charles were leaving at the same time. The two began to talk. Charles said to Brad: "I think I should give up this job; it is too hard for me. I guess I don't really want to work." If you were Brad, what would you say to Charles?

What you are to do:
Write or key a response to the question raised.

topic 3-2 review

Reading

127

topic 3-2 review

REINFORCING MATH SKILLS

Jan works for a financial advisor. Among her tasks are preparing figures for Betty Harman, the advisor. Below is a table that appeared in a local newspaper.

Performance Yardsticks

Investment Objective	Year-to-Date	Four Weeks	One Year	3 YRS (annualized)	5 YRS (annualized)
	On a Total Return Basis				
Capital Appreciation	+15.14%	+ 1.76%	+ 18.85%	+ 13.87%	+ 14.77%
Growth	+18.94	+ 4.08	+ 21.80	+ 16.43	+ 15.26
Small-Company	+15.47	+ 0.08	+ 19.97	+ 15.52	+ 16.28
Mid-Cap Stock	+15.72	+ 1.31	+ 19.70	+ 15.96	+ 16.00
Growth & Income	+20.36	+ 5.18	+ 23.85	+ 17.15	+ 15.69
Equity Income	+17.70	+ 4.41	+ 21.64	+ 15.14	+ 14.85
Global (inc U.S.)	+15.77	+ 3.02	+ 19.12	+ 10.93	+ 12.13
International (non U.S.)	+12.05	+ 2.85	+ 16.64	+ 7.73	+ 10.47
Stock/Bond Blend	+12.92	+ 3.50	+ 15.96	+ 11.45	+ 12.12
Short-Term Debt	+ 4.39	+ 1.06	+ 5.65	+ 5.05	+ 5.74
Intermediate Corp. Debt	+ 3.71	+ 2.19	+ 5.96	+ 5.48	+ 7.26
Intermediate Gov't	+ 3.30	+ 1.98	+ 5.25	+ 4.99	+ 6.51
Long-Term Corp.	+ 2.12	+ 2.80	+ 4.82	+ 5.10	+ 7.38
High-Yield Taxable	+11.69	+ 1.58	+ 13.38	+ 8.41	+ 12.05
Mortgage Bond	+ 4.46	+ 1.62	+ 6.13	+ 4.68	+ 5.88
World Income	+12.08	+ 2.82	+ 15.17	+ 6.39	+ 6.66
Short-Term Muni	+ 3.45	+ 0.85	+ 4.23	+ 4.09	+ 5.20
Intermed.-Term Muni	+ 3.54	+ 1.54	+ 4.84	+ 4.79	+ 6.38
General L-T Muni	+ 3.08	+ 1.82	+ 5.34	+ 4.86	+ 7.22
High-Yield Muni	+ 3.67	+ 1.37	+ 5.74	+ 5.26	+ 7.32
Insured Muni	+ 3.03	+ 1.96	+ 5.44	+ 5.06	+ 7.19

128

What you are to do:

1. Calculate the following for each column:
   - the average percentage rate (round to three decimal places)
   - the difference between the highest investment objective and the average for each column (round to two decimal places)
2. Verify the accuracy of the percentage differences calculated above.
3. Prepare the results of your calculations so they are easy to read by the financial advisor.

APPLICATION ACTIVITIES

ACTIVITY 1 Customer Service Agent in a Bank

Assume that you are an agent in the customer service department of a major bank. You spend a lot of time talking with customers by telephone. One area where questions are frequent is early withdrawal costs. Below are the rules for your bank.

What you are to do:

Assume that you respond to calls in which the following questions are raised. Prepare a written response to each of the customers.

Customer A: I have an account that has a term of 30 months, which I opened four months ago. I would like to withdraw about half of that money now. What will it cost me to do this?

Customer B: My one-year deposit will mature in eight months. Could I withdraw the money next month?

Customer C: I have an 18-month account that matures in six months. What penalty do I face if I withdraw all the money now?

Customer D: I would like to make an additional deposit to my account that I opened a year ago. May I do this?

129

topic 3-2
review

MINIMUM BALANCE REQUIREMENTS:

The following are the minimum balance requirements to establish an account:

Term to Maturity	Regular Certificate of Deposit	IRA/Keogh Certificate of Deposit
3 months	$2,500.00	$2,500.00
6, 7, or 9 months	$1,000.00	$1,000.00
1 year or greater	$1,000.00	$1,000.00

TRANSACTION LIMITATIONS AND EARLY WITHDRAWAL PENALTIES:

Additional deposits are not permitted to these accounts. Additional deposits will only be permitted on the maturity date at which time they become part of the principal of the account.

Principal or any part thereof may be withdrawn prior to maturity. There is an early withdrawal penalty on the amount of principal withdrawn. The penalty imposed will be as follows:

1. For an account with a term of less than 1 year, an amount equal to 31 days interest (whether earned or not) and calculated at the contract rate on the principal amount withdrawn;
2. For an account with a term of one year to less than two years, an amount equal to 90 days interest (whether earned or not) and calculated at the contract rate on the principal amount withdrawn;
3. For an account with a term of two years to less than three years, an amount equal to 120 days interest (whether earned or not) and calculated at the contract rate on the principal amount withdrawn.

ACTIVITY 2 Reading for Comprehension

In this activity you will apply techniques for improving reading comprehension. Choose a topic from one of your textbooks or another resource for use in this activity.

What you are to do:

1. Review the techniques for improving reading comprehension on page 118.
2. Carefully read the topic you chose, following the tips for improving comprehension.
3. Prepare a one-page summary of the topic.

130

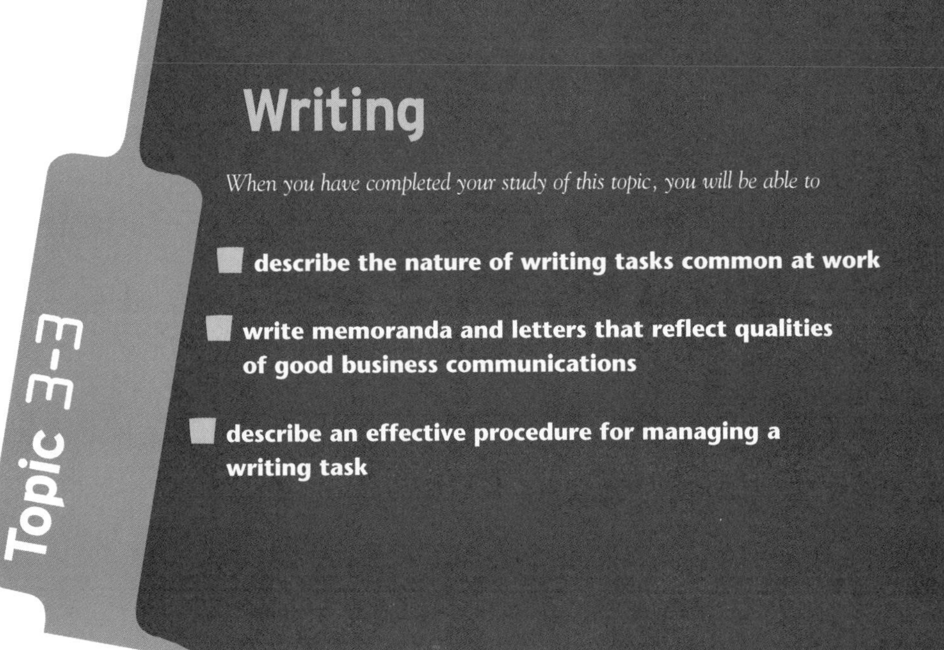

Writing

When you have completed your study of this topic, you will be able to

- **describe the nature of writing tasks common at work**
- **write memoranda and letters that reflect qualities of good business communications**
- **describe an effective procedure for managing a writing task**

Topic 3-3

getting started

From assignments in earlier chapters, you may have assessed students' writing skills. Classes vary in competencies. If basic English skills are good, limited attention can be given to that topic. If basic skills are weak, additional attention may be justified.

teaching tips

Ask students to collect e-mail messages, non-proprietary letters from businesses, and mail from charitable and political groups. As the characteristics of good writing are discussed, students can use such letters for illustrations of good and poor writing.

points to emphasize

When two employees know each other's work well, written communications between them can be brief. Detailed explanations are seldom required.

Most jobs in today's business world require writing. Talking with people in a wide range of jobs reveals considerable differences in their writing responsibilities. A reasonable conclusion is that those who work must have writing skills. You will want to be sure that you can write a memorandum, a letter, or a report following standards for such documents.

There is no single **model** for effective writing. All writing need not meet the same standard of quality. There are occasions, for example, when time is the critical factor, and you need to compose a message quickly to be transmitted by e-mail or by fax to someone within the company. Just getting the key points to the person who needs them is the goal of such a message. The recipient of your message will be grateful to you for forwarding the details requested quickly. At other times, your task may be to write a **diplomatic** response to a customer who is

model:
way in which something can be done

diplomatic:
skillful in dealing with others

Topic 3-3

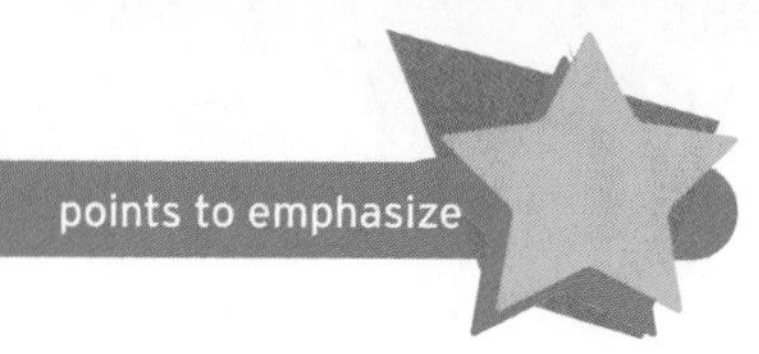

To know when you should write with care and when a quickly written message is sufficient is judgment that a good employee develops with experience.

Ask students to consider the kind of writing each of the following positions is likely to require: a manager in a bank, a teacher in a high school, a reporter with the local newspaper, the president of a company.

warranty: guarantee

complaining about a product after the end of the **warranty** period. You need to compose a response that conveys understanding, yet states the company's policy. In such a situation you hope to maintain the goodwill of the customer.

Illustration 3-3:1
Some correspondence requires a quick response.

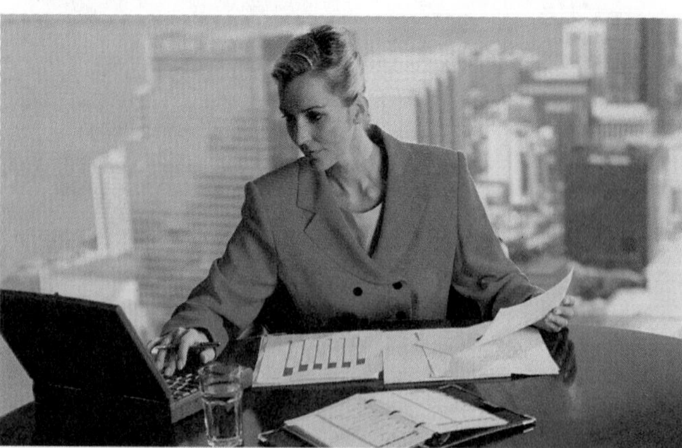

Common Writing Tasks

As noted, the extent and nature of your writing responsibilities are related to:

- the nature of your job
- the extent to which writing tasks are **delegated** to you
- your own interest and willingness to assume such tasks

delegated: assigned to another

Employees from senior executives to office workers are likely to need writing skills. Among the common writing tasks are these:

- summarizing written messages and meetings
- preparing drafts of communications for others to review
- revising others' writing and making changes
- composing communications and revising them before they are issued

Peggy is a technical writer for a software company. She was an English major in college. From her middle school days, when she began her study of the computer, she was aware of how important good instructions are. She enjoys her work, which requires that she understand thoroughly the procedures for using a new software so that she can write instructions for persons who want to learn on their own. She works in close cooperation with the developers of the software program.

When would summaries of written material be useful?

SUMMARIZING WRITTEN MESSAGES AND MEETINGS

A great deal of communication is required among employees and with outsiders. One person may gather information about a particular matter and communicate it to others involved in the decision-making process about the matter. Another common activity in organizations is a meeting that is followed up with a written report.

For what reasons might revising others' writing be an easier task than revising one's own writing?

Effective summarizing is a valuable skill. To do it well, the person assigned should:

- understand what is at issue or what is critical to those who are to read the summary
- listen and/or read attentively
- identify the critical points
- write a summary as concisely as possible
- review the summary to see if it actually reflects the written communication or the meeting

What do you think of Terri's response to the manager? What must she have known about the controller to respond as she did?

Terri is an assistant controller in a mid-size electronics manufacturing company. One plant manager called to talk with Jim, the controller, to discuss his need for more information than that provided in the current monthly report. Jim was at the company's Brazilian facilities. Terri asked: "George, what information would you like the report to include? Do you need information by product or for all products together? Why are you requesting this information?" George gave complete responses to Terri's questions. Terri took careful notes. She assured George that she would give his request to Jim when he returned to the office within a week.

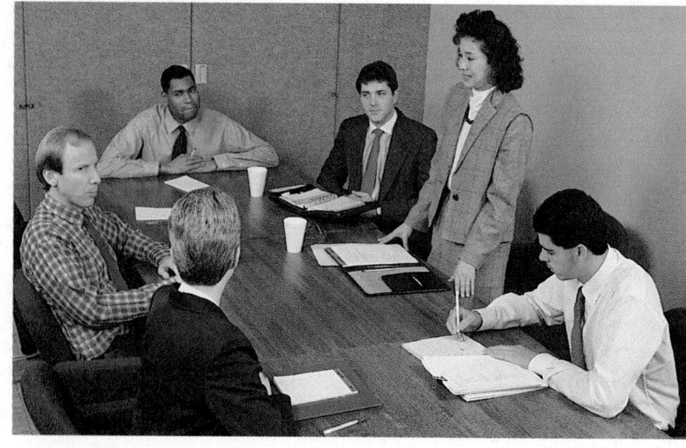

Illustration 3-3:2

This staff member takes notes to help him prepare the meeting summary.

Did Terri provide a valuable service? The controller thinks so. The controller wants to provide useful information to plant managers around the world. Can you imagine what the manager would think if Terri had responded: "Oh, George, would you call back when Jim is here?" Instead, Terri got information for the controller's use on his return.

PREPARING DRAFTS

Communications may reflect the point of view of a department or the company. Often, one person is assigned to prepare a draft, which is then reviewed by others. Staff at all levels may participate in writing tasks.

The staff of the Human Resources Department met to discuss the strategy for implementing a recently announced move to a new location, 2,000 miles away. A staff member, noted for her writing skills, was assigned the task of drafting a memorandum to be sent by e-mail to all employees. The staff member listened carefully to what had to be communicated. It was clear that many employees would be disappointed with such news, so an honest, carefully worded message was needed.

Why would a company want to communicate a single point of view to the public?

Administrative assistants and secretaries contribute to the efficiency of their managers by their help with incoming messages. In some offices, administrative assistants and secretaries prepare drafts of responses to messages received. Then the executive reads the incoming messages and the suggested response at one time. Often executives are satisfied with their assistants' suggestions. Little editing is needed. Final copies are prepared quickly. Recipients will have responses within a relatively brief period.

Illustration 3-3:3
An administrative assistant drafts replies to incoming mail.

REVIEWING THE WRITING OF OTHERS

Rewriting is often required for the preparation of an effective message. Administrative assistants are frequently asked to review the written communications of others. Some executives expect their assistants to act as editors. An editor is a person who reviews what has been written to suggest changes in wording, organization, and content. Workers with editorial responsibility are expected to:

- identify **precisely** what the writer's intent is
- focus on the purpose of the task—to assure that the message is meeting all requirements for effectiveness
- be candid in making suggestions
- review their own suggestions in an **objective** manner

precisely: exactly

objective: without bias

Note the draft prepared by a human resources manager shown in Illustration 3-3:4. Note the suggested changes made by a colleague. Consider the changes proposed. Do you think they improve the message?

What are some problems editors might encounter when doing their job?

Illustration 3-3:4
A paragraph from a communication to staff

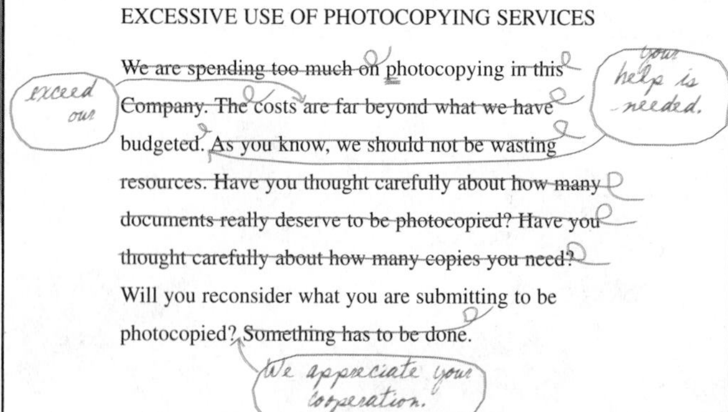

EXCESSIVE USE OF PHOTOCOPYING SERVICES

We are spending too much on photocopying in this Company. The costs are far beyond what we have budgeted. As you know, we should not be wasting resources. Have you thought carefully about how many documents really deserve to be photocopied? Have you thought carefully about how many copies you need? Will you reconsider what you are submitting to be photocopied? Something has to be done.

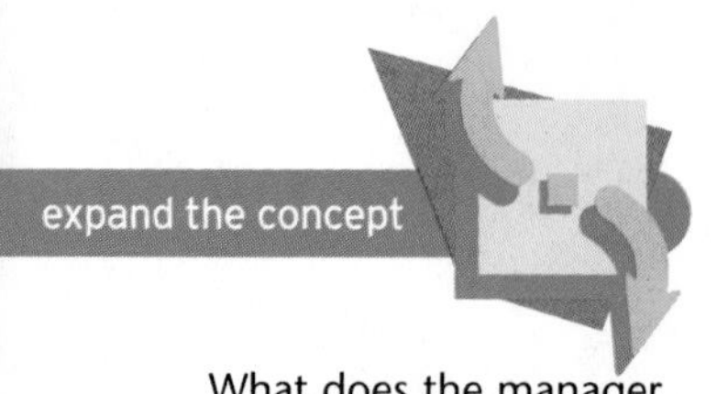

What does the manager mean when she says: "We are in the word business"?

Adele, manager of public relations in a large company, discussed how the staff viewed their work. She said: "We are in the word business, you might say. We prepare all press releases as well as a variety of communications for internal purposes. We strive to make all written communications as effective as possible. A **misstated** *message is difficult to erase. We believe the care we use initially in writing messages pays dividends later."*

misstated: not as it should have been

Ask students to recall when they wrote a message and forwarded it without any revision. Have the class make a list of generally unedited messages.

COMPOSING MESSAGES

You may have complete responsibility for certain writing tasks. You will want to be at ease when you write messages on your own. There may little time to get reviews from others and rewrite what you want to communicate. You will want to develop the skill of writing a message appropriately initially so little revision is needed. When you are doing the entire job of composing and signing memoranda and letters, you must be your own editor. If you are candid and objective, you will be a good editor of your own work.

provost: a top official in a college or university

The administrative assistant to the **provost** *in a state university had considerable responsibility for writing many responses to memoranda received in the provost's office. It was common for the provost to write*

To Jill:

TO: Provost Daniel T. Jacobson

FROM: T. W. Adams, Mathematics Department

DATE: October 5, xxxx

SUBJECT: Core Curriculum Changes

11/7/96 thanks!

As we discussed last week, it seems to me that we should have a meeting with representatives from the several colleges who have given some thought to what should be required mathematics courses for all entering freshmen. We also need to review the background of entering students to determine what kinds of remedial programs should be available.

agree with need

Tim Wallace in Arts and Sciences at the Elmwood Branch has done some interesting studies of his entering students. I think he would be a good one to head up a review committee.

Your attention to this matter is appreciated.

good recommendation, but I'd like you to take the job! your work on the core was great.

DTJ

Illustration 3-3:5

The notes that guide an administrative assistant

TO: Professor T. W. Adams, Mathematics

FROM: Daniel T. Jacobson, Provost

DATE: October 7, xxxx

SUBJECT: Reply to your memo of October 5

Your comments are appreciated. I agree that we need to review what is being done throughout the university in the teaching of mathematics.

I appreciate your recommendation for the head of the committee. However, I would like to see you serve as chairperson. Your work in designing the core courses reflected excellent ability to motivate a committee. Will you accept the assignment?

I hope you will say "yes."

Illustration 3-3:6

The memorandum written by the administrative assistant

a few words in response to an incoming memorandum. The administrative assistant then prepared a memorandum that was courteous and complete. The provost signed the memorandum quickly.

Business Writing is Purpose Driven

Most activity in business is purpose driven. Business writing, too, is purpose driven. The business office is not the place for literary writing—at least not during working hours! There is a practical reason for all writing activity at work. Some of the most common purposes are discussed in the following paragraphs.

expand the concept

How does consideration of purpose influence the writer of business communications?

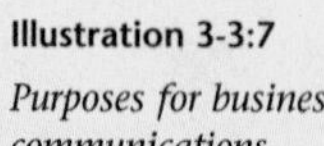

Illustration 3-3:7
Purposes for business communications

Purposes for Business Communications

- communicating policies and procedures
- communicating plans in progress
- seeking specific information
- providing specific information
- following up oral discussions
- sending messages to customers

Why would a company of chain restaurants want all managers to adhere to written policies and procedures?

COMMUNICATING POLICIES AND PROCEDURES

People must be informed about the company and their work. Many written messages relate to the policies and procedures in an organization. You can understand the need for written policies and procedures since many organizations have employees in many different locations. Yet employees must adhere to the policies and procedures established for the total organization. An executive vice president responsible for communications commented about the need for written communications in these words:

We are a high-tech company operating in the global community. Our customers use our services in a number of different countries. They expect our local units to behave toward them in the same way, regardless of where they are located. There is no way we could meet customer expectations without paying attention to communicating clearly the policies and procedures that guide all our efforts.

COMMUNICATING PLANS IN PROGRESS

There is much attention paid to the future in modern business. Numerous meetings are held within businesses to carefully think about what lies ahead. Many people in the organization, beyond those directly involved in the planning, must be kept informed. Written reports are invaluable in making everyone aware of progress.

Why is it common for many persons in an organization to participate in the development of plans?

SEEKING SPECIFIC INFORMATION

There are times when specific information required to make a decision is missing. Information is needed from outsiders who can provide the organization with equipment, supplies, and professional services. Often messages are exchanged within the organization for the purpose of seeking information. Illustration 3-3:8 on page 140 is a memorandum that seeks information from sales representatives throughout the company. All sales representatives interact with customers and have information about customer satisfaction—as well as dissatisfaction—in the use of the company's products or services. The sales representatives' observations are of critical value as those at headquarters plan for the forthcoming period.

PROVIDING SPECIFIC INFORMATION

Many written communications provide specific information. It is common in an organization for one department to need information from other departments. Furthermore, many messages from outside are requests for specific information. Customers and prospective customers make numerous inquiries to which companies give prompt and courteous attention.

Can you identify reasons the staff in the local banks might send written memos to each other?

Dan works in a management consulting firm that provides a wide range of services to companies in the banking industry. Dan works in the marketing department, where all correspondence related to inquiries

Why might a company want feedback from sales representatives throughout the country? Why is feedback from the local sales representatives not sufficient?

Discuss with the class the extent to which consultants are used in United States' businesses. Students may be able to identify reasons for this.

Why is a written communication prepared when all members of the group were present and expressed agreement about the decision?

Illustration 3-3:8

A memorandum forwarded to sales representatives

TO: Sales Representatives, USA

FROM: Ray O'Connor, National Sales Manager

DATE: October 11, xxxx

SUBJECT: Response to our 3-D Graphics Chip

In what ways are some of your key customers using our newest 3-D graphics chip? What disappointments do key customers have at this point? As you know well, our 3-D chip is speedier than any other available, and this speed is achieved without using more memory.

As you noted in the last report, our sales have grown dramatically in the first two quarters; and they are now exceeding our most optimistic forecasts. We continue to be the market leader, even though some giant companies are entering the business. We have good production capability to keep ahead, we believe.

Please e-mail your findings. Thanks.

about services are referred. Dan and his colleagues read incoming correspondence carefully and prepare responses related to the specific questions raised. Dan and his colleagues are careful to consider how what they say will sound from the inquirer's point of view. The marketing department is highly successful in gaining new clients. The responses of Dan and his colleagues are considered key to attracting clients.

FOLLOWING UP ORAL DISCUSSIONS

Much of the interaction among businesspeople is oral. Discussions may be in group meetings, person-to-person, by telephone, or by teleconferences. A written record of what was discussed is often required for those who participated and others who did not. Such a report serves as a summary of what happened and as a preview for further discussions.

A team of five managers met to consider quality management as it applies to their five departments. These five departments have the most interaction with the public. The purpose of the meeting was to review problems with telephone calls. Customers were encountering too much waiting time. One of the engineers in the group acted as recorder, keeping notes and preparing a report shortly after each meeting. The report was forwarded to the five people on the committee who then knew what had been decided and where the group would begin at the next session.

Illustration 3-3:9

One team member keys meeting notes for the group.

If students collected letters, have them review some that are advertising letters.

SENDING MESSAGES TO CUSTOMERS

Communications are a means of encouraging greater demand for the products and services of businesses. Letters, brochures, flyers, catalogs, and World Wide Web sites all require well-chosen words to communicate effectively.

Correspondence is also required to remind customers with **delinquent** bills of the actions that will be taken if payment is not forthcoming. Several employees may assist in preparing such correspondence. The credit department is responsible for following up with customers who have not paid on a timely basis. However, the letters mailed with the reminder are often reviewed by the director of customer services. Efforts to get payment are done in a friendly manner so that the customer will continue to patronize the company.

delinquent: past due

If a person is delinquent in making payments, why would a company want to continue having that person as a customer?

Characteristics of Effective Writing

Writing in the business world is expected to reflect basic concerns for efficiency and effectiveness. Unlike a poem, for example, where

obscure: not clear, hidden

meaning can be **obscure,** business writing is expected to be direct and meaningful to all who read it. Common characteristics of good business writing are discussed in the following sections.

Illustration 3-3:10
Effective writing gets high scores on all five factors.

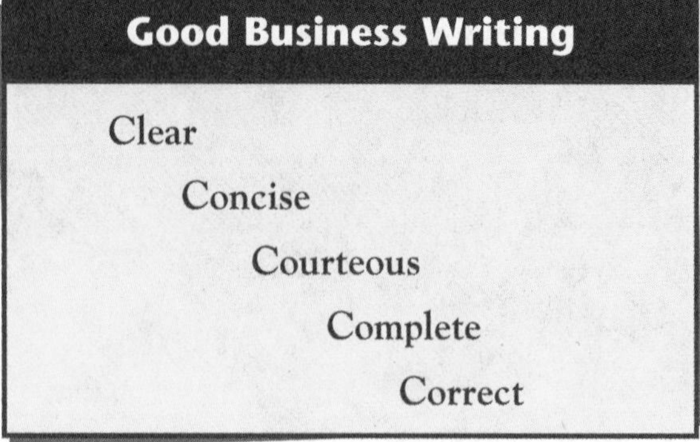

Good Business Writing
Clear
Concise
Courteous
Complete
Correct

How do clear messages contribute to productivity?

CLEAR

A clear message is logically arranged. This means the information is in an order that is natural for the recipient to follow. To prepare a clear message, you must know why you want to communicate, what you want to communicate, and who your recipient will be.

eliminates: removes

A clear message **eliminates** the need for requests for additional comment. A clear letter or memorandum allows the recipient to respond immediately and without hesitation. The person reading a clear message need not ask when finished: "What is the meaning of this message?"

The manager of computer services in a medium-sized firm learned about a book that would be of interest to his staff. Study the following sentences that the manager wrote to the publisher.

NOT CLEAR: *I noted in a recent copy of* BUSINESS TODAY *that you publish a handbook on* WISE USE OF SOFTWARE PACKAGES. *I would like a copy. What is the price of the book?*

The recipient of a letter with these sentences might raise questions such as: Does the writer of the letter want a copy of the book? Or, does he/she just want to know the price? Will he determine later whether the book will be purchased?

CLEAR: *In the September issue of BUSINESS TODAY, I noted that you publish a handbook entitled WISE USE OF SOFTWARE PACKAGES. Please send me one copy of the handbook. Enclose an invoice. Upon receipt of the book and invoice, I will send you a payment.*

CONCISE

A concise message states what you want to communicate in the fewest and most direct words possible. An efficient message is a concise message. The recipient will waste no time in reading words and thoughts that add nothing to understanding the message.

NOT CONCISE: *We have completed the first set of* **roundtable** *discussions held throughout the company. My thanks to everyone who attended (see list at the end of memo). The following is a list of many of the ideas raised. Please note that all the suggestions revolve around normal operations because we did not discuss anything else.*

roundtable: informal gathering

CONCISE: *Attached is the list of ideas raised at the first roundtable discussions held throughout the company. Normal operations was the topic of the discussions; other concerns will be topics for future meetings. Thanks to all participants (listed at end of memo).*

What does a writer have to consider when striving for a concise message? What knowledge of the recipient may serve as a constraint on conciseness?

COURTEOUS

Written communications are courteous when they conform to the expected polite, **considerate** behavior of the business world. Expressions such as "thank you," "please," and "you are welcome" are commonly used in business correspondence. As you know, most letters include salutations and complimentary closes that reflect courtesy. The so-called "you approach" is commonly recommended for the tone of

considerate: thinking of others

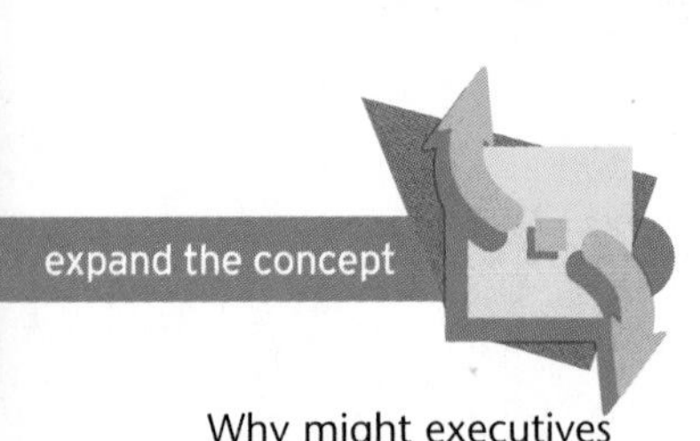

Why might executives strive to have all communications reflect the "you approach"?

messages. When you write with your attention on the recipient—using the "you approach"—you are likely to prepare a courteous message. Courteous messages encourage good relations and cooperation with your associates. Discourteous messages **alienate** people and can create strained relations and ill will.

alienate: turn away in feeling

DISCOURTEOUS: *You are unreasonable in your letter to us. You should realize that we were not responsible for the recent snowstorm that resulted in extended power* ***outages*** *in your area. Most customers understood the situation better than you did.*

outages: lack of service

COURTEOUS: *We regret the inconvenience you experienced during the recent power outage. The problem was widespread, making it necessary for our repair crews to work around-the-clock to restore power to you and our other valuable customers. As you undoubtedly noted in the local newspaper, our repair crews were* ***commended*** *for their devotion during this emergency.*

commended: noted for good job

COMPLETE

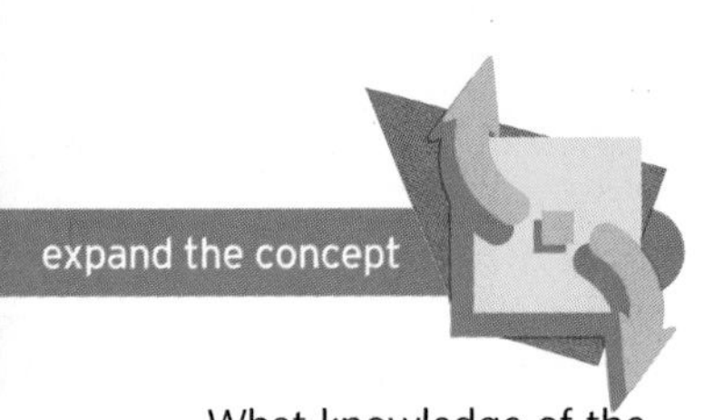

What knowledge of the recipient is important as the writer considers the completeness of a message?

A complete message provides all the information needed. Think of the recipient by asking yourself: "Does this answer all the questions the recipient might raise about this matter?"

NOT COMPLETE: *We will meet on Wednesday, November 3, at 9:00 a.m. at the Astor Hotel.*

The recipient is likely to ask: "How long is the meeting? In what room will the meeting be held? Who will be there? Is there an agenda?"

COMPLETE: *Our Community Environmental Committee meeting will be Thursday, November 3, from 9:00 a.m. to 3:00 p.m. at the Astor Hotel. The meeting will be in the Franklin Room, where we will have lunch from 12:00 p.m. to 1:00 p.m. The agenda will be forwarded to you within the next week.*

CORRECT

A correct message is accurate and up to date. Details provided in messages should be **verified** before the final form is prepared. You should not assume, for example, that a price in effect when you last wrote a message is still in effect. Changes are common in business, and any message must carry current information to be of value to the recipient.

verified: checked

In what ways do computer-accessed records aid an employee in being correct about details in messages?

Incorrect information causes many problems in business. Further correspondence often is required; the goodwill of customers is lost; and, at times, customers who expect accurate information may discontinue their association with the organization.

> *Part of Kathy's job was to answer inquiries about availability of products for future delivery. A prospective customer wanted to know whether a specified quantity could be shipped at four dates throughout the year. Kathy knew that the company maintained good inventories, so she responded by e-mail that there would be no problem in meeting the customer's order. Only after the customer sent the order with the specified dates for delivery did Kathy make an inquiry. At that point, she learned that the company was discontinuing the manufacture of the item within the next two months.*

English Skills for Business Writing

Why are English skills considered necessary for good business communication?

Effective business writing reveals good command of the English language. A review of such writing will show that:

- Sentences are complete.
- Grammar, punctuation, and capitalization follow standard rules.
- Words are spelled correctly.

CHECK SENTENCE STRUCTURE

A sentence is the basic unit of communications. It must contain one or more words identifying persons, places, objects, or ideas that serve as the subject of the sentence. It must also include a verb, which is a word or group of words that describes an action or a condition. At a

Further discussion of the illustrations may be warranted if students have problems with the basic concept. Students may be asked to give examples of nouns and verbs used in such a way that they do not create complete sentences.

Additional exercises, based on sentences student have heard, might be developed.

minimum, a sentence has one subject and one verb. For example, a sentence can be as brief as two words. "You write." is a sentence.

Some collections of words are just parts of sentences, since they lack one of the essential elements.

EXAMPLE 1:	*To reduce the glare on computer screens.*
Missing:	*one or more content words*
A complete sentence:	*Proper lighting will reduce the glare on computer screens.*
EXAMPLE 2:	*As noted, all new employees who meet the experience requirement.*
Missing:	*one or more verbs*
A complete sentence:	*As noted, all new employees who meet the experience requirement will be invited to the seminar.*

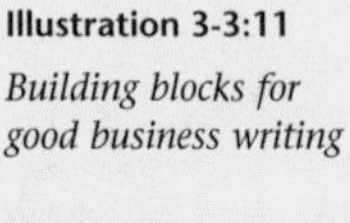

Illustration 3-3:11
Building blocks for good business writing

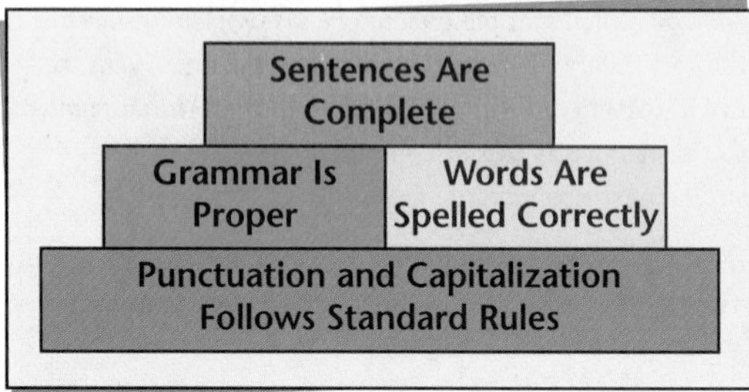

USE PROPER GRAMMAR

You may expect to experience some uncertainties about grammar while you are writing. Become acquainted with the grammar references available to you. Some references may be books, while others are databases accessed through your computer. Can you identify the errors in grammar in the following sentences? Can you explain the rule or rules that relate to the error(s)? If necessary, refer to a reference source.

1. You will want to know what computer program are available for your use.
2. The three accountants in our office works hard.

3. His knowledge of software programs are amazing.
4. Of the two word processors, Jeannie is the best.
5. Will you join Betty and I for lunch today?

FOLLOW RULES OF PUNCTUATION AND CAPITALIZATION

You have studied the basic rules of punctuation and capitalization. As you write or edit business messages, consider whether your marks of punctuation and use of capital letters are proper and add to the clarity of your message. Reference Sections B and C are valuable sources for answering questions about punctuation and capitalization. Can you determine what changes in punctuation and capitalization are needed in the following sentences?

1. Is jane going to join us for the demonstration at three.
2. More than three years ago the Company decided to have state-of-the-art equipment in all offices.
3. We expect to consolidate offices in St. Louis Kansas city and Springfield.
4. Can we be sure our customers get fast accurate information when they telephone us.
5. As you know our new Orleans office is the only office experimenting with the new tracking equipment.

SPELL WORDS CORRECTLY

Misspelled words are distracting to the recipient of your message. Such words are likely to give an impression of sloppiness and indifference to the writing task. Spelling errors may cause the reader to doubt the accuracy of what you are communicating.

Don't **undermine** the effectiveness of your message with misspelled words. Have a dictionary at hand or use the spell check program at your computer when you are not sure of the spelling of a word.

undermine: reduce

Are there spelling errors in the paragraph below? On a separate sheet, rewrite the short paragraph, correcting all spelling errors as you

A review of punctuation as it is used in one of the topics students have already studied might be helpful.

There are some arbitrary decisions relative to use of punctuation. (Example: the comma before *and* in a series.)

How do you find a word in a dictionary when you don't know how to spell it? (Consider the word *psychology,* for example.)

See Workbook pages 215–221 for Reference Sections B and C.

encounter each one. Please know, though, that few communications will have as many errors as are here!

> *Under seperete cover we are sending you, with our complements, a copy of our latest report. We believe you will be especially interested in the questionaire used as the bases of the report. The report* **underscores** *our committment to quality products. We will be happy to recieve your comments and sugestions.*

underscores: highlights

Illustration 3-3:12
A strategy for managing writing tasks

- ❖ Identify reasons for writing
- ❖ Secure information
- ❖ Compose draft
- ❖ Prepare outline for long message or key message directly
- ❖ Review
- ❖ Submit for review, if required
- ❖ Prepare final copy
- ❖ Proofread
- ❖ Sign and prepare for distribution

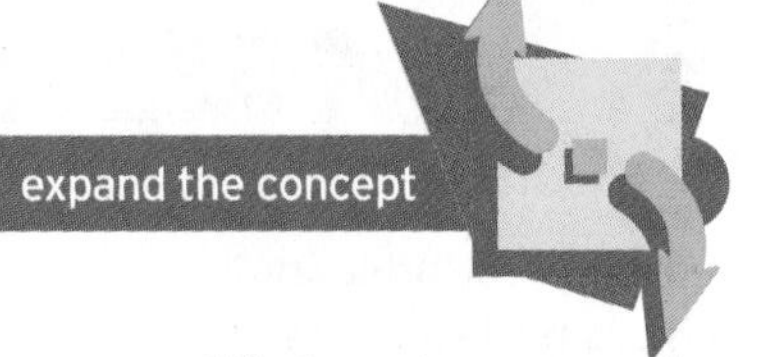

What must you assess in order to judge how long it will take to complete a writing assignment?

Management of Writing Tasks

Writing tasks must be managed wisely if they are to be completed successfully and on schedule. There are two aspects to managing writing tasks. One relates to the actual writing task itself; the other relates to scheduling the task properly to meet deadlines.

MANAGING THE TASK OF WRITING

The following steps will prove useful to you in completing a writing assignment:

1. Identify the reason for the written communication.
2. Secure all the information required for the message.

3. Compose a draft of your message.
   A. Prepare an outline of what you plan to say if the message is long.
   B. Key your message directly at your computer using your outline as a guide.
4. Review your message; make corrections if needed.
5. If required, submit your draft to a colleague or manager for review and approval.
6. Prepare a final copy of your communication.
7. Proofread carefully.
8. Sign and prepare the communication for distribution.

MANAGING THE SCHEDULE FOR WRITING TASKS

In most instances, there is a deadline for the completion of a writing task. It is important that deadlines be met. This means that when you accept a writing task, you must review how much time is required for each aspect of the work you must undertake.

One strategy is to review the steps in the preceding section, noting just how much time is needed to do the task well. For example, having required information at hand in a letter eliminates the need for time to search for information. A schedule may be needed for a major writing task to ensure that you work within the time period allowed. The time available must be **allocated** so that each aspect of the task can be accomplished properly.

allocated: set aside

Use one of the writing assignments as an example of scheduling time. (Suggestion: Integrated Activity at the end of this chapter)

Opportunities for Writing

You will have numerous occasions during your study of office procedures to develop your writing skills. Remember that all written communications do not need to be of the same quality. For example, a memorandum to the manager of the stockroom, whom you know personally, might be written informally and e-mailed without editing. On the other hand, a letter to thousands of customers might be rewritten several times, with others reviewing drafts to make sure the letter will attract customer attention.

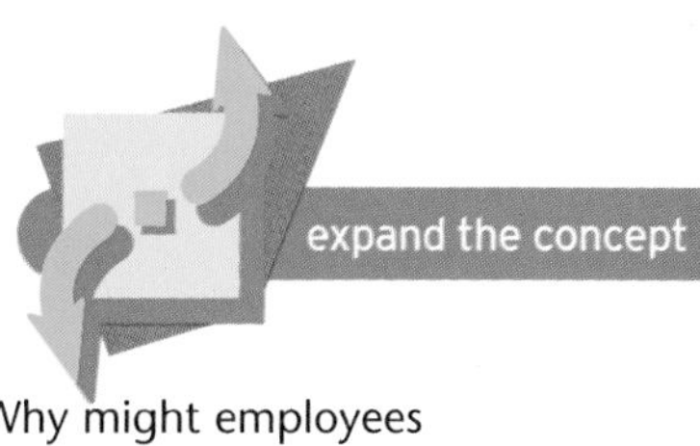

Why might employees postpone completing a writing task?

With practice, you will gain sufficient facility in preparing simple messages the first time you try. Also, you will gain a sense of what a good message should be and how to prepare one. You will develop skill in evaluating your own writing. You can become a good critic of your writing.

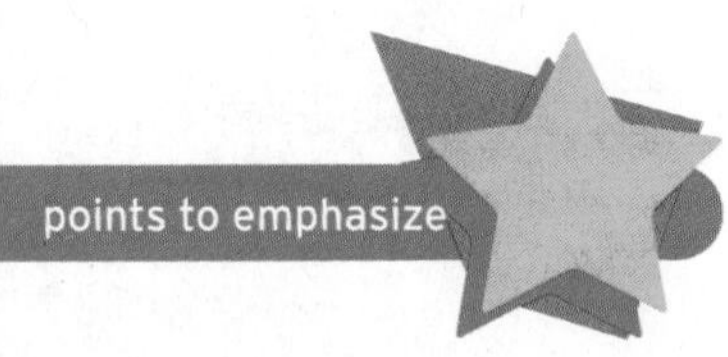

Common concerns of basic communications include awareness of recipient, understanding what is to be communicated, command of extensive vocabulary, and command of English skills.

The Interrelationship of Communication Skills

As you have studied the topics of this chapter, you undoubtedly noted that there is much overlapping of communication skills. Workers read to understand and talk with colleagues. Workers speak to a group about matters that require their reading a variety of materials. Workers read to search for information required for a writing task. Speaking, listening, reading, and writing all depend on high-level facility with words and continuing attention to what they mean and which ones are most effective in getting across a particular message. This means that an extensive vocabulary can be invaluable in oral and written communicating as well as in comprehending what you read. Therefore, attention to one aspect of your communications skills is likely to lead to improvement in a number of different ways. You will work in a world where communications are key to meeting your obligations with success. Use your classroom time and out-of-class experiences to enhance communication skills that have been the object of attention since you began your education.

Reviewing the Topic

topic 3-3 review

1. Is there a single model for effective writing? Why or why not?
2. What are common business writing tasks?
3. What are important skills for the person who is summarizing written messages or meetings?
4. What should a person keep in mind while reviewing a draft of a written communication?
5. Explain the attitude a person should maintain while reviewing his/her own writing?
6. What does it mean to say that business writing is "purpose driven."
7. Illustrate a situation where you would prepare a written communication to seek information.
8. For what purpose are written communications prepared after oral discussions?
9. Identify characteristics of good business writing.
10. Explain the importance of courteousness in business writing.

INTERACTING WITH OTHERS

The vice president named a committee of five, including you, to review employee communications. The vice president's charge was: Make an evaluation of internal communications and prepare a report.

You were happy to participate in this special project. You knew the others and you felt that the five of you could work well together. The group had an initial meeting. You were appointed chairperson. The project progressed with success and on schedule until the writing task began. Each person was to prepare a draft of a segment of the report. Everyone promised to review all the segments. As chairperson you had responsibility for coordinating the writing task. Two others and you met the deadline for drafts. The other two said that they did not realize that they really do not like to write. At this point they would like to resign from the group. As the chairperson of the group, what would you say to the two who are asking to resign?

topic 3-3 review

Writing

151

What you are to do:

Prepare a response to the question raised.

Writing

topic 3-3 review

REINFORCING ENGLISH SKILLS

The following sentences have errors in noun and verb agreement.

Simple rules of writing applies to e-mail. This type of writing seem informal, but it is still business communications. Experts points out that brisk and brief writing are fine. It is not wise to consider this type of communicating impersonal. Insensitive and discourteous statements should not be in your messages. The ease in corresponding via e-mail have led to many unclear and confusing messages. Reviews of e-mail has discovered all types of inappropriate and irrelevant material that are really clutter.

What you are to do:

Key the sentences correcting the errors in noun and verb agreement.

APPLICATION ACTIVITY

ACTIVITY **Press Release**

Assume that you are an assistant manager in the Public Information Department of your company, Laughlin & Mead Corporation, headquartered in Asheville, North Carolina. The Board of Directors met yesterday and elected Mr. T. W. Gomez to the company's new position of Vice President for Technology. The Public Information Director has asked you to prepare a draft of a press release to be sent to local newspapers as well as to business periodicals. The company address is 289 Westlake Avenue; Asheville, NC 28803; Telephone: 704-555-0101; Fax: 704-555-0102. Use your name as the contact person and these details you were given:

1. Mr. T. W. Gomez was elected by the Board of Directors at its meeting yesterday to fill the newly created position of Vice President for Technology.
2. Mr. Gomez has had ten years of experience in transforming the way work is done at Treadway Corporation in Boston, where he most recently served as Assistant Vice President for Technology.

152

3. Mr. Gomez is a graduate of Midwest University, where he earned a B.A. degree in mathematics and an M.B.A. in computer science.
4. Our company sees the need to introduce state-of-the-art technology throughout our facilities in the 12 countries where we have operations.
5. Mr. Gomez will assume his new responsibilities on the first of next month.
6. When Mr. Gomez accepted the position, he said: "I like the challenge of this large company that has a vision of what it can become. I want to be a part of that vision. I look forward to working with the fine group of people who lead the company."

What you are to do:

Compose and key a draft of a press release for review by the department manager. Consult Reference Section H, Sample Documents, for a sample news release format.

See Workbook page 235.

153

Chapter Summary

In this chapter, the communication skills of listening, speaking, reading, and writing were discussed within the context of responsibilities at work. Even though you have used these skills since you were very young, you can improve them for better performance on the job.

You studied a variety of strategies useful in improving your communication skills. Considerations for enhancing your basic communication skills include:

LISTENING

- develop the attitude of willingness to learn
- focus attention
- mentally summarize
- take notes
- ask questions

SPEAKING

- take an interest in communicating
- speak clearly
- use standard language
- express your ideas concisely
- consider your audience
- be aware of nonverbal communication
- be interested in listeners' response

READING

- follow techniques for increasing comprehension
- expand your vocabulary
- practice techniques to increase speed

WRITING

- write effective business communications to be clear, concise, courteous, complete, and correct
- apply rules of standard English
- manage the writing task efficiently to meet deadlines

There is considerable overlap among the four communications skills discussed in this chapter. The achievement of goals of all types of organizations is dependent on the communication skills of all employees. Persons who can communicate efficiently and effectively are valuable in any organization. Along with the development of other job skills, strive to develop good communication skills.

KEY CONCEPTS AND TERMS

clear
colloquialisms
complete
comprehension
concise
correct
courteous
editor
enunciation
nonverbal communication
slang
standard language

INTEGRATED CHAPTER ACTIVITIES

ACTIVITY 1 Report Presentation

You will be assigned to a group that will develop a report on the topic: The Significance of Communication Skills in the World of Work. Your group will present the report to the class.

What you are to do:

1. Identify sources of relevant material for all members to read and study. Possible sources include references in the library and websites.
2. Determine what, if any, information you might want to secure from surveys of persons at work on aspects of the topic.

155

3. Develop a schedule for the completion of the collection of information.
4. Determine assignments for writing the report, which should be approximately four to five pages long.
5. Consider as a group how the presentation will be made.
6. Determine assignments for the presentation, which is to include all members of your group.
7. Give the presentation to the class or another group.

ACTIVITY 2 Self-Evaluation of Communication Skills

In this activity, you will evaluate your own participation in Activity 1. You may find it helpful to keep a diary of your experience and your assessment of your own performance. When you rate your participation, use a scale of 1 to 5, with 5 being the highest point. Rate yourself on the following factors:

READING SKILLS

- identifying relevant materials
- identifying key points to be considered by the group
- understanding vocabulary
- reading at a reasonable speed

LISTENING SKILL

- listened to my group members as we discussed the issues that arose during our planning
- listened to persons interviewed (if interviewing was part of your group's plan)
- listened to presentations by other groups

WRITING SKILL

- wrote a draft of my segment of the report considering the characteristics of good writing

156

- edited my own writing with a critical attitude
- edited my group members' writing in an objective manner
- met the schedule set up by our group
- proofread final copy of the report with attention to details

SPEAKING SKILL

- considered the audience as I prepared my notes
- spoke clearly and to the topic
- responded thoughtfully to listeners' questions

What you are to do:

Key the list of factors listed above and indicate your own evaluation. Below your evaluation, indicate what you plan to do in relation to assignments in the future that require the use of basic communication skills.

157

Leslie Norwood
Director of Human Relations

Getting Acquainted with the World of Work

Should I Be Wasting My Time Attending Meetings?

Dear Ms. Norwood

Wasn't I hired because of my expertise in using computers? Now I find that I am to be part of a team. When I was in college, I spent all my time in the computer laboratory, learning, learning, learning. I enjoyed my studies very much. My teachers applauded my achievement. There were a number of companies that liked my résumé. I was offered several jobs. I chose the one that seemed to be the most challenging. It is in the research and development department of a major high-tech manufacturing company. I work as a programmer, which is a clearly defined position.

This is my problem. The head of the department expects me to attend all kinds of meetings that I believe are not related to what I do. Why do I have to take time to meet with people from marketing and accounting, for example? They don't know my job, and I really don't see why I need to interact with them. Do you agree with me that the department head is wasting my time?

Jill in Boston

Dear Jill

You are undoubtedly a master programmer. You are to be commended for giving your full attention to developing your knowledge and skills while in college. Those skills, as you found, were in great demand in the business world. With your attitude, I am sure you will continue to give attention to expanding your knowledge as new technology is introduced.

At the same time, Jill, your future usefulness in the company requires that you understand what is happening throughout the company. The head of your department is thinking ahead in relation to your career. She recognizes your competencies and dedication to work, I am sure. However, you must realize that your department head believes you have a great deal of potential for handling far broader responsibilities than you now have as a new programmer.

Your initial assignments are likely to be somewhat standard activity for new programmers. Your department head, however, wants programmers who know what the company's goals are and how key people are thinking ahead. Programmers who can respond to needs not yet identified by other units of the company are invaluable.

Jill, you aren't wasting your time. You are being given an opportunity to enlarge your understanding of the environment in which you work. Observe what is happening in your department. Listen to what is being discussed by senior members. Develop an interest in what the company plans to accomplish. Don't put aside your commitment to your specialization. You are in a company that is giving you an opportunity to grow. Accept it with a positive attitude. You will see how valuable your skills and knowledge of computers are to the whole company.

Leslie Norwood

Director of Human Relations

158

Simulation Parts 1 and 2

At Work at *Winston Human Resources*:

Winston Human Resources is headquartered in Atlanta, Georgia. The company was founded by Jill Bates and Steven Lacey five years ago. Both were directors of human resource services in large U.S. companies when they decided to open their own business. They began with one office in downtown Atlanta providing outplacement services for companies that wanted their employees, who were dismissed due to downsizing, to have assistance in preparing for new careers or finding new positions.

During the five years, the company has grown at a very rapid rate. Activities are just getting underway at the new branch in downtown Pittsburgh. A branch manager has been appointed and the office is now furnished and equipped. Five employees, including you, have been hired to staff the branch.

You will be an administrative assistant working primarily with the vice president, Mr. Todd Perenz, and the office manager, Jo Anne Keller. You are expected to complete assignments with little direct supervision. Your first task will be to complete a research project to learn about job projections for the next few years. This information will prepare you to deal more effectively with potential clients and employees. As you complete the project, you will develop:

- listening skills as you receive instructions regarding your assignments
- reading skills as you research information
- critical thinking and writing skills as you summarize and record information
- teamwork and speaking skills as you present information to coworkers and clients

Refer to your *Student Activities and Projects* workbook to learn more about your responsibilities and work assignments at Winston Human Resources.

159

See Workbook pages 105–120.

Simulation Parts 1 and 2

Managing Information to Enhance Productivity

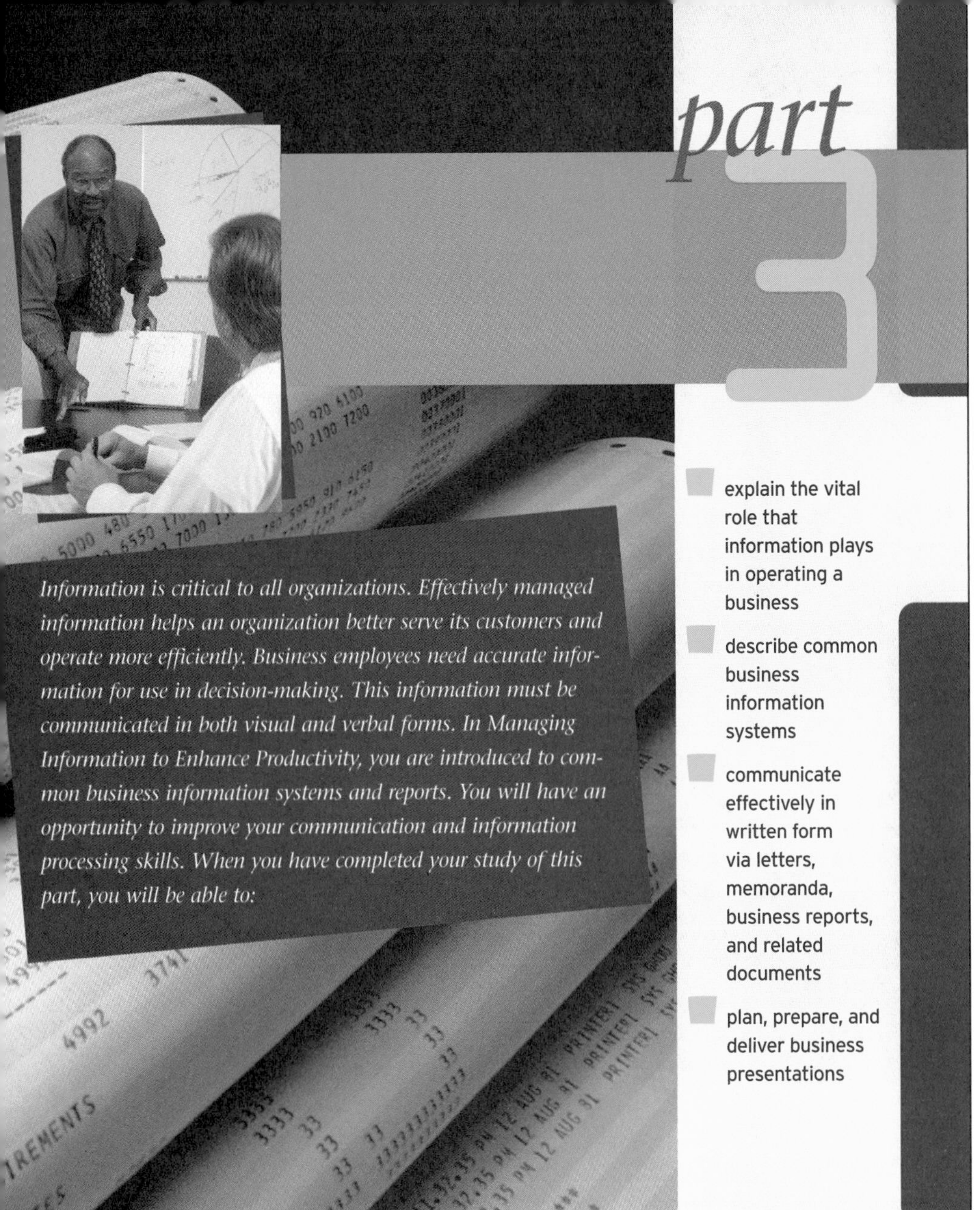

part 3

Information is critical to all organizations. Effectively managed information helps an organization better serve its customers and operate more efficiently. Business employees need accurate information for use in decision-making. This information must be communicated in both visual and verbal forms. In Managing Information to Enhance Productivity, you are introduced to common business information systems and reports. You will have an opportunity to improve your communication and information processing skills. When you have completed your study of this part, you will be able to:

- explain the vital role that information plays in operating a business
- describe common business information systems
- communicate effectively in written form via letters, memoranda, business reports, and related documents
- plan, prepare, and deliver business presentations

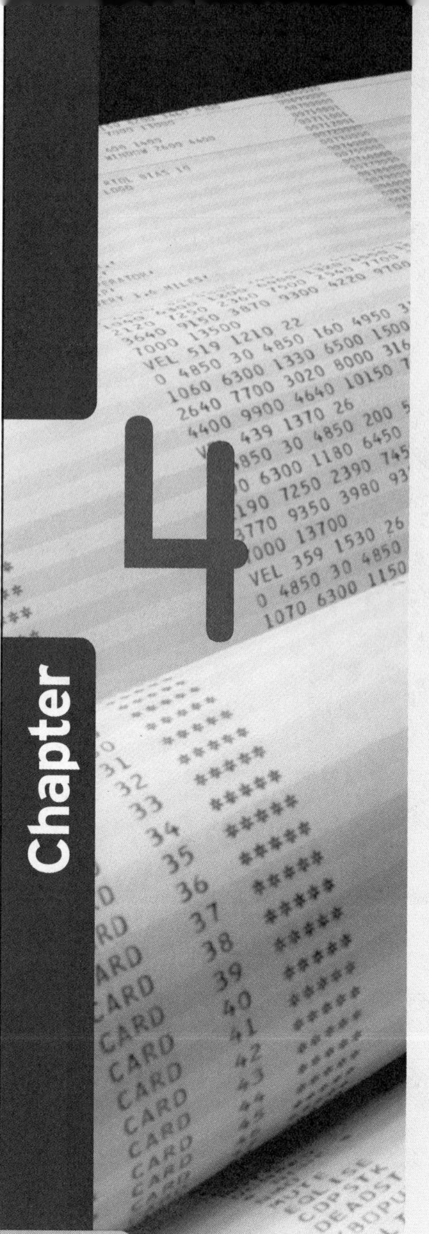

Information: A Vital Business Resource

To prosper and grow, an organization must make sound business decisions. To do this, the organization needs accurate, up-to-date information. Information is simply facts that are organized in a meaningful and usable form. Information is a vital resource that helps an organization serve its customers and operate efficiently.

As an office worker, you will help maintain the flow of information in your organization. You will find your work more interesting and more meaningful when you understand how it relates to the total information system of the organization. As you study this chapter, you will become acquainted with common information systems and resources found in businesses. You will also develop an understanding of how technology can enhance the effectiveness of the information system.

162

Information in Business

Topic 4-1

When you have completed your study of this topic, you will be able to:

- **define information**
- **explain how businesses use information**
- **describe information processing activities**
- **explain how information technologies enhance information systems**

Businesses use many resources in their daily operations—raw materials and equipment for manufacturing, workers to process orders and build products, investment money for expansion and improvements, computers and other technology for communication. The specific resources used will vary from business to business. Regardless of the nature of the business, however, information is an essential resource that affects how other resources are used and the overall success of the business.

How Businesses Use Information

Most of the work performed in offices involves the processing of information. Information starts as basic facts or raw data made up of numbers, symbols, and letters. This raw data becomes information when it is organized in a meaningful way.

getting started

Computers are critical to information management in many businesses. As a means of introducing this chapter, engage students in a discussion of how the computer directly affects their lives. After students have identified several examples (e.g., computer chips used in home appliances, computerized systems in cars), move the discussion to how computers are used in their school. Students should be able to identify examples such as their schedules, grades, attendance, and emergency information maintained in computer databases. Next, discuss how computers affect the functions of business offices they have visited or in which they have worked.

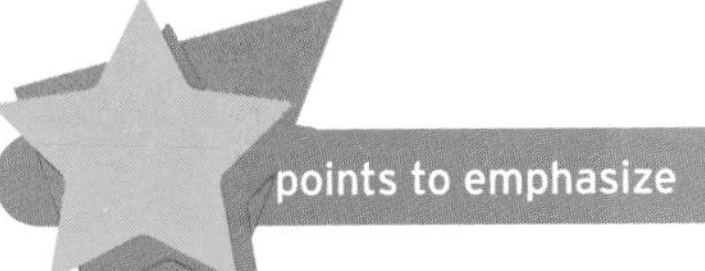

points to emphasize

Information is critical to every organization regardless of its size or purpose.

Topic 4-1

points to emphasize

Raw data becomes information when it is organized in a meaningful way.

> *A payroll manager prepares the weekly payroll checks. (The raw data used includes hours worked, rates of pay, and payroll deductions. When such data is arranged for individual employees, it becomes information to use in preparing the payroll.)*
>
> *An office worker in a shipping department answers a customer's inquiry about a shipping date. (The basic facts used are the customer's name, the invoice number, and the shipping date. Locating the specific invoice gives the office worker the information to answer the customer's question.)*
>
> *A sales associate in a real estate office prepares for a business trip. (The basic facts used are travel dates, destinations, and flight numbers and times. When the sales associate arranges the facts into a meaningful form, an itinerary is created.)*

In the examples above, basic facts have been organized to provide meaningful information: to prepare payroll checks, to answer a customer's inquiry, to prepare an itinerary. By processing or refining data or facts into a meaningful and usable form, you create information. Illustration 4-1:1 shows an example of how facts become information.

Illustration 4-1:1

Facts processed into a meaningful and useful form become information.

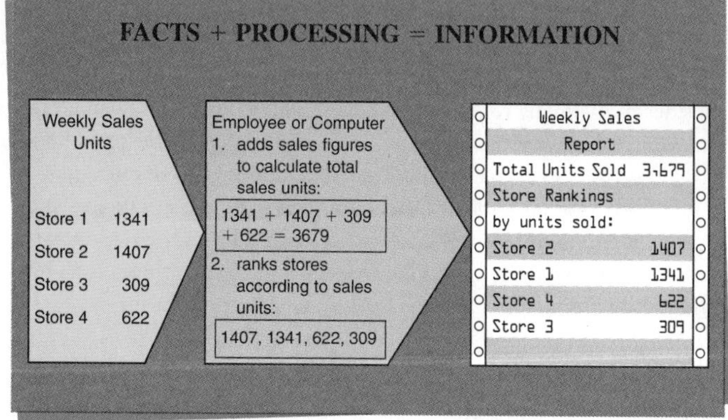

interwoven: mixed together

Information takes many forms. The most common types are identified in Illustration 4-1:2. In actual usage, these individual forms of information are often **interwoven.**

COMMON TYPES OF INFORMATION	
Type	**Examples**
numbers	amounts, quantities, sizes, weights, capacities, ages organized to convey meaning, as in a table or listing
text	words organized to convey meaning, as in letters, memoranda, or reports
image	charts, graphs, photographs
voice	messages conveyed in person; messages conveyed by telephone

Illustration 4-1:2

Common types of information include numbers, text, image, and voice.

Using information effectively is an increasingly important factor in achieving success. Information enables businesses to answer some of their most important questions:

- What do our customers want?
- How can we improve our product and deliver it faster?
- Who are our most productive employees?
- How much can we increase prices before we lose revenue?
- Where can we reduce costs?

Many businesses consistently gather data to use as the basis for making business decisions. Consider the questions listed below and the decisions that may be affected by information answering these questions.

Information Needed	Decisions Affected
What do our customers think of us?	Image to be built or points stressed through advertising Improvements to product quality or customer service
Who are our best customers and where are they located?	Placement of new branch locations Warehousing of goods to be shipped Areas targeted for advertising
What are our best-selling products? Why are these products successful?	Products to keep and products to discontinue Changes for less successful products to make them more popular

The most common forms of information in business offices are numbers, text, image, and voice.

Discussing the information needs of a local organization that is familiar to students can add much to their understanding of the content of the topic. You may find it helpful, therefore, to use any organization students know about—a supermaket, a video rental store—as a basis for a discussion on the types of information required to operate the business effectively.

Who are our best dealers?	Reward plans for dealers
Where are our most productive sales offices?	Strategies for improving sales in other offices
Who are our biggest competitors? What do they offer customers that we do not?	Points stressed through advertising Improvements to product quality, product features, customer service

Managing Information

transactions: business agreements or exchanges

The amount of data related to daily operations of a business can become unmanageable without procedures and technology designed to process the data efficiently. The complexity of running a business, the volume of **transactions** processed, and the need for accurate and up-to-date information make effective management of information essential.

COMPLEXITY OF BUSINESS

Operating even a small business can be quite complex. In a very small business, the owner may take care of all activities. In many small businesses, a few office workers handle all the daily business operations. Typically, all the information needed to operate the business is in one central location, usually the business office. For a small-business owner, efficient organization of information is necessary to maintain a competitive edge.

Illustration 4-1:3

To maintain a competitive edge, small businesses must manage information efficiently.

Efficient organization of information is even more critical in large organizations with many employees. The jobs of employees are often **interrelated.** Several workers may need to use the same information to process work or make decisions. Effective organization of information meets the needs of workers in all areas of the company.

interrelated: having something in common

VOLUME OF TRANSACTIONS

Some organizations must deal with thousands of transactions each day. Effective management of information allows these organizations to run smoothly. Consider the following examples:

Banks process millions of checks, receive millions of deposits, and issue millions of dollars in cash each day.

Manufacturing companies complete the production of millions of products, ship thousands of orders, and receive payments from thousands of customers each day.

Insurance companies receive thousands of premium payments, issue thousands of new policies, and send out notices to thousands of customers each day.

Illustration 4-1:4

A large insurance company may process thousands of communications each day.

Think of the problems that would occur if these organizations did not have adequate information management. The volume of transactions

Ask students: Does using a computer automatically mean that a company is accessing current and accurate information?

Help students understand that timely and accurate information is important to everyone. Relate this concept to a familiar experience, such as purchasing an item at a retail store. What would they think if the cashier could not successfully scan the product UPC code and, therefore, could not process the sale. How would they feel if the clerk told them it would be another day or two before the pricing information would be available? Ask them how they would feel if the clerk told them they had to wait 24 hours before a credit card purchase could be approved. Emphasize that the need for timely and accurate information is common in modern life.

would be overwhelming, and the access and retrieval of information would be slow and tedious.

CURRENT AND ACCURATE INFORMATION

For information to be valuable it must be current and accurate. Outdated or incorrect information can be useless, or worse, it can cost the organization money because poor decisions are made based upon the incorrect information. Coworkers and customers expect to receive information quickly, and they expect it to be accurate and up to date.

Consider the value of current and accurate information in the following examples:

> *Major airlines are able to provide an international network of service because current information is available. Travelers can request a reservation for a flight between two cities anywhere in the world and immediately receive information about the number of seats available on the flight. Customers making reservations are not willing to wait days for a response.*
>
> *A manager keeps detailed information about the company's cash-flow needs. The manager knows exactly how much cash is on hand. Cash not needed immediately is transferred to accounts that earn interest. The company earns money because accurate information is kept. Without this information, there would be no way to determine if some of the cash on hand could be invested temporarily.*

OBSTACLES TO MANAGING INFORMATION EFFECTIVELY

Information has unlimited potential for helping organizations operate effectively. Yet it can be difficult to manage. Data can be hard to organize, easy to lose, easy to alter, hard to locate, and even wrong. **Obstacles** to using information efficiently in an organization include:

obstacles: things that stand in the way

incompatible: unable to work together

- Uncoordinated procedures and files
- Duplication of information
- **Incompatible** databases
- Outdated or inaccurate information
- Missing information
- Limited access to information

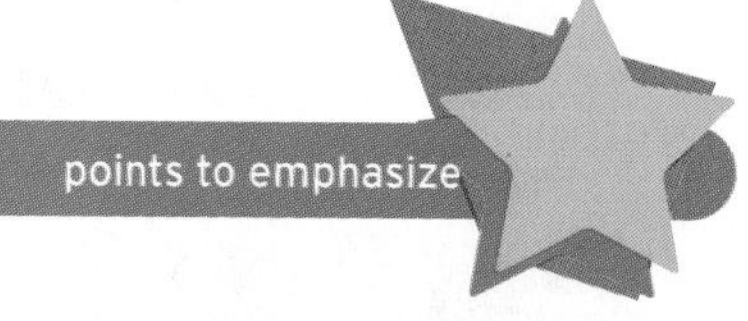

Recap this section by emphasizing that effective management of information is essential because of the complexity of business, the volume of transactions, and the need for current and accurate information.

An underlying goal of this section is to help students understand that all levels of office workers access information and depend on information to complete routine tasks and make decisions. Make sure students understand that regardless of the type of business, information is a vital resource at all levels of employment.

The office worker is often the company's first line of defense against these obstacles. The office worker is frequently the person gathering or processing the information—and therefore often the person who first recognizes that databases are incompatible or that critical information is missing.

If you experience difficulties in using information or technology efficiently, follow your company procedures for reporting the difficulties. If no procedures exist, inform your supervisor. Include a description of the problem in your report. If a company can move quickly to correct problems with its information resources, the negative effects of these problems are lessened.

Information Processing

Information processing is putting facts or numbers into a meaningful and useful form. It typically involves five types of activities or operations: input, processing, output, distribution, and storage. These operations are summarized in the table below.

Operation	Example
Input: Entering data into the the information system	Taking orders via phone and keying them into order entry system to generate shipment and billing for the order Entering data about a new employee to activate payroll and benefits Writing product features and benefits for an advertising brochure
Processing: Manipulating data to create meaningful information	Formatting and arranging text and graphics to create a newsletter Generating a report from a database Calculating and sorting data in a spreadsheet
Output: Retrieving information from the system	Viewing a list of out-of-stock items from the inventory database Printing labels and brochures for a customer mailing
Distribution: Sending information to the appropriate people	Faxing product updates to sales representatives Mailing price quotes to clients Sending a report to coworkers as an e-mail attachment
Storage: Saving information for future use	Filing paper documents Saving computer files

Why would duplication of information be costly to an organization? (Example: Customers would receive duplicate mailings, and the customer base would be overstated.) Could a business rely too much on computers? Illustrate such reliance. (Example: All payments are processed by computers, so a handwritten note by a dissatisfied customer is given no response.)

Field visits would be invaluable in introducing students to the total concept of an information processing system. A visit to a relatively small organization where a knowledgeable person could describe the processing system while students observe employees at work would be an especially useful introduction. Likewise, a visit to a large organization would be useful in showing students the variations to be found among companies.

If possible, arrange for a visit to a business where a network or intranet is utilized. Be sure to point out the flow of work throughout a department and throughout the entire organization. After such visits, a general discussion that focuses on the basic goals of an information processing system will be useful as students study the remaining chapters in the textbook.

As you perform your duties, you will often proceed directly through the input, processing, output, distribution, and storage operations. For example, you may enter numbers into a spreadsheet program, perform calculations and create a chart, print ten copies of the chart, distribute it to members of your department, and store the file and **hard copy.** At other times, you may complete only some of the operations. For example, you may receive a request from a coworker for another chart using some of the figures in the spreadsheet. You can proceed to the processing operation since the data has already been input earlier. As shown in Illustration 4-1:5, information can be stored and retrieved at any point.

hard copy: printed document

Illustration 4-1:5

Information processing typically consists of five operations: input, processing, output, distribution, and storage.

INFORMATION PROCESSING WORKFLOW

INPUT
Receiving text, numbers, image, and voice for processing.

PROCESSING
Transforming input into meaningful form through activities such as arranging, sorting, formatting, calculating, and comparing.

OUTPUT
Producing what was processed in a form that can be transmitted to others or in a form that updates computer-maintained records.

DISTRIBUTION
Forwarding the output to the appropriate people.

STORAGE
Saving/retrieving output according to the records management system. This operation can occur at any stage in the workflow, as shown by the dotted lines.

Information Technologies

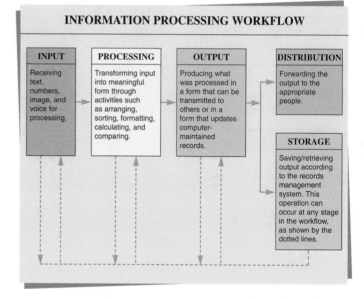

The information processing efforts of a business are aided by the information technologies it uses. Information technology refers to the equipment and software that allow the user to create, store, and retrieve information.

An underlying goal of this section is to help students understand that office workers do not work in a vacuum unrelated to the organization.

1. On a plain sheet of paper, have students prepare a quick sketch of the information processing workflow diagram labeling the five operations shown in Illustration 4-1: 5. Students should draw the boxes similar to the illustration, writing the box labels on their sketches but leaving the space below each label blank. Then ask students to compare their sketch with the illustration and make any necessary corrections.

2. Ask students to assume they have just been given a handwritten draft of a letter to key. After the letter is keyed, printed, and signed, it is to be sent by mail to the recipient. The letter will be stored on a floppy disk. Have the students fill in their diagrams as though they were completing the action in each phase of the workflow.

The information processing methods found in businesses vary according to the extent to which technology is used. The telephone is the most common piece of equipment that is found in almost all offices. Photocopiers, fax machines, and computers are becoming almost as common. Usually only small offices requiring few transactions or those that require highly individualized responses to customer needs rely heavily on manual processing methods.

> *Leah works in a small office for an importer of rare antique rugs. The importer specializes in one-of-a-kind rugs for select customers. Leah's workstation includes a typewriter, a calculator, and a telephone. Her primary duties are to serve as a receptionist answering the phone and greeting visitors to the office. She also maintains the rug inventory in a notecard file, prepares handwritten checks, and records orders by writing the information on a preprinted form.*

Using information technology increases the speed at which communications are processed. It allows for rapid processing of a huge quantity and variety of information. Many firms have enjoyed a competitive advantage by being the first to use a new technology within their industry. Consider this example.

> *Citibank, a leader in the banking industry, was the first bank to use automatic teller machines (ATMs) throughout its organization. Citibank tripled its market share within the first few years after introducing ATMs. By offering a needed service that other banks were not providing, Citibank achieved a competitive advantage over those banks slow to adopt the new technology.*

Illustration 4-1:6
Citibank gained a competitive advantage by its early use of new information technology.

Many offices use a combination of manual and automated processing methods. Ask students if they know of office employees who perform tasks using information technologies. If students know of such office employees, have them describe any additional duties these office workers may have beyond operating the technology. What are the types of offices in which the students' acquaintances are employed?

Ask students to cite other examples where companies have gained a competitive edge through the use of information technologies.

What advantages did Citibank gain? Citibank not only increased its number of banking transactions and earned ATM fees, but it also attracted many new customers from other banks. In spite of the fact that the number of transactions and customers increased, Citibank reduced the number of tellers and increased the accuracy and timely posting of customer banking information. Citibank held its competitive edge by using this new information to analyze customers' needs. As a result, it offered additional services based on those needs and explored new markets.

COMMON INFORMATION TECHNOLOGIES

Information technologies can be used to improve communication among the staff and between companies and their suppliers and customers. Examples of common information technologies used in offices include:

- Computers connected to networks, online services, and newsgroups—providing access to a wide range of resources
- **Electronic imaging** and transmission of documents—reducing paperwork, saving valuable time, and increasing customer satisfaction
- Electronic mail, online databases, and two-way video—increasing the flow of information and speed of responses
- **Interactive voice response** systems—eliminating repetitive manual processes for obtaining data and/or providing information
- Interactive CD-ROM reference media—making retrieval of data quick and easy
- Multimedia employee training programs—enhancing training effectiveness

electronic imaging: converting paper documents to pictures stored and displayed via computer

interactive voice response: recorded messages accessed and directed by the user to provide or record information

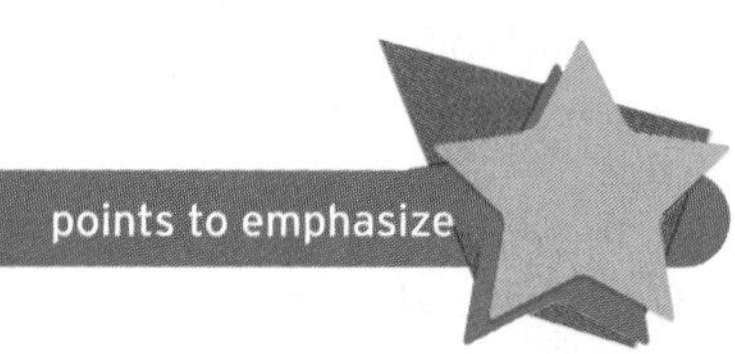

Technology can also improve the external communications among companies, their suppliers, and their customers.

American businesses are now in an era where larger quantities of information need to be precisely evaluated in increasingly shorter time spans. That is, businesses must respond more quickly and with more accurate and flexible approaches to market demands in order to remain competitive. Effective use of information and technologies helps businesses meet these challenges.

COMPUTERIZED PROCESSING

Computer-based systems are common in today's offices. Computerized processing relies heavily on equipment (the computer) and related software to transform facts into meaningful and timely information.

Hardware. While we often speak of the "the computer," many variations exist. Computers can be classified by their size, speed, and processing capabilities. With continued advancement in technology, however, the differences among computer categories have become more difficult to identify. Three major categories of computers are used in business: mainframe computers, minicomputers, and microcomputers.

Mainframe computers are large, multipurpose machines with very high processing speeds. Mainframes can handle many users and store large quantities of data. Mainframe computers use sophisticated programs to control their operation and require specially trained employees to operate the system. The mainframe computer has traditionally done tasks such as payroll, accounting, and personnel recordkeeping for large organizations.

Minicomputers are mid-sized computers capable of supporting a number of users. They are less powerful than mainframe computers but can perform a wide variety of processing tasks.

Microcomputers, also called *personal computers*, are the small, desktop variety. The system is made up of several components such as the central processing unit, a keyboard, mouse, and monitor. Microcomputers are designed for individual use and are used by people at all levels of business organizations. Laptop and notebook computers are other forms of microcomputers. As these computers can be battery powered,

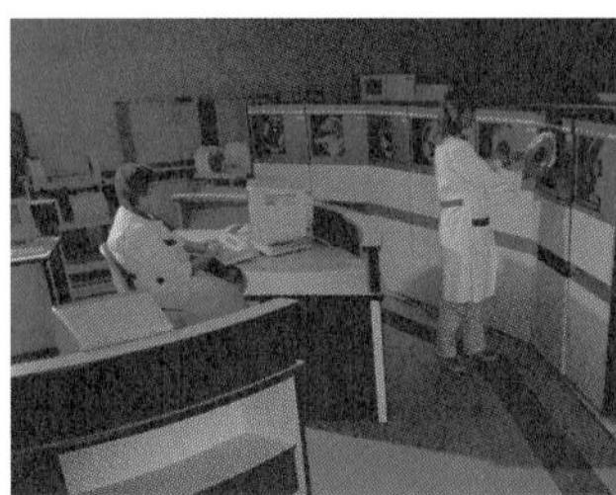

Illustration 4-1:7

Companies may use a mainframe (left) and personal computers (right) to fit their needs.

Have students identify the distinguishing features of the three categories of computers.

they are especially helpful to employees who must work on the road or at locations where desktop systems are not practical. Companies may have several types of computers to meet their processing needs.

Data from business transactions frequently consist of handwritten, keyed, or printed facts. Before these data can be processed, however, they must be entered into the computer system. Workers use input devices to enter data into computers. An input device is hardware that allows the computer to accept the data for processing. Common input devices that you probably use regularly include the keyboard and mouse. Other input devices include touch screens, light pens, and scanners. Touch screens and light pens are used to give commands, draw, or write input directly on the screen. Scanners are used to input text, graphics, and photos by "reading" hard-copy documents. Speech recognition is also a form of input for voice-activated systems.

Have students find photographs of input and output devices from magazines, catalogs, and newspapers. Students should label each example and be prepared to discuss its features. Use labeled examples to prepare a bulletin board display of computer system input and output devices.

Illustration 4-1:8

The most common input devices include the keyboard and mouse.

A computer system must have at least one output device. An output device prints, displays, or records information. The most common output devices are monitors and printers. Other output forms include floppy disks, tape drives, laser discs, and microfilm.

auxiliary: additional, supplementary

Since the amount of primary storage in a computer is limited, **auxiliary,** external storage is often needed to store data. Storage devices such as optical discs and magnetic disks and tapes allow large volumes of data to be stored and retrieved easily.

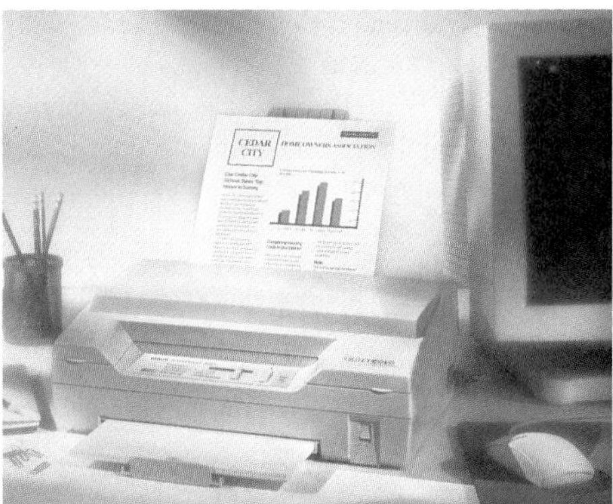

Illustration 4-1:9

Monitors and printers are the most common output devices.

Software. Thousands of **software** programs are available to meet information processing needs. Software may be divided into three broad categories: operating system software, application software, and utility software.

software: programs containing instructions for the computer

Operating system software contains programs that control the operation of the computer and provide the means for communicating with devices connected to it, such as a printer. Windows 95 is an example of a popular operating system software with multitasking features that enable the user to run two or more applications at the same time.

Application software directs the computer to carry out specific tasks. The application software may perform a single function, such as word processing. Other single-function software applications include inventory control and database management. Software that shares information (such as word processing, database management, spreadsheet, and presentation) between applications is known as integrated software. When these applications are packaged as one, they are commonly called a suite.

Application software can be quite powerful and provide numerous advantages for a business by improving the accuracy and efficiency with which it processes information. Software manufacturers continue to **upgrade** their products and add new features. As new applications

upgrade: acquire a new version

for discussion

Ask students to name the operating system and application software programs used in your classroom or your school's computer lab.

evolve, they become easier to learn and use with features such as onscreen help, tutorials, and templates, or "wizards," that automate common tasks. With the wide selection of application software available, the use of computers in offices continues to grow. Illustration 4-1:10 lists common application software categories you are likely to encounter in an office.

Illustration 4-1:10

A wide variety of software is available to meet specific information processing needs.

COMMON APPLICATION SOFTWARE	
Software Category	**Software Function**
Browsers	Search tools for locating information on the Internet
Communications	Modem connections; faxes; voice, electronic, and Internet mail; file transfers
Database Management	Records creation and maintenance, records updating and editing, report preparation
Desktop Publishing	Page composition, use of features such as type style and fonts to produce high-quality documents that contain both text and images
Development	Tools for authoring interactive applications including animations, and pages for the Internet
Graphics and Design	Clip-art images, photos, graphics, and drawing and design tools for use in word processing and desktop publishing documents as well as computer-aided design and special projects
Finance	Checkbook, online banking, accounts receivable/payable, billing, financial reports, financial forecasting, tax planning, inventory, job costing
Network	Server performance for networks, security management, directory services, intranets
Presentation	Create sophisticated presentations with graphics, sounds, and animation
Project Management	Timeline schedules, calendars, appointment reminders, travel guides, address books, prioritizing and task management, and employee performance evaluations
Specialized	Software developed for specialized needs such as medical, law, and real estate offices
Spreadsheet	Business calculations, number manipulation via input or formulas, and "what if" analyses
Utility	Scan and disable viruses, compress files, boost performance, recover lost files, repair disks, troubleshoot, data protection and backup
Word Processing	Document creation and editing; spelling and grammar checking; merging of text, data, and graphics into documents

Computer applications are designed around the capabilities of computer systems. With rapidly changing technology, the distinctions among application software change frequently as more powerful processing equipment becomes faster and cheaper than previous models. Manufacturers of application software continually upgrade existing products and introduce new ones that are designed to utilize the new features of the hardware.

Utility software carries out "housekeeping" duties, such as formatting a disk, making copies of data, deleting and organizing files, and protecting or recovering data. Many of the utilities you will use are included with the operating system. Many more features are available by purchasing utility software packages. As the use of computers has grown, utility software has become essential in preventing devastating data loss for businesses.

Another type of utility software are virus protection programs. This software identifies and clears files of hidden viruses, which if undetected could result in total loss of data and computer operations. Virus protection software is generally updated regularly to keep up with the new viruses that are introduced to computer environments.

MAINTENANCE AND SECURITY

Office workers in computerized environments are expected to be responsible users of information processing technology. They must be concerned with maintenance, security, and ethics related to information processing systems and software.

Whether a business uses a complex and diverse computer network or stand-alone computers, there will likely be a support plan for managing the maintenance, security, and controls of the system. With the increased dependence on technology, disaster planning is essential for uninterrupted computer service. The responsibilities can be so demanding that some companies hire security administrators and disaster recovery coordinators who handle plans for safeguarding the system and recovering quickly if data is lost or destroyed.

Maintenance. Computer systems are relied upon daily and are often used extensively, yet a surprising number of businesses neglect to conduct proper maintenance on the systems. For efficient operation and best performance levels, the systems must be serviced and maintained on a regular basis. Failure to maintain the equipment could result in lost data and even lost business.

Jan received a phone call from a new customer requesting a rush delivery on an important order. She checked the inventory system and found that the needed items were in stock and could be delivered the

The risk of losing data is a very serious consideration for businesses. Not only are backup copies common practice, backup tape drives and other auxiliary backup systems are frequently used to prevent such losses.

While not all viruses are harmful, many of them can be very destructive. They can wipe out entire databases or even cause total system failures. It is an ongoing challenge to keep computer systems virus free because new viruses are continually introduced to computer environments. You expose your system to viruses when you share data with other computers.

same day. Little did Jan know that the computer had been shut down for unscheduled repairs early that morning, preventing some shipments from being entered and deducted from the inventory count. The needed items were not really in the warehouse. Jan's company lost a customer because accurate inventory information was not available when needed.

malfunction: operate incorrectly, break down

When you use a computer, you will want to follow proper maintenance procedures. Read and follow equipment operation instructions so that you do not accidentally cause the equipment to **malfunction.** Many companies instruct employees in preventive maintenance procedures. If you are responsible for the maintenance of your computer, be sure you understand the procedures you are to follow.

Illustration 4-1:11
Regular cleaning is an important part of computer maintenance.

unauthorized: not approved

unintentional: not planned, accidental

Security. Businesses maintain sensitive information daily, and as a result, security measures are a critical issue. Security for computer information systems centers around two major concerns: (1) planning for potential loss and (2) protecting against **unauthorized** access to information. Loss of data can occur when a system fails. For this reason, backup copies are retained and stored in another location. Another potential area of loss is **unintentional** errors made by employees, such as deleting a file or incorrectly updating a customer database. Companies try to minimize potential losses of this nature through employee training.

Much of a company's information is confidential and vital to the continued operations of the organization. Companies must be careful to protect their interests. Security of computer-based information is of particular concern because an **unscrupulous** person can quickly and easily access and misuse or abuse the information. Security risks of this nature are handled in a variety of ways depending on the complexity of the system and the risk involved. Illustration 4-1:12 shows a checklist and description of typical security requirements for multi-user systems. It is important that all personnel be trained in security procedures and fully understand the security policy. Adequate policies, procedures, and precautions help to ensure that valuable information is safeguarded.

unscrupulous: dishonest, not responsible

TYPICAL SECURITY REQUIREMENTS

Security Measure	Purpose
Access control	Users limited to access information within their job responsibilities
Identification and authentication	Use of passwords or other identification to check for authorization
Accuracy	Guards against errors and unauthorized modifications
Reliability	Protection against control by any user
Data Exchange	Enables secure transmissions over communication channels
Accountability	Links all activities to the user's identity
Audit Trails	Maintains a log of all attempts to gain access to the system, all activity, unusual activity, and variations from established procedures

Illustration 4-1:12

Using appropriate security measures helps to minimize the risk of misuse, abuse, and theft.

Companies frequently assign passwords or access codes as a security precaution. In order to access certain information, an office worker must enter the proper password or access code when the prompt is displayed.

Reviewing the Topic

topic 4-1 review

1. Define information.
2. What are the most common types of information?
3. What effect might use of outdated or incorrect information have on a business?
4. List five obstacles to using information efficiently.
5. Explain why the office worker is the company's first line of defense against the obstacles to using information efficiently.
6. Describe the five operations of information processing workflow.
7. Describe five common information technologies.
8. Name the three broad categories of software and describe each one.
9. What are the two major security concerns for computer information systems?
10. List ways a business can safeguard information stored in their computer systems.

INTERACTING WITH OTHERS

Kristin and Tyler work together in a small office. One of Tyler's main responsibilities is updating customer account records. He enjoys completing the paperwork, but really dislikes filing. He is very prompt about updating customer account information, but not about filing the completed paperwork in the customer files. Kristin's main responsibility is customer service. When responding to customer concerns, she pulls the customer file to access the information. Kristin did not have up-to-date information available when she responded to three different customer calls, because Tyler had not yet filed the paperwork he completed two weeks ago.

What you are to do:

Explain why it is important for Kristin to have up-to-date information when she responds to customer calls. If you were Kristin, what would you say to Tyler?

topic 4-1 review

Information in Business

REINFORCING ENGLISH SKILLS

You work as an office assistant to the general manager of large service business. You were asked to research interactive voice response systems. A draft of your findings is shown in your *Student Activities and Projects* workbook.

What you are to do:

1. Locate the draft in your *Student Activities and Projects* workbook.
2. Identify the punctuation, spelling, capitalization, and word usage errors in the draft. Use proofreader's marks to indicate the needed corrections.

See Workbook page 19.

APPLICATION ACTIVITY

ACTIVITY **Virtual Meetings Memorandum**

Assume that you are an office assistant to Natalie B. McCardle, Information Systems Manager at Pacific-First Bank. The bank has several branches throughout the metropolitan area. Mrs. McCardle asked you to key a copy of the memo she drafted to all branch managers. On her way to a meeting, Mrs. McCardle stops by your desk and says: "Please compose a brief memo to Kenneth C. Withers, Vice President of Operations. Invite him to attend the demonstration and enclose a copy of the branch manager's memo. I'll initial the memos when I return."

What you are to do:

1. Key the memo to the branch managers as Mrs. McCardle requested. Refer to Reference Section A for information about standard proofreader's marks or Section H for a sample memo format if needed.
2. Compose a memo to Mr. Withers from Mrs. McCardle inviting him to the demonstration as requested.

See Workbook page 214 and page 235.

181

topic 4-1
review

To: All Branch Managers
From: Natalie B. McCardle, Information Systems [Manager]
Date: October 20, 19-
Subject: Virtual Meetings and Conferences

We think our experimental use of virtual meetings here in headquarters and at ~~one office~~ [our Seattle branch] supports its introduction throughout the organization.

A meeting [of all branch managers] is planned for November ~~14~~ [15] at 9:~~00~~ [30] a.m. in the conference room here at the Embarcadero Center. We hope you can join us. ¶There will be a discussion of this new technology and a demonstration of face-to-face communication with personnel at our [Seattle] branch ~~office~~ so you can experience virtual meetings firsthand. The meeting will end no later than 11:~~00~~ [30] a.m.

Please let me know by October 27 if you plan to attend.

182

Topic 4-2

Information Systems and Resources

When you have completed your study of this topic, you will be able to

- **identify typical information systems used in business**
- **describe traditional information resources**
- **describe electronic information resources**

You learned in Topic 4-1 that information technology refers to the computer hardware and software used to process information. Technology is only one part of managing information. Managing information effectively also includes people who follow procedures to run the information technology efficiently. An information system is composed of people, the information technology and resources, and procedures used to process information.

An information system is composed of people, the information technology and resources, and procedures used to process information.

Typical Information Systems

Information systems help workers perform business operations efficiently. The information systems found in business relate to typical business operations such as accounting or manufacturing. Four typical

information systems are described in the following paragraphs to help you understand how businesses use information systems. In reality, all the information systems of a particular business would probably be interrelated.

Ask students who may have work experience how their employee information, payments, or tax records were handled by the company's human resources information system.

HUMAN RESOURCES INFORMATION SYSTEMS

accrued: stored up, accumulated

Businesses must keep records on their employees. Specific data such as position, pay rate, hours worked, payroll deductions, **accrued** vacation, and sick leave are kept for each employee. The system is not limited to payroll functions, though. It also maintains information about medical records, retirement benefits, insurance benefits, and performance evaluations. The following list includes several examples of how various employees in a large service business are involved with the flow of data in a human resources information system:

- A data processing clerk enters the payroll data into the information system.
- A payroll department supervisor processes the payroll and prints the payroll checks.
- An accountant accesses the data to compile financial reports.
- An **auditor** examines the records for accuracy and makes sure the company complies with federal, state, and local income tax laws.
- A manager reviews an employee's work history and evaluates the employee's qualifications for promotion.

auditor: person who checks or verifies information

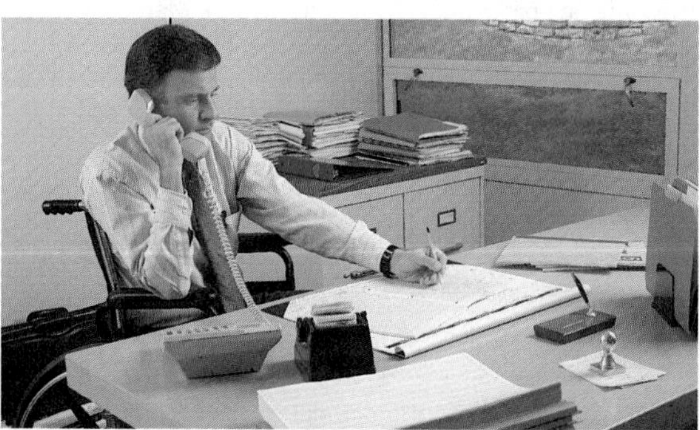

Illustration 4-2:1
Businesses must maintain accurate human resources information.

ACCOUNTING INFORMATION SYSTEMS

An accounting information system enables a business to record business transactions and report financial information. Information processed in an accounting system provides a variety of reports. These reports give information about many aspects of the business such as inventory, manufacturing costs, personnel costs, accounts receivable, and revenue. The following list describes how employees in a small retail business would use this information to make decisions or process work.

- An inventory clerk notes that stock of an item is low and decides that the item needs to be reordered.
- A billing clerk prepares invoices and computes amounts due.
- The credit department manager approves credit for an established customer.
- The **controller** prepares the annual budget and recommends ways to increase profits.
- A financial planner analyzes the information and recommends ways to invest the profits.

controller: person in charge of company finances

MARKETING INFORMATION SYSTEMS

A marketing information system is useful to a business that sells a product or provides a service. Such systems help the business keep track of the customer from an **initial** contact, to the point of the sale or service, to a customer satisfaction follow-up. The data provided by marketing information systems identifies whether or not:

initial: first, original

- a particular marketing approach is successful
- a customer is satisfied with the product or service
- a customer intends to make future purchases from the company

Illustration 4-2:2 on page 186 shows the flow of information throughout a software distributing firm:

PRODUCT INFORMATION SYSTEMS

If a business manufactures a product, the business must determine the cost of goods it sells. The activities that take place within the business to create the product are documented through the information system.

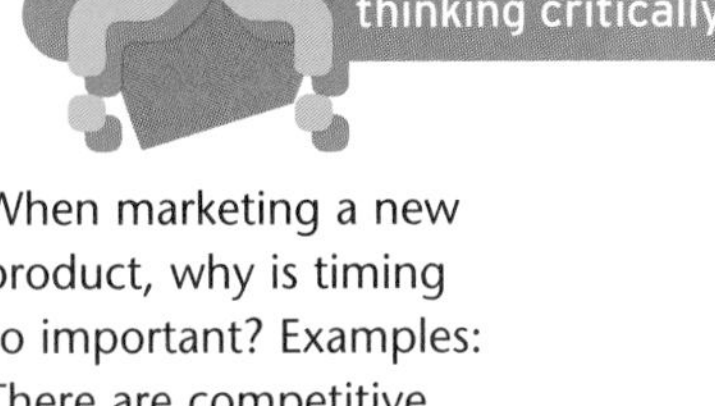

When marketing a new product, why is timing so important? Examples: There are competitive advantages to being the first to market a new product or idea. If you are the first to introduce the product, you don't have any competition. Sometimes products have a limited shelf life. If you take too long to bring the product to market, you miss the opportunity for sales.

The information system helps the business keep track of the customer. The data provided by the information system helps the business make decisions about future marketing efforts.

Illustration 4-2:2
Data provided by information systems can help businesses keep track of their customers.

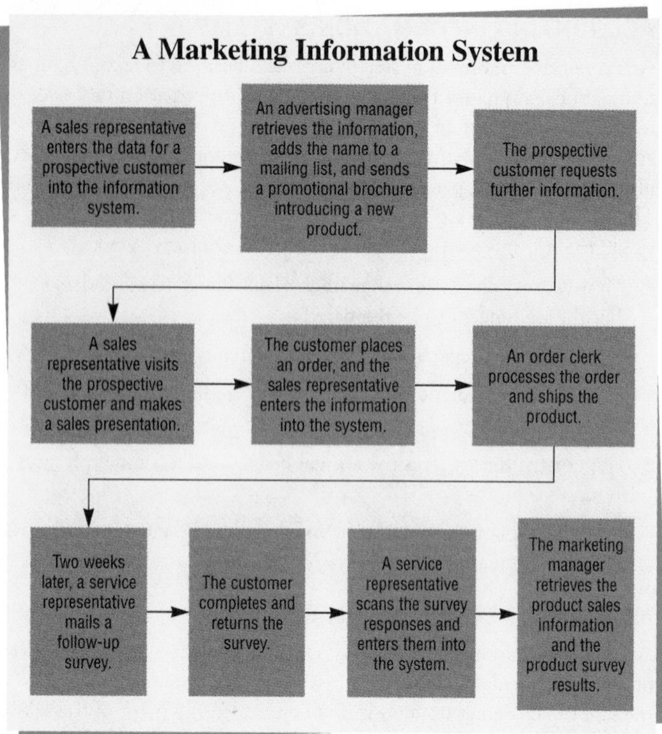
A Marketing Information System
A sales representative enters the data for a prospective customer into the information system.
An advertising manager retrieves the information, adds the name to a mailing list, and sends a promotional brochure introducing a new product.
The prospective customer requests further information.
A sales representative visits the prospective customer and makes a sales presentation.
The customer places an order, and the sales representative enters the information into the system.
An order clerk processes the order and ships the product.
Two weeks later, a service representative mails a follow-up survey.
The customer completes and returns the survey.
A service representative scans the survey responses and enters them into the system.
The marketing manager retrieves the product sales information and the product survey results.

overhead: business costs not directly related to a product or service

raw materials: parts or elements used to make a product

This system measures the cost of materials, labor, and **overhead.** The information maintained in this system is essential in helping determine the cost of the product. The following examples illustrate how different people access the information system in a manufacturing firm:

- A stock control clerk checks the inventory of **raw materials** and processes a purchase order to replenish stock.
- A receiving clerk scans bar code labels on incoming shipments to create a record of goods received.
- A production supervisor accesses purchase order data for goods used to determine production costs.

- A production worker completes an assembly operation, scans part-number information, and inputs quantity to register completed products in the system.
- An accounts payable clerk verifies invoices and receipt of goods before approving payment for purchases.
- A department manager uses prior months' financial data in creating a budget.

Information Resources

Information has never been more critical to businesses, large or small. It will continue to increase in importance as we move into the 21st century. A company's success may often depend on its source of information. Companies can get information from numerous resources. Naturally, much of the information a business uses comes from within the company. You have already learned about some typical internal information systems. Business can also get additional information through external resources. Some of these resources are described in the following paragraphs.

TRADITIONAL RESOURCES

Information is available to businesses from a variety of external sources. Some traditional information resources include marketing research firms, trade publications and associations, and government agencies.

Marketing Research Firms. Marketing research firms make data available in a variety of forms for business needs. They focus on the customer and the market. Marketing research firms use questionnaires and interviews to gather information about consumer behaviors and attitudes. They also look at marketing trends and collect valuable **demographic data.** Computer technology makes it possible for researchers to collect a variety of data, analyze huge amounts of information, and forecast market conditions.

demographic data: statistics that describe a population such as age or race

Organizations, both large and small, often rely on the information processed by these marketing research firms. It might be too expensive

Information has never been more critical to businesses, large or small. It will continue to increase in importance as we move into the 21st century.

Businesses get information from a variety of external sources. There are many more sources available that are not discussed here. Examples: Businesses can purchase mailing lists, get credit information about potential customers, and research historical data about individuals, just to name a few.

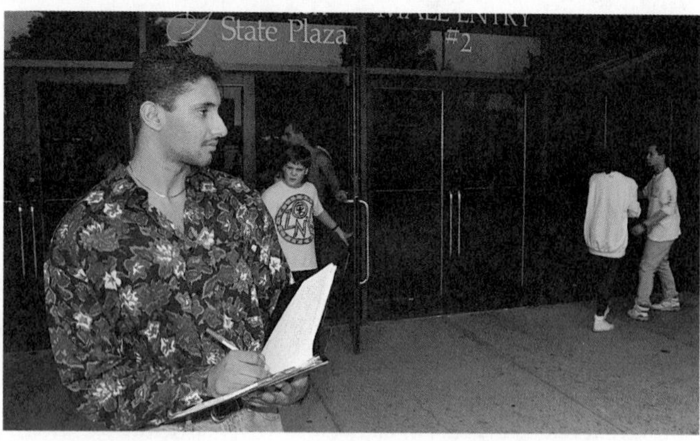

Illustration 4-2:3

Market researchers provide valuable customer information to businesses.

for a small-business owner to conduct market research. Even though a large corporation might be able to afford the investment for such research, it would save valuable time by accessing the information already compiled by the research firm.

Trade Publications and Associations. Many organizations look to trade publications, books, and journals for facts and forecasts about their industry. These publications include information about trade associations and provide good sources of information for the particular products, service area, or industry in which the business specializes.

Trade associations often conduct or sponsor research related to the industry. Association meetings and workshops provide an opportunity to **network** and share information with others. Conventions or trade shows provide an opportunity to view new products and services designed for the industry.

network: interact with others who have similar interests or concerns

Government Agencies. Information from government agencies is useful to many organizations. Government publications often include forecasts and results from research studies. The Small Business Administration and the U.S. Bureau of the Census are examples of sources that provide demographics, statistics, and other data useful in making business decisions. Consider the following example:

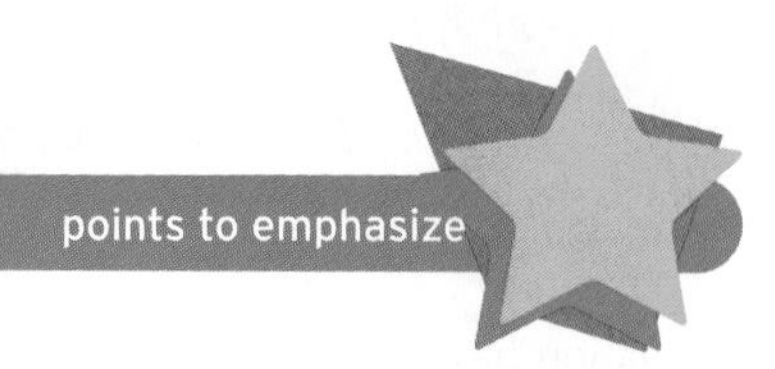

Even though a large corporation might be able to afford the investment for research, it would save valuable time by accessing the information already compiled by the research firm.

Demographic data are available from the U.S. Bureau of the Census in print, on CD-ROM, and via the Internet. Make the data related to your geographic area available to students. Have the class develop a list of three or four products or services and research demographic data related to the market for these items.

Illustration 4-2:4

Conventions and trade shows provide information about new products and services.

A cereal manufacturer is interested in the demographics of a particular region. By acquiring information about the number of individuals within a certain age range, the company can decide what types of cereal they could successfully market to the population in that region. If the demographics indicate a large population under the age of twelve, then cereal popular with children could be marketed successfully. On the other hand, if the adult population is small, cereals popular with adults may not be as successful.

Libraries. University libraries are an excellent information resource. Many offer research services as well as specialized publications not readily available elsewhere. It is estimated that there are about 6,000 corporate libraries nationwide. Many of these libraries also specialize in research.

Illustration 4-2:5

University and corporate libraries provide access to research data.

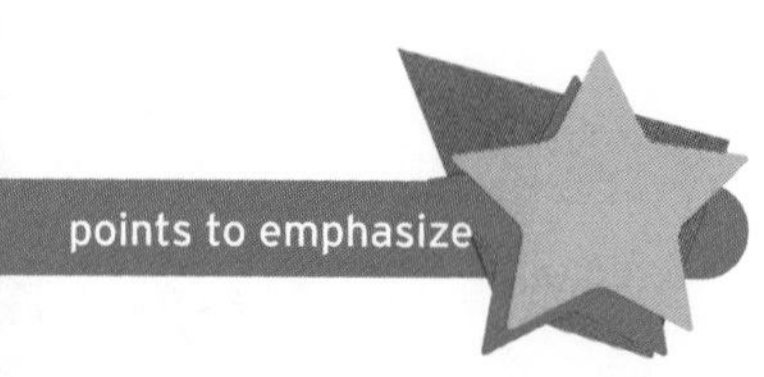

Most electronic databases have powerful search features. Using the search features effectively is important for saving time and producing relevant search results.

ELECTRONIC RESOURCES

With advancements in information technology come new sources of information and new ways to access the information. Electronic resources, often called online resources, are those available via the computer. Online resources are becoming more popular because of the wide range of available information, and the instant access to and timeliness of the information.

Electronic Databases. Use of electronic databases has grown rapidly in the past few years. A database is a collection of related information. Electronic databases are available on CD-ROM, the Internet, and online services such as CompuServe. These databases provide information on many topics useful to businesses. Most electronic databases have powerful search features that allow the user to find information quickly and easily.

Some databases support natural language searches. This means that the user simply enters a question in everyday terms and the database search feature interprets and answers the question. No special searching techniques or rules are needed.

Companies often maintain relational databases as part of their internal information system. Relational databases allow the user to link data from a number of database files or tables to find information or

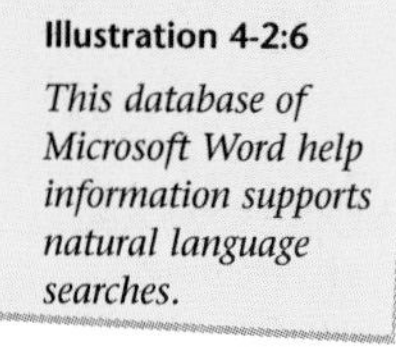

Illustration 4-2:6

This database of Microsoft Word help information supports natural language searches.

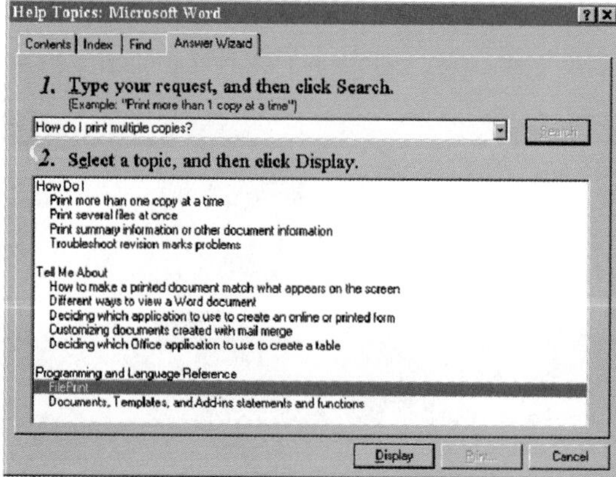

generate reports. This linking capability means that data can be stored in relatively small files that are easy to work with. It also means that data updated in one file can be used to update other files easily.

Data mining is a process that helps businesses analyze the wealth of information contained in databases. With automated data mining, the program searches for interesting and significant patterns of information in the database without detailed questions posed by the user. The information is then presented in graphs, reports, and so forth. The user can look at the data from several viewpoints, and the results may reveal **perceptions** the user never considered. Data mining can be used to help a business target consumers and predict market trends.

perceptions: insights, understandings

Personal Digital Assistants. The personal digital assistant (PDA) provides another means for retrieving information. PDAs are handheld **digital** organizers. They can be used to store a variety of data, from a personal diary of schedules and appointments to a reference text. Consider this example of how healthcare workers use PDAs:

digital: using numbers to perform logical calculations

Illustration 4-2:7

PDAs are used to store and access information.

Healthcare workers need to access not only clinical data, but also educational resources, decision aids, and other professional information. PDA technology stores several medical reference texts and clinical data. All of this information is stored on a memory card about the size

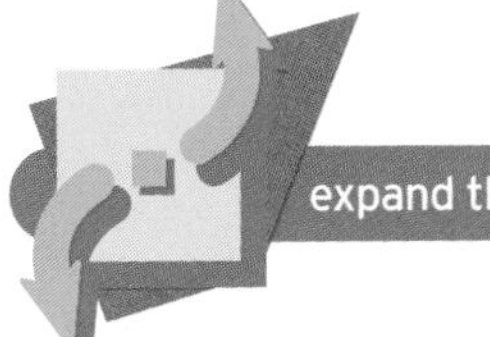

Ask students if they know individuals who own PDAs and how they use them for personal and business applications. Continue the discussion by asking students how they could use a PDA for personal needs.

Knowing where and how to look for information is basic to using electronic resources. With the increased use of the Internet, browser software has become very popular and almost a necessity for efficient and productive navigation through the wealth of information contained on the World Wide Web. Browser software programs provide search and navigation tools to help you search for topics and locations. Browsers enable you to customize searches and help you locate information from several indexes and information resources. They are easy to use and save you time in completing searches for information.

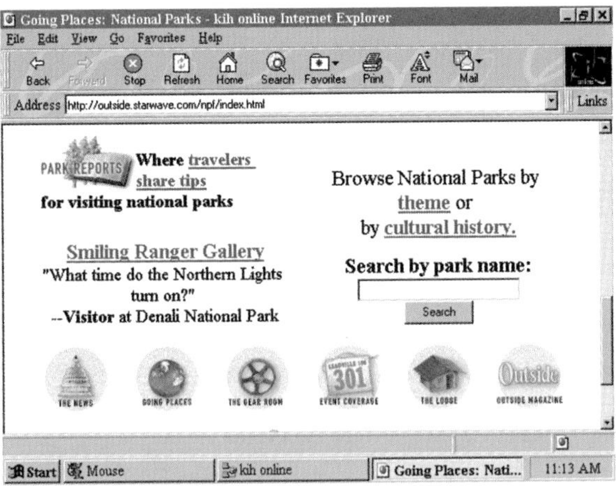

Illustration 4-2:9

Browsers enable you to customize searches and help you locate information.

Intranets. Online resource networks within a company are called intranets. Intranets are internal information networks based on Internet technologies and standards. Everyone in the organization has access to information and can communicate quickly and easily with each other. Intranets save time and money for businesses. Consider these examples of intranet use.

> *Using an intranet a distribution company sends sales information daily that was previously sent by overnight mail to 400 salespeople worldwide.*

> *Offices of an import firm from around the world feed data on product availability to the home office via the intranet.*

Ask students to describe browser software programs they have used. Discuss similarities and differences among the programs.

A technology firm links research efforts by engineers in Europe, Asia, and the United States via the company intranet.

Employees of a company can access the corporate policies and procedures manual, study computer-based training programs, read job postings, find answers to frequently asked questions about benefits, and apply for a parking pass all via the intranet.

modem: device that allows computer data to be transmitted via the telephone system

virtual: in effect but not in fact, nonphysical

The U.S. workforce is increasingly mobile. More workers than ever are on the road on a regular basis. With a laptop computer and **modem,** these workers can easily access the company intranet and interact with coworkers. Intranets also make **virtual** meetings possible.

Several people in a manufacturing business need to discuss some items reported on an electronic spreadsheet. A few of the workers are in the main office. However, one worker is at home, a second is away on business, and two more are off-site at other offices. A virtual group meeting can take place with all involved parties online. Not only can they communicate with each other, but they can also each access and work with the spreadsheet at the same time while the meeting is taking place.

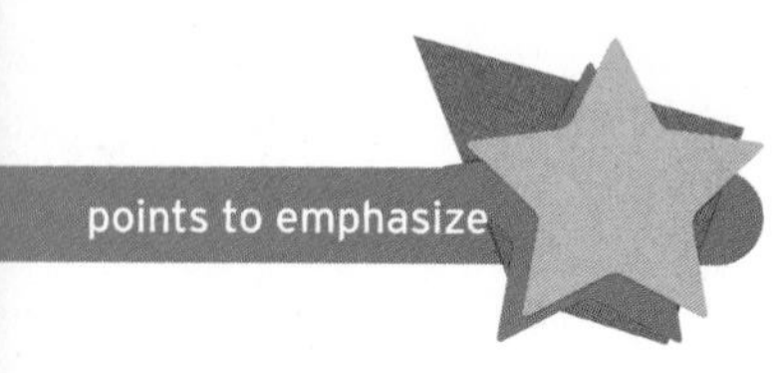

The ability to access information efficiently is an essential skill for office workers.

The development of corporate intranets is a growing trend. As the technology needed to develop an intranet continues to grow less expensive and easier to use, more and more companies will make an intranet part of their information system.

If you know what online resources are available to you via the Internet or your corporate intranet and how to access this information, your value to the company is increased.

Reviewing the Topic

1. What kinds of information do businesses keep about their employees?
2. What kinds of information does an accounting information system provide?
3. Describe how a marketing system can help a business identify if a particular marketing approach is successful.
4. List and briefly describe three traditional external resources where companies get information.
5. Why have electronic resources become so popular?
6. Describe relational databases and explain why businesses use them.
7. Describe how data mining helps businesses analyze information contained in databases.
8. List and describe four electronic resources where businesses can access information.
9. Describe the purpose of Internet browser software programs.
10. Distinguish between "the Internet" and an "intranet."

topic 4-2 review

THINKING CRITICALLY

Catherine, an office assistant in a recently established department, has had to learn much of what she does from oral instructions given by the department manager. Catherine is competent; she has been able to follow all the instructions given her by the manager. The work of the new department is done without problems. Catherine uses the technology and information resources effectively, but the workload continues to increase and Catherine is burdened with too much work.

One morning the manager approached her and said: "Catherine, I just received approval to hire two additional staff members. I will need you to train these individuals to perform the routine procedures in this department."

topic 4-2 review

Information Systems and Resources

195

topic 4-2 review

If you were Catherine, how would you plan the training? What information would you include? How would you provide this information? How could you organize the training for these new workers and any new workers who may be hired at a later date?

What you are to do:

Describe the steps you would take to plan for the training of the new employees.

REINFORCING MATH SKILLS

Assume that you are an office worker in the central office of a professional organization that sponsors training seminars for various information technologies. Recently, the company completed a series of seminars in five cities throughout the United States. The standard fee for each participant at one seminar was $1,000. However, two of the seminars (Update on Virtual Meetings and Using PDAs) had a $500 fee per participant. You were given the task of calling the manager of each seminar site and getting enrollment figures for the courses. The details you recorded from your telephone calls is shown below.

Seminar and Date	Participants				
	Boston	**New York**	**Washington**	**Chicago**	**San Francisco**
Data Mining January 6–10, 19—	125	245	110	117	97
Controlling and Managing Databases February 15–18, 19—	105	325	175	130	110
Security for the Internet March 1–4, 19—	78	110	45	72	70
Update on Virtual Meetings March 19–22, 19—	170	295	140	110	115
Using PDAs April 1–2, 19—	210	410	175	102	117

196

What you are to do:

1. Record the title of each of the five seminars on a separate line. Calculate and record the following:
   - the total number of participants for each seminar
   - the grand total number of participants for all seminars
   - the total revenue earned from each seminar
   - the grand total of all revenue received
   - the total number of participants in each city
2. Identify the seminar with the largest total number of participants and the seminar producing the largest total revenue.

APPLICATION ACTIVITY

ACTIVITY Interview Notes

Assume that you are employed in the office of a monthly magazine devoted to computers. One of the reporters gives you the rough draft that follows on page 198. The notes are from an interview with Lisa Holt, Manager of Information Services at Seagrove Pharmaceutical Co.

What you are to do:

Key a revised copy of the interview. Use your judgment with regard to line length. Make all corrections noted. If necessary, refer to Reference Section A for information about standard proofreader's marks.

The company is thinking of concentrating its seminar sites in the eastern portion of the United States and is considering the elimination of the San Francisco site. What is San Francisco's percentage of the total participants? How much revenue would be lost if the San Francisco site were closed? What is San Francisco's percentage of the total revenue?

See Workbook page 214.

topic 4-2
review

INTERVIEW WITH LISA HOLT

REPORTER QUESTION:	What is the priority of office automation in a giant company such as Seagrove Pharmaceutical?
LISA HOLT RESPONSE:	It's mixed. Obviously, when you have different operating companies, there are different priorities. We started more than a decade ago looking at office automation and personal computers. We actually bought our first personal computer about 15 years ago.
REPORTER QUESTION:	What services are presently available through your system?
LISA HOLT RESPONSE:	We offer a variety of services to all four five branches of our corporation. Communications, whether voice or data, are available anywhere, anytime. Within the company, all employees are connected to an intranet. There's electronic mail and electronic messaging. We can also transfer documents electronically—we do a great deal of that. Many of our employees who work in the field carry PDAs. We also have videoconferencing capabilities established among all of our branches. Many staff members also access online resources for global data.
REPORTER QUESTION:	Will you expand your information technology in the near future?
LISA HOLT RESPONSE:	As the need arises, we will respond. One of the reasons we started slowly was to give ourselves time to learn about available technologies. It was our belief early on that we would soon be doing work much differently than we'd done in the past. Things began to change as soon as we put in our first workstations with computer capabilities. We've learned a lot from those early experiences and have grown accustomed to the convenient and timely access to information. We will certainly expand those capabilities as the need arises, as long as the technology is affordable.
REPORTER QUESTION:	What specifically have you learned?
LISA HOLT RESPONSE:	One very important lesson is that all of our employees need to have easy access to current and accurate information. At all levels, and regardless of the employee's position, if the information is not available or accurate, the employee cannot make well-informed decisions. To maintain our competitive edge, we must manage our information effectively.

Use bold for the title and column 1.

198

Chapter Summary

Information is critical to every organization regardless of its size or purpose. Because organizations use information to make decisions, they give a great deal of attention to managing information effectively and to using technology for processing it efficiently. Managing information effectively, however, means more than using current technologies. To perform operations efficiently, businesses depend on information systems composed of people, information technology and resources, and procedures for processing the information. Key points in this chapter include:

- The common types of information found in businesses are numbers, text, image, and voice. The way office workers process this information varies depending on the nature of the business.
- When information is managed effectively, organizations can operate efficiently, regardless of the complexity of the business or the volume of transactions. If information is not current or accurate, a business may make poor decisions that could prove costly.
- There are several obstacles to using information efficiently, such as incompatible databases, duplicate or missing information, or limited access to information.
- The information processing workflow consists of five operations: input, processing, output, distribution, and storage.
- Information technologies improve the workflow and communication in companies both internally and externally, and technology can even give a company a competitive edge. Information systems found in business relate to typical business operations such as accounting or manufacturing.
- A company's success may depend on its sources of information. Traditional resources include marketing research firms, trade publications and associations, and government agencies.
- Advancements in information technology provide new sources of information and new ways to access the information, including electronic databases, personal digital assistants, the Internet, and intranets.

chapter 4 summary

Information: A Vital Business Resource

199

chapter 4 summary

KEY CONCEPTS AND TERMS

application software
browser software
data mining
electronic databases
electronic imaging
electronic mail
information
information systems
information technology
interactive CD-ROM
interactive voice response systems
intranets
managing information
online databases
online services and news-groups
operating system software
personal digital assistants
relational databases
the Internet
utility software

INTEGRATED CHAPTER ACTIVITY

ACTIVITY Research Videoconferencing

The company for which you work, Investments Diversified, is an international company that provides brokerage services. They are currently considering investing in new technologies that will enable them to conduct videoconferencing between branch offices. Your manager, John Garcia, has asked you to research the topic and provide a two-page summary of the latest advancements in teleconferencing technology.

What you are to do:

1. Access the resources available to you to find current information about videoconferencing technology and procedures. Consider researching traditional resources such as trade journals. If you have access to online resources, consider searching online databases including CD-ROM references, online services, or the Internet.
2. Once you have gathered the information, prepare a summary of your findings in a memo to your manager.

200

Mei-yu Liang
Office Supervisor

Getting Acquainted with the World of Work

Carpal Tunnel Syndrome: What Is It?

Dear Ms. Liang

For the past year, I've been working as an administrative assistant for a manufacturing business. I like the work and have learned a great deal about the company. I've learned to use the computer to complete many tasks. In fact, I spend much of my workday at the computer.

Because I spend so much time each day keyboarding text and numbers, I'm concerned that I could get carpal tunnel syndrome. I don't know much about CTS. What are the symptoms, what causes it, and how can I prevent it?

Paula in San Diego

Dear Paula

You have asked some good questions about carpal tunnel syndrome. Carpal tunnel syndrome was first diagnosed in 1713. At that time it was called scrivener's palsy because it was common among professional writers. Later it was also diagnosed among shoemakers, typesetters, and milkmaids.

CTS generally begins with a sore thumb or wrist, a tingling hand, or a numb finger. Pain then develops in the arms and hands, and eventually hands lose their strength and flexibility.

Even though it is not apparent what causes CTS, many researchers believe repetitive hand tasks such as keyboarding are to blame. Here are a few suggestions for preventing CTS:

- *If available, use an adjustable keyboard fitted for your comfort.*
- *Most keyboards have folding legs on the underneath side. Use these legs to adjust the height and angle of the keyboard to the most comfortable position for your keyboarding style.*
- *Be sure your chair is set at the proper height. Your forearms and hands must be at a comfortable angle to the keyboard. Your upper arms and forearms should form an approximate right angle, and your wrist and hand should be in a straight line.*
- *If the keyboard splits in the center, open the keyboard and experiment to determine the most comfortable position for you.*
- *Use palm rests to support the weight of your palms without moving from side to side. Move the keyboard toward you so you can reach it comfortably.*
- *Use a light touch and keep your hands, fingers, and wrists relaxed.*
- *Keep the mouse at the same level as the keyboard.*
- *Take frequent breaks to rest your muscles.*

If you are conscientious about these ergonomic techniques, you can probably avoid getting CTS.

Mei-Yu Liang
Office Supervisor

201

A reader judges a document first by its appearance—either positively or negatively. Next, the reader judges the contents. Appearance is important, but the document must also have substance. Office employees must be familiar with how to write and present common business documents such as business letters, memoranda, tables, and reports. The success of many businesses is influenced by the documents its employees produce.

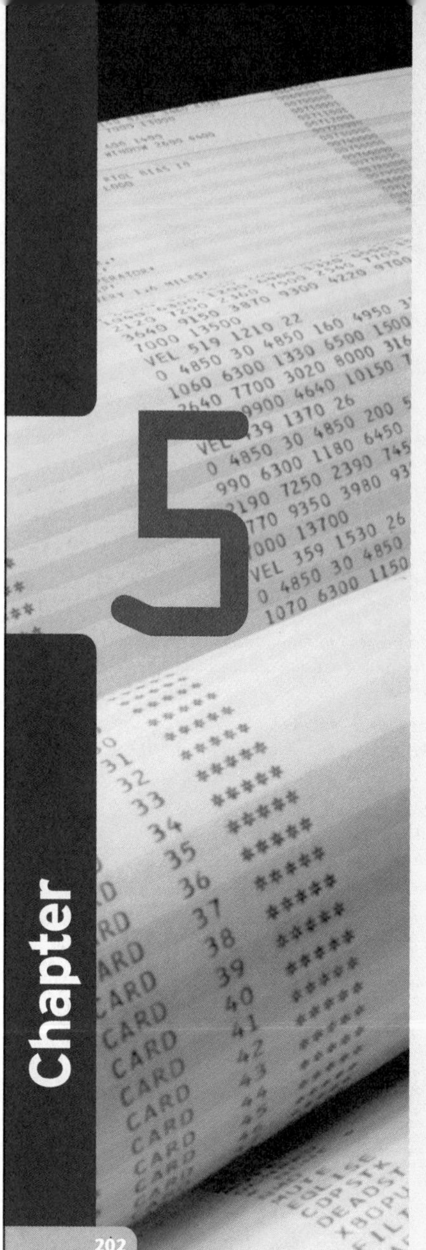

Chapter 5

Communicating in Written Form

Many business communications are in written form and their preparation is a time-consuming task that requires many competent employees. Millions of letters and memoranda are mailed each business day. Over 70 billion pages of other documents are prepared, processed, and distributed yearly. With this high volume of business documents, creating effective written communications is a critical task.

In this chapter you will learn to develop and process effective business documents. You will become acquainted with the procedures to prepare effective business letters, memoranda, reports, and related documents.

Chapter 5

202

Topic 5-1

Business Letters and Memoranda

When you have completed your study of this topic, you will be able to:

- **identify the characteristics of effective business letters and memoranda**
- **prepare effective business documents**
- **explain the function of business letters and memoranda**
- **identify and use appropriately the parts of business letters and memoranda**
- **choose appropriate formats for business letters**

Employees often **compose** business letters and memoranda. These documents may be prepared for a supervisor or coworker or written for the employee's own signature.

compose: write

Mike works in the office of a small plastics company. When the company president learned that Mike understood the business thoroughly, he was given the task of preparing responses to most letters and memos. Mike has learned how to individualize responses to most letters by selecting from appropriate paragraphs prepared and stored earlier. Because Mike works primarily on his own, he assumes full responsibility for making sure that all letters and memos requiring responses are answered as soon as possible. The president reads the responses Mike prepares and then signs all outgoing correspondence.

teaching tips

The extent of coverage on this topic will depend heavily on how much students have learned in prior courses. If there appears to be little understanding or retention from previous courses, you may wish to provide several laboratory experiences in which business letter writing and business formats are highlighted.

expand the concept

All offices are similar, yet no office is exactly like another. Likewise, office employees perform similar duties, yet the procedures and equipment used to complete these duties differ from company to company and even from office to office within a company.

for discussion

What appeals to you about Mike's position?

Topic 5-1

Composing and processing effective business letters and memoranda will make you a more valuable employee. As you study this topic, take time to review the document parts and standard formats thoroughly. By doing so, you will reduce the number of **occasions** when you must check references to determine how to format a document.

occasions: instances

thinking critically

As you proceed through this section, ask students to think about why each of these characteristics contributes to writing an effective document. Why is each characteristic important?

Characteristics of Effective Documents

Effective business documents are clear, concise, courteous, complete, and correct. These characteristics are known as the *five C's* of business writing. They are your guidelines to preparing business documents. You can quickly check the effectiveness of your documents by considering these factors.

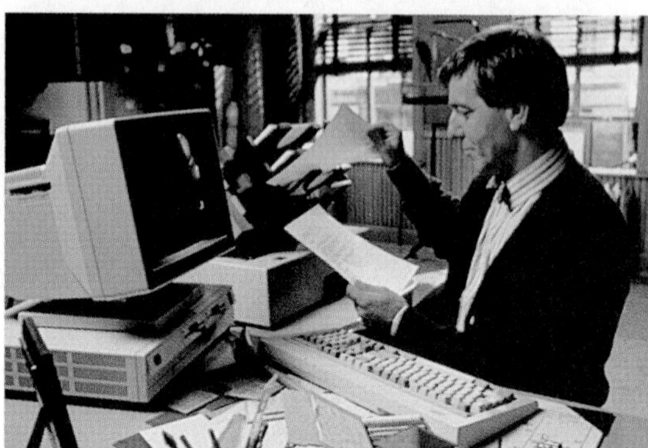

Illustration 5-1:1
Do your letters reflect the five C's of business writing?

teaching tips

If students have studied Chapter 3, present this section as reinforcement of the characteristics of effective writing discussed in Topic 3-3.

CLEAR

When your document is clear, the reader will have no trouble understanding what you are saying. Present your thoughts logically and use familiar words. Consider these example of unclear and clear writing.

Unclear:

> *I am concerned that we should cancel one of the meetings tentatively scheduled for Monday or Tuesday and reschedule it for Thursday or*

Friday. Don't you think we would acquire higher attendance levels by moving the meeting to Friday?

Clear:

Would we have better attendance if we rescheduled the meeting for Friday?

CONCISE

A concise message is brief and to the point. To make your message concise, avoid trite words and phrases. Use specific rather than abstract words. State your message without being wordy. Consider these examples:

Not concise:

We would like to advise you that your savings account will earn the highest possible interest rate bearable. Please be informed that we will advise you soon on these projections.

Concise:

Effective March 1, the interest rate on your savings account will be 6.5 percent.

CORRECT

A correct document provides accurate and current information. Check the content of your document to be sure is it correct and up-to-date. Verify all dates, numbers, and names. Make sure the document is technically correct by checking the spelling, punctuation, grammar, and word choice. Consider these examples:

Not correct:

Mrs. Spelding (sp?) said two weeks ago that she thought she would be finished with this project in about a month, of course, she is hoping for a quicker turnaround time.

Correct:

When I checked with Mrs. Spelling this morning, she told me she needed two more days to finish the project.

COURTEOUS

A courteous document helps present a positive image of you and your company. To make your document courteous, treat the reader with respect. Use polite expressions such as "thank you" and "please." Consider the reader's point of view. If the message relates to a problem situation, focus on the problem or behavior rather than the individual. Avoid using an accusatory tone as in the first example below.

Not courteous:

> *You did not send a check with your order. Our company policy precludes us from sending out merchandise without prepayment. This procedure is clearly stated on the order blank. If you want to receive the coat you ordered, you must pay for it in advance.*

Courteous:

> *Thank you for ordering your new fall coat from us. We know you must be eager to receive it. We did not find a check for the coat enclosed with your order. As soon as we receive your payment, we will ship your coat. For your convenience in responding, a postage-paid envelope is enclosed.*

COMPLETE

A complete document gives the reader all the needed information. To insure that your document is complete, include all necessary background and details. Try to anticipate questions that may occur to the reader. Include brief, related information that you think may be helpful as illustrated in the example below.

Not complete:

> *You asked if we had a 30-inch model available. Sorry, we do not. Thank you for asking.*

Complete:

> *The 30-inch model you requested is on back order until the end of February. We can have this model shipped to you directly from the factory to arrive at your home the first week of March. As alternatives, please consider our 25-inch and 40-inch models, which are in stock. If either of these models meets your needs, we can ship it to you immediately.*

for discussion

Is there any one of these five characteristics that is more important than the others? Why or why not? Can an effective document be created if any one of these characteristics is not used? Why or why not?

Preparing Effective Documents

An effective document is planned well and prepared carefully. The three stages of preparing effective documents are drafting the document, revising and editing the document, and proofreading the document for final **presentation.**

presentation: display or offering

expand the concept

To avoid writer's block, consider the first writing of a document a rough draft. People who try to write a perfect document on the first try will more likely encounter difficulty in expressing their ideas because of their unrealistically high expectations.

DRAFTING

Your first draft of a document will probably not be your final or finished version; it is considered a *rough draft.* Your goal in preparing the rough draft is to record your ideas. Do not try to make each sentence perfect. You will refine your document during the editing and proofreading stages.

Illustration 5-1:2
This woman is creating a rough draft of a letter.

To help **focus** your writing as you develop your document, ask yourself these questions:

focus: bring into clearer view

1. What is your purpose in writing?
2. What is your message?
3. Who and where is your audience?
4. What response do you want from the reader?

Purpose. Fix the purpose of the document clearly in your mind before you begin writing. Business documents are often written to inform. For example, you may want the reader to know about a new product or a new procedure. Business documents are also written to **persuade** or describe. Although these purposes may overlap, you need to have a clear understanding of why you are writing the document before you attempt your first draft.

persuade: influence, convince, urge

Message. Determine the points you need to make. What do you need to say to get your message across? What information do you need to include to build support for your position?

Preparing an outline actually saves time. Ask students to explain why this statement is true.

The tone of your message can be as important as the content. Keep these guidelines in mind as you draft your message:

- Prepare an outline of the document, particularly for longer documents. An outline will help you prepare the message in a logical **sequence.** The better you organize your points, the easier it will be for you to write the message and for your reader to understand your message.

sequence: order

- Focus on the reader as you write. Avoid using too many "I" and "we" words. Instead, use "you" and "your" frequently. This technique is called the *you approach*. Consider these examples:

Writer-focused approach:

> *We are happy to announce that The Traveler's Agency will now offer a full range of travel services. In addition to our regular travel services, we are now promoting three travel discount packages that we designed for the business traveler. Please contact our offices for more information.*

Reader-focused approach:

> *All your travel needs can now be met through The Traveler's Agency's full range of travel services. As a frequent business traveler, you are eligible for special travel discount packages. Three such discount packages have been designed for you, the frequent business traveler. Please return the enclosed postage-paid card to receive more information about these money-saving packages.*

- Give your message a positive tone. Avoid using negative words or a negative tone. Always be courteous. If your writing **demeans** the reader, you will build resentment in that reader. Be careful not to **inadvertently** insult the reader's intelligence or actions. Instead,

demeans: humiliates, degrades

inadvertently: unintentionally

make an extra effort in your writing to be helpful to the reader. Notice how the message below that is written in a positive tone sounds courteous while the message written in a negative tone does not.

Negative tone:

In the future, try not to wait so long to bring these delays to the attention of your supervisor. It is impossible to correct a situation if you cannot communicate with your supervisor in a timely fashion.

Positive tone:

In the future, please communicate with your supervisor immediately if you see a delay developing. Early reporting of potential delays will give us time to contact an alternative supply source.

Audience. Knowing certain characteristics about your reader(s) is important to how you develop your document. Is the reader already familiar with the topic? The reader's **familiarity** with the topic will help you determine how much information to include. Is your document going to one reader or to many? Is the document for external or internal distribution? These factors may influence how formal your writing needs to be, whether confidential topics may be mentioned, or how responses may be requested.

familiarity: detailed knowledge of

Response. How will the reader use this document? To make a decision? To gain information? If you want a response from the reader, let the reader know the specific action you want. Make it easy for the reader to respond by stating your message and the desired response clearly.

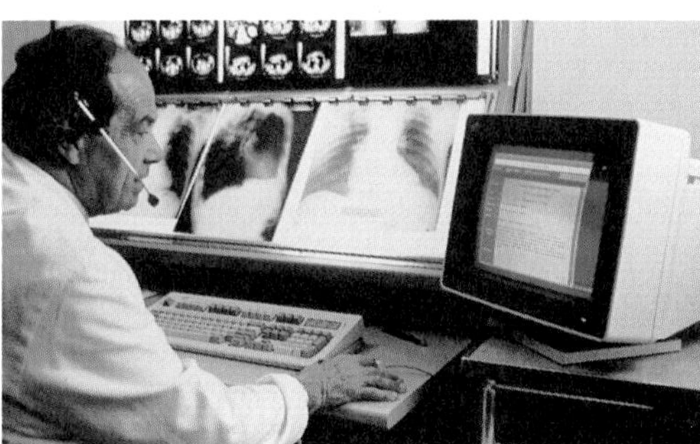

Illustration 5-1:3
Technical words should be used sparingly unless you know your audience is familiar with them.

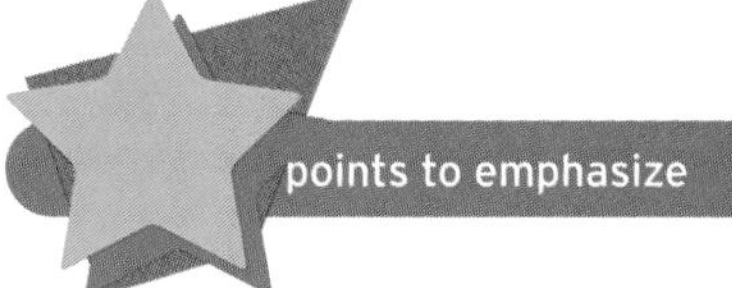

Review the four factors a writer should consider when drafting a document by asking students to restate each factor in their own words. Ask them what they think are the major points for each one.

REVISING AND EDITING

Most business documents are changed one or more times between the rough draft and the final document. This process of making changes to refine the document is known as editing or revising.

conveys: communicates, imparts

The primary purpose of editing is to make certain the message is accurate and **conveys** what the writer intends. In the editing stage of preparing your document, focus on the details of your writing. Read your draft carefully and consider the five C's of effective documents. Editing is your chance to polish your writing by making changes in response to these questions:

Finding inconsistencies takes attention to the detail in your writing. Using *Illus. 5-1:1* in some places and *Illustration 5-1:1* in other places is an example of an inconsistency. Inconsistencies are difficult to spot because the item is not wrong, simply different from the other uses of the item.

- Can you improve your word choice?
- Are your transitions smooth, flowing logically from one topic to another?
- Should the order of your points be changed?
- Are there **inconsistencies** in your writing that need to be corrected?

inconsistencies: differences

To make editing changes that can be understood easily by others, writers often use standard proofreader's marks as shown in Reference Section A. Once the changes are identified and marked, you can make the changes quickly using the editing features of your word processing software.

> *Steve works as an assistant to an engineer who prepares many reports. He has been instructed to prepare rough drafts of all reports. The engineer edits the drafts using standard proofreader's marks. After the engineer gives Steve the revised copy, he makes all text and formatting changes indicated. The engineer may revise complex reports several times. Steve's knowledge of word processing features allows him to make changes easily.*

PROOFREADING

Proofreading, the third phase of preparing a document, is your careful, overall check of the document. During this process, verify that the changes you marked in the editing phase have been made correctly. Check all numbers and unusual spellings against original documents. Use a spell checker and a grammar checker if available with your software.

Then complete a detailed **manual** proofreading. Remember that the spelling feature of your software is limited in the errors it can identify. For example, errors such as "there" for "their" will not be detected.

manual:
physical, not computer aided

Proofreading requires your complete attention to produce error-free documents. Depending upon the importance and complexity of the document, you may edit and proofread the document several times before it is finalized. Additional proofreading guidelines are shown in Illustration 5-1:4.

Proofreading Guidelines

1. Is the document technically correct? Check the following:
   - ____ grammar
   - ____ punctuation
   - ____ spelling
   - ____ word usage
   - ____ number usage
   - ____ capitalization
   - ____ word division
2. Is the document content accurate? Check the following:
   - ____ data accurate and complete
   - ____ directions followed
   - ____ all totals verified
   - ____ mailing notations followed
   - ____ enclosures assembled
   - ____ photocopies made
3. Is the document appearance professional? Check the following:
   - ____ stationery appropriate
   - ____ copy placement appropriate
   - ____ format consistent
   - ____ clean and smudge free
   - ____ type easy to read
   - ____ copy error free

Illustration 5-1:4
Proofreading guidelines provide a checklist for the careful writer to follow.

Discuss with students the importance of proofreading and their responsibility for proofreading. Students should be well versed in the guidelines for proofreading documents. You may wish to use transparency master TM5-1:1, Proofreading Guidelines, to introduce the discussion of this subject.

Message Types

Three message types are common in business correspondence: positive or neutral messages, negative messages, and persuasive messages. Each group of messages has unique characteristics that should be considered as you prepare documents. To determine which type of message your letter contains, consider the effect the message will have on the receiver.

"Common" does not mean unimportant, but emphasizes widespread standard use and acceptance.

POSITIVE OR NEUTRAL MESSAGES

The reader is not going to be disappointed with a positive or neutral message. The **strategy** for writing a positive or neutral message,

strategy:
plan

These letters are sometimes informally referred to as "good news," "bad news," and "please" messages. Emphasize the specific strategies in each message type.

therefore, is built on giving good news or neutral information to the reader in a straightforward way early in the document. Examples of positive or neutral messages include:

- placing or acknowledging an order
- placing or filling a request for information
- filling or extending a request for credit
- making, approving, or adjusting routine claims

To prepare good news or neutral messages, use the direct approach. Go directly to the main point of the message and give specific, complete information. Note how the message in Illustration 5-1:5 follows these general guidelines.

Have students identify the three strategy points used in preparing the good news message in Illustration 5-1:5.

Illustration 5-1:5
Use a direct approach to prepare a positive message.

Dear Mrs. Racine

Congratulations! Your request for a car loan was approved by our loan officers this morning.

Your loan for $10,000 is now being processed and will be available for your use within 24 hours. Please contact our loan officer, Jan Truong, at 555-0121 for an appointment to sign the final papers and to discuss your monthly payments.

Thank you for your business. We are pleased to serve you.

NEGATIVE MESSAGES

Negative messages typically involve a refusal or other news that the reader will find disappointing or upsetting. The strategy for preparing negative messages is based on having the reader understand why a request is being refused or other action is being taken while maintaining the reader's **goodwill.** Examples of negative messages include:

goodwill: friendly feeling

- refusing a request for an adjustment, a credit, or a favor
- canceling a service
- reporting unfavorable results

Negative messages require the writer to take considerable care in preparing the response. Use the indirect approach. Begin the message with a neutral statement that lets the reader know the message is your response to the request or to a situation that has arisen. Build your position by stating the reasons for your decision. State the refusal or other negative news. Close on a positive note and suggest alternatives if appropriate. Illustration 5-1:6 gives an example of a negative message.

Dear Mr. Roberts

Thank you for considering the Trust Bank for your car loan. Our loan officers met this morning to consider your loan application.

After a careful review of your application, they determined that your monthly income must be higher to support a loan of $10,000 with your current debt liability. Therefore, we cannot approve your loan at this time. Please consider resubmitting your loan application once your monthly payments of $250 on your existing loan are finished at the end of the year.

Your patronage is important to us, Mr. Roberts. We at Trust Bank hope you will continue to consider us for your future banking needs.

Sincerely

Illustration 5-1:6
Use an indirect approach to prepare a negative message.

Have students identify the four strategy points used in preparing the negative message in Illustration 5-1:6.

PERSUASIVE MESSAGES

In preparing a **persuasive** message, the writer wants to influence the reader to take a desired action. Sales letters, collection letters, and solicitation letters are all examples of persuasive messages.

persuasive: convincing

When you write a sales letter, for example, you want to influence the reader to buy your product or service. The basic steps to preparing a sales letter are as follows:

- Gain the reader's attention.
- Stimulate the reader's interest and desire.
- Give the reader opportunity to act.

Have students identify the three steps used in preparing the persuasive message in Illustration 5-1:7.

Note how these steps are used by the writer of the sales letter in Illustration 5-1:7.

Illustration 5-1:7
The writer of a persuasive message must first gain the reader's attention.

Dear Ms. Park

Would you let $2,000 slip through your fingers and do nothing about it? If you miss our big year-end sale this weekend at Don's Motors, that's exactly what you're doing!

This weekend, SATURDAY ONLY, from 6 a.m. to 6 p.m., you can take an extra $2,000 off selected vehicles.

Why not come by our sales lot this week to locate your bargain early. Sales associates will be available to assist you and answer your questions. Then, when Saturday comes—that $2,000 won't slip through YOUR fingers!

When you write a collection letter, you are trying to persuade the reader to pay his or her bill. Collection letters are typically a series of letters that move through different stages of persuasion: reminder stage, strong reminder stage, inquiry stage, and urgency stage. If collection messages are used at your job, you will probably have sample letters available for each phase of the collection-writing process.

Business Letters

A business letter is a written communication to a person(s) or an organization. It is usually written to someone outside the organization. As the writer of a business letter, you are your company's representative. Your letter helps the reader form an opinion about your organization.

Letters provide a long-lasting record of your message. Unlike verbal communications, a business letter can be read and reread many times and can serve different purposes. Reasons for writing business letters include:

- requesting information or an action
- giving information or fulfilling a request
- being courteous or maintaining goodwill (congratulations, thank-you's)
- explaining or stating a position or persuading the reader
- selling goods or services

PRESENTATION OF BUSINESS LETTERS

The primary purpose of a business letter is to convey a message. However, even before the message is read, the recipient makes a judgment about the letter and its sender. An attractively presented letter on quality paper will encourage the recipient to read the message with care. On the other hand, a carelessly presented letter on smudged paper may fail to get close attention.

A letter makes a good first impression if it has the following characteristics:

- The margins, indentions, and spacing are pleasing to the eye.
- Each letter part is correctly placed within the letter.
- Appropriate stationery is used.
- There are no obvious errors.
- The print is neat and clear.
- There are no smudges or fingerprints.

Make your letters as attractive as possible. If the appearance of the letter is pleasing to the eye, the receiver will be encouraged to read what you have written.

Why would a carelessly presented letter on smudged paper cause a reader to develop a negative attitude toward the sender?

LETTERS PARTS

Business letters represent a form of communication within the business world that follows a standard **protocol.** That is, those who receive business letters expect to see them written using **designated** letter parts. In Illustration 5-1:8 on page 217, you will find all the parts that could be included in a business letter. Of course, few letters will include

protocol: generally accepted customs or rules

designated: specified

all these parts. Some parts are included in most letters, while other parts are included only when needed. The standard letter parts that should be included in most business letters, as well as optional parts, are listed below.

Standard Letter Parts	**Optional Letter Parts**
Printed letterhead	Mailing notations
Date	Attention line
Letter address	Subject line
Salutation	Enclosure notation
Body	Separate cover notation
Complimentary close	Copy notation
Signature, printed name, and title	Postscript
Reference initials	Multiple-page heading

Occasionally, a letter will require more than one page. In such instances, a multiple-page heading is prepared to identify each page. As shown in Illustration 5-1:9, the heading includes the name of the addressee, the word *Page* and a page number, and the letter date.

BUSINESS LETTER FORMATS

Businesses want their written communications to represent them well. By using standard letter styles, businesses hope to achieve a high level of consistency in their documents. Using a standard arrangement for letters increases efficiency for both the writer and the **recipient.** For the writer, extra time is not needed to decide how to arrange the letter. For the recipient, the task of reading and **comprehending** is simplified because the arrangement of information is familiar.

recipient: receiver

comprehending: understanding

The arrangement of the letter text on the page is referred to as its format. Many companies have procedures manuals that contain standard format instructions and examples for frequently prepared documents. If examples are not available, you will be expected to make format decisions. These decisions should reflect your desire to produce attractive, easy-to-read documents.

Writers most frequently use the *block* and *modified block* letter formats. Refer to Illustration 5-1:10 on page 218 as you read about each format.

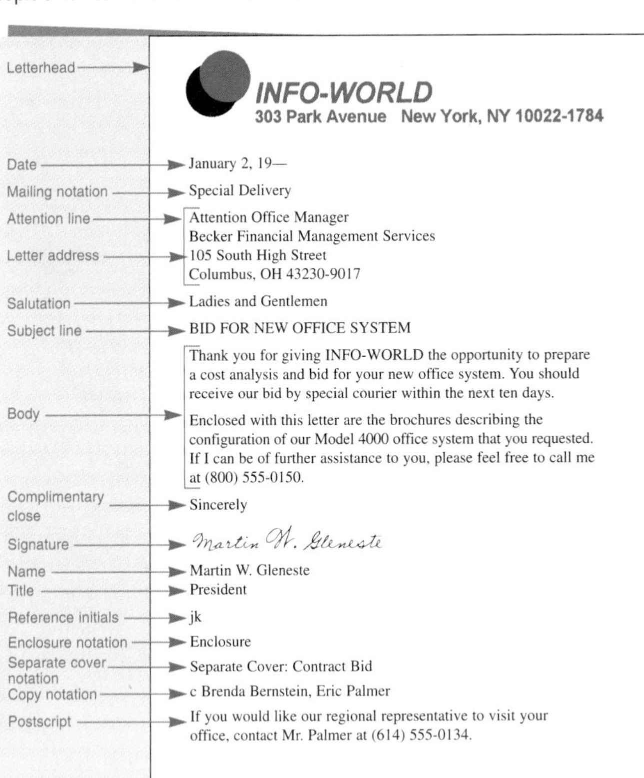

INFO-WORLD
303 Park Avenue New York, NY 10022-1784

January 2, 19—

Special Delivery

Attention Office Manager
Becker Financial Management Services
105 South High Street
Columbus, OH 43230-9017

Ladies and Gentlemen

BID FOR NEW OFFICE SYSTEM

Thank you for giving INFO-WORLD the opportunity to prepare a cost analysis and bid for your new office system. You should receive our bid by special courier within the next ten days.

Enclosed with this letter are the brochures describing the configuration of our Model 4000 office system that you requested. If I can be of further assistance to you, please feel free to call me at (800) 555-0150.

Sincerely

Martin W. Gleneste

Martin W. Gleneste
President

jk

Enclosure

Separate Cover: Contract Bid

c Brenda Bernstein, Eric Palmer

If you would like our regional representative to visit your office, contact Mr. Palmer at (614) 555-0134.

Illustration 5-1:8
Business letter parts

1 inch

Miss Laureen R. DiRenna
Page 2
February 2, 19—

apply this credit toward a future purchase. Be sure to include your membership number on the account credit form provided and return the form with the questionnaire. This will ensure that we credit your account properly.

Sincerely

Illustration 5-1:9
Multipage letter heading

The second-page heading is blocked at the left margin in Illustration 5-1:9.

Illustration 5-1:10
Business letter formats

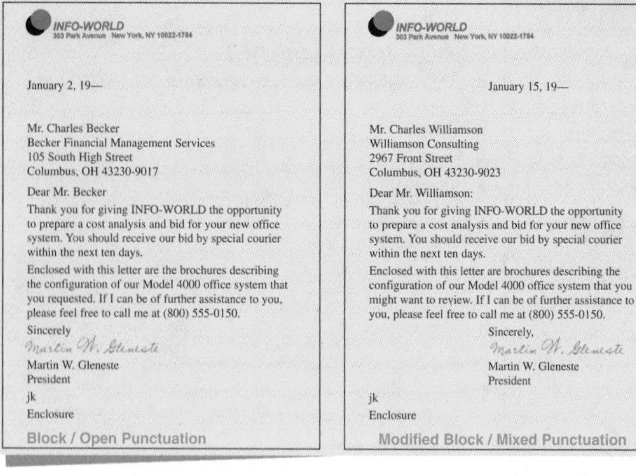

INFO-WORLD
303 Park Avenue New York, NY 10022-1784

January 2, 19—

Mr. Charles Becker
Becker Financial Management Services
105 South High Street
Columbus, OH 43230-9017

Dear Mr. Becker

Thank you for giving INFO-WORLD the opportunity to prepare a cost analysis and bid for your new office system. You should receive our bid by special courier within the next ten days.

Enclosed with this letter are the brochures describing the configuration of our Model 4000 office system that you requested. If I can be of further assistance to you, please feel free to call me at (800) 555-0150.

Sincerely

Martin W. Gleneste

Martin W. Gleneste
President

jk

Enclosure

Block / Open Punctuation

INFO-WORLD
303 Park Avenue New York, NY 10022-1784

January 15, 19—

Mr. Charles Williamson
Williamson Consulting
2967 Front Street
Columbus, OH 43230-9023

Dear Mr. Williamson:

Thank you for giving INFO-WORLD the opportunity to prepare a cost analysis and bid for your new office system. You should receive our bid by special courier within the next ten days.

Enclosed with this letter are brochures describing the configuration of our Model 4000 office system that you might want to review. If I can be of further assistance to you, please feel free to call me at (800) 555-0150.

Sincerely,

Martin W. Gleneste

Martin W. Gleneste
President

jk

Enclosure

Modified Block / Mixed Punctuation

As a review of the letter formats and punctuation styles, ask students:
1. In what ways are the two letter formats similar? How do they differ?
2. Which of the two punctuation styles would be more efficient? Why?

In the block format, all lines begin at the left margin; paragraphs and other letter parts are not indented. Block format is highly efficient because it saves time in moving from one part of the letter to another. In the modified block format, the date, complimentary close, and signature block begin at the horizontal center of the page rather than at the left margin. The first line of each paragraph may be indented one-half inch.

The two punctuation styles typically used in the special lines of business letters are open punctuation and mixed punctuation. In open punctuation style, no punctuation marks are used after the salutation and the complimentary close. In mixed punctuation style, a colon is placed after the salutation and a comma after the complimentary close. Either punctuation style may be used with a block or modified block letter format.

REPETITIVE LETTERS

Writing in the business office often involves preparing the same message or similar messages that are used again and again. Businesses often individualize letters even though similar letters may be sent to hundreds of people. If your responsibilities include preparing such documents, you may want to use form letters or paragraphs and features of your computer software to speed the preparation.

Prestored text, known as boilerplate text, can be combined to form a finished document, as shown in Illustration 5-1:11. In this instance, the writer assembled the document by combining custom text (the individual's name and address) with selected prestored sentences and paragraphs. Once the document is assembled, it is printed and saved in the same manner as other documents. A special feature of your word processing software, often called *merge*, may allow you to combine the boilerplate text and the custom text or variables automatically.

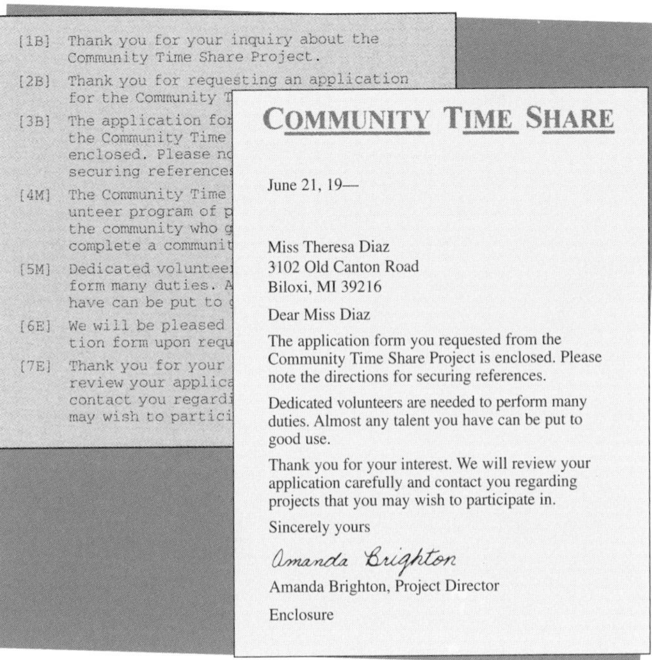

[1B] Thank you for your inquiry about the Community Time Share Project.
[2B] Thank you for requesting an application for the Community T
[3B] The application fo the Community Time enclosed. Please n securing reference
[4M] The Community Time unteer program of p the community who g complete a communit
[5M] Dedicated voluntee form many duties. A have can be put to
[6E] We will be pleased tion form upon requ
[7E] Thank you for your review your applica contact you regardi may wish to partici

COMMUNITY TIME SHARE

June 21, 19—

Miss Theresa Diaz
3102 Old Canton Road
Biloxi, MI 39216

Dear Miss Diaz

The application form you requested from the Community Time Share Project is enclosed. Please note the directions for securing references.

Dedicated volunteers are needed to perform many duties. Almost any talent you have can be put to good use.

Thank you for your interest. We will review your application carefully and contact you regarding projects that you may wish to participate in.

Sincerely yours

Amanda Brighton

Amanda Brighton, Project Director

Enclosure

Illustration 5-1:11

The writer selected paragraphs from the boilerplate text to prepare an individualized response.

ENVELOPES

Most business letters are written to individuals outside the company and require an envelope for mailing. Since the receiver begins forming

Certain word processing features permit the writer to individualize repetitive documents. Ask students: Have you ever received a letter that you identified immediately as one that probably hundreds of other received? Did you give it much attention?

Why would employees prefer to have carefully written paragraphs and statements already prepared for some of their more frequent writing tasks?

an opinion of the document when he or she views the envelope, the same care should be used in preparing envelopes as in preparing letters. The letterhead stationery and the envelope stationery should be of the same quality and color. The print should be clear and the envelope free of smudges.

In addition to making a good impression on the recipient, the envelope must be of a proper size and material acceptable to the U.S. Postal Service. To ensure prompt delivery, envelopes should include the following information:

- the recipient's name and address
- the sender's return address
- special addressee notation, if any
- special mailing notation, if any

The Postal Service recommends using all capital letters in the address with no punctuation marks except the hyphen in the ZIP code. Non-address data, such as a customer number or attention lines, should appear at the top of the address. Place special mailing notations that affect the cost of mailing, such as REGISTERED MAIL or SPECIAL DELIVERY, below the stamp area as shown in Illustration 5-1:12. Place special addressee notations that do not affect the cost of mailing, such as CONFIDENTIAL or HOLD FOR ARRIVAL, just below the return address.

Illustration 5-1:12

Recommended envelope format

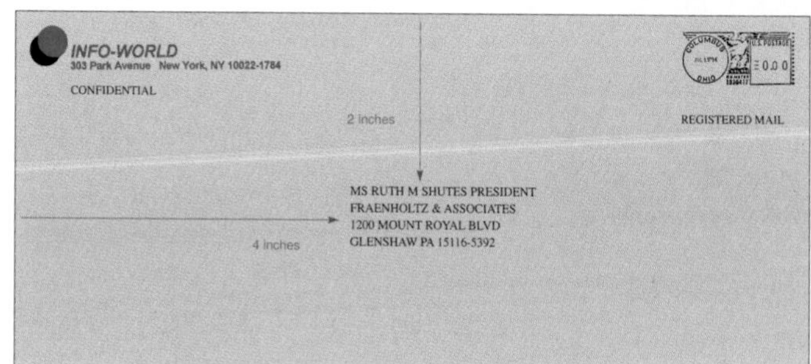

Computerized mail processing machines can increase the speed, efficiency, and accuracy of processing mail and help keep mailing costs down. These machines work best when envelopes use black ink on a white background. Certain other color combinations are acceptable if there is a high contrast between dark ink and a light background. There must be a clear vertical space between each character in the address and a clear horizontal space between lines for the address to be read properly by machine. Avoid script or other stylized fonts that do not meet these requirements. If you have questions about preparing mail for computerized processing, contact your nearest Postal Business Center.

Many companies have customers and/or subsidiaries in foreign countries. If you prepare correspondence to a foreign country, key the name of the country in all capital letters on a separate line.

Memoranda

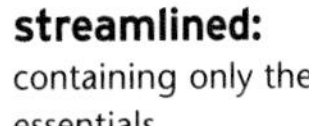

A memorandum is a **streamlined** business document used to communicate with an individual or a group within an organization. A memorandum may also be called an *interoffice memo* or just a *memo*. A memo that is transmitted electronically rather than delivered on paper is called *electronic mail* or *e-mail*. You may learn more about transmitting a memo electronically in Chapter 14.

streamlined: containing only the essentials

Whether memos are printed on paper or sent electronically, they are particularly useful for giving identical information to several people. They can be used effectively to give instructions, explain or clarify policy and procedures, or make announcements. Personnel directors, for example, send memoranda to inform employees of vacation and holiday schedules. Payroll department managers send memoranda to tell employees about new social security rates or income taxes. Credit managers send memoranda to sales representatives describing new terms for extending credit to customers.

People outside the organization who belong to the same task group or committee often exchange memoranda. For example, people from different businesses may join together to complete a community project. Correspondence among members of such groups often involves the exchange of memoranda.

Each memorandum you write makes an impression on the receiver whether the receiver is your coworker, your staff, or your supervisor. How you communicate with others in your organization influences their opinion of you. The more removed the recipient is from you, the more the memorandum represents you to that person. If, for example, a company official who does not know you reads a memorandum you have written, that memorandum may be all the official knows about

Ask students to interpret this statement: *The more removed the memo receiver is from you, the more the memorandum represents you to that person.*

you and the quality of your work. If the memorandum is prepared well, the reader forms a positive image of you as an employee.

GUIDELINES FOR WRITING MEMORANDA

An effective memorandum must be written clearly and concisely. The reader must understand why the memorandum is being written and what he or she is expected to do with the information. Often a memo must be developed and prepared under considerable time pressure because of the need for prompt decisions or sharing of information. Writers should exercise care to prepare an accurate, well-written message even though the memo is created quickly and the tone of the message is less formal than in a letter. Use these writing guidelines when preparing a memo.

in-house: within the company

- Give the writing your best effort. Consider **in-house** communications as important as correspondence to outside readers.
- Plan the writing of your memo and follow a logical sequence in presenting the information.
- Use discretion and tact when expressing personal opinions in your writing.
- Handle sensitive situations positively. Avoid using negative words; write using a positive tone.
- Check your memo carefully and apply the five C's of business writing. Ask yourself: Is my memo clear, concise, correct, complete, and courteous?
- Follow the same strategies as you would for a business letter to deliver positive, neutral, negative, or persuasive messages.
- Follow your company's standard format for a memo.

MEMORANDUM PREPARATION

A memo may be prepared on preprinted memo stationery or printed on plain paper with the company name and headings printed as part of the document. Memo stationery or headings with a special slogan or campaign logo may be used to provide updates on special events sponsored by the company.

A printed memo contains standard and optional parts as listed below and shown in Illustration 5-1:13. A memo transmitted electronically will contain the same information, but the format of the headings and the attachment or copy notations will vary depending upon the software used.

Standard Memo Parts	Optional Memo Parts
Headings: To, From, Date, Subject	Reference initials of typist
Body	Attachment or Enclosure notations
	Copy notations
	Distribution list

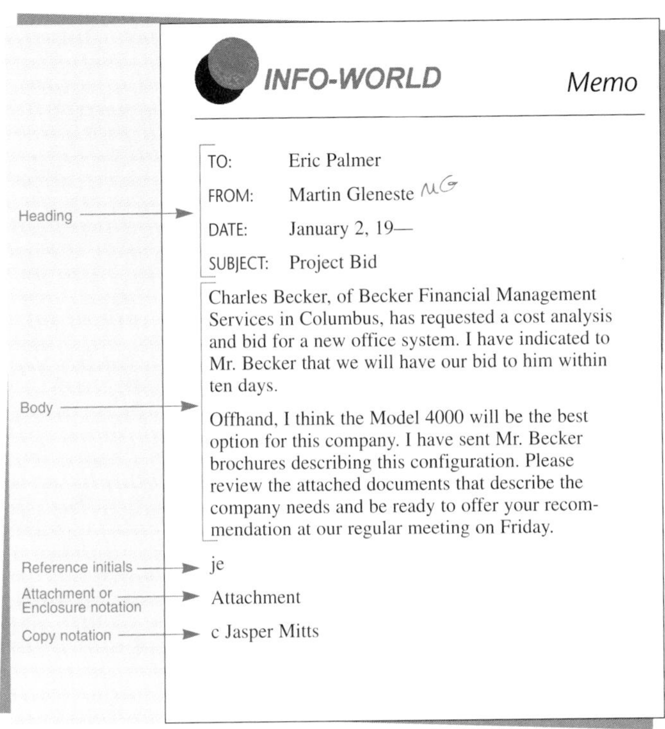
INFO-WORLD Memo

TO: Eric Palmer
FROM: Martin Gleneste MG
DATE: January 2, 19—
SUBJECT: Project Bid

Charles Becker, of Becker Financial Management Services in Columbus, has requested a cost analysis and bid for a new office system. I have indicated to Mr. Becker that we will have our bid to him within ten days.

Offhand, I think the Model 4000 will be the best option for this company. I have sent Mr. Becker brochures describing this configuration. Please review the attached documents that describe the company needs and be ready to offer your recommendation at our regular meeting on Friday.

je
Attachment
c Jasper Mitts

Illustration 5-1:13
Memorandum parts

Many office employees store memorandum forms that include the company name and logo, heading lines, and margin setting. The employee can recall the memo format and begin writing the memo immediately. The completed memo then can be printed on plain paper or sent electronically.

When a memo is sent to a group of people, it may be inappropriate to list all the recipients after the *To* headings. Instead, enter *Distribution List* after the *To* heading and list the recipients at the end of the memo under the heading *Distribution List*.

If the person receiving a printed memo is located nearby, the memo may be placed in the person's in-basket or mailbox. In this case, an envelope may not be needed. However, if the receiver is in a different location, the memo typically is sent in an interoffice envelope. A confidential document is always placed in an envelope and the envelope is marked *Confidential*.

Illustration 5-1:14

An envelope marked "CONFIDENTIAL" should be opened only by the addressee.

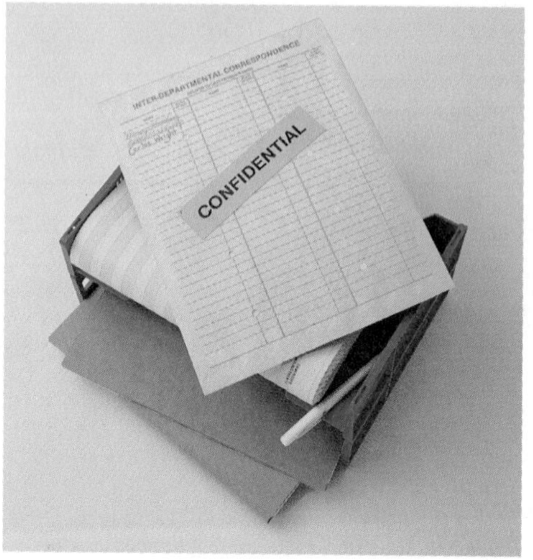

Reviewing the Topic

1. Describe the five characteristics of an effective document.
2. When creating the first or draft copy of a document, what four factors should you consider to help focus your writing?
3. Describe the three categories of messages common in business correspondence.
4. How can a writer use a reader-based approach in writing?
5. What reader characteristics are important for the writer to know?
6. Contrast the strategies used in preparing positive messages and negative messages.
7. What letter parts should be included in every business letter?
8. Identify the characteristics of a letter that make a good first impression.
9. Why do businesses use standard formats for their business letters and memoranda?
10. What is the purpose of a memorandum? How does it differ from a letter?

topic 5-1 review

INTERACTING WITH OTHERS

Andrea has been on the job for less than three months and has received a number of compliments from her supervisor. She feels she would be able to do a much better job if two problems were resolved. She finds the lighting at her desk inadequate. She also finds the music that is constantly provided in the office too distracting when she has to concentrate on more complicated tasks.

One day at lunch Andrea mentioned these two problems to a coworker. Her coworker quickly responded: "I think the lighting is fine, and the music is very relaxing. If you complain, there will be changes that the rest of us won't like." Later that same day, Andrea's supervisor stopped by her desk and asked, "How are things going?"

topic 5-1 review

What you are to do:

Prepare a response to the question raised. What do you think Andrea should say. Why?

REINFORCING ENGLISH SKILLS

The form letter that appears below has several errors in spelling, capitalization, and word usage. These errors must be identified and corrected before the form letter can be used to prepare responses to routine inquires for employment.

topic 5-1 review

Dear

Thank You for your inquiry concerning a position with our company as a(n) (position name). We do hve opeings available for (position name) from titme too time.

please complete and return the enclosed application from. The form will be keept on file and reviewed when an opening occurs.

If you decide to persue a position with our Company, you will find that we have very attractive workin conditins and an excellent promotion policy.

Sincerly

What you are to do:

Key the form letter, correcting all errors.

APPLICATION ACTIVITIES

ACTIVITY 1 Revise a Negative Letter

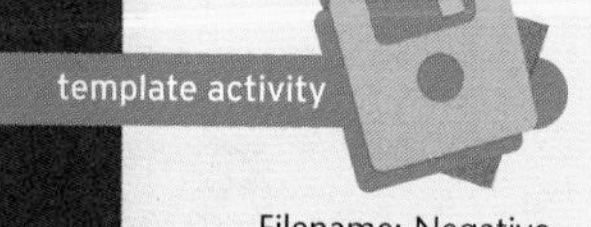

Filename: Negative

As part of an employee development plan, you are working your way through a business communications training program developed by your company to improve the communication skills of its employees.

Below is an excerpt you see on your computer screen from a draft of a letter from Computer Corner Furniture. Notice the antagonistic tone

226

of this response to a customer who was having difficulty assembling a computer workstation.

You obviously did not read the instructions that accompanied the computer desk, Model 122, which you purchased from our company. In case you misplaced or lost your instructions, I have enclosed another copy for you.

The instructions clearly state that you must assemble the base of the desk first, then the electrical wiring is inserted through the left front leg of the desk and through the slot in the top of the table. Obviously, it's too late to insert the electrical wiring once you have assembled the entire desk. You'll have to take the desk apart and start all over. This time, follow the instructions.

If you have any more problems with this desk, we do have a branch office in Independence. Please contact them; you should have sent your complaint to that office in the first place.

What you are to do:

Open the template file *Negative*. Revise the excerpt, making any changes necessary to prevent the response from conveying a negative or hostile attitude on the part of Computer Corner Furniture.

ACTIVITY 2 Standard Letter Format

Assume that you work for Western Security Systems. After several meetings, the support staff has recommended that a block style letter with open punctuation be adopted as the company standard for all business letters.

You have been asked to provide a sample of the standard letter format. You decide to use the body of the letter to describe the block format and open punctuation style so that everyone will understand how to prepare letters using this standard format.

Next, you will need to prepare a cover memorandum to all employees telling them that your company will implement this new procedure effective immediately. State in your memorandum that you are enclosing a sample letter using the block format with open punctuation as an example.

227

Business Letters and Memoranda

topic 5-1 review

What you are to do:

1. Compose and key a sample block letter with open punctuation. Use this information for the address and supply an appropriate salutation:

   Address: Customer's Name
   Street Address
   City, State ZIP

2. Prepare a cover memorandum to *All Employees*. Create a memorandum form for Western Security Systems to include the company name and heading lines to print on plain paper.

228

Topic 5-2

Business Reports and Related Documents

When you have completed your study of this topic, you will be able to:

- **identify the characteristics of business reports**
- **prepare reports in formal and informal formats**
- **create visual aids used in reports**
- **use software features effectively in creating and editing reports**

Reports are an important method of communication for a business. The business report is a presentation of organized information that will be used by the reader for a specific business purpose.

The extent of your involvement in the preparation of business reports will vary. It will depend not only on the size and type of your organization, but also on the nature of the report and your job duties. The smaller your organization, the more likely you are to be involved with writing, editing, assembling, and distributing business reports.

In this topic you will be introduced to two forms of business reports, the *informational* or procedural report and the **analytical** or persuasive report. These reports may be presented in formal or informal formats. In addition, you will explore special features of reports such as tables and graphs. Your ability to gather, organize, write, and present information

analytical: involving detailed study

To help illustrate the content of Topic 5-2, you may want to gather copies of business reports for the students to review. These reports could serve as a means to help students distinguish between informational and analytical reports. In addition, you could use these reports to identify the various report parts and formats used.

in a standard report format will allow you to adapt easily to specific reports you may encounter on the job.

Characteristics of Business Reports

The basic purpose of a report is to provide the reader with information. The reader, however, may need this information for different purposes, such as to make a decision or to keep up-to-date with company operations. Many reports are straightforward and informational. These may be referred to by their function or purpose, such as progress reports, quarterly or annual reports, financial reports, sales reports, or personnel reports. Others are more analytical, often covering more complex topics. They provide the analysis needed for critical business decisions. If the owners of a firm want to expand their product markets, for example, much of the information they need to make their decision will be presented to them in the form of reports.

Reports typically are more complex and longer than letters and memoranda. However, many of today's business executives prefer to use a memorandum format for shorter informational or procedural reports.

Ask students if they routinely fill out standard forms. Discuss with them some of the common forms used to collect data within the school. Talk about the importance of filling out the forms completely and accurately. Move the discussion to the next level of report preparation by asking them what they think happens to the data that is collected. Discuss the reports that can be generated from the forms they complete.

Informational Reports

Informational reports are typically based on data gathered within the normal operations of the company. Some reports are made so frequently that standard report forms, such as the one shown in Illustration 5-2:1, are developed. The company relies on employees to complete the forms accurately and neatly. Using printed forms saves time and ensures that data is collected uniformly across the company.

GATHERING DATA

Every organization requires some reports on a regular basis. Indeed, most businesses will establish procedures for gathering data needed to write these routine reports. In the example shown in Illustration 5-2:1, a completed copier repair form is submitted to the supervisor each week. The supervisor uses the weekly reports to write a repair summary

Cory's Copier Services

Person Reporting Problem	Leslie
Date	1/11 Time 9:15 am x pm
Customer Name	Amy's Hair Salon
Address	1538 South Elm Riverton
Copier Model	C-248 Number of Copies 235,687
Problem Reported	Lines across bottom of page
Action Needed	New Drum
Action Taken	Drum on order
Repair Person	Ryan Barnes

Illustration 5-2:1

Informational reports are often prepared from data collected in the day-to-day operations of the business.

report to the engineering department. One of the purposes of this report is to spot high maintenance trends and to anticipate when major maintenance will be needed on a copier.

WRITING THE REPORT

In addition to standard form reports, informal business reports are common. The supervisor uses the data shown in Illustration 5-2:1 to write a two-page memo report. The memo follows the same format each week. The similar data is summarized for each report using designated headings. The supervisor then adds comments and **interpretations** at the end of the report.

interpretations: explanations or views

In writing an informational report, follow the same guidelines used for direct correspondence. State your purpose early and clearly. For example, use the subject line in a memo report or the title in a formal report to help focus the reader to your purpose. Consider the audience in determining the level of formality needed and the appropriate use of technical terms or confidential information. Make certain the reader knows why the report is being written and what response or action is required. Provide complete and correct supporting information. Write the report in a positive and courteous tone.

Organize your report by outlining the points you need to make. If you are expected to follow a standard format, your organization is already determined. If, however, you can develop your own reporting format, organize your thoughts around a logical pattern or sequence.

Present only relevant data; do not clutter the report with unnecessary information. If you are expected to add your own comments or interpretations to the data, identify these comments clearly. Writers often use headings such as *Comments*, *Recommendations*, or *Implications* for their analysis and interpretation of the data.

Give attention to the formatting and final presentation of the report. As with letters and memoranda, the report represents you or your company and can make a positive or negative first impression affecting how the content of the report will be received.

Analytical Reports

The *analytical report* is generally a longer, more complex report than the informational report. It is normally prepared as a formal business report and often requires considerable research and information gathering. An analytical report takes more time to write and may require in-depth analysis of situations to persuade the reader.

The information and analysis presented in the analytical report is often used to make important company decisions. Typically, an employee or group of employees is asked to research a specific problem or situation. The employees gather data related to the problem and then write their report presenting the data they have collected along with their interpretations. They are often expected to draw conclusions and make recommendations.

GATHERING DATA

incorporated: brought into

Reports are often completed under the pressure of deadlines. Employees are expected to gather data quickly and accurately to be **incorporated** into reports in a timely fashion.

You may be asked to contribute to a formal business report. These guidelines will help you process data quickly, accurately, and with attention to detail:

- During the data-gathering stage, key information as it is collected. If information must be recorded manually, use notecards to allow for ease in rearranging the data while writing the report.
- Use a scanner, if available, to reduce the amount of time needed to enter large quantities of previously keyed data or technical material into the report. If scanning is not possible, photocopy the material (such as tables) to be sure that the details are accurate. Photocopying is faster and more accurate than copying the material by hand.

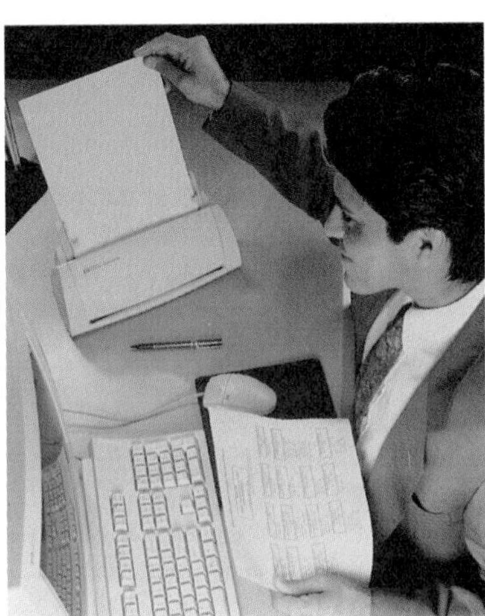

Illustration 5-2:2
Scanning text and graphics saves valuable time.

- Record complete source details for all data you locate (title of publication, author, publisher, date, and page).

USING ELECTRONIC INFORMATION SERVICES

By using a computer, modem, and communications software, your computer can connect with external online information services. Information services provide electronic access to accurate and timely data that otherwise may not be available to a business. Such services

Large volumes of information are available to users of information services. In those offices using information services, employees are highly valued who can identify the most useful source, select information relevant to the question, and organize the information into a meaningful form.

searches:
online database inquiries

external:
not located within the company

usually charge a connect fee, and then bill according to time used or the number of **searches** made.

Many businesses find an **external** information service is less costly than maintaining expensive journal subscriptions and more efficient than using staff time to search for information in libraries. By using an information service, volumes of information can be searched quickly. Over 8,000 online databases provide many services, such as financial and investment analysis, text of magazines and journals, and airline schedules.

WRITING THE REPORT

When the report data has been gathered, organized, and analyzed, you are ready to begin writing the report. Use the general guidelines presented in Illustration 5-2:3 to begin creating the report. If several drafts of the report are required, cycle through Step 4 as often as revisions are required. These steps are common to all business reports.

Illustration 5-2:3

Focus report preparations by using these guidelines to organize and write the report.

GUIDELINES FOR ORGANIZING AND WRITING REPORTS

1. **Focus the report.**
   - Know why you are writing.
   - Identify your readers.
   - Know why readers want to read the report.
   - Identify data needed for the report.
   - Identify information sources.
2. **Plan the writing.**
   - Identify the main topics and subtopics.
   - Prepare an outline of the report.
   - Identify potential visuals/graphics.
3. **Write the first draft.**
   - Write a draft of the text.
   - Develop related visuals/graphics.
4. **Revise your first draft.**
   - Revise the outline if necessary.
   - Edit/revise text of the first draft.
   - Verify and document sources used.
   - Finalize visuals/graphics.
5. **Present your report.**
   - Use standard formats.
   - Check headings/subheadings.
   - Prepare preliminary report pages.
   - Proofread the final copy.

As a writer, you will need to consider and use an appropriate tone and degree of formality in the report. If the report is for limited distribution to your coworkers, an informal style may be acceptable:

> *Jason, here is the information on the delivery routes and schedules you requested. You're right, two of the delivery schedules overlap, leaving the third route only partially covered on Tuesdays and Thursdays. No wonder we have had complaints from our customers on the third route. I'm taking immediate steps to correct this schedule.*

If the report is to be distributed to a broad audience or outside the company, however, your writing style should also be more formal:

> *In July, 19—, the Board of Directors authorized a study to determine the effect of downsizing on the production capability of the Houston plant. Several additional factors were determined to contribute to the 20 percent overall production drop.*

Using a more formal style is appropriate when the report will be read by a larger number of people or when the topic is complicated or critical. To achieve the formal style in the second example, note that the writer

- did not use first names (*The Board of Directors* vs. *Jason*)
- did not use contractions (for example, *you're* or *I'm*)
- used passive voice (*were determined* vs. *here is*)

Business Report Formats

Several acceptable formats are available for presentation of business reports. Your company, however, may have a preferred format that you can determine from previous reports or from the company procedures manual. Two common business report formats are the *unbound* and *leftbound* formats.

UNBOUND REPORT FORMAT

The *unbound report* is fastened together (generally in the upper left-hand corner) with a fastening device such as a paper clip or staple. No extra

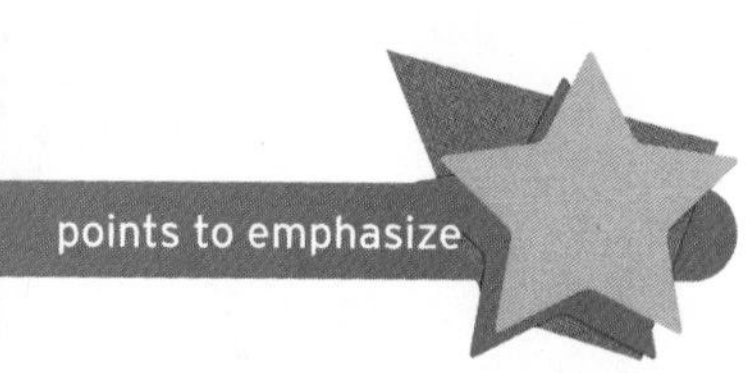

All margins except the left are the same for unbound and leftbound formats.

Business reports may be single- or double-spaced. Double-spacing provides copy that is easier to read. Single-spacing, however, reduces the volume of paper required.

space is provided in the margin of the unbound report for fastening the report together. Writers have found this format to be particularly useful for short informal reports that will be distributed internally.

LEFTBOUND REPORT FORMAT

The *leftbound report* format moves the left margin a half inch beyond the margin for the unbound report. The extra space allows for binding the report at the left. All other margins are the same as those of the unbound report. Writers use this format for longer, more complicated reports. It is also useful for reports that require a formal presentation or are being sent outside the company.

The formats presented to you in this topic represent acceptable business report formats. Refer to Illustration 5-2:4 for a summary of report formatting guidelines.

Illustration 5-2:4
Report Format Guidelines

BUSINESS REPORTS

Format	Top Margin	Bottom Margin	Left Margin	Right Margin
Unbound				
First page	2 inches	1 inch	1 inch	1 inch
Other pages	1 inch	1 inch	1 inch	1 inch
Leftbound				
First page	2 inches	1 inch	1.5 inches	1 inch
Other pages	1 inch	1 inch	1.5 inches	1 inch

Body of the report is usually double-spaced, but may be single-spaced.

Formal Business Reports

A *formal business report* includes standard parts that readers find valuable in helping them understand and interpret the report. Standard report parts are also an important **organizational** aid for writers.

organizational: arranging related parts into a whole

A formal report generally contains an explanation of the reason for the report, presentation of data, explanation of the meaning of the data, and conclusions and/or recommendations. The writer also documents the types and sources of information used to write the report. As such, a formal business report may contain all or some of the common report parts.

Typical report parts used in a formal business report include:

- title page
- table of contents
- summary
- body
- references
- appendices

TITLE PAGE

The title page contains the report title, the writer's name, the name of the organization, and the report date as shown in Illustration 5-2:5 on page 238. In addition to the writer's name, the writer's title and company address may be appropriate.

Pages **preliminary** to the body of the report are numbered with lowercase Roman numerals. Although the title page is considered the first of the preliminary pages, it is never numbered.

preliminary: coming before

TABLE OF CONTENTS

The table of contents presents an overview of the material covered in the report by listing the report headings and their corresponding page numbers. (Refer to Illustration 5-2:5.)

Writers prepare the final copy of the table of contents after the entire report has been completed. This procedure permits titles and page numbers to be verified, particularly if any last-minute changes were made in the report.

SUMMARY

The summary is a brief description that gives the reader an overview of the report. In the business office, you may hear the summary called by a variety of names, including *executive summary* or *abstract*.

Business reports represent an important form of communication for a business. Formal business reports are prepared using standard formats and parts.

Ask the students to distinguish between an executive summary and an abstract. Remind students that the summary is a preliminary page to the body of the report and is numbered with lowercase Roman numerals.

The heading, TABLE OF CONTENTS, is centered according to the format selected (unbound or leftbound). *Leaders* (periods and spaces alternated) extend across the page to guide the reader in finding the page number. If a table of contents follows the title page, it is numbered *ii.* If, however, the table of contents is the only preliminary page to the body of the report, the page may not be numbered.

Refer to Illustration 5-2:5. What would change on page 1 of the report if the report were unbound? Repeat the same line of questioning for all pages in the illustration.

Illustration 5-2:5
Leftbound report format examples

Title Page

Teleconference Feasibility Study

Sandra K. Marshall
Office Communications Consultants

February 16, 19—

Contents Page

TABLE OF CONTENTS

SECTION 1
TELECONFERENCING FACTORS

The factors involved in the decision to implement a teleconferencing network at National Enterprises, Incorporated, are presented in this section. The factors include equipment, facilities, personnel, management, supplies, and overhead.

Equipment
The success of the teleconferencing network is dependent in large part on the equipment the company uses. Most teleconferencing experts recommend a mix of teleconferencing equipment that is designed for the individual company. According to Ostendorf (1997, 152):

> Don't expect one type of equipment to handle all your needs. Conference calls differ. Some link three people, others connect thousands in many sites. They can last minutes or days. The location can be an auditorium or a phone booth.

Four terminal equipment groupings were considered for this study. The handset telephone, desk-top speakerphone,

Page 2

2

especially suited for the participant who needs to conduct long telephone conversations while referring to papers, files, online information, or other materials. The speakerphone can be effective for the small-group, two-location meeting.

References

REFERENCES

French, Alice. Teleconferencing—What You Need to Know. Baltimore, MD: Clearwater Press, 1996.

Hyde, Richard and Katerine Elrod. Teleconferencing in the Modern Office. 2d ed. Chicago: Torchbearer Publications, 1997.

Ostendorf, Virginia. "How to Buy and Set Up Teleconferencing Systems." Teleconnect. May 1997, 152, 154, 155.

An *executive summary* highlights the report's findings, conclusions, and recommendations. An *abstract*, however, is shorter and simply states the report's contents.

BODY

The body is the text or message of the report. Basically, the body of the report is used by the writer to define the purpose and scope of the report, present and evaluate alternatives, draw conclusions, and make recommendations. In long reports, the body will be divided into chapters or sections.

As you prepare a report, you may need to include quotes from the sources of information used. Quotations, which are excerpts from other sources, are identified in the body of the report. A quotation of more than three lines is set off from the rest of the text, as shown in Illustration 5-2:5, page 238.

Giving credit to the sources of information you used in a report is called documentation. Two common methods of documentation in addition to quotations are *endnotes* and *textual citations*. When the endnote method is used, a superior (raised) reference figure is placed at the appropriate point in the copy. The matching numbered reference is then listed at the end of the report with a separate page titled *ENDNOTES*.

> *When writing the report, credit must be given for material quoted either directly or indirectly from other sources.*[1]

When the textual citations method is used, the source information is placed in parentheses within the text. This information includes author(s), date of publication, and page number(s).

> *When writing the report, credit must be given for material quoted either directly or indirectly from other sources (Tilton, Jackson, and Rigby, 1996, 398).*

If the source is identified by name within the report copy, only the publication date and page number are used.

> *According to Tilton, Jackson, and Rigby, credit must be given for material quoted either directly or indirectly from other sources (1996, 398).*

The main heading of each of these divisions (chapters or sections) should begin on a new page as shown in Illustration 5-2:5. Insert a blank line before all side heads.

Single-space a long quotation in a report, and indent it five spaces from the left margin.

What do you consider to be the most distinguishing feature of each of the three documentation methods (quotations, endnotes, and textual citations). Under what circumstances might one method be preferable over another?

List report references in alphabetic order in appropriate bibliographic format. Consult a style manual, an office handbook, or a previously prepared report that you know has an acceptable format.

REFERENCES

The references section follows the body of the report and identifies the sources used in preparing the report. Include the sources for direct quotes, **paraphrased** sources, and sources used to obtain ideas or background information. This section may be titled REFERENCES, BIBLIOGRAPHY, or WORKS CITED.

paraphrased: stated in another form

An appendix can contain a variety of material, such as highly technical information, actual data used to prepare charts, questionnaires, or related correspondence. The appendix contains information that supports the report but is too long or too detailed to include in the report body.

APPENDICES

An appendix provides more detailed data (usually in the form of a chart, graph, table, or text) to support the body of the report. The appendix (or appendices if several are included) is placed at the end of the report for the benefit of interested readers. If more than one appendix is included, number or letter each in sequence.

Informal Business Reports

Like a formal business report, an *informal report* is also written to convey information in a clear, concise manner. Informal reports, however, often do not have as many parts as formal reports. How you organize an informal report will be based upon the purpose of the report. In presenting the informal report, you may wish to follow samples of previous reports.

The presentation formats discussed here are for informal, unbound reports of no more than five to six pages. For longer reports, you may wish to consider the formal report presentation format. Illustration 5-2:6 shows part of the first page of an informal, unbound report. The unbound report may fit on one sheet of plain paper or it may require several pages. Unbound reports do not allow extra margin space for fastening the pages together.

Informal reports include both a main heading (or title) and text, or body of the report. Informal, brief reports also may include the following parts:

- secondary heading
- reference list (or bibliography)

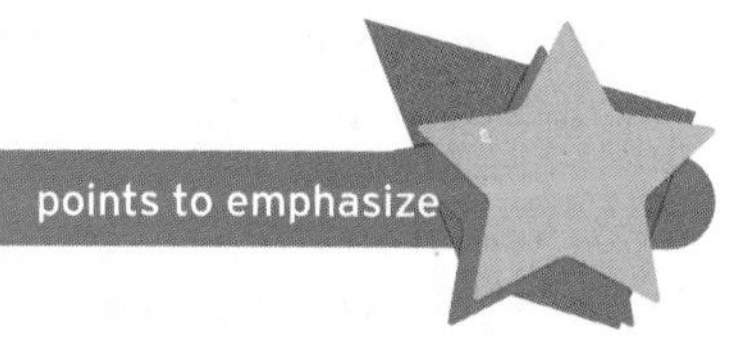

Because the report may be used as the foundation for an important decision, the report must be accurate and complete.

Informal reports often have fewer parts than formal reports.

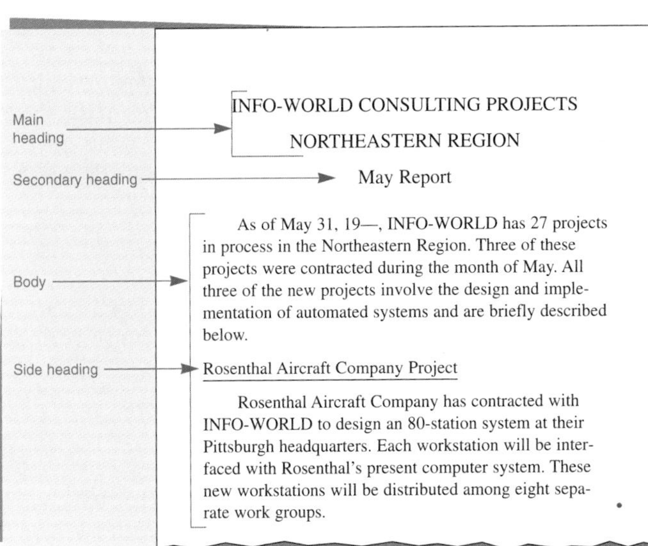

INFO-WORLD CONSULTING PROJECTS

NORTHEASTERN REGION

May Report

As of May 31, 19—, INFO-WORLD has 27 projects in process in the Northeastern Region. Three of these projects were contracted during the month of May. All three of the new projects involve the design and implementation of automated systems and are briefly described below.

Rosenthal Aircraft Company Project

Rosenthal Aircraft Company has contracted with INFO-WORLD to design an 80-station system at their Pittsburgh headquarters. Each workstation will be interfaced with Rosenthal's present computer system. These new workstations will be distributed among eight separate work groups.

Illustration 5-2:6

Informal, unbound report format

- side headings
- title page
- reference citations
- abstract

The number of additional parts a writer includes in an informal report will depend upon the nature of the report and the subject matter covered. Essentially, reports are organized to communicate information quickly and clearly. In this section, you will learn about the main heading, the secondary heading, the body, and side headings. Other report parts have the same function as in the formal report.

MAIN HEADING

The *main heading* is the title of your report. Use the heading to introduce your reader to the report's topic. Give the heading a **prominent** position in your report by using capital letters, bold type, a slightly larger type size, or a different complimentary font style.

prominent: important, easily recognized

If two lines are required for the heading, the lines may be either double- or single-spaced.

SECONDARY HEADING

The *secondary heading* provides additional, clarifying information. If a secondary heading is used, give it less prominence in your report than the main heading. Capitalize only the first letter of key words, as shown in Illustration 5-2:6, page 241. Use the same font style, perhaps in a smaller size, as used for the main heading.

BODY

The *body* of the report presents the information that you want the reader to know about the subject of the report. The body may be single- or double-spaced with a blank line between paragraphs.

SIDE HEADINGS

Use *side headings* to divide your main topic into subdivisions. Key side headings in capital and lowercase letters on a separate line beginning at the left margin. Insert a blank line before and after each side heading. Use underscore, bold, or the different font style used for the main and secondary headings for **emphasis.**

emphasis: a way of giving importance or directing attention

Refer to Illustration 5-2:7. Does one format appear to be more efficient than the other? Why? Does one format appear to be better balanced than the other? Why?

PAGE NUMBERS

An informal report frequently has more than one page. In such instances, number each page except the first. If a heading is used on the second and **succeeding** pages, the page number is part of that heading, as shown in Illustration 5-2:7. Use the header feature of your word processing software to automatically print the page number and/or heading at the top of succeeding pages.

succeeding: to come next after another

Visual Aids

Visual aids consist of the tables, graphs, and other illustrations, such as maps, which are used to present data in an appealing and efficient manner. The purpose of using visual aids is to help make the report easy to understand. They may also reduce the amount of text needed, presenting the data in a chart or table instead.

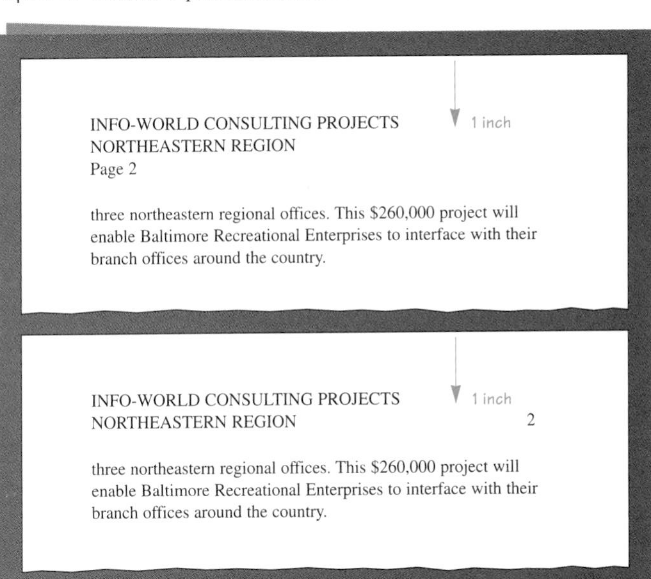
INFO-WORLD CONSULTING PROJECTS
NORTHEASTERN REGION
Page 2

three northeastern regional offices. This $260,000 project will enable Baltimore Recreational Enterprises to interface with their branch offices around the country.

INFO-WORLD CONSULTING PROJECTS
NORTHEASTERN REGION 2

three northeastern regional offices. This $260,000 project will enable Baltimore Recreational Enterprises to interface with their branch offices around the country.

Illustration 5-2:7
Heading for second and succeeding report pages

TABLES

A table is a **systematic** arrangement of facts, figures, and other information. Tables can be used to summarize information and to make comparisons. When developing a table to be used in a report, be certain that it relates directly to your report. The table should have a clearly defined purpose and should focus the reader's attention on a specific aspect of your report.

systematic: in an organized manner

A report table should be self-explanatory. That is, the reader should not have to refer to text that may **accompany** the table to understand the table contents. Look at the table in Illustration 5-2:8 on page 244. Is it self-explanatory? Which employee received the highest commission? How much were his or her total sales for the first quarter? Which employee received the lowest commission? How much were his or her total sales for the first quarter?

accompany: go with

Illustration 5-2:8 displays the standard parts of a table. Some simplified tables will not include all these parts. More complex tables will

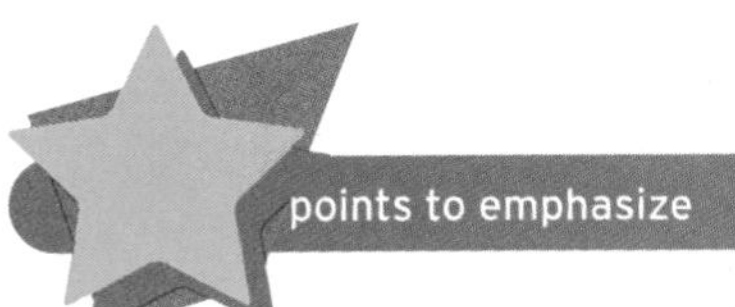

Tables are a systematic arrangement of facts, figures, and other information. Each table should be self-explanatory.

of a credit card. A medical calculator is also included for standard calculations. The healthcare workers have immediate access to reference material where and when they need it.

The Internet. The Internet is a giant network of computers and smaller networks that spans the globe. Via the Internet, businesses can connect with other people, businesses, and information resources around the world quickly and easily. The following examples describe how businesses use the Internet. More information about the Internet is provided in Chapter 14.

Through electronic mail, coworkers are able to communicate with each other. Workers can send and receive messages through computers used in the office, laptop computers used by employees working outside the office, and even computers used by employees working at home.

A sales representative plans an out-of-state trip, making the airline reservations using a travel service on the Internet.

An investment broker accesses information on the Internet to get up-to-the-minute stock quotes.

A small-business owner uses a site on the Internet to sell sports memorabilia such as baseball trading cards, league pennants, autographed products, T-shirts, and sports items.

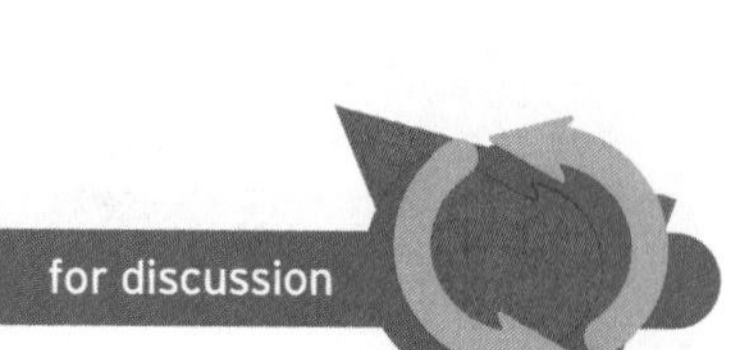

Ask students to share their experiences searching for information on the Internet.

Illustration 4-2:8

The Internet allows business to connect with people and information resources around the world.

Illustration 5-2:8
Basic table format

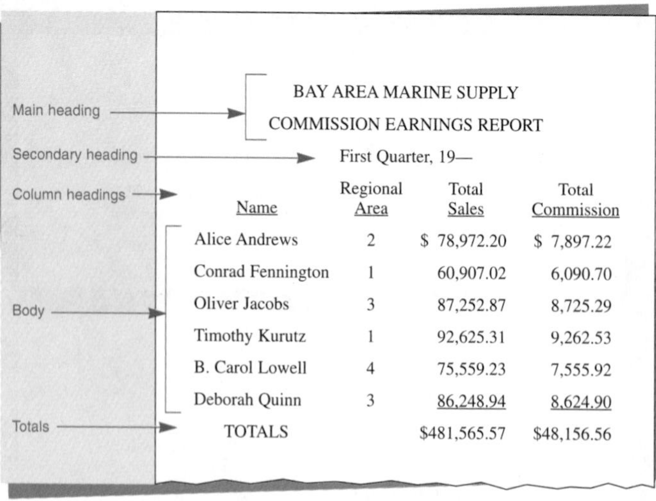

BAY AREA MARINE SUPPLY
COMMISSION EARNINGS REPORT
First Quarter, 19—

Name	Regional Area	Total Sales	Total Commission
Alice Andrews	2	$ 78,972.20	$ 7,897.22
Conrad Fennington	1	60,907.02	6,090.70
Oliver Jacobs	3	87,252.87	8,725.29
Timothy Kurutz	1	92,625.31	9,262.53
B. Carol Lowell	4	75,559.23	7,555.92
Deborah Quinn	3	86,248.94	8,624.90
TOTALS		$481,565.57	$48,156.56

include other parts such as a source note indicating the source of the data, ruled lines to separate the data visually, and dot leaders to aid in reading across the table from one column to the next.

Most word processing software packages have a table-generating feature that automatically determines column spacing and prepares the table layout. You may wish to start with the table layout that is generated automatically and then make adjustments as needed. Your goal is to create a table that is easy to read and highlights the appropriate information.

The secondary heading is centered below the main heading. Only the first letters of key words are capitalized.

Main Heading. The main heading is the title of the table and describes its overall content. A carefully written table title helps the reader focus on the table content. The main heading of a table is treated in the same manner as the main heading of an informal report. The heading is usually centered horizontally over the table data.

Secondary Heading. Some tables require a secondary heading such as the one shown in Illustration 5-2:8. A secondary heading gives the reader more specific information about the table contents.

Column Headings. Column headings identify the information provided in particular columns. A column heading may be centered above the longest line in that column or left-aligned even with the column data. Alignment of column headings may be mixed within the table as appropriate for the column data. For example, when using a spreadsheet program to create a table, the heading for a text column is often left-aligned while the headings for number columns are right-aligned to match the data alignment. Underscore column heads or use a bold or alternate type to set them off from the body of the table.

Body. The body contains the data indicated by the column headings and may be either single- or double-spaced. Tables are often double-spaced for improved readability. When the table is placed within the text of a report, use the space available on the page to determine how you will space the table body. The table width should not exceed the left and right margins of the report body.

Summary Lines. Data in a table is often summarized or calculated with the results shown at the end of the table. *Total*, *Average*, *Maximum*, and *Minimum* are common summary lines included on tables. The last entry in a column is often underscored to separate the table data from the summary lines. The summary line is typically labeled. For example, by using the word *Total*, the writer indicates that the figures in the column have been added.

GRAPHS

A graph is a pictorial representation of data. Graphs make the report more interesting and informative. In many cases, data is easier to interpret in a graph than when shown in columns of figures or blocks of text. Graphs, therefore, are used frequently in business reports to display supporting information.

As you prepare business reports containing graphs, study previous reports from the company to determine style preferences. If the graph is half of a page or less in size, include it in the body of the text. Leave enough space before and after the graph to separate it visually from the text. Position the graph as near as possible to the portion of the text in which it is mentioned, ideally on the same page. If the graph is larger than half a page, place it on a separate page and include a reference to the graph's page number.

Have students collect examples of graphs from newspapers, magazines, and reports. Have students label the graphs as to category (pie, bar, or line). Display the graphs by categories. Discuss with students the ways the graphs vary within the categories.

Three graphs commonly used in business reports are the circle graph or pie chart, the bar graph, and the line graph, shown in Illustrations 5-2:9, 10, and 11. Spreadsheet or charting programs are commonly used to convert numbers into percentages and prepare pie charts, bar graphs, and line graphs.

A pie chart (so called because the graph wedges look like pieces of a pie) is a display of how a part contributes to the whole. The whole circle represents 100 percent, and each wedge represents a portion of the whole. Each wedge should be identified with an appropriate label, color, or pattern.

Illustration 5-2:9

Pie charts show the relationship of a part to a whole. Color helps distinguish the individual parts.

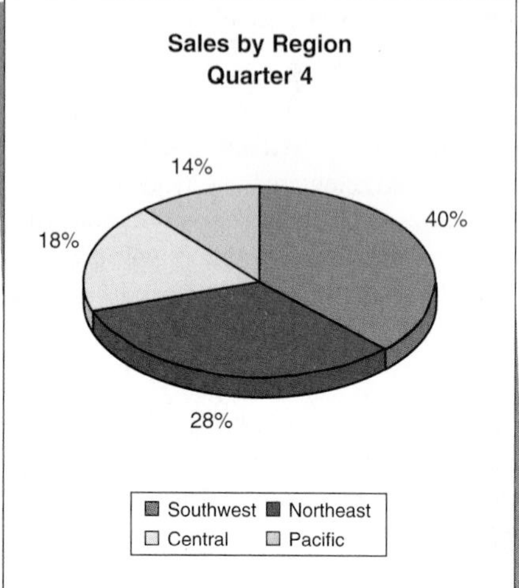

A bar graph is used to show comparisons, as seen in Illustration 5-2:10. Use bars of equal width and space the bars equally across the graph. If more than one set of data is included in the graph, use different colors or patterns to identify the sets of data. Stacked bars, three-dimensional bars, and gridlines may be used to make the data easier to read or understand. The number scale should be adjusted to show an appropriate range. For example, if the numbers graphed range from 75 to 103, the graph scale might begin at 70 rather than at 0. Consider carefully the point you intend to make with the graph. Adjusting the graph scale can make differences in the data appear smaller or larger.

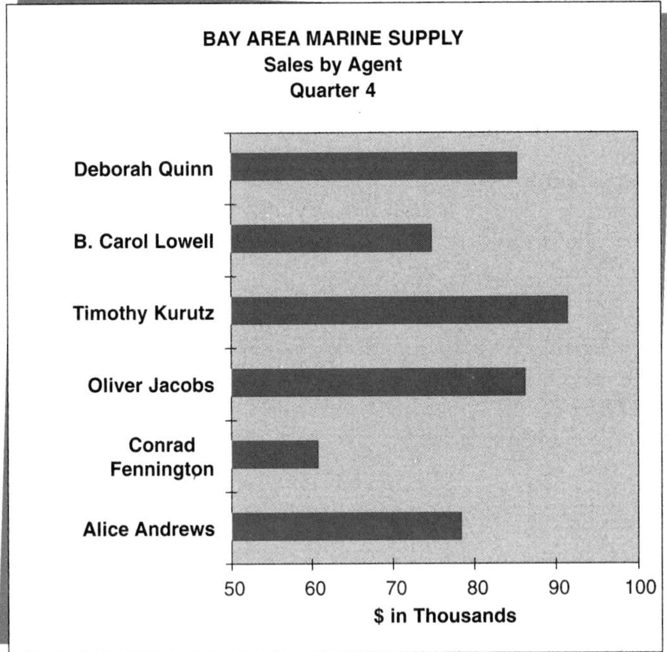

Illustration 5-2:10

Bar graphs are used to show comparisons between items.

A line graph, as shown in Illustration 5-2:11 on page 248, is used to display trends that emerge over a period of time. Monthly sales, for example, are frequently represented in line graph form. In preparing such a graph, place the time categories across the horizontal axis and the amounts along the vertical axis. If more than one set of data is shown on the graph, use different-colored lines to distinguish each set.

SPREADSHEETS

Many writers use spreadsheet software to perform calculations and analyze the data they use in tables. Tables, graphs, and charts used in business reports may be created easily using spreadsheet software.

points to emphasize

Graphs are often easier to interpret than columns of figures or blocks of text. Each graph has its particular function: pie, to show the relationship of a part to the whole; bar, to show comparisons; and line, to show changes over a period of time.

Illustration 5-2:11

Line graphs are excellent for showing changes over a period of time.

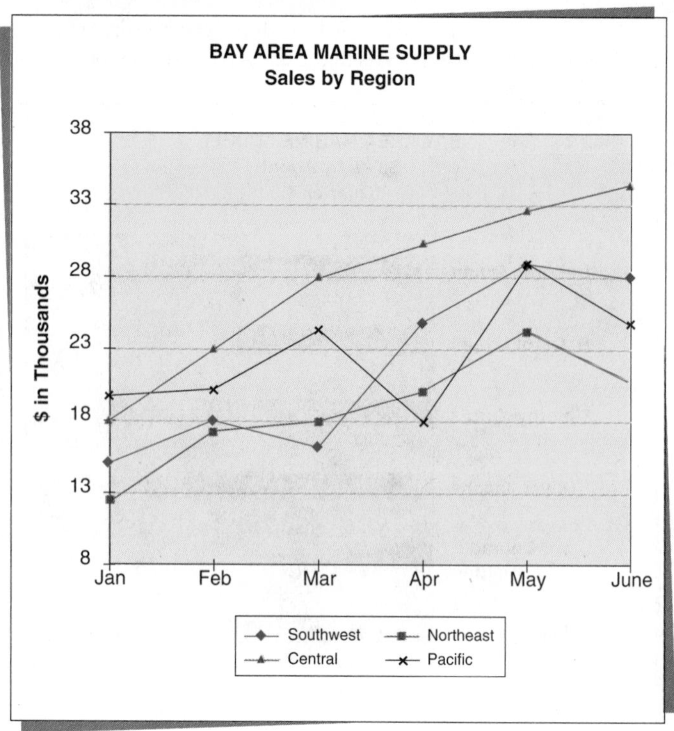

The documents can be integrated directly into the report or printed separately as attachments to the report.

Spreadsheets are commonly used to record and report current data (an income statement, for example) or create projections (of costs or sales, for example) and test alternatives. Calculations representing various scenarios can be made quickly and the results analyzed. Conclusions or recommendations for reports can then be made based upon the projections. For example, an executive might use a spreadsheet program to forecast income based on different sales forecasts or determine whether to rent or buy new equipment based on long-term costs.

Multi-Page Report Preparation

Preparing lengthy reports often involves **extensive** editing as the document goes through several revisions. Sections of the report may be revised, deleted or rearranged. Data to be included in tables or charts may change. Use your word processing and spreadsheet software effectively to save time in making these changes.

extensive: thorough, broad

PAGINATION

Pagination is the process of dividing the document into individual pages for printing. Page breaks are determined by the software inserting an automatic page ending as the page is filled or the user entering the command for a forced page ending. Use the automatic page numbering feature of the software to accurately record each page number. When revisions change the page endings, the repagination feature will adjust the text automatically and renumber the pages.

HEADERS AND FOOTERS

Use a header to place the same information above the text at the top of every page of a document. Page numbers and abbreviated report titles are frequently used as headers. Use a footer to place information below the text at the bottom of the document pages. Page numbers or the report date are commonly included in footers. Once activated, header and footer text will appear on every page of the document unless instructions are given to **suppress** its printing on a specific page. If changes are needed in the header or footer, you need only make the change once to correct all headers or footers.

suppress: keep from happening, prevent

WIDOWS AND ORPHANS

Because the pagination feature of your software merely counts lines before dividing a page, some paragraphs may be divided inappropriately. Paragraphs divided between pages should contain at least two lines on each page. A first line of a paragraph printed by itself at the bottom of a page is a *widow line*. The last line of a paragraph printed by itself at the top of a page is an *orphan line*. Avoid widows and orphans by reviewing the page breaks in the report and adjusting them as needed.

What is the purpose of the widow/orphan feature? How will using this feature improve the quality of a document? the efficiency of the writer?

FOOTNOTES OR ENDNOTES

Use the footnote feature of your software to automatically place footnotes at the bottom of the proper page or endnotes in order at the end of the report. If a text segment that has a related footnote is moved to another part of the document, the footnote will also be placed on the new page and renumbered automatically. If the moved text contains an endnote reference, the endnotes will be renumbered appropriately. Footnote and endnote numbers will also be adjusted when new footnotes or endnotes are inserted.

Reviewing the Topic

1. What is a business report? What do all business reports have in common?
2. How does the analytical report differ from the informational report?
3. What guidelines should a writer of an informational report follow?
4. Why would an office employee use a scanner to gather data for a report?
5. Why do some businesses use information services?
6. When is a formal writing style appropriate for reports?
7. Distinguish between unbound and leftbound reports.
8. How does the informal report differ from the formal report? What are the common parts of a formal business report?
9. Identify visual aids commonly used in business reports. Why are visual aids useful?
10. Describe the best uses of pie charts, bar graphs, and line graphs.

INTERACTING WITH OTHERS

Beth is the new office assistant to Mr. Hope, supervisor of the Customer Service Division. This morning Mr. Hope called Beth into his office and asked her to arrange for dinner reservations for himself and two clients at a local restaurant. When Beth returned from Mr. Hope's office, she looked upset. "I don't think I was hired to be a social secretary," she said. "I guess rank has all the privileges. Don't you agree?"

What you are to do:

Prepare a brief response to Beth's question. What is Beth's professional responsibility in this situation?

REINFORCING MATH SKILLS

You work in the accounting department of The Computer Depot, a small retail computer store. Your supervisor, Mrs. Lowell, hands you the page from a report shown on page 252 and asks you to determine

topic 5-2 review

Business Reports and Related Documents

topic 5-2 review

the total sales, the cost of units sold, and the gross profit on the sales of each product. "We'll need this information to fill in the figures for the revised quarterly earnings report," Mrs. Lowell says.

What you are to do:

1. Using the headings *Product Number*, *Total Sales*, *Cost of Units Sold*, and *Gross Profit*, list each product by its product number.
2. Compute the total sales for each product. (Multiply units sold by the selling price.)
3. Compute the cost of units sold for each product. (Multiply units sold by the wholesale price.)
4. Compute the gross profit for each product. (The gross profit is the difference between the total sales and the cost of units sold.) Add the gross profit column to determine the total gross profit figure.
5. Refer to your figures to determine the information Mrs. Lowell needs to complete the portion of her draft shown on page 253. Include the completed statement at the bottom of your page. Save your work; you will use it in another activity.

Product Earnings Report

Product Description	Product Number	Units Sold	Wholesale Price	Selling Price	Total Sales	Cost of Units Sold	Gross Profit
Monitor	M2021	15	$173.90	$ 248.50	$?	$?	$?
Keyboard	K001	5	126.18	180.25	$?	$?	$?
CPU	C3011	82	995.60	1,422.32	$?	$?	$?
Disk Drive	D8929	111	145.55	207.93	$?	$?	$?
Computer Desk	K3723	15	134.40	192.00	$?	$?	$?
Diskettes (box)	T5221	722	20.65	29.50	$?	$?	$?
Computer Paper (box)	P0010	57	13.30	18.98	$?	$?	$?
TOTAL GROSS PROFIT							$?

252

Our gross profit for this earning period was $________. The three products (by product number) that produced the highest total sales are _?_ ($_?_), _?_ ($_?_), and _?_ ($_?_) the three products that produced the greatest gross profit for the store during this period are _?_ ($_?_), _?_ ($_?_), and _?_ ($_?_).

APPLICATION ACTIVITIES

ACTIVITY 1 **Table and Memo Report**

Refer to the Reinforcing Math Skills activity for this topic. You previously calculated the Total Sales, Cost of Units Sold, and Gross Profit columns for your supervisor, Mrs. Lowell. The two of you have been working on the quarterly earnings report, and she has asked you to prepare a table using your computations to include with the short memo report.

"Please include the Product Description, Units Sold, Total Sales, and Gross Profit columns," Mrs. Lowell said. "We also need a secondary heading to identify the reporting period. I suggest you use 'Reporting Period January 1–March 31'."

What you are to do:

1. Refer now to your computations. If you did not complete the math exercise before, do so now. Prepare an appropriately formatted table using the columns Mrs. Lowell requested.
2. Prepare a short memo report for Mrs. Lowell's signature. Address the memo to Mr. Carlos J. Morales, Vice President of Sales. Use an appropriate subject heading. Begin the body of your memo report with the lines of the completed handwritten draft (above). Next, inform Mr. Morales that you are including a complete product sales breakdown in the enclosed table.

253

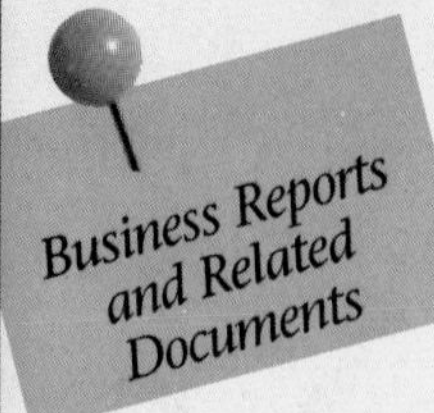

topic 5-2
review

ACTIVITY 2 Graphs

Mrs. Lowell has asked that you prepare charts using data from the table you created earlier. She requests a pie chart showing total sales dollars for each product and a bar chart that compares both wholesale and retail prices for monitors, keyboards, and disk drives.

What you are to do:

1. Use the data from the table you created in Activity 1.
2. Create the pie chart as requested. Show total sales dollars for each product as a percentage of the total sales for all products. Include a chart legend to identify the products. Use the chart titles:

   THE COMPUTER DEPOT
   Product Sales $

3. Create the bar chart as requested to show bars for wholesale prices and retail (selling) prices for the products. Include a chart legend to identify the products. Adjust the chart scale for appropriate minimum and maximum dollar figures. Use the chart titles:

   THE COMPUTER DEPOT
   Wholesale vs. Retail

254

Chapter Summary

People who work in offices are often responsible for preparing written communications such as letters, memoranda, reports, tables, and graphs. In this chapter, you were introduced to guidelines for planning, preparing, and presenting written business documents. From your study of this chapter, you should be able to discuss the following points:

- Effective documents are well planned. They are clear, concise, courteous, complete, and correct. These characteristics apply to all documents.
- The three stages of planning effective documents are creating/drafting the document, revising/editing it, and proofreading it for final presentation.
- When writing a document, know your purpose, your message, your audience, and the response you want from your audience.
- Several categories of messages are common in business correspondence: positive or neutral, negative, and persuasive messages.
- Business letters are generally written to people outside the organization. Memoranda are generally written to people inside the organization.
- Business documents have standard formats, or protocol, that are commonly used in business communications. Using standard formats provides greater efficiency for both the writer and reader of business documents.
- Business reports are a source of information for making business decisions. They are basically either analytical or informational in nature and may follow either a formal or an informal format and presentation.
- Visual aids are commonly used in business reports to make the report more understandable. They not only add interest to the report but may reduce the text needed to explain the information.

chapter 5 summary

Communicating in Written Form

255

- Electronic resources are helpful aids to the business report writer. Preparing long business reports often involves extensive research and many revisions. Electronic-based aids can be used in different phases of report preparation, such as conducting electronic data searches, using spreadsheets to calculate and graph data, and using pagination aids to revise multipage documents with ease.

KEY CONCEPTS AND TERMS

appendix
block format
business letter
business report
clear
complete
concise
correct
courteous
direct approach
documentation
graphs (pie, line, bar)
indirect approach
information services
memorandum
modified block format
pagination
positive tone
quotations
references
spreadsheet
table
visual aids
writer-based approach

INTEGRATED CHAPTER ACTIVITY

ACTIVITY Formal Report

Filename: Legal

You are employed by East Coast Office Consultants. You have been writing a report on legal documents for a client to distribute to the legal secretaries in her firm. You have finished your first draft. (See the template file *Legal.*) You now need to edit your draft and prepare your final copy. Once you are satisfied with the copy, you need to prepare the preliminary and reference pages. The assembled report and a letter of transmittal will be sent to your client.

(At your teacher's direction, you may do research and prepare additional chapters on different types of legal documents.)

256

What you are to do:

1. Retrieve the rough draft report from your template disk. Edit the report and format it as a leftbound report. Although you are a careful writer, you know your first draft is never your final draft. See if you can improve the wording or make the document easier for the readers to understand. Side heads are indicated by an underscore.
2. Prepare these additional report pages:
   - Title page that gives (a) the title of the report, LEGAL DOCUMENTS; (b) your name; (c) the name of your company; and (d) the current date
   - Table of Contents
   - Abstract of the report no longer than 100 words
   - Reference page. The source you referred to in Chapter 1 is: Rita Sloan Tilton, J. Howard Jackson, and Sue Chappell Rigby. <u>The Electronic Office: Procedures and Administration.</u> Cincinnati: South-Western Educational Publishing, 1996, p. 603.
3. Prepare a short cover letter to your client, Hilda Treanor of Treanor Legal Assistance, 3435 Adelphia Blvd., Hastings, NE 68901. This is the first work you have done for Ms. Treanor, and you are hoping she will use your services again.

257

Mei-yu Liang
Office Supervisor

Getting Acquainted with the World of Work

New Job Jitters

Dear Ms. Liang

I definitely am doing something wrong! I'm embarrassed to admit that although I've been working in an office for almost a month, yesterday I didn't prepare one document that wasn't returned to me for corrections. As I made the corrections, I realized that I should have caught the errors—but I didn't. I have a very understanding supervisor; she thinks I can do the work but feels I'm too nervous and am not concentrating. I am nervous. I want to do a good job, but I keep asking myself, "Can I do this job?"

Is there any hope for me? I don't know where to begin. Can you help me?

Beverly in Baltimore

"***Dear Beverly***

You seem sincere about wanting to be a good employee. It takes courage to admit that every document required corrections. You also realize that you do not edit or proofread as you should. You are facing the situation in an honest manner, and that is a basic requirement for solving any problem. Here are some suggestions:

- *Try to put aside the constant questioning of how well you are doing.*
- *Begin acting like a competent worker by giving full attention to the job at hand. Make sure what you are keying makes sense. If you have a question, ask your supervisor.*
- *Practice being calm. Take care not to put too much pressure on yourself to complete the job too quickly.*
- *Carefully proofread what you have prepared. Ask questions like: Is my writing clear, concise, and courteous? Is the document complete and correct—grammar, punctuation, spelling? Imagine that there must be a mistake somewhere in what you have written and search for it. Inexperienced writers often assume that there aren't any mistakes in the copy. Such an attitude leads to overlooking errors.*

Yes, there is hope for you. The fact that you want to improve is the first big step.

Mei-yu Liang
Office Supervisor"

Communicating via Presentations

Regardless of your position, you will need to express yourself clearly so others will understand you. Even though presentations may not be a part of your daily work, there may be many occasions when you need to present information to others, formally or informally.

In most cases, you will speak either to motivate and influence or to inform and educate. The situation may require that you speak one-to-one, to a small group of your peers, or even to a large audience. Regardless of the size of your audience and whether the presentation is to be formal or informal, you must keep your goals and your listeners' needs and wants clearly in mind as you develop your presentation.

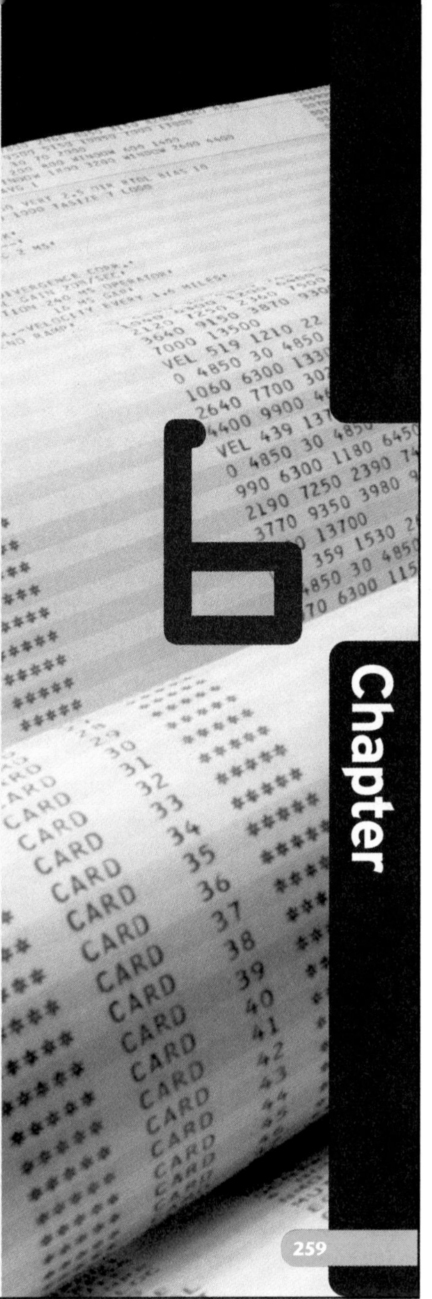

Chapter 6

Chapter 6

Planning and Preparing the Presentation

Topic 6-1

When you have completed your study of this topic, you will be able to:

- **profile your listeners**
- **identify the message you want to provide**
- **address the interests of your listeners**
- **develop ideas for your message and organize them in a storyboard**
- **create effective visuals and handouts**
- **organize team presentations**

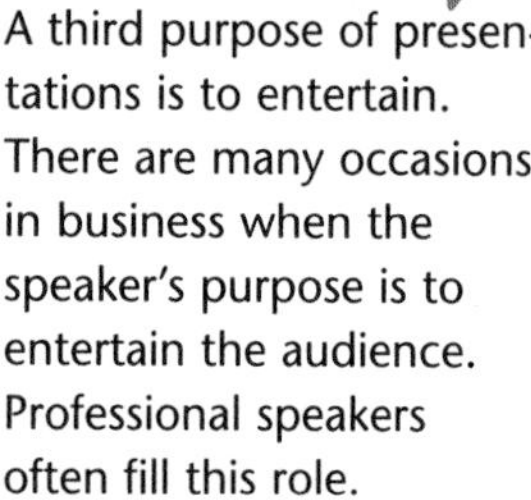

A third purpose of presentations is to entertain. There are many occasions in business when the speaker's purpose is to entertain the audience. Professional speakers often fill this role.

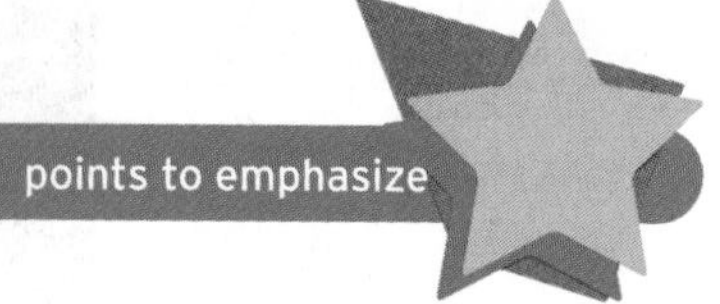

A speaker's goal may be to teach an audience about new ideas, to create a good feeling or entertain an audience, persuade an audience to accept new opinions or take certain actions, or provide information about a topic. In all cases, the message is meant to accomplish a purpose.

When you have an opportunity to prepare a presentation, it will likely be for one of two purposes. You will either want to motivate and influence your listeners, or you will want to inform and educate them. The message of your presentation will include the main ideas and supporting details you want to present. When you are speaking to motivate or influence, your message needs to be persuasive. Your purpose is to get your listeners to take a course of action. When you are speaking to inform, your message should be clear and concise. Your purpose is to communicate the information so your listeners can understand and use the information.

Regardless of your purpose, in order to hold your audience's attention, your message must be important to them. You need to determine your listeners' interests or needs. Then you need to convince them that

what you have to say can satisfy those needs or relates to those interests. The important key, therefore, is to present your ideas with the listener in mind. For example:

> *Robert is planning a presentation for office personnel in his department. The purpose of his presentation is to inform the personnel about new office procedures that are to be implemented throughout the department. The new procedures have been adopted to increase productivity and efficiency within the department. However, Robert's message to the office staff must address their concerns and interest. Robert needs to present the information in a way that addresses the needs of the office personnel. He will explain that the new procedures will make their jobs easier.*

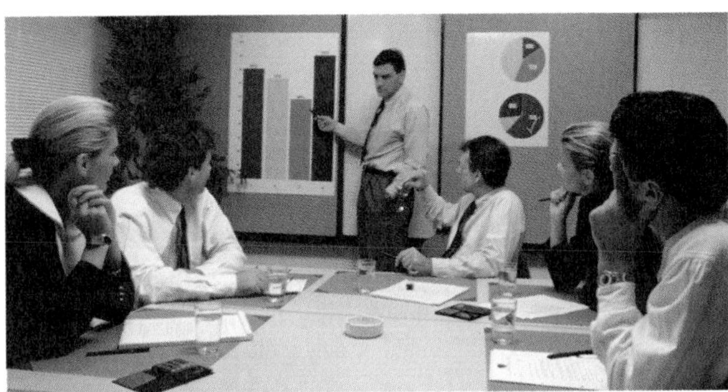

Illustration 6-1:1
Your message must be important to your listeners.

Identify the Purpose of the Presentation

Speakers often make the mistake of communicating only what is important to them. You might wonder why this is a mistake. Obviously, the speaker should be able to choose the topic. However, knowing what moves, inspires, and persuades his or her listeners is what makes a speaker effective. Few speakers can be successful if they do not analyze their listeners before speaking.

PROFILE YOUR LISTENERS

Developing a **profile** of your listeners and knowing what is important to them is a critical beginning to preparing a presentation. If the listeners

profile:
description, picture

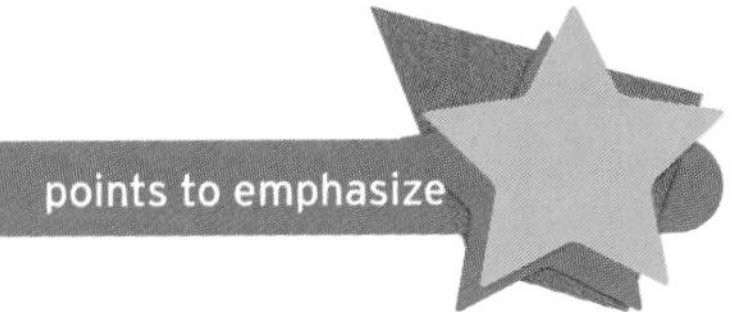

An effective speaker studies the psychological makeup of the people listening to the presentation. The speaker tries to determine what may excite or anger the listeners and what might provoke them to take action.

Even though speaking is not a part of our daily work, many of us find ourselves in situations where we are asked to make presentations. Ask students to give examples of these situations. Answers may include speaking at a graduation ceremony, making a toast to the bride and groom at a wedding reception, or addressing clubs or other organizations.

Rev. Martin Luther King, Jr., delivered one of the most effective speeches in American history. He knew the deeply felt values of his audience and identified the dream of civil rights with those values. He was able to reinforce those values through his own credibility as a speaker. Ask students for other examples of effective speeches from history.

do not think the topic of your presentation is important to them, they will not listen to your message. If you are communicating one idea and your listeners are thinking about something different, you will not successfully communicate your ideas.

To avoid this situation, you need to first determine what is important to your listeners so the message will be something they want to hear about. To determine what is important to them, you must first describe them in as much detail as possible. Put yourself in their shoes. Write down everything you know about them:

- What do the listeners like or dislike?
- What do the listeners need?
- What is the expertise of the listeners?
- What **biases** do the listeners have?
- What responsibilities do the listeners have?
- Are the listeners decision-makers?

biases: prejudices

ADDRESS THE LISTENERS' INTERESTS

After developing a listener profile, the second step is to identify the interests of your listeners. At first this may seem difficult, but if you try to think as they think, you should be able to do so. For example:

> *Robert knows that several office personnel are responsible for updating the company customer database. As a result, efforts are often duplicated. Further, some customer records are overlooked because one office employee assumes another employee took care of it. As a result, office personnel are never sure customer records are accurate. There needs to be a more efficient procedure for updating customer records.*

Develop the Message

Your ideas, or the main message of your presentation, must relate to your listeners' needs or interests. The first step in developing an idea for your message is to identify a listener interest. Then you develop the idea with that interest in mind. Be sure that each interest you identify is stated from the listeners' point of view and that your ideas provide advantages for them.

ORGANIZE YOUR IDEAS

After you have identified the ideas or main points to be included in the presentation, organize them in a logical way so that your listeners can see that your ideas are consistent with meeting their interests. Describe your ideas in terms that your listener will understand and relate to. For example:

> *Robert will describe the problems with the current procedures for updating customer records. Then he will describe the new procedure that will ensure efficiency and accuracy.*

Organizing your thoughts is the most important part of planning a successful presentation. It lays the foundation for how you will communicate your thoughts to your listeners. Sketching out and organizing your thoughts is called storyboarding. Essentially, storyboarding involves brainstorming several ideas and then organizing them to create an outline and notes for your presentation. The notes can be just words or phrases, or they can be complete sentences.

To create a storyboard, you can complete a worksheet page for each element or idea for your presentation. Illustration 6-1:2 on page 264 shows a sample of a storyboard worksheet. The worksheet helps you organize your thoughts about a specific idea.

Notice in the illustration that the worksheet page provides an opportunity to **formulate** ways of explaining each idea. You begin by stating the purpose of the presentation. Then you identify a listener interest. Next, you describe your main idea and provide information that supports your idea. You also list listener advantages. Don't be concerned right now with the worksheet box labeled "Visual Element." You'll learn about that shortly.

formulate: draft, express

To complete the storyboard, you fill out a worksheet for each idea in your presentation. Once all your ideas are written down, you can improve the flow by rearranging the pages. The storyboard provides the basic organization of the presentation. Through this planning process, you organize your key concepts and define the overall presentation.

Speakers often know well in advance when they are scheduled to make a presentation. As a result, they are able to prepare their message before they deliver it. However, there are occasions when speakers must deliver a message without advance preparation. This is called extemporaneous, or impromptu, speaking.

Although most speakers write their own speeches, it is common for business executives and politicians to employ professional writers who help them prepare their speeches. The speaker generally has some input into the contents of the speech, but the professional writer usually has a great influence over the opinions expressed.

Illustration 6-1:2

A storyboard worksheet helps you organize your presentation.

STORYBOARD WORKSHEET	
Purpose of Presentation: Motivate and influence sales staff to increase sales during the fall campaign	
Listener Interest	Commissions and bonuses that may be earned during the campaign
Main Idea	Commission and bonus opportunities will increase
Support for Idea	Commissions on sale items raised from 10% to 15% $500 bonus for top ten total sales
Listener Advantage	More income for the staff member
Listener Objection	Large number of clients to be handled during the sale Counter: The extra effort required will be rewarded with higher income
Visual Element	Growing dollar sign

An alternative to completing storyboard worksheets is to use a software outline feature to create the storyboard pages. Create the main topics (or ideas), and then break down each main topic into subtopics. Once you key your ideas, you can edit and rearrange them quickly and easily. Be sure to include listener interests, support for your ideas, and listener advantages for each idea.

INCLUDE SUPPORTING DETAILS

credibility: confidence, integrity

analogies: comparisons

Whenever possible, add **credibility** to your presentation by providing evidence or details that support your ideas. For example, you can state facts or offer statistics to back up a proposal. You can use examples and **analogies** to confirm a need. You can use expert opinions to endorse a recommendation. You can relate a situation to personal experiences of your listeners or experiences of your own. For example:

> *Robert will describe an embarrassing situation he experienced recently. He was talking with a customer on the phone, and the information in*

the database was not up to date. As a result, he was not able to handle the customer's inquiry satisfactorily. The office staff easily identifies with this problem.

CONSIDER LISTENER ADVANTAGES AND OBJECTIONS

Once you have developed your ideas and have found solutions for your listener's interests, list the advantages for your listeners if they accept your ideas. If possible, prioritize these advantages in order of importance to the listener. For example:

Robert will explain that the new procedures will assure accuracy and efficiency. When office personnel access customer records, they can be sure the records are up to date. Further, because of the new procedure, fewer persons are responsible for updating customer records. Everyone's job is easier.

Consider all the **objections** your listeners may have regarding your ideas. It is critical that you anticipate the listeners' objections so you can counter them before they become a problem. When you anticipate the objections, you can minimize them so the listener no longer sees them as a problem. For example:

objections: reasons to disapprove or reject ideas

Robert anticipates objections from some employees. They are accustomed to the current procedures, and they don't like change. Robert will also explain that the new procedures will be easy to learn.

Choose Visuals and Audio

Images are very powerful. A **visual aid** stimulates the listener and keeps the listener's attention. Studies show that we retain about 10 percent of what we hear in a presentation and about 20 percent of what we see. However, we retain about 50 percent of what we both see and hear.

visual aid: picture, chart, graphic

Even in one-to-one communications, visuals are extremely effective. Not only will the visuals help you present your content, they will also make your listeners feel important because you took the time to create them.

Create a visual for each main idea (each page in your storyboard). This will help provide direction for your presentation. Each visual you create

A presentation should have a defined logic. If the purpose of the presentation is to inform, the information presented should be complete, explicit, and clear. If the purpose of the presentation is to persuade, the order of the reasons presented should provide support for convincing the audience to accept that opinion.

Ask students to recall a recent dream. Typically, they will recall the dream with pictures. In order to describe their dream, they will visualize the events.

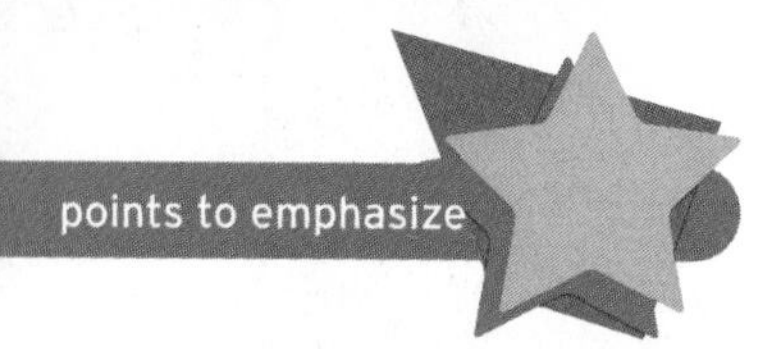

Use your visuals to guide you through the outline presentation. If all your key ideas are presented in the visuals, you won't overlook them.

Illustration 6-1:3
Visuals help us retain information.

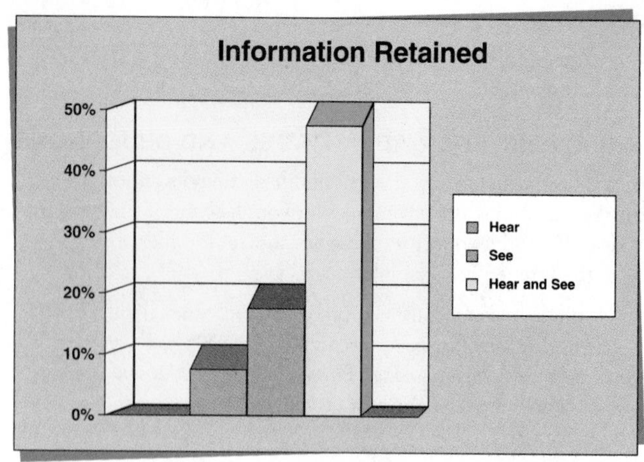

should be designed for consistency and simplicity. Carry out the theme of the presentation in all visuals. For example:

> *Robert's slide show provides information about the new office procedures. Each slide reflects an image of simplicity to project the idea of efficiency.*

Illustration 6-1:4
This slide reflects the image of simplicity and efficiency.

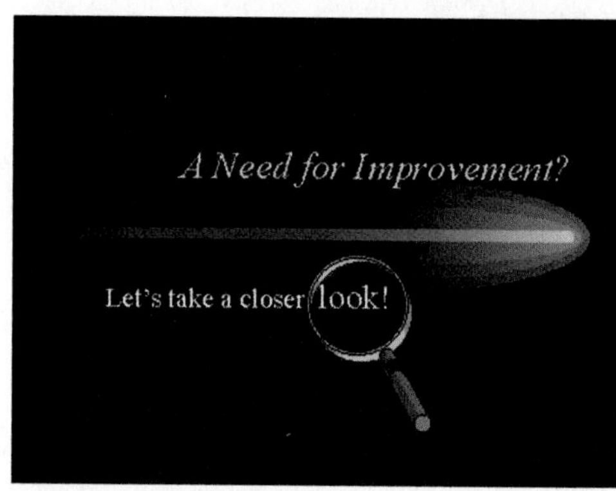

The first visual should introduce the topic and set the tone for the presentation. All visuals should support the overall message and should address the interests and advantages of the listeners.

CHOOSE THE MEDIA

The media you choose for your visuals will depend on your budget and the equipment you have available. It will also depend on the size of your audience and whether the presentation is formal or informal.

Flip charts are very effective for small, informal groups. They are inexpensive and easy to create and use. For one-to-one communications, desktop easels can be effective.

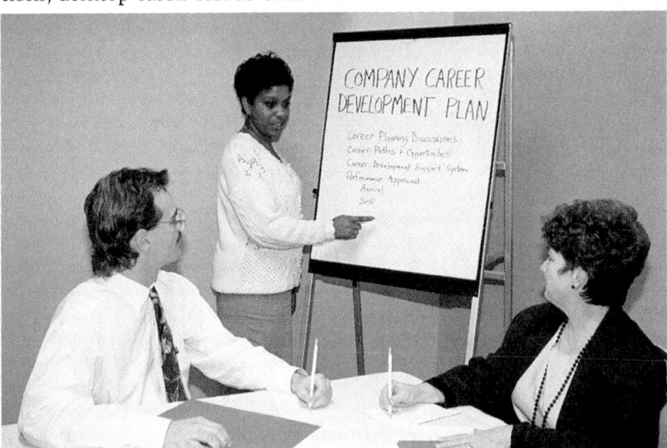

Illustration 6-1:5

Flip charts are inexpensive and easy to use.

Overhead transparencies are effective for small or large groups and for formal and informal presentations. Overhead transparencies are inexpensive to create. They can be created in black and white or in color. If you have access to a copier that can handle transparency film, you can copy text, photos, and illustrations and turn them into transparencies quickly and easily. If the copier can produce color copies, you can create four-color transparencies inexpensively.

Transparencies are easy to use. If you reorganize your presentation, you can quickly and easily rearrange the **sequence** of the transparencies. You can write on them and add to them during a presentation. You can overlay them to build a concept or to add special effects or emphasis.

sequence: order

Slide shows are effective for both large and small groups, and they enhance formal presentations. With the many commercial software

Illustration 6-1:6
Overhead transparencies are effective for a variety of presentations.

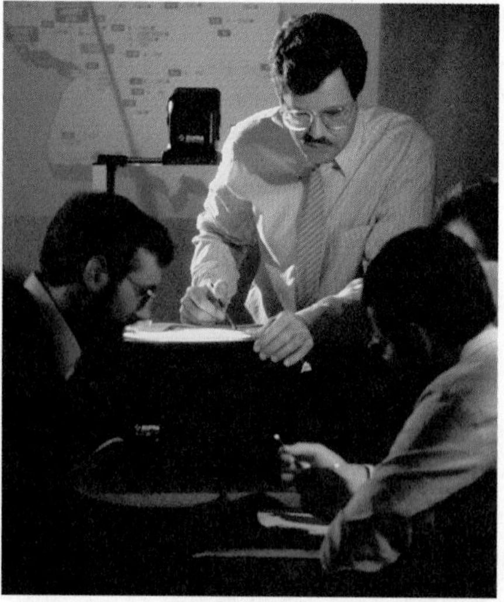

LCD panel: equipment that works with an overhead projector to display images from a computer

packages available that create professional slides quickly and easily, slide shows have become very popular. If an **LCD panel** is available, you can display your slide show directly through a computer. This, of course, would be the most economical and easiest method for presenting your slides.

Your needs may require you to create individual slides that are to be displayed through a slide projector. Perhaps you are adding slides to an existing set of slides, or you do not have the equipment available to utilize the LCD technology. You can have individual slides created commercially at photo centers. The slides can be produced from photos or illustrations, or they can be developed from the presentation you create using computer software applications. The cost for creating these slides varies greatly depending on the media, turnaround time for development, and the vendor.

Traditional presentations have generally included static visual aids. In other words, the visuals don't move. Advancements in technology enable you to add motion to your visuals. You can add creativity to your presentation by incorporating video clips in your slide presentations.

Illustration 6-1:7

Commercial software packages enable you to create professional slide shows.

teaching tips

Commercial packages provide some powerful design tools. Multimedia, animation, and sound options can enable you to create glamorous and sophisticated presentations. However, the key to effective visuals is to keep them simple and related to the purpose of the presentation. If possible, demonstrate some of these programs and advanced features to students.

Most computers today have the built-in capability to display photographic-quality images and to play high-fidelity sound. You can enhance your presentations by importing animation clips and audio.

CREATE THE VISUAL ELEMENTS

Think of your favorite book. Do you remember the story with visual elements or with words? Most of us mentally picture things we remember. When we recall previous experiences, we generally remember them visually.

You can remember graphics better than words. Whenever possible, use a graphic or picture instead of words. Keep the graphics simple. Effective visuals enable the communicator to maintain the listener's attention. In return, the listener can stay involved in the presentation and retain more of the message. Make sure the visual element you choose reinforces what you want to communicate. Remember, the storyboard worksheet includes a box for describing your visual element(s) as you plan and organize your presentation.

Computer technology provides us with a multitude of applications for using clip art, graphs, illustrations, and photographs. However, the graphics you incorporate in your presentations do not need to be elaborate. They can be simple creations that you draw. For example:

Robert uses a flip chart to identify the reasons for new office procedures. He uses an up arrow to represent "increase" as he discusses productivity. He uses a stopwatch to represent "time" when he talks about efficiency.

Illustration 6-1:8
Simple graphics illustrate presentation ideas.

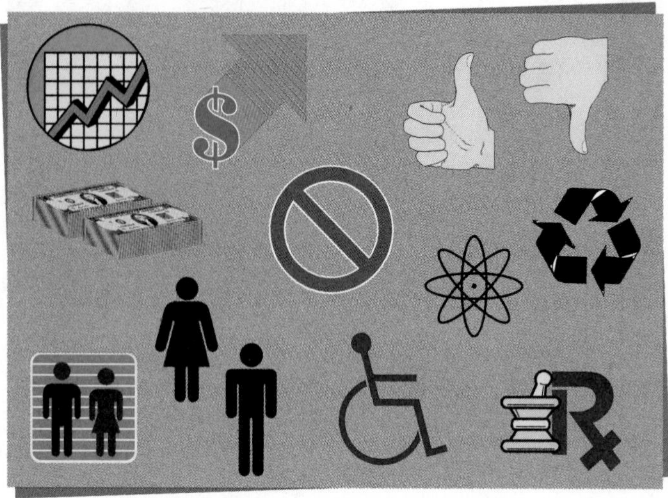

DESIGN STRATEGIES

white space: blank area

Limit your design to one idea per visual, and use plenty of **white space.** Slides and transparencies are usually created in landscape orientation (as opposed to portrait orientation) because that better utilizes the space. We are accustomed to reading from left to right, and in landscape orientation you can fit more words in a line. It is important, however, that you keep the orientation consistent throughout the presentation.

Keep the design of your visuals simple. Remember that the purpose of the visual is to help you maintain your listeners' attention and to help your listeners remember your message. You don't want your visuals to be complicated and difficult to read or understand.

Text. Keep text on visuals to a minimum. If the text on a visual is crowded, it results in a confusing appearance. If you have too much text, the audience becomes involved in reading the content of the visual instead of listening to what you are saying.

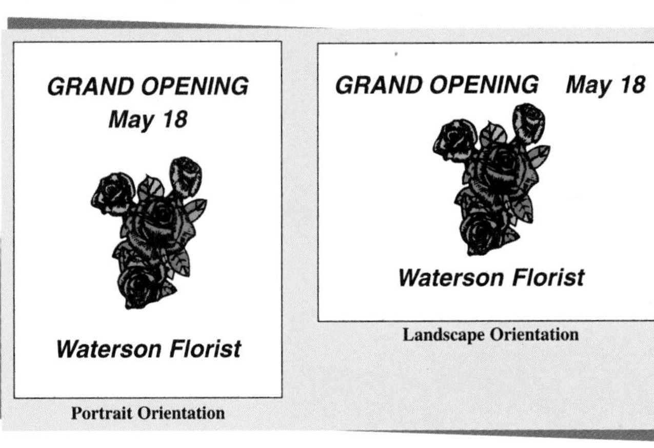

Illustration 6-1:9
Portrait and landscape orientations

Limit the use of different text styles, sizes, and colors throughout to avoid a confusing appearance. For example, you might choose to use Arial, 24 point, blue text for main points or headings and Times Roman, 18 point, black text for subheads or supporting details. Lowercase text is easier to read than all caps. As a general rule, avoid having more than seven consecutive words in uppercase.

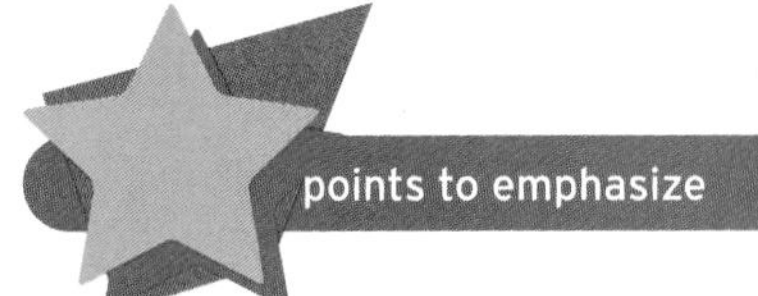

As a general rule, use no more than 15 to 20 words per slide or transparency.

Use **bullets** to help the audience follow the presentation. Bullets are effective for presenting important points and specific terminology. Indent bullets to establish a hierarchy of points or details.

bullets: small graphics, such as circles or diamonds, used to draw attention to a line of text

Make the wording on all visuals parallel in verb tense. Use strong, active verbs. Whenever possible, limit the use of adverbs, adjectives, and prepositions.

Color. Use color effectively for maximum impact. Just because color is available does not mean it has to be used extensively. In fact, it is often best to use color sparingly.

Know the generally accepted associations of colors. For example, in business, red usually relates to cost and green usually relates to profit. In general, red draws the most attention and evokes excitement. Blues and greens are relaxing; earth tones suggest environmental consciousness. A blending of colors or graduated colors instead of a solid background can help to guide the viewer's eyes to a focal point.

Borders are effective for adding and using color wisely. They help to guide the viewer's attention and give the visual a professional touch.

The colors you choose will depend on the media you are developing. Overhead transparencies are most effective with dark text on a light background. Computer slides and 35mm slides are most effective with light text on a dark background.

Illustration 6-1:10

Choose your background colors based on the media.

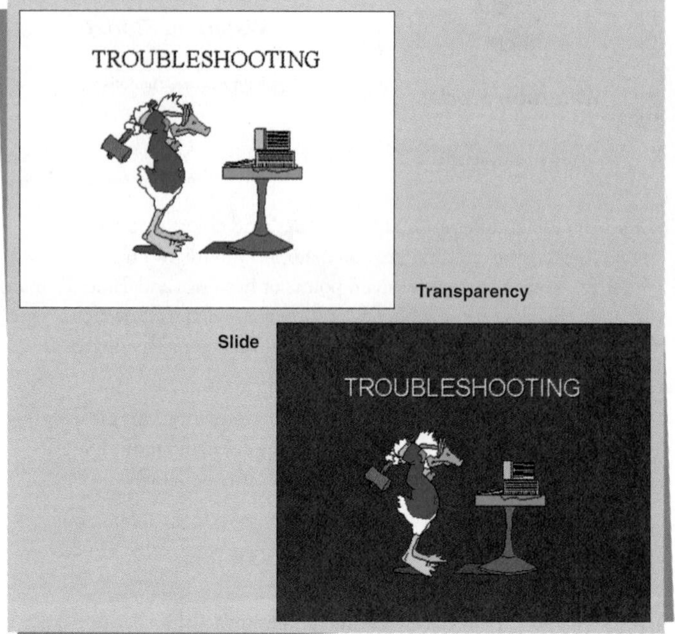

BUILD VISUALS

You can also build visuals for effective communication. In other words, you continue to add to your visuals during the presentation so your listeners can see the building process. For example:

> *The slides Robert will use in his slide show illustrate the development of a list of new office procedures. In the first slide introducing the new procedures, only one new procedure is illustrated in bright yellow on a*

dark blue background. In the succeeding slide, a second new procedure appears below the first one that has already been illustrated. The new procedure is illustrated in bright yellow for emphasis; the first procedure is now illustrated in light blue since it was previously illustrated. Each new procedure will be introduced in a similar manner, showing the gradual progression of the list.

When using transparencies or flip charts, it is very effective to write on the visual as you use it in your presentation. Not only does this draw the listeners' attention to the visual, but it also enables you to create a visual memory for your audience. For example, you can fill in key points or you can underline or circle important information.

USE AUDIO EFFECTIVELY

From soft music playing as your audience gathers to resounding applause to stress a job well done, audio can enhance your presentation. Like clip art and other graphics, audio collections are readily available and contain a wide variety of music, sound effects, and common phrases. If you require specific music or text, you may wish to record your own audio or have it prepared professionally.

If you add audio to your slide or multimedia presentation, make sure it is appropriate. The audio should enhance the presentation and not be overbearing or distracting. Sound can be used effectively to introduce a topic, build excitement, or add special effects. If you decide to incorporate sound, be sure you are not competing with it when you are talking. Like color, use sound wisely. Make sure it serves a purpose.

Create Handouts and Posters

The audience will only remember a small portion of the content of your presentation. Provide handouts for your listeners so they can be used later for reference and as reminders of the key points in your presentation. The handouts need not be limited to text. Consider including some of the visual elements you've displayed in your presentation. Even if they are small, icon-like images, these visual elements will serve as reminders of the message you provided.

If you have several handouts to distribute during a presentation, consider printing them in different colors. That will make it easy for you and your listeners to distinguish between them. Also, although it may be more expensive, consider using a color copier to reproduce four-color handouts that will add impact to your presentation.

Handouts can also be useful in guiding your listeners through the presentation. The intent of the handouts will determine how you design them and when you distribute them to the audience.

OUTLINE THE PRESENTATION

Sometimes it is helpful to prepare handouts containing the outline of your presentation. The outline will help your audience follow your presentation and stay involved. Throughout the presentation, the handout can be used for notetaking. For example:

> *Robert provided a handout containing the outline of his presentation. He removed the details of the outline and replaced them with blank lines. As he presented the new office procedures, the staff members took notes to fill in the missing information.*

PROVIDE DETAILS

Another reason to provide handouts is to supply your listeners with specific, detailed information that is too lengthy to provide on visuals. You may also want to provide additional information not contained in your presentation. For example:

> *One of the handouts Robert plans to provide during his presentation contains detailed descriptions of the new office procedures. The office staff will use this information later when they begin implementing the new procedures.*

SUMMARIZE MAIN POINTS

The information included in your handouts can also summarize the main points of your presentation. It is important, though, to use different words and examples in your summary handout so that the information does not simply duplicate your presentation. Obviously, you would not want to distribute a summary of your presentation until you have given the presentation.

There is nothing more embarrassing than distributing a handout that contains errors or typos. Such mistakes reflect negatively on the credibility and image of the speaker. Ask students to give examples of handouts or other materials that contained errors and made a negative impact on them.

TEN WAYS TO EXCEED SALES QUOTA

GENERATE NEW BUSINESS

1 ____________________

2 ____________________

INCREASE DAILY SALES CONTACTS

3 ____________________

4 ____________________

REDUCE COSTS

5 ____________________

6 ____________________

7 ____________________

IMPROVE CUSTOMER SERVICE

8 ____________________

9 ____________________

10 ____________________

Illustration 6-1:11

An outline of your presentation can also be used for notetaking.

DISPLAY POSTERS

Another way to reinforce the content of your presentation is to enlarge a slide, photo, or handout into a poster-size print. Display the poster to restate key points, introduce a new product, or review a visual element.

You can have posters created at photo centers. The cost will vary depending on the vendor, the poster size, and the turnaround time for development. Standard poster sizes include 16" × 20", 20" × 30", and 24" × 36". The positive impact a poster can have can justify the expense of creating it.

Plan Team Presentations

There may be occasions where you will be involved in a team presentation. For a team presentation to be successful, each member of the team must be committed to accomplishing the task. When the individuals within the team work together to prepare the content and deliver the message, they can utilize the expertise of all the individuals involved. Not only can this expertise add credibility to the presentation, but it can also provide diversity and comprehensive coverage of a subject.

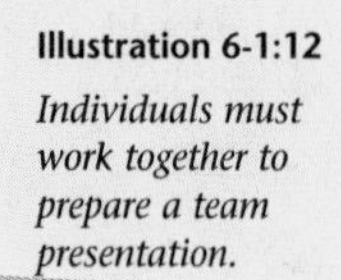
Illustration 6-1:12
Individuals must work together to prepare a team presentation.

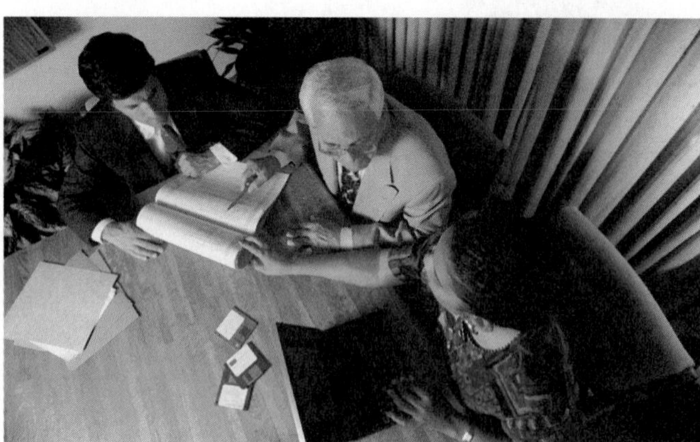

teaching tips

Use some cooperative learning activities to help introduce students to working in teams. Assign some short, team presentations regarding topics familiar to the students. For example, have them make presentations to inform the class about new school policies or to persuade the class to support a club event or fundraiser.

DETERMINE ROLES OF INDIVIDUALS

The first step in preparing a team presentation is to select a leader. The leader will ensure that the team stays focused on accomplishing its objectives.

Each team member must have a valid role. It may not be necessary for all team members to present, but it is essential that each make significant contributions. Those contributions can vary. For example, one or more team members may research and develop content for the presentation; another may create the visuals. One or more members may deliver the presentation.

WORKING AS A TEAM

Once the team has been formed and each individual's role is established, all members of the team must agree on the purpose or objective of the presentation. All their contributions to the team presentation must be directed toward accomplishing this objective. Through sharing of ideas and brainstorming, the team can develop an outline of the presentation that will incorporate everyone's ideas.

Developing the content of the presentation takes some extra effort. Because several individuals have contributed, the team needs to make sure the tone and the terminology is consistent throughout the presentation. Further, all the content must be presented from the listeners' point of view, and it must provide clear listener advantages.

The development of the visual aids must also be consistent in style and content. Using compatible media for visual aids can help to create a smooth transition from one presenter to another. For example, all presenters use slide shows with similar designs.

Consider the confusion it would create for listeners if one presenter used a slide show, a second used flip charts, and a third used overhead transparencies. It would appear as three separate presentations. Following the first and second speaker, the presentation would halt with an equipment change as well as a change in lighting. It would almost be like a break. The listeners would lose their train of thought and the **continuity** of the presentation would be lost.

continuity: smoothness, flow

Once the content and visuals have been developed and organized, the team should review the entire presentation to make sure all the elements flow together well. The team can then determine time allowances and the content to be presented by each person.

Reviewing the Topic

topic 6-1 review

1. What are the two primary purposes of presentations?
2. What kind of information can you gather to profile your listeners?
3. What kinds of evidence can you use to support your ideas?
4. Describe a storyboard and its purpose.
5. When would you use a flip chart to display visuals in a presentation? an overhead projector?
6. Explain how audio may be used effectively in a presentation.
7. Why should you consider listener advantages and objections in planning your presentation?
8. List three design considerations relating to text on visuals.
9. Would you use the same colors and design on a transparency as on a slide? Explain.
10. What are the advantages in a team presentation?

REINFORCING ENGLISH SKILLS

Your colleague Elaine has asked you to review her ideas for a presentation she will give to train the staff in using the new company e-mail system. She plans to create some transparencies for her presentation. A partial list of her ideas is provided below. Help Elaine restate her ideas so they can be displayed on transparencies.

> *This new e-mail system offers many advantages that will improve your efficiency and reduce the amount of time you are online. For example, you have lots more options that you can preset. You can customize these settings for your particular needs. You get faster delivery times.*
>
> *The new features include the following: You can upload and download files. You can automatically retrieve new incoming mail and send new outgoing mail. You can also get to the address book and retrieve data quicker and easier.*

topic 6-1 review

Planning and Preparing the Presentation

278

Let's take a close look at the new address book. Now you can store multiple e-mail addresses within an individual record. You can sort the records in the address book in alphabetical order. Or you can organize the address book to first display the addresses you use most frequently.

What you are to do:

1. Restate Elaine's key ideas in short, concise phrases. Remember to use strong, active verbs and to limit the use of adjectives, adverbs, and prepositions.
2. Identify the text that is to be contained on each transparency. Use bullets to help organize the information.
3. Plan the flow of the presentation and place the material in logical order.

INTERACTING WITH OTHERS

Assume that you are part of an office team assigned the task of improving the companywide schedule for employee breaks and lunch times. The schedule was revised to eliminate overcrowding in the cafeteria at various times throughout the day. The team recently submitted a proposed schedule to management and has just received approval. The new schedule will be effective the first of the month.

You have been asked to present this new schedule to the personnel in your department. You have worked with the individuals in your department long enough to know that many of them are reluctant to accept change. You also realize that some of the employees in your department currently enjoy sharing their breaks and lunches with employees from other departments. Unfortunately, this may no longer be possible for some. Obviously, before you present the new schedule, you must be ready to address the concerns and needs of the personnel in your department.

What you are to do:

1. Describe how you would introduce this new schedule with the listener in mind. What listener needs or interests would you address? What listener advantages would you present?

279

Students have the option of using the template file STORYBD to create their worksheets. If a computer is not available, duplicate transparency master TM6-1:1 in the *Teacher's Resource Guide* for the students to complete manually.

Remind students that this is to be a five-minute presentation. They need to be realistic about the amount of information they can present in that time frame. Students will be preparing visuals for their presentation in an activity at the end of Topic 6-2. It is appropriate for them to plan to bring in props or objects (such as sports equipment or craft items) to display or demonstrate concepts or ideas. However, they will also be expected to create visuals to enhance their presentations.

2. List some complaints and objections you might expect to hear from your colleagues in the department.

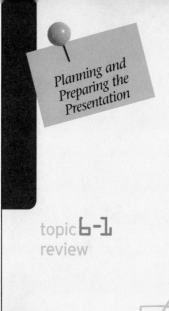

topic 6-1 review

APPLICATION ACTIVITIES

ACTIVITY 1 Visual Aids

Appropriate visual elements can greatly enhance a presentation while inappropriate ones can detract from it. In this activity, you will practice creating visuals to convey these ideas:

1. Profits have increased by 25 percent.
2. Expenses have decreased by 10 percent.
3. We need a cooperative effort between the distributors and the warehouse.
4. Since 1990 our savings have doubled.
5. We need a reduction in staff.

What you are to do:

Create a visual such as a slide, transparency master, or small poster to communicate each of the ideas. Use clip-art images or software drawing tools to create the visual elements if available. If these tools are not available, draw images on paper or paste images clipped from magazines and newspapers.

ACTIVITY 2 Plan and Organize a Presentation

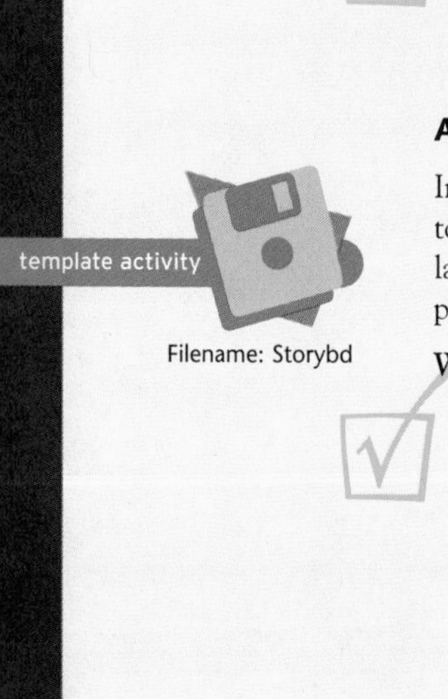

Filename: Storybd

In this activity, you will plan and organize a five-minute presentation to inform and educate your classmates on a topic of your choice. In a later activity, you will prepare the visuals you plan here and give the presentation to your class.

What you are to do:

1. Choose a craft, sport, or activity that you really enjoy and about which you are knowledgeable.
2. Complete a storyboard worksheet for each main idea in your topic using the file *Storybd*. Complete all parts of the storyboard worksheet, including ideas for the visual elements. (You will create the actual visuals in a later activity.)

Topic 6-2

Delivering the Presentation

When you have completed your study of this topic, you will be able to:

- **apply methods for practicing and preparing for a presentation**
- **describe appropriate appearance for making presentations**
- **apply proper techniques for communicating with your audience**
- **use visuals effectively**
- **conduct question-and-answer sessions**

Now that you've prepared your message, it's time to put your ideas in motion. You may think that with all this preparation, you are ready to deliver the message. The content of your presentation may be right on target, but if you cannot communicate the content effectively, your efforts will not be rewarded. There are several factors to consider that can help you communicate your message with confidence, enthusiasm, and professionalism.

Practice and Prepare

The more experienced you become in speaking to others, the less practice you will need. But if you're new at making presentations, you'll definitely want to practice. You can practice before friends or colleagues, or you can rehearse the presentation on your own.

Practicing the delivery of the presentation is just as important as the time and effort spent in planning the content of the presentation. It can be very intimidating for students to speak before a large group. Initially, you may wish to pair students with others they are comfortable working with, or divide the class into small groups. Encourage students to first practice in front of a mirror; then have them present to their partner or their small group.

Recommend that students:

- Use 4" x 6" or 3" x 5" index cards for their notes.
- Use a card for each idea to be presented.
- Write brief notes as reminders of key points.
- Write in large letters so the text is easy to read.
- Consider drawing pictures as reminders instead of using words.
- Number the cards so they can be quickly reorganized if they get out of order.

Review each of your visuals and the notes you have created to accompany them. Rehearse out loud exactly what you plan to say. Make sure you state each idea from the listeners' point of view. Also be sure to provide listener advantages.

For team presentations, each presenter must know the content he or she is presenting. Although each member should use his or her own style of presentation, the overall theme should be reflected by everyone. All team members should be there, even if some of them do not present. Most importantly, the team should practice the presentation as a group.

PREPARE NOTES

One of the best ways to assure that you will make a successful presentation is to prepare well. The visuals you have prepared will guide you through the outline of the presentation. Use notes to remind you of the key points and the facts relevant to your presentation. You can use notecards to record details, ideas that each visual presents, content prompts, and reminders. If you've practiced **extensively,** you'll probably find you no longer need to look at your notecards because you are knowledgeable about the content and know what you plan to say. When you have done a thorough job of preparing your message, you can feel confident and remain calm during the presentation.

extensively: at length, completely

Illustration 6-2:1

Notes help the speaker explain the information that each visual presents.

VIDEOTAPE YOUR PRESENTATION

Videotape your presentation so you can evaluate and critique yourself. Review your presentation and consider ways you can improve the delivery of your message. If necessary, practice and videotape yourself again and then reassess your presentation. Remember, you will most likely be much more critical of yourself than anyone in your audience will. Also, consider getting constructive criticism from friends and coworkers.

PREPARE THE MEETING ROOM

There are many factors to consider regarding the meeting room. Make sure the seating arrangement is appropriate. A semicircular or inverted U arrangement is good for an audience that will focus on visuals at the front of the room. This arrangement also enables the presenter to control the focus of the group. If the presenter is standing before the audience, a rectangular seating arrangement also works well. A circular or oval arrangement is **conducive** to group discussions and shared communications, but does not work well if the presenter will be standing to address the group.

conducive:
helpful, favorable

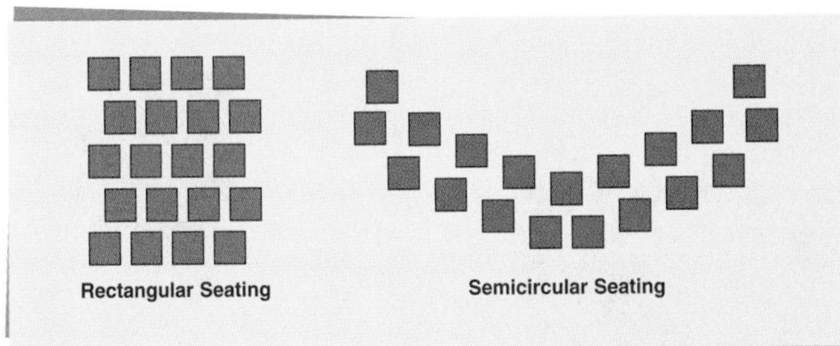

Illustration 6-2:2
These seating arrangements help the presenter hold the audience's attention.

Arrive early to set up equipment and support materials. Practice ahead of time with the specific equipment to be used in the presentation, such as a computer or projector. Even if you are familiar with operating a similar piece of equipment, make sure you practice on the one you plan to use. This will allow you to discover any differences or problems with the equipment. Test the audio equipment and get comfortable with the microphone. Know whom to call if you should need a technician.

Videotaping is a valuable tool for teaching techniques and style. Allow students to privately review their videotapes first. This will give them an opportunity to become more comfortable watching themselves. When reviewing the tape with each student, be sure to point out all the positive techniques the student demonstrates. Identify only one or two areas for the student to improve.

Experiment with different seating arrangements in your classroom. Ask students for their opinions about what works well and what doesn't. Allow students to determine the seating arrangements they would prefer for their presentations.

Check the lighting in the room and determine the best light level to use for the presentation. Even though your visuals may look good in a dark room, you want the lighting sufficient so your audience can clearly see you as you speak. Also, check the room temperature. Remember that bodies heat up a room. Setting the temperature to about 68 degrees will usually provide a comfortable environment when the room is filled with people.

CONSIDER YOUR APPEARANCE

Your appearance makes an impression on your audience and can influence how they receive your message. Dressing appropriately can help you gain their respect and hold their attention. When inappropriate, your appearance can distract your listeners or **detract** from your credibility.

detract:
take away from

Obviously, good grooming is critical. Be neat and clean in your appearance. Get a good night's rest before the presentation so you can look and be alert. For formal presentations, business suits are appropriate. For informal presentations, your attire can be more casual depending on the audience. Dress comfortably but conservatively.

for discussion

Ask students to collect examples of both appropriate and inappropriate appearance for speakers. Have them gather pictures from newspapers and periodicals. Discuss the pictures in class and point out the positive and negative factors for each.

Illustration 6-2:3
Business suits are appropriate for formal presentations.

Present Opening Remarks

In a small- or large-group presentation, it is likely that another person will introduce you to your audience. It is appropriate, however, for you to introduce yourself. In your opening remarks, be sure to state your purpose. Your opening remarks help to set the tone for your presentation. You may choose to use a visual for this introduction.

Always remember that your remarks should be appropriate for the occasion. For example, some people like to begin with a joke or with a note of humor. This helps to break the ice and gets you more comfortable with your audience. However, if the topic of your presentation is very serious in nature, a joke may not be appropriate.

Communicate With Your Audience

To deliver your message effectively, you must communicate with your audience. Although you will not be carrying on a two-way conversation with members of your audience, there still needs to be a sharing of ideas and information. You will not be able to successfully communicate your message to your listeners until you have established a meeting of the minds. To do this, you must get your audience involved.

Your listeners will likely be involved in your presentation if you appear relaxed and comfortable. It's normal to be nervous. Naturally, you want to do well, and you may experience some nervousness. Take deep breaths, concentrate on talking slowly, and think about what you're going to say next. It may seem to you that you are talking too slowly, but that is generally not the case. The listeners will find you to be more credible because they can tell you are giving thought to what you are about to say. Lastly, maintain a positive self-image and an upbeat attitude. Remind yourself that you are well prepared and can deliver the message effectively.

MAINTAIN EYE CONTACT

Making eye contact with one person in the audience helps all members of the audience feel like you are talking to them. Until you become experienced, you may find it difficult to make eye contact

Have students practice the five-second rule for maintaining eye contact. Designate a timekeeper in the audience who will actually time and record the speakers' eye contact with listeners.

with your listeners. If this is a problem for you, try to maintain the eye contact with one individual for at least five seconds before making eye contact with another person in the audience. Not only will maintaining eye contact help you involve your listeners, but it will also help you know your audience is following you. You can judge their reactions to what you are saying. It will make your listeners feel more involved and important.

Illustration 6-2:4

Establishing eye contact with someone in the audience makes all your listeners feel more involved.

AVOID NON-WORDS

Sounds or words that do not contribute to the meaning of the presentation are often called non-words. The use of non-words is a habit many of us need to break. Often we don't realize we say non-words such as "uhh," "OK," or "you know." Review your videotape or have a friend help you identify non-words that you use. Count the number of non-words you say throughout your presentation. You may be surprised to find how frequently you use non-words.

Usually we say non-words because we are thinking about what we want to say next, and we don't want to allow a period of silence. Actually, a non-word does not fill up much time as we speak, and it doesn't hurt to have quiet pauses between our statements. The non-words can be much more annoying to listeners than a pause with silence.

If you know you use too many non-words, videotape your presentation a second time. This time, consciously pause instead of saying a non-word. Review your videotape and count the occurrences of non-words again. Hopefully, you were able to reduce them significantly. Don't be concerned if you cannot eliminate all non-words initially. Habits are difficult to break. Consciously work on avoiding non-words in your daily communications as well. You'll soon see you can speak without them.

NON-WORDS

ah	uh-huh
all right	well
and	yeah
and ah	you know
okay	you see

Illustration 6-2:5

Avoid the use of non-words in your presentation.

SHOW ENTHUSIASM AND SPEAK CONVINCINGLY

Speak with enthusiasm and conviction. A sure way to get your audience involved is to convince them that you are excited about the topic. If you believe in what you are saying, let your listeners know. Let your enthusiasm be genuine, however. Most listeners will know if you're not being honest, and that is a sure way to lose their attention.

Show a sincere interest in helping your listeners meet their needs. This is where knowing your listeners can be very helpful. Use keywords that your listener wants to hear to which they can relate. Describe experiences or examples with which your listeners can identify. In doing so, you can be very convincing as you share your ideas.

CONTROL YOUR POSTURE AND GESTURES

It is distracting to watch speakers who pace and walk back and forth or who shuffle their feet and shift weight from one leg to the other. Instead of becoming involved in your presentation, listeners start concentrating on your posture and gestures. You only want them to think about your message.

Ask students to watch TV news programs and write down the non-words they hear during interviews. Who generally uses the non-words, the newscaster or the lay person? Do the students notice the professional newscaster purposely pausing instead of using a non-word?

Let students have some fun with posture and gestures. Ask them to describe or demonstrate posture and gestures they think are distracting. After demonstrating the inappropriate gesture, they must offer an appropriate gesture or posture to replace it.

Stand with your feet slightly apart and firmly planted. Leave your hands at your sides until you use them for natural gestures that enhance your words. For example, if something is really big, show it by opening your arms really wide. If something is minor, use a gesture with your hands to show the problem is small. Make sure your gestures don't **contradict** your words. When your hands drop below your waist, your gestures are not effective.

contradict: deny, counter

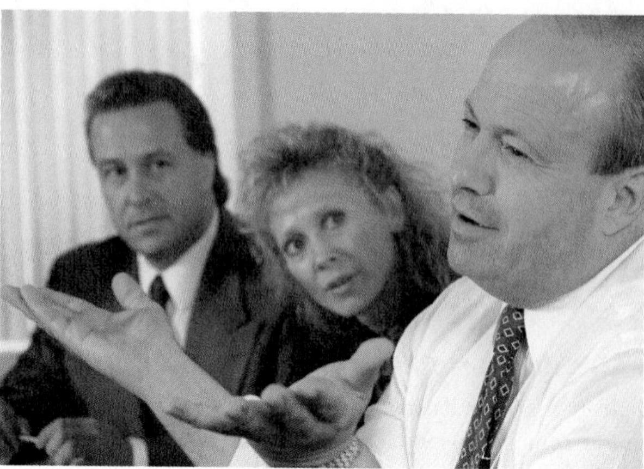

Illustration 6-2:6
Gestures enhance a speaker's words.

Avoid other distracting gestures such as rubbing your hands together or crossing your arms. These forms of body language communicate nervousness. Your listeners will be watching your body language as they listen to you speak. Make sure your posture and gestures are not communicating something different than the message you want them to receive.

USE GOOD INTONATION

No one likes to listen to a person speaking in a monotone. As you review your videotape, close your eyes and listen to your voice. Do you use good **intonation?** Does your voice reflect enthusiasm? Is it easy to listen to? With practice, you can learn to speak with a pleasant voice that is neither too high nor too low. Your voice should sound relaxed and have an even tone.

intonation: the rise and fall in voice pitch

Learning to relax can help you control your voice. If you are tense, your voice may sound shaky and high-pitched. Concentrate on speaking loudly enough without straining your voice or shouting. Vary your **inflection** to help you sound more interesting. Enunciate clearly, and don't speak too quickly.

inflection: tone of voice

KEEP THE AUDIENCE FOCUSED

Watch the reactions of your audience. Make sure they are focused on what you are saying. If they seem confused or distracted, back up and rephrase your point. If you sense that your are losing their attention, try to focus again on listener interests and advantages.

Don't panic, however, if the audience does seem to lose focus. Keep in mind that this topic is something that you know and understand very well. It may be that your listeners need more time to think about the information and ideas you are presenting.

Use Visuals Effectively

If you've prepared well, you have some great visuals to help you communicate your ideas. These visuals, however, are not the key to your presentation. You are the key element. Begin by drawing the listeners' attention to yourself. Then, when appropriate, direct their attention to the visuals to make your message more powerful.

One way visuals can make your message more powerful is by creating anticipation. Don't reveal the visual too soon. Set it up before you introduce it. For example:

> *In his presentation, Robert has a visual that summarizes data collected in a survey of office staff members. To set up the visual, Robert says, "You'll recall that last month we requested your input regarding our current office procedures. We received some interesting insights from many of you." Then Robert reveals the slide that summarizes the findings.*

As you display your visuals, look at your listeners, not at your visuals. Continue to maintain eye contact. Stand to the left or right of the display of your visuals. Don't let the visuals replace you. Be sure your listeners can see you *and* the visuals.

Demonstrate improper use of visuals. For example, stand in front of the visual to block the view. Or stand at the back of the room so the listeners can see only the visual and not you. Ask students to comment as to why your methods are ineffective.

Illustration 6-2:7

The audience should be able to see the speaker and the visuals.

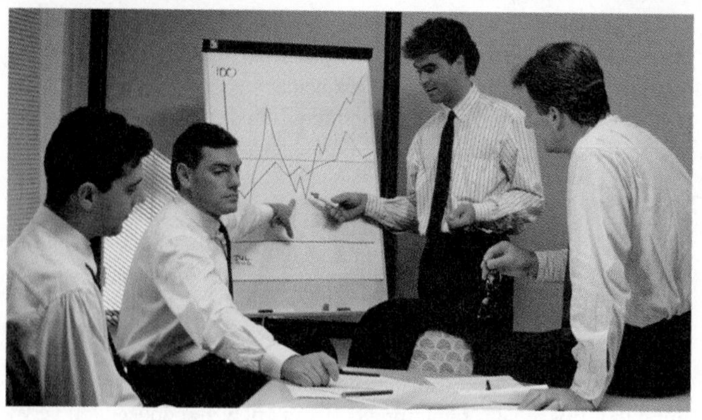

Pause to allow listeners time to view and think about your visuals. You've seen them and studied them, but your listeners have not. Also, use pauses to allow for listener reaction. Allow them time to laugh if it is a humorous visual, or give them an opportunity to read and evaluate a proposed solution displayed on a visual. During this pause you can study their reactions to your visual. For example, look for nods of agreement or expressions of disagreement. If appropriate, **solicit** their feedback before continuing.

solicit:
seek, request

Answer Questions

It is important to allow your audience time to ask questions. Question-and-answer sessions are valuable to you as well. They provide you an opportunity to hear from your listeners and to share what they are thinking.

ANTICIPATE LISTENER QUESTIONS

Many speakers become anxious about receiving questions from an audience. They're afraid they won't be able to answer the questions or that they will lose control of the situation. As with the overall presentation, the key to feeling calm and confident when receiving questions is preparation. Anticipate what your audience will ask you following your presentation. If you've prepared well, you've probably addressed many of their concerns in the content of your presentation. However, you may get questions about content you have already covered. This means that the listener either did not understand or did not retain that information.

Perhaps when you give your audience the opportunity to ask questions, no one will raise their hand. This happens frequently. Initially, you may think they are not interested in the topic and just want to leave. The truth is, if you've been effective as a speaker, they've been listening and thinking about your ideas. You've been directing their train of thought. Perhaps they haven't had time to think about their own ideas and questions to ask. Just in case no one in the audience asks a question, have some questions ready. This will help to fill the time you have allotted for questions, and it may help to **initiate** some questions from the audience.

initiate: begin, launch

RESTATE THE QUESTION

When you receive a question from the audience, the entire group needs to hear the question. Generally, the person asking directs the question to the speaker and the entire audience does not hear the question. Restate the question for everyone to hear. Doing so gives you time to think about the answer and enables you to confirm to the listener that you understand his or her question.

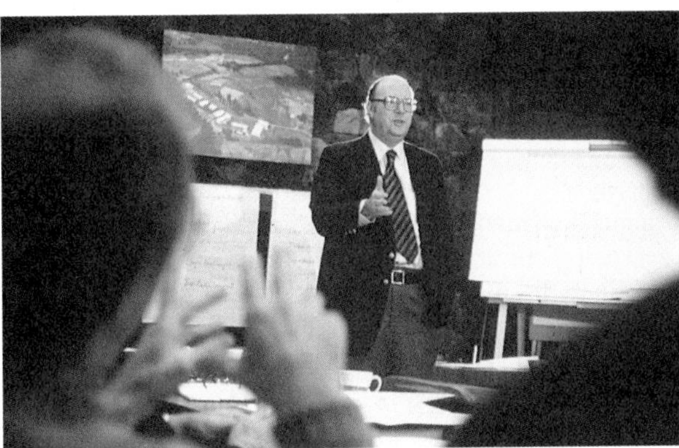

Illustration 6-2:8
In question-and-answer sessions, the speaker should direct the focus of the discussion.

In one-to-one situations, you may wish to rephrase a question or incorporate part of the question in the beginning of your answer to let the listener know you understood it. However, be careful not to offend your listener by rephrasing all the questions. Instead, allow yourself time to think about the answer by making comments such as, "I can understand your concerns" and "I, too, have experienced that and here is what I've learned."

RESPOND TO THE QUESTION

Respond to all questions in a courteous and sincere manner. Keep your answers brief to maintain the exchange between you and the audience. Direct your answer to the entire group, not just the person who asked the question. Maintain eye contact to keep the audience focused on the discussion. When appropriate, provide supporting details or evidence to back up your answer.

Be honest if you don't know the answer to a question. You will gain more credibility with your audience if you are honest than if you try to bluff your way through the answer. If appropriate, offer to find the answer and communicate it to the individual later.

Don't become frustrated if the question relates to information already covered in your presentation. If one listener missed details or became confused, chances are that others did, too. Provide the details or explain the point again briefly, perhaps using different words. Offer to provide more details on an individual basis later if appropriate.

Sometimes one individual will ask more than one question and begin to dominate the question-and-answer session. The other listeners often become aggravated when this happens, and they can begin to feel unimportant or unnoticed. If this happens, you can quickly lose the audience's attention. If one individual begins to **dominate** the questions, break eye contact with the individual before he or she has an opportunity to ask another question. Or upon giving an answer to that individual's question, establish eye contact with another person and ask, "Does anyone else have a question they would like to ask?"

dominate: command, take over

teaching tips

Have students role-play question-and-answer sessions. Ask the listeners to purposely try to dominate the questions. Have the speaker focus on maintaining control by rephrasing the questions and by not permitting one individual to dominate the questions.

HANDLING TEAM QUESTIONS

In a team presentation, the team members should decide in advance how they will handle questions from the audience. For example, they may decide that one team member will direct the questions to the appropriate person for an answer. All presenters should be included in the question-and-answer session.

Present Closing Remarks

Following the question-and-answer session, you have one last chance to get your point across. Your closing remarks should be a concise review of the major points in your presentation, but be careful to word your closing so that you do not repeat exactly what you have already said. Restate the specific points. Then close the presentation, thanking your audience for listening.

Evaluate Your Presentation

After the presentation is completed, evaluate yourself. Consider the strong points of your presentation and what seemed to be effective. Think about what you could do to improve it. Did you forget to mention something? Could you have used more visuals, or did you use too many? What would you do differently the next time?

Ask your audience to evaluate the presentation also by providing an evaluation form. Evaluation forms are valuable tools that can help you improve your communication skills. To be effective, though, the evaluation form has to gather appropriate information from your listeners. Be specific about the feedback you are soliciting. Illustration 6-2:9 on page 294 shows a sample evaluation form. For example, ask listeners the following questions:

- Have you convinced them to take a course of action?
- Have they learned something from your presentation?
- Was the length of your presentation appropriate?
- Could they relate the content of your presentation to their personal experiences?

You will get the most accurate feedback if you ask your listeners to complete the evaluation immediately following your presentation. Their reactions are fresh and their comments will be more specific.

Illustration 6-2:9

Evaluation forms provide valuable feedback.

EVALUATION FORM

Please check one of the boxes at the right for each of the statements below.	Very Much	Somewhat	Not at All
The coverage of the topic met my expectations.			
The topic was of interest to me.			
I can use the information presented.			
The length of the presentation was adequate.			
The presenter addressed the topic effectively.			
Following the presentation, I feel more comfortable about the topic.			
I was able to clearly understand all concepts presented.			
I can relate the information that was presented to my personal experiences.			
I am convinced that I should adopt this new procedure.			

Comments:

Learn from the evaluation comments and use the information constructively to improve the content and/or the delivery of your message. Each time you speak before a group, you will grow in confidence and ability. If you have the opportunity to give the same presentation again, you can refine and improve it based on the evaluation and feedback you receive.

Reviewing the Topic

Delivering the Presentation

1. What seating arrangement is appropriate when the audience will be viewing visuals?
2. Describe four considerations in preparing the meeting room.
3. What risks are involved if a speaker dresses inappropriately?
4. Why is it important to maintain eye contact with the audience during the presentation?
5. What are non-words? Why do many of us use them?
6. List some distracting gestures and explain why they can be a problem for a speaker.
7. Describe intonation.
8. How can you use a visual to create anticipation?
9. Why should you restate or rephrase a question before you answer it?
10. How can you discourage an individual who is beginning to dominate the question-and-answer session.

topic 6-2 review

REINFORCING MATH SKILLS

Assume that you work as an office assistant to a manager of a small company that sells interactive software. Your manager, Norm Schehl, will be discussing the recent successes and growth of the company at a business luncheon next month. Norm has not yet decided what type of media he will use for his presentation. He has asked you to explore the costs of creating visuals for his presentation. He plans to use approximately 25 different visuals.

You did some checking with some local vendors and found the following prices to have four-color transparencies, four-color copies, four-color slides, and four-color posters made.

Slides created from a negative	$6 for first slide; $1.12 for each additional slide
Slides created from a print or a hard-copy illustration	$5.25 each

topic 6-2 review

Delivering the Presentation

Slides created from disk	$4.95 each
Posters	16" × 20" $9.99 20" × 30" $14.99 24" × 36" $19.99
Color transparencies	$2.49 each
Color copies	$1.49 for the first 25 copies; $.99 for additional copies

What you are to do:

Determine the total cost for each of the following options:

1. Create 25 slides (from a disk) and three 20" × 30" posters.
2. Create 25 slides (from a print or hard-copy illustration) and three 20" × 30" posters.
3. Create 25 color transparencies and one 24" × 36" poster.
4. Create 35 ten-page, four-color handouts.

topic 6-2 review

INTERACTING WITH OTHERS

Assume you just completed a presentation before a group of colleagues about how to operate a new copier in your department. You just opened the question-and-answer session. One individual in your audience is very knowledgeable about the topic. During one of his questions, he implies that you are not correct in the information you have presented.

What you are to do:

Explain how would you respond to this individual.

APPLICATION ACTIVITIES

ACTIVITY 1 Prepare and Practice with Visuals

In this activity you will prepare some simple visuals for the five-minute presentation you planned for Topic 6-1.

What you are to do:

1. Choose the media you will use to create the visuals depending on the equipment and materials available for use in your classroom. Ask your instructor for the media options available to you.

296

2. Create a visual for each storyboard worksheet you prepared earlier.

3. After your visuals are complete, practice your presentation in front of a mirror. Or, if possible, videotape your practice session. Focus on using your visuals correctly so they help to emphasize the key points in your presentation. Notice your posture and gestures, and concentrate on using a pleasant voice.

ACTIVITY 2 Deliver a Presentation

In this activity, you will deliver the presentation created in Topic 6-2 to a group of your classmates.

What you are to do:

1. Work with two or three students from you class as assigned by your instructor.
2. Deliver your five-minute presentation to the group. Be sure to include a question-and-answer session at the end of your presentation. If possible, videotape your presentation.
3. Complete the self-evaluation form in your *Student Activities and Projects* workbook.

Have the students create simple visuals using flip charts, posterboard, or large sheets of paper. Encourage them to use color markers, color pencils, or crayons.

For their first presentation, let students present to one person or to a small group as opposed to the entire class. Assign partners or small groups of three or four. If possible, videotape each student's presentation and allow the student to complete a self-evaluation. This first presentation should not be graded. Do not use the videotape to evaluate the student and assign a grade.

See Workbook page 31.

Do not involve the small group listeners in the evaluation of the student's delivery or the content of the presentation.

If students work in pairs, it may be appropriate for the listener to provide positive feedback and constructive criticism. Student feedback should be closely monitored.

Chapter Summary

To prepare an effective presentation, you must know your listeners. It is critical that you develop your presentation with them in mind. Practicing the delivery of a presentation can take as much time and thought and is as important as planning and preparing the content of the presentation. The following key points will reinforce your learning from this chapter.

- It is important to know the interests of your listeners and to address those interests in the content of your presentation. As you do so, you describe the advantages the listeners can gain from the information you will provide. When a listener understands these advantages from your presentation, you have that person's attention.
- A storyboard can help you organize and illustrate your ideas.
- Finding a logical sequence for presenting your ideas will help your listeners stay interested in what you have to say.
- Much of what we remember is in the form of pictures. Visual elements can help you communicate your message and provide a picture that will help your listeners recall the information you have provided. Handouts are also effective for providing your listeners with a summary of the key points in your presentation.
- Practicing your presentation out loud is important. Videotaping your practice sessions can also be very helpful.
- Knowing how to communicate with your audience and keeping them involved is essential for a successful presentation.
- Question-and-answer sessions are important for both the speaker and the audience. Handling questions effectively helps you direct the focus of the session.
- Evaluations provide valuable feedback for improving your performance in future presentations.

chapter 6 summary

Communicating via Presentations

KEY CONCEPTS AND TERMS

avoid non-words
evaluation form
gestures
intonation
listener advantages
listener interests
listener profile
maintain eye contact
practice and prepare
question-and-answer session
storyboard
visual elements

INTEGRATED APPLICATION ACTIVITY

ACTIVITY Team Presentation

You work in the accounting department for a large insurance company. There are approximately 25 coworkers in your department, of diverse ages and lifestyles. During the past year you actively participated with several other employees in writing a proposed plan for employee flex-time options. Recently, management decided to test the flex-time schedule with employees in your department only. They have agreed to run a pilot program with the personnel in your department for two months. If the pilot is successful, management will offer the flex-time options company-wide.

You and a team of coworkers have been asked to prepare and deliver a ten-minute presentation to motivate coworkers in your department to participate in the flex-time pilot program. Specific details about the flex-time schedule are provided below.

- Employees must work a minimum of an eight-hour day.
- Employees must work five days a week.
- An employee's workday must begin no earlier than 6 a.m. and no later than 10 a.m.
- The employee's workday must end no earlier than 3 p.m. and no later than 7 p.m.

299

- Employees may schedule their own lunch hours and break times; they must not abuse this privilege.
- Employees may vary their work schedule from day to day, but the employee must keep a regular schedule from week to week. (For example, an employee may choose to work from 9 a.m. to 6 p.m. on Monday, Wednesday, and Friday and from 8 a.m. to 5 p.m. on Tuesday and Thursday.)
- The employee's supervisor must be informed in advance; and the supervisor must agree to the proposed work schedule.
- Employees must submit a request form for the flex-time option to their immediate supervisor. On the form, the employee will indicate the desired weekly work hours.

What you are to do:

Work with a team of classmates as assigned by your instructor to develop a team presentation as described above:

1. Determine the objective of the presentation.
2. Develop the outline of the presentation.
3. Develop the content of the presentation.
4. Develop the visual aids.
5. Practice with your team, and then deliver the presentation to your class.

Use available media to have students create transparencies or slides. For example, have students use the computer to create transparencies and print them on transparency film. Or have them create a slide show using presentation software and display the slides with a LCD panel. However, visuals using flip charts, posterboard, or large sheets of paper will also be effective.

Emphasize to the students to work as a team. The success of their presentation will depend on the efforts and contributions of each team member.

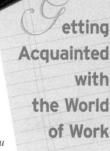

Blake Williams
Office Manager

Getting Acquainted with the World of Work

Presentation Panic!

Dear Mr. Williams

I've been working as an office assistant for a pharmaceutical company for six months. Today my supervisor asked me to prepare a sales meeting presentation. I am to demonstrate to all the company sales representatives the new system we've adopted for company e-mail. I know the system well, and I've presented it to my coworkers. The sales meeting is to be held in two weeks. I'm in a panic because I've never presented at a sales meeting. I've never even met any of the sales representatives!

Duane in Long Beach

Dear Duane

A little anxiety about a presentation can be good, but don't panic! The secret to remaining calm for a presentation is being prepared. It sounds as though you have already done some of the preparation because you presented the new E-mail system to your coworkers. You can approach the presentation with confidence because you already know the system and its features. You're well on your way to putting together an effective presentation for the sales representatives.

Reflect on your previous presentation and make any necessary changes to improve the content or delivery. Most importantly, remember that you have been chosen to train the sales representatives. Obviously, your supervisor is confident that you can do a good job.

Perhaps your anxieties exist because you will be presenting to people you do not know. Previously, you presented the new e-mail system to your coworkers, and perhaps you were more comfortable because you were talking to your peers. What you have to say and what you can explain about the system is important. Once you convince the sales representatives that what you have to say will help them, they will eagerly listen to the information you plan to share.

Good luck with your presentation, and enjoy the sales meeting. It will provide a wonderful opportunity for you to meet the sales representatives with whom you do not get to work on a daily basis.

Blake Williams

Office Manager

301

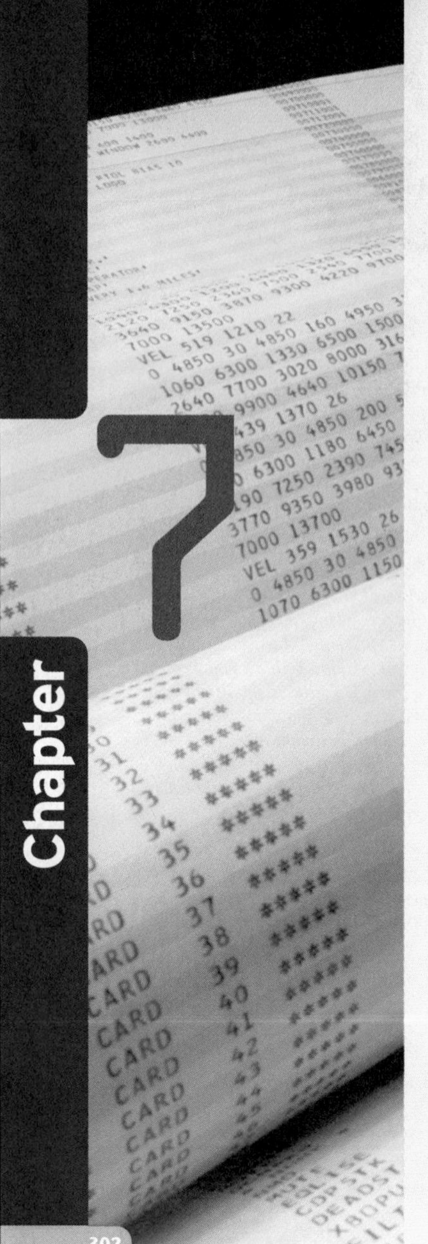

Processing and Understanding Financial Information

Can you imagine a business that needs no financial information? Of course not. Sound financial information is critical to successful organizations. Many day-to-day business decisions are based on financial information:

> *What is the price we must pay for our next purchase of raw materials? Will this expenditure exhaust our budget allowance? How much do we owe our suppliers? What is the amount owed us by customers? How much overtime will we need to complete this order? What will it cost us?*

If this information is not correct or not received in a timely manner, unwise decisions may be made.

In this chapter, you are introduced to concepts and procedures used in cash and banking activities and to basic financial procedures and reports used in financial management.

Chapter 7

302

Topic 7-1

Cash and Banking Procedures

When you have completed your study of this topic, you will be able to:

- **explain the value of internal control for cash handling**
- **explain procedures for receiving cash and making cash payments**
- **prepare a bank account reconciliation**
- **prepare entries for a petty cash fund**

Careful control of cash receipts and cash payments is necessary for a business to succeed. Most businesses have developed procedures to help assure that the processing of cash is done securely, accurately, and efficiently.

In the business world, cash refers both to actual cash (coins and bills), **checks,** and money orders, and to funds in checking accounts in banks. Some companies, such as supermarkets and retail stores, may handle large volumes of currency. In other companies almost all transactions are paid by check, credit card, or electronic funds transfer. Still others will accept only currency or money orders.

checks: written orders to a bank to make payment against the depositor's funds in that bank

If you work in a small office, you are likely to have some responsibility for cash-related transactions. If you work in a large company, you may work in a department where many cash-related transactions are

processed. In either case, you should understand the safeguards for cash and procedures for processing cash transactions used in your company.

Safeguarding Cash

negotiable: easily exchanged for cash

Currency is easily transferred without identifying the owner. Checks can be transferred with some ease because they are **negotiable.** Therefore, businesses must carefully guard the flow of cash, regardless of its form, through their organizations.

fraud: deceit, dishonest act

You will find that companies organize tasks to minimize the possibility of **fraud** and theft of cash. For example, in a small company, the owner may open all incoming mail, remove all cash, and make all deposits at the bank. The owner also may personally sign all checks issued. Furthermore, the owner may directly supervise all the employees. This provides additional assurance that company **assets,** including cash, are not being **misappropriated.** The overall organization for safeguarding assets is a component of a company's *internal control.*

assets: resources available for use

misappropriated: used for purposes other than those authorized

DIVISION OF RESPONSIBILITY

In processing cash transactions in large organizations, direct supervision by the owner-manager is not possible. Most companies develop procedures to safeguard cash and other assets. In Illustration 7-1:1, note the separation of tasks designed to ensure that all checks received by the company are actually added to the company's cash account.

Illustration 7-1:1

Separation of duties helps assure internal control of incoming checks.

Processing Of Incoming Checks

Mail Clerk

- opens and sorts mail
- places checks in one pile
- stamps endorsement on checks
- prepares multiple copies of a listing of all checks
- forwards checks and a copy of listing to the cashier
- forwards a copy of the listing to accounts receivable or the accounting office
- files one copy of the listing

Cashier

- receives the listing of checks prepared by the mail clerk
- verifies the listing by comparing each check with the listing
- prepares deposit slip
- makes deposit in person or by mail
- receives a copy of receipted deposit slip from bank
- forwards a copy of receipted deposit slip to accounting office

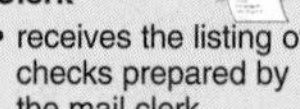

Accounting Clerk

- receives the listing of checks prepared by the mail clerk
- receives copy of the receipted deposit ticket prepared by the cashier
- verifies the listing prepared by the mail clerk by matching each check with the deposit slip received from the cashier
- makes entries in customers' records

expand the concept

Use a local business (such as a theater, grocery store, or fast-food restaurant) to explain how absentee owners (or on-site managers) organize, for internal control, the handling of cash. In some fast-food establishments, the order clerk does not take the customer's money but fills out or rings up a prenumbered slip. A cashier near the exit takes the slip and the payment. In this procedure, it would be somewhat difficult for the order clerk to get the money. The cashier must account for the amount of cash listed on the slips filled out by the order clerk. (Some fast-food restaurants reward cashiers who have a perfect till at the end of their shift. The reward may be a free meal or other incentive.)

expand the concept

What control would be missing if mail were opened by the cashier, who also performed the duties listed? For what control purpose is the cashier not assigned the task of making entries in customer records?

INTERNAL AUDITS

In some companies, an *internal audit* department establishes and oversees the system for safeguarding assets. Staff in such a department perform **audits** to determine if the procedures for control are actually being followed. You may be expected to assist the personnel responsible for internal auditing.

audits: the verifying of facts or procedures

Jill, a staff member in the internal audit department, was assigned the task of determining the efficiency of the mail procedures. She arrived unannounced early in the morning just as the mail was being opened. She observed the work of two office assistants, Tom and Rica, who had the task of recording all checks received. Tom and Rica knew the procedures they were expected to follow. They followed the procedures at all times, so the audit revealed no problems.

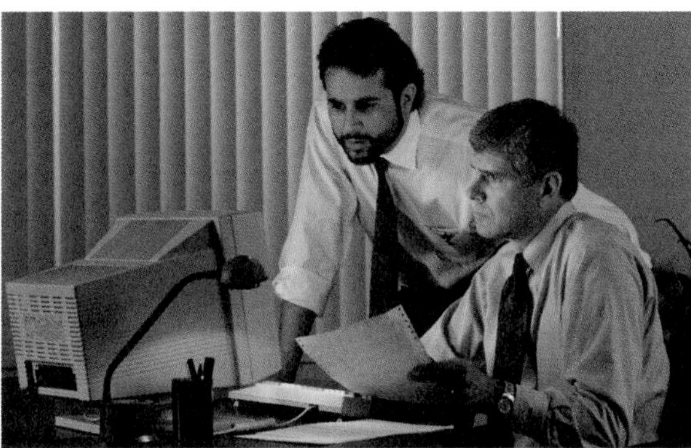

Illustration 7-1:2
Internal audits are performed regularly to determine if procedures are being followed.

BONDED EMPLOYEES

To safeguard resources, companies strive to hire honest employees who will **adhere** to the policies and rules pertaining to their jobs. To protect against possible loss, a company may require some employees to be bonded. Bonding is insurance for financial loss due to employee theft or fraud.

adhere: follow closely

The company that insures bonded employees makes a search of the employee's work history and criminal record. They check with former employers and other references. This search, which is generally more thorough than that done by the company at the time employees are hired, is considered another advantage of bonding.

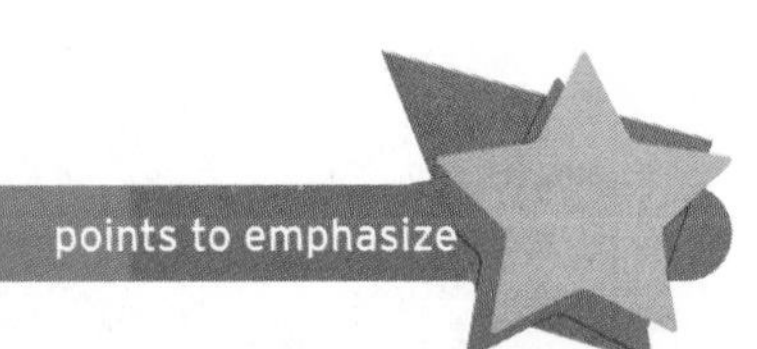

Cash and checks are easily transferable. Therefore, companies must depend on the integrity of employees to be sure cash and checks are properly processed for company purposes.

Receiving Payments

Many sales are made on account with payment to be made at a future date. This payment frequently comes in the form of a check. In large companies, the payments are processed by employees in the accounts receivable department. Accounts receivable are the short-term debts owed to your company by others, such as its customers.

When payments come in the form of currency or checks, specific procedures are followed for processing the payment into the firm's accounts. Three such procedures are handling the cash drawer, preparing bank deposits, and making bank deposits.

HANDLING THE CASH DRAWER

entrust: give employees use of valuable assets

If you are responsible for receiving payments and making change, you will probably do so using a cash drawer. By using a cash drawer, a business can **entrust** an exact amount of money to an employee to conduct financial transactions. This money is placed in a cash (currency, coins, checks) drawer from which the employee removes cash for making change and receives cash from the customer. The employee is personally responsible for this money.

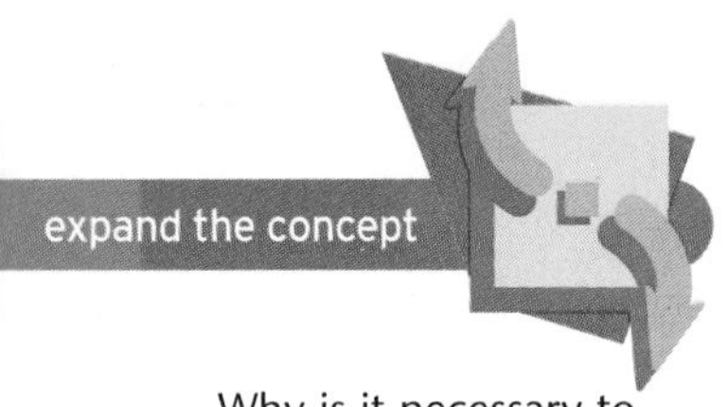

Why is it necessary to actually count the cash in the drawer when a cash register report is generated?

verify: prove to be true

Employees issued cash drawers are required to **verify** the amount of cash in their cash drawers at the beginning and end of the business day. The procedure for verifying cash is known as proving cash. Employees generally verify the cash drawer amount by using a form designed for proving cash similar to the form shown in Illustration 7-1:3. Another method of checking the accuracy of cash handling is the cash register report generated electronically at the register, also shown in Illustration 7-1:3.

PREPARING DEPOSITS

It is a common policy to deposit all cash in a bank as soon as possible. In some organizations where many payments are received, deposits

CASH PROOF

Date: 1/15/xx Register 2

Employee: Glenn Rae

Quantity	Denominations	Amount
15	Pennies	.15
25	Nickels	1.25
13	Dimes	1.30
9	Quarters	2.25
0	Half-Dollars	--
11	$1 Bills	11.00
4	$5 Bills	20.00
4	$10 Bills	40.00
3	$20 Bills	60.00
1	$50 Bills	50.00
--	$100 Bills	--
	Checks	
	Total Cash in Drawer	185.95
	Cash Paid Out	5.50
	Total Cash	191.45
	Less Beginning Cash	100.00
	Actual Drawer Count	91.45
	Register Cash Reading	91.45

Proved x Short ____ Over ____

Signed: Glenn B. Rae

Register Totals Report
1/15/XX 16:35
Store: 001 Register: 002

Description	#	Register Totals
ASH	9	91.45
/R CHARGE	3	84.86
ISA	1	26.45
ASTER CARD	1	28.38
	14	231.14
OTAL MERCHANDISE		219.44
OTAL NON-MERCHANDISE		0.00
OTAL BUY BACK		5.50
OTAL PAY IN		0.00
TAL PAY OUT		(5.50)
TAL TAXES		11.70
		231.14

shier Using This Register:
GBR

Illustration 7-1:3

The cash proof form and the cash register tape report become the source documents for recording cash sales.

may be made several times a day. In other companies, a deposit is made on any day when payments are received.

Common Endorsements. If you have the responsibility of preparing a bank deposit, your first task will be to see that all checks are properly **endorsed.** An endorsement is a signature or instructions, stamped or written on the back of a check. An endorsement is required before a check is transferred from the company or person to whom the check is written to another person, company, or bank. In many companies, office workers who prepare deposits also endorse the checks using a stamp.

endorsed: authorized for transfer

Endorsements vary. Some provide more protection or instruction about the **disposition** of the check than others. The most commonly used forms of endorsements are *blank*, *restrictive*, and *special*. Look closely at Illustration 7-1:4 on page 308 as you read about each form of endorsement:

disposition: settlement

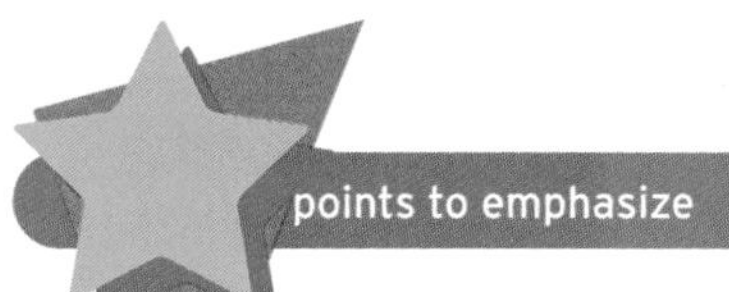

"Protection" means safeguarding against transferring funds to an unauthorized person.

Which endorsement provides the least protection? Why?

Illustration 7-1:4

Endorsements can be stamped or handwritten and provide varying levels of protection.

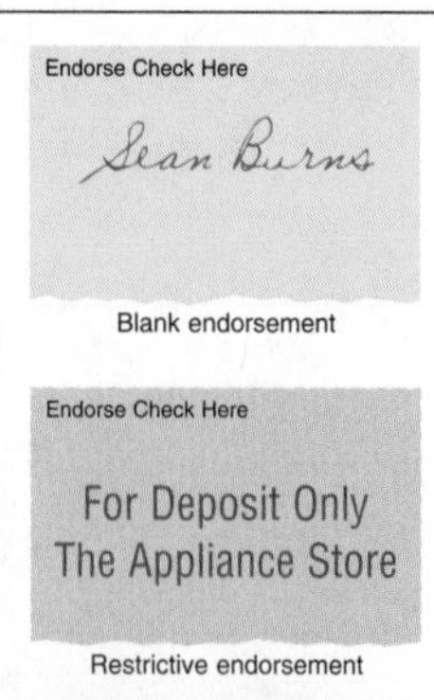

Endorse Check Here
Sean Burns
Endorse Check Here
For Deposit Only
The Appliance Store

Blank endorsement

Only the signature is used. The signature must be in ink. This endorsement provides little protection, since anyone who gains access to a check with a blank endorsement can readily transfer it to another person or to a bank. Generally, you will not want to use this endorsement unless you are in the bank and will be depositing the check immediately.

Restrictive endorsement

The purpose of the transfer of the check is indicated in the endorsement. Note in the illustration that the check is marked *for deposit only.* Restrictive endorsements are often made with a rubber stamp or a stamping machine.

Endorse Check Here
Pay to the Order of Baylor Florists
Drew L. Westwood

Special endorsement

The signature of the endorser is preceded by the name of the person or company to whom the check is being transferred. In some instances a special endorsement is referred to as an *endorsement in full.*

To prepare a check for endorsement, place the check face up. Grasp the left edge of the check and turn it over, keeping the same edge at the left. Carefully stamp or write each endorsement on the left edge of the check or other marked endorsement area.

Deposit Slip. A deposit slip is a form used to record cash and checks to be added to a bank account. As shown in Illustration 7-1:5, the deposit slip requires the following details:

- the current date.
- the amount of each item to be deposited. For each check, identify the bank on which the check is drawn. This is done by recording the bank's number, which is the upper portion of the fraction noted on each check.
- the total amount to be deposited. This amount includes all checks listed on both the front and back of the deposit slip.

To verify the accuracy of the total deposit, compute the total by adding the checks and currency. Verify that this total is exactly the

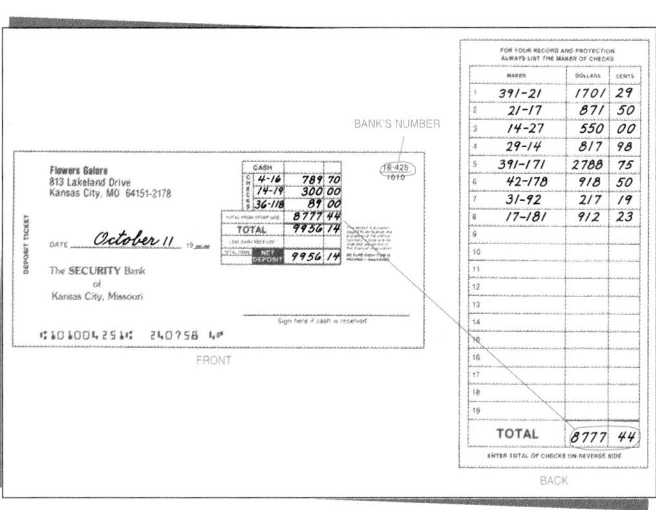

DEPOSIT TICKET

Flowers Galore
813 Lakeland Drive
Kansas City, MO 64151-2178

DATE October 11 19__

The SECURITY Bank of Kansas City, Missouri

		Dollars	Cents
CASH			
CHECKS	4-16	789	70
	14-19	300	00
	36-118	89	00
TOTAL FROM OTHER SIDE		8777	44
TOTAL		9956	14
LESS CASH RECEIVED			
NET DEPOSIT		9956	14

18-425
1010

Sign here if cash is received

⑆101004251⑆ 240758 4⑈

FRONT

BANK'S NUMBER

FOR YOUR RECORD AND PROTECTION ALWAYS LIST THE MAKER OF CHECKS

	MAKER	DOLLARS	CENTS
1	391-21	1701	29
2	21-17	871	50
3	14-27	550	00
4	29-14	817	98
5	391-171	2788	75
6	42-178	918	50
7	31-92	217	19
8	17-181	912	23
9			
10			
11			
12			
13			
14			
15			
16			
17			
18			
19			
	TOTAL	8777	44

ENTER TOTAL OF CHECKS ON REVERSE SIDE

BACK

Illustration 7-1:5

On the front of the deposit slip, record the total amount of the checks listed on the back.

same as the total listed on the deposit slip. If so, you are assured that your listing is correct and includes all items.

One of Inez's daily tasks is preparing deposit slips for all items to be taken to the local bank. Inez works in a systematic fashion so that she makes no errors. She verifies that each deposit slip is correct by totaling the amounts carefully. She is proud that the bank has never sent the cashier a notice that an error had been made in a deposit!

MAKING DEPOSITS

Office workers may have the task of making deposits in local banks on a regular basis. If your tasks include going to the bank with deposits, be sure all checks, currency, coins, and deposit forms are in proper order and in an envelope before you leave the office.

Deposits can be made electronically at automatic teller stations at the bank and at other convenient locations. If you make this type of deposit, follow instructions and get a receipt. Verify that the receipt shows the amount of your deposit.

In many companies, payments from customers are made directly to a bank lockbox, a postal address maintained at the company's bank to

Obtain copies of a deposit slip (or photocopy) used in a local bank and have students complete the form neatly and accurately. Follow up with a discussion of the purpose of each item of information on the slip.

What kind of record of deposit will this worker have of this transaction?

Illustration 7-1:6

This worker is making a deposit at an automatic teller machine conveniently located near the office.

collect payments. A worker in the bank's office typically processes the deposit and updates the company's bank balance. The bank may transfer updated information electronically to each company for which lockbox payments are received.

Making Payments

In larger firms, processing payments is the responsibility of employees in the accounts payable department. Accounts payable refers to the short-term debts your company owes to others. In a smaller business, however, one individual may be responsible for all aspects of financial transactions, including receiving and making payments.

Illustration 7-1:7

Accounts payable workers review documents related to company purchases.

If it is your responsibility to make payments for your company, you will be involved in several related tasks: reviewing purchase-related documents, preparing vouchers, and preparing checks.

REVIEW DOCUMENTS

Companies want to be sure that payments are made only for **goods** purchased and received. The task of the accounts payable department or the individual responsible for making payments is to review all the documents related to each purchase.

goods: raw materials, merchandise

Several related documents may be generated with each purchase. The documents and their usefulness in making payments are as follows:

- Purchase requisition: Shows that the purchase item requested was authorized by someone with the authority to do so
- Purchase order: Shows exactly what was ordered and to what address it was to be shipped
- Receiving report: Shows that goods were actually received by the company
- Invoice from **vendor:** Shows what is owed for the purchases
- Credit memorandum (if applicable): Shows the reduction in amount owed due to return of goods or to **allowance** for goods not received or of poor quality

vendor: agency that provides goods or services

allowance: credit given on account

The review of purchase-related documents is essentially a task of determining if all the appropriate documents are present for each purchase and that all the details on the documents are the same.

You will not arrange for payment until all documents are accounted for and agree with each other or until there is a reasonable explanation for missing documents or **discrepancies** in information.

discrepancies: differences , contradictions

PREPARE VOUCHERS

In many offices a voucher system is used for payments. This system requires the preparation of a voucher before a check is written. A voucher is a document that shows the vendor name, invoice date, terms, and amount owed. The approved voucher serves as the authorization to make the payment. Illustration 7-1:8 is an example of a

What documents support the voucher?

voucher. If you have the responsibility for preparing vouchers, you should follow these general steps:

Illustration 7-1:8

Can you name the documents that are needed before this voucher can be written?

VOUCHER

The Lampshade Store
426 Monroe Street
Cedar Falls, IA 50613-3467

VOUCHER NO. 4379

DATE: October 17, 19--

PAY TO: Just Shades
135 Green Street
New York, NY 10003-4689

For the following: . (All supporting documents are attached.)

INVOICE DATE	TERMS	INVOICE NUMBER	GROSS AMOUNT	DISCOUNT	NET PAYABLE
October 17	2/10,n/30	5479	$4,560.90	$91.22	$4,469.68

PAYMENT APPROVED
Helen Northcutt

1. Check that all the documents related to the purchase are present. Often an envelope-type file folder is used to collect all the documents for a payment. A listing of collected documents is placed on the outside of the folder.
2. Prepare the voucher, checking every detail required on the form.
3. Obtain the authorized signature.
4. File the vouchers appropriately. Vouchers typically are filed by the dates on which they must be processed in order to meet the payment due dates. Filing vouchers in this way creates a tickler file—a file that is reviewed daily for the purpose of taking action to clear the items from the file. In companies where the policy is to take all discounts allowed, the voucher is filed in the tickler file by the discount date.

The terms of the voucher in Illustration 7-1:8 are 2/10, n/30. If the invoice is paid within ten days of the invoice date, a 2 percent discount can be taken from the invoice amount. If the invoice is paid after the 10th day and before the 30th day, the full amount of the invoice is paid. If payment is made after the 30th day, a penalty may be applied. Therefore, many businesses try to pay their bills in time to take advantage of the discount and to avoid being charged late fees.

PREPARE CHECKS

If you are responsible for preparing checks for payments due, you should inspect your tickler file daily to retrieve all vouchers for which checks are to be prepared.

In some offices, especially small ones, a checkbook similar to one an individual uses for personal check writing is the source of checks for paying business **obligations.** If you are responsible for writing checks using a checkbook, these suggestions will be helpful:

obligations: legal debts

1. Read carefully the name of the company or individual to whom payment is to be made as well as the amount of the check. If you are writing a check in time to take advantage of a discount, compute the discount using a calculator.
2. Fill in the checkbook stub or the check register. (See Illustration 7-1:9 for the way in which an item is listed in a check register.)

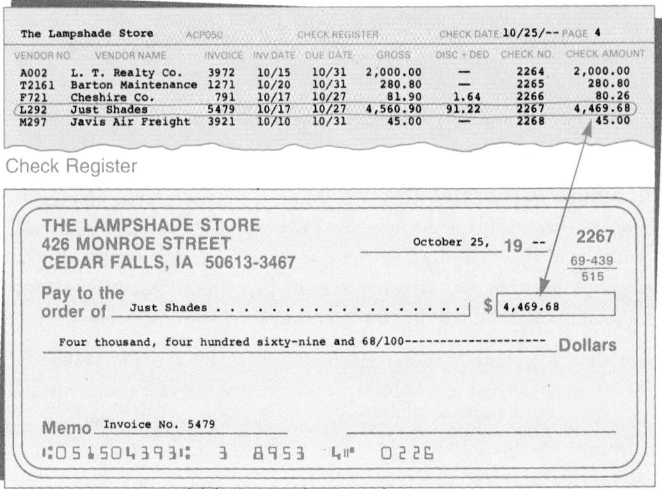

The Lampshade Store ACP050 CHECK REGISTER CHECK DATE 10/25/-- PAGE 4

VENDOR NO.	VENDOR NAME	INVOICE	INV DATE	DUE DATE	GROSS	DISC + DED	CHECK NO.	CHECK AMOUNT
A002	L. T. Realty Co.	3972	10/15	10/31	2,000.00	—	2264	2,000.00
T2161	Barton Maintenance	1271	10/20	10/31	280.80	—	2265	280.80
F721	Cheshire Co.	791	10/17	10/27	81.90	1.64	2266	80.26
L292	Just Shades	5479	10/17	10/27	4,560.90	91.22	2267	4,469.68
M297	Javis Air Freight	3921	10/10	10/31	45.00	—	2268	45.00

Check Register

THE LAMPSHADE STORE
426 MONROE STREET
CEDAR FALLS, IA 50613-3467

October 25, 19 --

2267

69-439
515

Pay to the order of Just Shades $ 4,469.68

Four thousand, four hundred sixty-nine and 68/100 Dollars

Memo Invoice No. 5479

:051504393: 3 8953 4" 0226

Ordinary Check

Illustration 7-1:9

(Top) Check register. (Bottom) Completed check.

Companies put enormous trust in employees who write checks against company funds. This trust must be respected.

Why is the amount of the check written in numbers and in words? Which amount is considered to be the legal amount—the numbers or the words?

3. Prepare the check. (See Illustration 7-1:9.) Note that the amount is written in numbers as well as in words. Notice how the space between the name and the dollar sign and the space between the amount in words and the word "dollars" is filled in so that changes cannot be made easily. Notice that the purpose of the payment is shown on the face of the check on the *Memo* line.

Can you think of a purpose for which a business might use a certified check? a cashier's check? a bank draft?

perforated: having a series of tiny holes for separation

Voucher Checks. Voucher checks are ordinary checks with an additional portion that gives a description of the payment. The two parts are **perforated** so that they can be separated easily. The voucher is detached before the check is deposited. The procedures for preparing voucher checks are the same as those for ordinary checks, except that you also fill in the voucher portion rather than merely indicating the purpose of the check.

Special Checks. From time to time, special checks that provide guarantee of payment are used by businesses.

- **certified check**: An ordinary check that the bank marks "certified" after establishing that the funds are in the account of the party drawing the check. The funds are immediately subtracted from the depositor's account.
- **cashier's check**: A check written by a bank on its own funds. Such a check can be purchased with cash or with an ordinary check.
- **bank draft**: An order drawn by one bank on its deposits in another bank to pay a third party. Such a draft can be purchased with cash or with an ordinary check.

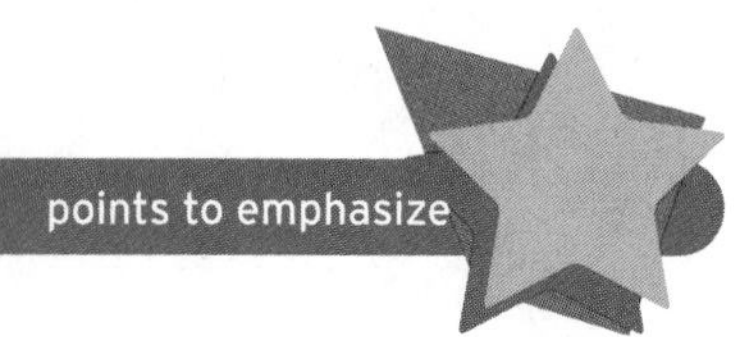

Although accounts payable tasks may be accomplished faster with computers, the accounting clerk must ensure that the data are accurately entered to reap the benefits of the increased processing speed.

Computer-Generated Checks. Many companies use computers to prepare checks. If you are authorized to prepare checks, you likely will be issued a password to access the company's accounts payable system. Security measures are taken to safeguard both the information used to prepare the checks and the printed checks.

Refer to each vendor's file in the accounts payable system to obtain information needed to complete the checks, such as vendor name and address, amount to be paid, and the purpose of payment. Then, by selecting a menu option such as Print Checks, checks will be printed as shown in Illustration 7-1:10.

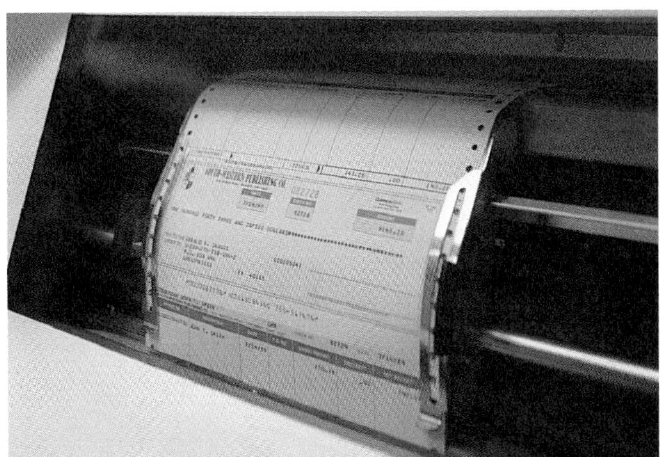

Illustration 7-1:10

Many companies use computer-generated checks such as the ones shown here.

Electronic Funds Transfer

Payments, as well as deposits, can be made electronically. With electronic payments or deposits, there is no physical exchange of currency or checks. Electronic funds transfer (EFT) is the use of a computer and a telecommunications network to transfer funds from one party to another.

Some companies transfer funds electronically to the vendor's bank. The vendor's bank electronically processes the deposit and credits the vendor's account. Also, many companies electronically deposit wage and salary payments to employees' designated banks where the funds are credited to the employees' accounts.

Telecommunication networks make it possible to electronically transfer money to all parts of the world in a matter of minutes. In addition, electronic funds transfers can be accomplished with ATMs and in many stores at the point of sale.

Reconciling a Bank Account

Companies need to be sure that receipts and **disbursements** shown in their records are reflected also in the bank's records. If you have the task of comparing these records, you will need a bank statement as well as your own company's records. This task is called **reconciling** the bank statement balance with the company's cash account records.

disbursements: payments

reconciling: bringing into agreement

Use Illustration 7-1:11 to guide the discussion of a bank statement. Questions might include:

1. What is the overall purpose of this statement?
2. What is the time period covered by this statement? What is the checking account number?
3. What was the customer's beginning balance?
4. What was the document (or documents) that resulted in the bank's recording the deposit of 7/23?
5. Were any checks deposited that did not clear because of insufficient funds?
6. Did the total amounts added to the customer's checking account exceed the amounts deducted from the account?
7. Was there a service charge? If so, how much was it?
8. What is the ending balance?

BANK STATEMENT AND COMPANY RECORDS

Banks send statements that show the activity in each account on a regular basis, usually monthly. As you will note in Illustration 7-1:11, a bank statement gives the following information:

Illustration 7-1:11

Find the beginning and ending account balances on this bank statement.

NECHES BANK
Cincinnati, Ohio

ADLER KNITTING MANUFACTURING CO
658 TEAKWOOD AVENUE
CINCINNATI OH 45224-4578

CHECKING ACCOUNT NUMBER
32921-6

DATE OF STATEMENT
08/31/--

BALANCE FROM PREVIOUS STATEMENT	NUMBER OF + CREDITS	AMOUNT OF DEPOSITS AND CREDITS	NUMBER OF DEBITS	AMOUNT OF WITHDRAWALS AND DEBITS	TOTAL ACTIVITY CHARGE	STATEMENT BALANCE
22,890.75	4	26,962.10	20	29,255.96	25.00	20,596.89

DATE	CODE	TRANSACTION DESCRIPTION	TRANSACTION AMOUNT		ACCOUNT BALANCE
07-22	AW	0248 634	200.00		22,690.75
07-23		DEPOSIT	6,790.40		29,481.15
		CHECK 187	3,750.00		25,731.15
		CHECK 189	1,890.25		23,840.90
07-27	AW	0248 634	2,500.00		21,340.90
07-28		CHECK 190	6,590.70		14,750.20
07-29	PD	RAE'S SWEATER CORNER DEPOSIT	7,980.70		22,730.90
08-03		CHECK 191	3,875.00		18,855.90
08-04		CHECK 192	1,870.70		16,985.20
		CHECK 194	580.90		16,404.30
08-05		CHECK 193	450.00		15,954.30
08-06	AC	OWL DEPOSIT	4,280.90		20,235.20
08-09	AW	0248 634	1,000.00		19,235.20
08-10		CHECK 197	2,975.25		16,259.95
		CHECK 195	1,800.00		14,459.95
08-11		CHECK 196	290.20		14,169.75
08-12	PD	RAE'S SWEATER CORNER DEPOSIT	7,910.10		22,079.85
		CHECK 198	378.28		21,701.57
08-16		CHECK 202	150.50		21,551.07
		CHECK 201	95.70		21,455.37
		CHECK 199	110.98		21,344.39
08-17		CHECK 206	525.00		20,819.39
08-18		NSF CHECK	197.50	NSF	20,621.89
08-19		SERVICE CHARGE	25.00	SC	20,596.89

- the balance as of the opening date of the statement
- checks listed by number and amount that the bank has received and **honored**

honored:
accepted and paid

- automated teller machine transactions and miscellaneous charges
- deposits
- the balance on the closing date of the statement

On the bank statement shown in Illustration 7-1:11, the automated teller transactions are coded AW for ATM withdrawals, AC for ATM deposits and credits, and PD for preauthorized electronic deposits.

In addition to the bank statement, the bank may return **canceled** checks and any *advices* (notices) reporting increases or decreases in the bank balance. Other banks may provide only the statement. Copies of checks that have been **scanned** may be provided upon request.

canceled:
already paid by the bank

scanned:
"read" by electronic equipment into a computer's memory

The *advice* shown in Illustration 7-1:12 reports that a check deposited was returned by the bank on which it was drawn. Because the person writing the check did not have sufficient funds to cover the amount of the check, the check was not honored. Such checks are referred to as *NSF (not sufficient funds)* checks. Illustration 7-1:12 shows that Adler Knitting's balance was reduced by the amount of the check that was not honored.

ADVICE OF CHARGE ☑ Checking (82) ☐ Savings (78) — ADVICE OF CREDIT ☐ Checking (32) ☐ Savings (27)
NECHES BANK — BANK ENTRY
ACCOUNT NUMBER: 32921-6 — AMOUNT: $197.50
YOUR ACCOUNT HAS BEEN ☑ CHARGED ☐ CREDITED
FOR THE REASON DETAILED AT RIGHT →
1. TRANSFER FROM ... TO
2. CORRECTION OF MISPOSTED ☐ DEPOSIT ☐ CHECK
3. MONEY MARKET
4. INSTALLMENT LOAN ACCOUNT #
5. REFUND FOR:
6. STOP PAYMENT FEE
✓ 7. OTHER insufficient funds
NAME AND ADDRESS
Adler Knitting Manufacturing Co.
658 Teakwood Avenue
Cincinnati, OH 45224-4578
DATE 8/18/-- — AUTHORIZED APPROVAL *Lisa Olmstead* — BR #
⑆04 20004 24⑆

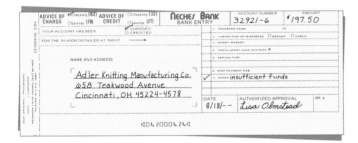

Illustration 7-1:12
This advice informs the depositor (Adler Knitting) that a customer's check for $197.50 was returned.

Generally, there are no documents included that relate to automatic teller machine (ATM) transactions. These are deposits and withdrawals made at electronic machines. Keep the slips generated at the time these transactions are made. They provide your receipt of the transaction.

To complete the reconciliation, you will need the company's checkbook or check register, which records all checks written and all deposits made. You also will need last month's reconciliation.

expand the concept

Provide students with a statement from a local bank. Compare and contrast the presentation of codes for ATM transactions, service charges, listing of canceled checks, and beginning and ending balances.

thinking critically

What is the purpose of an advice? How will the company use the information provided in the advice?

PURPOSES FOR RECONCILIATION

Cash is a valuable resource for all business organizations. It is important, therefore, to know the exact status of the cash account. A monthly reconciliation is completed to:

- determine that all deposits made have been recorded by the bank, as indicated on the bank statement
- verify that all the checks that cleared the bank were written by authorized persons in the company
- determine which checks have not yet cleared the bank
- identify additional bank charges, as indicated on the bank statement, that need to be recorded in the books of the company
- determine the cash balance as of the date of the bank statement

STEPS IN PREPARING A RECONCILIATION

The company in which you work will have an established procedure for preparing bank reconciliations. You will want to learn these specific procedures.

Assume that you are working in an office where a bank statement is received monthly and a reconciliation is prepared at that time. The steps described here are likely to be similar to the ones you will learn on the job:

1. Compare the ending balance on last month's bank reconciliation with the beginning balance on this month's bank statement. Under normal circumstances, these two balances will be identical. If there is a difference, record the two figures on a sheet of paper. Investigate any differences before completing the reconciliation.
2. Record on your reconciliation worksheet the balance in your check register as of the last day of the month. (See Illustration 7-1:13.)
3. Record the ending balance as shown on the bank statement.
4. Compare each deposit shown on the bank statement with the deposits recorded on the check register.

points to emphasize

Keeping neat, accurate records and following established procedures will mean fewer problems encountered in preparing a bank reconciliation.

Adler Knitting Manufacturing Co. Reconciliation of Bank Statement August 31, 19__			
Balance in check register		Balance on bank	
August 31, 19__	18711 50	Statement, August 31, 19__	20596 89
Deduct:		Add:	
Service Charge 25.00		Deposit in Transit	
NSF 197.50	222 50	August 30, 19__	2851 10
		Total	23447 99
		Deduct:	
		Outstanding Checks	
		No. 188 198.70	
		No. 200 110.10	
		No. 203 347.29	
		No. 204 82.50	
		No. 205 4220.40	4958 99
Adjusted check stub		Adjusted bank balance	
balance, August 31, 19__	18489 00	August 31, 19__	18489 00

Illustration 7-1:13

Preparation of a bank reconciliation worksheet will help determine the exact status of the cash account.

- Put a small check mark in both places if the amount and date agree.
- Record on your worksheet any deposits shown in the check register that are not on the bank statement. Deposits made near the end of the month are not likely to have been processed by the bank by the date of the statement. Such deposits are referred to as *deposits in transit*.

5. Arrange in numeric order the checks returned with the bank statement. (Skip this step if it is not the bank's policy to return checks.)
6. Compare the amount of each check with that shown on the bank statement. Use small check marks by the items on the statement to show that there is agreement. Record any differences noted. Follow up on any discrepancies before preparing your final reconciliation.
7. Compare each canceled check with related information in the check register. Place a small check mark in the register if there is agreement. (See Illustration 7-1:14 on page 320.)

expand the concept

Reproduce copies of a reconciliation form provided by a local bank. Guide the students in completing the form with details shown on the chalkboard or on an overhead projector. Use the following questions to be sure students understand the sources of the figures:

1. Where do you find the beginning balance?
2. Where are deposits recorded?
3. Where is the record of checks written?
4. Where do you find charges for checks or automatic teller transaction fees?
5. If your ending balance differs from the balance on the bank statement, what may be the reason(s) for the difference?
6. What steps may lead to reconciling the two balances?

What is the status of check #188 on this check register?

If related computer software is available, have the students set up a reconciliation statement using the data from the bank statement in Illustration 7-1:11.

Illustration 7-1:14

One item on this check register does not have a check mark. What is the status of check #188?

PLEASE BE SURE TO DEDUCT ANY PER CHECK CHARGES OR MAINTENANCE CHARGES THAT AFFECT YOUR ACCOUNT

ITEM NO.	DATE	PAYMENT ISSUED TO OR DESCRIPTION OF DEPOSIT	AMOUNT OF PAYMENT	✓	AMOUNT OF DEPOSIT OR INTEREST	BALANCE FORWARD	
							28681 15
187	7/17	To Taylor Brothers For	3750 00	✓		Payment or Deposit Balance	3750 00 24931 15
188	7/18	To Elman and Stone Co. For	198 70			Payment or Deposit Balance	198 70 24732 45
189	7/18	To Marshall Gomez For	1890 25	✓		Payment or Deposit Balance	1890 25 22842 20
190	7/25	To Leitz Mfg. Co. For	6590 70	✓		Payment or Deposit Balance	6590 70 16251 50
	7/29	To Deposit For		✓	7980 70	Payment or Deposit Balance	7980 70 24232 20
191	8/1	To Yarns, International For	3875 00	✓		Payment or Deposit Balance	3875 00 20357 20

8. Record on your worksheet the number, date, and amount for each check that was written but had not cleared as of the bank statement date. These checks are referred to as *outstanding checks*. The total of the outstanding checks will be subtracted from the bank statement balance.

9. Review last month's outstanding checks as listed on the bank reconciliation to determine which ones are still outstanding. List these on your worksheet also.

10. Record on your worksheet any charges shown on the statement that are not recorded in your company's records. For example, any checks returned for insufficient funds (NSF checks) must be subtracted from the balance in your check register. Bank charges, such as ATM fees, also must be subtracted.

11. Complete the computations required on your worksheet. Note that the two balances are the same in the reconciliation shown in Illustration 7-1:13. Having the same balances means that your cash account has been properly reconciled.

12. Prepare a clean, correct copy of the bank reconciliation. Print the reconciliation on plain paper or use the reconciliation form provided on the back of the bank statement.

When you have completed a bank reconciliation, obtain any required approval signatures. Once the reconciliation is approved, file it so that it can be readily retrieved. When you receive the next bank statement, you will refer back to this completed reconciliation to determine which checks were outstanding and should be in the next batch of canceled checks.

Recordkeeping tasks in many large offices are computerized. Therefore, you may use a computer and software to prepare a bank reconciliation worksheet. The advantage of an electronic reconciliation is that the program automatically makes all calculations.

Maintaining a Petty Cash Fund

There are occasions in many offices when cash is needed to pay for small expenditures, such as delivery services, postage due, and taxi fares. To facilitate such payments, departments are given a small sum of money, which is called a **petty cash fund.** Amounts in such funds can range from $20 to as much as $1,000.

In the office of a small insurance broker, a petty cash fund of $75 is maintained to pay for taxis and special delivery services needed from time to time.

The sales office of a women's fashion manufacturing company has a petty cash fund of $500, primarily to provide money for lunch ordered at a local coffee shop for visiting buyers and for late dinners when staff members must work or entertain major buyers from around the world.

ESTABLISHING THE FUND

The department head establishes how much money is to be maintained in the petty cash fund. Once this amount is approved by the officer responsible for payments, a check is written payable to **Petty Cashier,** the person in charge of the petty cash fund. This check may be cashed by the company cashier in the treasurer's office or at the bank. The petty cashier will keep the cash in a locked cash box. Only the petty cashier has access to the key.

In some organizations, petty cash funds are maintained in a separate checking account. However, the discussion here will be limited to a

for discussion

1. What are the qualities needed by a petty cashier?
2. Why is each quality important?
3. Would you like to be a petty cashier? Why?

cash box system only. Regardless of the petty cash system used, the petty cashier must adhere to the highest ethical behavior as he or she makes payments from the fund and maintains appropriate records.

MAKING PAYMENTS

To assure control of funds, records must be maintained for all disbursements from petty cash. The petty cashier keeps a complete and accurate record for every payment made from the cashbox. Petty cash receipt forms are filled out each time cash is given out. Here is a procedure that is commonly followed in offices:

reimbursement: payment for an outlay of cash already made

1. Ask each person who seeks **reimbursement** to submit a sales slip, statement, or receipt that indicates what was purchased, what the price was, and that payment was made. Generally, reimbursement should not be made without some kind of document. Occasionally, cash payments are made even though no sales slip, statement, or receipt is provided. On such occasions, the employee being reimbursed should present a brief memo describing what was spent and the purpose of the expenditure.
2. Prepare a petty cash receipt for each reimbursement and ask the person who will receive the cash to sign the receipt. Note the receipt shown in Illustration 7-1:15. It indicates the amount paid out, to whom payment is made, and the purpose of the payment.

Why should a receipt be issued for each disbursement from the petty cash fund?

Illustration 7-1:15

What is the value of a petty cash receipt issued for each reimbursement from the petty cash fund?

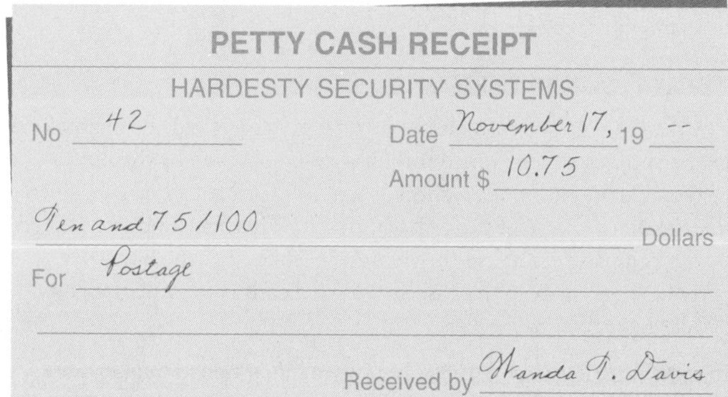

PETTY CASH RECEIPT

HARDESTY SECURITY SYSTEMS

No 42 Date November 17, 19 --

Amount $ 10.75

Ten and 75/100 Dollars

For Postage

Received by Wanda T. Davis

3. Attach the sales slip or other document to the receipt and place these papers in the cash box.

KEEPING A RECORD

In offices where many transactions require petty cash, an organized record is justified. In some departments, a *petty cash book* is maintained for recording receipts and disbursements. A page from such a record is shown in Illustration 7-1:16. Note the headings of the columns under which the expenditures are recorded. In each office the same types of expenditures are likely to occur again and again. However, the column headings for your office may be different from the ones shown here. By classifying the expenses as indicated in Illustration 7-1:17 on page 324, the task of preparing a report at the end of the month or at the point when the fund must be **replenished** will be simplified.

replenished:
restored to original level

MONTH OF November, 19__ PETTY CASH RECORD PAGE 12

Date		Explanation	Petty Cash Form No.	Receipts	Payments	Distribution of Payments: Art Supplies	Books/Other Publications	Messenger Services	Office Supplies	Taxi/Bus Fees	Postal Services	Miscellaneous
Nov.	1	Balance		25000								
	6	Books	39		1295		1295					
	8	Taxi	40		850					850		
	8	Office Supplies	41		770				770			
	11	Postage	42		1075						1075	
	14	Messenger	43		645			645				
	17	Art Supplies	44		1250	1250						
	18	Art Supplies	45		3015	3015						
	19	Books	46		1875		1875					
	19	Messenger	47		1420			1420				
	20	Office Supplies	48		1050				1050			
	20	Art Supplies	49		660	660						
	21	Taxi	50		2190					2190		
	21	Office Supplies	51		970				970			
	21	Messenger	52		1455			1455				
	22	Taxi	53		1040					1040		
	23	Taxi	54		1170					1170		
	24	Taxi	55		1635					1635		
	24	Postage	56		1145						1145	
	27	Miscellaneous	57		1210							1210
		Totals		25000	24720	4925	3170	3520	2790	6885	2220	1210
		Cash Balance			280							
		Totals		25000	25000							
	30	Cash Balance		280								
	30	REPLENISHED FUND # 3721		24720								

Illustration 7-1:16

In the petty cash record pictured here, what was the purpose for the expenditure reimbursed most often?

What category had the highest amount of expenditures reimbursed?

Why are expenditures classified and summarized? How is the summary information recorded in the accounting system?

Illustration 7-1:17

This petty cash summary report answers the question: "For what purposes were funds used?"

PETTY CASH SUMMARY REPORT
November 1 to November 30, 19--

Balance, November 1		$250.00
Expenditures:		
Art Supplies	$49.25	
Books/Other Publications	$31.70	
Delivery Services	$35.20	
Office Supplies	$27.90	
Taxi Fees	$68.85	
Postal Services	$22.20	
Miscellaneous	$12.10	
Total Expenditures		$247.20
Balance, November 30		$2.80

REPLENISHING THE FUND

You will need to note the amount of cash in your cash box and to replenish your fund according to established company procedures. In some offices, the fund is replenished when a certain balance is reached. In others, the fund is restored to its original amount at the end of each month regardless of the level of funds.

In the process of replenishing the fund, you also will prepare a summary report of the expenditures. Here is a procedure that is commonly used in offices:

1. Count the money in the cash box.
2. Total the columns in the petty cash book. (See Illustration 7-1:16.)
3. Total the receipts in the petty cash box.
4. Compare the petty cash box total to the petty cash receipts total. They should be the same. If they are not, determine why there is a difference. Did you fail to include a receipt in your total? Did someone fail to turn in a receipt?
5. Add the amount of the petty cash receipts to the amount of petty cash remaining in the cashbox, as in the following example:

   Petty cash on hand $2.80
   Petty cash receipts $247.20
   Total of petty cash fund $250.00

The total, in this case $250, should equal the amount of petty cash you had when you last balanced and/or replenished the petty cash fund.

6. Investigate any discrepancy. Careful attention to managing the petty cash fund will result in few, if any, discrepancies. If, after your investigation, you find that you are over or short by a few pennies, note this difference in your calculation. For example, if in Step 2 you found only $2.75 in cash, your calculation would indicate:

   Cash on hand $2.75
   Receipts $247.20
   Cash short $.05
   Total $250.00

   You also will indicate the *shortage* (the missing amount for which there is no explanation) in your summary report.
7. Prepare a report of the activity in the petty cash fund for the period beginning with the last replenishment or the last time you balanced the records. Note the portion of the report shown in Illustration 7-1:17.
8. Prepare a request for a check for the amount of the receipts plus any shortage (or minus any *overage*).
9. Submit your report, the accompanying receipts, and your request for a replenishment check for approval.
10. Once approved, follow up by sending a copy of the report to the accounting department and by sending the request for a check to the proper office.
11. Exchange the check for cash in the treasurer's office or at a local bank. Immediately place the cash in the cash box.

COMPUTERIZED PETTY CASH RECORDS

You may work in an office where all petty cash records are maintained electronically. If you use a financial software package to record petty cash transactions, enter the beginning balance when the fund is established, funds paid out, explanation of expenditures, and petty cash receipt numbers. When a summary report is needed, you will be able to generate one by using the appropriate software commands. Attention to detail and keying all data accurately are critical when maintaining petty cash records.

Role-play petty cash fund procedures to give students the confidence to handle different and varying requests for small outlays of cash in the office from various levels of employees. The "Interacting with Others" activity at the end of this topic could be used for role playing.

Reviewing the Topic

topic 7-1
review

1. What is included in the general category referred to as cash?
2. In processing incoming checks, what tasks generally are handled by the cashier?
3. Explain why a company might bond an employee.
4. How does a blank endorsement differ from a restrictive endorsement?
5. What is the function of a voucher?
6. What is an EFT?
7. Why is a deposit slip prepared?
8. What information is included on a bank statement?
9. Why is a bank account reconciliation completed?
10. Why are departments given petty cash funds?

INTERACTING WITH OTHERS

Assume that you are the cashier for the petty cash fund in your department. The fund is maintained at $1,000 because of the many small payments that must be made during the month. One Wednesday, shortly after the fund had been replenished, one of your friends in the department says to you: "I certainly didn't budget my money very well this week; I'm down to my last $5. You know that I'm dependable. Would you let me borrow $25 from the petty cash fund? You have almost $1,000 just lying there! And if I had only $25, I'd be able to take care of my expenses until Friday, which is payday."

You wonder why your friend didn't plan better. You know that you can depend on him or her to repay the fund as soon as paychecks are distributed in two days.

What you are to do:

Explain what you would do if you were faced with the situation described above. Give the reasons for your actions.

topic 7-1 review

Cash and Banking Procedures

326

REINFORCING MATH SKILLS

Your tasks include opening the mail and making a list of all checks received. Below is the list of checks you made as you opened the mail. These checks will be deposited later in one of two banks. The checks from Mills, Olsen Corp., Yaroff Bros., Susi & Karlin, Rice Corp., Caputa & Zinn, and Prevetti Co. are deposited at the Penn Avenue Bank; the remaining checks are deposited at the Smithfield Bank.

What you are to do:

1. Find the total of the amounts of all checks received.
2. Determine what the total deposit would be at the Penn Avenue Bank.
3. Determine what the total deposit would be at the Smithfield Bank.

Receipts 10/15/—

L.T. Mills	4200.50	Rice Corp.	781.18
Olsen Corp.	7592.70	Rabinowitz & Sons	2768.71
Mars, Linwood & Co	2540.15	Caputa & Zinn	848.88
Gomes & Co.	985.40	Beilens, Lutz & Co	129.50
Yaroff Bros.	1975.95	Prevetti Co.	8912.50
O'Brien & Wickes	3791.21	Jay F. Sterling	819.19
Susi & Karlin	7297.45	W. N. Neeley	7819.12

APPLICATION ACTIVITY

ACTIVITY **Reconciliation of Statement**

You work in the office of the cashier. You have been given a Reconciliation of Statement form and the bank statement for the month ending October 31. You have checked all the deposits and all the checks shown on the statement. You also have compared the checks returned with your check register. Your worksheet shows the following information:

The bank statement balance is $4,467.03.
The check register balance, before adjustment, is $3,560.58.

327

Cash and Banking Procedures

One deposit is in transit for $1,256.50.

The following checks are outstanding: #457 for $356.76, #481 for $125.00, #482 for $890.65, and #483 for $790.54.

What you are to do:

Prepare a bank reconciliation using the information above. Create the reconciliation using spreadsheet software or the form provided in your *Student Activities and Projects* workbook.

See Workbook page 35.

topic 7-1 review

328

Topic 7-2

Financial Reports and Payroll

When you have completed your study of this topic, you will be able to:

- **explain the purpose of a budget, income statement, and balance sheet**
- **participate in preparing a budget, income statement, and balance sheet**
- **explain concepts and procedures related to payroll payments**

The success of any business rests largely on how well the **resources** of the business are managed. Businesses use financial reports to aid in the management process. Financial management begins with the preparation of an annual budget and ends with the issuance of financial statements. Budgets represent the financial decisions made about resource allocations and are typically prepared for a 12-month period. Businesses report their financial progress through financial statements such as the income statement and the balance sheet. Investors and lenders use these reports to make judgments about the financial health of the business.

resources: property, goods, or wealth

In this topic, you will be introduced to common financial reports—budgets, income statements, and balance sheets. Additionally, you will learn about concepts and procedures related to payments for wages and salaries.

Gather copies of business and financial reports for students to review. Use these reports as references as you discuss and interpret various financial documents. Encourage your students to bring copies of business reports from home if their parents receive such reports. Your public library is also a possible source of such reports. Ask students why a business needs a financial plan. Is a financial plan less important to a smaller firm than to a larger firm? Why?

Why is it important to have a reasonable budget for employees to follow?

Financial Reports

Many reports relate to financial aspects of businesses. Some financial reports, such as budgets, are typically for internal use only. Others are provided to those outside the company, including shareholders in publicly owned corporations. Financial statements provide information about a company's financial status and results of operations. Publicly owned companies must provide financial statements to shareholders at the end of each quarter and at the end of the **fiscal** year.

fiscal: period for financial recordkeeping

In this section you will examine commonly prepared financial reports—budgets, income statements, and balance sheets. You will also be given guidelines for preparing these important financial documents (also known as *financial statements*).

BUDGETS

A budget is a financial plan for allocating business resources for the coming year. In a small business, much of the budget planning and control is handled directly by the owner. In a large business, many people will provide information and suggestions about needs for resources in their departments. Preparing a budget for the coming year is a critical task. All employees are affected by the budget whether or not they actively participate in the budget process.

Planning the Budget. Typically, the budget process begins with a review of last year's data to determine past expenses. The purpose of reviewing the financial history of a business is to prepare a budget with **attainable** goals.

attainable: reachable

To determine attainable goals, managers use documents such as financial statements, tax returns, summary worksheets, and income and expense reports from previous years. In addition to the financial data from the business, budget preparers often use statistical and financial references to determine financial **ratios** and industry averages that may be useful in projecting budget figures. Many of these references are available in local libraries.

ratio: proportion of one quantity to another

cycle: completion of a series and return to the starting point

Monitoring the Budget. The budget is generally developed for an annual **cycle.** Budgets for shorter periods are developed from the annual budget. As the year progresses, budget performance reports are **generated** that compare the money spent in each category to the budgeted amount. Budget performance reports are typically prepared monthly or quarterly. If expenses in any category are too high, steps are taken to limit spending. Consider the example below.

generated:
produced, prepared

Pitzer Corporation budgeted $15,000 for staff training and development for the year. More training than anticipated was needed in the new order entry and inventory software. By August 1, $12,750 of the $15,000 budgeted had been spent. As a means of controlling this budget item, Greg Tapier, Vice President of Human Resources, issued a memo stating that all staff training for the remainder of the year must receive his prior approval as well as the usual approval from the department head.

A periodic (monthly or quarterly) budget performance report is often combined with a year-to-date budget report. The year-to-date report shows the amount spent in each category from the beginning of the budget cycle to the date the report was prepared.

Combining both a periodic and a year-to-date report provides a better view of expenses as they relate to the entire budget cycle. Some expenses, such as insurance or taxes, for example, may be paid quarterly. When the payment is made, the amount of the payment may be larger than the monthly or quarterly budgeted amount. Yet the payment may be within the total amount allotted annually. An example of a budget performance report for Dandy's Delights is shown in Illustration 7-2:1 on page 332.

Preparing the Budget. Procedures for preparing the budget will depend upon the size and nature of the business. In businesses large enough to have several units, many employees may be involved in planning the budget. Budget preparation often begins at the departmental level. Department heads and members may keep notes during the year about where they believe additional funding will be needed or where funds could be reduced during the next budget period. If you participate in the budget process, these suggestions will be helpful to you:

1. Learn all you can about the company's budget process including the forms used, data needed, terminology, documentation needed for requests, and deadlines.

What budget categories need to be reviewed based upon this budget performance report?

Illustration 7-2:1

The monthly budget report shows actual and budgeted expenses.

DANDY'S DELIGHTS
BUDGET PERFORMANCE REPORT
For the Month Ending June 30, 19xx

June Actual	June Budget	Variance Fav. (Unfav.)	Variance %	Category	Year-to-Date Actual	Year-to-Date Budget	Year-to-Date Variance Fav. (Unfav.)	Variance %
				Operating Expenses				
$4,850	$4,850	$0	0.0%	Salaries	$29,100	$29,100	$0	0.0%
1125	375	(750)	−200.0%	Payroll Taxes	2250	2250	0	0.0%
45	42	(3)	-7.1%	Advertising	245	250	5	2.0%
210	42	(168)	−400.0%	Delivery	610	250	(360)	−144.0%
60	67	7	10.4%	Office Supplies	395	400	5	1.3%
280	333	53	15.9%	Utilities	1400	2000	600	30.0%
35	42	7	16.7%	Miscellaneous	255	250	(5)	−2.0%
$6,605	$5,751	($854)	−14.8%	Total Expenses	$34,255	$34,500	$245	0.7%

2. Begin the preparation of your *preliminary* budget as soon as the budget information and instructions are received. You will often receive some guidelines, such as an overall 10 percent increase or decrease anticipated in expenses. Use your financial records to help you determine what effect such guidelines will have on your unit.
3. Consider the department's needs in relation to the company financial priorities for the coming year. How does your department contribute to current and proposed priorities?
4. Collect data to support your requests such as the costs for installation of a new telephone system. Information about other companies' success with the equipment you are requesting is often useful to those who review budget requests.
5. Realize that budgets are reviewed by company executives at various levels. There is generally communication up and down the organization during the budget preparation. The company's overall goals and limited resources are considered in making the final budget decisions.
6. Once final budget figures have been given to you, prepare a document showing your unit's final budget figures. Your final budget is actually the company's approval for your unit's work and for the resources to do that job for the coming year.

Assume you are preparing budget suggestions for the first time in your new job. How would you begin to develop your preliminary budget requests?

INCOME STATEMENTS

An income statement is a financial report that details the results of operations for a certain period of time. It answers the question, "How successful was the business during the time period?" In this report you will find **revenues,** expenses, and the income or loss of a business for the reporting period.

revenues: earnings realized for goods and services

The income statement lists the amounts and sources of revenues, as well as expenses, for the reporting period. A *net income* results if revenues are greater than expenses. A *net loss* results if expenses are greater than revenues. This equation expresses the formula for income:

Income = Revenues − Expenses

Dandy's Delights' (a single **proprietorship**) income statement for the recently ended fiscal year is shown in Illustration 7-2:2.

proprietorship: legal ownership

Illustration 7-2:2

An income statement reflects the results of operating the company during a specific time period.

DANDY'S DELIGHTS
INCOME STATEMENT
For Year Ended December 31, 19xx

Sales		$200,000
Cost of Goods Sold	100,000	
Gross Profit on Sales		$100,000
Operating Expenses		
Advertising Expense	$500	
Delivery Expense	1,000	
Office Supplies Expense	800	
Payroll Taxes Expense	4,500	
Salaries Expense	58,200	
Utilities Expense	3,500	
Miscellaneous Expense	500	
Total Operating Expense		69,000
Net Income from Operations		$31,000
Other Expense		
Interest Income		2,000
Net Income Before Income Tax		$29,000
Less Income Tax		8,200
Net Income After Income Tax		$20,800

Samantha is the office assistant to Dan Burls, the owner of Dandy's Delights. Mr. Burls's cookies and baked goods are sold in most local supermarkets, and he is planning to expand soon into nearby towns. One of Samantha's duties is to prepare the financial statements. These statements will be used to help secure funds for expansion.

Illustration 7-2:3

A balance sheet represents the financial condition of a company as of a specific date.

DANDY'S DELIGHTS
BALANCE SHEET
For Year Ended December 31, 19xx

Assets			
Current Assets			
Cash		$12,000	
Accounts Receivable		3,500	
Baking Supplies Inventory		2,000	
Office Supplies		500	
Total Current Assets			$ 18,000
Fixed Assets			
Delivery Van		$ 7,000	
Baking Equipment		5,000	
Building and Land		95,000	
Total Fixed Assets			107,000
Total Assets			$125,000
Liabilities			
Current Liabilities			
Notes Payable		$ 1,500	
Accounts Payable		1,000	
Salary and Wages Payable		200	
Total Current Liabilities			$ 2,700
Fixed Liabilities			
Long-term Note Payable		$ 5,000	
Mortgage Payable		35,000	
Total Fixed Liabilities			40,000
Total Liabilities			$42,700
Owner's Equity			
Dan Burls, Capital January 1, 19xx		$63,500	
Net Income for 19xx	$20,800		
Less Withdrawals	2,000	18,800	
Dan Burls, Capital December 31, 19xx			82,300
Total Liabilities and Owner's Equity			$125,000

BALANCE SHEETS

A balance sheet is a report that presents the financial condition of a company as of a specific date. The balance sheet reports the assets, liabilities, and owner's equity or capital. The *assets* of a company include all the goods and property owned by the firm as well as the amounts due the company from others. *Liabilities* are the debts of the company—what the company owes. The owner's equity or *capital* is the owner's share or the worth of the firm—the difference between assets and liabilities.

On every balance sheet, the total assets must equal the total liabilities plus the owner's equity. Thus, the accounting formula shown below applies to every balance sheet, whether the balance sheet is for a giant corporation or a small, individually owned business.

Assets (A) = Liabilities (L) + Owner's Equity (E)

FORMATTING FINANCIAL DOCUMENTS

When you are responsible for keying and formatting financial documents such as budgets, income statements, and balance sheets, study earlier copies of the documents. If possible, use the same formats as in the previous documents. Continuing to use the same formats allows easier comparison of data from year to year. Such guidelines may be included in a company's procedures manual.

Although the financial statement formats may vary, the following format guidelines represent the generally accepted style of presenting financial statements in the absence of any company standards:

- Leave at least a one-inch margin at the top and bottom and on both sides.
- Center the lines in the statement heading—company name, statement name, and the date(s) covered by the statement.
- Double-space before and after headings in the body of the statement.
- Use a single line (extending the width of the longest item in the column) keyed underneath the last figure to indicate addition or subtraction.

expand the concept

The annual or quarterly reports of corporations provide examples of how businesses actually report financial conditions and results of business activities. In addition, the annual report is now considered a means of educating the reader about many other aspects of the business, such as its managers and leaders, the mission of the business, product changes, and new subsidiaries.

expand the concept

If you have business reports available, have students review them for different report formats. In what ways are the formats the same? different? Why?

- Use double lines underneath the final figure in a column.
- Use the dollar sign with the first figure of each new column of figures to be added or subtracted or with every sum or difference if the figure is keyed directly underneath a single line.

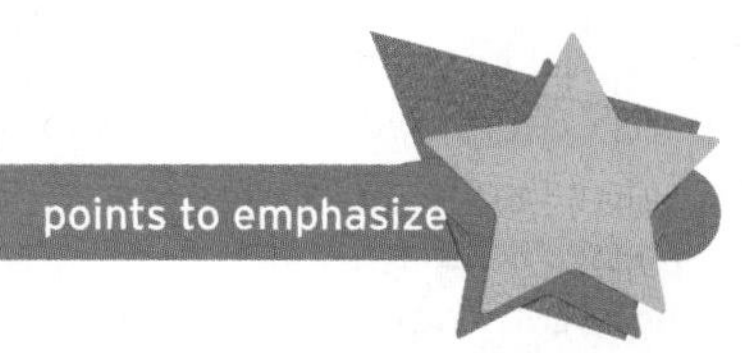

Proofread copy slowly and carefully. Give attention to detail. When working with numbers you calculated manually, recalculate all totals.

transposing: changing the order of

prove: check the correctness of

Proofread the documents carefully, even if you have used a computer to prepare the statements. Give attention to detail. If another worker is available to help you, proofreading can be made easier with one person reading aloud from the original document while the other person proofreads the prepared copy. In addition to the words and figures, the person reading aloud should indicate details such as capitalization, punctuation, underscores, vertical spacing, indentions, and dollar signs. Be particularly alert to **transposing** figures (for example, keying $1,245,385 for $1,254,385). As a final proof, recalculate or **prove** all totals and compare them with the original. If you are using a computer software program to prepare the statement, check the accuracy of any formulas used in the statement.

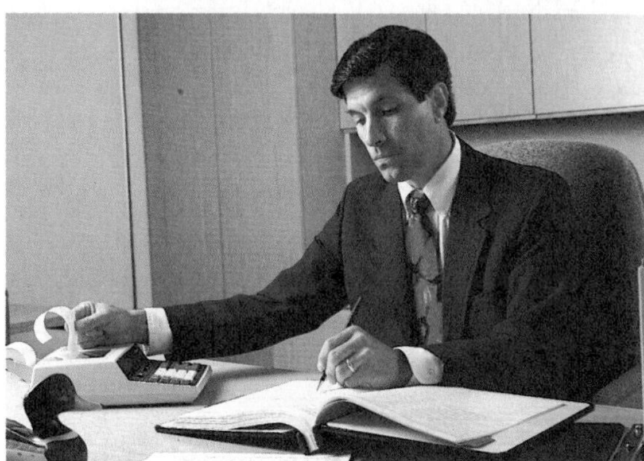

Illustration 7-2:4
Carefully check financial documents and prove all totals.

Payments for Wages and Salaries

Typically, the processing of earnings is the responsibility of the payroll department. The procedures used within the payroll department will vary depending upon the size of the workforce and the degree to which the recordkeeping is automated. However, common tasks completed by the payroll department include:

- ensuring that employee payroll records are kept up to date
- using special software to automatically figure deductions and changes in salary, commissions, or overtime
- updating attendance, vacation, and sick leave data
- processing, printing, and distributing paychecks
- creating tax reports that must be submitted to local, state, and federal agencies

Some companies use time and attendance recording systems where employees register their attendance at a computer terminal. Attendance data goes directly into the company's computerized payroll system.

Payroll employees understand that it is extremely important to be accurate and to keep salary information confidential. By following standard procedures, carefully verifying their work, and maintaining orderly records, payroll employees help ensure accurate employee records.

COMPENSATION PLANS

In some companies, all employees are **compensated** in the same way. In other companies, however, several different plans may be used for different groups of workers. The typical ones include salary, hourly, commission, and combination plans.

compensated: paid

Salary. Under this plan, the employee is paid an amount that is quoted on a weekly, monthly, or yearly basis. The gross salary, which is the salary before any deductions, is the figure quoted. A salary quoted on a yearly basis is **subdivided** into the number of pay periods per year. Thus, a person who earns $22,000 yearly and is paid twice each month will have a gross salary of $916.67 each pay period.

subdivided: separated into several parts

Hourly. In some jobs, employees are paid on the basis of a **wage** rate per hour. The hourly rate applies to the hours considered standard. The standard workweek may be 35, 37½, or 40 hours. When workers paid on an hourly basis work more hours than those specified as their

wage: payment based on number of hours worked

Determine an amount to be paid to each student for each day spent in class. Then keep a payroll register during one week or month. Require students to sign in at the beginning of each class and sign out at the end. Issue simulated voucher checks and have students verify payments and deductions.

overtime:
hours worked over the standard work week

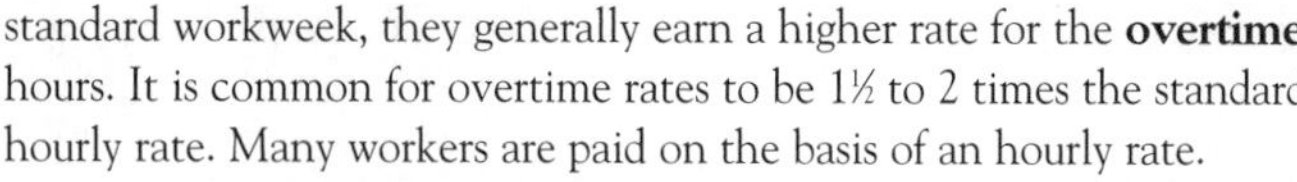

standard workweek, they generally earn a higher rate for the **overtime** hours. It is common for overtime rates to be 1½ to 2 times the standard hourly rate. Many workers are paid on the basis of an hourly rate.

Illustration 7-2:5
This employee works a standard 40-hour week and is paid an hourly rate.

for discussion

What kinds of jobs might be paid on a salary basis? on an hourly basis? on a commission basis? On which basis would you prefer to be paid? Why?

Commission. Some workers' earnings are based on a percentage of the value of what they sell or process. The percentage may vary by volume of sales or amount of production. This method is commonly used for the payment of sales representatives. For example, sales representatives of a computer supplies company are assigned territories to service. Since their earnings depend on the sales they generate, they are motivated to please customers and secure new orders. For example, if the salesperson earns a 10 percent commission on each sale, a $1,000 dollar order would result in a $100 commission.

Combination Plans. In some jobs, a combination plan is used. For example, a commission, referred to as a *bonus*, may be given to employees who are successful beyond some established standard. Such a bonus is often a percentage of additional sales or production. For example, a salesperson may earn a weekly salary of $500 plus a 5 percent commission on weekly sales exceeding $5,000. If sales for the week were $8,000, the salesperson would earn $500 in salary plus $150 ($3,000 × 5%) in commission for a total of $650.

DEDUCTIONS FROM EARNINGS

As you have learned, salaries and wages are quoted at their gross figures, which is before any **deductions** are considered. The earnings actually received will be less than the gross wages or salaries. Some payroll deductions are required by law; others are voluntary as requested by the employee.

deductions: items that reduce gross pay

Deductions Required by Law. Deductions required by law include the following:

- federal income tax
- Federal Insurance Contributions Act tax (referred to as *FICA* or *social security tax*)
- state income tax (where applicable)
- city income tax (where applicable)

Federal income tax deductions vary depending on gross amount of wages or salary, the employee's marital status, and the number of **exemptions** claimed. Each employee must complete a Withholding Allowance Certificate (known as a W-4 form), which is kept on file by the employing company. The employee is responsible for notifying the human resources department of any changes in the number of exemptions. Illustration 7-2:6 is an example of a W-4 form.

exemptions: withholding allowances

FICA deductions are a percentage of gross wages or salary, up to the maximum amount of wages or salary taxed. The employee's contribution

Cut here and give the certificate to your employer. Keep the top portion for your records.

Form **W-4** Department of the Treasury Internal Revenue Service — **Employee's Withholding Allowance Certificate** — ▶ For Privacy Act and Paperwork Reduction Act Notice, see reverse. — OMB No. 1545-0010

1 Type or print your first name and middle initial / Last name: Jeffrey C. Hunter
2 Your social security number: 321-22-4697
Home address (number and street or rural route): 45 Newland Place
City or town, state, and ZIP code: Matawan, NJ 07747-6321
3 Marital Status: Single ✓Married Married, but withhold at higher Single rate.
Note: *If married, but legally separated, or spouse is a nonresident alien, check the Single box.*
4 Total number of allowances you are claiming (from line G above or from the Worksheets on back if they apply) .... 4 | 1
5 Additional amount, if any, you want deducted from each pay .... 5 | $ —
6 I claim exemption from withholding and I certify that I meet **ALL** of the following conditions for exemption:
• Last year I had a right to a refund of **ALL** Federal income tax withheld because I had **NO** tax liability; **AND**
• This year I expect a refund of **ALL** Federal income tax withheld because I expect to have **NO** tax liability; **AND**
• This year if my income exceeds $500 and includes nonwage income, another person cannot claim me as a dependent.
If you meet all of the above conditions, enter the year effective and "EXEMPT" here .... ▶ 6 | 19
7 Are you a full-time student? (**Note:** *Full-time students are not automatically exempt.*) .... 7 Yes No
Under penalties of perjury, I certify that I am entitled to the number of withholding allowances claimed on this certificate or entitled to claim exempt status
Employee's signature ▶ Jeffrey C. Hunter Date ▶ July 5, 19 --
8 Employer's name and address (Employer: Complete 8 and 10 only if sending to IRS): Modern Software, Inc. 29 Exchange Place New York, NY 10038-0630
9 Office code (optional)
10 Employer identification number

Illustration 7-2:6

How many deductions does Jeffrey Hunter claim?

Where would a payroll employee find the withholding tables needed to compute the deductions from gross pay?

How many deductions does this employee claim?

to social security is matched by the employer. Each year the rates are reviewed by Congress, which has the authority to change the rate as well as the maximum amount taxed. The payroll office in your company can provide you with the up-to-date percentages for deductions and the amount of earnings subject to FICA tax. This information also is available from your local office of the Social Security Administration.

State and local government units that tax the earnings of citizens issue instructions regarding the taxes to be withheld. Your payroll office will have this information on file for your reference.

Voluntary Deductions. Voluntary deductions vary considerably. In some companies, employees voluntarily make deductions for health insurance, savings plans, retirement plans, and other purposes. Employees who work in the payroll office have the responsibility of keeping the records up to date for employees' individual deductions. Payroll workers follow standard company payroll procedures to complete their tasks.

RECORDS FOR PAYROLL

Companies maintain careful records of all payments made to employees. Employee earnings records are prepared for each pay period and for the

What are this employee's net earnings for the year? What percentage of Jefferey Hunter's gross salary is deducted each year?

Illustration 7-2:7

What are Jeffrey Hunter's net earnings for the year?

EMPLOYEE EARNINGS RECORD

Employee: Jeffery Hunter
Employee No.: 3415
SS No.: 321-22-4697
Marital Status: M
No. Allowances: 1
Year Ending: December 31, 19xx
Position: Data Entry Clerk
Rate of Pay per Year: $19,200

Pay Per	Ended	Regular	Total	Inc Tax	FICA	Hosp	St Tax	Total	Net Pay	Acc Earnings
1	31-Jan	$1,600.00	$1,600.00	$242.00	$122.40		$37.59	$401.99	$1,198.01	$1,600.00
2	28-Feb	1,600.00	1,600.00	242.00	122.40		37.59	401.99	1,198.01	3,200.00
3	31-Mar	1,600.00	1,600.00	242.00	122.40		37.59	401.99	1,198.01	4,800.00
4	30-Apr	1,600.00	1,600.00	242.00	122.40		37.59	401.99	1,198.01	6,400.00
5	31-May	1,600.00	1,600.00	242.00	122.40		37.59	401.99	1,198.01	8,000.00
6	30-Jun	1,600.00	1,600.00	242.00	122.40		37.59	401.99	1,198.01	9,600.00
7	31-Jul	1,600.00	1,600.00	242.00	122.40		37.59	401.99	1,198.01	11,200.00
8	31-Aug	1,600.00	1,600.00	242.00	122.40		37.59	401.99	1,198.01	12,800.00
9	30-Sep	1,600.00	1,600.00	242.00	122.40		37.59	401.99	1,198.01	14,400.00
10	31-Oct	1,600.00	1,600.00	242.00	122.40		37.59	401.99	1,198.01	16,000.00
11	30-Nov	1,600.00	1,600.00	242.00	122.40		37.59	401.99	1,198.01	17,600.00
12	31-Dec	1,600.00	1,600.00	242.00	122.40		37.59	401.99	1,198.01	19,200.00
Totals		$19,200.00	$19,200.00	$2,904.00	$1,468.80		$451.08	$4,823.88	$14,376.12	

PAYROLL REGISTER FOR MODERN SOFTWARE, INC.

January 31, 19xx

Emp No.	Emp Name	Regular	Overtime	Total	Inc Tax	FICA	Hosp	St Tax	Total	Net Pay
4568	Acota, B.	$2,150.00		$2,150.00	$236.00	$164.48		$58.98	$459.46	$1,690.55
4321	Beres, W.	1,088.00		1,088.00	131.00	83.23		19.64	233.87	854.13
3457	Cantrell, T.	2,840.00		2,840.00	635.00	217.26		103.97	956.23	1,883.77
3921	Evans, T.	2,010.00		2,010.00	249.00	153.77		55.32	458.09	1,551.92
3415	Hunter, J.	1,600.00		1,600.00	242.00	122.40		37.56	401.96	1,198.04
3401	Hutchins, W.	3,445.00		3,445.00	854.00	263.54		135.83	1,253.37	2,191.63
4563	Jacobs,S. L.	1,810.00		1,810.00	193.00	138.47		43.30	374.77	1,435.24

year-to-date. The earnings records show earnings, deductions, and net pay. Many companies issue payroll checks that have an attached voucher showing similar information.

At the end of the year, the company is responsible for issuing to each employee a Wage and Tax Statement (commonly called a W-2 form) for the calendar year. The information needed to prepare the W-2 form is found on the payroll register, which records all the earnings and deductions for the payroll period. Additionally, the company makes weekly, monthly, or quarterly reports to government agencies of taxes withheld and taxes the employer must pay. Periodically, the company makes deposits of the amounts withheld and the taxes owed.

PAYROLL CHECK DISTRIBUTION

Procedures for distributing paychecks will vary from company to company. A company may distribute checks in person or mail them to employees. Other companies use direct deposit. That is, they electronically deposit wage and salary payments to employees' designated banks where the funds are credited to the employees' accounts. The company provides the employee with a voucher that details the deposit. In some companies, employees may choose their payment method.

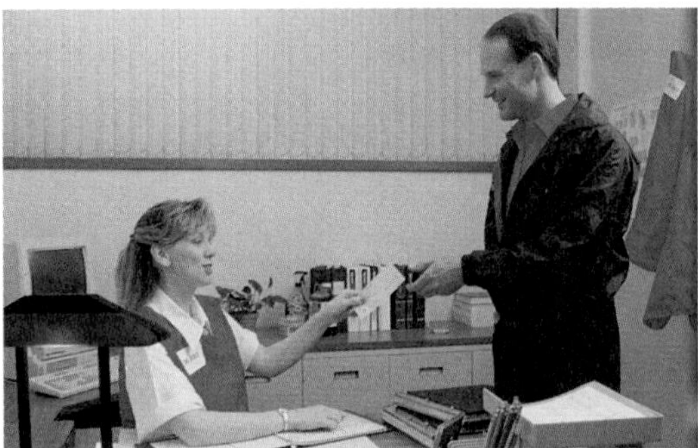

Illustration 7-2:8

In this company, payroll checks are delivered in person.

expand the concept

An office worker in the payroll department discovers a difference between the hours reported by the supervisor and the hours reported by an employee. What might the office worker do at this point? What department typically provides the payroll department with information about salary changes?

Reviewing the Topic

topic 7-2 review

1. Give an example of a financial report that is typically for internal use only and of other reports that are typically distributed outside the company.
2. What is a budget and what is its purpose?
3. What report can a business use to help monitor its budget, and what information does it typically include?
4. What suggestions will be helpful if you participate in the budget process?
5. What is an income statement? What information does it typically include?
6. What is a balance sheet? What information does it typically include?
7. What tasks do employees in the payroll department perform in processing the payroll?
8. How does the hourly method of payroll payment differ from the salary method? How does the salary method of payroll payment differ from the commission method?
9. What deductions from earnings are required by law?
10. Describe the information recorded in a payroll register.

MAKING DECISIONS

Valerie's job responsibilities include filing all vendor invoices and purchase orders in the accounts payable department. Janie's job responsibilities include checking the accuracy of vendor invoices against purchase orders. From time to time, Janie must retrieve these documents from the files. Recently, Janie has had difficulty in locating specific documents. Often she must search through practically an entire file drawer to find what she needs. Janie noted that others seem to be spending too much time looking through the files also.

Janie has no authority to supervise Valerie. The supervisor has said nothing to Valerie about the matter as far as Janie knows. "Since the

topic 7-2 review

Financial Reports and Payroll

342

supervisor doesn't use the files, the supervisor may not be aware of this problem," thinks Janie. She believes the work of the department would be far more efficient if the filing were done carefully.

What you are to do:

If you were in Janie's position, how would you handle this situation? Describe the action you would take and what you might say.

REINFORCING ENGLISH SKILLS

You are helping a colleague prepare an announcement to be published in a professional accounting journal. Your colleague hurriedly prepared the following rough draft, which must be faxed this afternoon to the journal offices to meet their publication deadline. You find five misspelled words in the rough draft. In addition, there are six words (in parentheses) whose definitions you want to check. You want to be certain the words convey the meanings you want them to convey in the announcement. Likewise, your colleague asked you to edit the copy if you feel you can improve the announcement.

What you are to do:

Prepare a final copy of the announcement, correcting all spelling errors. On a separate sheet of paper, give an appropriate definition for each of the six words in parentheses. If you feel a better word could be used for any of the six words, replace that word with another. If you use another word, add the new word to your list of definitions. Edit the copy if you feel you can improve the announcement.

The Business Accountants Association has formed a new (advisory) group on small businesses which will (fund) independantly any of the Board's specific (projects). It will help the Board identafy the (implications) of Board decisions to small businesses. Also, it will help identify any (implementation) problems small businesses may have with those decisions. The executive director of the Association is one of the members of the new panal. Any member who wants to coment on an (issue) envolving small business may write to the national office.

343

topic 7-2
review

APPLICATION ACTIVITY

ACTIVITY **Calculating Gross Salaries**

You are an office employee in a retail furniture company store in a suburban mall. You have been given the following schedule of salaries. Employees are paid twice monthly, on the 15th and on the last day of the month.

What you are to do:

Determine the gross salary for each of the employees for the two-week period ended November 30. Commissions for employees who receive them are based on their net sales for the two-week period preceding the current pay period. Prepare an appropriate chart or table to show this information.

Administrative and Office Employees	Salary	Base
Agins, Richard	$18,000	Annually
Birin, Otto	1,400	Monthly
Dalla, Sarah	19,500	Annually
Flynn, Julia	34,500	Annually
Kramer, Elsie	1,200	Monthly
Phillip, Michael	1,550	Monthly

Sales Employees	Monthly Salary	Net Sales November 1–15
Chase, Eric	$ 600 plus 6% commission	$16,000
Hayward, Louise	1,000 plus 6% commission	21,000
Majia, Dora	1,000 plus 6% commission	15,560
Myers, James	600 plus 6% commission	12,436
Pedro, Silvia	1,000 plus 6% commission	10,500
Saha, Eunice	1,000 plus 6% commission	17,540

344

Chapter Summary

In Chapter 7 you were introduced to concepts and procedures for processing financial information. Although procedures may vary from company to company, employees have responsibility for maintaining accurate, up-to-date financial records at all times. From your study of this chapter, you should be able to discuss the following key points:

- Companies generally separate responsibility for tasks in processing cash, and they may also bond employees in order to have good internal control.
- Employees assist in the processing of cash by seeing that checks are endorsed properly, filling in deposit slips, preparing bank reconciliations, and maintaining petty cash funds.
- In larger firms, processing cash payments is often the responsibility of employees in the accounts payable department. Employees who make cash payments review purchase-related documents, prepare vouchers, and prepare checks.
- Bank accounts are reconciled to be sure that receipts and disbursements shown in company records match the bank's records.
- The petty cash fund is used in many offices to pay for small expenditures such as postage or delivery services.
- Sound financial management includes planning, analyzing, and reporting financial information.
- The budget is the financial plan for allocation of the resources of the business. It is a tool for planning and monitoring expenditures.
- Companies design payroll procedures to ensure that employees are paid accurately and on time.
- Financial statements provide information about a company's economic resources and the results of the company's operations.

chapter 7 summary

Processing and Understanding Financial Information

chapter 7
summary

KEY CONCEPTS AND TERMS

accounts payable
accounts receivable
ATM
balance sheet
bank draft
bonding
budget
budget performance report
cash
cashier's check
certified check
check
deposit slip
EFT
endorsement
financial management
gross salary
income statement
lockbox
net income
petty cash fund
proving cash
tickler file
voucher
voucher check

INTEGRATED CHAPTER ACTIVITIES

ACTIVITY 1 Payment of Invoices

You have been given invoices that are to be paid within the discount period. The information shown below has been taken from the invoices. Also, the terms for payment are given.

Vendor	Amount Owed	Terms
Jim's Imports	$2,345.00	2/10, n/30
Premier Associates	5,678.50	3/15, n/30
Poteet Stationers	3,450.00	2/10, n/30
C. M. McDougal & Co.	10,650.65	3/15, n/30
Handex Corporation	12,450.00	2/10, n/30
Meyer & Sons	9,456.43	1/10, n/30
Caprock Spas	7,789.42	1/10, n/30
CCC Cotton Co-Op	4,569.23	2/10, n/30
Mullenax, Inc.	5,908.00	2/10, n/30

346

What you are to do:

1. Compute the amount that should be sent to the vendor in each instance. For example: 2/10, n/30 means that a 2 percent discount is allowed if payment is made within 10 days of the invoice date. If not paid within 10 days, the total due is to be paid within 30 days of the invoice date. Assume that all payments will be paid within the discount date.
2. Prepare a short table or chart showing the names of the vendors, the amounts owed, terms, discounts, and the amounts of the checks.

ACTIVITY 2 Evaluating Discounts

Your department head, Mary Roberts, mentioned to you that some payments are being paid after the discount period because personnel are so busy with other tasks. "It's only 2 or 3%" she said, "but I know we must be losing considerable money by not taking the discounts. Please figure out just how much we can really save with the discounts and give me some findings that I can use when I request additional staff."

What you are to do:

Using your completed work from Activity 1, prepare a response to your department head's request in the form of a memo. Add the amount owed to vendors as well as the applied discounts. Determine the cost differences between paying without using the discounts and the amount owed using the discounts. Use those figures in your response.

347

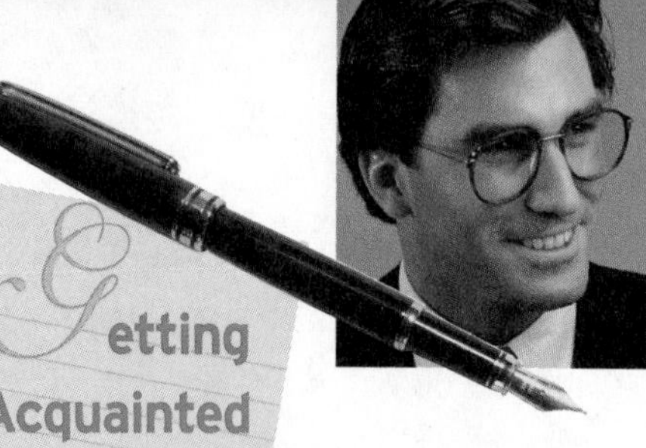

Garth Howells
Vice President of Finance

Getting Acquainted with the World of Work

Are They Speaking A "Foreign" Language?

Dear Mr. Howells

I am really enjoying my first full-time job but, at times, I have a problem with understanding what people are saying to me. It's as though they are speaking a foreign language. When they discuss a project with me and use technical words I don't know, I lose my confidence and become quiet. I have to concentrate so hard on the words they are saying that I'm afraid I won't understand what I am supposed to do. At other times, I'm not really sure what people mean when they say "We have spent the total allocation," or "The company has no money left."

I know I have good skills and am qualified for my job, but this problem seems to be keeping me from doing my best and from feeling comfortable at work. Do you have any suggestions?

Kathi from New York City

Dear Kathi

You're absolutely right! A special, or "foreign" language is often spoken in offices. Each office has a technical or specialized vocabulary that relates to the activities of the business. For example, people in the construction industry use a specialized vocabulary that differs from the specialized vocabularies used in banks or advertising agencies. In addition to using industry-specific terms, businesspeople who are very familiar with the company operations often speak in abbreviated terms assuming that everyone else knows what they mean. For example, "we have no money left" probably means that the amount budgeted for a particular expense category has been used—not that the company is bankrupt.

There are a number of ways you can learn the specialized language you face at work and gain command of the new vocabulary you hear.

Listen attentively to the context in which an unfamiliar word or phrase appears to determine if you can guess what it means.

Write down words or phrases that puzzle you and investigate them as time allows. If you believe you need to understand them to complete a current task, seek help from a coworker or supervisor. Otherwise, use memos and correspondence, reference materials and magazines, or specialized newspaper columns to see if you can discover the proper meanings.

Take time to think about the new words and phrases as you encounter them in your daily work. Use the words as you discuss matters with your coworkers and supervisor.

Best wishes in gaining command of your "foreign" language.

Garth Howells

Vice President of Finance

348

Simulation Part 3

At Work at *Maple Valley Chamber of Commerce*:

Maple Valley Chamber of Commerce is located in Geneva, Illinois. Like all chambers of commerce, Maple Valley Chamber of Commerce serves area businesses in many ways. For example, it sponsors special events designed to promote the products and services of local businesses to the general public.

You just accepted a part-time administrative assistant position with Maple Valley Chamber of Commerce. You will work from 3:30 to 5:30 p.m. Monday through Friday. Because the Chamber sponsors many weekend events, you may also be asked to work on a Saturday. You are sure to find your work both interesting and challenging as you help with the many office tasks that must be completed in order for the Chamber to operate effectively and meet the needs of its members and the local community.

You will quickly see that your knowledge of integrated software can help you increase your efficiency and productivity. You will use word processing, spreadsheet, database, and presentation software as tools for completing your work assignments.

You will be working closely with all the members of the office staff, and you will receive your assignments from Patti Petruci, the Assistant Director. Refer to your *Student Activities and Projects* workbook to begin your first day on the job at Maple Valley Chamber of Commerce.

See Workbook pages 121–147.

Managing Time, Tasks, & Records

part 4

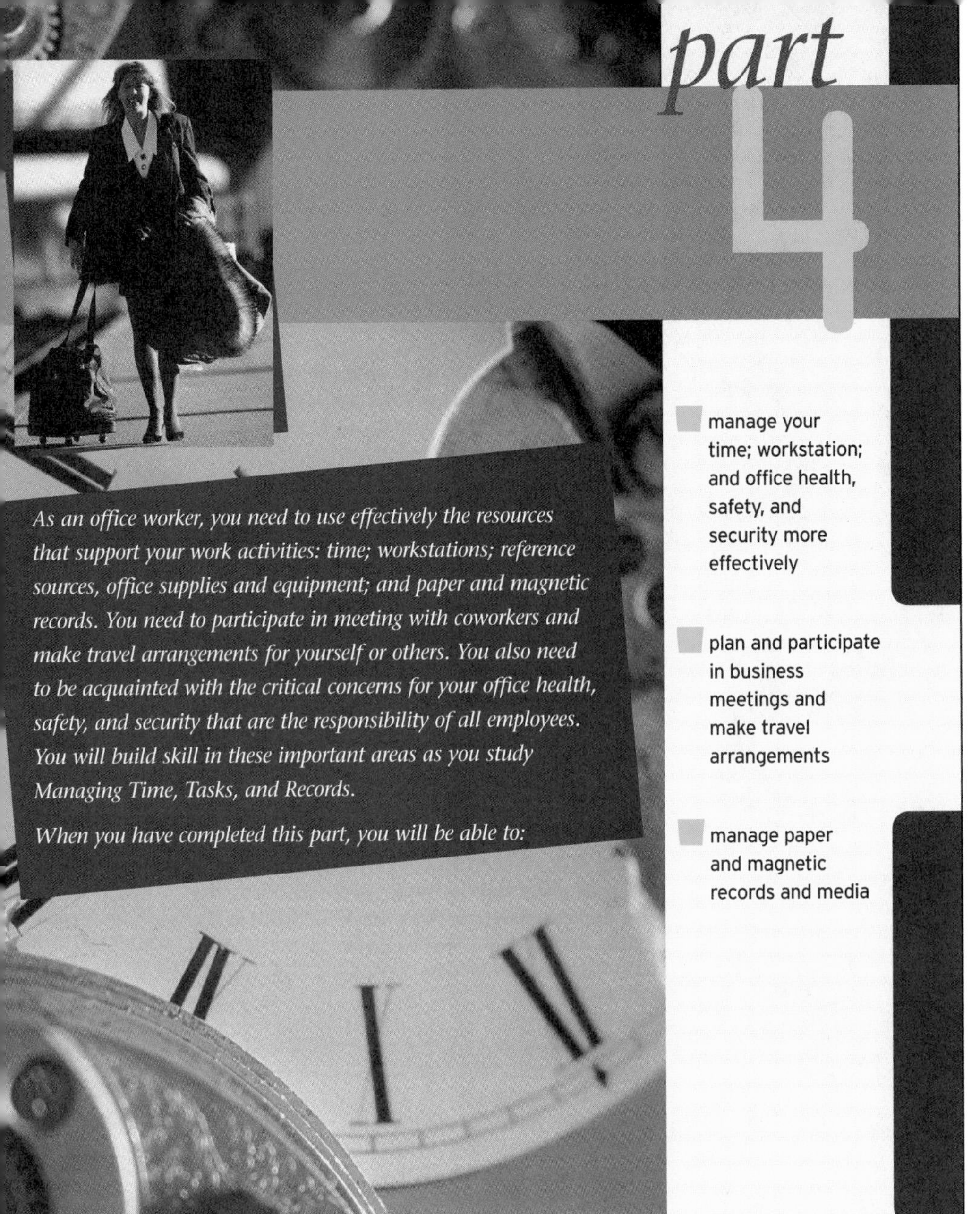

As an office worker, you need to use effectively the resources that support your work activities: time; workstations; reference sources, office supplies and equipment; and paper and magnetic records. You need to participate in meeting with coworkers and make travel arrangements for yourself or others. You also need to be acquainted with the critical concerns for your office health, safety, and security that are the responsibility of all employees. You will build skill in these important areas as you study Managing Time, Tasks, and Records.

When you have completed this part, you will be able to:

- manage your time; workstation; and office health, safety, and security more effectively
- plan and participate in business meetings and make travel arrangements
- manage paper and magnetic records and media

Office employees are managers of their time, work, workstation, and work environment. Help students realize that being a good worker requires more than technical competencies. Discuss with them how the basic job requirements relate to the topics that are included in this chapter.

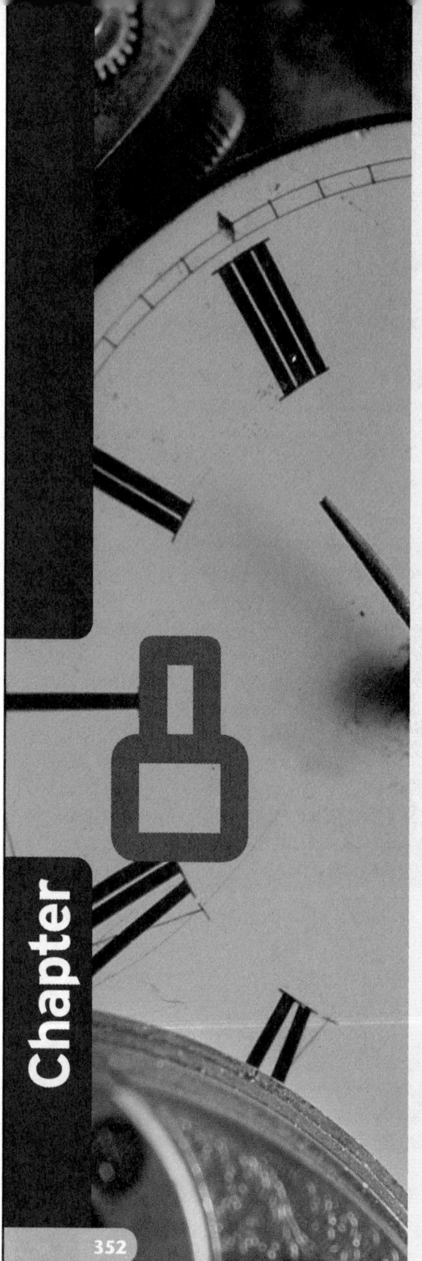

Time and Workstation Management

The concept of time management is actually misleading—none of us can manage the clock. All of us have the same 24 hours in a day. It is how we manage *ourselves* in relation to time that is important. In this chapter, you will learn time management techniques and tools that will help you work productively.

Effectively arranging and managing the furniture, equipment, files, supplies, and other resources used in your work is as critical as managing your time wisely. Arranging furniture and equipment in your work area can enhance your feelings of comfort and contribute to your overall productivity. Having files, supplies, and other resources within easy reach of your work assures that you have the right information at the right time.

To work effectively and efficiently, you must have a safe environment. In this chapter, you will learn about the critical concerns for safety and security that affect office workers. You also will learn about ergonomic factors, such as lighting, color, sound, office equipment, and furniture, that affect how you feel and how productive you are in the office environment.

Chapter 8

Topic 8-1

Time Management and Reminder Systems

When you have completed your study of this topic, you will be able to:

- **identify common time wasters**
- **analyze how you spend your time**
- **plan your work activities**
- **use common reminder systems**
- **compare and contrast manual and electronic reminder systems**

Time management is a major factor in your productivity and feelings of job satisfaction, your reputation as an effective worker, and opportunities for advancement. Managing your time at the office is a process of choosing the most effective way to do your job. The creative use of techniques to manage time will enrich your work life.

Calendar and other reminder systems are helpful in bringing to mind events, tasks, and other office-related activities. These reminder systems assist you in scheduling activities for the most efficient use of time and resources.

Manage Your Time

Time management is the process of planning your activities to gain better control over how you spend your time. Managing your time

You may want to engage students in a brief discussion of the importance of time-management skills. Studies show effective time management to be a factor common to highly successful people. Ask students, "What does the management of oneself in relation to time have to do with success?"

Topic 8-1

Students can begin now to establish efficient time-management procedures in their daily lives. Time-wasters that are common in the office also may be common in students' personal and academic lives. Ask them:

1. How would you define "wasted time"?
2. Have you ever wasted time in telephone conversations? Why do you conclude that time was wasted as you think of a particular telephone conversation?

obligations: commitments, duties, responsibilities

effectively is critical to your success on the job. You will want to learn how to eliminate time wasters and handle time **obligations** efficiently. Analyzing how you spend your time will increase your effectiveness in managing your work. One of the first steps in learning how to use your time is to recognize how it can be wasted.

COMMON TIME-WASTERS

All time spent at work is not productive. You can waste time without realizing it. Some common time-wasters, along with suggestions for overcoming them, are discussed in the following paragraphs.

Unnecessary Telephone Conversations. The telephone can be either a time-saver or a time-waster, depending on how you use it. Often, a telephone call that starts out saving time can end up wasting it. For example, if an office worker takes ten minutes to verify price information and five minutes to discuss the latest episode of a favorite television program, a conversation that began productively ends up being a time-waster. If this happens two or three times a day, the time wasted can add up rapidly.

deterrent: barrier, obstacle

Frequent Interruptions. Interruptions in your work can come from many sources—unplanned visits or questions from coworkers or customers, phone calls, and delays in receiving work or material from others are common ones. On the surface, each of these interruptions may appear to be a **deterrent** to completing your tasks. However, it is important to remember that working with coworkers and customers is an important element of most jobs and that the telephone is a tool that helps you do your job more efficiently. True time-wasters do occur when materials, reports, or other work is late in reaching you. Evaluate the interruptions by determining whether they contribute to better relations with coworkers and customers or whether they are actually causing a delay in meeting established deadlines or producing a quality product.

misuse: abuse, an improper use

Excessive Socializing. Although some socializing will help you maintain good working relations with your coworkers, too much is **misuse** of company time. Some workers may socialize excessively, and you will be wise to avoid engaging in long conversations with them. When a talker tries to involve you in idle conversation, offer a simple response like: "I really must get back to work. Maybe we could discuss this at lunch." You will maintain good working relations while excusing yourself to continue your work. If you are consistent in your responses, the talker will soon learn that you are not easily distracted from your work. Be careful to limit your lunch and breaks to the planned or approved times.

Illustration 8-1:1

Socialize with co-workers at appropriate times such as lunch or during breaks.

Ineffective Communication. As an office worker, you will receive information in both written and oral form from customers and coworkers. You also will give information in written and oral form to others. If the information that is given or received by you is inaccurate or incomplete, lost time and money can be the result of the poor communication. Be certain the information you give others is specific and accurate. Ask for feedback from those to whom you give information to be sure you have communicated the information clearly and completely. Likewise, be sure that you understand any instructions or information you receive. Ask questions to clear up any misunderstandings and to gain all the needed information.

Disorganization. Being disorganized can be a major time-waster. Searching for the paper you just had in your hands, missing important deadlines, and shifting unnecessarily from one project to another are

Emphasize to students the importance of being aware of how they spend their time. Ask them:

1. Have you ever wasted time on excessive socializing?
2. What specifically can you do to eliminate this time-waster in the future?
3. Describe the kind and extent of socializing that is considered appropriate in an office.

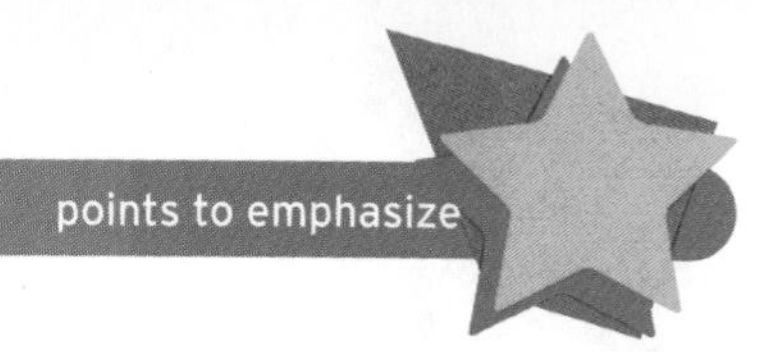

Time on the job must be channeled to assure that time obligations are handled effectively and that time-wasters are eliminated or at least minimized.

Have students interview an office worker to learn what techniques he or she uses to manage time on the job. Students may want to ask:

1. Have you ever used a time-use log to determine how you spend your time on the job?
2. If so, did the log help you manage your time better?
3. What tips might you have for me when I become an office worker in helping me manage my time, work, workstation, and work environment efficiently and effectively?

Ask students to share the results of their interviews with the class.

all signs of a disorganized person. Take the time to organize your work area and prepare a daily plan for your work. Think through and plan complicated jobs before starting them. Group similar tasks together and avoid jumping from one project to another before finishing the first one. Do not **procrastinate.** If unpleasant or difficult tasks are needlessly delayed, they can become potential crises just waiting to erupt.

procrastinate: delay intentionally, put off

TIME ANALYSIS PROCEDURES

Time is a valuable resource that should be used wisely; it cannot be replaced. You have learned about common ways time can be wasted. One of the smartest things you can do for yourself is to analyze how you spend your time on the job. Time analysis aids you in determining how effectively your time is used. By keeping a written account of what you do, you can determine whether or not you are using your time effectively. With this information you can then develop a plan of action to correct or redirect the use of your time.

Keep a Time Inventory. Start by keeping a written record of what you do and how much time is used. Record all activities in a time-use log: tasks accepted and completed, telephone calls, meetings, discussions, receiving and responding to e-mail messages or other correspondence, and so forth.

You may choose to keep a time-use log for a day, for several days, or even a week. The longer you keep it, the more representative it will be of how your time is spent. A partial time-use log is shown in Illustration 8-1:2 on page 357.

Analyze How You Spend Your Time. When you have completed your time-use log, you are ready to analyze the results. By studying your time-use patterns, you will be able to spot problem areas quickly. Be alert to the following points as you analyze:

- During what time of the day was I most productive? least productive? Why?
- How did I lose (or waste) my time? Was it because of unnecessary interruptions, visitors/socializing, crises, telephone? Who and what was involved in each case?

Time-Use Log

Name Michele Fitch

	Day 1 Monday	Day 2 Tuesday	Day 3 Wednesday	Day 4 Thursday	Day 5 Friday
8:45 a.m.	arrived early opened office	arrived early opened office	arrived early opened office	arrived early opened office	arrived early opened office
9:00 a.m.	checked calendar, tickler & To Do list	checked calendar, tickler & To Do list	checked calendar, tickler & To Do list	checked calendar, tickler & To Do list	checked calendar, tickler & To Do list
9:15 a.m.	met with supervisor	met with supervisor	keyed meeting notes and report	met with supervisor	met with supervisor
9:30 a.m.	keyed report	keyed letter		organized trip reports	memo to staff
9:45 a.m.		took notes at meeting		keyed trip expense forms	made copies and distributed
10:00 a.m.					
10:15 a.m.			coffee	handled phone call	coffee
10:30 a.m.	coffee break		checked supplies and completed requisition form	coffee break	talked to Nancy
10:45 a.m.	telephone call to confirm Wed. travel	mail arrived:	mail arrived:	mail arrived:	filed
11:00 a.m.	mail arrived:	opened/sorted/distributed	opened/sorted/distributed	opened/sorted/distributed	
11:15 a.m.	opened/sorted/distributed	coffee	talked to Nancy	keyed report	mail arrived:
					opened/sorted

Illustration 8-1:2

A time-use log will aid in determining how effectively your time is used.

- Is there a pattern emerging that might indicate the times when there are more interruptions? Is there a pattern that indicates that more time is needed to handle crises or emergency tasks that may arise? Do I need more time to complete specific tasks?
- Do I feel that I have used my time wisely?

Develop a Plan of Action. After you have analyzed how you spend your time, determine how well the tasks you complete contribute to meeting your work goals.

For each activity you have listed in your time-use log, ask yourself if that activity contributed to the satisfactory completion of your work.

1. In Illustration 8-1:2, during what time of the day was Michele most productive? least productive? Why?
2. Did Michele lose (or waste) time? If so, how?

Why do you think writing or keying tasks in a calendar or a To Do list or other time-management tool helps to ensure those tasks will be completed on time?

Emphasize to students that planning their daily activities will help them prioritize tasks and complete assignments on time. Ask them to:

1. Take five or ten minutes each day to plan their day's activities.
2. Prepare a To Do list similar to the one shown in Illustration 8-1:3.
3. Complete the tasks according to their order of importance.
4. Cross tasks off as they are completed.
5. Carry uncompleted tasks over to the next day's To Do list.

systematic: methodical, well organized, orderly, efficient

If not, you need to develop a **systematic** approach to your work that will increase the effective use of your time.

Manage Your Work

peak: a period of increased work activity

slack: a period of decreased work activity

Using time efficiently requires developing an organized approach to your work. Calendars and time-management systems can help you identify **peak** and **slack** work periods. Once you know when to expect such periods, you can plan your work to allow for more productive use of your time as well as for a more even workload. To accommodate a peak period, think ahead to determine what jobs could be completed in advance. Then the peak period will not place undue pressure on you. Planning for the slack periods is equally important. During these times, you can catch up on those tasks that do not have deadlines but nevertheless must be done. Follow the suggestions described below for handling your time obligations more effectively.

PLAN YOUR WORK ACTIVITIES

Planning your daily work activities will help you avoid forgetting tasks that need to be completed. Take five or ten minutes either at the beginning or the close of the workday to plan the coming day's work. Prepare a To Do list similar to the one shown in Illustration 8-1:3 on page 359, and complete the tasks according to their order of importance. Keep the list accessible as you work. Check it frequently. This list should guide you through your daily activities. As tasks are completed, cross them off. Tasks not completed can be carried over to the next day's list. Be alert, however, to any item that seems to be carried over too many times. Perhaps it should be broken down into smaller segments, or perhaps you are procrastinating in completing the task. Your list may be part of a calendar system that allows you to set work and career goals. Stay alert for opportunities or work assignments that will help you meet, expand, or develop new goals.

SET PRIORITIES

Once you have identified tasks for the day, rank them on your To Do list and complete the most important ones first. To determine the priority of the tasks, ask yourself these questions:

TO DO

Thursday, January 13

Priority	Task	Completed
A-1	Prepare and distribute memo announcing a staff meeting for this Monday	
A-2	Prepare minutes from 1/10 regional sales meeting; distribute to participants	
B-1	Call McPhetter to coordinate travel dates to sales meeting	
B-2	Call travel agency for flight times	
B-3	Prepare draft of contract for Roberts	
B-4	Call Karen to get dates for Perez conference	
C-1	Delete backup copies of old short-term vendor agreements	

Notes: Karen is taking a vacation day on Friday.

Illustration 8-1:3

A To Do list shows tasks that need to be completed for the day.

- How much time will the task require?
- By what date (time) is this needed?
- Are others involved in completing the task?
- What will happen if this task is not completed on time?
- Do I have all of the information (or materials) I need to complete the task?

At times you may need to discuss your priorities with coworkers or a supervisor to be certain that you agree on the order for doing tasks. Once you set your priorities, finish the tasks in their priority order. Remain **flexible,** however, about revising your priorities as circumstances change.

flexible: able to adapt or change as necessary

You may want to demonstrate and compare a couple of commercial time management systems available or require students to use a student version, which is available for a nominal cost.

Ana Maria's To Do list for tomorrow is shown in Illustration 8-1:3. Notice that she has identified the tasks as A, B, or C. The A-level tasks need immediate attention or completion. If the item is a long-term project, the portion of the task that should be finished that day is listed. B-level tasks can be done once the A-level tasks have been completed. C-level tasks have no specific deadline, but can be done when the A and B tasks have been completed.

pertinent: to the point, relevant

Before Ana Maria left work, she jotted down the tasks she needed to complete the next day at work. She checked her To Do list for any unfinished items to be carried over to the current list. She also checked her calendar and her supervisor's calendar for any **pertinent** *notes. Her calendar contained a reminder notation that the national sales meeting would be held three weeks from tomorrow. Jim McPheeter, a regional sales manager, is to accompany her to the meeting.*

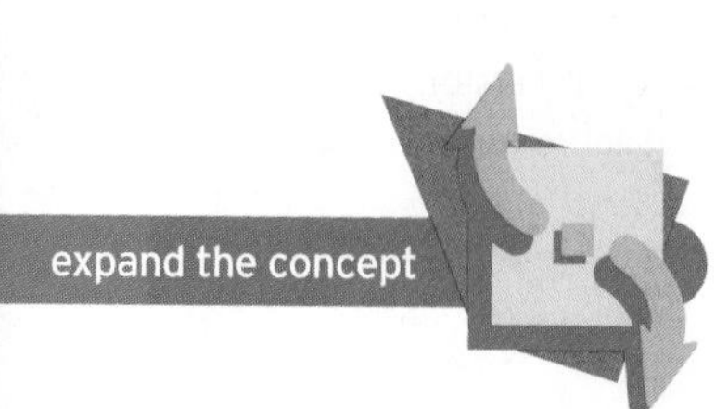

Students may have difficulty knowing how to get started on a large project. Share with them how you plan for and complete long-range projects. Then, ask them to follow the guidelines presented in this topic to complete the application activity on page 372.

CONTROL LARGE PROJECTS

Sometimes it is difficult to get started on a large project even though it may be very important. Smaller tasks can be checked off your To Do list with ease; a large task may seem overwhelming. Do not let the size of a project keep you from getting it under control and moving toward satisfactory completion. Here are several suggestions for handling a large project:

- Break the large project into smaller tasks.
- Determine the steps to be taken in each of the smaller tasks.
- Establish deadlines for each section or smaller task and stick to those deadlines.
- Look for ways to improve your procedures and simplify the completion of the project.
- If the large project is one that will be repeated periodically, record your procedures and suggestions you want to follow in the future for improvements.

SIMPLIFY YOUR WORK

Work simplification is the process of improving the procedures for getting work done. It often involves streamlining some steps and eliminating others. Your goal is to use the most efficient procedure for completing a task. As you complete a task, be aware of the steps you are going through. Eliminate any unnecessary steps and/or details. Consider alternative methods for completing the task. Are they more efficient than those you are using? Look at the task and your procedures objectively to find ways to improve your productivity.

Analyze the workflow. Consider the information and work assignments you receive and those you forward to others. Ask yourself the following questions:

- Does the flow of work to my desk make good use of my time and effort? of everyone's time and effort?
- Does the flow of work provide the right information to customers or others outside the company in a timely fashion?
- Are the materials and equipment needed to complete my work readily at hand or nearby?
- Am I using the capabilities of my office equipment and software to their fullest extent?

Your answers to these questions should provide clues to simplifying your work. Incorporate these suggestions into your workflow analysis:

- Group and complete similar tasks together. For example, if you need photocopies of the letters you are preparing, do them all at once rather than making several trips to the copier. If you have several related phone calls to make, try to make them in sequence.
- Combine tasks if doing so will increase your efficiency. For example, if you plan to leave a request at the Records Center for a series of files you need to complete a report and the Records Center is near the company cafeteria, stop by the Records Center on your way to lunch.
- Determine how to best organize and arrange the equipment and supplies you use to complete a task. For example, if you cross a room every few minutes to retrieve pages from a printer, perhaps you can reorganize the placement of the equipment to provide a smoother flow of work.
- Enlist the help of others when you have an important deadline to meet and the workload is overwhelming. Be sure to **reciprocate** when the roles are reversed.

reciprocate: repay in kind

1. How can you simplify, or streamline, tasks that you are responsible for completing either at home or on the job?
2. Do you have a large project now? Describe it and detail procedures that will help you meet the deadline.

How does knowing the flow of work enhance the use of time?

Have the class list the kinds of documents or messages an office worker may receive daily. These might include reports, original letters from managers or customers, e-mail messages, phone messages, magazines, memos, minutes of meetings, photocopies of letters forwarded from other workers, flyers, and announcements. Ask students: How can an office worker handle all of this information efficiently and effectively so that it does not become overwhelming?

Handle information overload. When the amount of information you receive on a daily basis becomes overwhelming, you are experiencing *information overload*. Being able to provide timely information to the right person at the right time means that you will be responsible for effectively handling many types of records and documents you encounter. You will save time (yours and others') by trying to handle each file or piece of paper just once. Take any needed action immediately if that is appropriate, or note the task on your To Do list for completion at the proper time. In this way, the amount of information you receive will not become overwhelming. A good rule of thumb is to make a decision about how to handle every piece of paper or file the first time you view it.

Reminder Systems

As an office worker, you must keep track of appointments, meetings, travel dates, and deadlines. Perhaps the most widely used device for keeping track of such items is the calendar. A reminder file, arranged **chronologically,** also can be helpful by providing a convenient place to keep notations of tasks to be performed on specific dates.

chronologically: arranged in order of time

CALENDARS

Calendars, time-management systems, and electronic organizers are useful tools for recording deadlines, appointments, telephone numbers and addresses, and daily or monthly reminders.

Manual systems. A well-maintained desk calendar can assist you in keeping track of the many tasks and deadlines in your job, as well as being helpful to others who may have access to it. Illustration 8-1:4 shows a commonly used manual desk calendar in which appointments, deadlines, meetings, or other important data can be written.

Wall calendars also are useful when large projects or those involving a number of people are broken into various small tasks with many deadlines. By displaying the wall calendar, you and others can keep track of deadlines and materials and equipment that may be needed.

Illustration 8-1:4

Time management systems can help you plan and organize tasks.

Electronic systems. Electronic organizers may be used in the same way as paper-based systems to keep track of project deadlines, appointments, and work schedules. Rather than recording information on paper, the information is entered into a computer program.

Electronic calendar programs have various features. Some programs allow only **minimal** information to be entered. Others include To Do lists, additional notes regarding appointments or projects, deadlines, and completion dates. Some calendar programs sound an alarm to remind users of specific engagements or deadlines. Programs that include more advanced features for planning large or long-term projects are sometimes called scheduling programs.

minimal: smallest or least possible

> *Donna uses a calendar program to track her weekly schedule. The calendar shows an 8:30 a.m. staff meeting that the supervisor has scheduled for Monday of this week as well as several other appointments. She can print the information, make a paper notation, or forward the message electronically to a coworker as a reminder.*

Personal Digital Organizers. Personal digital organizers fall under a variety of names: electronic calendars or schedulers, personal information managers (PIMs), personal data managers, and personal digital assistants (PDAs). Basic features of personal digital organizers include storing telephone numbers and addresses, appointments, To Do lists, and **recurring** events. The more sophisticated electronic organizers can:

- recognize handwriting
- automatically track telephone calls

recurring: repetitive, ongoing, regular

Have students compare and contrast the differences between manual and electronic calendars or scheduling systems. What is the best use for each one?

- record notes of telephone calls
- recognize schedule conflicts
- sound alarms as reminders of meetings or deadlines
- create labels from address lists
- provide space for writing memos

Some personal digital assistants can share data with calendar computer programs, allowing the user to coordinate the schedules easily.

Illustration 8-1:5

Personal digital assistants provide a variety of calendar features.

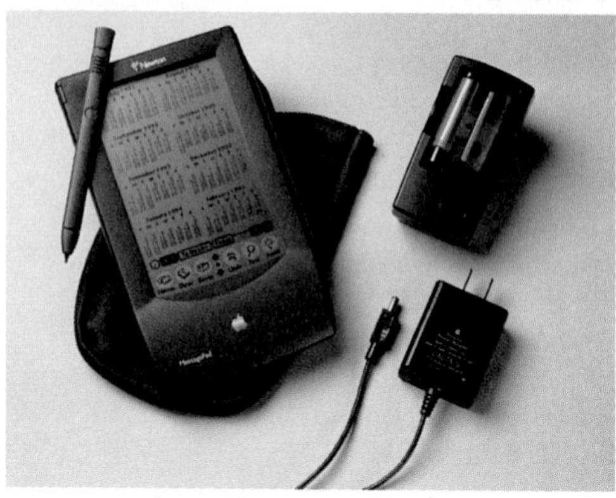

SCHEDULING APPOINTMENTS

Typically, you will have your own calendar to maintain. You also may make appointments and schedule meetings for coworkers. People request appointments in different ways: in person, by telephone, by letter or memorandum, or by electronic message. Although the manner in which you respond to these requests may vary, the basic information you need will be the same:

WHO:	name and telephone number of the individual requesting the appointment
WHEN:	date, time, and approximate length of appointment
WHERE:	location of the appointment
WHY or WHAT:	purpose of meeting

Responding to Appointment Requests. When you receive a request for an appointment, check the calendar to determine that the date and time requested are available. If not, you may suggest alternative appointment dates and times. By knowing the purpose of the meeting, you can determine and provide all **backup materials** needed. To maintain the calendars properly, clarify the following points:

backup materials: related or supporting documents

- To what extent do you have authority to make appointments?
- When should you check with others before making appointments?
- Are there regular times when appointments are not to be made, such as the first half-hour of the day?
- To what extent will the manager or coworkers make appointments without checking with you?
- Does the person for whom you work want to know the purpose of each appointment you schedule?

The authority you have to make appointments will depend in great part on the nature of your business. For example, if you work in a doctor's office, most of the appointment requests would be from patients. You would be expected to schedule appointments without having to verify each one with the doctor. On the other hand, you may work in a general office where both you and your coworkers make appointments. You must agree on procedures that will allow you to operate effectively. Follow these guidelines when making appointments:

1. Do not schedule overlapping appointments. Try to determine the amount of time needed for each one. Some time may be left unscheduled to return telephone calls or prepare for the next appointment.
2. Keep a complete calendar. Record names, telephone numbers, and other pertinent information.
3. Use legible handwriting to record entries on handwritten calendars. Avoid crossing out and rescheduling over scratched-off entries. To make changes easily, write appointment information in pencil.
4. Determine a symbol to designate confirmed appointments. As appointments are confirmed, record the symbol. Commonly used

Have students consider what difficulties an office worker might encounter if these points were not clarified with a manager or coworkers.

The office calendar is a widely used reminder system for scheduling the activities and resources of the business office. Office workers often maintain office calendars and manage appointment requests.

Illustration 8-1:6

Your desk calendar can be easily seen, so avoid writing confidential entries.

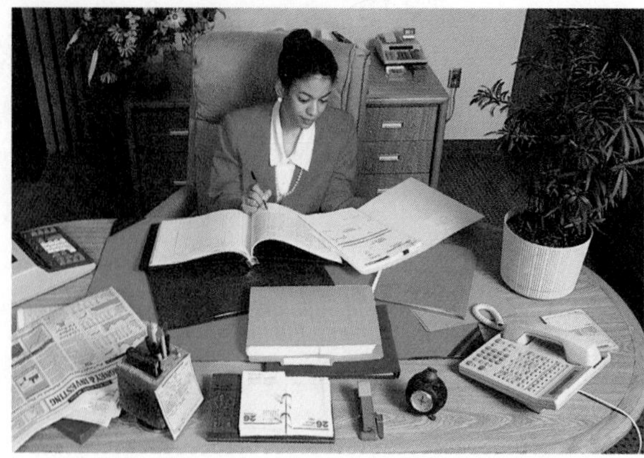

symbols include a check mark, an asterisk, or an underscore of the individual's name.

5. If you are responsible for keeping a calendar for others, provide a daily listing of appointments and reminders at the beginning of the workday. Show the appointments for the day in chronological order.
6. Keep the previous year's appointment calendar. You may find it necessary to refer back to a calendar to reconstruct or retrieve needed information. If you use an electronic calendar, print a copy of the calendar before deleting the data, or save the information in an electronic file.

Entering Recurring Items. Some meetings and tasks are performed weekly, monthly, quarterly, or annually. As you set up your calendar at the beginning of the year, enter the recurring meetings and tasks on both your calendar and your coworkers' or work group's calendar as appropriate. If you block out the times for these recurring items, both you and others will know what time is available for scheduling other appointments.

Coordinating Calendars. If both you and your coworkers schedule appointments using desk calendars, you need to coordinate appointment calendars so that they are consistent and up to date. Adjustments to schedules are usually made at the beginning or the end of the workday.

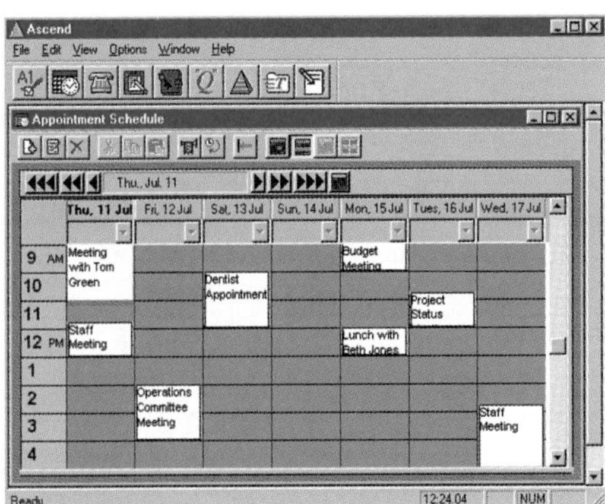

Illustration 8-1:7

Scheduling software can be used to set up a meeting with coworkers.

They include confirming tentative appointments, rescheduling appointments, deleting canceled appointments, changing time allotments, and preparing materials for the appointments.

You may use an electronic calendar program for your individual schedule or to set up group activities. An electronic calendar that resides on the computer network often can be updated by everyone using the calendar. Changes made are reflected instantly and may be viewed by anyone accessing the calendar.

> *Donna needs to schedule a meeting with six other people. She can access a program on the company's computer network to check the schedules of the six people for times available for the meeting. She can either check all of the schedules herself or she can enter the names of the people she wants to attend the meeting and a general time frame. The program then will look at everyone's schedule and the other* **parameters** *she entered to find a meeting time. Depending on the program available to her, she also might be able to schedule a meeting room.*

parameters: guidelines, criteria

TICKLER FILES

A tickler file is a chronological system for keeping track of future actions. Such a file is divided into 12 monthly divisions with 31 daily parts for each day of the month. Tickler files can be set up using cards,

Embarrassing conflicts can be avoided by coordinating and regularly updating the appointment calendar with a manager or coworkers.

a pocket file (an accordion-like file), or a file drawer with file folders. A tickler file also can be maintained on a computer.

Store or record in a tickler file items requiring future action. Assume your employer says to you, "Please call the Morgan Company on Monday and make an appointment for us to discuss our purchasing contract with them." You would prepare a reminder to make the phone call and place it in your tickler file under next Monday's date.

As soon as you become aware of a deadline or a detail that needs to be checked in the future, place a notation in your tickler file under the relevant day. Check your tickler file each morning and remove those items requiring attention for the current day. Complete the appropriate action for each item. Between your tickler file, your calendar, and your time management system, you will be aware of what must be done to keep your work flowing smoothly.

Reviewing the Topic

1. Define time management. Why is time management important to the office worker?
2. Identify and describe common time-wasters in the office.
3. Describe the procedures you can use to handle your time obligations effectively.
4. Define workflow analysis. What steps can you take to complete an analysis of your workflow?
5. What are reminder systems?
6. What steps do you complete to analyze how you spend your time?
7. What is a personal digital organizer? Name some common features of a digital organizer.
8. Define work simplification.
9. What guidelines should you follow in scheduling appointments?
10. To maintain calendars effectively and efficiently, what points should be discussed and clarified with your manager or coworkers?

MAKING DECISIONS

Ana Maria arrived at the office a few minutes early to review the items on her To Do list for the day. Just as she was about to begin, her supervisor arrived and told Ana Maria she had received a call at home last night. The national sales meeting scheduled for three weeks from today had been moved to the day after tomorrow because of an emergency. Ana Maria said to Ms. Baldwin: "This definitely changes the priorities for today." Here are the items that Ana Maria had on her To Do list for today. She had not prioritized them:

- Revise sales contract for national sales meeting in three weeks
- Complete weekly sales report due in three days
- Start planning monthly sales meeting two weeks from today

topic 8-1 review

- Call Tom about the Patterson report for the monthly sales meeting
- Call Lisa for lunch
- Look in tickler file
- Check e-mail messages
- Schedule room for monthly sales meeting in two weeks
- Make airline and hotel reservations for national sales meeting
- Verify travel expense vouchers
- Replenish desk supplies

What you are to do:

1. In groups, discuss the changes Ana Maria needs to make in her To Do list. List the items that will be affected by the supervisor's news.
2. In your group, prioritize the items to reflect the change in the date and time of the national sales meeting. What other items on her list will be affected?
3. Decide if other items will be added to or deleted from her To Do list.
4. Decide who else is affected by the news from the supervisor.
5. Review the discussion of To Do lists on page 359, if necessary.
6. Create a To Do list form and prepare a revised To Do list.
7. Share your group's new To Do list and its priorities with your class. Be able to justify and defend your newly revised list.

topic 8-1 review

REINFORCING ENGLISH SKILLS

You work in the Human Resources Department of Raleigh Corporation, a manufacturer of modular business furniture. Your supervisor, Florita Langford, has prepared a punctuation test to be administered to job applicants. She asks you to complete the punctuation test to be sure

370

that the instructions are clear before she has large quantities of the test printed.

What you are to do:

Refer to Chapter 8, Reinforcing English Skills, in your *Student Activities and Projects* workbook. Follow the instructions to complete the test. If necessary, refer to Reference Section B, Punctuation.

See Workbook page 41 for Punctuation Test and pages 215–219 for Reference Section B.

APPLICATION ACTIVITIES

ACTIVITY 1 Maintaining and Analyzing a Time Log

As you have learned in this topic, managing your time on the job and developing an orderly approach to your work are important for your success on the job. In this activity, you will complete a daily time log. After you have charted your activities, you will use your chart to help you determine your most and least productive time periods.

What you are to do:

1. Prepare a time-use log similar to the one shown in Illustration 8-1:2 on page 357, using the appropriate software. Print the number of copies you think you will need to complete this activity. Use 15-minute time intervals, and prepare the chart to cover your entire waking day; for example, 6:30 a.m. until 11:00 p.m. for one to two weeks.
2. Complete your time-use log. If you start Day 1 on Monday, for example, write Monday in the blank following Day 1. Try to record your activities every 15 minutes as you progress through each day and evening. Record all your activities: studying, attending class or going to work, watching TV, talking on the telephone, eating, and so on.
3. Analyze your time log and then summarize your analysis: Identify the hours where you used your time most productively as well as those hours where you wasted your time. During what hours do you get the most accomplished? During what hours do you tend to waste your time?

371

4. Summarize your time spent by hours into categories; for example, school, work, leisure, sleep, hobbies, etc.
5. Create a pie chart showing the percentages of time spent in each different category as part of your total time.
6. Write a two- or three-paragraph summary of the analysis of your time-use log. Include the pie chart in your written summary. Describe what you intend to do differently as a result of your time analysis.

ACTIVITY 2 Long-Term Portfolio Project

In this activity, you will plan, schedule, and complete a long-term project: a portfolio to display your work. This project should be completed four to six weeks from now.

You and your teacher should agree on the specific timeline for this activity. Consult your teacher and others to help you build a realistic schedule.

topic 8-1 review

What you are to do:

1. Consulting with your teacher, determine the deadline for completing the project.
2. List the steps to complete the portfolio. For example, define clearly the purpose for your portfolio, research portfolio layouts, schedule time to work on the portfolio, collect materials (classroom and other), create a tentative layout, and plan initial documents to go into the portfolio.
3. List the materials and resources you will need to complete the portfolio, such as folders, time, money, computer supplies, dividers, notebooks, classroom projects, and so forth.
4. List the people you need to contact to complete the project: teachers, administrators, students, parents, businesspeople, etc.

372

5. Construct a tentative long-range schedule, using spreadsheet software to list the dates and tasks in Items 1–4 above, to be completed by specific dates. (Hint: Enter your ending date or deadline first.) Enter a title and beginning date on your schedule to make it uniquely yours.
6. Print a copy of your schedule to use as you complete your portfolio project. Enter each date and task into your To Do list.
7. Make a note of the changes that had to be made to your original schedule as you complete your project: Was your deadline realistic? Were the people available at the times you listed? Did you find the materials and resources available when you needed them? Did you follow your schedule? If no, why not?
8. Write an evaluative summary of your experience, using the factors listed above and your own observations. Include in your summary a copy of your beginning and ending schedule for comparison purposes.
9. Display or share your portfolio with other class members.

373

Workstation Management and Office Safety

Topic 8-2

When you have completed the study of the information in this topic, you will be able to:

- **explain the importance of an organized workstation**
- **identify factors related to ergonomics and its importance to the office worker**
- **describe significant safety and security procedures for the office**

getting started GO

Office workers are managers of their time, activities, and work environment. Students should realize that being a good office worker requires more than technical skills. Discuss with them the relation of basic job requirements to the information presented in this topic.

As an office worker, you must be able to manage your work effectively to be productive. Proper lighting, the arrangement of your materials, and the design of your workstation contribute to your productivity. Most companies strive to provide physically comfortable and safe environments for their office employees. It is your responsibility to keep your work area well organized and to be aware of safety and security issues that affect you in the office environment.

Workstation Management

Your workstation is a key component of your work environment. A workstation is the physical area in which a worker performs his or her job. A typical workstation provides a work surface and space for equipment and supplies.

MANAGE YOUR WORKSTATION

The workstation shown in Illustration 8-2:1 is arranged so that the worker has easy access to the items used frequently, such as the computer keyboard, telephone, supplies, and reference materials. This is called a modular workstation, because it is made up of interchangeable components, such as sound-absorbing wall panels, storage areas, and a desktop surface. Interchangeable components permit the workstation to be arranged to meet the company's and the worker's individual needs. Modular workstations are generally used with the open office plan; however, they can be adapted for use with any office plan.

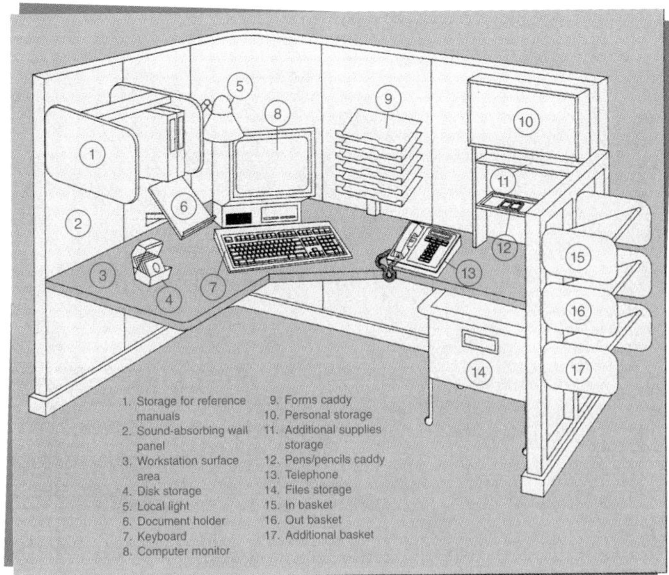

Illustration 8-2:1

Many companies provide flexible workstations that can be arranged to meet specific user needs.

1. What factors were considered to determine the proper location of each item shown in Illustration 8-2:1?
2. Would any item be better placed in a different location? If so, where should it be placed? Why?

The effective organization of your workstation increases your efficiency. A functional work area is one that is well maintained, well equipped, well organized, and efficiently managed. Illustration 8-2:2 on page 376 displays a work area that is **conducive** to productivity and efficiency. Specific attention should be given to managing

conducive:
favorable, helpful

the desktop area; your desk drawers; reference materials; and office equipment, supplies, and accessories.

Desktop Area. Keep your workstation's surface clear. Clutter on the desktop can cause unnecessary delays as you search for papers or objects. Remove materials that do not relate to your current project. Put descriptive labels on file folders, and place documents that are not needed in the folders. Place the folders in your file drawer.

Arrange your equipment and supplies to allow easy access so that you avoid making unnecessary movements. Keep frequently used supplies, such as pencils and paper clips, in a caddy on the surface of your work area. Reaching for the caddy is more efficient than opening and closing a drawer each time you need an item.

for discussion

Do you think the office employee who works at this workstation is organized or disorganized? Why?

Illustration 8-2:2

An organized desktop area will enhance productivity.

Drawers. Reserve your center drawer for frequently used supplies that are not needed on the surface area, such as a letter opener, scissors, and paper clamps. Arrange the contents of the center drawer so that the most frequently used supplies are toward the front where you can reach them easily.

accessible: easy to locate, reachable

The top side drawer may be used to store stationery supplies or to lay file folders containing current work so that they are readily **accessible** when you need them. You avoid cluttering the desktop by putting the file folders in a specific location in your desk. In this way, you also can protect any confidential items.

Illustration 8-2:3

Top, side drawer with files (left). Center drawer with supplies (right).

A desk also may contain either a file drawer or additional side drawers. A file drawer can be used to store files that are referred to often but are not in current use. Other drawers can be used to store supplies.

Reference Materials. The nature of your job will determine which references you will use most often. Some items may be in print form, while others may be accessed via your computer. Reference materials that should be accessible at your workstation may include a dictionary, a **thesaurus,** telephone directories, company and office reference manuals, safety handbooks, and equipment and software manuals. Other reference items used less often may include an almanac, atlas, and vendor supply catalogues.

thesaurus: book of words with synonyms

Office Equipment, Supplies, and Accessories. Office employees use a variety of equipment, supplies, and accessories to do their jobs. In fact, the right resources help you perform your job more efficiently. What you need at your workstation will depend on your particular job. Some of the more common equipment, supplies, and accessories are shown in Illustration 8-2:4 on page 378. Although this is not a **comprehensive** list, it is typical of what you may find at an office workstation.

comprehensive: complete

Using Office Supplies and Accessories. An adequately stocked workstation is essential to your productivity. If you run out of supplies in

expand the concept

A well-organized workstation increases worker productivity, since time is not wasted searching for a needed item. This concept can be applied to students' personal lives as well. Ask them to arrange the items in their school lockers or in a closet at home for maximum efficiency.

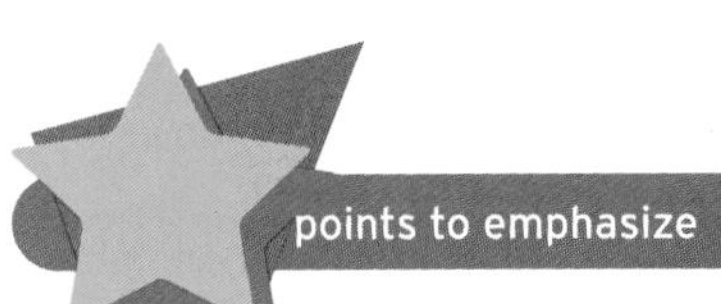

points to emphasize

The typical office employee uses a variety of office supplies and accessories. Correctly selecting, using, and caring for office supplies are factors in the economical use of resources. How an employee handles and utilizes office supplies also demonstrates whether he or she is a good steward of a company's resources.

challenge option

Provide various equipment, supplies, and accessories typically found on a workstation surface or in the drawers of a workstation. Ask two students to demonstrate before the class how they would organize the workstation for maximum efficiency. Ask the class to discuss and critique the arrangement.

You may want to bring two or three brands of various office supplies for students to compare—such as plain paper of different weights and for different types of printers, letterhead, forms, notepads, ribbons, plastic and metal paper clips, markers and pens, self-stick notes and tape flags, file folders, and so on. Cover the brand names and let students test and examine the products. Discuss the possible uses, strengths, and weaknesses of the office products. This activity will help students realize that the quality and designated uses of office supplies vary. Selecting the right supply item for the task often affects how successfully the task will be completed. (Alternative exercises might include a visit to an office supply store near your school or asking students to visit the store in groups and compare quality and cost of the products.)

Illustration 8-2:4

A variety of equipment, supplies, and accessories are commonly needed at a workstation.

WORKSTATION EQUIPMENT, SUPPLIES AND ACCESSORIES		
	workstation equipment	microcomputer, computer monitor, keyboard, input device (mouse or trackball), printer, scanner, transcription unit, electronic calculator, telephone, modem
	basic supplies and accessories	calendar and/or daily planner, scissors, paper clips, stapler and staple remover, pencils, pens, tape and tape dispenser, notepaper and message pads, in and out baskets
	communication-related supplies	date stamp and ink pad, stationery, envelopes, forms, reference materials
	information processing supplies	diskettes and CD-ROMS, diskette and CD files, software and hardware manuals, computer paper, data binders, printer ribbons, toner cartridge
	peripheral supplies	typewriter and ribbons, correction supplies, printwheels or elements

the middle of a critical task, you could lose valuable work time by stopping to **replenish** needed supplies. Also, you run the risk of not completing the task on time. Use supplies properly for best results and to save money. Here are four guidelines to follow:

replenish: make full, restock

- Select the quality of the supply according to the nature and importance of the task. For example, if you are preparing a rough draft of an important letter, don't use expensive letterhead paper. Use a lower-quality paper for the rough draft and the letterhead paper for the final copy.
- Learn to read product labels for the correct use of a product. For example, paper designed for use in a laser printer may not work well in an inkjet printer.

- Look for ways to conserve supplies. For example, reuse file folders by placing new file folder labels over the old ones. To save paper, preview documents carefully onscreen before printing.
- Do not **hoard** supplies in your workstation. It is a work area, not a storage space. Check your workstation periodically. If you have not used a supply item in several weeks, perhaps it should be returned to the supply cabinet.

hoard:
collect in great numbers

Illustration 8-2:5
To work efficiently, keep adequate supplies at your workstation.

Using and Maintaining Office Equipment. Since the condition of your equipment affects the quality of your work, you will want to keep your equipment in top working order. To get dependable service from your equipment, you will need to practice preventive maintenance. This involves servicing equipment and replacing parts while the equipment is functioning properly in order to prevent failure. Fewer repairs are necessary when equipment is cared for properly on a daily basis. By practicing preventive maintenance, you can extend the life of your equipment over a longer period of time. You will want to follow these three maintenance guidelines:

- Learn how to use and care for the equipment properly. Read and understand the manufacturer's operating instructions. Follow the **troubleshooting** guidelines so that you are able to recognize and prevent minor problems.

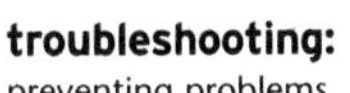

troubleshooting:
preventing problems

Office workers are expected to learn how to use office equipment properly and to do their part in keeping it properly maintained, including anticipating and trouble-shooting potential minor problems.

adhere:
follow closely

- Inspect and clean equipment regularly. Know the basic care routines your equipment requires. Establish a regular inspection schedule. **Adhere** to the preventive measures (such as cleaning and replacements) recommended by the manufacturer.
- Report problems immediately. When you spot a potential problem, take steps to prevent it from occurring or report it to the appropriate person. Many minor problems can be corrected before they become serious and require costly repair.

How does the work environment affect an employee's health and feelings of job satisfaction? Use Illustration 8-2:6 to expand this discussion.

MANAGE ERGONOMIC FACTORS

Ergonomics is the study of the effects of the work environment on the health and well-being of employees. How well a workstation and its components—chairs, desks, lighting, and computer equipment—are designed can influence your productivity, efficiency, and physical well-being. Illustration 8-2:6 focuses on the height and angle dimensions of

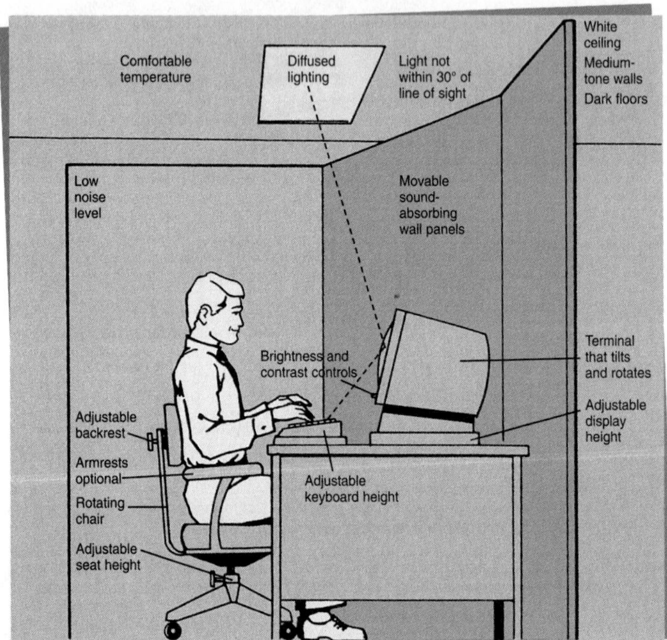

Illustration 8-2:6
Ergonomic factors affect productivity.

an ergonomically sound workstation. This workstation allows the user to adjust the chair, desk, lighting, and computer equipment.

A well-designed chair is essential since many office workers spend much of their time sitting. However, ergonomic seating involves more than just quality. An ergonomic chair must be adjustable, like the one shown in Illustration 8-2:7. Office workers should be able to adjust their chairs to fit individual physical requirements for comfort and good posture.

The height of the desktop should allow your elbows to be parallel to the computer keyboard and floor as shown in Illustration 8-2:6. This arrangement prevents unnecessary strain on the arms and wrists. Keep the desktop clear of materials not related to the current task.

Two kinds of lighting are often found in workstations: ambient and task. **Ambient** lighting is provided by overhead light fixtures for the entire work area. Although you may not be able to adjust the overhead lighting, you can adjust the arrangement of your workstation. Task lighting focuses on the immediate work area and should be adjustable for your specific needs. Adjust the task lighting so that there are no glares on your computer monitor or from the desktop. Ensure that there are no dark or dimly lit areas where you may have to retrieve files or work away from your desktop.

ambient:
surrounding, on all sides

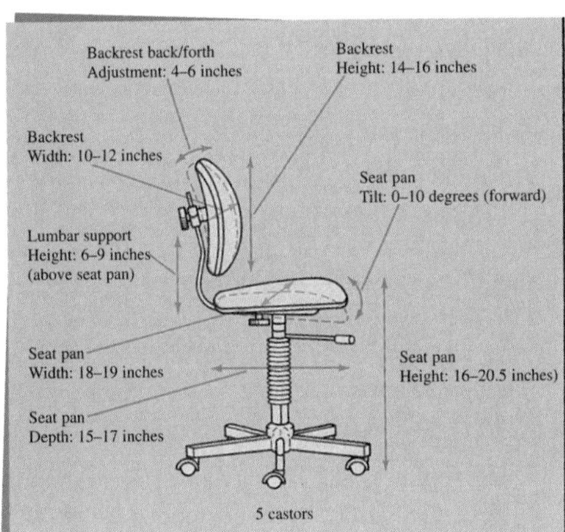

Illustration 8-2:7

Some experts believe a chair is a workstation's most vital component.

teaching tips

You may want to have current catalogs, equipment and furniture brochures, and business magazines readily available so students can become acquainted with typical equipment and furnishings found in offices. You may want to ask students to equip an office that you describe (e.g., an office of an assistant to an executive, a home office, or an office for eight customer service representatives). Have the students cut out or draw the furniture and equipment and office layout. Ask them to list the key elements they considered in designing their offices, including ergonomic and aesthetic factors. The final layouts with explanations can be used for a bulletin board display.

Illustration 8-2:6 can be used to reinforce the ergonomic factors that are critical to employee productivity, health, and well-being.

Demonstrate relaxation techniques, hand and finger exercises, and correct posture. Then have students practice them.

Your computer monitor should be placed at eye level, as shown in Illustration 8-2:6, to help reduce eyestrain and neck pain. Glare on the monitor often contributes to eyestrain. Common symptoms of eyestrain are teary or burning eyes, blurred vision, and headaches. Glare from outside light can be prevented by placing the computer monitor so that you do not face a window or have your back to a window. Peripheral input devices, such as the mouse, should be located next to the computer keyboard. The movement of the arm from the keyboard to the input device should be natural and without strain.

MANAGE YOUR OFFICE HEALTH

Being aware of the physical responses your body has to your work procedures and habits will enhance your job satisfaction, comfort, and productivity. The following guidelines may help you complete your work without feelings of strain, fatigue, or other physical discomforts:

- Learn to adjust the workstation components for the best fit to your work habits and procedures. Follow the manufacturer's recommended work postures and practices even if at first they feel unnatural.
- Take rest breaks often—at least 15 minutes every two hours. Do not sit in front of your computer monitor or at your desk for long uninterrupted periods of time. Arrange your work so that you have to get out of your chair and walk to the copier or to the supply cabinet. If you feel yourself becoming **fatigued,** stop working and do simple breathing or relaxation exercises.

fatigued: tired, weary

- Learn stretching exercises for your hands, wrists, arms, and fingers to relieve pressure on them. Carpal tunnel syndrome is a repetitive strain injury that occurs when stress is placed on the hands, wrists, or arms while working at the computer keyboard or using the computer input device for prolonged periods of time. Again, taking breaks from the computer keyboard will give your hands, wrists, and arms a chance to relax. Simply dropping your arms to your side and dangling them will relieve tension. Squeeze a handgripper to strengthen and relieve tension in hands and wrists.
- Focus your eyes away from your computer monitor often. Do not stare at the monitor for an extended length of time. Remember to

blink your eyes. If possible, face your computer monitor against a wall to avoid looking directly out of a window or into glare from other bright light sources. Place antiglare filters similar to the one shown in Illustration 8-2:8 over the monitor screen. Filters reduce glare, static electricity, and dirt and smudge buildup on the screen. Adjust the screen brightness to a contrast level that is comfortable for you. Adjust the screen angle so that it is at eye level or slightly lower. Remember to occasionally clean the screen with an antistatic cloth to remove dust, dirt, and fingerprints.

Illustration 8-2:8

Antiglare screens reduce glare and reflection from computer monitors.

- Learn and use good posture: back straight against the back of your chair, feet flat on the floor, and computer monitor at the proper height and angle so that it is level with your eyes. To enhance your posture, adjust your chair so that your feet do not dangle off the floor; use a footrest if your feet don't touch the floor; use a back pad to keep your back in a straight line; and adjust your computer monitor to the right height and angle for you.
- Arrange your work materials so that you do not have to overreach for the telephone or supplies, lift heavy binders or boxes, bend or stretch to reach files, or strain to use staplers or paper punches. Avoid repetitive motions for extended periods of time without taking a break.
- Report any prolonged physical discomfort that affects your work performance to your supervisor.

Filters reduce glare, static electricity, and dirt and smudge buildup on the computer monitor screen.

In developing this information with the students, you may want to begin with a brief discussion of accidents in general. Ask students if they have ever had an accident, and let one or two describe the events of the accident. Tell them that accidents occur in the office as well and that they will learn how to make themselves and their coworkers safer in the office by studying this information.

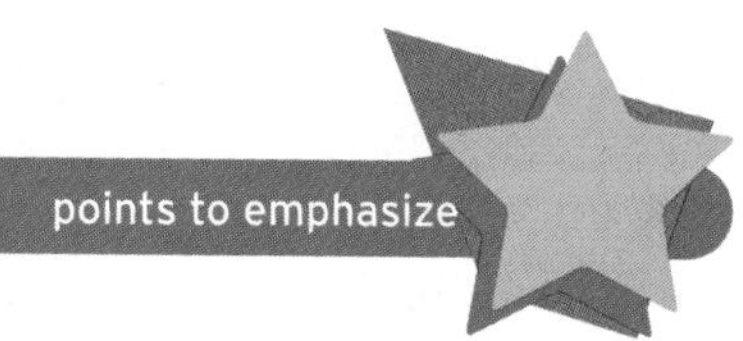

It is important to understand how accidents can be prevented in an office. Many companies have a formal accident prevention program.

What might Molly have done to prevent this accident from occurring? What could Laverne have done to prevent her coworker from being injured?

Office Safety

Most of us think of the office as a safe place to work. Office workers are not required to use heavy equipment or power tools. They are seldom exposed to poisonous chemicals or dangerous working conditions. Yet, thousands of them have disabling accidents each year. Falling, tripping, or slipping account for many office accidents. Common causes of falls include drawers partially open, slippery floors, torn or loose carpeting, obstructions on stairs or in walkways, and dangling telephone or electrical cords.

Other causes of office accidents include faulty or poorly maintained equipment, collisions and obstructions, falling objects, fire and electrical hazards, and human carelessness. Potential safety problems can exist in any office. With knowledge of correct safety procedures, however, you can learn how to correct and report potential safety problems and prevent injury to yourself and your coworkers.

ACCIDENT PREVENTION

To many people, the office seems to hold little danger. Becoming aware of the potential safety hazards in an office is the first step to gaining control over unsafe procedures and conditions. Unfortunately, accident control often is imposed only after an accident occurs. An *accident prevention approach* should be used to decrease the chances that an undesirable incident will occur. Workers who develop positive safety attitudes are able to detect potential safety problems and take steps to eliminate them.

Molly came around the corner with her arms full of supplies for the supply cabinet. She could not see where she was going very well since her arms were so loaded down. She should not have been trying to carry so much, but she was trying to save a few steps and not have to make a second trip.

Laverne looked up from the phone to see Molly just a few feet from her open file drawer. When Laverne realized that Molly could not see where she was walking, she called, "Watch out!" Too late—Molly fell with a loud crash over the bottom file drawer. X-rays showed that Molly had broken her wrist while trying to catch herself in the fall. She was unable to resume her full duties for eight weeks.

This accident could have been prevented if Molly and Laverne had acted responsibly. Laverne should have closed the file drawer, and Molly should have carried the supplies in two trips rather than in one.

WORKSTATION SAFETY

Most office employees spend the majority of their working time at their workstations. The wise safety practices you use at your own workstation will repay you in personal safety benefits. Remember the following safety pointers.

Desktop Area. As you work, you will occasionally use scissors and other sharp objects. Place them away from the edge of your workstation so they will not be knocked off easily. Avoid eating or drinking at your desk. An overturned drink can ruin hours of hard work! Pencils stored on the top of your desk with the sharp points up are dangerous; they are best stored flat or with points down. Use a staple remover, rather than your fingernail, to remove staples. Never examine a jammed stapler by holding it near your eyes or testing it over your finger.

Drawers. Keep your workstation drawers neat. Do not allow papers to **accumulate** to the point of clutter. If the drawers are cluttered, your hands could easily be punctured by hidden scissors, pins, or pencils. Sharp objects such as pins and thumbtacks should be placed in closed containers.

accumulate: collect

Even with these precautions, never reach blindly into a desk drawer or file drawer. Take time to look where you are placing your hands, even if you are rushed or are talking to someone. Close workstation and file drawers by the handle. Don't push a drawer shut by placing your hand at the top or side of the drawer. You may lose a fingernail or suffer a crushed finger or hand.

Chairs/Mats/Static Control. Most office chairs have casters, which are small wheels that provide ease of movement for the worker. This same ease of movement can produce painful injury unless you look at the chair and hold onto its arms or seat as you sit down. When seated, be careful not to lean too far forward or backward to prevent falling out of the chair.

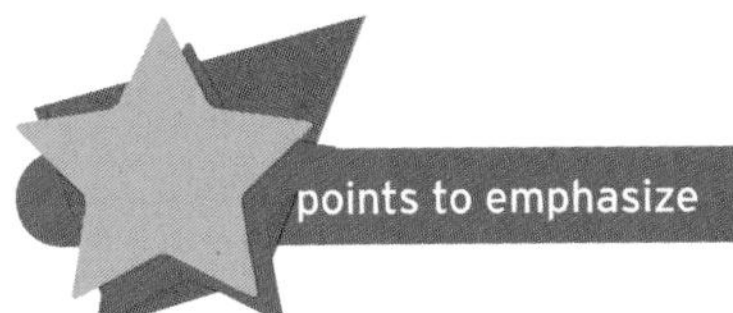

Organizations strive to maintain a safe and secure environment for all their employees by encouraging them to adhere to safe practices at their workstations.

After covering the material on potential safety hazards in the office, ask students: What would you suggest to this office worker to correct the obvious safety problems? Are there any safety hazards that are not so obvious?

Many of the suggestions for work area safety presented here can be implemented in the classroom and in the home to make those environments safer. Ask students to conduct a short safety inspection of your classroom and to offer suggestions for correcting any safety concerns they find. Also, they may want to conduct a safety inspection of their homes.

Illustration 8-2:9
Extension cords often present a tripping hazard.

A chair mat is a vinyl pad placed underneath the chair to eliminate wear on the carpet from rolling the chair. Static control mats are designed for use on floors underneath workstations and computer monitors. The static control mat safeguards valuable computer data and electronic equipment from possible harm from a charge of static electricity.

Chair mats and static control mats can cause you to trip, particularly if the edges are beginning to curl. Replace worn mats when they become a hazard.

WORK AREA SAFETY

In addition to your workstation, other objects in your immediate work area can either add to your comfort and work productivity or become a source of injury.

Office Furnishings. Learn how to use small furnishings, such as a step stool and paper cutter. In using a step stool with casters, step firmly in the middle of the stool. Never step to the side because this can cause the stool to slide out from under you. When using the paper cutter, keep your fingers away from the blade and never leave the blade up. Furniture with rough or sharp edges should be sanded or taped to prevent injury to employees and to prevent clothing from being torn.

Report to the appropriate person tears in carpets, burned-out lights, broken handles or mechanisms on equipment, and other potential hazards related to office furnishings.

File drawers should be filled beginning with the bottom drawer of the cabinet and moving to the top drawer. **Conversely,** they should be emptied from the top drawer down. When working with file cabinets, pull out only one drawer at a time so that you do not change the cabinet's center of gravity and cause it to tip over. Avoid placing objects that have the potential to harm you or your coworkers on top of filing cabinets. Coffeemakers or heavy plants can slip off the cabinet and cause serious injuries.

conversely: reversed in order, on the other hand

Electrical Equipment. Office equipment, such as electric staplers, electric pencil sharpeners, electric hole punchers, deskside paper shredders, computers and related peripherals, adds to the convenience of office workers. With the increase in electrical and computer equipment in the office, many cords and cables become a safety hazard. Cables and cords should never extend into traffic areas. Do not overload electrical outlets. If necessary, purchase a power strip or **surge suppressor** made specifically for multiple appliances. An extension cord should be used only to extend the position of the electrical appliance, not to increase the power load.

surge suppressor: electrical outlet that controls unexpected sharp increases in electricity

Electrical cords to power strips, surge suppressors, and extension cords should be placed behind equipment or within the walls of the workstation. If cords must be placed where people walk and they present a tripping hazard, tape them down or cover them with materials made specifically for this purpose.

General Office Equipment. You will want to keep the following safety procedures in mind when you use office equipment:

- When operating office equipment, follow the manufacturer's directions for safe and efficient equipment use.
- When you are operating equipment, avoid other activities that will distract you from the operation of the equipment.
- If you feel a tingling sensation, notice smoke, or smell something burning while you are operating the equipment, turn it off and

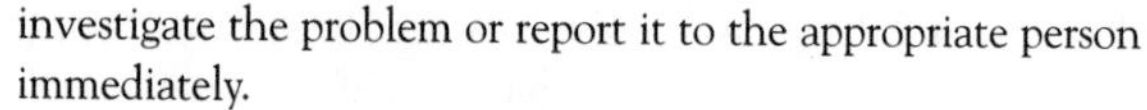

investigate the problem or report it to the appropriate person immediately.

- Know where the power switches are located on the equipment in your general area. In the event of an emergency, power surge, or power outage, you may need to turn off the equipment.

Ask students to identify emergency numbers that should be posted by their home telephone.

KNOW EMERGENCY PROCEDURES

Learn emergency procedures immediately upon beginning a new job. If your office does not have established procedures, do what you can to help initiate practices such as those described in the following paragraphs.

Emergency Telephone Numbers. Emergency telephone numbers are used to seek help for an immediately dangerous situation. The most important are those of the company medical and security personnel, police and fire departments, paramedics, and the general emergency number for your area, such as 911.

Emergency numbers should be posted beside each telephone or, ideally, stored in each telephone's memory. The memory feature saves valuable time in an emergency. You press only one or two buttons, and the number is automatically dialed.

Encourage students to attend first aid or CPR classes offered in the area. The life-saving techniques they learn will be a valuable asset in both their personal and professional lives. You might ask them to make a list for future reference of the agencies or organizations that offer first aid or CPR training in their area.

First Aid Procedures. First aid kits should be located conveniently within the office. They should be inspected frequently and restocked whenever supplies are used from the kit. Some firms will send an employee from each floor or work group for first aid training and/or CPR (cardiopulmonary resuscitation) classes. These courses are given periodically by the American Red Cross. Each employee should know who has completed first aid training and who is qualified to help in the critical first minutes of an emergency. First aid posters can be put in **conspicuous** places to further assist employees.

conspicuous: easily seen, out in the open

Fires. Some companies prohibit the use of appliances, such as cup warmers and space heaters, because of their potential fire hazard. If appliances are allowed in your office, always unplug them when they are not in use and before leaving the office. Know the location of the nearest fire exit, fire alarm box, and fire extinguisher. Large office buildings generally have the fire alarm boxes and fire extinguishers in

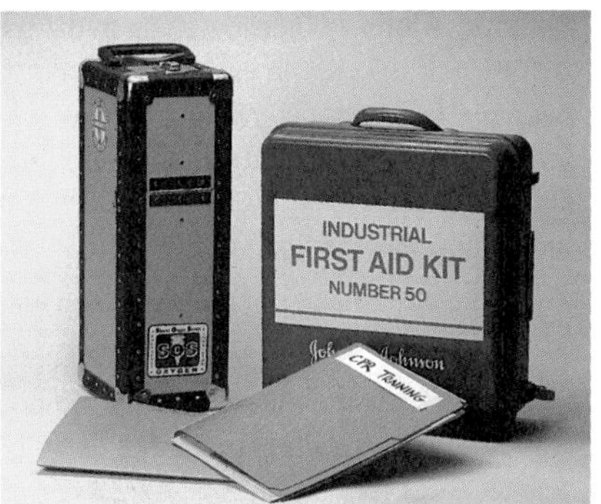

Illustration 8-2:10

First aid kits, oxygen, and CPR manuals should be easily accessible.

the same location patterns on each floor. Learn how to use the fire extinguisher and what type of fire it is intended to put out. Never attempt to fight a fire alone. Always have someone report it to the proper agency.

Building Evacuation Plans. Learn the established escape routes and **evacuation** procedures for your building. Emergency exit routes should be posted in conspicuous places throughout the building. Employees should know their individual responsibilities during a drill or evacuation. Who, for example, is responsible for checking conference rooms, restrooms, and other areas where the alarm may not be heard?

evacuation: leaving, clearing the area

1. Do you know the proper evacuation procedures for leaving the school building in an emergency?
2. For leaving your home in an emergency?

PERSONAL SECURITY ON THE JOB

Protection for yourself and your property requires a continuous **vigil** on your part. Most businesses strive to provide a safe and secure work environment for their employees. To **complement** the company's effort in providing for your safety and security on the job, you should always use good common sense.

vigil: watch

complement: make complete, support

Protecting Personal Property. A purse left at a workstation, a jacket slung over the back of a chair or left in an unoccupied office, cash left out in plain sight—all are invitations to a would-be thief. Keep personal belongings out of sight and locked in a drawer, file cabinet, or employee locker or closet. The key to this drawer or other receptacle should be issued only to the employee who is assigned its use.

Ask students how they would react in the following situations:

1. You work in an office that is located in a large office building. You decide to work late to finish a project. Because you are alone, you lock the door to your office. You are about to "call it a day" when someone knocks on the door and says, "Open up, please. I'm with the cleaning service, and I need to get in so I can clean your office." You know the custodial staff usually cleans the offices in the building earlier in the evening. What specifically would you do in this situation?
2. You work for an insurance company that has its own building in a business office complex. Again, you are working after-hours to complete the monthly report, which must be sent to the regional headquarters the next day. You hear the fire alarm in an adjacent office go off. What specifically would you do in this situation?

abide: stay

Working Alone. Sometimes you may find it necessary to stay late at the office or to come in early. If your company has established security measures, follow the company procedures for being in the building during non-working hours. If no after-hours procedures exist, establish your own security routine and **abide** by it. Follow these security procedures when you work alone:

- Always work near a phone and keep emergency telephone numbers handy.
- Lock all doors to your work area. Do not open the door to anyone you are not expecting or cannot identify.
- Get to know the cleaning staff and when to expect them.
- If you use the elevator to leave the building, do not enter the elevator if anyone is in it whom you find suspicious.
- Avoid using a restroom that is located away from your work area.
- When working late, phone home before leaving the office to let someone know what time to expect you. If you live alone, call a friend before leaving the office and again when you get home to let her or him know you've arrived safely.
- Park your car near the building entrance and/or in a lighted parking lot. Check the parking lot visually before leaving the building. Have your car keys in your hand and ready to use. If security personnel are available, ask to be escorted to your car.

KNOW BUILDING AND OFFICE SECURITY

safeguards: protection

Building and office security measures are necessary **safeguards.** Casual consideration of security measures today has been replaced by a more serious approach to planning and analyzing security needs. Discontented workers, theft, sabotage, and fire are major security concerns of a business.

instituted: established, initiated

disgruntled: discontented, upset

Many companies today have **instituted** security procedures to guard against employees who have been fired or who are experiencing pressures from work. These **disgruntled** workers pose a hazard to themselves and to their fellow workers. Be alert to changes in your coworkers' behavior and to statements they may make that sound like threats against supervisory personnel or the company. Know the procedures for protecting yourself from these workers:

- Do not get involved in a verbal exchange.
- Leave the work area if you are feeling threatened and proceed to an area designated as safe.
- Report any unusual behavior to your supervisor and/or company security personnel.

The protection of computer-generated information and records is an issue in many companies. Entrance to secure areas is carefully controlled. In addition, privacy and protection for employees while on company property are important concerns.

Controlling Outsider Access. Although businesses cannot operate without being open to the public, the public does not need uncontrolled access to all parts of most office buildings. Businesses use varied security means to safeguard their personnel and assets. In large metropolitan areas, for example, the presence of a highly visible, centrally located security station with personnel in the lobby has proved effective.

Some companies have security personnel who make sure each visitor signs a log and gives his or her name, address, and the name of the person or office being visited. (See Illustration 8-2:11.) Other companies find it more convenient to send an employee to the lobby to escort the visitor back to the office. In smaller offices, the receptionist may be the controlling agent simply by being present in the front office.

Illustration 8-2:11

Office security guards provide protection for workers and office property.

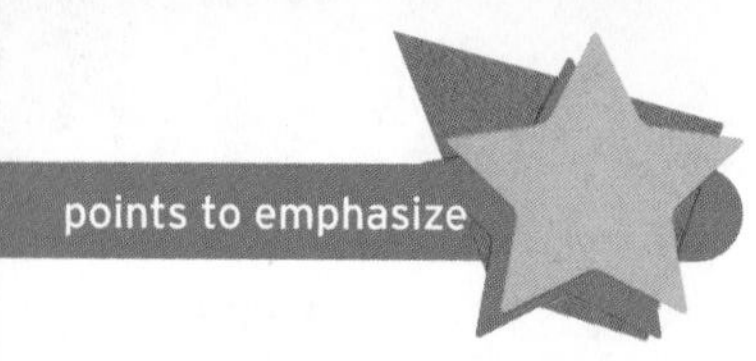

As an office worker, you will want to understand and abide by all security measures established by the company in which you work.

Do you know someone who uses an identification (ID) card to gain access to buildings or grounds at his or her place of employment? Discuss the procedure this person follows.

Controlling Employee Access. Many medium- and large-sized businesses require positive identification of those employees who should have access to the buildings and grounds through the use of identification (ID) cards or badges. Photo ID cards, like the one shown in Illustration 8-2:12, are issued by many companies. Your cooperation in wearing your ID helps assure your personal safety and security on the job.

Businesses that must restrict employee entry to selected areas of a building often use a magnetically coded card as a substitute for keys. This card can be inserted by the employee into a magnetic card reader to gain access. If the card is authorized for entrance, the door opens.

Some companies use magnetically coded badges that can be sensed by electronic readers, referred to as proximity readers. As the wearer approaches a controlled access point, the electronic reader reads the code on the badge and transmits the information to a computer. This information provides a record of who enters and leaves designated areas, the time of entry, and in some instances, the time of exit—all valuable security information.

Illustration 8-2:12

Some companies issue their employees photo IDs or magnetically coded access cards.

Olivia looked up to see a repairman coming through the doorway. "I'm here to check your computer. Apparently, you had a large electrical surge last night. Here's the order," he said, as he flashed a copy of a repair order in front of Olivia. "This will take a few minutes— why don't you just take a short break?"

Olivia got up from her terminal, but she was puzzled. She hadn't heard that an electrical surge had occurred. "Besides," she thought, "we have surge suppressors for the equipment." Olivia felt she should check this with her supervisor, Ms. Calibre.

Ms. Calibre was not aware of an electrical surge occurring either. "Let me check on this before we do anything," she said. Olivia stepped back into her office to see the repairman disconnecting the computer.

Repairman: Looks like I'll have to take your computer back to the shop for repairs.

Olivia: You'll have to wait until my supervisor authorizes you to take the computer.

Repairman: Well, I have several other computers to check. Why don't I come back after I've checked them and pick this one up.

The repairman left hurriedly, and a minute or so later Olivia's supervisor appeared at the door: "No one authorized a computer repair check. We had better report this."

Ms. Calibre called the police immediately to report the incident. The police sergeant told her that several businesses had recently lost computers and other electronic equipment in this manner. "You're lucky to have an alert employee," the sergeant told Ms. Calibre. "None of the others questioned an unexpected repair check. When the employees returned from their 'short breaks,' their equipment was gone."

Would you have done what Olivia did in this situation? If not, what would you have done?

Detection Systems and Alarms. Companies often choose to use a combination of security systems and procedures. Detection systems and alarms reinforce other security measures. A detection system consists of **monitoring** devices and alarms that sense and signal a change in the condition of an area being protected. Some detection

monitoring:
warning, watching

You may want to arrange for students to visit a building that is monitored by closed-circuit television or other detection systems. Perhaps the building security guard could discuss the types of detection systems used in the building and how they operate.

systems detect entry into the area while others are designed to detect movement in the area.

Detection systems and alarms are designed to reduce a firm's reliance on an on-site security guard. Even if a firm has security officers, they cannot be at all stations at once. Closed-circuit television, as shown in Illustration 8-2:13, can be used to provide continuous monitoring of corridors, entrances, or other sensitive areas. When used with a videotape recorder, closed-circuit television provides the firm with a record of significant events for review.

Illustration 8-2:13
Closed-circuit television provides continuous monitoring of the premises.

Reviewing the Topic

1. What is the guiding principle you should follow in planning the arrangement of any workstation?
2. Describe how you can organize your workstation (both desktop areas and drawers) to increase your productivity.
3. Discuss the guidelines an office worker should follow when using office equipment, supplies, and accessories.
4. What are the safety practices you should follow in maintaining your own workstation?
5. What are the safety practices you should follow with regard to office furnishings and electrical and electronic equipment?
6. What are the safety practices you should follow with regard to general office equipment?
7. Describe the emergency office procedures you should learn immediately upon starting a new job.
8. Describe some of the precautions you may take as an office worker to protect yourself and your personal property on the job.
9. How can you help assure your personal security when you are working alone?
10. Explain procedures businesses use to control access to their property and employees by other employees and by outsiders.

THINKING CRITICALLY

At a department meeting your manager, Mr. Petersen, discusses a memo regarding company security. He shakes his head and says: "This is the second memo the managers have received about security leaks. One of our competitors has just introduced a new product, and it's identical to a product we have been working on. Apparently they discovered our plans. The president wants our thoughts on how to improve our product security. In addition to the main shredder in the reprographics center, he is suggesting a shredder for each office. Well,

topic 8-2 review

Workstation Management and Office Safety

395

I'm just glad everyone in our department can be trusted."

As you hear this, you remember several situations you have observed in the office:

- You have seen poor photocopies—even photocopies of confidential material—discarded in the wastebasket.
- Computer printouts with product-testing results are left stacked next to the filing cabinets rather than being locked inside them.
- Workers often talk about current projects during their breaks.
- Workers have a habit of using the offices of other workers who are out of town or on vacation.
- Workers too freely give out unnecessary information to callers, such as telling a caller exactly where the individual is.

"Tell me," Mr. Petersen says, "do you think we need a shredder? What other measures can we take to tighten security? Please give this matter some thought and send me your ideas."

How do you respond to him? What suggestions can you make for tightening office security?

topic 8-2 review

See Workbook page 235.

What you are to do:

Prepare a response to the questions in a memo to Mr. Petersen. Include suggestions for correcting the problems mentioned above as well as other security measures that you think would be effective. Refer to Reference Section H, Sample Documents, for a sample memo format.

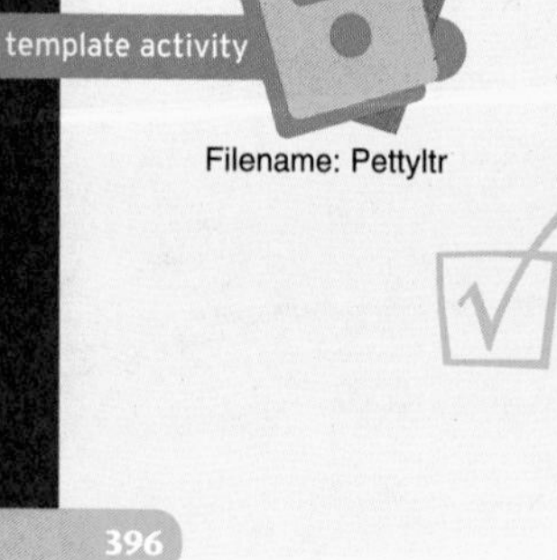

Filename: Pettyltr

REINFORCING ENGLISH SKILLS

In this exercise, you will edit and format a rough draft letter to Ms. Joan Petty at Officeware, Inc. You will also design a letterhead for your company.

What you are to do:

1. Design a letterhead for a company that is a retail outlet for office furniture and supplies. Make up a company name, address, and phone number to include in the letterhead. Use clip art or drawing tools to place a

396

graphic in the letterhead design. You may use any template, wizard, or macro file available with your word processing software to create the letterhead.

2. Open the template file *Pettyltr*. Cut and paste the body of the letter into your letterhead file.
3. Correct all grammatical, spelling, number/word usage, capitalization, and punctuation errors in the letter. Insert paragraphs and reword the letter to correct errors where appropriate.
4. Arrange the letter in an acceptable format, adding any missing letter parts. Use your name in the signature block. (Refer to Reference Section H, Sample Documents for a sample letter format.) Print one copy and sign your letter.

APPLICATION ACTIVITY

ACTIVITY **Office Safety Guidelines**

Your supervisor, Mr. Petersen, is concerned that each employee take an active interest in good safety practices. He is considering an employee's suggestion that a safety committee be formed for each floor of the building. He would like you and your committee members to develop a safety guidelines checklist for your floor of the building. The checklist will be submitted to the company safety department for final approval.

What you are to do:

1. Work as part of a group assigned by your instructor. Compose a list of 15 to 20 office safety guidelines. Use your textbook, magazine articles, online resources, or safety handbooks as your sources.
2. Open the template file *Safety*. Key your guidelines to complete the table.

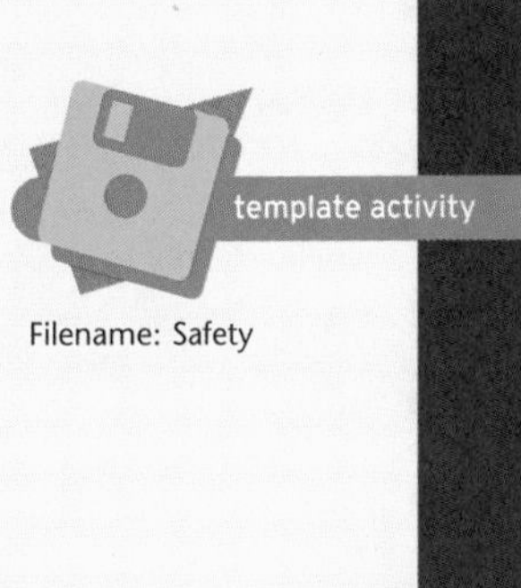

Filename: Safety

challenge option

Consider your classroom to be an office. Ask students to compose safety guidelines for your particular room. Instruct them to key a draft of the guidelines for your review.

See Workbook page 236.

thinking critically

Ask students to complete these additional sentences:

1. A workstation should be organized so an employee can work efficiently and productively throughout each workday. As a future office employee, I plan to arrange my workstation...
2. Using time efficiently involves developing an orderly approach to work. I plan to handle time obligations effectively by...

Chapter Summary

In this chapter, you learned the importance of managing your time and workstation effectively. The roles of both employee and employer in establishing and following office safety and security procedures also were discussed. Consider the points listed below as you reinforce your understanding of the topics in this chapter:

- Task management is vital to your success on the job. Although what you actually do in your job will depend upon the nature of the business for which you are employed, you will need to be able to plan and organize your work activities, whatever they may be.
- You will need to manage effectively the resources that support your work activities. The basic resources for this are your workstation and your time. Your workstation provides the physical space for you to do your job. By correctly organizing the equipment and supplies at your workstation, you can increase your productivity.
- Your time on the job must be channeled to assure that time obligations are handled effectively and that time-wasters are eliminated.
- The typical office employee uses a variety of office supplies and equipment. Correctly selecting, using, and caring for office supplies are important cost reduction factors in an office. Office workers are expected to learn how to use office equipment properly and to do their part in properly maintaining it.
- Ergonomic factors related to the office contribute to your physical comfort and well-being, as well as to enhancing your productivity and efficiency.
- Organizations strive to maintain a safe and secure environment for all their employees. As an office worker, you should follow safe practices at your workstation. You should understand and follow all security measures established by your company.

chapter 8 summary

Time and Workstation Management

398

KEY CONCEPTS AND TERMS

accident prevention approach
carpal tunnel syndrome
ergonomics
functional work area
information overload
office health
preventive maintenance
time analysis
time management
time-management tools
time-wasters
work simplification
workstation

INTEGRATED CHAPTER ACTIVITIES

ACTIVITY 1 Getting Ready for an Office Equipment Sale

Your manager has asked you to plan and submit a tentative schedule for advertising a sale of office equipment to begin two months from today. She wants your tentative schedule one week from today. She hands you a rough draft of the inventory list of the products that will be included in the sale. Items marked with an asterisk (*) will have to be ordered from the suppliers so that they arrive in time for the sale.

What you are to do:

Filename: Todosale

1. Create a To Do list for the sale. A partial list is included in the template file *Todosale*. Create a form that includes these columns: Priority, Task, Completed. Place the items on the form in the Task column. Next, rank each item in order of importance:

   A Most Important

   B Medium Importance

   C Least Important item

   Key the rank in the Priority column. If an item is listed as a C item, does it need to be completed at all? If not, delete the item. Are there other items that need to be added to this list? If yes, add these items.

399

2. Create a long-term schedule for the office equipment sale. Use spreadsheet software to complete the exercise.
   - List tasks to be completed from your To Do list in order by date using the dates when a task should be begun. Start with your ending deadline and work backward to create your schedule. For example, if a task should be completed one week before the sale and the task takes two weeks to complete, then list the task on the date three weeks prior to the sale.
   - Show dates when each task should be completed.
   - Include a column to check off tasks and confirm that they have been completed on time.

ACTIVITY 2 Create a Safety Presentation

Ms. Perez has asked your work group to present a short safety presentation based on the safety guidelines checklist you have completed. The presentation will be made to your peers and the company safety department. The presentations are to be used to promote office safety during the company Safety Month.

What you are to do:

1. Work in a small group as assigned by your instructor to complete this activity.
2. Use the list of safety guidelines you created for the Application Activity, Office Safety Guidelines, in Topic 8-2. Rank the items on the safety guidelines list in order of importance, with Item 1 being the most important and Item 15 being the least important. Prepare a list of your ranked items.
3. Still working in your group, create a short safety presentation for your peers and the members of the company safety department. Your group may choose to include all 15 items in the safety presentation or choose to focus on the 5 most important items according to your list. Be guided by your instructor.

400

4. Your presentation should include the major points about safety as well as clip art, tables, graphs, or other visuals to support and enhance the presentation. Use presentation software, if available, to prepare your safety presentation.
5. Make the presentation to another work group or to the entire class.

401

Getting Acquainted with the World of Work

Blake Williams
Office Manager

Safety First—All the Time!

Dear Mr. Williams

My supervisor arrived this morning and found that the empty coffeepot had been plugged in overnight. Last week, someone forgot to lock up an expensive projection system at the end of the day. My employer is becoming concerned that the safety and security practices of our office are too lax.

Although we have no formal safety program, we do try to practice good work habits. We are all very busy, and we won't have a lot of time to listen to presentations on safety and security. Do you have any suggestions for us?

Fred in Tulsa

Dear Fred

Safety and security instruction should not be left to formal presentations alone. Try the following ideas:

- *Establish a safety committee. Rotate membership to get maximum involvement from all employees. Get first aid training for committee members to increase their value to the employees.*
- *Use bulletin boards, posters, brochures, booklets, films, online shows, checklists, and the company newspaper to communicate safety messages.*
- *Use a checklist with specific safety and security pointers so that employees know exactly what is expected of them under various circumstances.*
- *Assign particular duties, such as unplugging the coffeepot or locking up the calculator, to specific individuals. Post the list of assignments. Rotate the assignments on a weekly or monthly basis.*
- *Hold periodic fire drills. With over 18,000 office fires a year, according to the National Safety Council, this can be time well spent.*
- *Designate specific employees to help handicapped workers in an emergency.*
- *Devise an evacuation plan and practice it together.*
- *Write the National Safety Council, PO Box 11933, Chicago, IL 60611, for information on office safety and security.*

Good luck in developing a sound program for your office.

Blake Williams

Office Manager

402

Meetings and Travel

The purposes of business meetings range from getting acquainted to exchanging information to solving complex issues. Formats for meetings can be informal or formal, with many participants or only a few. Learning to be an active, interested participant in a meeting aids in reaching viable group decisions. Employees often travel to attend meetings. Travel arrangements might include setting up air travel, hotel accommodations, and car rental; confirming appointments; preparing an itinerary and gathering supporting items; and handling work while away from the office.

In this chapter, you will learn about planning and participating in meetings, about making travel arrangements, and about supporting activities related to business travel.

Chapter 9

403

teaching tips

Ask students to identify the kinds of meetings they attend—for school or organizations—and to identify the purposes of the meetings. Ask if an agenda is prepared for the meetings or how business is conducted; if minutes are taken by someone in the meetings; and how minutes are distributed after the meetings. Share the kinds of meetings you attend and the documents associated with the meetings. Discuss the various roles in meetings, from chair to member.

for discussion

The size of an organization determines how meetings and travel are handled. In a small office, individuals may arrange their own accommodations for meetings and travel; in larger organizations, a separate department may be available to manage the details.

Chapter 9

Planning and Participating in Meetings

Topic 9-1

When you have completed your study of this topic, you will be able to:

- **plan business meetings**
- **prepare documents related to business meetings**
- **participate effectively in meetings**

Meetings provide an important communication link in business. They have many purposes: to give and receive information, solve problems, change attitudes, determine priorities and objectives, explore new ideas, and make decisions.

interdependence: mutual reliance or dependence on others

Business meetings bring people together to communicate or receive information, make decisions, and solve problems. Meetings provide an important communication link in business because of the increasing **interdependence** of tasks. Without meetings, it would be difficult for employees to keep up to date on company matters, changing business conditions, and procedures.

Meetings may range from an informal chat in a manager's office to a formal gathering of the board of directors in the company boardroom. While many meetings are held in person, technology allows people in different locations—even on different continents—to conduct and attend meetings without leaving their offices. Well-organized meetings, whether held face to face or by electronic means, are necessary for businesses to run smoothly. Your role in assisting with these meetings

will vary, depending upon the degree of formality, purpose, size, and location of the meeting. In this topic, you will learn how to plan and participate in meetings efficiently and effectively.

Types of Business Meetings

The nature of the organization, the function of the department in which you may work, and the purpose of the meeting will determine whether the meeting is small or informal, formal, or multinational in scope. You will want to understand the differences in the nature of the meetings and your role in planning and participating in them.

INFORMAL AND SMALL GROUP MEETINGS

Many of the meetings in which office workers are involved will be informal discussions and small group meetings. Many times small, informal meetings are set up as committee meetings that address a specific topic or ongoing concerns and issues, such as safety and security. The following example shows how one office worker carried out her responsibilities for setting up and participating in a small, informal meeting:

> *The manager sent an e-mail message to Carla, as follows: "Carla, see if you can get the other four Pikesville Project engineers together tomorrow at three o'clock for about an hour to discuss the status of the Pikesville project ... and see if the conference room is available." As she read through the message, Carla wrote down the instructions. She noted the materials she needed to bring to the meeting, as well as the arrangements she needed to make for special equipment. Immediately after reading all of the instructions, Carla inquired about the availability of the other engineers through the company's electronic calendaring system; she noted that all four of the other engineers were free at that time and added the meeting to their calendars. Then she arranged for the conference room by electronically accessing the schedule for the room. Finding it free at the hour requested, she added her name as the person requesting the meeting and her telephone number as a reference. She sent an e-mail message to each of the engineers,*

Illustration 9-1:1

Informal, small group meetings are held frequently in many organizations.

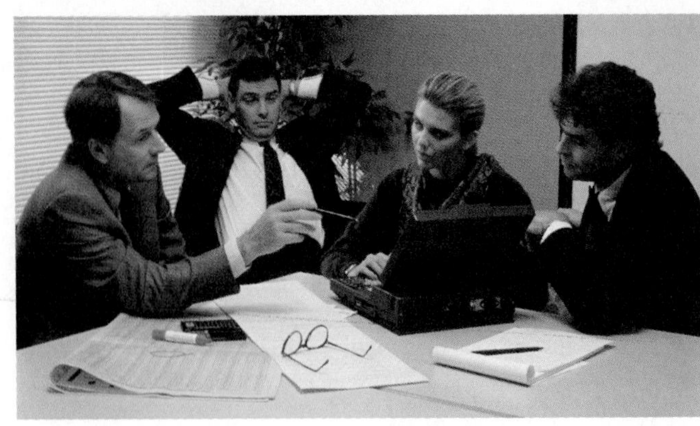

noting the time, place, and approximate length of the meeting and telling them she had added the meeting to their electronic calendars. She then arranged for the necessary equipment and photocopied her materials for the meeting. To follow up the request, she sent an e-mail message to the manager to confirm her arrangements. She noted the meeting on her own calendar. The next day, Carla checked the conference room before the meeting to see that everything was in order.

FORMAL BUSINESS MEETINGS

A formal meeting follows a definite order of business, involves a specific audience, and requires a high degree of coordination and preparation. Many organizations set up formal staff meetings at a specific time on a weekly or monthly basis. Other formal business meetings, such as conferences or quarterly sales meetings, may be planned for longer periods of time. Your skills as organizer, scheduler, and **facilitator** for formal business meetings are critical to ensure that the meeting is planned properly, materials are available, and follow-up items are noted and carried through.

facilitator: one who assists, makes easy

MULTINATIONAL MEETINGS

Many companies are conducting meetings where all participants do not speak the same language or may not be in the same physical location. Multinational meetings are likely to be very formal, requiring detailed long-range planning and preparation. Knowledge of international and business etiquette, time differences, technology troubleshooting (if an electronic conference room is utilized), and the role of **liaison** among all participants in the meeting will be critical. Your liaison role may include working with hotel personnel (if the meeting is held away from company offices), equipment providers, and the participants themselves.

liaison: acting as go-between for two or more groups of people

Planning the Meeting

Regardless of the size of the meeting, documents prepared for meetings require organization and planning. These may include:

Agenda	A list of the topics to be discussed during the meeting
Minutes	The written, historical record of the official business of a meeting
Follow-up items	Reminders to participants of tasks to do before the next meeting

You may have responsibilities before, during, and after a formal meeting for preparing the agenda, taking the minutes, writing and distributing the minutes, and noting the follow-up items from the minutes.

BEFORE THE MEETING

The following suggestions will be helpful to you in your planning. You may not use all the suggestions for each meeting. However, these guidelines will be helpful as you plan for most business meetings.

Establish a Meeting Folder. Once you are aware that a meeting will take place, set up a folder for it. Use this folder to collect items related to the meeting, such as the list of attendees, the agenda, notes, and copies of materials to be distributed.

Reserve the Meeting Room. When you are given the date, time, and location of the meeting, check immediately to see if the desired meeting room and time are available. Many times the purpose of the meeting will determine the kind of equipment that will be needed.

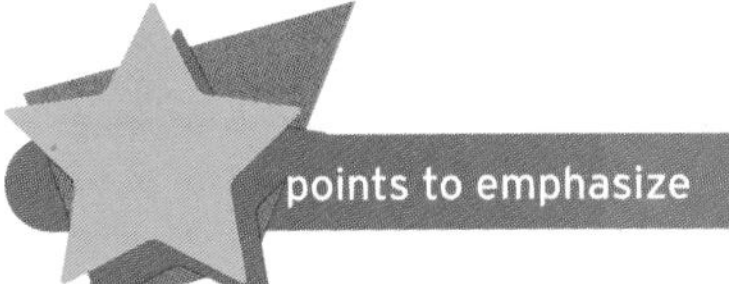

The person who has responsibility to complete meeting arrangements will ensure that everyone's time is used efficiently and effectively. Such arrangements typically involve procedures that must be completed before, during, and after the meeting.

The last meeting of the Pikesville Improvement Council was June 30. It is now time to update the agenda for the next meeting of the Council:

1. Determine the agenda's date for the next meeting, which will be three weeks from today.
2. The new business item (under No. 7) from the June meeting should be moved to unfinished business. Unfinished business will now have two items.
3. The new business to be discussed at the coming meeting will be Funding Alternatives.
4. The date of the next meeting for item No. 8 is to be three months from the coming meeting.

Give your instructions orally and have students make notes of the changes they are to make on a plain sheet of paper before preparing the new agenda.

Rooms may be equipped with overhead projectors, but more sophisticated LCD projection systems may be required—especially if sharing sales or production figures is involved or if the information will be sent to an off-site location.

Notify the Meeting Participants. Notify the participants as soon as possible of the time, place, approximate length, and purpose of the meeting. Identify any materials or supporting documents they should bring.

Use Your Reminder Systems. Mark your and others' calendars with the meeting time and place. Use your tickler file to help you control the preparation details. For example, if you must prepare 20 copies of a report to present at the meeting, place a note in the tickler file as a reminder.

Key the Agenda. All participants and the recording secretary should receive a copy of the agenda prior to the meeting. An agenda typically contains many of the items shown in Illustration 9-1:2.

Illustration 9-1:2

An agenda is a list of the topics to be discussed during a business meeting.

AGENDA
PIKESVILLE IMPROVEMENT COUNCIL
June 30, 19—

1. Call to Order:
   Nancy Hollingshead, Pikesville Improvement Council Chair
2. Roll Call: Troy Jones, Secretary
3. Reading of the Minutes: Troy Jones, Secretary
4. Treasurer's Report: Sean Petersen, Treasurer
5. Committee Report:
   Recognitions Committee: Briana King, Chairperson
6. Unfinished Business:
   Telecommunications Improvement Project
7. New Business:
   East Pikesville Drive Improvement Project
8. Date of Next Meeting
9. Adjournment

Organize Meeting Materials and Handouts. You may be expected to gather certain materials such as extra notepads, pencils, file folders, and courtesy identification badges and parking stickers. Also, organize any materials and handouts such as reports, letters, and statistical data that will be distributed at the meeting. Review any material to be presented at the meeting on the equipment that is available in the meeting room.

Prepare the Meeting Room. The room temperature should be comfortable and the seating arranged to fit the meeting style. A room arrangement in which all participants can be seen and heard will facilitate the discussion. Any presentation aids should be positioned so that they are near the leader and can be seen by all in the room. Check to be sure that requested equipment is present and working properly.

Illustration 9-1:3
Careful planning and organization should be done before a meeting begins.

Have students study this illustration. What details has the meeting organizer taken care of prior to the meeting?

DURING THE MEETING

The degree to which you participate during the meeting will depend upon the purpose of the meeting, where it is held, and the preplanning to be done. You may be responsible for the minutes or for leading part of the discussion.

The minutes detail the action taken by the group, and they provide the reader with a concise record of what took place at the meeting. The minutes should not be a **verbatim** transcript of the meeting.

verbatim: word for word

Do all of these items appear in the minutes shown in Illustration 9-1:4 on page 411?

However, the recorder must make note of all pertinent information. The minutes must give a clear, accurate, and complete accounting of the happenings of the meeting. Although various reporting formats are acceptable for recording minutes, the following items appear in most of them:

- name of group, committee, organization, or business holding the meeting
- time, date, place, and type of meeting (for example, weekly, monthly, annual, called, special)
- name of presiding officer
- members present and absent (In a large organization, only the number of members present needs to be recorded to verify that a **quorum** was present.)
- reading and approval of the minutes from the previous meeting
- committee or individual reports (for example, treasurer's report, standing committees, special committees)
- unfinished business (includes pertinent discussion and action taken)
- new business (includes pertinent discussion and action taken)
- time, date, and place of next meeting
- time of adjournment
- signature of the individual responsible for the minutes

quorum: minimum number of members necessary to conduct business

The following suggestions will be helpful to you when it is your responsibility to prepare the minutes of a meeting:

1. Have at the meeting copies of the agenda, the minutes of the previous meeting, and any report or document that might be referred to during the meeting.
2. If you record and transcribe minutes frequently, a **parliamentary procedure** reference source (such as *Robert's Rules of Order Revised*) will help you better understand the meeting proceedings and the correct terminology to use when taking and preparing minutes.

parliamentary procedure: guide for conducting meetings

PIKESVILLE IMPROVEMENT COUNCIL
Meeting Minutes
June 30, 19—

Time and Place of Meeting	The regular weekly meeting of the Pikesville Improvement Council was held on Tuesday, June 30, 19—, in the Meeting Chambers of City Hall. The meeting was called to order by President Nancy Hollingshead at 7:30 p.m.
Attendance	Present were Improvement Council members: Elizabeth Larkin, Rodger Aycock, Douglas Ivey, Laura Johnson, Steven Minnhausen, Briana King, Sean Petersen, Troy Jones, and President Nancy Hollingshead. Absent was Kelly Pearce. Guest: John Byrd, City Manager.
Approval of Minutes	The minutes of the June 23, 19—, meeting were read and approved.
Treasurer's Report	Treasurer, Sean Petersen, reported that with the receipt of the State Improvement Funds check, the Improvement Projects Account has a balance of $359,450.
Report of Recognition Committee	Briana King, chair, submitted the committee report (attached to the minutes) recommending that the name of Jane Ann Adamson be submitted to the City Council as a candidate for Employee of the Month. Ms. Johnson moved and Mr. Minnhausen seconded that the committee report be accepted. President Hollingshead directed the secretary to prepare the Resolution of Recognition for submission (attached to the minutes).
Unfinished Business	President Hollingshead reported that the three recorded bids for the Telecommunications Improvement Project have been forwarded to the city engineering department for evaluation.

Pikesville Improvement Council
Meeting Minutes for June 30, 19—
Page 2

Date of Next Meeting	President Hollingshead declared the next regular meeting of the Pikesville Improvement Council to be held on July 7, 19—, at 7:30 p.m. in the Meeting Chambers at City Hall.
Adjournment	Mr. Ivey moved and Ms. Johnson seconded the motion that the meeting be adjourned. The motion carried, and President Hollingshead declared the meeting adjourned at 8:45 p.m.

Troy Jones, Secretary

Nancy Hollingshead, Pikesville Improvement Council President

Attachments: Recognition Committee Report
Resolution of Recognition

Illustration 9-1:4

Minutes are the official record of a meeting.

thinking critically

Assume that a mistake has been made in the minutes in Illustration 9-1:4. Under the treasurer's report, the amount of the State Improvement Funds check ($250,000) was omitted and the balance in the Improvement Projects Account is incorrect. It should have been $349,550. How should the minutes be changed to reflect these corrections?

teaching tips

If students belong to school clubs, you might find out if minutes are prepared for these meetings. If they are, ask students to obtain copies and review them. Ask them to suggest ways to improve the presentation and the formatting of the information.

3. Record the important points of discussion during the meeting and identify the individual making a comment. Often, only the action taken or the conclusion reached is recorded without identifying the persons involved.
4. Record the names of the persons making a motion and seconding it. Motions should be recorded verbatim, and a statement should be made in the minutes as to whether or not the motion was adopted.
5. Correct minutes of the previous meeting. Sometimes at the following meeting, corrections must be made to the minutes before they can be approved. If only a few words are affected, lines may be drawn through the incorrect words and the proper insertions made above them. If more than a few words are affected, lines may be drawn through the sentences or paragraphs to be corrected and the changes written on a new page. The page number of each correction should be indicated on the original minutes. The minutes should not be rewritten after they have been read and approved at the meeting.

Meetings are a fact of business life. As jobs and duties become more interrelated and as more employees choose to work away from the main office, more meetings will be needed to share and make changes in work procedures and goals. It is critical that office workers be prepared to participate in and become a contributing member of a meeting. Also, when it is appropriate, knowing how to lead a discussion or help participants make effective decisions are important career skills.

AFTER THE MEETING

Once the meeting is over, you will need to complete certain follow-up activities. Make calendar notations for any item from the meeting that will require future attention. Prepare the minutes as soon as possible. This will be easier if you do them while the details of the meeting are fresh in your mind. Use examples of previous minutes for appropriate format. Ask the chair of the meeting to proofread the typed minutes before they are distributed to be sure there are no omissions or errors.

Complete any correspondence associated with the meeting, such as thank-you letters to speakers or resource persons or letters requesting information. Items to be added to the agenda for the next meeting also should be noted.

Participating in Meetings

Meetings are a permanent part of the business world that will continue to grow in number and importance. Individuals, departments, and divisions need to communicate with one another on a daily basis to complete the work of the organization. Whether they are called staff, marketing, committee, **ad hoc,** or sales meetings, they are designed to discover problems, exchange information, and make decisions. As an office worker, you should be prepared to lead, participate in, contribute to, and feel a part of any meeting you attend.

ad hoc:
created temporarily to solve a specific problem

LEADING

All employees lead in their jobs: that is, they lead by knowing the elements of their jobs, meeting deadlines, improving how the tasks are completed, and working with people to get their jobs done. These same leadership skills are important in meetings. A good meeting leader is aware of his or her style of leadership and conducts the meeting in a way that makes everyone feel comfortable. A good leader knows the objectives of the meeting, is familiar with the background material, and has relevant documents at hand. While offering suggestions and asking questions during the meeting, a good leader is always willing to listen to others' suggestions. A good leader keeps the meeting on topic and moving toward a solution or a **consensus,** ensures that all participants are taking part in the discussion, and remains open to new and creative approaches.

consensus:
common agreement, mutual understanding

BRAINSTORMING

Brainstorming is a group technique used to facilitate and generate ideas that lead to making decisions or solving problems. The objective is to come up with as many ideas as possible to solve a problem. During the brainstorming process, the following rules are usually observed:

- All ideas are recorded, no matter how unrealistic they may appear.
- Criticism of ideas is not allowed until all ideas have been expressed. Comments such as "that will never work" or "we tried that once already" may **inhibit** the flow of ideas—the main purpose of brainstorming.
- Explanations and combinations of ideas are encouraged. The value of brainstorming is that one idea may build upon another.

inhibit:
hinder, limit, get in the way of

To encourage brainstorming, a meeting leader must be willing to give time to the process and encourage everyone to participate.

teaching tips

Ask students for specific examples of when they have "led" in their classes or on their jobs. Expand the topic by discussing what makes an effective leader in a meeting.

expand the concept

Use the brainstorming technique in your classroom. Ask students to brainstorm (or come up with) as many ideas as they can about a new idea to take school attendance, to register for classes, to purchase football or basketball tickets, to raise funds for a school organization, etc. Ask a student to record the ideas as they are offered by other students. Does a workable idea emerge from the list? Evaluate the process with the students.

The traditional classroom arrangement (chairs in rows facing forward) does not lend itself to group interactions, exchanges, or communication. Why? Is it possible to arrange your classroom so that each of the configurations in Illustration 9-1:5 can be evaluated? Did the group dynamics change with each configuration? How? Which arrangement did the students prefer?

GROUP DYNAMICS

Group dynamics refers to the interactions, communications, exchanges, and relationships among the members of a group. Within the meeting environment, group dynamics can play an important part in reaching group consensus and decisions. The following discussion may help you focus on the three critical components of group dynamics:

Interactions. Interactions among group members will depend on the purpose of the meeting. In almost all meetings, communications will be enhanced when group members can see one another, when eye contact can be used to gain attention or control a participant, and when all participants can see the leader and the visual aids. Illustration 9-1:5 displays possible seating arrangements. Each of these arrangements can be appropriate. The purpose of the meeting should determine the seating arrangement.

Illustration 9-1:5
Using the appropriate seating arrangement can contribute to the purpose of the meeting.

The round table or circle may be used when the leader is seeking a true cooperative form of decision making. This format also reduces the appearance of status differences between the participants.

The U-shaped arrangement accommodates larger meetings—those that include 10 or 12 participants. In this arrangement, the leader may sit in the middle of the U to maintain eye contact with all participants. At the same time, all participants can see each other and side conversations are less likely.

The center table layout, with the leader at one end of the table, allows the leader to control the discussion and communications of the meeting. In this arrangement, all communication tends to flow toward the head of the table (where the leader is seated).

Exchange of information. Exchange of information can be enhanced by the seating arrangement and the willingness of the leader to encourage and facilitate communication. Pre-meeting planning by the leader can set up the open exchange of information among group members by:

- providing in advance materials that will be discussed
- arranging the room and seating to meet the needs of the meeting
- preparing visual aids that guide the discussion
- using the appropriate leadership style

Relationships. Relationships among the group's members will play a critical role in the quality of the decisions made. A good leader listens, asks questions, accepts criticism, keeps the meeting on topic, negotiates, and resolves conflicts. Conflicts arise when participants have strong opinions or *hidden agendas* (their own private objectives). The following guidelines may be helpful when a leader wants to create an atmosphere of mutual trust and cooperation in meetings:

- Use neutral language in the discussion.
- Avoid placing blame.
- Ask open-ended questions.
- Use terms that all participants understand; define those that are controversial.
- Allow all participants to speak completely with no disruptions.
- Maintain a pleasant facial expression.
- Pay particular attention to the physical arrangements.

INVOLVING EVERYONE

Questions or statements, such as those listed below, may encourage group participation and give each person at the meeting the opportunity to express his or her opinion:

- What do you think about …?
- What approach can we use to solve this problem?
- Jane, what do you think about Jim's idea?

Ask students to observe the dynamics among the group members at a meeting they may attend. How were the exchanges, interactions, and relationships either encouraged or discouraged? Share with the class.

- Ron, we haven't heard your ideas about. . . .
- That's an interesting question, Mary. What would be a good answer?
- Are we ready to make a decision or is there still more discussion?
- Let me summarize what I think I have heard so far.

DEVELOPING THE ACTION PLAN

Unless stated otherwise, it is important that a concrete, specific plan of action comes out of the meeting and that each participant has a voice in the outcome. The written *plan of action* can replace the traditional minutes of a meeting, because it focuses on the actions to be taken after the meeting rather than simply recording the proceedings (see Illustration 9-1:6). The following basic information about the meeting is included in the action plan:

- subject, date, name of chair, and recorder
- specific actions to be taken and the person(s) responsible
- the deadlines for the actions and completion dates
- key issues discussed and the participants
- the meeting length
- announcement of the next meeting

To arrive at a plan of action, the meeting leader should ensure that:

- all meeting participants understand the plan
- all meeting participants have input into the final outcome
- all meeting participants have definite assignments to put the plan into action
- the plan of action is implemented and assignments are completed

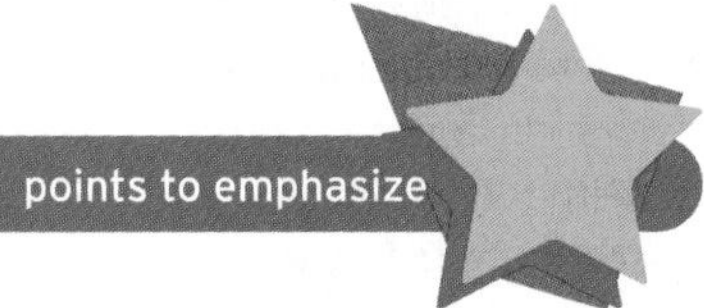

Teleconferencing can be an expensive means of communicating. Individuals planning and participating in teleconferences should be aware of the cost factor and use time wisely.

Teleconferences

A *teleconference* is a meeting of people in different locations connected by a telecommunications system. Teleconferences can be used to deliver training, exchange information, or solve problems and make

PIKESVILLE IMPROVEMENT COUNCIL
Plan of Action
April 30, 19—

Subject	The sole purpose of the meeting of the Pikesville Improvement Council on Wednesday, April 30, 19—, was to discuss the Downtown Improvement Project. President Hollingshead called the meeting to order at 7:30 p.m. and declared a quorum present. Ms. Hollingshead called the members' attention to the information that was delivered to them during the week prior to the meeting.
Attendance	Present were Improvement Council members: Elizabeth Larkin, Rodger Aycock, Kelly Pearce, Troy Jones, and President Nancy Hollingshead. Guests: John Byrd, City Manager; Sharon Young, City Surveyor.
Key Issue	Downtown Improvement Project The Pikesville Improvement Council discussed the plans to acquire an additional piece of property that abuts on the downtown area. The additional property has been set aside to develop a park area to include an outdoor amphitheater and petting zoo for children. Three specific pieces of property are under consideration, as follows: East Pikesville Drive (owner, Martin Victor Wolfe) North River Drive (owner, Hancock Industries) West High Street (owner, The McFaddin Family Group) President Hollingshead asked the City Manager, John Byrd, and City Surveyor, Sharon Young, to provide details on each piece of property. At the conclusion of their remarks, President Hollingshead appointed the following ad hoc groups to study and make recommendations to the Council on which piece of property to purchase: Larkin, Aycock, and Ivey: East Pikesville Drive Johnson, Minnhausen, and King North River Drive Petersen, Pearce, and Jones West High Street President Hollingshead and John Byrd will be ex-officio members of each work group.
Deadlines	Work groups will have initial reports ready to present on May 14, 19—. The final reports will be made to the Council meeting on June 1, 19—.
Meeting Length	The meeting was adjourned at 9:00 p.m.
Next Meeting	May 14, 19—.

Troy Jones, Secretary

Nancy Hollingshead, Pikesville Improvement Council President

Illustration 9-1:6

Compare the action plan illustrated here with the minutes in Illustration 9-1:4.

teaching tips

Discuss the similarities and differences between the minutes in Illustration 9-1:4 on page 411 and the action plan in Illustration 9-1:6 on page 417. When is it appropriate to use an action plan rather than minutes of a meeting?

decisions, just as face-to-face meetings can. A variety of telecommunications systems are available, as described below.

AUDIO CONFERENCES

The telecommunications system may involve only audio (sound) exchanges among the participants, as in a telephone conference. An audio conference room is equipped with microphone-speakers, arranged on tables at certain intervals, so that all participants can talk to and hear from other participants. Audio-graphic conferences, using a microphone-speaker system, a computer terminal, and an *electronic tablet*, make it possible to hear the other participants and see written information at the same time. A speaker at one location can explain material on the speaker system and **concurrently** write on the electronic tablet. The information appears on the computer terminal at the receiving end along with the audio explanation. Since the tablet is electronic, with the touch of a button the information can be printed for all participants.

concurrently: at the same time

All teleconferences include the use of computer networks—whether it is the telephone network, a local area network, or a wide area network. Refer to Chapter 14 to review and reinforce the discussion of computer networks.

VIDEO CONFERENCES

The teleconference may be more sophisticated when an **interactive video** system is used than when audio alone is used. Video conferencing permits people to meet at two or more locations with visual and audio contact (through television cameras, microphones, monitors, and other equipment) almost as if they were in the same room.

interactive video: two-way exchange of sound and video pictures

COMPUTER CONFERENCES

In a computer conference, people communicate information through computer networks, allowing them to have "meetings" by writing messages to each other on their computers. No audio message accompanies the written message. Computer conferences are similar to telephone conference calls—with the exception that these conferences are on the computer and the written messages appear on computer screens. Another term applied to computer conferences is *interactive computer conferencing*.

Technology allows flexibility in planning, setting up, preparing for, and participating in meetings. However, teleconferencing can be expensive so the meeting time should be used wisely. Much assistance is often necessary in preparing for a teleconference. Your role may include the following responsibilities:

1. Reserve the conference room and necessary equipment.
2. Notify the participants of the date, time, length, and purpose of the meeting. Include a telephone number and the name of a contact for participants in the event of technical difficulties.
3. Prepare and distribute any related materials well in advance of the meeting. If several documents are to be sent, use different paper colors to copy different reports. That way, it will be easy to identify reports during the teleconference.
4. Prepare and distribute to the participants the **online** agenda well in advance of the teleconference. The online agenda is a listing of the events and topics of discussion planned for the teleconference, with the estimated time for each item.
5. If the teleconference room is equipped with a fax machine, telephone, electronic tablet, or other electronic systems for exchanging information during the meeting, be sure these systems are in operating condition and are available for use during the teleconference.
6. If the services of a telecommunications technician or coordinator are needed, arrange to have that person available or in the room during the conference in the event of technical difficulties. Take it upon yourself to learn the less complicated technical characteristics of computer teleconferencing, so that you can expand your skills and knowledge in this area.

online:
connected to an electronic system

Illustration 9-1:7

A video conference permits both voice and video communication.

Have students study Illustration 9-1:7. What specific technology can they identify in this illustration?

Reviewing the Topic

topic 9-1 review

1. List at least four reasons why meetings are held in business.
2. What types of meetings may occur in business? Give an example of each.
3. What kinds of documents are prepared for meetings? What is the purpose of each?
4. What guidelines should you follow before, during, and after a meeting?
5. As an office worker, how can you prepare yourself to participate in business meetings?
6. What items generally appear in minutes of a meeting?
7. What guidelines should you follow to prepare the minutes of a meeting?
8. Compare and contrast a plan of action with meeting minutes. What are the similarities? the differences?
9. What preparations need to be made for a teleconference?
10. What guidelines should you follow to create an atmosphere of trust and cooperation during a meeting?

INTERACTING WITH OTHERS

Crystal's manager, Mr. Burrell, is meeting with union leaders to discuss delicate labor-management relations pending the renewal of the employees' contract. The meeting has been underway for about half an hour when Mr. Burrell's brother appears in the office and asks to speak to Mr. Burrell. Even after Crystal tells him that Mr. Burrell is in a very important meeting, the brother still insists on speaking with him. He is becoming upset with Crystal for attempting to prevent him from entering his brother's office.

What you are to do:

Write a paragraph explaining how Crystal might handle this situation. How could it have been avoided?

topic 9-1 review

Planning and Participating in Meetings

420

REINFORCING ENGLISH SKILLS

In this exercise, you will review pronouns. Pronouns are words that serve as substitutes for nouns. Pronouns must agree with their antecedents (nouns for which they stand) in person, number, and gender. Practice choosing the correct pronoun in each sentence below taken from reports keyed by an office worker.

What you are to do:

Write or key the sentences below selecting the proper pronouns.

1. The executive (that, who) directed the meeting is considered an effective business leader.
2. Neither Jack nor Jim feels that (his, their) itinerary should be changed.
3. The executives said that (them, they), along with a group from another company, would attend the seminar in Paris.
4. Office workers who take the minutes of meetings need a parliamentary procedures resource available to (them, they).
5. The committee has promised to have (its, their) findings ready for review at the departmental meeting next week.
6. The executives traveling on business from that office often use (its, their) company's credit cards.
7. The executive and her associate were uncertain how (she, they) should reschedule the trip.
8. The members of the group attending the meeting wanted (its, their) opinions aired before a final vote was taken.
9. The oval table (that, who) was placed in the meeting room will be there only a short time.
10. Joy and Wendy reviewed the meeting agenda before (it, they) was sent to the participants.

421

topic 9-1
review

APPLICATION ACTIVITIES

ACTIVITY 1 Preparing for a Meeting

Ms. Burris has asked you to take charge of preparations for a meeting with union leaders and company officials on April 2. In addition, she has asked you to sit in during the meeting and take minutes. You know from the agenda that the meeting has been scheduled for her conference room.

What you are to do:

1. Key a list of the preparations you may need to make for the conference room.
2. Key a list of questions you have for Ms. Burris regarding the meeting preparations. For example: Will there be breaks for refreshments? If yes, how many and when?
3. Key a list of the preparations you need to make for someone to cover your desk during the time you will be in the meeting.
4. What items will you need to take to the meeting with you?
5. Key a list of your responsibilities before, during, and after the meeting.

ACTIVITY 2 Agenda for a Teleconference

You work in Atlanta for Ernest L. Fogg, Director of Marketing. Mr. Fogg is in the process of finalizing arrangements for a teleconference with regional marketing vice presidents located in five different regional offices. The teleconference will originate in Atlanta.

Mr. Fogg hands you an edited copy of the online agenda for the teleconference and says, "Please key this agenda in final form. Open up the spacing as I've indicated and list the participants in alphabetic order according to city. Proofread very carefully. It's vital that all times and telephone numbers are correct."

422

What you are to do:

Key the final agenda following Mr. Fogg's oral and written instructions.

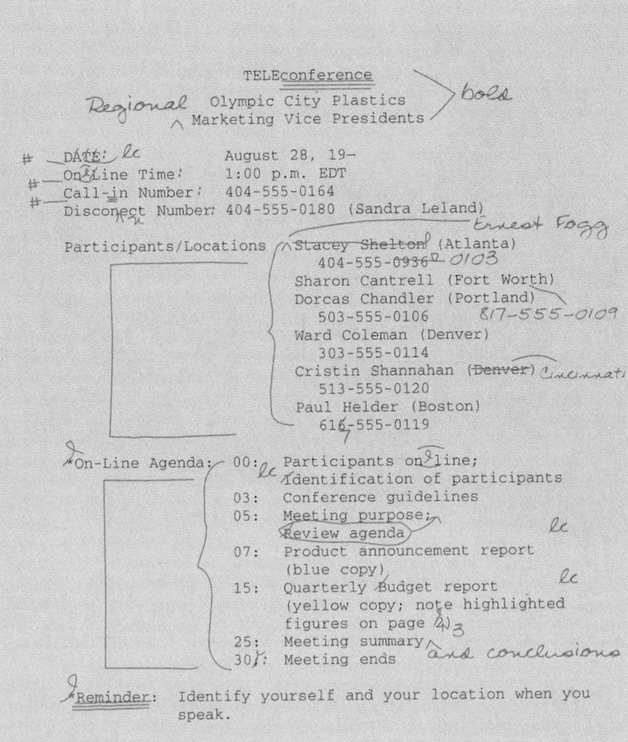

TELEconference
Regional Olympic City Plastics
Marketing Vice Presidents

DATE: August 28, 19–
On-Line Time: 1:00 p.m. EDT
Call-in Number: 404-555-0164
Disconect Number: 404-555-0180 (Sandra Leland)

Participants/Locations
- Ernest Fogg ~~Stacey Shelton~~ (Atlanta) 404-555-~~0936~~ 0103
- Sharon Cantrell (Fort Worth) 817-555-0109
- Dorcas Chandler (Portland) 503-555-0106
- Ward Coleman (Denver) 303-555-0114
- Cristin Shannahan (~~Denver~~) Cincinnati 513-555-0120
- Paul Helder (Boston) 617-555-0119

On-Line Agenda:
- 00: Participants on line; Identification of participants
- 03: Conference guidelines
- 05: Meeting purpose; Review agenda
- 07: Product announcement report (blue copy)
- 15: Quarterly Budget report (yellow copy; note highlighted figures on page 3)
- 25: Meeting summary and conclusions
- 30: Meeting ends

Reminder: Identify yourself and your location when you speak.

Filename: Agenda

423

teaching tips

You may want to collect common travel references, such as train, bus, and airline schedules. Travel agencies are an excellent source of travel brochures that describe all modes of travel and various accommodations. Also, students may have brochures from family vacations that can serve as a basis for discussions of making travel arrangements. If time permits, have students plan a business trip to several different offices of a national or international company, using the travel references you have collected.

Arranging Travel

Topic 9-2

When you have completed your study of this topic, you will be able to:

- **use appropriate procedures for planning business travel**
- **explain procedures for obtaining a passport and visa**
- **prepare appropriate travel documents, including an itinerary**
- **describe the factors involved in travel etiquette and travel safety**
- **complete pertinent follow-up travel activities**

Business people travel for various reasons: to supervise company operations, to meet with clients or company associates, or to attend meetings and conferences. Increasingly, large and small organizations conduct business on an international scale. Telecommunications technology and accessible air travel have combined to make business travel convenient and worthwhile.

Travel arrangements are made in accordance with company policy. Large firms may have a travel department for this purpose. Smaller firms, however, may rely on the services of a travel agency or an office worker to make the travel arrangements. In addition, some companies have special agreements with travel agencies, hotels, and transportation companies for designated services. You should follow company procedures and instructions to complete any travel arrangements you must make.

Preparing for Business Travel

You may have an opportunity to choose the **mode** of travel, the time of departure or arrival, and the overnight accommodations for a business trip. When such choices are available, you will need to know your personal preferences or those of the person traveling if you are making the arrangements for that person.

mode:
manner or way of doing something

When you travel on company business, you must be able to meet your business obligations scheduled away from your office. You must arrive at meetings on time and with the necessary supporting materials. You will find that carefully planned travel arrangements are crucial to the success of a business trip.

A travel folder (or trip file) will help you organize the details of an upcoming trip. Use the folder to collect background information and details about the trip, such as notes on reservations, tickets, accommodations, and meeting or appointment confirmations. The information in the travel folder will help you prepare an itinerary, complete company travel documents, and serve as a reminder system for tasks related to the trip.

As you plan the trip, set aside time to:

- Schedule meetings and appointments to be held during the trip. Shortly before the trip, contact each individual with whom you plan to meet to confirm the appointment date, time, and meeting place.
- Organize the names, titles, company names, addresses, and telephone numbers or e-mail addresses of the individuals with whom meetings are scheduled.
- Make reservations for transportation and overnight accommodations.
- Prepare an itinerary and gather supporting materials for the trip.

COMMERCIAL AIR TRAVEL

Time is money for the busy business traveler, and the popularity of air travel among businesspeople reflects this point. Often, the only way to manage a tight schedule is by air travel. An extensive network of airline routes is provided by national, regional, and commuter airlines. If you

Making travel arrangements requires accuracy and attention to detail. For example, an incorrect flight time or flight number could cause a business traveler to lose considerable time and the company to lose potential business.

The OAG is available in North American, Worldwide, Europe/Middle East/Africa, Pacific/Asia, and the Latin American/Caribbean editions. Other information related to travel may be accessed electronically from the government and other sources, such as The Virtual Tourist, *http://wings.buffalo.edu/world/;* GNN Travel Center, *http://nearnet.gnn.com/*; the U.S. State Department: gopher to: *gopher.stolaf.edu*; or by entering the names of specific airlines and travel agencies.

Display a large map of the United States and/or the world to help students gain a sense of travel distances and times involved in traveling. Highlight the time zones on the map.

are a frequent flyer on one particular airline, an updated airline timetable provides a convenient way to determine travel information such as flight schedules, services offered (meals, snacks, movies), and toll-free reservation numbers. Airline schedules are available free of charge at ticket counters in airports, at airline offices in major cities, at large hotels, and from travel agents.

If you use several airlines, you will find the *Official Airline Guide* (OAG) a valuable source of flight information and schedules. Your company may have a copy of this publication for your reference. If not, a travel agent can provide you with the same information.

Many businesses subscribe to an online travel information service. This service allows you to scan information for various airlines, make the selections, and have the tickets prepared for mailing or pickup at the airport.

You may make flight reservations by calling a travel agent or by calling an airline directly via a toll-free number. If you use the services of a

Illustration 9-2:1

An Official Airline Guide listing shows many details about a flight.

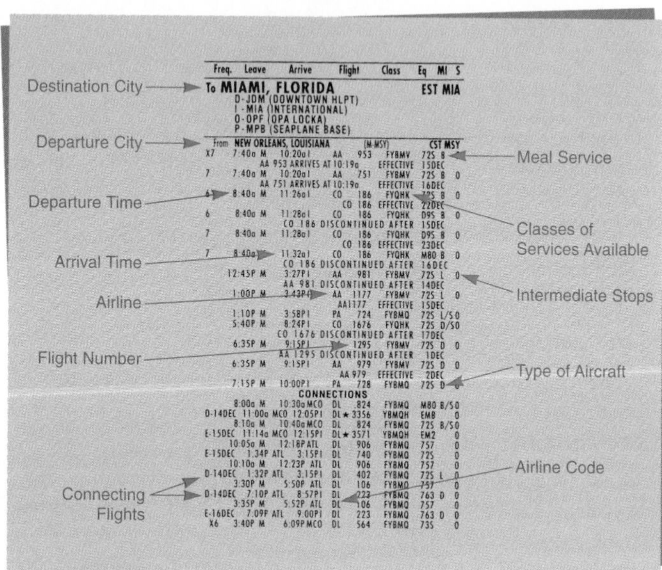

travel agent, your flight itinerary, invoice, and boarding pass may be received with the airline tickets. Each of these documents serves a specific purpose. The flight itinerary is checked against your records and used to create the traveler's itinerary. Many travelers attach a copy of the flight itinerary to the overall itinerary for the trip. The invoice is retained to attach to the travel expense report. The boarding pass is given to the airline attendant prior to boarding the plane.

Illustration 9-2:2

Some businesses prefer to make all travel arrangements through one travel agency.

OTHER FORMS OF BUSINESS TRAVEL

Rental cars and trains provide **alternative** forms of business travel. You may have occasion to make travel arrangements using one of these forms of transportation.

alternative: another choice

For short trips, particularly in a local area, many people prefer to rent cars. A rental car may also be suitable when you fly to a city and have appointments in outlying areas. Rental cars are available at most airports and other convenient locations. Rental fees vary in price according to the size of the car, the length of time the car is needed, and the miles driven. Follow any established company guidelines for renting a car.

Train travel is popular in some sections of the country, particularly in areas with high population concentrations. Train stations are located in the centers of cities and can provide an alternative to air travel on

teaching tips

Another approach to augment the travel topic is to have students visit local travel agencies to find out what services they provide and then report the results to the class. Another benefit of doing this is to become acquainted with the telecommunications technology (hardware and software) travel agencies use to plan and make travel accommodations.

for discussion

For businesspeople who work in the community, what towns and cities are within the range that could be reached in reasonable time by car? What cities or towns would be outside the range?

Have students consider what services offered by a large hotel in a major city might be of importance to a person traveling on business. Students may name airport limousine service, wake-up calls, fax/reprographic services, overnight delivery services, business services (complete with telecommunications capabilities), restaurants, meeting rooms, and physical fitness centers.

Ask students: If you were making a hotel reservation directly with the hotel, what information would you need to know before you placed the call? What information should you ask for during your call?

Illustration 9-2:3

Some business trips require the use of a rental car.

certain routes. Overnight trains have sleeping and dining accommodations on board. Check with a travel agent or look in the yellow pages of your telephone directory for information on the railway lines serving your area.

HOTEL/MOTEL ACCOMMODATIONS

Many business travelers must stay overnight at their destinations and will need hotel or motel accommodations. You may specify a particular hotel or motel, especially if you are familiar with the city or if a convention or meeting is being held at a specific hotel. In other cases, you may rely on a travel agent or office assistant to select the lodging.

When you make reservations by telephone, use toll-free telephone numbers whenever possible. Write down the names of the persons who make and confirm reservations. Always make a note of the rates you are quoted. Record the confirmation number and repeat it to the reservation agent to assure the accuracy of the number. The confirmation number should be included on the itinerary. A written confirmation from the hotel or motel is helpful.

The OAG's *Business Travel Planner* provides names, addresses, telephone numbers, room rates, and other information about hotels and motels throughout North America. For international travel, consult the OAG's Worldwide, European, Latin American/Caribbean, or Pacific/Asia editions. Your company may have a copy of these publications. If not, a travel agent can provide you with the information.

ITINERARY AND SUPPORTING MATERIALS

Once the travel plans are set, prepare an itinerary and assemble travel documents and related materials for meetings or appointments. If the plans for the trip change, alternative arrangements may need to be made. These can generally be made at the time you cancel the first trip. Have your confirmation numbers and other pertinent reservation details available when you call to change reservations or appointments.

Prepare an Itinerary. An itinerary is a detailed plan of a trip that serves as a guide for the business traveler away from the office. The itinerary includes travel arrangements, appointments, hotel or motel reservations, and reminders or special instructions. Allow enough travel time between appointments to avoid having to rush to make the next appointment.

You may need several copies of the itinerary: one to carry, another to be carried in the baggage, and possibly one for family members. The itinerary should be in an easy-to-read format that gives the day-by-day schedule for the complete trip, as shown in Illustration 9-2:4 on page 430.

Gather Supporting Items. Before the trip, gather the travel documents, supplies, and supporting materials, such as those listed below, that are needed for the trip.

- itinerary
- travel tickets
- travel funds
- hotel/motel and car rental confirmations
- maps of cities or states as appropriate
- directions to offices or other meeting locations
- speeches, supporting correspondence, reports, or files for each appointment/meeting

Use a current flight schedule to update the itinerary for Ms. Stanford. Schedule the trip beginning one week from this coming Wednesday. (Note: All meeting times, hotel reservations, and rental car reservations should not change.) Use a current flight schedule to find flights that leave and arrive in time to meet Ms. Stanford's appointment schedule (Wednesday's 2:30 p.m. meeting and Thursday's afternoon plant tour). A second option is to change one or more of the cities from which Ms. Stanford departs or arrives and have students change the airline, flight numbers, and flight times on the itinerary. Students should key a completed copy of their revised itineraries.

Illustration 9-2:4

A comprehensive itinerary contains relevant travel details, as shown here.

ITINERARY FOR CHARLENE B. STANFORD
May 17 to May 19, 19—

WEDNESDAY, MAY 17	Atlanta to Dallas
9:43 a.m.	Leave Hartsfield Atlanta International airport on Delta Flight 17. Breakfast served.
10:50 a.m.	Arrive Dallas/Fort Worth International Airport. Pick up rental car keys at Sun Rentals counter; confirmation number 388075.
	Hotel reservations at Fairmont Hotel, 1717 W. Akard Street, 214-555-0102. Confirmation number: 7K4995F.
2:30 p.m.	Meeting with George Thatcher, Vice President, Marketing, Fabric Wholesalers, 1314 Gaston Avenue, 214-555-0196, to discuss fabric purchase agreement.
7:00 p.m.	Dinner with staff at hotel to review plans for Apparel Fair.
THURSDAY, MAY 18	Dallas to San Diego
12:02 p.m.	Leave Dallas/Fort Worth International Airport on Delta Flight 444. Lunch served. Drop rental car and keys at counter and take shuttle bus to airport terminal.
12:55 p.m.	Arrive at Lindbergh Field International Airport. Richard Stanley (619-555-0152) will meet you at the airport and drive you to the Naples plant for the tour and return you to your hotel.
	Hotel reservations at the Seven Seas Lodge, 411 Hotel Circle South, 619-555-1300. Confirmation number: 4478S84.
FRIDAY, MAY 19	San Diego to Atlanta
7:55 a.m.	Leave San Diego Lindbergh Field International Airport on Delta Flight 880. Breakfast served. Richard Stanley will meet you in the lobby of your hotel at 6:45 a.m. to drive you to the airport.
3:52 p.m.	Arrive Hartsfield Atlanta International Airport.

- forms for recording expenses
- extra notepaper, pens, and business cards
- electronic equipment, such as a calculator, laptop computer and modem, or portable phone

If the supporting materials, such as a large number of handouts, will be too heavy or bulky to carry with you, arrange to have them shipped to your hotel or meeting location. Arrange for special packaging for equipment, such as computers and projection panels, to prevent damage to these items while en route. Confirm the safe arrival of critical supporting materials immediately upon arrival and have a backup plan to follow in case items are lost or damaged. For example, you might carry one set of handouts with you so that copies can be made at your destination if necessary.

Travel Etiquette

The behavior of a business traveler reflects on more than the traveler alone. Your behavior also reflects on your company and your home area. Proper dress and travel **etiquette** will contribute to a successful business trip.

etiquette: manners, code of behavior, conduct

U.S. companies of all sizes have extended their operations internationally. This global perspective is handled differently in each company. Many companies have international divisions to deal with their branch offices in other countries. The personnel in these departments can provide valuable advice about dress, etiquette, travel documents, health considerations, and other information for the business traveler while abroad.

DRESS

Remember that you represent your organization when you travel. Your dress will contribute to that most important first impression you make on others. Follow these guidelines for appropriate travel attire:

- Dress appropriately for the type of meeting or function you are attending. Many companies send employees to training sessions in which the attire is less formal than while on the job. If the meeting is to take place at another company's site, the attire may be more formal.
- Dress for travel. Many times, employees need a day to travel to a business destination. Dress in this case will be less formal on the airplane or in a car. However, if a short plane or car ride is all that is necessary to reach your destination, dress more formally in order to be ready to conduct business upon arrival.

To reinforce and expand the material presented in the textbook related to travel etiquette, you may want to invite a guest speaker into your classroom from a local business or travel agency to discuss the dress and customs of domestic and foreign travelers. Ask students to read the materials and have two or three questions ready to ask the guest speaker. Students also may share their experiences with traveling.

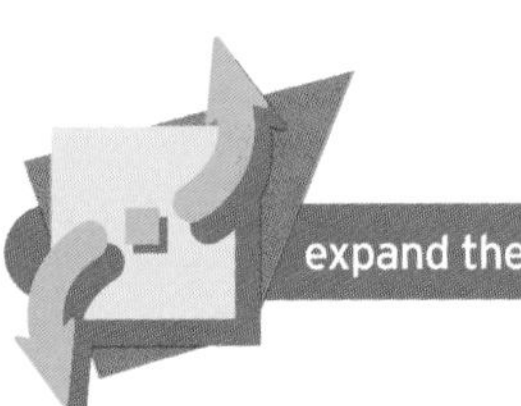

It is impossible for this chapter to cover all of the customs that may be observed by the international business traveler. Ask students to research a specific country and share with the rest of the class the information about doing business in that country.

- Dress to impress. Consider the persons with whom you will be doing business and the impression you want to leave about your organization. Many companies may permit less formal dress while on the job; however, while on business in another city or country, more formal business dress is expected. Proper dress is especially important when traveling in foreign countries or meeting with persons from a culture different from your own. Be aware of the dress customs for the country in which you will do business and dress accordingly.

Illustration 9-2:5

Dressing appropriately for a meeting will contribute to a successful business trip.

CUSTOMS

Proper etiquette plays an important role in conducting business successfully, both in the United States and in foreign countries. The etiquette will vary from country to country. Various print and electronic resources are available to provide in-depth information about business and travel etiquette. For information about a specific country, consult a travel agent or someone who has lived or done business there. Consider the following customs and **protocols** related to business travel:

protocols: rules, etiquette

- Be on time for appointments. Arrange your schedule to allow time for unexpected delays in travel.

- Take an ample supply of business cards. Business cards are always presented by a caller and serve the purposes of introducing the person who is visiting and providing an easy future reference. Business cards should include your name, your company's name, your position, and your title. Avoid using abbreviations on the card. For international travel, have the same information printed in the local language on the reverse side of the card.
- If and when appropriate, provide a gift that is company-associated, such as a pen or sweatshirt with a company logo. Flowers are generally a safe and appreciated gift in almost every country.
- Paying for meals and tipping for clients is generally accepted as the role of the host—the person who initiated the meeting.
- The universal business greeting in the United States is the handshake. When you offer your hand or reach out to take another's hand, be sure your grasp is firm but not painful. Establish eye contact with the person at the same time.

Illustration 9-2:6

The universal business greeting in the United States is the handshake.

- Know the body language and gestures that may be offensive or have different meanings in other cultures. The universal form of communication that all people recognize and appreciate is the smile. Use it often to break the ice and ease tense situations that may arise.
- Know how to pronounce the name of the person you are visiting, as well as how to address the person. Use academic or honorary titles when appropriate.

expand the concept

Information to share with students:

In most of Southeast Asia, Africa, and the Middle East (except Israel), never present the business card with your left hand.

In Japan, present the business card with both hands, and be sure the type is facing the recipient and is right side up.

What other tips might students be able to find about using business cards in another country?

expand the concept

Have students practice shaking hands with fellow students in class. Stress that handshakes leave an impression with the other person. Practice giving a firm, warm handshake. Ask students: Is it always necessary to shake hands?

1. Have telephone directories available so that students can locate the listing for the nearest passport office in your city or community.
2. Obtain a copy of a passport application from a travel agency or the nearest passport office at a post office so that students can become familiar with the kinds of questions asked and the process involved in applying for a passport. Many students travel with parents or join tours sponsored by schools; ask them to bring their passports for demonstration purposes.
3. Invite a travel agent into the classroom to discuss the passport application process.

- Taste any food that is offered by the host. Many hosts will proudly present the best delicacy the area has to offer.
- Speak standard English. Avoid using slang terms and **colloquialisms.** This is especially important when meeting with people for whom English is a second language.

colloquialisms: phrases known only in the local area

DOCUMENTS FOR FOREIGN TRAVEL

Two documents are required for foreign travel in most countries: a passport and a visa. Other documents, such as work permits, tourist cards, prescriptions for medicine carried, and health records may also be needed. These documents are discussed below.

Passport. A passport is an official document granting permission to travel. Issued by the United States Department of State, it **authenticates** a person's right to protection in the foreign country. A passport is needed for travel in most foreign countries.

authenticates: approves, confirms

To secure a passport, application forms may be obtained from designated post offices and local federal buildings. Look in the white pages telephone directory (under "Government Agencies") to find the passport office nearest you.

The requirements to obtain a passport for the first time are listed on the passport application. Since processing the application can take up to six weeks, you should allow enough lead time to avoid having to delay travel plans. After the passport is received, it should be signed and the information requested on the inside cover completed. A passport is **valid** for ten years from the date it is issued. To replace an expired passport, obtain a renewal application from the nearest passport office or designated post office.

valid: in effect, authorized

A passport should be carried or kept in a hotel security box or safe and never be left in a hotel room. Make a photocopy of the identification page so that the passport can be replaced if it is lost. Report the loss of a passport immediately to the nearest passport office or, if traveling abroad, to the United States Embassy.

Visa. A visa is a permit granted by a foreign government for a person to enter its country. The visa usually appears as a stamped notation in a passport, indicating that the person may enter the country for a certain purpose and for a specific period of time. Be sure to note the effective dates of a visa. Illustration 9-2:7 displays a passport and a page of the passport with a visa stamp.

Illustration 9:2-7

A passport and visa are often required for travel in foreign countries.

If you are unsure whether it is necessary to obtain a visa for the country in which travel is planned, contact the consulate or embassy of the country or a travel agent before leaving the United States. Addresses and telephone numbers of consulates of most foreign countries in the United States can be obtained through an online search, using the term "embassy," or by looking in the yellow pages of telephone directories in major cities under "Consulates." Again, allow lead time to obtain the visa stamp from the appropriate consulate prior to traveling to that country.

Health Documents. When traveling to some countries, certain vaccinations and inoculations may be required to protect against a variety of diseases. A travel agency or the consulate of the country to be visited can supply information about required immunizations. Records of the vaccinations and inoculations must be signed by a physician and validated by the local or state health officer on a specific form that may be obtained from a travel agent, the passport office, the local health department, or some physicians. Even if the country to be visited does not require immunizations, the international traveler is well advised to carry a written record of childhood vaccinations and booster shots.

Other health considerations for international flights and travel may include medicine for air sickness, documentation from a physician verifying special prescription medicines that must be taken by the traveler, and permission to carry over-the-counter medicines that might not be available in the country to be visited. Check with a travel agent or the country's consulate to see what arrangements must be made for these medicines.

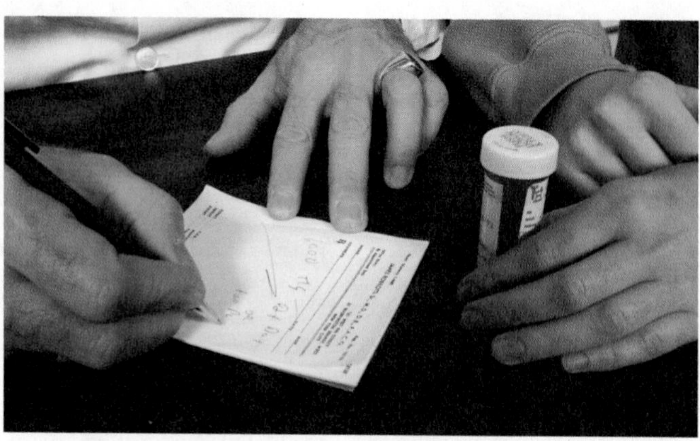

Illustration 9-2:8

Medicines carried in foreign countries may need to be accompanied by the doctor's prescription.

Other Travel Documents. The foreign consulate of the country to be visited can tell you whether other travel documents, such as a work permit, are required. A work permit registers the presence of the person as a visitor on specific business. Several destinations—Mexico, Canada, Bermuda, the West Indies, or Central America—do not require a U.S. citizen to have a passport, but it is a good idea for a visitor to these countries to have a tourist card and to carry proof of citizenship. A tourist card authorizes a person to travel throughout the country. Proof of American citizenship can be provided with a passport or birth certificate.

Travel Safety

Many airlines, hotels and motels, and travel agencies provide tips for travelers to ensure personal safety. Follow these safety suggestions as you travel:

- Do not leave your luggage or other items unattended in hotel lobbies or in waiting areas in airports. Unattended luggage may be stolen or have illegal or unsafe items placed in it.
- Keep your passport and travel funds in a safe, secure place.
- Do not agree to carry items in your luggage for another person.
- Use all locking devices on doors and windows in your hotel room.
- Do not leave valuables in your car and be sure to lock your vehicle.
- Be observant and look around before entering parking lots late at night. Always return to your hotel through the main entrance after dark.
- Protect your credit and calling card numbers at all times.

Illustration 9-2:9

Never leave your luggage unattended.

Many motels and hotels place safety guidelines on specially printed cards in rooms. Read and follow their guidelines for your personal safety.

Handling Work While Away from the Office

Business travelers may depend on an office assistant to handle routine tasks and facilitate communications while away from the office on business. Before the traveler leaves for the business trip, it is important for the office assistant to understand how to deal with routine matters, crisis situations, and out-of-the-ordinary occurrences.

DURING THE TRIP

Answers to the following questions may be helpful to the traveler in keeping work flowing and situations under control during the trip:

- Who will handle crises that may arise while you are out of the office? What kinds of emergencies or crises have occurred in the past that you need to be prepared for?
- Who will be making routine decisions while you are out of the office?
- What kinds of messages or documents should be forwarded to you?
- How many times will you be in touch with the office during the trip?
- What kinds of documents will be forwarded to the office prior to returning to the office?

To keep the office running smoothly, the following suggestions may be helpful to the office assistant:

- Keep up your regular duties and use your time wisely.
- Keep an itemized listing of incoming mail.
- Answer any routine mail that you can.
- Keep a log of faxes, telephone calls, and office visitors.
- If possible, avoid making appointments for the first day the traveler is back in the office.
- Keep notes of matters you want to discuss with the traveler upon his or her return.

STAYING IN TOUCH

instantaneously: immediately, at once

Telecommunications technology makes it possible to take the office anywhere. Business information can be sent and received **instantaneously** with the appropriate equipment. Portable or laptop computers, internal and wireless modems, software with print/fax capabilities, and cellular telephones allow you to do business from any location. In addition, some hotels provide secretarial services and fully equipped business centers for travelers. Airlines provide in-flight telephones and conference rooms in airports. Having access to telecommunications technology allows the traveler to:

- send and receive business data
- access messages (voice or electronic mail)
- transfer travel expense records to an office assistant
- check availability of products for clients
- place orders and receive confirmation of orders placed by clients
- stay up to date with policy or procedural changes that occur while the person is out of the office
- participate in audio conferences

Illustration 9-2:10
Today's technology allows business travelers to use their travel time efficiently.

Technology will continue to play an increasingly important role in how work is handled while traveling on business.

Business Travel Follow-Up Activities

Certain follow-up activities should be completed as soon as possible after the trip. These include determining travel expense reimbursement, generating a variety of reports, and writing thank-you letters.

Ask students to identify the technology this business traveler is using. Without this technology, how could work be accomplished while away from the office?

EXPENSE REPORTS

incurred: generated, brought about

advanced: given ahead of time

A complete record of travel expenses **incurred** while on company business is reported on a specific form provided by the company. The expenses listed on a travel expense report may include hotel or motel accommodations, meals and tips, ground and air transportation, entertainment expenses, and other approved business expenses. If company funds were **advanced** to the business traveler, they are accounted for on the travel expense report. Receipts may be required for travel expenses. Follow the company procedures manual to prepare expense reports, obtain the necessary signatures, and submit the completed forms.

MEETING REPORTS

Examples of meeting reports include sales summaries, client visit logs, project progress updates, or other communications that present the results of the business trip. The completed reports provide written evidence of decisions that were made, goals that were set, complaints or suggestions from customers or clients, or ideas that needed to be discussed. Reports are forwarded to persons who will be affected by the decisions, goals, complaints, or ideas.

THANK-YOU LETTERS

Thank-you letters may be sent as a result of the business contacts and activities encountered on the trip. The need for thank-you letters will depend on the purpose of the travel and business etiquette guidelines. Other follow-up letters may provide a written record of agreements made during the visit or items that need to be accomplished to support organizational goals.

Reviewing The Topic

1. In planning a business trip, what activities should you set aside time to complete?
2. What procedures should you follow in making hotel reservations by phone?
3. What items might be collected in a trip folder?
4. Identify five important travel safety tips.
5. Identify and describe three common forms of business travel.
6. Where can airline schedules be obtained?
7. What items generally appear in a travel itinerary?
8. Define travel etiquette. Describe five etiquette tips related to domestic and international business travel.
9. Where can you obtain forms to apply for a passport? How much time should you allow for processing the passport application?
10. What suggestions should the office assistant follow to keep the office running smoothly while the traveler is away from the office?

THINKING CRITICALLY

A local travel agency is organizing a study tour in England, scheduled for June or July. Your assignment is to make a list of questions to ask the travel agent about travel to England.

What you are to do:

- Work in small groups to develop your list of questions.
- Review the international travel information in this chapter to develop your list of questions.
- Use a map to identify the cities your group would like to visit in England.
- Share your list of questions with the class.
- If possible, visit a travel agency and ask your questions.

topic 9-2 review

Arranging Travel

441

See Workbook page 236.

topic 9-2
review

REINFORCING ENGLISH SKILLS

Thank-you letters are important follow-up activities after the business traveler has returned to the office. The goodwill generated by these letters is invaluable. In this exercise, you will revise, edit, and key a thank-you letter.

What you are to do:

1. Key the letter below correcting the grammar and punctuation mistakes. Rewrite and revise as needed to make the letter clear and concise. Use an appropriate letter style and the current date. See Reference Section H, Sample Documents, to review letter formats.
2. Create a letterhead for the document, adding an appropriate graphic if you wish. Choose a company name and address for Mr. Miller's company to include in the letterhead.

Send the letter to: Dr. Debra Huntington at Dearborn Manufacturing, 8888 Highland, Dearborn Park, Illinois, 45599.

Dear Debra

Thanks for inviting the other members and I of our dept. to visit your new manufacturing process and to learn more about your comapny. We were very impressed with your training program and hope that we can profit by ourvisit.

The warm reception and touryour people gave us at the plant was very edifying. You must have spent a long time getting ready for us. We thought it was great! Everyone said how much they liked it and how much they learned. Especially the demo of the new training program. Your people were really prepared and knew their stuff.

Thanks again. I have noted that you and some of your peopleare interested in returning the favor. I will be in touch with you to set up a date.

Fred J. Miller, Vice President, Manuffacturing

442

APPLICATION ACTIVITIES

ACTIVITY 1 Travel Itinerary

Your manager has handed you a note and a handwritten itinerary for you to create in final format. Follow the directions in her note and answer her questions.

What you are to do:

Locate your manager's conference schedule notes in your *Student Activities and Projects* workbook. Follow the directions in the note your manager has handed to you.

See Workbook pages 49–50.

A NOTE FROM . . . Patti Stanford

Here are my notes regarding my upcoming trip to the Chambers of Commerce National Convention trip to Orlando, Florida. Please use this information to create and key an itinerary for me. Use your own judgment with regard to format. I need the itinerary tomorrow.

Several people may be calling to confirm conference session and appointment times. Please provide the information I need by answering these questions:

1. The session Successfully Surveying Local Communities is held on what day and at what time?
2. The session Networking with Other Chambers is held on what day and at what time?
3. When is my appointment with Robert Mansehund?
4. Which sessions are held on Wednesday?
5. On what days am I available by 12 noon?
6. What is Melinda Carreros' phone number?

Thanks
Patti

443

ACTIVITY 2 Travel Etiquette And Safety Brochure

Ms. Stanford has asked your work group to create a brochure of travel etiquette and safety tips for business travelers in your company. Many managers are traveling to domestic and international destinations, and she feels that the brochure would be helpful to them and their office assistants.

What you are to do:

1. In small groups, create a list of travel etiquette and safety tips that both domestic and international travelers need to know. The textbook information may need to be supplemented with information you can find from magazines or from an online search. If available, use a search engine to find information by keying in *travel etiquette*, *etiquette*, *travel tips*, *travel safety tips*, or other terms.
2. Still working in your group, decide on the format for your brochure. Lay out your brochure on paper before you create it on the computer. The answers to the following questions may be helpful to your group: What is the name of your brochure? What kind of clip art will you need? What clip art is available to you in your classroom? What software is available to you to create your brochure?
3. Use word processing or desktop publishing software to complete your brochure. Your finished brochure should include clip art, bulleted items, or other graphics to support and enhance the brochure.
4. Save your brochure with the filename *Brochure*.
5. Present your group's brochure to your class.

444

Chapter Summary

In this chapter, you learned about the important role office workers play in planning and conducting meetings, participating in meetings, arranging travel, and conducting business away from the office. You also learned about travel etiquette and travel safety. Review the chapter by reading these key points:

- Office workers spend a significant portion of their time in meetings and traveling on business. Your ability to complete meeting and travel arrangements efficiently and accurately adds to your effectiveness. Such arrangements typically involve procedures that must be completed before, during, and after the event.
- Travel etiquette and safety guidelines for domestic and international travel are becoming increasingly important to the business traveler.
- The office assistant plays a critical role in the office while coworkers travel on business trips. The scope of the activities the assistant will handle must be agreed to by both the assistant and the business traveler.
- Telecommunications technology has made it easier for the business traveler to stay in touch with the office, thus ensuring that the office continues to run smoothly.
- After returning to the office from a business trip, certain follow-up activities must be completed. Thank-you notes, reports, travel expense forms, and other travel-related documents will provide a record of the business that has been completed during the business trip or needs to be completed after the trip.

chapter 9 summary

Meetings and Travel

KEY CONCEPTS AND TERMS

ad hoc
advanced
agenda
alternative
authenticates
colloquialisms
concurrently
consensus
etiquette
facilitator
incurred
instantaneously
interactive video
interdependence
itinerary
liaison
minutes
mode
online
parliamentary procedure
passport
protocols
quorum
teleconference
valid
verbatim

chapter 9 summary

INTEGRATED CHAPTER ACTIVITY

ACTIVITY Teleconference on International Travel Etiquette and Safety

Your manager has asked your work group to plan an interactive teleconference to present a training program on international travel etiquette and safety. The teleconference will last about one hour. She indicates that the teleconference should be planned for three weeks from today in the company's interactive teleconference room. Those who will be attending the teleconference include executives who will be traveling to a new company site abroad and office assistants who will make travel arrangements.

What you are to do:

Work in small groups to complete these steps:

1. Decide on the date and time for the teleconference. Key a paragraph describing the procedures and information

446

you would use to schedule and arrange the meeting room.

2. Choose a country where the company has the new site. Research customs and etiquette a business traveler would need to know for that country. To begin your research, review the material in the textbook. If available, complete an online search for customs, etiquette, and travel trips for the country you have chosen. Key a list of customs and etiquette guidelines for a traveler to that country.
3. Obtain the address of the U. S. consulate for the country you have chosen. You can find this information by completing an online search. For example, if the country you have chosen is Japan, you might search using the term *U. S. consulate Japan*. Write a letter to the consulate asking for information about traveling and doing business in the country. Since it may take some time for your request to be processed, search for this information from other sources also.
4. Research the travel documents needed to travel in that country. Key a list of travel documents a traveler needs for the country. In your training program, include an example of each of the documents. Contact a travel agency, your local post office, or other sources to obtain samples of or applications for the documents.
5. Plan the content of the interactive teleconference based on the information you have collected.
6. Create and key an agenda for the meeting. Review Activity 2 from Topic 9-1 to familiarize yourself with the contents and format of a teleconference agenda.
7. Use presentation software to create your training presentation so that it reflects the information your group has found about the country. Your audience will be eager to have this information. Be sure that it is easy to read and understand.

447

8. Present your training program to your class.
9. Submit to your instructor the following items: the agenda; list of customs, travel tips, and etiquette guidelines; travel documents; the letter you have written to the consulate; and the outline (or a disk with the slides you created) of your training program presentation.

448

Mei-yu Liang
Office Supervisor

Getting Acquainted with the World of Work

Is It Any of My Business?

Dear Ms. Liang

I have been worrying about something that happened last week, and I still am not sure what I should have done. You see, I work as an assistant in the office of one of the division managers in our company. One of the staff members asked me to prepare a draft of minutes of the monthly meeting where income figures were discussed. I left the draft on the staff member's desk. A few hours later, the division manager called me into his office. He said, "I've just reviewed the figures in this draft. These revenues aren't right; the profit isn't high enough. Some of these figures must be changed. Please prepare another draft." I said nothing. I took the draft and changed the figures as indicated.

Now I wonder what I should have done. Did the division manager dishonestly change numbers to reflect false profits? Should this have been done? Did I have any responsibility?

Lynn Litchfield

Dear Lynn

As an office assistant, it was your job to prepare the drafts as instructed. From what you say, I am guessing that you were not at the meeting when the income figures were discussed. Therefore, it is possible that income estimates were discussed because final figures for the month were not available. The division manager may have had access to the final figures and used this information to revise the estimated numbers. The figures you were asked to use in the revision may have given a more accurate presentation of the month's activity than the figures you had keyed initially. Of course, there is the possibility that the manager was deliberately distorting the figures in order to show a more favorable performance record.

I would advise you not to worry about having done the wrong thing. You were not in a position to challenge the manager. However, in the future, become familiar with your company's ethical standards. There may be a printed code of ethics available to all employees. Ask about such a code and read it carefully. Be careful to understand a situation fully before you make judgments about the ethical behavior of others. Always strive to reflect high ethical standards in all aspects of your own work.

Lynn, companies need employees with high ethical standards. Your sensitivity to such matters is a valuable trait.

Mei-yu Liang
Office Supervisor

449

getting started **GO**

Students have probably seen people locating and checking records: tellers providing balances in banks, their parents preparing for taxes, clerks looking for receipts in stores, and so on. Ask students to give their observations of how well organized the people who were seeking records seemed to be. Ask if they have ever heard someone express dismay at being unable to find a record. Why do the students think such a problem may have occurred?

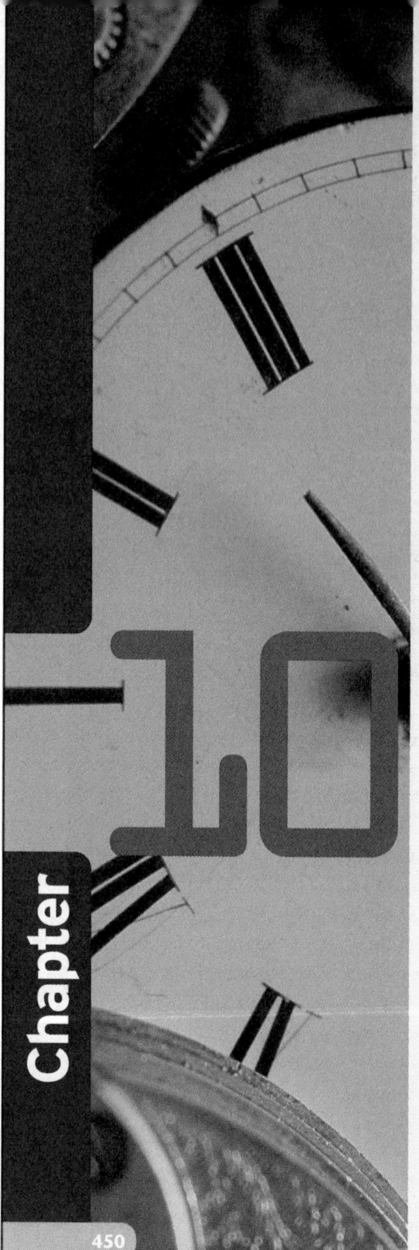

Records Management Systems

Information is important to the operation of an organization. However, a large amount of information alone is not enough to make an organization successful. A system is needed for organizing, storing, and retrieving records and for removing outdated records.

As an office worker in a small department or organization, or in the records management department of a large one, you will need to follow procedures carefully. These procedures include how to organize, store, retrieve, remove, and dispose of records. This series of steps is known as the record life cycle. You will learn in this chapter that organizations keep records on a variety of media. They use paper, magnetic tapes and disks, optical discs, and micrographics. You will also learn that there are advantages and disadvantages to each. You should know about these media so that you can maintain records properly.

This chapter will give you the latest information about the various media and the skills to use the most common filing systems. Additionally, topics such as disaster recovery and cost-saving techniques will be covered.

Chapter 10

Topic 10-1

Maintaining Office Records

When you have completed your study of this topic, you will be able to:

- **explain the purposes of records management**
- **identify the benefits of records management**
- **describe types of media on which information is kept**
- **identify the cost factors involved in a records management system**
- **describe the phases of the record life cycle**
- **describe the process for the removal and archiving of records**
- **describe disaster recovery**

An office cannot operate without records. For example, each time an item or service is purchased or sold by an organization, a record of the transaction is made and kept in the files. When you work in an office, you will keep a copy of correspondence you mail or transmit. You will also keep items that you receive from other individuals or companies, such as letters, memos, reports, and advertisements. You may even keep a written record of important telephone conversations.

Records are kept so that you and others in the office can refer to the information later or use it to complete another task. That is why many businesses and other organizations have a records management system. Such a system will help you store and retrieve records efficiently and keep the files current.

As an office worker, you need to realize how vital an efficient records management system is to the smooth operation of a organization. In this topic, you will learn how organizations use such a system to maintain office records.

Overview of a Records Management System

A record is any information—text, data, image, or voice—kept for future reference. A records management filing system is a set of procedures used to organize, store, retrieve, remove, and dispose of records.

The main purpose of a records management system is to make sure records are available when needed so that the organization can operate efficiently. Such a system fulfills this purpose in several ways by:

- using storage media
- providing proper storage equipment and supplies
- outlining procedures for filing
- developing an efficient retrieval procedure
- setting up a schedule for when records should be kept or discarded

An employee of a records department who has a good understanding of the services the department provides for the entire company and of how the records management system works may be a valuable guest speaker for your class. He or she could be asked to discuss the organization of his or her department and the responsibilities of entry-level employees.

CHOOSING APPROPRIATE STORAGE MEDIA

medium or media: form(s) on or in which information may be stored

An organization may keep records on a variety of **media**: paper, magnetic media such as computer disks or tape, and micrographics (documents reduced and placed on film). A good records management system includes a program for analyzing the needs of the company to determine which storage **medium** or combination of media is best. As an office worker, you may be expected to work with all of these media. Each medium has particular advantages and disadvantages, and you will learn more about these in this topic.

PROVIDING PROPER STORAGE EQUIPMENT AND SUPPLIES

Storage equipment, such as filing cabinets, should be chosen with specific storage media in mind. For example, if your records are on paper, you might use a filing cabinet similar to the one shown in

Illustration 10-1:1. However, this cabinet would not be appropriate for filing micrographic records. You may use supplies such as file folders to hold paper records, but you would not use them for storing computer tapes. Chapter 12 discusses the various equipment and supplies appropriate for each type of storage medium.

You should keep certain especially valuable records in fireproof cabinets or vaults. A good records management system includes policies that help you determine which records require special protection. For example, you may be instructed to protect original copies of contracts by storing them in a fireproof vault.

Illustration 10-1:1
Filing cabinets are ideal for storing paper records.

ESTABLISHING PROCEDURES FOR FILING

Filing is the process of storing office records in an orderly manner within an organized system. The procedure you follow to file records will vary according to the storage media used and the manner in which the files are organized. Topic 10-2 explains the various paper filing systems. Chapter 11 presents specific filing procedures for managing hard copy and electronic media files.

DEVELOPING AN EFFICIENT RETRIEVAL PROCEDURE

You need an orderly way to retrieve records. An efficient retrieval procedure will include specific instructions for removing or charging

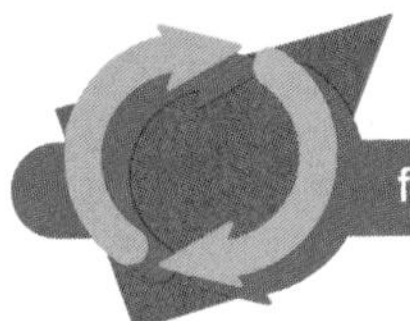

for discussion

Ask students to think of and name five equipment or supply items that are used to store records. Answers may include: metal cabinets, tape reels, file folders, diskette sleeves, shelves, and so on.

for discussion

The efficiency of the filing system shown in Illustration 10-1:1, enables this office worker to store and retrieve paper records quickly. Ask students: From what you can see in the photograph, what do you think are some specific features of this filing system that help make it efficient?

out records. Charging out a record usually means that the following information is recorded when the record is removed from the file: the name and department of the worker who is taking the record, the date the record was retrieved, and the date it will be returned. This information is kept on file in case someone else must locate the record. A retrieval procedure also should indicate whether all workers or only designated staff members have free access to the records. Chapter 11 explains retrieval procedures in more detail.

SETTING UP A RECORD RETENTION AND DISPOSITION POLICY

policy: an overall plan describing goals and acceptable rules or procedures

Each record has a life cycle. A records management system should include a statement of the **policy** on how long records are kept and how they are to be disposed of. Most companies use a retention schedule, which lists how long each type of record should be kept. You should follow this schedule to be certain that the files are free of outdated or unnecessary records so that you can work efficiently. Proper disposition of records, or how they are discarded, can be equally important. Later in this topic, you will learn more about this aspect of records management.

Benefits of an Effective Records Management System

Ask students to identify ways in which an efficient records management system might make workers more productive. (Possible answers may include not having to waste time searching for records.) Ask them how such a system might create and maintain customer goodwill. (Possible answers may include not having the customer get angry at being kept waiting during a search.)

goodwill: a good feeling of approval and support

compile: put together

An effective records management system benefits the organization in two ways. First, workers are more productive. Second, customer **goodwill** is maintained.

To make an intelligent decision or complete a task well, you need accurate, current information. For example, to **compile** a monthly sales report, you need to have the sales figures for each sales representative. Also, before you pay an invoice, you should check your records to be sure the charge is correct. And, certainly, before you can mail a package, you need to know the recipient's complete address.

You must be able to access needed records easily and quickly. An effective records management system will enable you to be more productive since you will not waste valuable time searching for information that should be easily available.

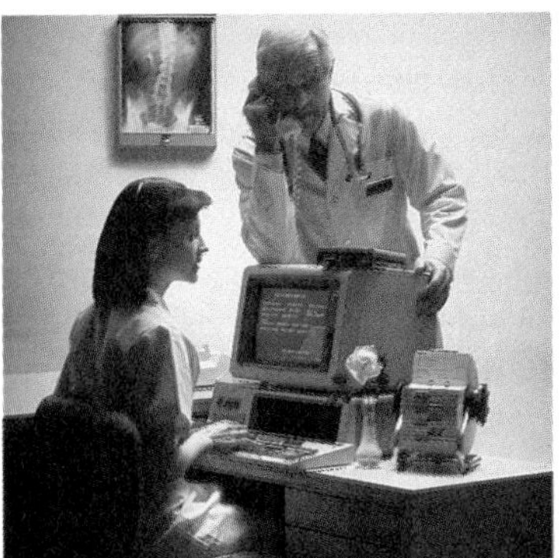

Illustration 10-1:2

This medical assistant can quickly access important patient information.

Customers and business associates may not fully appreciate efficient records management in your organization even though they like the results of such management. They are pleased when you retrieve pertinent information quickly. Yet they may take the smooth operation of the records management system for granted.

Imagine a customer's reaction if he or she called to ask a question and the customer services representative reported that there was no record of the account! The customer would be furious and probably would tell others about this frustrating event. This action could have a devastating effect on the business. Customer goodwill and confidence would have been **eroded.** On the other hand, if a customer called and received a prompt and courteous response to questions, he or she would be pleased and probably tell others about the good service. Goodwill between the customer and the business would be maintained or even improved.

eroded: made less; worn away

An effective records management system will describe procedures for accessing records quickly and for keeping records current. If you follow these procedures, the system will help you maintain customer goodwill.

Storage Media for Records

Businesses and other organizations typically store records on a variety of media. The most common storage medium continues to be paper. Although paper records will remain a major part of the filing system for years, businesses are recording more and more information on magnetic media and micrographics. These systems require less space to store the records and allow them to be accessed more quickly.

PAPER

Each time you print a copy of a letter, record an address on an index card, complete a telephone message form, or print a statistical report or complicated graph from the computer, you are recording information on paper. These paper records are referred to as hard copy.

The advantage of keeping paper records is that you can immediately read the information recorded. With magnetic media, on the other hand, you need a display screen or printer to access the information. Two disadvantages of storing records on paper are that such records take up a great deal of space and can be easily misfiled.

thinking critically

Ask students: Why might a company choose to maintain some records on paper even though other storage media are available? Answers may include access in easily readable form, legal reasons, and so on.

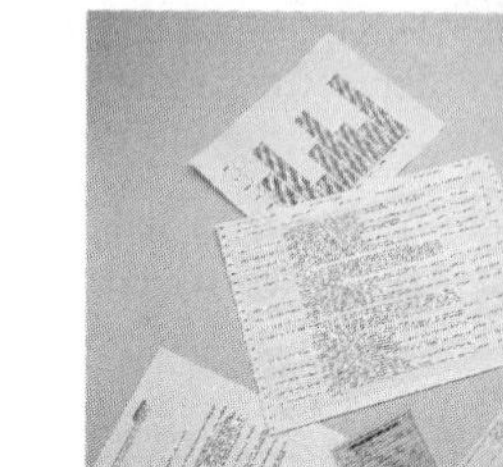

Illustration 10-1:3
A record may be stored using a variety of media.

Minimizing Paper Records. The best records management system is one in which a mixture of paper and other storage media are used. You may keep those records that are vitally important in more than one medium. You might keep records that must be seen all at once or are signed, legal documents in paper form. Records that are no longer needed daily but, perhaps, occasionally may be kept in electronic form. Whatever the needs of your office, you should consider keeping paper records to a minimum. Follow these rules:

- Do not be a pack rat. It is essential to know what paper to save and what to throw away.

for discussion

Ask students to identify the items shown in Illustration 10-1:3. Ask them to decide what items would be best stored in each medium.

- Do not wait until you are afloat in a sea of paper or have a large number of electronic files to store or organize. Set aside time for records management in your day.
- Keep a file directory. Maintain a written directory for files.

Accessibility Is Key. When paper records are maintained, they must be accessible. Topic 10-2 offers an explanation of the various filing systems used. Chapter 11 covers the equipment you will need for filing. A good office designer and a manager can coordinate the most efficient combination of systems and equipment so that you will know where to go to find records easily. For instance, moveable filing racks are great for quick access; an alphabetic filing system may be just right for an office with lots of files of patient names.

MAGNETIC MEDIA

Magnetic media are reusable and contain information that is stored electronically. The most frequently used forms of magnetic media are hard computer disks (hard drives), flexible (floppy) disks, and tapes. Hard disks are metal disks that are specially magnetized to hold the information put onto them and are usually internal to a computer. These disks vary in size and may hold up to nine gigabytes (9,000,000,000 bytes) of information. Floppy disks are bendable disks placed inside a hard casing to protect them. They work in the same way as hard disks but hold less information and are less durable. Their main use is portability. Information can be placed on a floppy disk in one computer and transported by that disk to be read or used in another computer. These disks hold up to 1.44 megabytes (1,400,000 bytes) of information. Tape is used primarily for backing up (making a copy of the files on) hard drives and for holding large amounts of information that is not used on a regular basis. Because tape may be of great length, it has a large storage capacity. However, with the invention of the compact laser disc, tape may become a thing of the past. Compact discs are far more portable than tape and hold equally large quantities of information.

Advantages of Using Magnetic Media. Four major advantages to the use of magnetic media are:

What kinds of records would be best kept on paper? best kept electronically? Would their answers change for a used auto parts dealer? for a medical office? Help students see that the filing system and equipment should vary based on the type of office and purposes for records.

Ask students to name all of the advantages and disadvantages that they can think of for storing records on magnetic media.

- Records can be retrieved quickly and easily.
- The storage space required for housing records on magnetic media is much less than that required for paper media.
- Records stay in the same sequence on the magnetic media even after being retrieved several times.
- Records can be updated easily.

Disadvantages of Using Magnetic Media. Three disadvantages to using magnetic media to store records are:

- An output device such as a monitor or printer is needed to read the information recorded on the magnetic media.
- Electrical power surges and failures can erase or **alter** the information recorded on magnetic media.
- Magnetic media require special protection from extreme heat and cold and should be kept away from magnetic fields.

alter: change

COMPACT DISCS (CDs)

The CD, or compact disc, is an optical storage form. (See Imaging Systems on page 463.) Information is put on the disc by laser and read by a CD drive in the computer. These discs are in many ways better than most magnetic media, such as floppies, because they can hold more information than any but a hard disk. The disadvantage is that most older computers only have a drive to read CDs and cannot write (or save) information to these discs. New computers and stand-alone drives are available that write to CDs. However, these drives are expensive and are not yet in wide use. Eventually, though, as prices fall and old computer systems are replaced, CDs will be used more and more by businesses. The biggest advantage of CDs over magnetic media is their ability to hold large files needed for graphic information, including moving pictures with stereo sound.

> *When Joyce walked by Ken's workstation, she noticed that several floppy disks and a CD out of its protective jacket were lying on top of the monitor. Ken was working at the computer and seemed unconcerned about the situation:*

Joyce: Ken, did you know you could be destroying all your hard work right now?

Ken: What do you mean?

Joyce: Floppy disks are sensitive to magnetic forces such as those found in the computer and even the telephone. You should never place them on top of the monitor! And, by leaving the CD out of its jacket you risk scratching it or dropping something on it that will mar the surface and make it unreadable.

Ken: I guess you're right. (He removes the floppy disks from the top of the monitor and places the CD in its jacket.) I'd hate to lose everything I just worked on.

MICROGRAPHICS

Microimaging systems, also called micrographics, photographically reduce documents to a fraction of their original size to fit on film or **microfiche.** You will want to understand the equipment, supplies, and procedures used to record micrographics. The following steps are involved in the process:

microfiche: a small rectangular sheet of microfilm that contains a series of records arranged in rows and columns

1. Records are gathered so they can be imaged to film. (Chapter 11, Topic 11-3, describes methods of organizing records for micrographic storage.)
2. A special camera is used to take pictures of the hard copies.
3. The film is developed. Each record then appears as a tiny picture—a *microimage*—on the film or fiche, as shown in Illustration 10-1:4 on page 461, and Illustration 10-1:6, on page 462.
4. A device called a reader is used to display the microimage for reading. Some readers, referred to as reader/printers, will also print a hard copy of the microimage.

Computer Output Microfilm (COM) is the process of transferring computer files directly to microfilm or fiche. The computer reads information recorded on magnetic media and outputs it as microimages on film rather than as paper printouts. Computer Input Microfilm (CIM) is the process of converting data to electrical impulses stored on magnetic media and using the data as input to the computer to

You may want to arrange a trip to a company or library where students can observe a micrographics system in use.

create files. Microimages take less space to store than paper and will not, if properly stored, deteriorate after long periods of time.

Best Uses. Micrographics are used when paper or computer files would be inappropriate or less feasible. For instance, an automobile dealer usually will keep parts lists for past-year vehicles on microfiche. Because the list is unchanging, it is not necessary to keep it on magnetic media that can be updated. Because the fiche is less bulky, it is easier to store and retrieve than paper records. Also, libraries keep back issues of magazines and newspapers on microfilm because it is much easier and less costly to store rolls of films than huge stacks of periodicals.

Microforms. You may use micrographics in different forms, collectively called microforms. The most frequently used microforms are described here along with the advantages and disadvantages of using microfilm.

Roll Microfilm. Microfilm is similar to motion picture film and is available in different widths. Roll microfilm is usually a roll of 16mm or 35mm film that contains a series of pictures or images. The film, which usually comes in 100- or 215-foot lengths, is the most inexpensive microform. A 100-foot roll can hold up to 4,000 images. Typically, roll microfilm is used to store records that are not used frequently or do not require changes. Roll microfilm is usually housed in a protective cassette or cartridge as described in the table below.

ROLL MICROFILM

Reels	Reels are the spools upon which microfilm can be wound. These make for easy storage but have the drawback that it is difficult to locate a particular record or item on any given reel.
Cartridges	Cartridges are more convenient than reels for filing in that each roll of film may be wound onto a single cartridge, thus making retrieval easier. They also protect against fingerprints and touch damage.
Cassettes	Cassettes are often used for filing microfilm. Each cassette holds two spools—the feed spool and the uptake spool, much like a film cassette. Viewing of the film is easier than with rolls and damage from touching the film is kept to a minimum.

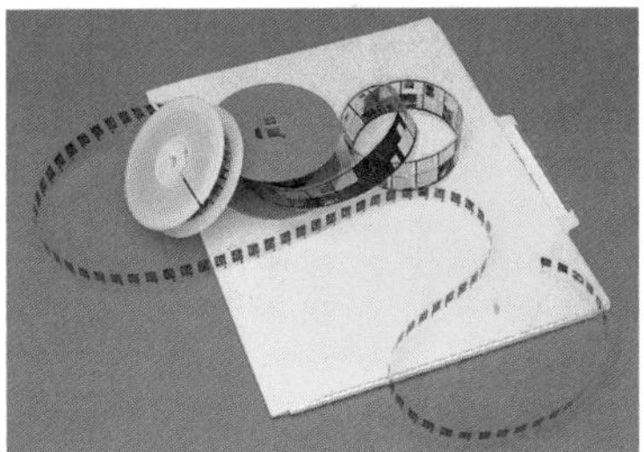

Illustration 10-1:4

Roll microfilm is a good way to store records that would be bulky in paper form.

Aperture Cards. An aperture card is a paper card that holds a piece of microfilm that is visible through an opening in the card. The most commonly used aperture card contains one microimage from 16mm or 35mm film. You may be asked to keep images of large-format drawings, such as engineering drawings or land surveys, on aperture cards. Identifying information about the microimage can be printed on the card.

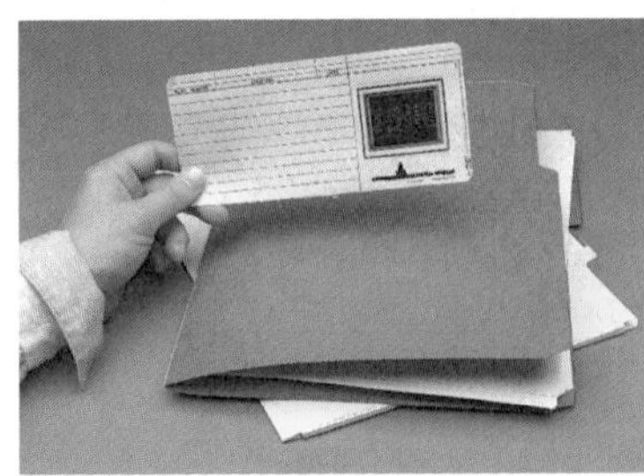

Illustration 10-1:5

An aperture card contains one microimage.

Microfiche. Microfiche, as noted previously, is a small rectangular sheet of microfilm that contains a series of records arranged in rows and columns. Although microfiche is available in a variety of sizes, the 6" x 4" size is the most commonly used. You might be asked to store directories or manuals on microfiche. Identifying information about the records appears at the top of each microfiche, as shown in Illustration 10-1:6 on page 462. Thus, individual records are more easily located on microfiche than on roll microfilm.

Ask students for examples of records that might be stored on roll microfilm. Answers may include back issues of newspapers and magazines.

Ask students for examples of records that might be stored on aperture cards. Answers may include landscape and architectural drawings.

Ask students for examples of records that might be stored on microfiche. Answers may include parts listings for prior-year cars. Ask students for examples of records that might be stored in microfilm jackets. Answers may include photo records of art pieces on exhibit at a museum.

Ask students for advantages and disadvantages of using microform storage. Advantages include reduced storage space. Disadvantages include the inability to update records in this form.

Illustration 10-1:6
Microfiche is a popular, economical, and practical method for storing records.

Microfilm Jackets. A microfilm jacket is a plastic holder for strips of 16mm or 35mm microfilm. The most common jacket size is 4" x 6". Strips of microfilm or single microimages are inserted into sleeves or pockets, as shown in Illustration 10-1:7. You can easily update a microfilm jacket by removing a microimage or an entire strip of film from a sleeve and replacing it with another. Some companies use microfilm jackets to store personnel records. With a microfilm jacket, records can be added easily. Space at the top of the jacket is reserved for identifying the contents.

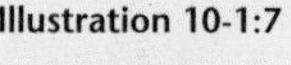

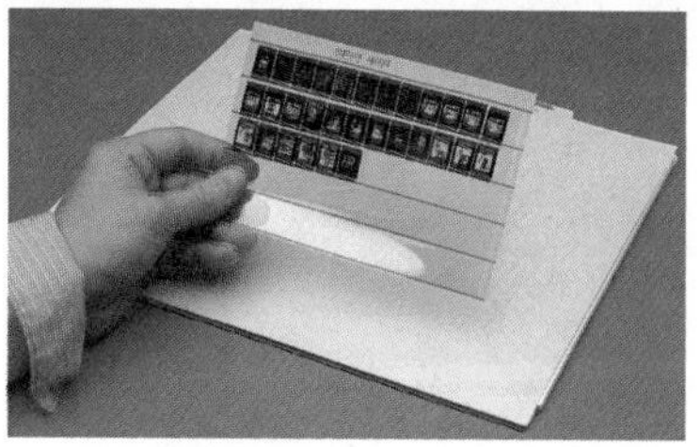

Illustration 10-1:7
A microfilm jacket is used to hold strips of microfilm or single microimages.

Advantages of Using Microfilm. There are several advantages of storing records on microfilm. These advantages include:

- A microimage takes up less space than a record stored on paper.
- In a microimaging system, the image is viewed but not removed from the film. The microimages are always in the same sequence on the same microform, regardless of how often the microform is retrieved and filed. In a paper storage system, the record is usually removed from the folder for reference and then returned later.

- Hard copies of microimages can be produced on reader/printers when needed.
- Microimaging is an inexpensive way to **archive** important records. Microimages are usually accepted in courts as legal evidence just as paper records are.
- Retrieval devices available for use with microfilm make it easy to access needed records.
- Microfilm can be easily duplicated and stored in a separate, protected location.

archive: keep permanently in inactive files

During their break, Mario and Carolyn began discussing the new microimaging system their company had recently implemented:

Mario: At first, I wasn't sure that microimaging would be helpful. But now, I'm glad we have the system.

Carolyn: I was looking forward to having our records on microfilm! Our file cabinets were so crowded and the file drawers so high that I had difficulty just filing and retrieving records.

Mario: What I've enjoyed is being able to refer to a record without cluttering my workstation with more paper. But if I need a hard copy, I can make one by using the microfilm reader/printer.

Disadvantages of Using Microfilm. Three disadvantages of storing records on microfilm are:

- The initial cost may seem high since a camera, reader/printer(s), and microfilm must be purchased to record information on film.
- Office workers must be given special training so they can operate the microimaging equipment.
- Records stored on microfilm cannot be updated or altered.

IMAGING SYSTEMS

Imaging is a relatively new process of handling information and the media on which it is kept. An imaging system converts all types of documents to **digitized** electronic data that can be stored on CD-ROM or rewritable CDs (see Compact Discs on page 458) and retrieved immediately. Electronic image systems include:

digitized: converted to digital form that can be read by a computer

Both Mario and Carolyn have positive attitudes toward the changes taking place at their company. Ask students how Mario's and Carolyn's attitudes will help them adjust to the new microimaging system.

- a scanner to convert the paper documents to a digitized form
- a processor that compresses the image
- a storage medium to retain the image
- a retrieval mechanism to convert the image for viewing on a monitor
- an output device that processes the image to hard-copy format

Imaging systems, as they are adopted, are dramatically altering the workplace by reducing paper processing, speeding up workflow, and making files instantly accessible. Because of the relatively high cost of these systems, they are not prevalent. However, as the cost decreases, the number of companies employing the systems will increase. The best use of imaging is in organizations that:

- have a high volume of documents
- have high activity in files
- cannot afford a misfile or lost file
- require a high level of security for documents
- need to maximize personnel efficiency

Cost Factors Associated with Records Management

inevitable: unavoidable

Costs are **inevitable** with any records management system. The cost factors involve buying equipment and supplies, leasing storage space, and paying office workers to file and retrieve records.

EQUIPMENT, SUPPLIES, AND STORAGE

conservative: not wasteful

Major equipment purchases such as filing cabinets and shelves, as well as periodic purchases of filing supplies, contribute to the cost of maintaining a records management system. Proper care of equipment and **conservative** use of supplies on your part will help control costs.

When businesses lease office space, they lease by the square foot. The company pays for the space occupied by records every time it writes a rent check. By keeping that space to a minimum, the room available for work is increased. Using microfilm to store records is one way to reduce the amount of space required to house records.

HUMAN RESOURCES

Workers are a key element in an effective records management system. Efficient procedures are worthless unless they are put into practice. Thus, the salaries a company must pay its human resources (workers) to manage records are a cost factor of records management.

Illustration 10-1:8

A tape librarian contributes to the efficiency of the overall records management system.

Because the Information Age is generating a need for capable workers who understand and can apply sound records management principles, the field offers many career opportunities.

Large companies often have an entire staff of records management personnel. There may be a manager who is in charge of the records management department. The staff may include an analyst, a records center supervisor, and several clerks. Since records management is a field growing in importance, more and more businesses are looking for workers who specialize in this area. Records management is a major career opportunity.

DESTRUCTION COSTS

There are several costs associated with destroying records. Paper must be shredded, removed from the business in bulk, and placed in a landfill in an ecologically sound manner. Some paper records may need to be placed on micrographic or optical media first, and storage of those resulting records will be an additional expense. Some of the costs can be reduced. Small businesses may take advantage of commercial records centers for destruction of records and of micrographics services if such imaging is needed. Large businesses may find it more cost effective to establish these services for themselves.

Use transparency master TM 10-1:1, Record Life Cycle, found in the *Teacher's Resource Guide,* to enhance a discussion of the record life cycle. The flowchart shown in the transparency is designed to provide students with a visual representation of how a records management system functions within a company. As you review the flowchart, emphasize the phases of the life cycle as presented on this and the following pages.

Record Life Cycle

Records come from many sources. Some originate outside the organization (correspondence from other businesses and industry surveys, for example). Others originate within the organization (interoffice memorandums, records of sales and purchases, computer printouts, and copies of outgoing correspondence, for example).

The usefulness of each record has a beginning and an end. Therefore, each record has a life cycle. The phases of the record life cycle are the same regardless of whether the records are kept on paper, magnetic or optical media, or micrographics. Sometimes, however, records will change media in the process. For example, in moving a paper record to inactive storage, it might be microfilmed. A record life cycle is shown in Illustration 10-1:9. Refer to this illustration as you read the following brief description of each phase.

Phase 1 *Collect the Records*
The cycle begins when you collect or create the records. The two arrows at the top of Illustration 10-1:9 indicate the source of the records—either from outside or inside the organization.

Phase 2 *Categorize the Records*
Next, you need to **categorize** the records as to how important they are to the operation of the organization. A records management policy will help you do that. How records are categorized will affect how you store the records and how long you keep them. Refer to Illustration 10-1:10 on page 467.

categorize: assign to a group of similar items, arrange by type

Phase 3 *Prepare the Records for Storage*
The exact procedure you use in this phase will vary. The specifics of the procedure will depend on whether the record is on paper, magnetic media, or micrographics. You also need to know whether the record should be filed alphabetically, numerically, or chronologically—as discussed in Topic 10-2.

Phase 4 *Maintain the Records in Active Storage*
When a record is in active storage, you probably will store and retrieve it many times. A good records management system will specify procedures for retrieving records and for returning them to the files efficiently.

Phase 5 *Reevaluate the Records*
Each record's importance should be reevaluated regularly. Some records may remain in active storage while others are transferred to inactive storage or to a different media. Some records may be removed from the files altogether and destroyed. Records in inactive storage are still retrieved and refiled, but not as frequently as those in active storage.

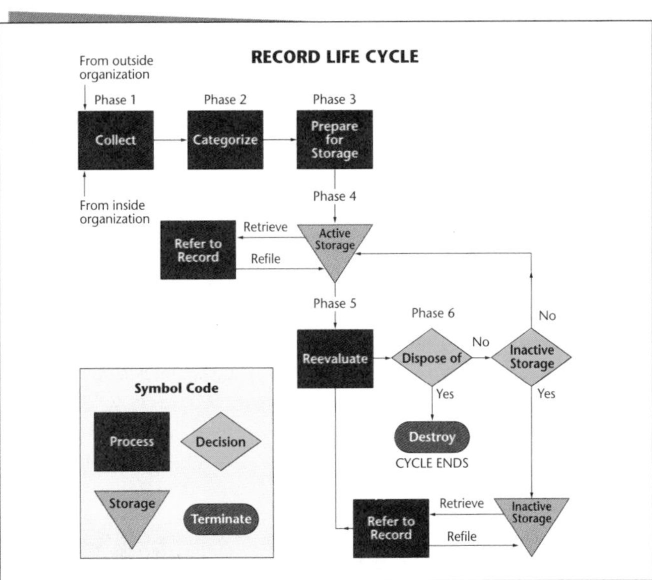

Illustration 10-1:9

These six phases make up the life cycle of a record.

Ask students to name the six phases of the record life cycle. Then ask them what skills an office worker needs in relation to each phase.

Phase 6 *Dispose of the Records*
Disposing of a record involves transferring it to inactive storage or destroying it. When a record is no longer needed and will not ever be needed again, you should destroy it to make room for current records. The cycle ends when a record is destroyed.

RECORD CATEGORIES

Category	Description	Examples
Vital Records	Essential for the company to survive	Original copies of deeds, copyrights, mortgages, trademarks
Important Records	Needed for business to operate smoothly; expensive to replace	Tax returns, personnel files, cancelled checks
Useful Records	Convenient to have, yet replaceable	Correspondence, purchase orders, names and addresses of suppliers
Nonessential Records	Has one-time or very limited usefulness	Meeting announcements, advertisements

Illustration 10-1:10

Records must be categorized as to their importance to the company.

Records must be categorized as to their importance to the company. Choose some of the "examples" from Illustration 10-1:10, and ask students to decide quickly which category these records fall into.

Removing Records from Active Storage

When records are outdated, or needed only infrequently, you should remove them from the active storage area. An effective records management system will include a policy for such removal.

RETENTION SCHEDULE

A retention schedule, shown in Illustration 10-1:11, is a valuable records management tool that identifies how long particular types of records should be kept. The retention schedule has columns for a description of the type of record, the retention period (how long the record should be kept), and the authority who regulates how long the record should be kept. Government authority dictates how long you should keep certain records, such as tax returns. Company executives may also establish policies for keeping records such as bank statements, expense reports, and budgets.

A retention schedule outlines how long particular types of records should be kept. Choose some of the items in the "Records Description" column of Illustration 10-1:11, and ask students to decide quickly how long the retention period for each is.

Illustration 10-1:11

Can you determine from this retention schedule how long bank statements must be kept?

RECORDS RETENTION SCHEDULE

Record Description	Retention Period	Authority
ACCOUNTING RECORDS		
Accounts Payable Ledger	5 years	Company Policy
Accounts Receivable Ledger	5 years	Company Policy
Balance Sheets	Permanent	Company Policy
Bank Statements	3 years	Company Policy
General Ledger Records	Permanent	Code of Federal Regulations
Payroll Registers	3 years	Fair Labor Standards Act

INACTIVE STORAGE AND COMMERCIAL RECORDS CENTERS

Records that are needed by the organization but are not often referred to are inactive. Inactive records should be stored separately from active ones. For example, assume you are required to keep company bank statements for three years. Since it is not likely that you will often refer to the past years' statements, you should remove them from active storage. You do not want inactive records to take up valuable active storage space. It is easier to retrieve and file active records when the inactive ones are in a separate location.

The most cost-effective way for many businesses, particularly small ones, to store inactive records is to use commercial records centers. Most of these centers offer a number of services and charge on a unit-cost basis per month. These centers base the unit on a standard-sized box that fits their shelving and that customers are required to use—thus maximizing storage space. Other costs may include pickup and delivery, receiving and handling at initial storage, and destruction costs at the end of the record's life cycle.

Special records of historical value are stored apart from active records. An archive is a storage area that is dedicated to organizing and preserving such historical records. These archived records may be in the form of paper, optical media, or microimages.

Disaster Recovery

A disaster recovery plan is the procedure that is to be followed in case of **catastrophe,** such as an earthquake, fire, flood, or other situation that results in a partial or total loss of records. Important records and a disaster recovery plan must be kept current and vary depending upon the needs of the organization. Special removable files may be used for taking out records in the event of an emergency. In an earthquake-prone area, special below-ground vaults may be used to store irreplaceable records. Some companies may use electronic imaging to send essential data to an off-site storage facility where it will be safe.

catastrophe: major disaster

Reviewing the Topic

topic 10-1 review

1. Why is an effective records management system vital to the smooth operation of an organization?
2. How does an effective records management system result in greater productivity by office workers?
3. List one advantage and two disadvantages of using paper to store information.
4. What are the three most frequently used forms of magnetic media?
5. Identify four types of microforms.
6. List four advantages of storing records on microfilm.
7. What are four cost factors that affect the efficiency of a records management system?
8. List the six phases of the record life cycle.
9. What is a retention schedule?
10. What is disaster recovery and why is it important?

INTERACTING WITH OTHERS

An important folder is missing from the central files. You discover that someone in your department has signed it out. You go to this person, who is above your level in the company, and he says that he does not have it. The folder is essential for your work. What should you do?

- Confront the higher-ranking person and insist that he give you the file?
- Go to your supervisor and ask her to help resolve the situation?
- Attempt to do your work without the folder and make mistakes since you do not have the information you need?

How could you have prevented this awkward situation?

topic 10-1 review

Maintaining Office Records

470

What you are to do:

Prepare a written response to the questions asked.

REINFORCING MATH SKILLS

ACTIVITY 1

A single file drawer contains 75 folders. Documents from 15 of these folders were converted to micrographic form, then destroyed. The microforms were transferred to inactive storage. Of the remaining active folders, six had their contents divided into two folders each.

What you are to do:

Calculate how many active folders are now in the file drawer. Show your calculations. Also, calculate the percentage of decrease in the number of folders in the active file. Refer to Reference Section D, Math, if necessary.

See Workbook pages 222–226 for Reference Section D, Math.

ACTIVITY 2

Seven departments have requested additional file folders. Folders are ordered from the supply company in boxes, each containing 25 folders. The number of folders each department needs is given in the following list:

Accounting	21
Finance	48
Human Resources	99
Marketing	125
Production	175
Public Relations	100
Word Processing	260

How many folders are required to meet the needs of the seven departments? How many boxes of folders should be ordered? How many folders will be left after each department has received the number of folders it requested?

What you are to do:

Calculate the answers to the above questions. Show your calculations. Refer to Reference Section D, Math, if necessary.

471

APPLICATION ACTIVITIES

ACTIVITY 1 Purchase Order

In this activity, you will prepare an order to purchase filing supplies from:

Folders For You, Inc.
4141 Industrial Road
San Jose, CA 95066
(408) 555-0118 FAX (408) 555-0119

What you are to do:

1. Prepare Purchase Order No. 7893 to order the filing supplies listed below using the spreadsheet template file *Porder*. Use today's date and request that the items be shipped via UPS. The terms are Net 30.
2. Use a rate of 6 percent to compute the sales tax and use a formula to calculate the tax on the subtotal. Shipping costs are $136.00.
3. Refer to your answer from REINFORCING MATH SKILLS, Activity 2 above for the number of folders needed. Leave the *Authorized by* and *Date* signature lines blank for your supervisor to complete.

topic 10-1 review

Items to order:

Qty.	Order No.	Description	Unit Price
?	FOL298	File Folders, box of 25	$12.95
5	PEN542	Black Pens, 1 gross	$ 5.99
2	LBL641	Labels, 50	$ 4.89

ACTIVITY 2 Records Management Job Descriptions

Your supervisor, Ms. Suzuki, asks you to update the records management section of the office manual. She approaches your workstation and says: "Here is my edited draft of the updated material for the office

472

manual. Please prepare a final copy, making the changes I've indicated on the draft. Correct any errors I may have overlooked."

What you are to do:

Prepare a final copy of the draft shown below using the word processing template file *Jobs*. Print the document on plain paper.

JOB DESCRIPTIONS
FOR RECORDS MANAGEMENT

RECORDS MANAGEMENT DIRECTOR

Education: Bachelor's Degree with intensive course work in business administration; minimum advanced degree helpful.

Duties: Responsible for developing and implementing all company records management policies and practices; coordinates personnel and resources.

Experience: Five years experience as a records management supervisor or consultant.

RECORDS SUPERVISOR

Education: Two years of college or vocational training in business.
Experience: Too to five years in records center.
Duties: Maintain and oprate corporate records center; hire and supervise staff; responsible for protection, storage, and disposal of vital records.

MICROIMAGING TECHNICIAN

Education: High school diploma plus technical training in Microfilming.
Experience: Previous experience helpful but not necessary.
Duties: Operate cameras and film processors; test developed film for quality; conform operations to meet production standards.

RECORDS CLERK

Education: High school diploma with courses in office procedures.
Experience: Entry-level position; experience not required.
Duties: Sort, file, an retrieve records; classify materials and records; transfer records to inactive storage.

473

Paper Records Systems

When you have completed your study of this topic, you will be able to:

- **identify the components of a paper filing system**
- **describe four alphabetic filing systems**
- **explain how a numeric filing system is organized**
- **explain terminal-digit and middle-digit filing systems**
- **explain how a chronologic filing system is organized**

Topic 10-2

In Topic 10-1, you learned that each record has a life cycle. In this topic, you will become acquainted with systems for organizing paper files while the records are in the storage phase of the life cycle.

Although there is a definite move toward computerized filing systems, paper filing systems continue to be the most common. In today's rapidly changing offices, it is typical for a company to use both. Systems for organizing magnetic and optical media and micrographic files are presented in detail in Chapter 11.

In a paper filing system, individual records are stored in folders. These folders are labeled and organized alphabetically according to names of individuals, organizations, businesses, subjects, or geographic locations. Files may also be organized numerically and by date.

As an office worker, you will be expected to understand your organization's filing system so that you can file and retrieve records efficiently. You may even have an opportunity to suggest ways to improve the system.

Some organizations use only one filing system for all their paper records. Other organizations may use more than one. For example, purchase orders may be filed numerically by order number, while records about customers are filed alphabetically. In this topic, you will learn how each type of paper filing system is organized and used.

Components of a Paper Filing System

A filing system requires equipment, procedures, and supplies. You need to understand the various types of each. You also need to understand the use of guides that apply to all of the systems.

EQUIPMENT

Various types of equipment—cabinets and shelves—are used to **house** paper records. Lateral file cabinets like those shown in Illustration 10-2:1 are used in many offices. In this topic, we will assume that all records in your organization are stored in lateral file cabinets. Chapter 11 describes other equipment used in a paper filing system.

house: store

Illustration 10-2:1
Lateral files are frequently used to store medical records.

Most companies (even those using state-of-the art technology) maintain some of their records in paper filing systems. Therefore, understanding such systems is critical to students seeking employment in office occupations.

Collect and display magazine and catalog clippings of various storage equipment for paper records. Ask students to collect other examples and bring them to class to add to the display.

Ask students what other kinds of records, besides medical ones, would logically be stored in lateral files.

PROCEDURES

Before placing records in folders, you should index and code each record. Chapter 11 explains in detail the procedures for indexing and coding. However, a brief introduction is included here to help you understand why these procedures are an important component of a filing system.

Indexing. Indexing is the process of deciding how to identify each record to be filed—either by name, subject, geographic location, number, or date. In a name file, for example, you would index a record by a specific individual, organization, or company name. In a numeric file, on the other hand, you would index a record by a specific number.

Coding. Coding is the process of marking a symbol or other identification on the record to indicate how it was indexed. Colored pencils often are used for coding.

You may code a record by circling the appropriate name, subject, geographic location, or number that appears on the record. Or you may write the identification in the upper right-hand corner of the record.

As you learned in Topic 10-1, you may retrieve and refile a record many times while it is in active storage. By coding a record, you help ensure that it will be filed correctly each time it is returned to the files.

SUPPLIES

Each drawer in a file contains two different kinds of filing supplies: guides and file folders. The *guides* divide the drawer into sections and serve as *signposts* for quick reference. They also provide support for the folders and their contents. File folders hold the papers in an upright position in the drawer and serve as containers to keep the papers together. *Labels* are attached to file folders to identify the contents of each folder. Labels are also attached to file cabinet drawers to identify the contents of each drawer.

Guides. Guides are heavy cardboard sheets that are the same size as the file folders. A *tab* extends over the top of each guide, and a notation is marked or printed on the tab. This notation is called a *caption*. By reading the captions, you can quickly identify divisions within the

teaching tips

Collect and display samples of various storage supplies for paper records—such as file folders, guides, and labels. You may wish to take a file drawer and set it up with the samples in it organized properly with primary and special guides and labeled file folders.

file. For example, a guide may carry the caption "A," which tells you that only records starting with the letter A are found between that guide and the next one.

Guides are classified as primary or special. *Primary guides* indicate the major divisions, such as letters of the alphabet, into which the filing system is separated. *Special guides* indicate subdivisions within these major divisions. Illustration 10-2:6 on page 481 shows how primary and special guides are arranged in an alphabetic filing system. Behind primary guide "C" you may have a special guide such as "Cooper Temporaries." For quick retrieval of files, place no more than ten folders behind a guide; and place only about 15 to 25 guides in a file drawer.

Labels. You need labels on file drawers so that you can identify the contents of each drawer without opening it. You also need labels on file folders to likewise identify them without digging through the contents. The information on the drawer label should be specific, easy to read, and current. When the contents of a cabinet are changed in any way, the drawer label should be corrected immediately.

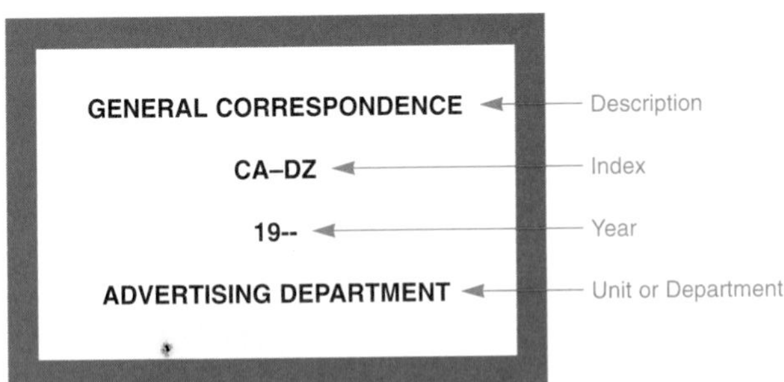

Illustration 10-2:2
Drawer label

Folder labels are gummed strips of paper you attach to the folder tabs. The caption on the label identifies the contents of the folder. It is important to format the captions in a consistent manner, usually at the top, left-hand corner of the label.

Many companies use color-coded labels to improve filing efficiency. There are several ways to use these labels. One simply involves assigning a specific color to each alphabetic or numeric section of the files.

Students can benefit from seeing how the concepts presented in this topic are applied in the work world. You may want to arrange for students to visit a company with paper records systems to view the supplies and equipment used.

Illustration 10-2:3
Folder labels

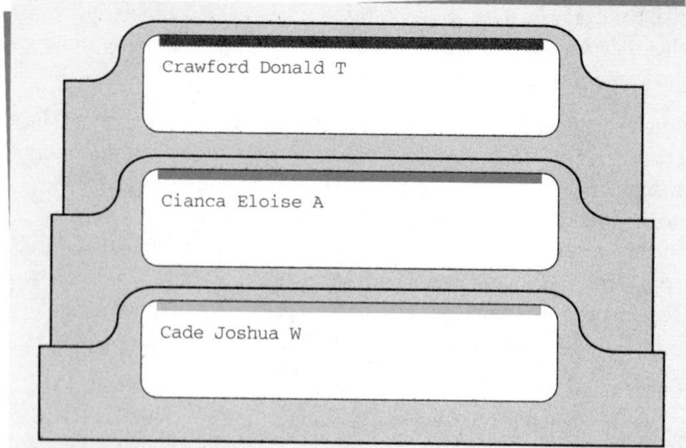

In Illustration 10-2:6, on page 481 notice that all the fourth/fifth position folders in the drawer labeled "CA-DZ" have labels coded with the same color.

A more complex coding system is shown in Illustration 10-2:4. You can see the color pattern formed by the labels. Such a pattern helps you file and retrieve records quickly and accurately. If a folder were misfiled, you would know immediately because the color pattern would be interrupted.

Ask students to describe the pattern created by the color-coding system in the photo of file folders shown in Illustration 10-2:4. Have them name some advantages to color-coding labels.

Illustration 10-2:4
A color-coded filing system helps office workers file and retrieve records efficiently.

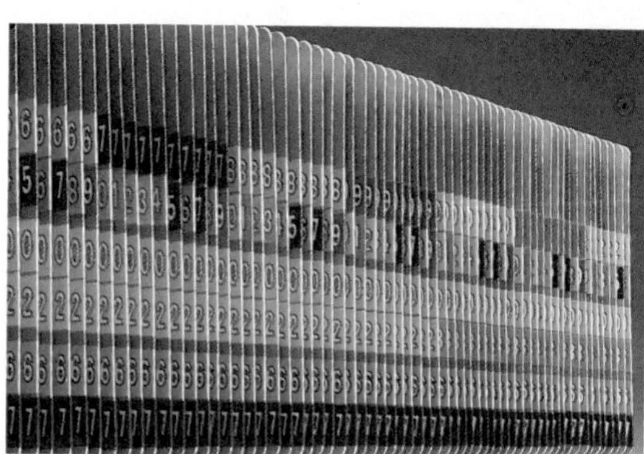

Folders. A folder is made of strong, durable paper called *manila*. Each folder is larger than the papers it contains so that it will protect the contents. Standard folder sizes are designed for papers that are $8\frac{1}{2}$" x 11", $8\frac{1}{2}$" x 13", or $8\frac{1}{2}$" x 14".

Folder cuts are made in the back of a folder, which is higher than the front, to create a tab. You attach labels to the tabs to identify the contents. Folder tabs vary in width and position, as shown in Illustration 10-2:5. Sometimes the tab is the full width of the folder. This is called a *full-cut* or *straight-cut folder*. *Half-cut tabs* are half the width of the folder and have two possible positions. *Third-cut folders* have three positions, each tab occupying a third of the width of the folder. Another standard tab has five positions and is called a *fifth-cut folder*. Some folders hang from metal frames placed inside the file drawer. Removable tabs can be attached to these folders at appropriate positions.

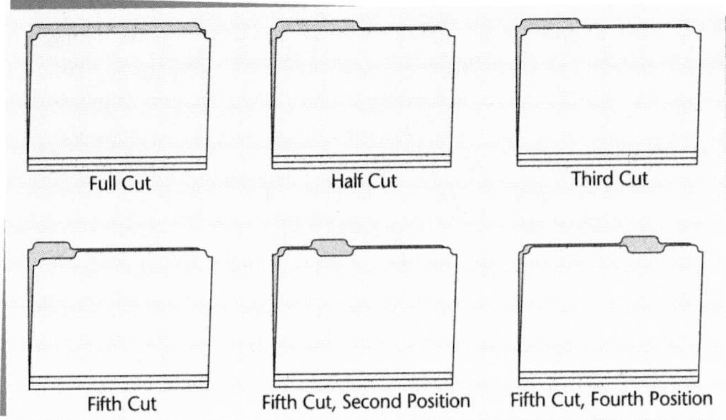

Illustration 10-2:5

There are four standard folder cuts. Note that the folder tabs vary in width and position.

Display several file folders with varying cuts and ask students to identify each cut. Ask them which cuts might be best suited for various filing needs that they can envision.

Costs. The costs associated with paper filing include paper, folders, labels, organizers, indexing products, printing supplies for labels, equipment maintenance and upgrades, and other essentials. It is not surprising, therefore, that the largest budget item for records management systems is often for active files. The cost is ongoing because of the new files added to the system regularly. Thus, a department is constantly purchasing new paper supplies as well as equipment such as storage cabinets.

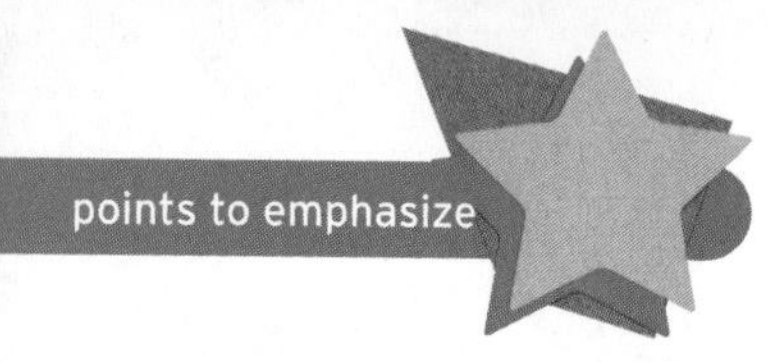

The positioning of guides and folders within filing systems will vary from office to office. Regardless of the system used, the guides and folders should be arranged so that they are easy to see and are in a logical order.

Use transparency master TM 10-2:2, Drawer Label, found in the *Teacher's Resource Guide.* Ask students to identify the guides and folders and their positions.

To give students practical experience with records management systems, ask them to establish a filing system for their personal records. Students will gain experience determining appropriate label captions and folder cuts for their records. Some records they might consider organizing into a filing system include:

1. correspondence from friends and family
2. certificates and awards
3. information from colleges, universities, technical schools, or other institutions they may plan to attend
4. magazine and newspaper articles
5. information about career options
6. work-related materials, such as pay stubs
7. information about a personal interest or hobby, such as photography or baseball

You may wish to have on hand used folders, with the labels removed, in various cuts for students who cannot afford to purchase their own.

POSITION OF GUIDES AND FOLDERS

in-house: within the company or organization

A variety of filing systems are used in offices today. Some systems (especially color-coded ones) are purchased from commercial manufacturers of filing supplies; other systems are developed **in-house.** Therefore, the positioning of guides and folders within filing systems will vary from office to office. Regardless of the system used, the guides and folders should be arranged in such a way that they are easy to see and in a logical order. You can see that the arrangement in Illustration 10-2:6, allows your eye to move easily from left to right.

Guides. When you open a file drawer, you look first for the appropriate primary guide. Since you read from left to right, the tab on the primary guide should be at the far left, where it will be easy to locate.

Special guides are used to pinpoint the location of a specific fourth/fifth position individual folder. In Illustration 10-2:6, they are located in the third position. For example, the special guide "Dorcey Electronics" was added because of frequent requests for the Dorcey Electronics folder. Because of the special guide, this folder can easily be located. Sometimes a special guide is used to pinpoint the location of a series of folders relating to a specific subject. In Illustration 10-2:9, on page 484, for example, the special guide "Film" marks the location of two individual folders relating to the subject *film*.

Folders. There is usually a general folder for each primary guide. This second position folder bears the same alphabetic caption as the one shown on the primary guide. For example, the general folder that goes behind the primary guide "C" also will bear the caption "C." These folders are given the name *general* because they are used to accumulate records that do not justify the use of an individual folder. When you accumulate five or more records relating to one name or subject, prepare an individual folder for those records.

Using individual folders helps you locate records more quickly. In Illustration 10-2:6, individual folders are shown in the combined fourth/fifth position. Notice the width of the tabs on the individual folders. This extra width allows ample space for labeling personal, company, or subject names.

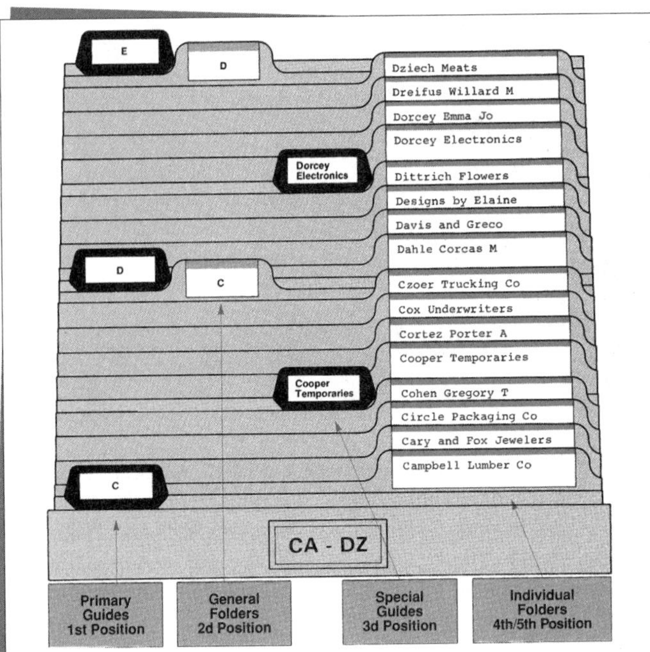

Illustration 10-2:6

Note the positions of guides and folders in this portion of a CA–DZ name file.

Alphabetic Filing Systems

In an alphabetic filing system, letters and words (names, subjects, or geographic locations) are used as captions on the guides and folders. Both guides and folders are arranged in alphabetic order according to the captions. Reference Section F, Alphabetizing Procedures, presents rules for filing alphabetically.

Four common alphabetic filing systems use name, subject, a combination of name and subject, and geographic location.

FILING BY NAME

If a name file is used, records are indexed according to the name of an individual, organization, or company. The folders are arranged in alphabetic order within the file drawer.

The alphabetic indexing rules presented in Reference Section F, Alphabetizing Procedures, reflect the guidelines published by the Association of Records Managers and Administrators (ARMA). (See Workbook pages 228–233.) Refer to the ARMA rules while reading the text and completing certain end-of-topic and end-of-chapter activities.

expand the concept

Compare retrieving records filed by name to finding names and phone numbers in a phone book. Provide each student with a telephone directory or with pages extracted from one. (Outdated directories can be used.) Give students a sheet with 20 names of local residents and/or businesses and ask them to record telephone numbers for each name. Have students raise their hands when they have all numbers recorded. Note the accuracy of the responses recorded.

Illustration 10-2:7

Efficient records management systems allow quick and easy records retrieval.

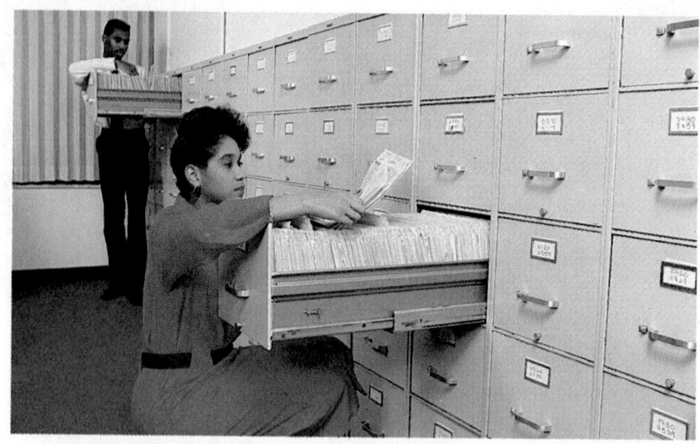

Illustration 10-2:8 shows how alphabetic primary and special guides are used in a name file to help you file and retrieve records efficiently. If you were looking for a folder labeled "Burns Jewelers," you would find the primary guide "B," scan the special guides until you found "Bu," and search for the individual folder for Burns Jewelers. By using the guides, you should be able to locate the folder quickly without having to thumb through all the folders.

If you do not find an individual folder for the record, file the record in the appropriate general folder.

> *Carrie: Roy, there is no folder labeled "Burton Real Estate" in the file. Where do I file this letter?*

> *Roy: If there is no individual folder for Burton Real Estate, file it in the general folder behind the "Bu" secondary guide. When we have several more letters to or from Burton Real Estate, we'll set up an individual folder for those records.*

FILING BY SUBJECT

When a subject filing system is used, you index records according to particular subjects—such as marketing, office machines, and public relations. A subject file is used when you request records by their contents more often than by the names of individuals or companies.

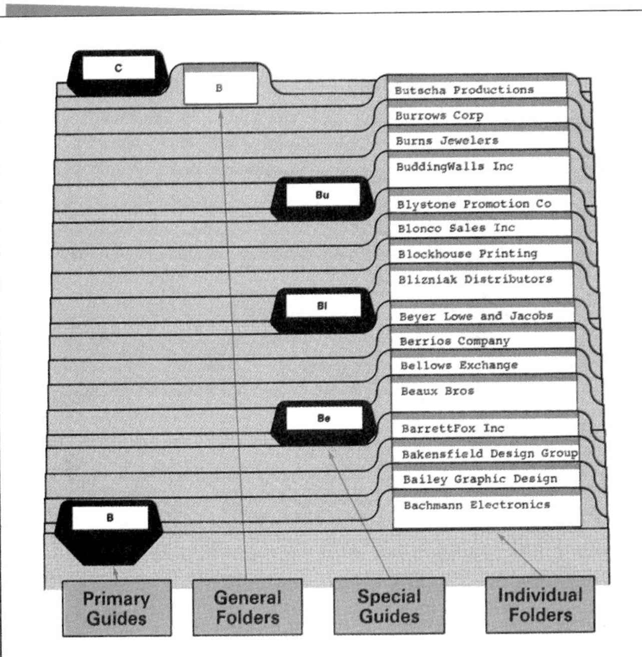

Illustration 10-2:8

Locate the alphabetic primary and special guides in this name file.

Use subject titles as captions for primary guides. In Illustration 10-2:9, you can see that the primary guides are "Advertisers," "Applications," and "Audiovisual Equipment."

You may use special guides to identify subdivisions within the main subjects. In Illustration 10-2:9, the main subject "Audiovisual Equipment" is divided by special guides into subdivisions of "Film" and "Overhead Projectors." You may use names, geographic locations, numbers, or subjects as captions for special guides.

As you can see in Illustration 10-2:9, the label for an individual folder behind a primary guide includes:

- the primary guide caption ("Advertisers," for example)
- the caption for the folder ("Gebhart Glassware," for example)

Ask students the names and positions of the guides and folders shown in this name file.

Have students develop the captions for a subject file you might maintain in the classroom that would be available to both the teachers and students.

Ask students to name the primary guides and the special guides.

Refer students to Illustration 10-2:9. Ask them what information is included on the individual folders behind the primary guides and on those behind the special guides.

Ask students how a real estate agency might maintain files on properties for sale, how such a file might be organized, and why it might be useful.

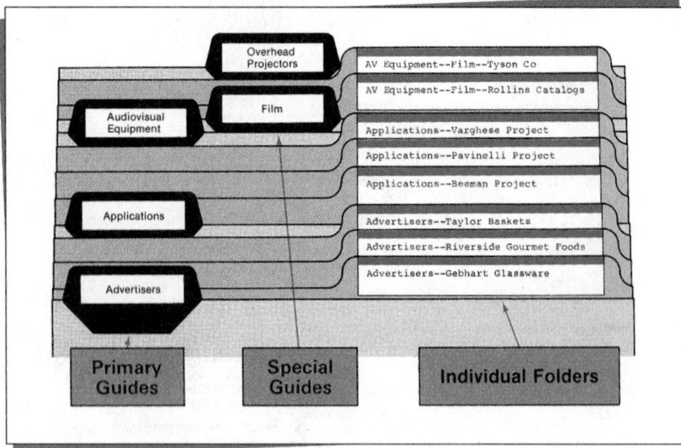

Illustration 10-2:9

In subject files, the special guides identify subdivisions of the main subjects.

The label for an individual folder behind a special guide should include:

- the primary guide caption ("AV Equipment," for example, and note that you may abbreviate "Audiovisual" as "AV")
- the special guide caption ("Film," for example)
- the caption for the folder ("Rollins Catalogs," for example)

FILING BY COMBINATION NAME AND SUBJECT

Many offices do not have enough file space for separate name and subject files. When this is true for your office, you may file name and subject folders together.

FILING BY GEOGRAPHIC LOCATION

When using a geographic file, you index records according to geographic location. You may base a geographic file upon sales territories, states, or cities in a single state.

Typical users of geographic filing are publishing houses, mail-order houses, radio and television advertisers, real estate firms, and organizations dealing with a large number of small businesses scattered over a wide area. The human resources in these small businesses may change frequently. Therefore, the name of each individual owner or manager is often less important for filing purposes than the location of the business. Refer to Illustration 10-2:10 as you read about the components of a geographic filing system.

Guides and Folders. The primary guides in a geographic file are named for the largest geographic divisions below the level of the key units. For example, in Illustration 10-2:10, the primary guides are based on cities. The key unit ("Alabama") appears on a location name guide positioned in the center front of the file. The special guide ("Capitol") is used to **pinpoint** the location of certain individual folders.

pinpoint:
identify precisely

You need a general folder behind each location name guide. In the illustration, the general folder and the location name guide bear the same caption ("Alabama"). When you prepare labels for individual folders, give the geographic location on the first line ("AL Birmingham," for

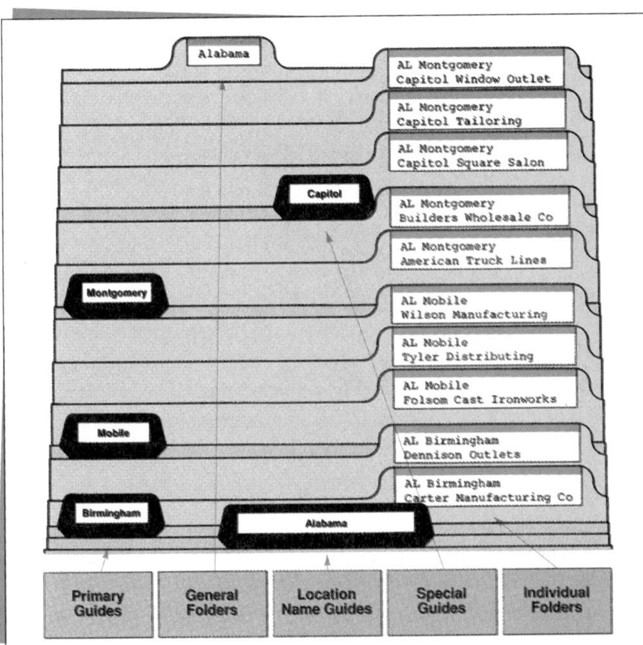

Illustration 10-2:10

In a geographic file, the primary guides identify the largest geographic locations within each key unit.

Ask the students the names and positions of the guides and folders shown in Illustration 10-2:10. Ask them to explain the components of the system.

example). On the second line, indicate the caption for the individual folder ("Carter Manufacturing Co," for example). These complete labels tell you behind which primary and special guide to refile the folder.

Index Card Control File. To retrieve a specific record in a geographic file, you must know the geographic location of each person or business. Since you may not remember all this information, you will find it helpful to keep an *index card control file*. This is usually a file that includes a 3" x 5" card for each individual or business record in the geographic file. The cards containing names and addresses are filed alphabetically. This index control file might be kept on a computer database rather than on index cards.

pertaining: relating

The firm where Carlota works uses a geographic filing system based on states. This morning, her supervisor needed a record **pertaining** *to Wonderland Toy Company. To retrieve the record, Carlota first checked the card index. She learned the toy company was located in Richmond, Virginia. She scanned the drawer labels and opened the drawer labeled "Virginia." She then searched through the primary guides until she came to the city of Richmond. It was then easy to locate the individual folder for Wonderland Toy Company. Carlota's supervisor appreciated her ability to locate the record so quickly.*

Numeric Filing Systems

In a numeric filing system, records are indexed by number. This method of filing is frequently used when records are already arranged in numeric order. For example, insurance companies may arrange their records according to policy number. Utility companies often index customers' accounts by account number. The Internal Revenue Service indexes tax returns by social security number.

Some companies may ask you to index records numerically even though they are not already numbered. For example, you may be asked to assign a number to each name or subject in a file. The caption on the individual folder would then be a number (for example, "3877" for "Global Security Systems" or "8551" for "West Coast Development Project") rather than a name or a subject.

Have students ask a parent, guardian, or family friend how paper records are organized at her or his place of business (alphabetically, numerically, or chronologically). Ask students to volunteer to share findings with the class. This activity will help students gain practical knowledge of paper records systems.

GUIDES

The guide captions in a numeric system are numbers instead of letters or words. Look at the numeric file shown in Illustration 10-2:11. Notice how the numbered special guides highlight divisions within the primary guide category. This helps you retrieve records quickly.

GENERAL FOLDERS

In a numeric system, you do not provide a general folder behind each numeric guide. Instead, you maintain a separate *alphabetic general file*.

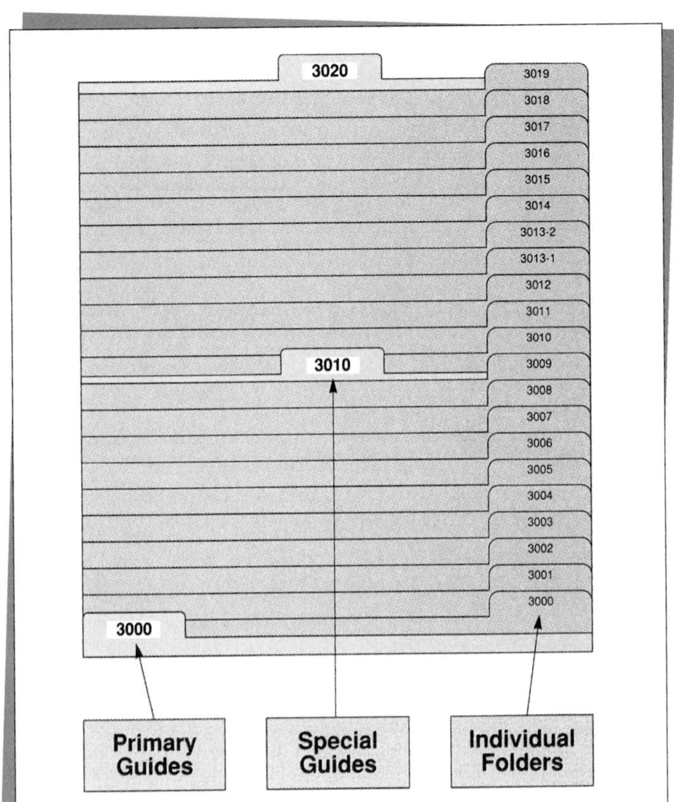

Illustration 10-2:11
Insurance companies often arrange records by policy number using a numeric file.

Ask students what businesses other than insurance companies might use a numeric filing system such as the one shown in Illustration 10-2:11.

Have students list, in alphabetical order, the names of all students in the class. Then, have them list all of the students in the class in order by locker number. (If there are no locker numbers, have students count off down each row and use the number they sound off as their number.)

In a numeric system, you do not provide a general folder behind each numeric guide. Instead, you maintain a separate alphabetic general file.

Records that do not have an individual numeric folder are filed in the general alphabetic file by name or subject. When you collect enough records related to one name or subject, you create an individual numeric folder.

INDIVIDUAL FOLDERS

To set up an individual folder, you first refer to the accession book. An accession book is a record that lists in numeric order the file numbers already assigned and the name or subject related to each number. In Illustration 10-2:12, you can see that the last number, 3877, was assigned to Global Security Systems. The next number you assign will be 3878. By keeping an accession book, you avoid assigning the same number to more than one name or subject. Such a book might be maintained by hand or on a computer database.

Ask students to explain why it is necessary to keep an accession book. Have the students suggest problems that might arise if such a book were not kept or not used every time a file was created?

Illustration 10-2:12

This is a portion of a page from an accession book.

NUMBER	NAME	DATE
3873	Payroll Register	Jan. 1, 19--
3874	Joseph E. Fuline Co.	Jan. 3, 19--
3875	Monthly Production Reports	Jan. 3, 19--
3876	Rogers Collection Agency	Jan. 4, 19--
3877	Global Security Systems	Jan. 10, 19--

INDEX CARD CONTROL FILE

After you have assigned a number to an individual folder, you need to record both the name or subject of the folder contents and the folder number on a 3" x 5" card. Just as you need an alphabetic index with a geographic file, you need one with a numeric file as well. It is extremely difficult to remember the number for each name or subject in the files. When you must retrieve a record, you refer to the index control file to learn the correct file folder number. Illustration 10-2:13 shows how the index corresponds to individual records. This index file might be kept on a computer database rather than on index cards.

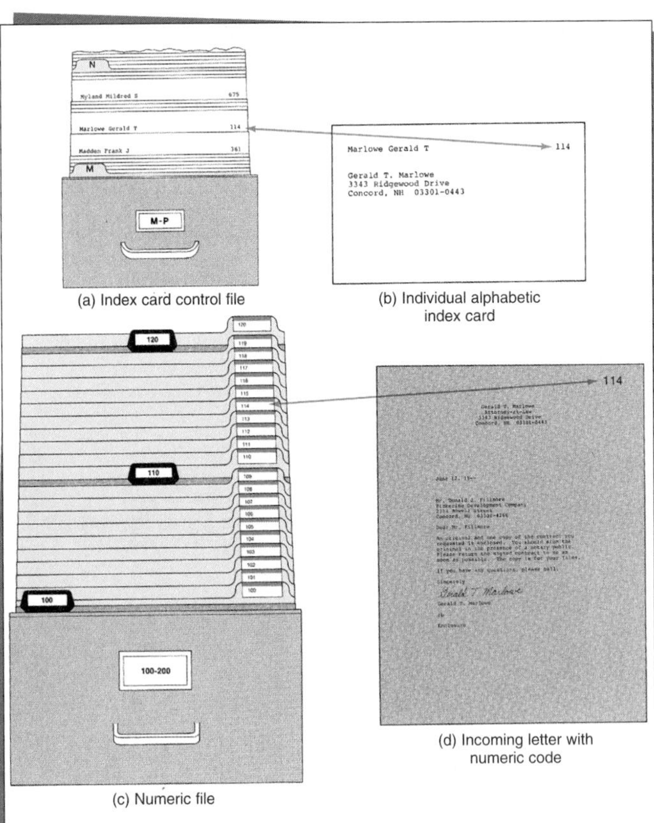

(a) Index card control file

(b) Individual alphabetic index card

(c) Numeric file

(d) Incoming letter with numeric code

Illustration 10-2:13

An alphabetic index must be used in conjunction with a numeric file.

Ask students to identify the alphabetically labeled parts of Illustration 10-2:13. Then have them explain how the system might be streamlined by using an index control file on database rather than as written cards. Ask them the possible drawbacks of using a computer database. (Possible problems include computer failure, cost, and training time.)

You also need to prepare a card for each name or subject in the general alphabetic file. Instead of including a folder number on the card, type the letter "G" as shown in Illustration 10-2:14 on page 490. The G indicates you filed the record in the general alphabetic file instead of in an individual numeric folder.

An advantage to a numeric system is that it helps you keep records confidential. Scanning the numeric captions on folders will not tell a casual observer or an **intruder** much about the contents.

intruder:
unwelcome or uninvited person, burglar

Today is Carlos' first day of work. Mimi Dibbern, Carlos's supervisor, briefed him on the filing system they use: "Carlos, the records in our department are confidential. We use a numeric filing system so that unauthorized people cannot locate specific records easily. To keep these files secure, we have a policy that allows only workers in our department to have access to the index control file and the accession file."

Have students look over Illustration 10-2:14. Ask them which company's records would be found in the general file. Ask how they know this. (The company is Centrex Systems. They should know because of the G that appears in the upper right-hand corner of the card.)

Illustration 10-2:14

Alphabetic index cards show if an individual numeric folder has been assigned.

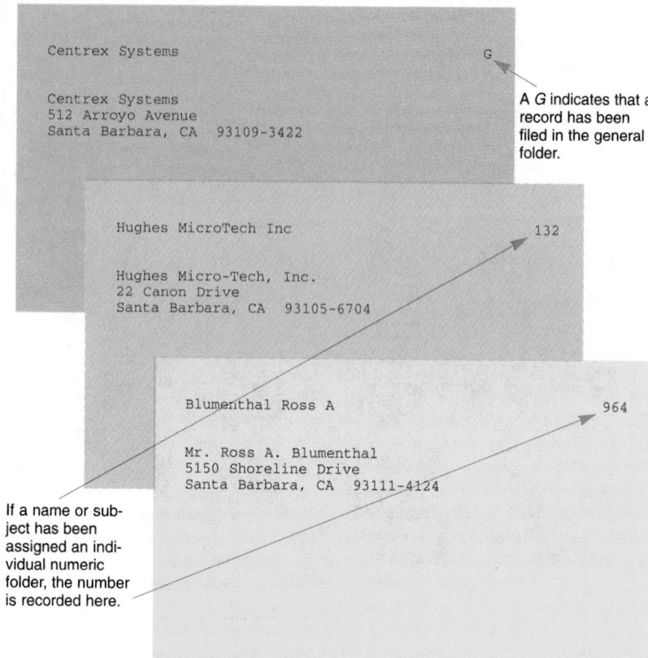

Terminal-Digit and Middle-Digit Filing Systems

Sometimes in a numeric filing system numbers can get quite long. A social security number, for instance, is nine digits. Some insurance policy numbers might be fifteen or more digits. To improve the accuracy of numeric filing systems, terminal-digit or middle-digit numbering methods are often used.

TERMINAL-DIGIT FILING

Terminal-digit filing is a kind of numeric filing in which the last two or three digits of each record number serve as the primary division under which a record is filed. Numbers are assigned consecutively, just as in numeric filing; however, they are read from *right to left* in small groups beginning with the terminal (final) group of numbers.

Record numbers are divided into three groups of two or three digits each. If numbers have too few digits for three equal groups, zeros are added to the *left* of each number. These groups of digits are called primary, secondary, and **tertiary.** The right (terminal) group of digits is primary, the middle group is secondary, and the left group is tertiary. The primary number (right group) is used as the number of the file section, drawer, or shelf. The secondary number (middle group) is used for the guide. The tertiary number (left group) is the folder/record number.

tertiary:
third in level

Just as in regular numeric filing, an index card control file or index control database is used.

MIDDLE-DIGIT FILING

Middle-digit filing is a method of numeric filing in which the middle two or three digits of each record number are used as the primary division under which each record is filed. Numbers are assigned consecutively; however, for filing, numbers are read from *middle to left to right*.

Just as in terminal-digit filing, groups of digits are identified as primary, secondary, or tertiary. In this system, the middle group is primary, the left group is secondary, and the right group is tertiary. Drawer, file, or shelf numbers are from the primary (middle) group. Guide numbers are from the left group. Folder numbers are from the right group. As in other types of numeric filing, an index card control file or index control database is used.

Chronologic Filing Systems

In a chronologic filing system, records are filed according to date. Chronologic files primarily help you keep track of tasks you need to

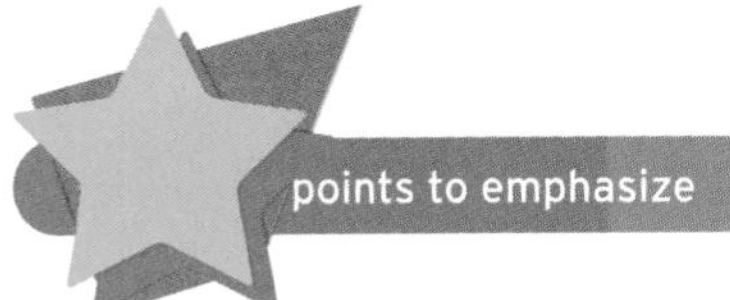

Numbers are assigned consecutively, just as in numeric filing; however, they are read from *right to left* in small groups beginning with the terminal (final) group of numbers.

Numbers are assigned consecutively; however for filing, numbers are read from *middle to left to right.*

complete each day. A desk calendar and a tickler file are two kinds of chronologic files used for this purpose.

You may also use chronologic filing in combination with name, subject, geographic, or numeric systems. In these situations, individual folders are all coded in the normal way of that system. However, records within the individual folder are organized by date, usually with the most recent document placed at the front of the folder.

Reviewing the Topic

1. What are the three components of a filing system?
2. What are two methods of coding a record? Why is coding helpful?
3. Why are guides used in a filing system?
4. Describe an advantage of using color-coded labels.
5. Where should the tabs on primary guides be located? Why?
6. What are four frequently used alphabetic filing systems?
7. Why do you need an index control file in a geographic filing system?
8. What is an accession book or file? Why is it necessary to use an accession book or file?
9. In what direction are the numbers read in a terminal-digit filing system? in a middle-digit filing system?
10. When would you most often use a chronologic file?

THINKING CRITICALLY

For three months you have worked in the office of Davis-Rider, Inc., a company with 12 employees. When you began the job, your supervisor, Mr. Davis, told you that you would be generally in charge of the files as well as having other duties. While everyone has access to the files, he explained that you need to make sure the files are neat and that materials do not stack up.

Although the task seemed simple when Mr. Davis explained it to you, it has become a source of frustration. Some employees remove records and do not return them for several weeks. Other employees open file drawers and place folders on top of the other folders instead of inserting them in their proper places. Needless to say, the files are not being managed well.

Since you are generally in charge of the files, you are being held accountable for the situation.

topic 10-2 review

Paper Records Systems

493

Paper Records Systems

What you are to do:

Remembering that you are a relatively new employee, how would you handle this problem? Prepare a written description of the steps you would take.

REINFORCING ENGLISH SKILLS

Using *it's* and *its* incorrectly are common writing mistakes. *It's* is a contraction of *it* and *is* or *has*. *Its* is a possessive pronoun. To help you know which term to use, ask yourself: "Could I substitute the words 'it is' or 'it has' in the sentence and have it make sense?" If you can, use *it's*; if not, use *its*.

What you are to do:

Rewrite the following eight sentences, inserting either *it's* or *its*, whichever is appropriate.

1. You need to put the folder back in ____ place.
2. ____ time to remove the inactive files from active storage.
3. He replied, " ___ necessary to charge out each record."
4. This folder has lost ____ label.
5. ____ been returned to the files.
6. Please let me know when ____ ready.
7. The company improved ____ image.
8. ____ on the top shelf of the bookcase.

topic 10-2 review

APPLICATION ACTIVITY

ACTIVITY Accession Book

You work for a management consulting firm in Miami, Florida. In order to keep the records confidential, a numeric file system is used. You find that enough records have accumulated in the general files to necessitate creating individual folders for several Miami businesses. You need to complete a card for each business to be placed in the index card control file.

494

What you are to do:

1. In your *Student Activities and Projects* workbook, locate the index cards that show the names and addresses of the new businesses. Consult the accession book shown below to find the file number assigned to each business. Write the file number assigned to each business in the blank on the upper-right corner of the index card.

See Workbook pages 55–57.

2. Arrange the cards alphabetically according to business name in preparation for filing them in the control file. Refer to Reference Section F, Alphabetizing Procedures, for filing rules.

See Workbook pages 228–233.

ACCESSION BOOK — **Page 10**

Number	Name	Date
1009	Rosewood Import Company	12/3/9-
1010	Peninsula Savings & Loan	12/3/9-
1011	Juline's Delivery Service	12/3/9-
1012	Nico's Fine Seafood Restaurant	12/3/9-
1013	Gomez, Jackson, & Associates	12/4/9-
1014	Trade Winds Travel Agency	12/4/9-
1015	Citrus Growers' Association	12/4/9-
1016	Executive Helicopter Service	12/4/9-

495

Chapter Summary

An effective records management system improves office efficiency and customer goodwill. In this chapter, you learned about the equipment, procedures, and supplies used in paper filing systems. As an office worker, you will probably be involved in some aspect of records management. You should be knowledgeable about the following key points:

- A records management system is the manner in which an organization chooses to organize, store, retrieve, remove, and dispose of its records.
- You may be called upon to manage records on various media such as paper, magnetic or optical media, and micrographics.
- The phases of the record life cycle are as follows:

  Phase 1: Collect the records.
  Phase 2: Categorize the records.
  Phase 3: Prepare the records for storage.
  Phase 4: Maintain the records in active storage.
  Phase 5: Reevaluate the records.
  Phase 6: Dispose of the records.

Records can be filed alphabetically by name, by subject, by a combination of name and subject, or by geographic location. Records can also be filed numerically using a consecutive, terminal-digit, middle-digit, or chronologic system.

Each organization will choose a filing system that best suits its individual needs.

KEY CONCEPTS AND TERMS

accession book
archive
coding
Computer Input Microfilm (CIM)
Computer Output Microfilm (COM)
filing
indexing
microforms
microimaging systems
record
records management filing system
retention schedule

chapter 10 summary

Records Management Systems

496

INTEGRATED CHAPTER ACTIVITIES

ACTIVITY 1 **Filing Cards**

You work for Midwestern Mutual Life Insurance Company. Records of policyholders are placed in an alphabetic name file and also in a chronologic file set up according to the dates the policies are accepted. Your supervisor has given you index cards showing the names, addresses, and policy dates for new policyholders (also shown below) whose records must be added to both filing systems.

What you are to do:

1. Locate the index cards for this exercise in your *Student Activities and Projects* workbook. Arrange the cards alphabetically by policyholder name. Prepare a list of card numbers. (Use the numbers shown in the upper-right corner of each card.)
2. Rearrange the cards in chronological order. Prepare a list of card numbers.

See Workbook pages 59–61.

(1) Ms. Jessica P. Cohen
5414 Highland Drive
Denver, CO 80215-5632
Policy: 11/21

(2) Mr. Thomas Parker Hill
253 Gary Court
Stockton, CA 95212-2131
Policy: 1/20

(3) Miss Kathleen A. Young
34 East Mercer Place
Denver, CO 80237-7114
Policy: 1/29

(4) Miss Susan J. Caldwell
8254 Willow Road
Syracuse, NY 13212-2023
Policy: 8/14

(5) Mr. Christopher Thomas Privett
6333 South Hudson Street
Seattle, WA 98108-2184
Policy: 6/12

(6) Ms. Felicia M. Rodriguez
8731 First Avenue
Memphis, TN 38109-8830
Policy: 2/10

(7) Mr. Miles D. Ulberg
3212 West 53rd Street
Little Rock, AR 72209-2433
Policy: 5/18

(8) Mr. Ryan Baker
3600 Linden Avenue
Pittsburgh, PA 15234-2770
Policy: 10/2

(9) Mr. Clayton W. Ingraham
334 Madrid Lane
Santa Fe, NM 87501-3434
Policy: 9/4

(10) Mrs. Jolene C. Ward
122 Oak Street
Rutherford, NJ 07075-8122
Policy: 2/15

497

ACTIVITY 2 Records Management Survey

The president of Brooks Advertising Agency has appointed a committee to determine whether or not to establish a separate records management department. The committee has drafted a survey designed to identify how hard-copy records are currently being managed. The chairperson hands you a draft of the survey instrument and says, "Please prepare this questionnaire in final form. Use your judgment regarding spacing so that the page does not appear so crowded. Lines for answers should be added after each question. Also, make sure the questionnaire fits on one page."

What you are to do:

Prepare a final copy of the survey instrument shown below.

Records Management Survey

1. How many filing cabinets are in your particular department?
   a. How many letter size drawers are used?
   b. How many legal size drawers are used?
2. How are records organized in your department?
   alphabetically? numerically? chronologically?
3. Do you house records in locations other than file cabinets?
   If yes, how do you house them?
4. Do you follow a schedule for removing inactive files and destroying outdated records?
5. Do you use a standardized procedure for charging out records?
   If yes, what procedure do you use? stet
6. What percentage of your records would you classify as:
   vital? important? useful? nonessential?
7. How frequently do you refer to active files?
8. How frequently do you refer to inactive files?
9. What method is most often used to destory records?
10. Who in your department has responsibility for managing the files?
    is responsible

Department Date
Name and title of person completing the survey

chapter 10 summary

498

Blake Williams
Office Manager

Getting Acquainted with the World of Work

Looking to the Future

Dear Mr. Williams

I recently graduated from high school and found a job at a local insurance agency. A good deal of my time on the job is spent filing and retrieving customer records. From my experience, I see that management puts a high priority on maintaining good records. I wonder, therefore, if there would be any future for me in the records management field?

Karla in Portland

Dear Karla

You have made a good observation. Even though you are a new employee, you are able to see the value of the customer records you handle each day. Records management is a vital part of every company, not just the insurance agency for which you work. If a business is to operate efficiently, up-to-date records must be available when needed.

I heartily recommend that you pursue your interest in the records management field. The practical experience you are getting on the job today will provide a firm foundation upon which to build a career in this rapidly growing field.

There are several professional organizations for records management personnel that you might wish to contact for additional information. One organization is the Association of Records Managers and Administrators (ARMA). Another is the Institute of Certified Records Managers (ICRM). The ICRM administers a professional exam. If you pass the exam and meet the qualifications, you earn the title of Certified Records Manager.

Approximately 90 percent of all office workers perform some records management tasks. So, whether or not you plan to pursue a records management career, your interest in maintaining good records and your desire to learn more about the field of records management will be a definite aid to you on this job or any job you hold in the future. Best wishes.

Blake Williams

Office Manager

499

While teaching this chapter, you will want to introduce students to real-world records management systems. To achieve this goal, you may want to take students to local companies that have effective records management systems to see how workers use and manage files in a business environment.

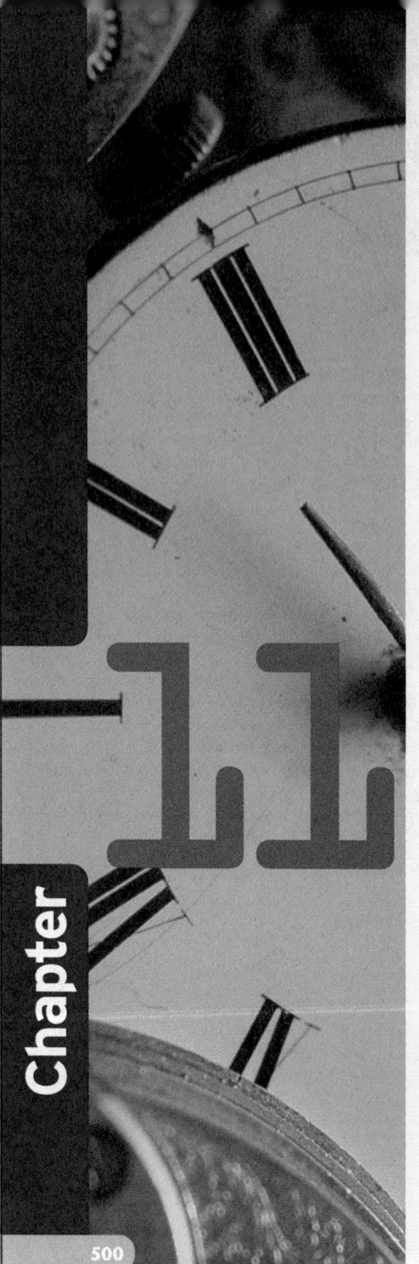

Managing Records

Office records are stored on a variety of media. These storage media have different storage requirements. For example, magnetic media must be protected from other magnetic sources that could erase or change the stored information. Equipment and supplies specially designed to protect magnetic media should be used. Special storage equipment and supplies also are available for micrographic files as well as for paper records. All records that relate to a particular topic, regardless of the storage media used, are often stored together. For example, a floppy disk containing a project proposal and the paper correspondence relating to the project are placed in a folder together.

This chapter describes the principles, procedures, equipment, supplies, and technology available to help you manage various forms of records efficiently. The second topic of the chapter describes reprographics and its use in the modern office. The third topic is devoted to the expanding field of managing magnetic and microimaging media.

Topic 11-1

Managing Paper Records

When you have completed your study of this topic, you will be able to:

- **explain how to prepare records for filing**
- **apply efficient filing procedures**
- **describe the use of requisition cards, out guides, and out folders in charge-out procedures**
- **describe how inactive files are transferred and stored**
- **describe storage plans for vital records protection**

Wherever you work—whether in a small advertising agency or in a large manufacturing company—you probably will store some records on paper. Even in offices where magnetic media and micrographics are used extensively, there often is a need for certain paper (hard-copy) records.

> *Kerry works for O'Roark & Sullivan, a law firm of four attorneys. She keeps form documents, such as leases and wills, on her computer hard drive and backed up on floppy disks. But for a legal transaction to be valid, the document must be signed. These signed paper documents are stored so that the signatures can be kept on file.*

Because paper is a major medium for storing records, it is important that you understand how to maintain paper files. Once you have a clear understanding of the principles and procedures for managing

points to emphasize

Paper is a major medium for storing records. Even in offices where magnetic media and micrographics are used extensively, paper records are still used for much information and are necessary in many instances.

To involve students in actively managing records, you may want to have them complete a filing practice set as a supplement to this text because is offers such extensive instruction in records management. Such a practice set could be assigned as a one-day-a-week in-class group project or a grading-period-long outside project that you offer help with on certain days.

these files, you can easily adapt this knowledge to maintaining records stored on other media.

In this topic, you will learn about preparing individual records for storage. You will study methods for locating and removing individual records as well as entire folders. You also will become acquainted with the equipment used to store paper records.

Preparing Records for Storage

Before filing a record for the first time, you need to prepare it properly for storage. By doing so, you speed up the filing process and insure that the record is filed correctly. Follow these five steps to prepare paper records for storage:

1. Collect the records.
2. Inspect the records.
3. Index/code the records.
4. Cross-reference the records.
5. Sort the records.

Illustration 11-1:1

Office workers must be familiar with the procedures for managing paper files.

COLLECT RECORDS

Throughout the workday, you will **accumulate** records that need to be filed. Instead of preparing and filing each record as you are finished with it, collect the records in a **designated** place such as a tray labeled *TO BE FILED*. Then at scheduled times, such as after lunch or at the end of the day, you can prepare a batch of records for storage at one time. You will not need to index, code, or cross-reference records that have been filed before. But, you will still need to inspect and sort them before they can be refiled.

accumulate: gather, collect

designated: set apart for a specific purpose

Ask students why it is not a wise practice to prepare and file each record as you are finished with it. Answers may include the understanding that tasks grouped together are faster in the long run than when done separately, since the tools needed are gotten out once rather than many times.

INSPECT RECORDS

After you collect a batch of records to prepare for storage, you next need to inspect each record by following these procedures:

- When you are preparing a record for the first time, look for a release mark, an official authorization to file a record. The initials of someone authorized to release the record, written in the upper left-hand corner of the record, often serve as the release mark.
- Remove all paper clips or rubber bands from the records.
- Staple all related materials together.
- Repair any torn records with **transparent** tape.
- Attach small records to a full sheet of paper so that they will not be lost or crumpled in the file. Alternatively, you may copy the small record onto a full page—unless the original must be kept.

transparent: see-through

Ask students to read the bulleted items that describe how to inspect records. Then ask them to consider what would happen if these procedures were not followed. Next, ask them to suggest further safeguards that might be added to the list.

INDEX/CODE RECORDS

Indexing a record means deciding how to identify it for filing purposes. The name, subject, geographic location, or number used to identify a record is called the filing segment. You should code the record by the filing segment for two reasons:

- You can quickly tell how to file a record by glancing at it.
- You will file the record the same way each time it must be refiled.

Records may be coded by hand, the **conventional** method, or by bar-coding.

conventional: customary, standard, usual

Illustration 11-1:2

These are the five steps to take when preparing paper records for storage.

STEPS INVOLVED IN PREPARING PAPER RECORDS FOR FILING	
COLLECTING	COLLECTING means gathering records in a designated place such as a tray labeled "TO BE FILED."
INSPECTING	INSPECTING means observing a record to be sure that it has a release mark, paper clips are removed, materials are stapled together, and tears are repaired.
INDEXING/CODING	INDEXING means deciding how to identify a record. CODING means marking on the record how it was indexed.
CROSS-REFERENCING	CROSS-REFERENCING means providing a way to retrieve a record by more than one name or subject.
SORTING	SORTING means arranging all the records in alphabetic, numeric, or chronological order before placing them in files.

Conventional Coding. Some companies prefer that you code records with a blue, nonreproducing pencil. This way, if you must copy the record, the code markings will not copy.

To code a record indexed by subject, geographic location, or number, write the filing segment in the upper-right corner of the record.

Coding a record indexed by individual or company name involves three steps:

1. Identify the filing segment. Underline or circle the name the first time it appears on the record. If the name is not contained in the record, write it in the upper-right corner.
2. Identify the indexing units of a name, which include each word, initial, or abbreviation within a name. For example, there are three indexing units in the name "Grady P. Hill." Use slash marks to divide the filing segment into separate indexing units:

   Grady/P./Hill

3. Number the units in proper indexing order, which is the order in which units are considered when a record is filed alphabetically. For example, individual names are filed alphabetically by last names, not by first names. Therefore, in the case of Grady P. Hill, you would number the indexing units this way:

2 3 1
Grady / P. / Hill

Reference Section F presents standard rules for identifying indexing units and for alphabetizing names. You will use these rules to complete the activities at the end of this topic. Illustration 11-1:3 shows a record properly indexed and coded.

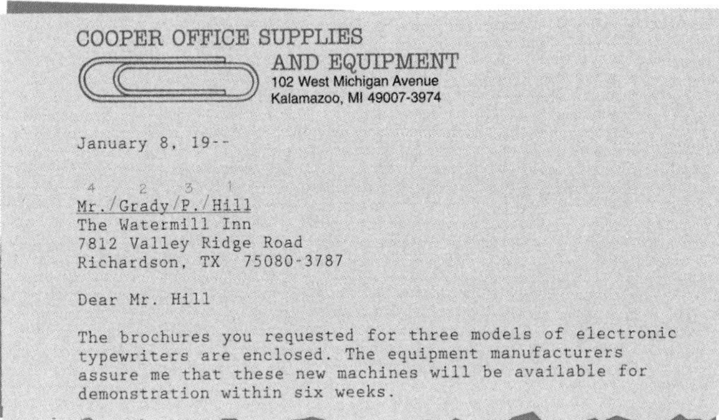
COOPER OFFICE SUPPLIES
AND EQUIPMENT
102 West Michigan Avenue
Kalamazoo, MI 49007-3974

January 8, 19--

4 2 3 1
Mr./Grady/P./Hill
The Watermill Inn
7812 Valley Ridge Road
Richardson, TX 75080-3787

Dear Mr. Hill

The brochures you requested for three models of electronic typewriters are enclosed. The equipment manufacturers assure me that these new machines will be available for demonstration within six weeks.

Illustration 11-1:3
This letter has been indexed and coded for filing.

Bar-Coding. A bar-code is a label, usually self-adhesive, that is preprinted or manually created and attached to an item to identify it electronically. The advantage of preprinted labels is that an office worker will not accidentally assign the same bar-code number to two files. When the bar-coding system is used, card indexes and manual logs—discussed in Chapter 10—are replaced by automated indexing and tracking systems. Bar-codes can be used not only for filing and refiling, but also for tracking files, documents, and correspondence.

In the bar-code system, the code on the record is scanned into the electronic tracking system, much as grocery prices are scanned at the register of a large supermarket. The computer will add the date and

challenge option

You may want to give students copies of a variety of actual business correspondence and ask them to index and code the pieces by subject, geographic location, number, and individual and company name, as applicable. To safeguard the anonymity of the correspondents, opaque important information and make photocopies for students to use.

time the record is filed or retrieved. When an item is refiled, the computer identifies the date and time of the return. A bar-coding system allows less margin for human error, and fewer files are lost.

CROSS-REFERENCE RECORDS

Some records may be requested by more than one name or subject. For example, in Illustration 11-1:4, the record may be indexed by the name of the company sending the letter or by the subject of the letter. In this case, you would first index and code the record by the name or subject of primary importance, which is Boyer Wholesale Groceries (the name of the company sending the letter). Then you would code the name or subject of secondary importance, which is SPRING BONANZA OF VALUES (the subject of the letter). Note that you code the subject by underlining it, numbering the indexing units if appropriate, and placing an X in the margin. The X is a signal that the record is cross-referenced under that particular subject.

Ask students how they can tell that the record in Illustration 11-1:4 has been cross-referenced. (They should identify the *X* in the right margin of the letter.) Next, ask them under what name this letter has been cross-referenced. (They should say, "SPRING BONANZA OF VALUES.") Finally, ask them why that name was chosen. (They should understand that it is the subject of the letter.)

Illustration 11-1:4

This letter has been properly indexed and coded by name and subject.

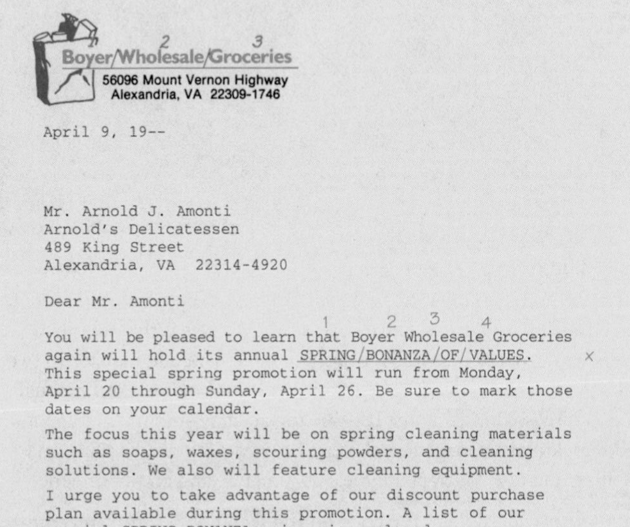

2 3
Boyer/Wholesale/Groceries
56096 Mount Vernon Highway
Alexandria, VA 22309-1746

April 9, 19--

Mr. Arnold J. Amonti
Arnold's Delicatessen
489 King Street
Alexandria, VA 22314-4920

Dear Mr. Amonti

1 2 3 4
You will be pleased to learn that Boyer Wholesale Groceries again will hold its annual SPRING/BONANZA/OF/VALUES. X
This special spring promotion will run from Monday, April 20 through Sunday, April 26. Be sure to mark those dates on your calendar.

The focus this year will be on spring cleaning materials such as soaps, waxes, scouring powders, and cleaning solutions. We also will feature cleaning equipment.

I urge you to take advantage of our discount purchase plan available during this promotion. A list of our special SPRING BONANZA prices is enclosed.

Cross-Reference Sheet. A *cross-reference sheet* includes information about the record and is filed in the cross-referenced folder. The following information is recorded on the cross-reference sheet as shown in Illustration 11-1:5:

a. the name or subject under which the record was cross-referenced

b. the date the record was originated

c. a brief description of the record

d. the location of the record in the files

e. the name of the authorized person who released the record and the date it was released

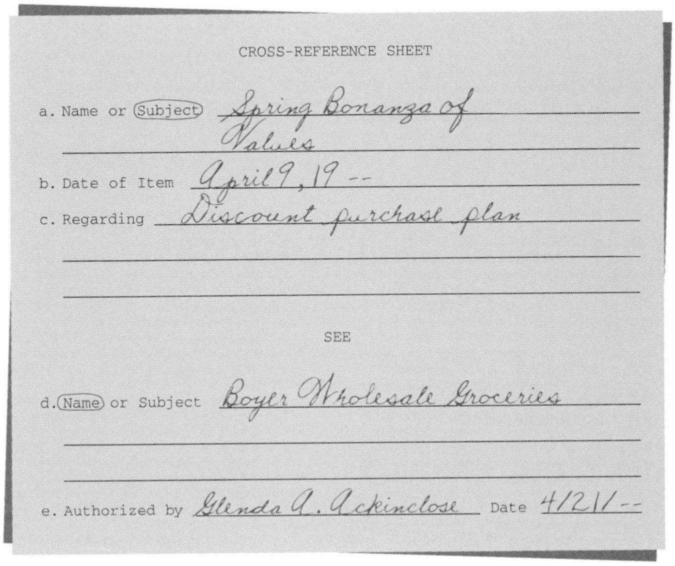

CROSS-REFERENCE SHEET

a. Name or (Subject) Spring Bonanza of Values

b. Date of Item April 9, 19--

c. Regarding Discount purchase plan

SEE

d. (Name) or Subject Boyer Wholesale Groceries

e. Authorized by Glenda A. Ackinclose Date 4/21/--

Illustration 11-1:5

This is a cross-reference sheet for the letter in Illustration 11-1:4.

File the cross-reference sheet in the SPRING BONANZA OF VALUES folder and the record in the BOYER WHOLESALE GROCERIES folder.

Copies of Records. Some companies do not use cross-reference sheets. Instead, they copy the original record and place the copy in the cross-referenced folder. This speeds retrieval since a complete copy of the record is available at each file point, and the process does not often slow filing since it may take the same or less time to make a copy as to complete the cross-reference sheet. If you are instructed to use this method, be sure to code the copy for cross-referencing so you will file it in the proper folder.

Ask students to differentiate between a cross-reference guide and a cross-reference sheet. (They should explain the different uses for the two as well as the differing appearances.)

Cross-Reference Guides. If a permanent cross-reference is desired, you will need to prepare a *cross-reference guide*, a stiff board the same size as a file folder. A typical situation requiring a permanent cross-reference guide might occur when a company with which you do a great deal of business changes its name. You would first label a fresh folder using the new company name and place in it all materials from the old folder. Then you would replace the old folder with a permanent cross-reference guide showing the necessary retrieval information on the tab. The cross-reference guide remains in the file as long as the name or subject is still active.

Illustration 11-1:6

Prepare a permanent cross-reference guide for a company that changes its name.

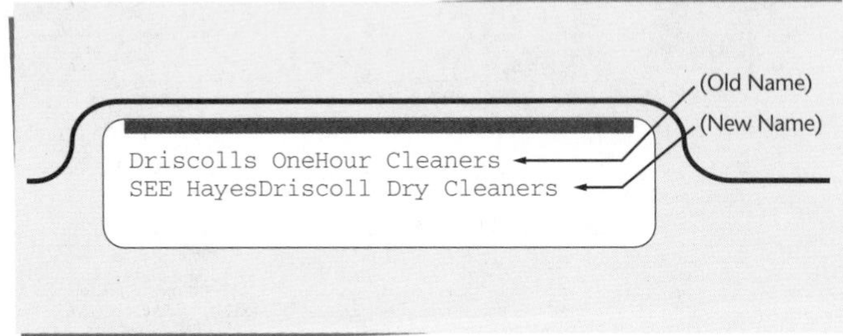

When to Cross-Reference. As a general rule, you should cross-reference a record if doing so will save you time when you need to retrieve the item later. Too much cross-referencing, however, will hinder your ability to retrieve records quickly. An effective records management program will include guidelines to help you know when to cross-reference.

You usually will cross-reference only records filed in name or subject filing systems. Geographic and numeric filing systems have alphabetic card indexes that lead you directly to the item you need.

SORT RECORDS

After you have coded the records and cross-referenced them, if necessary, you are ready to sort them. Sorting is the process of arranging the records alphabetically or numerically before placing them in the folders.

Sorting serves two important purposes. First, it saves you filing time. Since records are in proper sequence, you are able to move quickly from file drawer to file drawer as you place the records in folders. Second, if records are requested before you file them, you can find them quickly.

Charlotte Running-Bear is training Henry Davis, a new office worker. This afternoon they are preparing the records collected that day for storage. They have already indexed, coded, and cross-referenced the records that had never been filed before. Henry thinks they are ready to place the records in the folders. But Charlotte explains they have one more step to complete first.

Charlotte: Henry, we need to sort these records alphabetically before we file them.

Henry: It will take forever to sort this stack of records. Let's just file them in the order they are in, now.

Charlotte: Sorting doesn't take that long. First, we'll rough-sort.

Henry: What does that mean?

Charlotte: It means we'll group all the A records together, all the B records together, and so forth. Then we'll fine-sort. That means we'll place all the A records in alphabetic order, then all the B records, and so on.

(Charlotte and Henry quickly sort the records and begin to file. Their supervisor, Ms. DeRosa, approaches them and asks a question.)

Ms. DeRosa: Charlotte, I placed the Norris letter in the TO BE FILED tray, but I need it again. Have you filed it yet?

Charlotte: No, Ms. DeRosa. We've only filed up to the C's. (Charlotte flips through the records, which are in alphabetic order, and quickly retrieves the Norris letter.)

Charlotte (after Ms. DeRosa leaves): Well Henry, now you see why I believe sorting is worth the time it takes!

To involve students actively in filing, you may want to place a stack of random correspondence (appropriately depersonalized) on a desk in the classroom and have students see how quickly they can accurately sort the correspondence alphabetically, chronologically, or numerically.

Ask students what two purposes sorting serves.

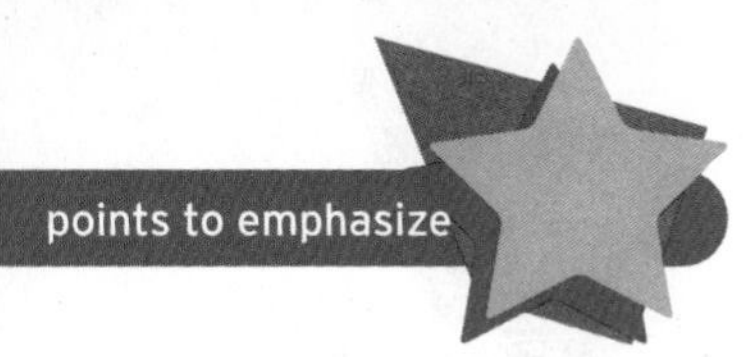

Do not underestimate the importance of filing. You must allocate time each day to file just as you would allocate time to any other office task.

Filing Records

clogged: cluttered, overloaded

You need to set aside time each day to file. This may seem simple to do, but it is not. Many other tasks often seem more important. But if the rest of your work is to go smoothly, the records management system cannot become **clogged** with stacks of unfiled records. If you have followed the five steps for preparing records for storage, you can file the records easily and quickly by following these points:

1. Locate the proper file drawer by reading the drawer labels.
2. Search through the guides in the drawer to locate the desired alphabetic or numeric section.
3. If an individual folder has been prepared for the record, place the record in the folder with the front of the record facing the front of the folder and the top of the record at the left side. You should arrange records in an individual folder according to date, with the most recent in front.
4. If no individual folder is available, file the record in the general folder for that section. You should arrange records in a general folder alphabetically by name or subject. If there are two or more records for the same name or subject, they are arranged according to date with the most recent in front.

USING SPECIAL FOLDERS

Some companies use special folders as well as general and individual folders. A *special folder* is a type of general folder that is used for a variety of purposes. For example, you may remove all the records coded *Smith* from the general folder and place them in a special folder, thus permitting material filed under *Smith* to be found more quickly. You also may prepare special folders to collect miscellaneous information about a particular subject or project, such as *ARMA Convention Travel Plans*. You arrange records alphabetically in a special folder. Within each group of names or subjects, arrange the records by date.

AVOIDING OVERCROWDED FILES

Never allow folders to become overcrowded. Usually, a folder has score lines at the bottom. Creasing the *score lines* widens the folder and increases its capacity. A folder should not contain more than an inch of filed material.

When a folder becomes too full, **subdivide** the records into two or more folders. The labels of each should accurately reflect the contents of the new folders. For example, they could be labeled by date or subject:

subdivide:
separate into smaller parts

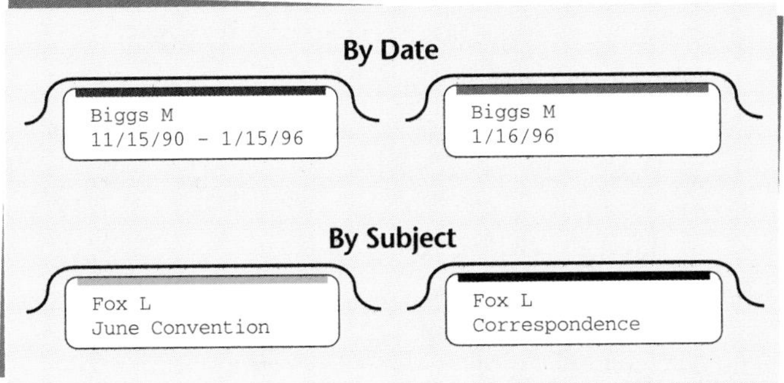

Illustration 11-1:7
Subdivide records by date or subject when folders become full.

Be sure to examine general folders often so that you can prepare individual and special folders when necessary. It is best not to fill a file drawer to capacity. You should have enough room in the drawer to move the folders easily.

Storage Equipment

Since paper is the oldest and most commonly used storage medium, equipment and supplies for filing paper are plentiful. Each business must decide what system works best to fit its particular filing needs. Each office must balance the costs of replacing their current system of filing cabinets against the advantages of using the **optimal** one. The following descriptions will give you a general idea of the equipment that is available to help you maintain paper files and the best uses of each.

optimal:
that which will work best

VERTICAL FILE CABINETS

Vertical file cabinets contain one to five drawers. Of this kind of system, five-drawer cabinets use storage space most economically, providing

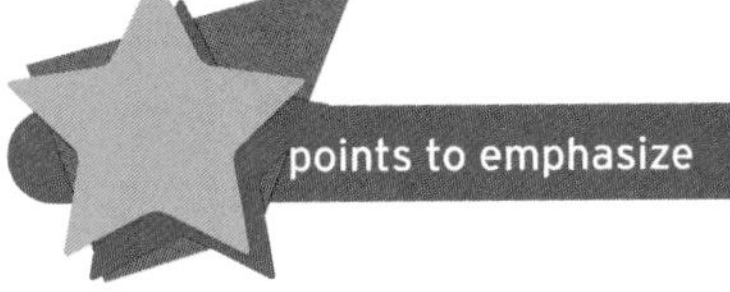

Never accumulate in a folder more than one inch of filed material. An overcrowded folder is unmanageable and should be subdivided into two or more folders.

Ask students to ask family and friends what types of equipment are used to store paper records at their places of employment. You may want to ask students to share their findings with the class—via a written, anonymous poll. (The purpose of the anonymous poll is not to embarrass or offend students who have no friends or family who work in offices.)

the most filing space for the amount of floor space used. Vertical file cabinets must be arranged so there is space in front of each one to allow drawers to be opened fully. Although vertical files are used by many businesses, they have significant disadvantages. These disadvantages include:

- using a great deal of floor space (especially when the drawers are extended)
- making visual access to files difficult
- being unsuitable for use with bar-code labeling or color-coding
- being incompatible with records in media other than paper

LATERAL FILE CABINETS

Lateral file cabinets are also common storage equipment. Fully opened drawers in such a cabinet do not open as far out into the room as do drawers in a vertical file cabinet. Lateral files are manufactured in a variety of drawer heights, widths, and depths to fit different office needs. These cabinets have many of the same drawbacks as traditional vertical file cabinets.

Illustration 11-1:8
Vertical file cabinets are standard equipment in many offices.

Illustration 11-1:9
Lateral file cabinets are available in a variety of sizes to meet specific space needs.

HORIZONTAL (FLAT) FILES

Horizontal files are used in offices that store large-format documents. Such documents include architectural plans, advertising layouts, engineering drawings, and geographic surveys.

Illustration 11-1:10

Horizontal files come in a variety of drawer depths and widths for storing large documents.

STORAGE DRAWERS

Storage drawers are interconnected, stackable file drawers that work like traditional vertical files but may be put together in any **configuration** needed. These drawers come in a variety of heights, widths, and depths. Some storage drawers, often used for temporary storage, are made of cardboard; others are made of metal.

configuration: setup

SHELF FILES

Shelf files store records on open shelves instead of in drawers. They come in a wide variety of configurations: self-contained units, box-on-rails units, high-density mobile-aisle units, and electric elevating units. Records on open shelves are immediately accessible, as you can see from Illustration 11-1:11 on page 514. Since no drawers need to be opened, central file departments often use shelf files to conserve space.

Shelf filing is most appropriate for filing and retrieving entire folders and is ideally suited for numeric filing systems. Since folders on open shelves are readily visible, many companies use color-coded folder labels to improve filing efficiency. Bar-coding may be used with shelf filing systems. Shelf files are generally the most efficient and modern system. The advantages of shelf filing are:

- easy visual and hand access
- maximum use of space

Ask students where in the school each of these types of file storage equipment might be found: vertical file cabinets, lateral file cabinets, horizontal files, shelf files, and drawer files. Then ask what types of records might be stored in each.

- simultaneous availability of files to multiple workers
- compatibility with bar-coding and color-coding systems

Illustration 11-1:11

Open shelf files provide easy access for office workers.

MOBILE FILES

Mobile shelf files have many shelves but only one aisle. The shelves are arranged next to each other on a track. To form the aisle in front of the desired shelf, the shelves are moved along the track manually or electronically. Mobile files take up less floor space than either fixed shelf files or cabinets holding the same number of records.

Illustration 11-1:12

The sections of a mobile file are mounted on rollers and can be moved quickly and quietly.

CARD FILES

Although numerous businesses are moving to computer databases for storing information, paper card files are still used in many offices. Office workers keep card files containing the names, addresses, and telephone numbers of the people with whom they communicate regularly. Such files can be used in many ways, depending on the needs of particular offices.

The devices for housing card files are varied. Cards can be stored vertically in plastic or metal boxes. They can also be stored in vertical file cabinets designed to house cards. When information on cards is referred to often, an open card file is used. In this system, the cards are on special trays or wheels that make it easy to locate specific cards quickly.

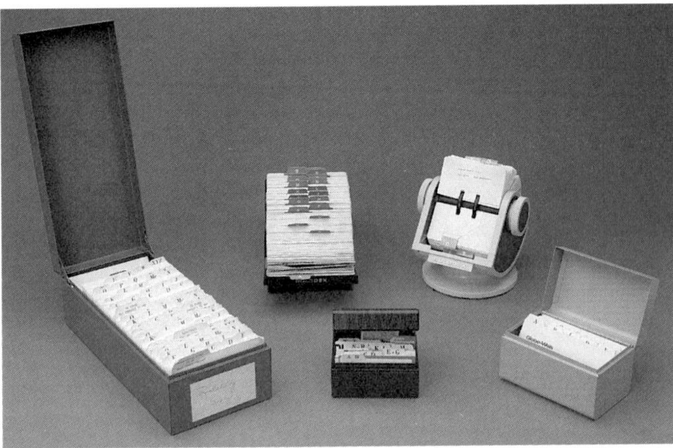

Illustration 11-1:13

A variety of card files are used in many offices.

Ask students what types of records might be best suited to storage in mobile files and what type in card files.

PRINTOUT STORAGE

With the increasing use of computer information processing, more and more computer printouts are generated each day. These printouts vary in size but are often too bulky to store in traditional filing cabinets. Most companies prepare printouts for storage by placing them in binders made of thick cardboard or plastic. The binders have thin, flexible metal posts that fit through the holes on the sides of the printouts. Printouts can be:

- placed on shelves horizontally
- hung on racks or cabinets using binders with special hooks or handles
- filed in a frame that accommodates hanging binders

Some storage units for printouts are mobile so that they can be rolled from one location to another. Most binders are indexed by tabs or labels that attach to the binder. Color-coded binders are frequently used to help you locate specific groupings of printouts.

Illustration 11-1:14

Bulky materials, such as computer printouts, are often stored in binders and hung on racks.

STORAGE BOXES

Storage boxes are fiberboard cartons that are often used to hold files temporarily while moving them. These boxes are also used by some companies for the storage of inactive files. Refer to Illustration 11-1:16 on page 519 to see an example of storage boxes.

Retrieving Records

Once records are in active storage, you may retrieve and refile them many times. An effective records management program includes charge-out procedures that help you keep track of records when workers remove them from the files.

Ask students what problems might arise if a company had no formal procedure for retrieving records and simply allowed any worker to remove records or an entire folder at any time.

REQUISITION CARDS

Many companies that use central files have a staff of trained records management personnel to file and retrieve records. In companies using this arrangement, other office workers do not have direct access to the files. To retrieve records, you must submit a requisition card. A requisition card is a form that has space for all the charge-out information needed, such as:

- a description or file number of the record
- the name and contact information of the person taking the record
- the current date
- the date the record is to be returned

If you work in the central files, you will keep a copy of each requisition card in a tickler file. When a record has not been returned by the expected date, you need to take appropriate follow-up action. This is an important part of an effective records management program. A records manager also may use requisition cards to analyze how often the files are used and which records are most active.

OUT GUIDES

When you remove a record from the files, you must replace it with a record of the charge-out information. This can be accomplished by using an out guide, which is a sheet of thick cardboard that has the word *out* printed on the tab. On some out guides, you write the charge-out information on ruled lines. On other out guides, there is a pocket where you insert the completed requisition card. You usually use out guides when individual records within a folder are removed.

OUT FOLDERS

An out folder is used when an entire folder is removed from the file. When an out folder is used, you may temporarily file additional records in the out folder until the regular folder is returned.

When Lakisha removed the Brandon-Mills folder from the files, she provided the charge-out information on the printed lines of an out folder. Later, when Chin Lu was filing, he placed two letters in the

teaching tips

You may want to obtain from a local office supply store requisition cards, out guides, and out folders so that students can conduct a hands-on examination of the materials they are reading about.

for discussion

Ask students when it is necessary to use an out guide and when it is necessary to use an out folder. (Students should be able to explain that an out guide is used when a *record* is removed and an out folder is used when a *folder* is removed.)

Illustration 11-1:15

A ruled out guide (left) or an out guide with a pocket containing a requisition card (right) may replace a folder that has been retrieved.

OUT

NUMBER, NAME, OR SUBJECT	CHARGE OUT DATE	NAME OF BORROWER	DUE DATE
Forest Park Florist	4/22/--	Ruth Carson	5/1/--
Spanish Village Apartments	5/6/--	Jerry Ahmed	5/14/--

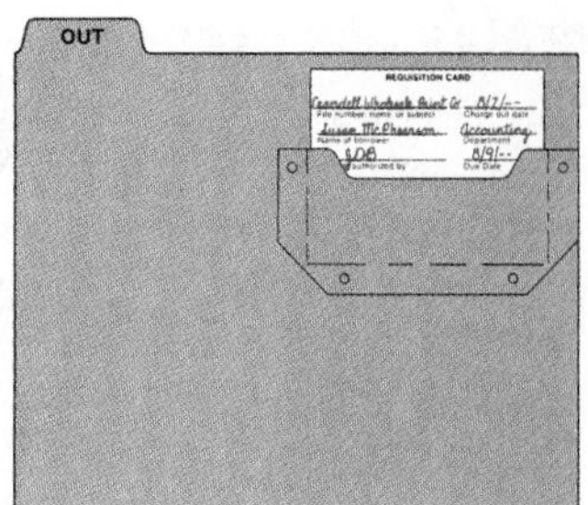

Brandon-Mills out folder. If Lakisha had not provided the out folder, Chin Lu would not have been able to file the two letters. This way, Chin Lu could file the records. Lakisha then would insert those records into the Brandon-Mills folder when she returned it to the files.

Removing Records from Active Storage

An efficient records management system will have a retention schedule that identifies which records should be removed from active storage and on which dates. Whether they are sent out to a storage facility or kept in-house, records that are placed in inactive storage usually are put into cardboard or fiberboard storage files like the ones shown in Illustration 11-1:16 on page 519 rather than in metal cabinets. The boxes are sturdy and provide a place to identify the contents. Some storage boxes can be stacked, saving storage space. Color-coded storage boxes can help you locate inactive records quickly. As discussed in Chapter 10, some companies store inactive records in off-site locations, which range from rented storage space to underground vaults.

Vital Records Protection

Vital records are those of significant importance to maintaining the operations or fulfilling the legal obligations of an organization. There are numerous methods of storage that can be used to protect vital records:

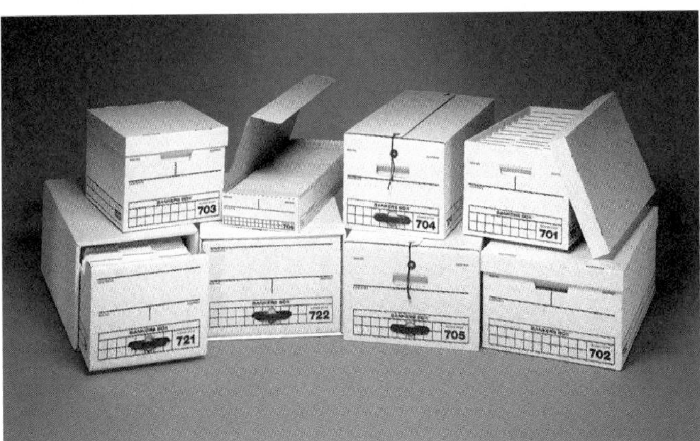

Illustration 11-1:16

Inactive records may be stored in cardboard or fiberboard boxes designed for that purpose.

- Multisite storage. If a company has two or more locations, it may choose to keep duplicates of vital records at each of its locations.
- Planned dispersing. Some companies use a secure vital records storage center and have a plan to disperse records there on a regular basis.
- Duplication. A number of organizations place vital records in micrographic media that is placed in a disaster-proof facility.
- Vaulting. Some businesses have special fire-resistant vaults, safes, or filing cabinets in which they store vital records. Other companies use an off-site facility with such protection.

Any combination of these methods may be used. Since the cost involved in storing vital records can be significant, records should be reviewed regularly. Those that are no longer of use should be removed and destroyed. The subject of vital records and disaster recovery is also discussed in Chapter 10.

Reviewing the Topic

1. List the five steps involved in preparing paper records for storage.
2. What is the purpose of a release mark?
3. How would you code a record indexed by name?
4. Why is it necessary to cross-reference some records?
5. Give two reasons for sorting records before filing them.
6. How should you arrange records in an individual folder?
7. What is a special folder and how might it be used?
8. Why are shelf files the overall optimal filing equipment?
9. Under what circumstances might a requisition card be used?
10. What is the difference between an out guide and an out folder?

MAKING DECISIONS

Professional Support Services, Inc., is a small personnel agency that places workers in both permanent and temporary jobs. The office is staffed by two placement officers and one general office worker, Eileen. The office is a busy place, and Eileen has many responsibilities. She greets the clients who visit each day, answers the telephone, prepares correspondence, handles incoming and outgoing mail, orders office supplies, and files records.

Although Eileen is considered a competent office worker, she sometimes gets behind in her filing. This morning, one of the placement officers says to her, "I can't even see the top of the filing cabinet because it's so cluttered with file folders. Don't you think you should take time to file them?" Eileen thought to herself, "I don't even have time to take a coffee break during the day. When am I going to find time to file all these folders?"

Why do you think Eileen puts filing so low on her priority list of things to do? How might she find time to file and fulfill her other responsibilities as well?

topic 11-1 review

Managing Paper Records

What you are to do:

Prepare a response to the questions raised.

REINFORCING ENGLISH SKILLS

For written communication to be clear to the reader, you must use commas correctly. Test your skill in using commas in these sentences.

What you are to do:

Prepare a copy of the sentences below, inserting commas in the correct positions. Refer to Reference Section B, Punctuation, if necessary.

1. Records can be organized alphabetically numerically and chronologically.
2. You will however be responsible for preparing paper records for storage.
3. As a general rule you should cross-reference a record if doing so will save you time when you need to retrieve it later.
4. Before filing a record for the first time you need to prepare it properly for storage.
5. Records may be coded by hand or bar-coding may be used in the computer-oriented office.

APPLICATION ACTIVITY

ACTIVITY **Alphabetic Filing**

In this activity, you will place the following twenty-five names of individuals and organizations in alphabetic order. Reference Section F, Alphabetizing Procedures, presents the rules you will need to follow. You will need twenty-five 3" × 5" cards or twenty-five pieces of plain paper cut to that size.

What you are to do:

1. Write or key each name at the upper-left corner of the card, placing the units in correct indexing order (see the sample card that follows). Place the number of each name in the upper-right corner of the card.

challenge option

Have students create a memo that Eileen could send to her boss. In it, they should outline (based upon information found in the topic) what steps Eileen plans to take to improve her filing and should request help from the boss in arranging the workload so that the proposed system will work. Answers should be grammatically correct and written in proper memorandum form.

See Reference Section B, Punctuation, on Workbook pages 215–219.

See Reference Section F, Alphabetizing Procedures, on Workbook pages 228–233.

topic 11-1 review

2. Arrange the cards alphabetically. Prepare a list of the card numbers as they are arranged in alphabetic order to submit to your instructor. Save these cards to use with the Integrated Chapter Activity at the end of this chapter.

Edlestone Devorah R Ms 13

(1) Albert P. Sweeney
(2) The Art Center
(3) Nico's Italian Restaurant
(4) Clayton J. Pierce, Jr.
(5) Javier Gomez, M.D.
(6) Mrs. Angela T. Light-Runner
(7) Del Norte Manufacturing
(8) Melissa K. Jackson
(9) Grayson Oil & Gas Company
(10) Jefferson, Riggs, & Associates
(11) Sister Margaret
(12) Papa's Pizzas
(13) Ms. Devorah R. Edlestone
(14) O'Reilley Motors
(15) Albright Aviation
(16) Mrs. Clayton J. Pierce, Sr.
(17) Petite Dress Shop
(18) Mrs. Thomas G. Ramirez
(19) Gerald M. Von Hagen
(20) Allied Builders
(21) Bonnie's Bakery
(22) S&D Marina
(23) Sweeney & Company, Inc.
(24) Wm. S. De Palma
(25) Dependable Pest Control

522

Topic 11-2

Reprographic Systems and Procedures

When you have completed your study of this topic, you will be able to:

- **describe reprographic processes**
- **explain how office copiers are classified**
- **identify copier features and operating procedures**
- **explain how to control copier supplies**
- **prepare materials to be copied**
- **describe phototypesetting/imaging and its uses**

Reprographics is the process of making copies of graphic images, such as hard-copy documents, and also includes other image processing such as scanning images into computer files. Reprographics plays an important role in the records management system. Although technology is bringing changes to records management systems, paper is still the most common medium for storing documents and for sharing information with others. Businesses have different needs for reprographic services, depending upon the size of the organization and the types of documents to be reproduced. Large businesses frequently have a reprographics center. In this setting, you would prepare the original from which the copies are made. You would use special forms to give detailed copying instructions to reprographics personnel. Organizations often have a minimum number of copies that will be made by the reprographics center. Smaller copying jobs are handled

As a part of your presentation on reprographics, you may want to ask a person working in a reprographics center of a company, a copier salesperson, or a company work group member using convenience copiers to speak to your class.

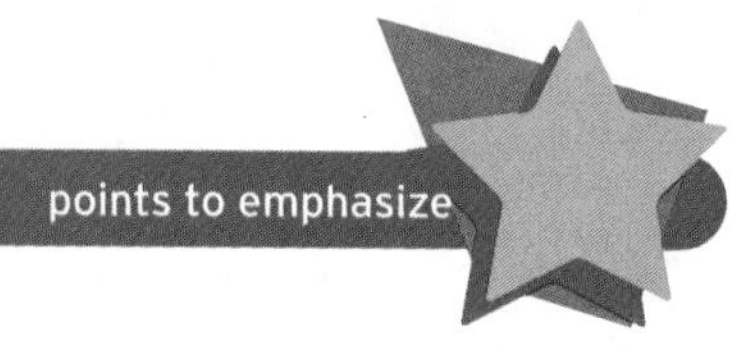

Much of the activity in the business office involves preparing, distributing, and storing copied materials.

by individual employees using convenience copiers located throughout the business.

Small organizations do not usually have a reprographics center. In this setting, you would be responsible for preparing the original and making the copies. Even many larger organizations have done away with their reprographics centers. Instead, copiers are placed throughout the offices.

No matter what size the organization is, you need to know the capabilities of reprographic equipment you are likely to find on the job. You should also be familiar with advances in reprographics technology, including phototypesetting/imaging, multiuse machines, and desktop publishing.

Office Photocopiers

Photocopiers, often simply called copiers, produce copies directly from an original. The original can be handwritten, printed, or drawn. You can produce copies quickly using a photocopier. The quality of the copy is excellent if the machine is in good condition and the original is of high quality.

Photocopiers are found extensively in business offices, and they are used by almost all employees. In fact, much of the activity in the business office centers around preparing, distributing, and storing copied materials. Photocopiers like the one shown in Illustration 11-2:1 are found in many offices because they are convenient and versatile. For example, many models reproduce onto one or both sides of a sheet of paper and can copy onto letterhead paper, mailing labels, bond paper, and colored paper. Some machines copy in color as well.

ELECTROSTATIC COPYING PROCESS

photoconductive: sensitive to light

The most commonly used copying process is the electrostatic one. This method involves copying the image of the original onto paper by means of an electrical charge to a **photoconductive** surface. The electrical charge produces a magnetic field that attracts an ink (toner) to the image of the original.

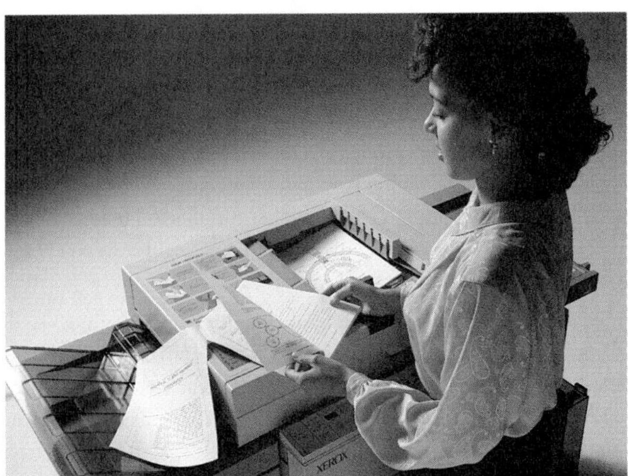

Illustration 11-2:1

Many businesses have convenience copiers located throughout the business for employee use.

REPROGRAPHIC TECHNOLOGY

Advances in technology continue to improve the reprographic process. Advances include optic fibers, laser beams, and microprocessors. Optic fibers are thin glass rods that transmit light. Laser beams are highly focused streams of red light. In both processes, the light is used to transfer the image of an original onto a photosensitive surface and, finally, to paper. Scanners are another part of the technological revolution. These devices allow photographs and text to be scanned into computer files.

Microprocessors select the sequence of operations and proper paper arrangements based on the copier function chosen by the machine operator. Microprocessors also perform **diagnostic** functions such as alerting the machine operator to paper jams and low levels of paper. The latest generation of microprocessor-equipped copiers have routines for detecting common problems written into them. The machine is actually able to tell the repair technician what is wrong with it and will notify the selling dealer of the problem before the operator does so. This advancement goes beyond the usual self-diagnosis discussed later in this topic, which merely indicates via a symbol that a specific problem (such as a paper jam) has occurred.

diagnostic: determining the nature of a problem

Electronic Copiers/Printers

Electronic copier/printers, sometimes called intelligent copiers, can receive, transmit, store, print, and copy data. Microprocessor technology enables these copier/printers to produce copies from sources such as word or data processors, graphic scanners, or even pictures. For example, you may key material at your computer terminal, proofread the copy, and then transmit it electronically to the copier/printer in a reprographics center or at a nearby location, where the copies will be printed.

Electronic copier/printers can easily be commanded to use specific print fonts, justify lines, number pages, or insert graphics within the text material. These machines can merge data from various electronic sources. They can also communicate with other intelligent copier/printers. Electronic copier/printers are available with speeds ranging from 10 to 200 pages a minute. Companies that **generate** reports and forms in large quantities find the electronic copier/printer to be cost effective.

generate: produce

Illustration 11-2:2
Files can be transmitted electronically to an intelligent copier/printer.

Copier Classifications

Copiers can be classified according to their capacity: low, mid, high, and duplicating (see Illustration 11-2:3). Copier capacity is usually determined by two factors: speed (copies produced per minute) and volume (copies produced per month). As an office worker, you should know the capacities of your company's copiers so that you can select the best copier for the task at hand when more than one machine is available to you.

Daisuke is a new employee at Textron, Inc. His supervisor, Lakisha, is explaining the features and capacities of each copier available for Daisuke's use. Lakisha emphasizes that choosing the most appropriate copier for each copying job is an important step. She hands Daisuke two copying jobs. One is a ten-page proposal requiring one photocopy. The other is a 55-page report requiring six photocopies. Lakisha asks Daisuke to choose the copiers that will complete each job most efficiently. Based on what Daisuke has learned about the company's copiers, he knows it is most efficient to copy the ten-page proposal on the low-capacity copier and the 55-page report on the high-capacity copier.

COPIER CAPACITY	SPEED Copies per Minute	VOLUME Copies per Month	COPIER USAGE
Low	up to 20	up to 20,000	Low-capacity copiers are frequently the desktop convenience copiers located close to the employees who use them. A low-capacity copier may be the only copier needed by a small business. A selection of these copiers may be the only copying resources for employees in other companies as well.
Mid	21–60	up to 60,000	The trend in mid-capacity copiers is to allow companies to select those features that meet the needs of the work group. Thus, by using a modular approach, a company can develop a custom-copying system by selecting from a group of available special features.
High	61–125	50,000–100,000	High-capacity copiers typically are found in centralized locations such as reprographic centers. The copiers are floor-console models and generally have a full range of special features as standard components.
Duplicating	over 90	50,000–200,000	Copier/duplicators produce excellent copies and do not require the specialized labor that the more traditional process requires. As with high-capacity models, special features are standard components to reduce labor needs and to increase productivity.
Multiuse	10–200	variable	Low- to mid-capacity copiers can be networked or connected to an individual computer. These copiers are often used in home and personal offices. They are not as suitable as other copiers for networks in office groups.

Illustration 11-2:3

Select the most appropriate copier for the task at hand.

Ask students to get the following information from their parents or acquaintances who work in offices:

1. Do you work for a company with a reprographics center? If so, are there also convenience copiers? If not, was there once a reprographics center?
2. Where are the copiers located?
3. Does any part of your job include copying or requesting copies?

Some multiuse machines function as printers for computers, as copiers, and as fax machines. Some even include telephones with answering capabilities. These devices are most often used in small offices and home offices. Because of the cost of multiuse machines and the difficulties of having a work group's copier function as its printer, these machines are usually not commonly used in work group settings.

Copier Features

Special features designed to meet specific copying needs and to increase the user's productivity are available on many copiers. Most of the copiers you will use will offer several of the following features, which are only a few of those available. The symbols in Illustration 11-2:4 are standard ones used on copiers to represent a specific function or activity.

Illustration 11-2:4

You will quickly learn to interpret these standard copier symbols.

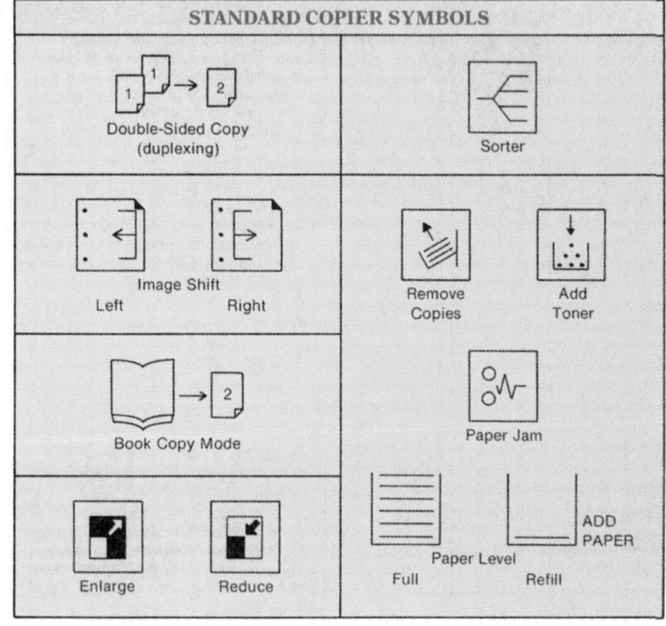

AUTOMATIC DUPLEXING

The duplexing feature allows you to copy on both sides of the paper. This saves materials and lessens the weight and, therefore, postage costs of mailings.

AUTOMATIC IMAGE SHIFT

This feature creates a margin on one or both sides of the copy paper to allow space for three-hole punching or for binding the copies (both single-sided and duplexed copies). For example, if you have a letter that needs to be copied and included in a bound report, the automatic image shift feature will provide the space for the extra left margin without losing any portion of the letter. This is, of course, provided the lines of text are not too wide themselves. Many quality document processing programs allow you to print with a gutter margin; this makes image shifting unnecessary because the original has already been created with the necessary margins.

BOOK COPY MODE

The book copy mode allows you to copy both pages of an open book or magazine onto the front and back of a single sheet of copy paper. This feature allows rapid copying of bound material and saves paper.

IMAGE ENLARGEMENT AND REDUCTION

Most copiers allow you to make a photocopy larger or smaller than the original document. For example, some copiers are capable of 102 to 140 percent enlargement, which produces a copy 2 to 40 percent larger than the original. A range of 66 to 88 percent reduction produces a copy 12 to 34 percent smaller than the original.

SORTER

The sorter feature enables the copier to automatically collate the copies. Collating is the process of integrating or arranging the copies in order. Copiers with 10-, 15-, or 20-bin sorters are typical. Using a copier with a sorter to collate ten copies of a 50-page report is much more efficient than collating the copies by hand.

Students will understand the various copier features better if they see these demonstrated. You may want to take them to the school library or to an office to see equipment in use. If neither of these is an option, you might try to arrange a demonstration by a copier representative.

AUTOMATIC AND SEMIAUTOMATIC DOCUMENT FEED

On some copiers, you must lift the copier lid, place each original on the glass surface, close the lid, and instruct the copier to make the required number of copies. With automatic document feed, you place the stack of originals in the receiving tray, and the copier automatically feeds the originals into the machine. With semiautomatic document feed, you feed one original at a time through the receiving tray. However, the copier lid can still be lifted for easy copying of books, three-dimensional objects, and oversized originals.

SELF-DIAGNOSIS

Most copiers can self-diagnose common technical problems. When a problem occurs, a symbol or message indicating the nature of the problem is displayed. For example, if copy paper jams as it feeds through the machine, the copier may display a paper jam symbol similar to the one shown in Illustration 11-2:4. If the paper supply drawer is not closed properly, the copier may display a message similar to the one shown in Illustration 11-2:5. With the self-diagnosis feature, the operator knows immediately the cause of a problem and does not waste time **troubleshooting.**

troubleshooting: determining the cause of a problem

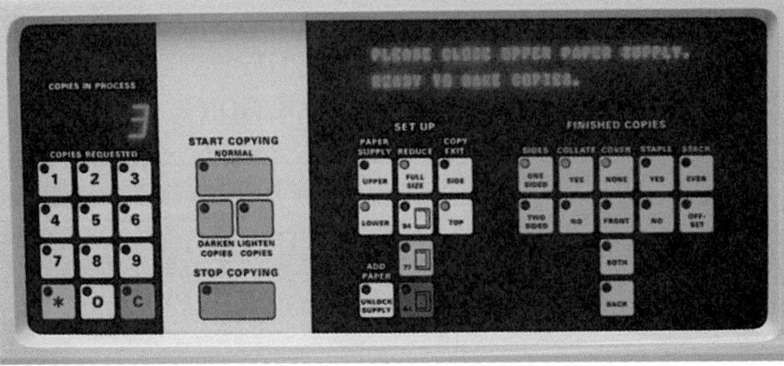

Illustration 11-2:5

Most copiers can self-diagnose common technical problems.

AUTOMATIC EXPOSURE CONTROL

Most copiers allow the user to adjust the darkness or lightness of copies. Many will sense the density of the original and will make the adjustment themselves. This latter feature is called *automatic exposure control*.

COPY COUNTER

A copy counter allows the user of the machine to select how many copies of each original she or he wishes to create.

ROLL FEEDING

Some copiers have a roll of continuous-feed paper fitted to the machine so that copies of varying sizes can be made at one time. The paper is cut by the machine to match the sizes needed. This feature is called roll feeding.

JOB RECOVERY

Job recovery is a device on a copier that allows an interrupted print job to be picked back up at the place where the user left off. Since interruptions in copying occur frequently in the workplace, such a function is very useful. Many times someone has an emergency high-priority job that must take precedence over yours.

COLOR

Some copiers can make color copies using removable toner cartridges of different colors. Color copiers can prepare colorful graphs, charts, brochures, and transparencies. Some advanced color copiers can produce high-quality copies from photographs, slides, film negatives, and transparencies. The latest advance is the longer-lasting laser toner cartridge.

IMAGE EDITING

The image editing feature allows you to change images on a photocopy without permanently changing the original document. You can select a block of text or an illustration and highlight it, add color to it, or delete it. These modifications will appear in the photocopy only; the original will remain the same. Image editing uses digital technology to electronically "cut and paste." Cutting and pasting is the process of manually cutting a block of text with scissors and pasting it with tape or rubber cement to the desired location on the page. A photocopy is then made of the page to get a clean copy.

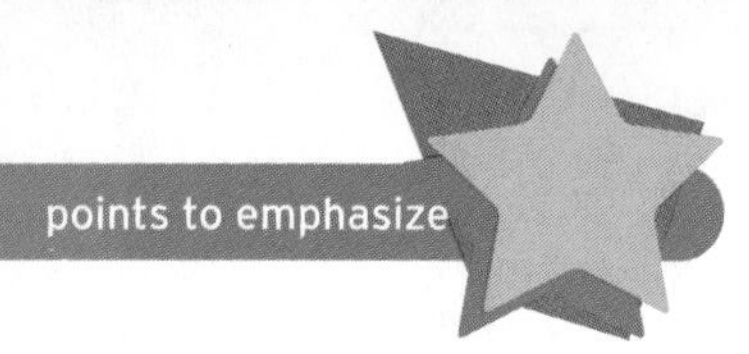

All employees are expected to follow closely the recommendations of the vendor or manufacturer and company guidelines when using copier supplies in order to control costs.

Controlling Copier Supplies

Office employees need to be knowledgeable about the proper use and selection of reprographic supplies. You will find that the selection of paper, toner, and other materials can significantly affect the per-copy price of reproduction. All employees are expected to follow closely the recommendations of the vendor or manufacturer and company guidelines when using copier supplies in order to control costs.

Various kinds of paper can be used in the photocopier. Copier paper typically is purchased by the *ream* (500 sheets of paper). Several reams should be kept on hand. You will need to know the proper paper to use for the copiers you have in your office and for the particular copying job you need to do. Instructions for using special-purpose paper products—such as address labels, reinforced binder paper, and nontear sheets—are provided with the product. Follow these operating instructions for the best results when using any special-purpose copying product.

Most copiers display a message when it is time to replace supplies such as the toner cartridge or developer cartridge. For supplies such as these that are replaced infrequently, a general practice is to keep only one or two of each item on hand. That way, valuable storage space can be used for more frequently used supplies such as various sizes and colors of paper.

Illustration 11-2:6

Use copier supplies that are recommended for your type of copier.

Controlling Operating Procedures

Without adequate controls, copying costs can rise dramatically. If a company has convenience copiers located throughout the building, it is easier for copy misuse to occur. Employees who do not know how to operate the equipment properly may damage the copier or misuse supplies.

> *When Larry found that there was no paper in the copier, he added two reams to the paper bin. Before he had run three copies, the machine was jammed. He was upset and sought help from Robin, a coworker. When Robin checked the paper bin, she said, "You haven't inserted the paper under the guides correctly." Larry responded, "Oh, is there a special way to place the paper in the bin?" Robin then showed Larry how the paper should be placed in the bin so that it will be guided into the copier correctly.*

Management often takes steps to control copying procedures. The steps most often instituted are the use of centralized copying, monitoring devices, a copy log, and individual user guidelines.

CENTRALIZED COPYING

Companies with large reprographic needs have traditionally centralized the equipment to control the number of copies made and to make the best use of the equipment. In today's competitive market, many organizations have chosen to use convenience copiers in work groups as a cost-saving measure. However, some companies still find centralized reprographic centers cost effective. Companies provide guidelines for using centralized reprographic services to assure quality production, proper equipment use, and economy of use. Companies often use a chargeback procedure to **allocate** copying costs to the individual or department requesting the copying.

allocate: assign

MONITORING DEVICES

To gain better control over their copying equipment and to reduce the number of unaccountable copies, management will place monitor devices on their convenience copiers. You cannot operate the copier without the monitoring device. Various types of monitors are available, from simple mechanical counters to electronic recorders.

Illustration 11-2:7

This copy monitor can be accessed by keypad or credit card.

COPY LOG

A common copier control procedure is the copier log book or, more commonly, a computerized log based upon a code or card used by each employee or department. When a copier log book is used, you are expected to record information pertaining to your copy job. This function is done automatically when a code or card is used, as shown in Illustration 11-2:8. To complete the log, you would:

1. Record your name as the person making the copy.
2. Record the name of the person/department for whom the copies are being made.
3. Record the number of originals.
4. Record the number of copies per original.
5. Record the total copies made.
6. Record any special features used.

USER GUIDELINES

Another way to control copying is to establish guidelines for employees who use copiers. As a responsible employee, you should adhere to these general guidelines:

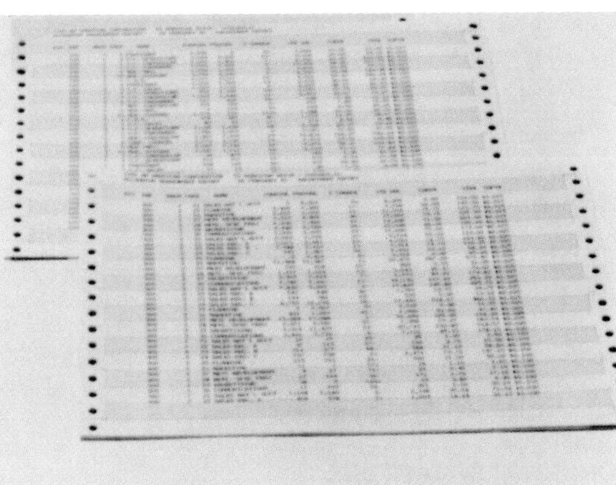

Illustration 11-2:8

A computer-generated copier log can help monitor and control costs.

1. Follow company policy regarding the maximum number of copies to be made at convenience copiers. Large copier needs are best handled through centralized reprographic services, when available.
2. Be cost conscious when planning to use the copier. Use the copier's economy features, such as duplexing, to save file space, postage costs, and work time. Never make more copies than you need.
3. Comply with copyright laws. Copyright laws describe those documents that cannot be legally copied. These documents that should not be copied at their original size and with the intent to represent the original include money, postage stamps, United States securities, birth certificates, passports, draft cards, drivers' licenses, automobile registrations, and certificates of title. Many books and other documents may also be copyrighted and should not be reproduced.
4. Do not use company resources to make copies for personal use.
5. Follow good housekeeping rules. Always clean up the area after you have completed your copying project.
6. Practice common courtesy when using the copier. If you have a long copy job and another worker needs a priority copy, stop at a convenient point and let the other person have access to the

Ask students to respond on paper to the following scenario: You are working for a company that gives you a code for the copier so that a count can be kept for your department's use of the machine. One day, without thinking, you begin to copy and discover that no code is needed to make the machine work. The counter/processor is obviously broken. You have some originals of a charity poster that need to be copied. You were going to stop at a photo shop on the way home. Would you just copy them on the office machine? Why or why not?

Student answers should explore the ethics of the situation. Students should understand that this unauthorized use is a form of stealing.

machine. If you need a few copies and someone else is near the end of a long copying job, wait until the other person is finished to make your copies.

7. Never run the copier with the lid open. The excess light causes caking of toner on the drum, which can eventually ruin this very expensive part.

Copy Preparation Procedures

To obtain quality copies, care must be taken when preparing documents to be reproduced. The following guidelines will help you achieve professional-looking copies.

ORIGINALS/MASTERS

Even the most attractive format can be ruined if you do not give attention to the preparation of the original document. The printer should be checked to see that its cartridge is not in need of replacing and that the paper is properly installed. Use white bond paper and select black as the color for printing. Handle your original carefully. Smudges and smears can show up on the copy. Unless your copier reproduces to the edge of an original, leave at least a one-fourth-inch margin on all sides of your original.

CORRECTION TECHNIQUES

Proofread the original carefully. One mistake on an original from which you make 100 copies magnifies that mistake a hundred times. Check the spelling carefully an any document to be copied. Verify all figures in the document, and check the document format. Use the spell check feature of your software, but do not assume that it will find all errors. A spell checker will not catch the use of an incorrect word. For instance, if you use *from* when you mean *form*, the spell checker will not detect the error since both are correctly spelled words.

EQUIPMENT CHECKS

To achieve excellent copies, you must keep the equipment operating at peak performance. Know your copier and follow the directions for using it. If the copies are too light or too dark, adjust the exposure control. If your copier does not have an automatic feed, position the original carefully so that copies do not appear to be run at an angle. If spots appear on your copies, check the glass surface to see if it is clean. Do not remove paper clips and staples over the machine, because they may fall into a machine opening.

Illustration 11-2:9

An occasional paper jam is easily remedied by an employee knowledgeable about the equipment.

Do your share to keep the copier in excellent condition. If the *add paper* indicator comes on, fill the paper bin properly before leaving the copier. If you use special paper, remove it when you finish the copying job and return the regular paper to the paper tray. If you have a paper jam and are not authorized to remove the paper, get the key operator (person knowledgeable about the equipment). Do not leave the copier in a **down** condition without informing the key operator or your supervisor.

down:
not operating

Imaging

Imaging is a general term that refers to the process of producing or reproducing the image of a page. It is replacing the specific terms *phototypesetting* and *photocompositing*, which constitute one type of imaging process. This new wording is an example of how modern technology creates changes in terminology.

PHOTOTYPESETTING

Phototypesetting is a photographic process used to set text and art into special columns and widths. Businesses use phototypesetting to create items such as newsletters, pamphlets, and advertisements.

A phototypesetter workstation is shown in Illustration 11-2:10. The operator types text and uses command keys and codes to input format instructions and place artwork. This process of arranging text and artwork on the page is called page composition. Today, phototypesetters, also called photocompositors, can complete the page composition process electronically with no need for manual cutting and pasting of text or art.

DESKTOP PUBLISHING

Businesses that have large printing jobs, such as newspaper or magazine publishers, usually have their own photocompositors. Businesses that have occasional typesetting jobs may use commercial services or in-house desktop publishing systems.

Documents can be prepared on microcomputers using one of the many popular desktop publishing software programs available today.

expand the concept

Obtain and bring to class materials created on a photocompositor and on desktop publishing software. Have students compare and contrast the two. Ask which jobs are appropriate for each type of device.

Illustration 11-2:10
Phototypesetting combines text and art to produce items such as pamphlets and advertisements.

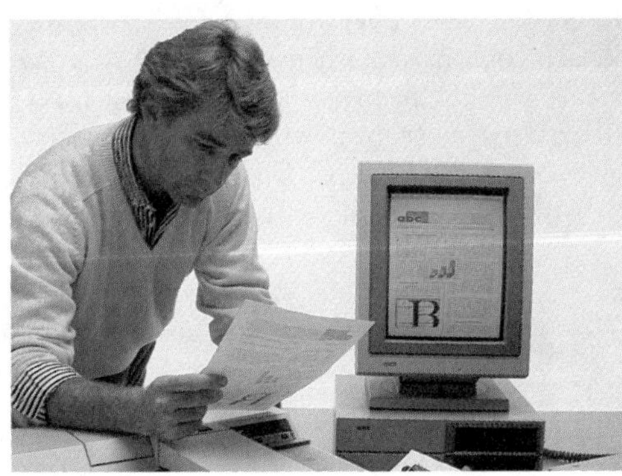

Companies are finding that desktop publishing is an economical way to create a variety of documents, including letterhead, forms, and newsletters. The cost of desktop publishing is low compared to traditional photocompositing, and interest in desktop publishing is increasing rapidly as costs decrease. Also, using desktop publishing to create, arrange, and print documents in-house is much faster than using commercial services.

Illustration 11-2:11

Newsletters are a common desktop publishing application.

Desktop publishing programs allow you to create a page **layout** for text and art. The art may be photographs that are electronically scanned, **clip art,** or original art created using a computer. The document is viewed in WYSIWYG (What-You-See-Is-What-You-Get) format so that you can tell exactly what it will look like when printed. The software provides you with guides, rulers, and design tools to help you create professional-looking results.

layout: placement of text and artwork on a page

clip art: computer files containing drawings or illustrations that can be placed in a document

Desktop publishing cannot produce the super high-quality and high-resolution color photographs offered by print companies with composition machines. However, very fine text and reasonably good graphics make desktop publishing the best option for doing many jobs.

As an office worker, you may have an opportunity to use a photocompositor or desktop publishing software on your computer to prepare documents for your company. When preparing documents such as newsletters or brochures, you can use your creativity as well as your writing and software skills.

If possible, have students create a class newsletter on desktop publishing software.

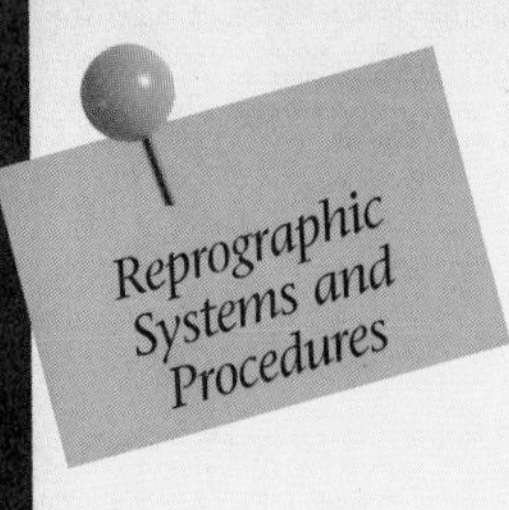

Reviewing the Topic

topic 11-2 review

1. What is reprographics?
2. Explain the electrostatic copying process.
3. Name two technological advances that have improved the reprographic process.
4. Why are convenience copiers more popular than reprographics centers today?
5. List five common features found on office copiers.
6. Would you use a low-, high-, or medium-capacity copier to make ten copies of a 35-page document?
7. Describe two methods of controlling copier operating procedures.
8. Identify and describe two user guidelines you should follow to help control copying operations.
9. Describe the modern photocompositing process.
10. What are advantages of using desktop publishing rather than commercial services or traditional photocompositing?

INTERACTING WITH OTHERS

Marie Little Fox, office manager, is concerned about the large increase in copier expenses in her office. She has asked you to help determine the reasons for the increase.

For several days you have observed the traffic flow to the copier and the types of documents copied. You found that employees made more copies of documents than were needed. They also copied on only one side of the paper when duplexing could have been used. Also, some employees used the more expensive colored paper when white paper would have been sufficient. You further discovered that employees made copies of personal documents.

To overcome these problems, Ms. Little Fox suggested, and the company president agreed, that everyone be given a code for copier use.

topic 11-2 review

Reprographic Systems and Procedures

540

You have been asked to manage the copy log printout, review the data, and present a monthly report on your findings.

From reviewing the log, you see that certain employees have very high numbers of copies logged on their code. What should be considered in determining whether or not these workers are making excessive copies or using company resources inappropriately? Should you evaluate the types of jobs these employees do in considering the number of copies made?

What you are to do:

Prepare a brief response to the questions raised.

REINFORCING MATH SKILLS

You work in the reprographics center of Del Sola Productions. Management is in the process of preparing a budget for the upcoming year. Your task is to provide data regarding the operation of the office copiers. This information will be useful in determining next year's budget for the reprographics center or if it would be more cost efficient to phase out the center in favor of convenience copiers with work group user codes.

Del Sola Productions bought the copiers in the center five years ago. During that time, 763,978 copies were made at an average cost of $.043 per copy plus $.576 per copy for employee overhead.

What you are to do:

Using spreadsheet software, enter or calculate the data described below. Use formulas and functions to make the calculations. Print your results.

Number of Copies

Total Copies in 5 years = 763,978
Average Copies per Year = (Total Copies/5 years)
Average Copies per Month = (Average Copies per Year/12 months)
Average Copies per Day = (Average Copies per Year/365 days)

Cost of Copies

Average Cost per Copy = ($.043 + $.576)
Average Cost per Year = (Average Cost per Copy x Average Copies per Year)
Average Cost per Month = (Average Cost per Copy x Average Copies per Month)
Average Cost per Day = (Average Cost per Copy x Average Copies per Day)

Total 5-Year Cost = (Average Cost per Copy x Total Copies)

541

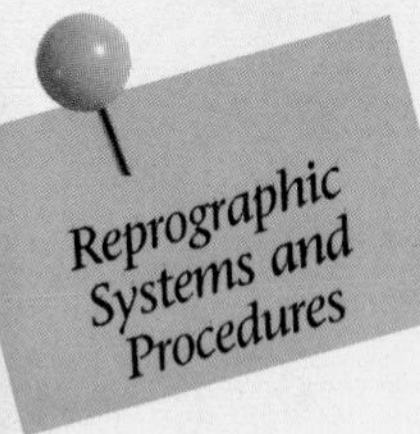

topic 11-2 review

APPLICATION ACTIVITIES

ACTIVITY 1 Reprographic Equipment in Your School

Schools, as well as companies, have reprographic equipment to help employees complete tasks efficiently. For example, your school administration may prepare a packet that explains school regulations, class registration procedures, and school holidays. The packet would be reproduced for each student. A letter announcing an open house at your school may be photocopied and mailed to your home. A schedule listing school activities, such as student council meetings and sporting events, may be photocopied and posted in each classroom. Also, teachers may use reprographic equipment to reproduce student handouts and tests.

What you are to do:

Prepare a one-page report about the reprographic equipment available in your school. For each piece of equipment, include the brand name, location, features, and controls or other procedures used (such as monitoring devices and copy logs).

ACTIVITY 2 Copier Log

In this activity, you will use database software to create a copier log. Fields should include the work group copier code, the number of originals, the number of copies per original, the total copies, and the date.

What you are to do:

1. Create the database as described above. Enter the copy data for two days as shown on the next page.
2. Sort the data first by work group code and then by date.
3. Print a list or report showing the sorted data.

542

Work Group Code	Originals	Copies per Original	Total Copies	Date
4040	2	20	40	3/2
3450	1	50	50	3/2
3450	3	15	45	3/2
2952	7	30	210	3/2
4040	32	5	160	3/2
1029	20	3	60	3/2
1029	45	2	90	3/2
3450	5	5	25	3/3
3450	6	5	30	3/3
3450	8	5	40	3/3
4040	100	5	500	3/3
1029	20	1	20	3/3
2952	32	2	64	3/3

543

Managing Magnetic and Microimaging Media

Topic 11-3

When you have completed your study of this topic, you will be able to:

- **explain how to store individual records on magnetic media**
- **describe supplies used to store and organize magnetic and optical media**
- **explain why databases are useful in businesses**
- **describe two ways to produce microfilm files**
- **explain how computer-assisted retrieval systems are used to speed the record retrieval process**

Advancements in technology affect almost every aspect of office work, including records management. As an office worker, you will need to know how to store and access information recorded on magnetic media such as tapes, floppy disks, hard disks, and on optical discs.

Unlike paper records, records stored on magnetic and optical media are not readable by simply looking at the storage medium. These records must be accessed via a computer. For this reason, it is especially important to properly organize and manage these media with great care. The procedures presented in this topic are used to store and access information recorded on magnetic and optical media.

Organizations that keep many records for an extended period of time frequently use microforms to store records conveniently and safely. Many companies use this medium for active records as well.

Topic 11-3

As an office worker, you should know how micrographic records are created and maintained and how to use computer-assisted retrieval systems.

Stored information is useful only if it can be accessed when needed. A carefully designed and implemented records management system is essential for the efficient operation of an organization.

This topic provides an overview of the technology, procedures, and supplies used to manage magnetic and optical media and micrographic files.

Records Management Software

Records management software is the computer software that allows electronic management and control of records from receipt or creation, through processing, storage and retrieval, to disposal. The advantage of such a system is that it allows all of the records management tasks to be performed with limited personnel. Records management software is an efficient tool that allows companies to become more competitive in the worldwide economy.

When records management software is used with a network of computers, the entire organization has access to inventory, record research, and retrieval. Thus, a reduced number of records management clerks is required. Some software can also perform the library-like function of retrieving records, avoiding the need for human management of requisition cards and records. All records management software performs the following functions:

- tracking of all records from creation/reception to destruction
- tracking stored records, whether on-site or off-site
- creating and maintaining a retention schedule
- archiving and managing record archives
- identifying and managing vital records as part of a disaster recovery program

To familiarize students with magnetic and microimaging media, you may want to invite a product representative to your classroom to demonstrate the media and equipment. Be aware that a store owner may be more willing than a salesperson to give her or his time since the latter may work strictly on commission. If a field trip is possible, it may be preferable to visit a company in your area that uses magnetic and microimaging media.

You may want to obtain various samples of magnetic and microimaging media from manufacturers' representatives to display in the classroom. Samples should include $3^1/_2$" floppy disks, CD-ROMs, tapes, microfilm, microfiche, and aperture cards.

Explain to students the evolution of secondary storage media. You may want to bring in an old $5^1/_4$" floppy disk and explain how this item was replaced with the $3^1/_2$" floppy. Also, show them a CD-ROM and explain its enormous capacity and how it is replacing even the $3^1/_2$" disk as a device for loading software programs because of the capacity. You will want to note that the $3^1/_2$" disk is still the most portable medium for transferring files you create.

Storing Files on Magnetic or Optical Media

Storage media used for information stored outside the internal memory of a computer system is referred to as *auxiliary* or *secondary storage*. Each collection of related information treated as a unit is called a file. Common auxiliary media used for storing files include magnetic tape, magnetic floppy disks, hard disks, and optical media such as CD-ROM. CD-ROM stands for *Compact Disc-Read Only Memory*. Records can be stored on the CD only once, but they can be accessed many times. Since CD-ROMs can hold many more records than a floppy disk or magnetic tape, this medium is a good choice for archiving records or for records that do not need to be updated frequently. At present, drives that store data on CDs are expensive. However, as they become more affordable, their use for storing data will become more common.

Illustration 11-3:1

A variety of secondary media is available for storing files.

CONVERTING TO ELECTRONIC MEDIA

For many large businesses, the need to automate their systems has become very important because the totally paper-based system has become unmanageable. However, decisions beyond which records management software will be used have to be made. What computer system will be used? What will be on individual hard drives or network drives? What will be stored on secondary media and which media will be used?

Illustration 11-3:2
An internal hard disk is the computer's main storage medium.

Converting to electronic media or updating the current electronic records management system involves several stages:

1. Evaluation.
   - Make a careful study of the current system.
   - Determine the number of workers employed to operate it and the equipment used.
   - Evaluate the efficiency of the system.
2. Development.
   - Examine the records management software available.
   - Determine the kinds of computer equipment that may work best and be most cost efficient.
   - Determine the types of storage media best suited to the software, the equipment, and the organization.
   - Determine the number of employees and the training required.
3. Implementation.
   - Install the equipment and software.
   - Train the employees.
   - Institute evaluation procedures.
4. Evaluation.
   - Evaluate the system on an ongoing basis.
   - Alter the system as necessary so that it will continue to meet the organization's needs over time.

THE IMPORTANCE OF SECONDARY STORAGE

back up:
make a copy of

The internal storage medium for most computer systems is a hard disk. The hard disk is used to store programs that run the system and data files as they are being created and processed. While it is possible to store files permanently in internal storage, many companies use secondary storage to **back up** files or for freeing hard disk space of files that are not used regularly.

If an electronic records management system is to be efficient, the files stored on the system should be examined periodically. Inactive files should be saved onto a secondary storage medium and then deleted from the internal memory of the system.

STORING ELECTRONIC FILES

One company stores its mailing list for the city of Austin, Texas, on a floppy disk. This mailing list is stored in a single file, and it must be assigned to a folder or directory and given a name so that it can be identified and accessed when needed. While some operating systems limit the length of a filename to eight characters, other systems allow longer, more descriptive names to be used. Some systems allow you to add a three-character extension (such as "DOC" for document) to further identify your file. Naturally, you will want to assign a name that reflects the type of information stored in the file. For example, the name assigned to the Austin mailing list file could be "AUSTINML.DOC" or "Austin TX Mailing List."

The following guides may be used in storing electronic files:

- Create folders or subdirectories to group related files. When a large number of files accumulates in the folder or directory, reorganize files into two or more new folders or directories.
- Give each file a different name even if it is stored in a different folder or directory than a similar file.
- Use abbreviations that are commonly recognized, for example, "DEPT" for *department*.
- Use as many characters as allowed since more characters make the filename more readable and the file more identifiable.

- Leave out minor words and leave out vowels if your system limits filenames to eight characters plus a three-character extension, for example, "MLNGMN.DPT" for "Mailing to Main Department."
- Use numbers to label versions of a file. For example, your fourth letter to the accounting department might be labeled "ACCT-DPT4.LTR" or "ACCT. DEPT. LETTER 4." Or use numbers to date such a file. For example, the letter to the accounting department might be the one of April 7, and the file might be named "ACTDP407.LTR" or "ACCT. DEPT. LETTER 4/19."
- Use the file extension to identify the type of document. For example, all letters might use the file extension "LTR."

You must understand the system of drives and folders or subdirectories on your computer system or network in order to store and retrieve files efficiently. The filename alone may not be enough information to retrieve the file quickly. You need to know the drive designation and folder or directory name where the file is stored. Illustration 11-3:3 shows a list of files and subdirectories on the C: drive (hard drive) of a

~msstfqf.t	Netcom	Config.bak
Access	Program Files	Config.dos
Aol25	Pwralbm	Config.ins
Aol25a	Qa4	Config.syd
Books94	Ufu	Config
Btw	Vgawin	Config.win
Cie	Windows	File0000.chk
Comitw	Winfax	File0001.chk
Cserve	Winworks	File0002.chk
Dos	Wq40	File0003.chk
Exchange	Autoexec.000	File0004.chk
Inset	Autoexec.bak	File0005.chk
Medvsn	Autoexec	File0006.chk
Moneynet	Autoexec.dos	Netlog
Mouse	Autoexec.ins	Qa
Msmoney	Autoexec.syd	Scandisk.log
Msoffice	Chklist.ms	Wbide
Msworks	Command	
msworks4	Command.dos	
Navimage	Config.000	

Illustration 11-3:3

This directory shows the subdirectories, files, and programs on the C: drive (hard drive) of a computer.

Show students how to differentiate among subdirectories, folders, files, and software. Explain that the little folder icons indicate a subdirectory, some of which are applications software (such as, Microsoft Office). Explain that the icons that look like tiny sheets of paper are files and the ones with borders on top are systems software.

hierarchy:
a ranking by level

computer. Another way to look at the directories and subdirectories on a computer hard drive or secondary media is to examine them in tree form. A tree is a display that shows the **hierarchy** of directories or folders. Illustration 11-3:4 shows part of the tree for the C: drive of a computer. The C: directory is the "root" directory. Other directories or folders "branch" from C.

Illustration 11-3:4

This is a partial tree for the C: drive of a computer.

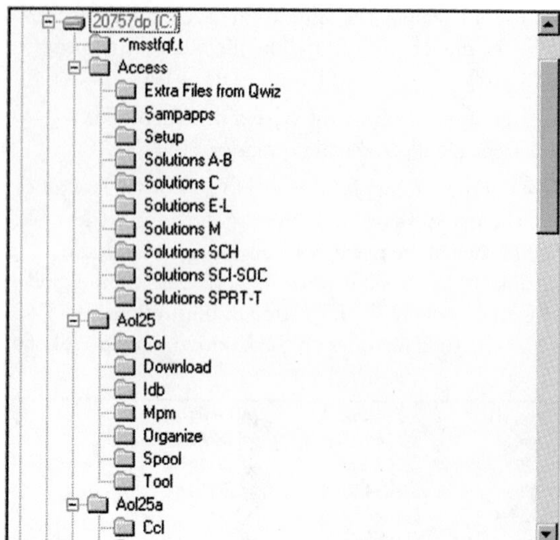

Businesses must develop policies and procedures for storing files on secondary storage media. For example, will all letters be stored in one folder or directory? all mailing lists in another? all business forms in another? Will various files related to one project be stored in the same folder? Will documents be stored in chronological order? by the name of the originator? by the name of the department? The type of records management system a company uses will determine how and where files will be stored.

IDENTIFYING INDIVIDUAL DISKS AND TAPES

Magnetic media can be organized alphabetically or numerically. Label each disk, tape, or CD so that you can locate it quickly. Use captions that are as descriptive as possible, just as a folder label caption is

Draw an upside-down tree on the chalkboard. Be sure to include the root ball, a trunk, branches, and smaller branches off of each branch. Label the root ball "C:". Label each branch as a directory and each smaller branch as a subdirectory—refer to Illustration 11-3:4. Help students understand why this illustrated diagram is called a *tree*.

descriptive of the folder's contents. Often, the labels are color coded to indicate how long the data on the disk or tape should be **retained.**

retained:
kept

The Petro-Davis Company has classified all information placed on its floppy disks as permanent, semipermanent, or temporary in nature. Illustration 11-3:5 further describes these categories. To aid in distinguishing the disks by their retention category, disk labels are color coded. Permanent storage disks are labeled in red, semipermanent in blue, and temporary in green. Look at the disks shown in Illustration 11-3:6. Label A identifies the type of information that will be placed on the disk. Label B tells what operating system (Windows 95 in this case) and computer program were used and the retention category.

Retention Category	**Label A** Information on Disk	**Label B** Operating System Computer Program Retention Category
Permanent	Balance Sheet 12/31/— Income Statement 12/31/—	WIN95 Word 6.1 Permanent
Semipermanent	Expense Forecast 5/8/— Alcorn Proposals 5/10/—	WIN95 Excel 6.1 Semipermanent
Temporary	Correspondence	WIN95 Word 6.1 Temporary

Illustration 11-3:5
It is important to maintain a retention schedule for records stored on magnetic media.

Illustration 11-3:6
These 3 1/2" floppy disks are properly labeled for storage.

Ask students to put themselves into the following scenario:

You are an office worker in a small company. Your supervisor approaches your workstation and says, "Please label this disk for storage. The disk contains correspondence that was keyed using Word 6.1 for Windows 95." Determine the appropriate information to include on LABEL A and LABEL B according to the retention schedule shown in Illustration 11-3:5. Use Illustration 11-3:6 as a guide.

Ask students what information is stored on the disks shown in Illustration 11-3:6. Then ask what applications software was used. Finally, ask them to identify the retention categories of each disk.

MAKING BACKUP COPIES

Data files can be expensive to recreate or replace if they become damaged and are no longer useable. Loss of important data files, such as customer, payroll, and personnel records, can cause serious problems for the organization. Make a backup copy of each file, disk, or tape if the loss of the data would have serious consequences. *Backing up a hard drive, tape, or disk* means making a copy of all the data onto another tape, disk, or CD. *Backing up a file* means making a copy of an individual file onto a different tape, disk, or drive.

Applications software, such as records management, spreadsheet, and word processing programs, can be expensive to replace if damaged. Store the original disks or CDs in a safe location after the programs have been loaded onto the computer. If the programs come preloaded on the computer, original disks may not be included. Make backup copies of the programs for use in restoring the software if the programs on the computer should become damaged.

In many offices there are individual computers for each employee. Often these computers are linked together in a local area network or via a modem to a wide area network of computers. In some cases, files may be backed up automatically or by command to a network location before the user exits the network. In other cases, each employee is responsible for backing up her or his own files. High-capacity external disks, such as ZIP or SyQuest cartridges, are popular choices for backups from individual computers.

Most computer operating systems provide easy-to-follow procedures for making backup copies of tapes and disks. Research and practice the backup or copy commands for your particular system if you are not familiar with them. Backup disks should be labeled in the same manner as their original with the word *backup* added to the label. Backup copies of tapes and disks should be stored in a separate, safe location.

points to emphasize

It is a good practice to make backup copies of hard drive files, disks, and tapes and to store them in a separate, safe location.

CONTROLLING FILE SECURITY

The security of confidential files stored on magnetic media is a concern to you as an office worker. You would not want a competitor to have access to a customer mailing list or a sales report that you keyed. Some companies use security measures such as access logs and passwords, which allow only authorized employees to access certain files. You should, however, take steps to safeguard all files you use. For example, clear a document from the computer screen when you are not working on it, and store disks in a concealed location rather than on the surface of your workstation.

Many companies have a policy manual that outlines the procedures for handling files. In addition to security and backup procedures, such a manual often includes policies regarding:

- **e-mail**
- downloaded files
- internal audits for proper use and storage of files
- retention schedules
- accessing or storing files at home or other offsite locations

e-mail:
electronic mail; letters and other communications sent via telephone modem or hardwired lines from one computer to another

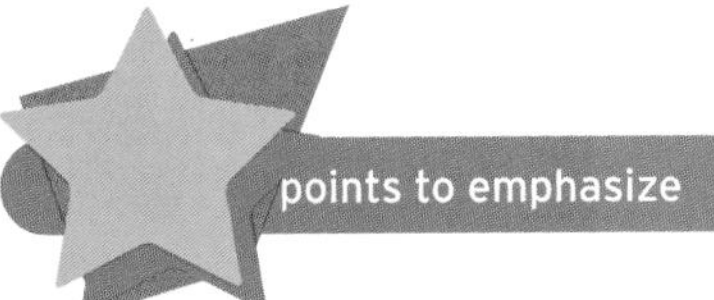

File security is every worker's responsibility.

Storing Magnetic Media

Magnetic and optical media require special care to protect the valuable information they contain. Magnetic media, such as floppy disks, must be protected from extreme heat or cold, moisture, dust, and magnetic fields. Optical media, such as a CD-ROM, should be protected from dust, moisture, and rough surfaces that may scratch the CD. By becoming familiar with the wide variety of equipment and supplies available, you can adequately protect the media that you handle and organize.

You may want to obtain various samples of floppy disk storage devices from manufacturers' representatives. Such samples may include boxes, cases, and trays.

FLOPPY DISK AND CD-ROM STORAGE

Floppy disks and CDs can be organized and stored in a variety of ways. The way selected will depend on the number of items you need to store, the frequency with which you use the disks or CDs, and the storage space available. Many companies color code the labels to **expedite** the storage and retrieval process. The hard protective covers for floppy disks also are available in various colors.

expedite:
speed up

Floppy disks and CD cases are often filed in plastic boxes, cases, or trays designed to protect the disks. Within the cases are guides in which to slide the disks; these guides also make storage and retrieval simpler.

Illustration 11-3:7

Plastic trays with lids are one way to store floppy disks. Notice the handy guides and color coding.

CDs and floppy disks may be stored in plastic pockets designed to fit a ring binder or folder. Each disk is protected by the pocket into which it slides. Some plastic pockets can hold hard copy as well as disks; others are designed to allow disks to be placed in a standard paper file.

Illustration 11-3:8

These disks are stored in plastic sleeves in a 3-ring binder.

Ask students if they have ever seen or used the disk storage devices shown in Illustration 11-3:7, and Illustration 11-3:8. Ask them what other disk storage devices they have seen.

REEL TAPE STORAGE

Reels of tape are stored in round, protective cases. These cases are usually hung for easy access or stored on wire racks. Sometimes the cases have handles or hooks that allow the reels to be attached to frames or cabinets. Other times the cases rest on a backward-slanting shelf. Labels on the protective cases can be color coded for easy reference.

Illustration 11-3:9

Magnetic tapes are stored in protective cases, which can be color coded.

Database Management Systems

A database is any collection of related records. An electronic database is a collection of records accessible by computer. Electronic databases are useful to businesses because thousands of files can be searched in only a few seconds to locate the specific information needed. If you had to go through the same number of files stored on paper, the search would be overwhelming! Electronic databases are often accessible to many employees via a computer network. Accessibility to a central electronic database helps decrease the need to have information filed in several different departments within the organization. Electronic databases can be very flexible and may be designed especially to meet the needs of a particular organization.

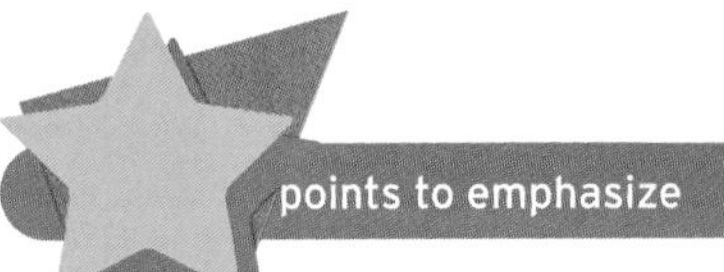

Database software enables you to search through thousands of files in seconds to locate alphabetic, numeric, and alphanumeric data (25521W, for example). Such software allows you to create reports that outline records with matching data as well.

Organizations collect large amounts of data that office workers and managers may want to access in different ways. The strength of a database management system is that it enables the user to select, sort, calculate, and retrieve data according to her or his particular needs. A DBMS also allows the user to organize that data into a meaningful printed report.

You may want to schedule a field visit to a company that utilizes image processing technology. If that is not possible, you may wish to invite a manufacturer's representative or company owner to demonstrate image processing equipment or supplies in your classroom. If neither of these is possible, you will want to have a display of CDs on hand. If students are not familiar with CD drives and the equipment is available, show them how the CD-ROM drive works.

The more efficiently you can retrieve files from a database, the more productive you will be. A database management system (DBMS) organizes and manipulates large numbers of files in a database. A major advantage of a DBMS is that information can be compared and shared among the files in the database. For example, the Internal Revenue Service uses a DBMS to compare information on a person's current income tax return with information on past tax returns.

A DBMS helps you keep database files up to date. If you change information in one file, the system may be designed to update all files affected. Suppose you work in a company that uses a DBMS to manage its personnel and payroll files. If an employee's last name changes, you need only make the change in the personnel record and the system will automatically update the payroll record.

A DBMS eliminates repetition in the database. Because the system can automatically locate information requested, the information needs to be stored only once. Another advantage of a DBMS is file security. Access to parts of the database can be limited to authorized employees who have been issued passwords.

Image Processing Systems

Manufacturers continue to research and develop new products in order to satisfy the ever-changing needs of business and industry. One technological development that has affected records management is image processing. An image processing system uses software and special equipment, including scanners and optical discs (CDs), to store an exact reproduction of a paper document. The images may be very complex and sound files may be used to annotate the images. These systems are like **enormous** electronic filing cabinets linked together that allow the user to quickly access and review the images of original documents. A computer is used to display a document on the screen or to print a hard copy of it.

enormous: extremely large, huge

Optical discs (CDs), which are an important component of image processing systems, offer large storage capacity. A 4¾" optical disc can store about the same number of documents as two file drawers, a 14" disc about the same number as six four-drawer file cabinets.

Illustration 11-3:10

Documents, visual images, and sound files can be stored on optical discs.

For ease of access, discs can be stored in a retrieval system called a *jukebox*. An image processing jukebox contains many optical discs and allows records to be retrieved quickly. Image processing jukeboxes can be linked together electronically, which further increases storage capacity and speed of record retrieval.

An imaging system may use various platforms: an imaging computer system; stand-alone computers, or networked computers. In choosing a system, the organization must consider:

- the organization's imaging needs
- the number of employees that will use the system
- employee training
- cost to implement and maintain the system

A large business with training funds and a significant budget for equipment would likely choose an entire imaging computer system. A small company with limited employees and budget might pick a stand-alone computer. A medium-sized company would likely decide to use networked computers.

Regardless of the system chosen, certain basic components are required—the imaging software, the scanning device, and the reading device. If cost makes buying the scanner impossible, an organization may choose to purchase document scanning services.

Image processing is an effective way to store documents that must be seen in their original form to verify information. For example, American Express™ utilizes image processing to store the individual charge slips received from businesses. Copies of the charge slips are merged with the monthly statements that are mailed to cardholders.

Ask students how the management system at Sharmane's company will help the employees be more productive. Next, ask how the system will improve customer goodwill. Finally, initiate a discussion about other advantages of image processing systems.

Sharmane is a customer service supervisor at a savings and loan company. All questions and comments from customers regarding their mortgage accounts are directed to her. The company stores all its customer accounts on optical discs. Sharmane is describing the features of the image processing system to Dewey, a new employee.

Sharmane: Our new image processing system lets me retrieve documents quickly. When customers call with questions about a mortgage payment, I just key the customer's name at my computer. The system almost instantaneously locates the account and displays it on my screen. I can even get a printout if I want.

Dewey: That's certainly efficient.

Sharmane: Right! Before, it took so long to locate document files that I'd have to tell customers that I'd call them later after I'd pulled the folder.

Creating Microfilm Files

The space required to keep records on micrographics is greatly reduced from the space needed to keep the same number of records on paper. Images on micrographics can be created in two ways:

- Paper records are photographed and developed as images on microfilm.
- A computer is used to convert information stored on magnetic media into images on microfilm. Some microfilm images can also be converted to electrical impulses and stored on magnetic media.

PHOTOGRAPHING RECORDS

A company that chooses microfilm as a storage medium may purchase photographic equipment so that the microfilm can be produced in-house. Some businesses offer microimaging services and will photograph a company's records for a fee. Paper records are photographed and are developed as images on roll microfilm, microfiche, or aperture cards. Reduction ratio is a term used to describe how small the microimage is compared to the original record. For example, if the reduction ratio is 48:1 (also written 48x), the microimage is 48 times smaller than the original record.

COMPUTER OUTPUT MICROFILM (COM)

Microfilm produced by computer is *computer output microfilm,* usually referred to as COM. The most common form of COM is microfiche. By using a COM recorder in **conjunction** with a computer, information stored on magnetic media is converted directly into readable images on roll microfilm or microfiche. Illustration 11-3:11 shows how records on computer-produced magnetic tape are converted into images on microfiche. When a record is needed, it can be retrieved quickly and viewed on a microfilm reader.

conjunction: in combination with, along with

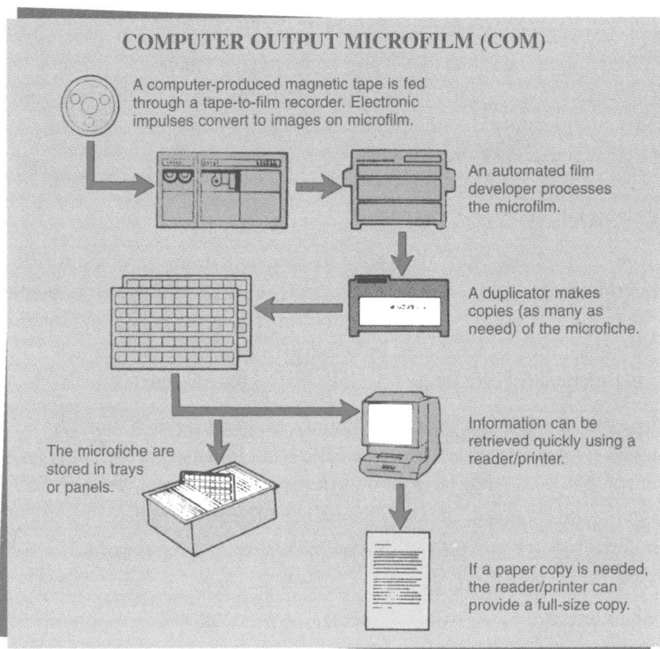
COMPUTER OUTPUT MICROFILM (COM)
A computer-produced magnetic tape is fed through a tape-to-film recorder. Electronic impulses convert to images on microfilm.
An automated film developer processes the microfilm.
A duplicator makes copies (as many as neeed) of the microfiche.
Information can be retrieved quickly using a reader/printer.
The microfiche are stored in trays or panels.
If a paper copy is needed, the reader/printer can provide a full-size copy.

Illustration 11-3:11
Follow the flow of the computer-produced magnetic tape as it is converted into images on microfiche.

for discussion

Ask students to identify the equipment and supplies used in the Computer Output Microfilm (COM) process shown in Illustration 11-3:11.

COMPUTER INPUT MICROFILM (CIM)

Microfilm that can be converted to electrical impulses and stored on magnetic media is *computer input microfilm*, usually called CIM. CIM is really taking the process used in COM and reversing it. The greatest use is in updating information from a microform. Images stored on microfilm cannot be updated. CIM allows microfilm to be converted to magnetic media so that changes can be made and new microfilm produced.

Organizing Microforms

In a paper system, you file individual records in folders. You label each folder so that you can identify the contents and file the folder alphabetically, numerically, or chronologically with other folders. A microform is similar to a folder because it contains many records.

Microforms should be labeled and organized alphabetically, numerically, or chronologically so that they can be retrieved easily. How you label and organize the microforms will depend on the particular filing system used in your organization.

You may want to obtain various samples of microform storage devices from manufacturers' representatives. These samples should include trays, rotary stands, cases, and boxes for microfiche, roll microfilm, and aperture cards.

ORGANIZING MICROFICHE

A microfiche is a transparent sheet of film containing several rows of microimages. At the top of each microfiche (or *fiche*) is space to label the contents of that particular microform. The caption on a microfiche is similar to the caption used on a folder in a paper filing system. Microfiche labels are frequently color coded for easy retrieval.

Microfiche is the microform commonly used for active (frequently used) storage. Fiche can be stored efficiently in panels, which are pages of paper or vinyl that have several slots into which you insert the microfiche. The slots are deep enough to protect the fiche, yet shallow enough to allow the caption to be read easily.

Microfiche can also be stored in trays where guides and color-coded labels are used to organize the media.

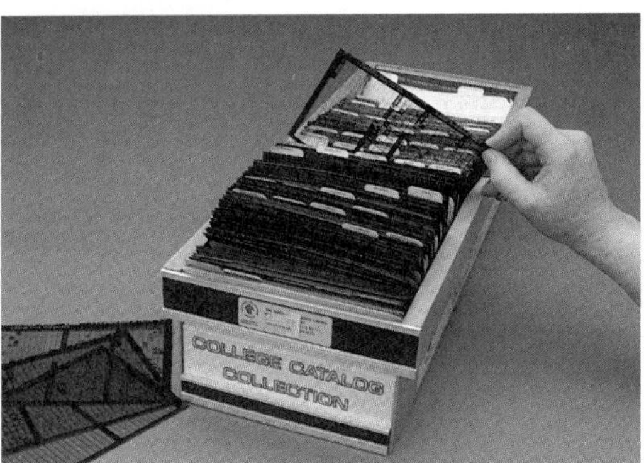

Illustration 11-3:12

Microfiche is easily stored in plastic trays.

ORGANIZING ROLL MICROFILM

Roll microfilm is kept in protective cases or boxes. A label is attached to the case or box to identify that particular roll of microfilm. The roll is filed alphabetically, numerically, or chronologically with other rolls in a drawer or cabinet.

ORGANIZING APERTURE CARDS

The most commonly used aperture card contains only one record or image. Because identifying information can be printed along the top edge of the card, you may file and retrieve aperture cards much as you would file and retrieve paper records. Aperture cards are often housed in trays.

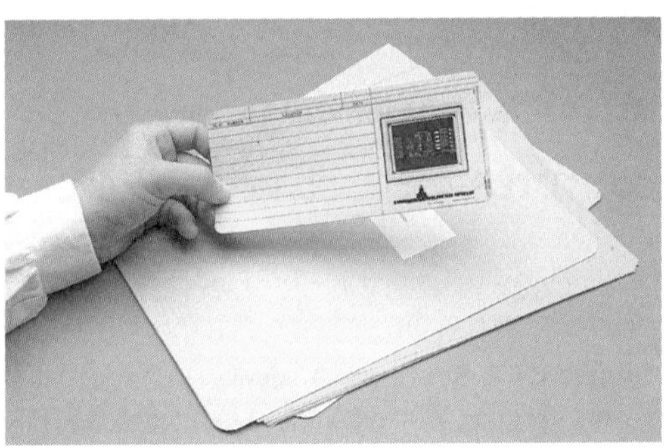

Illustration 11-3:13

Aperture cards can be easily filed and retrieved.

Retrieving Records on Microfilm

When you find it necessary to refer to a record on microfilm, you must know on which roll, fiche, or aperture card the record is stored. If the record is on roll microfilm or microfiche, you also must know the specific location of the record on the film. An index provides you with the information you need by listing an address for each microfilm record. The first step in retrieving a specific record is to consult the index to determine the exact location of that record. Next, a reader is used to view the record. Finally, print a full-sized hard copy of the record if needed.

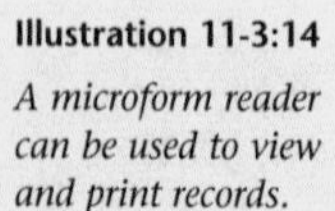

Illustration 11-3:14

A microform reader can be used to view and print records.

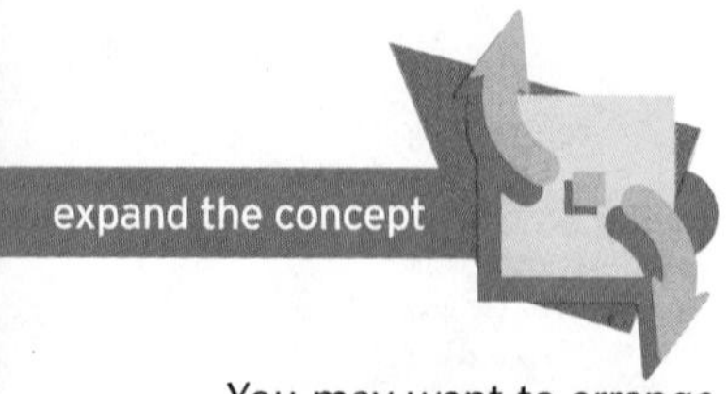

expand the concept

You may want to arrange for students to visit a company or library where they can see how records stored on microfilm are retrieved.

challenge option

You may want to give students experience in retrieving records on microforms by having them retrieve specific articles from back issues of newspapers and magazines on microfilm or microfiche in the library. Students could either write certain information obtained from each article or print a copy of each.

COMPUTER-ASSISTED RETRIEVAL (CAR) SYSTEMS

Computer-assisted retrieval (CAR) is the process of locating records on film by using computer-stored indexes. A CAR system may be very simple or very sophisticated.

Simple CAR Systems. A simple CAR system uses a computer and a reader/printer. When you need to refer to the index, you use the computer to print or display the index. Then you consult the index and manually locate and load the proper microform into the reader.

Advanced CAR Systems. Advanced CAR systems use computer software to maintain an index that is similar to an electronic database. An advantage of a database index is that you can search for a record by name, subject, or date. The address of the needed record will be displayed on the screen. Then you place the microform into the reader/printer and view the record.

Some CAR systems automatically locate the correct image and display it on the reader screen by using a *film autoloader*. A film autoloader is a piece of equipment that not only loads and scans the film but also houses the microfilm rolls until they are needed. These systems allow microform records to be viewed from **remote** locations via a computer network or modem.

remote: distant

While the use of microforms and magnetic/optical media for record storage is growing, most industry experts do not believe that paper will be obsolete any time soon. Paper usage in this country continues to grow at 4 to 5 percent per year.

Reviewing the Topic

topic 11-3 review

1. What is the advantage of records management software?
2. What restrictions are there on naming a computer file?
3. When labeling individual disks or tapes, what descriptive information should appear on the label(s)?
4. Why should you make backup copies of disks and tapes?
5. Why are databases useful to businesses?
6. What is one major advantage of using optical disk (CD) storage?
7. Describe two ways in which images are created on microfilm.
8. What does the reduction ratio 48x tell you about the size of the microimage?
9. What are the components of a simple CAR system?
10. List an advantage of a film autoloader.

INTERACTING WITH OTHERS

You and two of your coworkers, Tom and Paula, are working late one evening. All the other employees have gone for the day. During a brief break, Tom says to you: "I hear the company is about to close some pretty big real estate deals. Since you know the access code for the financial database, let's look and see what's going on." Paula agrees, saying, "Sure! No one else is here. What difference will it make? We won't tell anyone you let us see the information." How would you react in this situation? What would you say to your coworkers?

What you are to do:

Prepare a response to the questions asked.

REINFORCING MATH SKILLS

Your company estimates that it takes you 20 minutes less to file each day using folders with color-coded file labels than using folders without them.

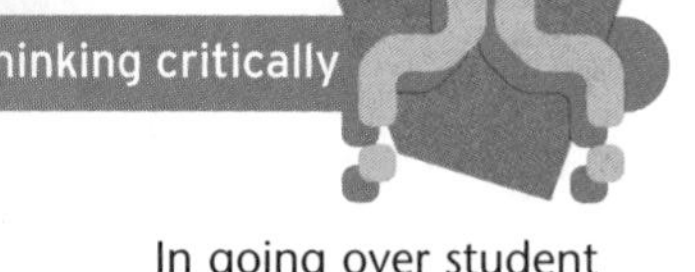

In going over student answers to "Interacting With Others," initiate a discussion about business ethics. Ask student if they believe that Tom and Paula are acting ethically and why or why not.

topic 11-3 review

Managing Magnetic and Microimaging Media

564

What you are to do:

1. Calculate how many hours the use of color-coded file labels saves you each 7-day week, each 4-week month, and each 52-week year. Show your calculations.
2. There are 8 file folders with captions that have "Randolph" as the first indexing unit, 6 with "Reynolds" as the first unit, and 2 with "Rogers" as the first unit. There are 130 folders filed under the letter *R*. Of the total *R* folders, calculate what percentage are "Randolph" folders, what percentage are "Reynolds" folders, and what percentage are "Rogers" folders. Round your answers to the nearest whole percentages. Show your calculations.

APPLICATION ACTIVITY

ACTIVITY **Document Retention**

template activity

Filename: Cookiej

The Cookie Jar, a well-known producer of 34 varieties of cookies, classifies word processing documents as Permanent, Semipermanent, or Temporary for retention purposes. Complete a procedures manual page that contains descriptions and examples of the three categories.

What you are to do:

1. Access the template file *Cookiej.*
2. Add the description for Temporary documents shown below.
3. Complete the table of document examples. For each document shown in the first column, enter the proper Retention Category in the second column.
4. Proofread, correct all errors, and print one copy.

Temporary

Documents that are saved for a very limited period of time (for example, routine correspondence) are stored on floppy disks with green labels bearing the caption TEMPORARY. Each of these documents will be deleted after it has been fully processed and a photocopy has been made.

565

Chapter Summary

In this chapter, you learned about the procedures, equipment, supplies, and technologies available to help you manage records stored on paper, magnetic, optical, and microimaging media, and about reprographics. You should be knowledgeable about the following key points:

- Use these five steps to prepare paper records for storage: collect, inspect, index/code, cross-reference (if necessary), and sort the records.
- Although vertical and lateral file cabinets are still used most frequently in offices to house folders, shelf files are overall the optimal choice. Other equipment includes horizontal (flat) files and mobile files.
- Supplies such as requisition cards, out guides, and out folders are used to manage records efficiently.
- Reprographics is the process of making copies of graphic images such as documents. Photocopiers are found extensively in business offices and are used by almost all employees.
- Advances in technology that continue to improve the reprographic process include the use of optic fibers, laser beams, microprocessors, and scanners.
- Measures used to control copier use include monitoring devices, copy logs, user guidelines, and centralized copying centers.
- Many businesses store records on magnetic disks and tapes. Since you cannot read the information on magnetic media without using a reader, it is necessary to identify individual records appropriately and to organize the media carefully.
- A company that has many records to maintain may use a database. A database management system simplifies and speeds up the retrieval process by organizing and manipulating large numbers of files.

chapter 11 summary

- Image processing systems allow users to quickly access and review images of original documents. The documents are stored on optical disks. Advantages of optical disk storage are high-storage capacity and speedy record retrieval.
- Records may be stored on microfilm. Microimages produced by a computer are referred to as computer output microfilm (COM). Microimages transferred to a computer are referred to as computer input microfilm (CIM).
- Many companies use computers to retrieve microimages. A computer-assisted retrieval (CAR) system can be very simple or very sophisticated.

KEY CONCEPTS AND TERMS

bar code
collating
computer-assisted retrieval (CAR)
database management system (DBMS)
desktop publishing
duplexing
file
filing segment
image processing system
imaging
indexing order
indexing units
LAN
out guide
phototypesetting
records management software
reduction ratio
reengineering
release mark
reprographics
requisition card
scanner
sorting

INTEGRATED CHAPTER ACTIVITY

ACTIVITY Alphabetic Filing

At the end of Topic 11-1, you completed an application activity that involved indexing names of individuals and organizations and placing them in correct alphabetic order. That application activity dealt with Rules 1–7 of Reference Section F. The names presented in this activity relate mainly to Rules 8–14. You will need thirty-five 3" x 5" cards or thirty-five pieces of plain paper cut to that size.

challenge option

You may wish to have students select several words from the "Key Concepts and Terms" list and use them in writing a paper on one of the following topics: "What All Office Workers Should Know About Filing"; "What Equipment Is Best Suited to the Medium-Sized Office"; or "How a Records Management System Can Benefit the Average-Sized Company." Papers should be graded for grammar and syntax as well as for content; proper sentence, paragraph, and report form should be used.

See Workbook pages 228–233.

See Workbook pages 228–233.

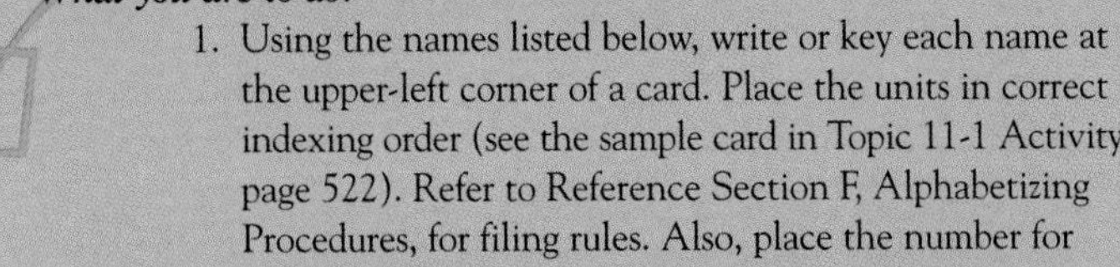

What you are to do:

1. Using the names listed below, write or key each name at the upper-left corner of a card. Place the units in correct indexing order (see the sample card in Topic 11-1 Activity, page 522). Refer to Reference Section F, Alphabetizing Procedures, for filing rules. Also, place the number for each name in the upper-right corner of the card.
2. Arrange the cards alphabetically, combining them with the cards you prepared in Topic 11-1.

(26) North Side Florist Shoppe
(27) McCullum Printing Co., Augusta, Georgia
(28) Collin County Department of Human Services
(29) Lightner & Bagwell, Inc.
(30) 39 and Holding Club
(31) Republic National Bank
(32) Louann D. Grayson
(33) The First Bank of Topeka
(34) Parker-Smith Real Estate
(35) Northside Dry Cleaners
(36) Saint John's Hospital
(37) Omaha Savings and Loan
(38) California Department of Public Safety
(39) Bonny Brite Industries
(40) Carl Michael Collin
(41) Carrollton Department of Engineering and Planning
(42) East Texas State University
(43) North Trails Inn

568

(44) Strickland-Hall Photography

(45) United States Government Department of Labor

(46) X-Cel Interiors

(47) Lou Ann Grayson

(48) Health Science Center

(49) 16th Street Cafe

(50) Anderson Paint Store, Paris, Tennessee

(51) McCullum Printing Co., Atlanta, Georgia

(52) American Institute of Architects

(53) Clarence C. Bonner

(54) 16th and Grand Shoe Repair

(55) City of Richardson Department of Parks & Recreation

(56) E-Z-Rest Motel

(57) 18th Avenue Apartments

(58) McCullum Printing Co., Savannah, Georgia

(59) 39 Palms Hotel

(60) Anderson Paint Store, Paris, Texas

569

Getting Acquainted with the World of Work

Mei-yu Liang
Office Supervisor

Halting Hackers

Dear Ms. Liang

I am a computer operator for a large chemical company that manufactures prescription drugs. My supervisor constantly stresses the need to keep the files confidential. Each week we use a different password to access the files. Only those who are authorized are told the new password.

Recently, on the news I've been hearing about hackers—those who gain access to computer files without permission. What other types of security measures besides passwords are available to keep hackers out?

Ernest in Santa Fe

"***Dear Ernest***

You might be surprised at the variety of security systems that are used. For example, an access control may use fingerprints, voice recognition, or even palm geometry to verify your identity.

One interesting access control is referred to as random personal identification. Stored with the computer are personal history questions about each authorized user. When you try to access files, the computer will randomly choose several personal history questions to ask such as, "Where did you live in 1993?", "What is your mother's maiden name?", or "When did you begin working for the company?" It is very unlikely that someone other than the person seeking access could successfully answer these questions.

Another access control is an error lockout, which means that after a certain number of unsuccessful attempts to gain access, the terminal's power shuts off. A company may also choose a time lock to restrict the use of the computer to regular office hours.

These are only a few of the security control measures available. As technology advances, even more sophisticated methods of security control probably will be invented. But the best security "device" of all is people who recognize and respect the need for companies to maintain confidential files. I'm glad you realize the importance of protecting your company's files!

Mei-yu Liang
Office Supervisor"

570

Simulation
Part 4
At Work at *Maple Valley Chamber of Commerce:*

The Maple Valley Chamber of Commerce offers various services and sponsors special events to promote local businesses in the Geneva, Illinois, area. The Business Expo, held annually at the Maple Valley Convention Center, was attended by more than 5,000 people over a two-day period last year.

As a part-time administrative assistant at the Chamber, you will complete many office tasks to help it operate effectively and meet the needs of its members and the local community.

Patti Petruci, the assistant director, will provide direction for your projects. Your knowledge of integrated software will be invaluable as you work with word processing documents, spreadsheets, and databases in completing your assignments. Prioritizing tasks and managing your time well will be essential in meeting deadlines.

Refer to your *Student Activities and Projects* workbook to learn more about your work at Maple Valley Chamber of Commerce.

See Workbook pages 149–169.

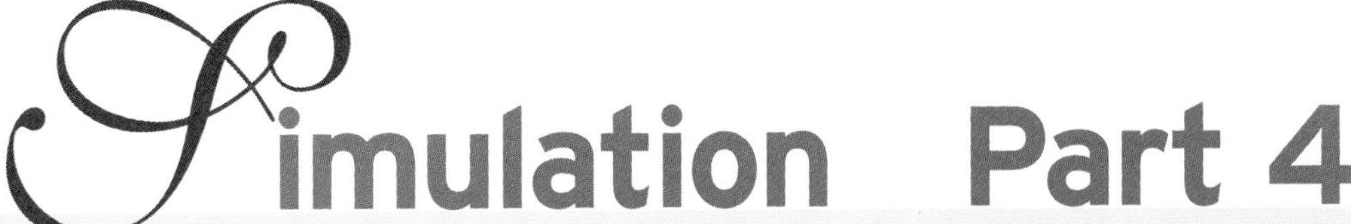

Mail & Telecommunication Systems

RECALL

part 5

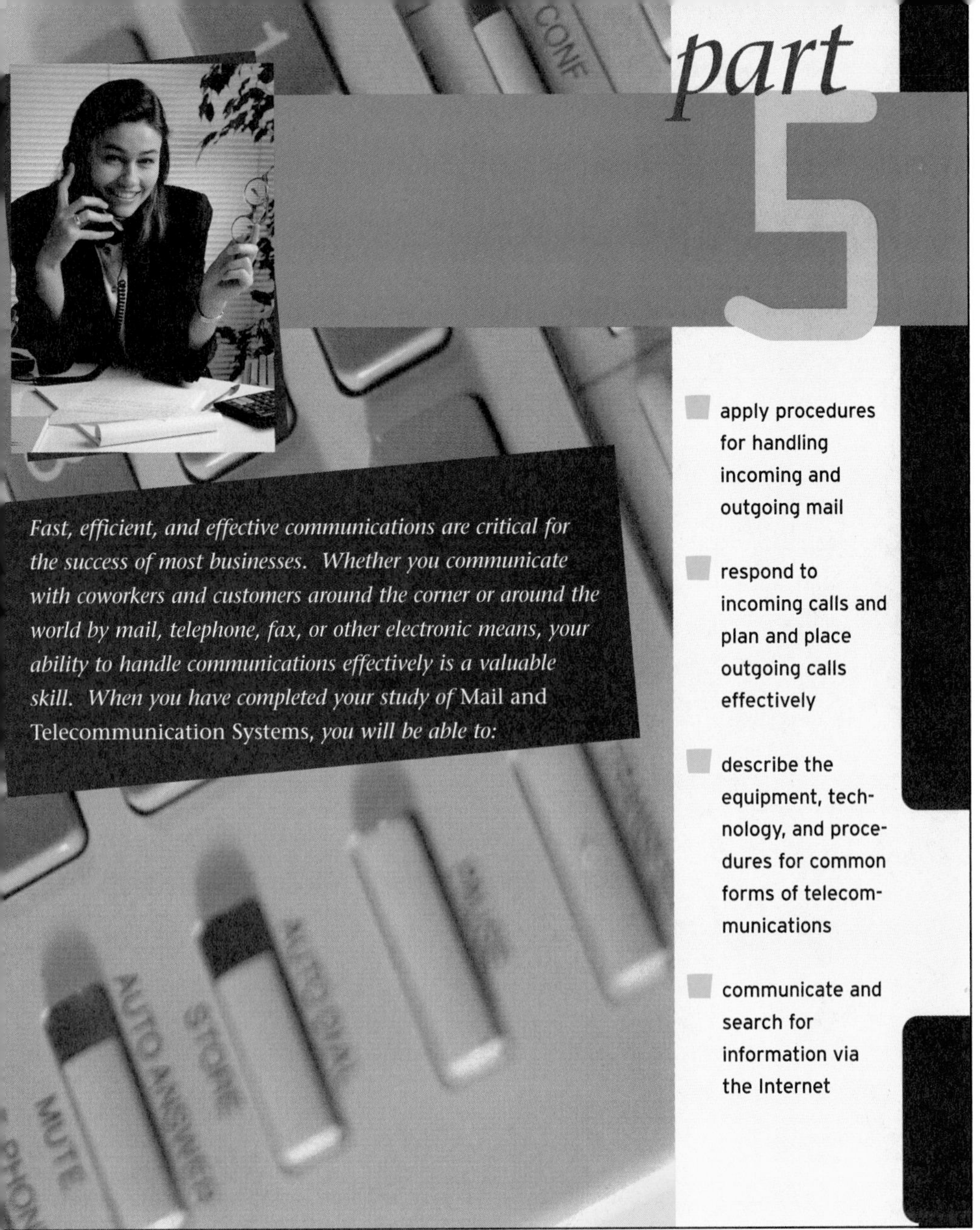

Fast, efficient, and effective communications are critical for the success of most businesses. Whether you communicate with coworkers and customers around the corner or around the world by mail, telephone, fax, or other electronic means, your ability to handle communications effectively is a valuable skill. When you have completed your study of Mail and Telecommunication Systems, *you will be able to:*

- apply procedures for handling incoming and outgoing mail
- respond to incoming calls and plan and place outgoing calls effectively
- describe the equipment, technology, and procedures for common forms of telecommunications
- communicate and search for information via the Internet

You may want to emphasize to students that even though there are many means of communicating—telephone, mail, e-mail, and facsimiles—the use of the U.S. Postal Service, as well as mail services provided by private companies, remains the delivery method of choice for most businesses.

Stress how important it is for a company to have systematic procedures for prompt distribution of incoming and interoffice mail.

Chapter 12

Processing Mail

Workers frequently use written messages to communicate with coworkers as well as individuals outside the company. For example, Jane, a worker in the marketing department, sends a memo to Dan, in the research & development department, requesting information about a new product. Shana Fields, an architect, sends a set of plans to Gayle Morton, an electrical engineer, to have them approved. Juanita Ramirez, the advertising director for a furniture store, sends announcements of an upcoming sale to all customers. In all these situations, information may be sent and received by mail. Mail must be processed as efficiently as possible so that communication is not delayed.

The size of a company and the amount of automated equipment available affect the procedures used for processing incoming and outgoing mail. In a small company, one worker may handle incoming and outgoing mail (as well as perform other office tasks) using limited automated equipment. In a large company, a full-time mailroom staff often uses specialized equipment to process mail. Even in large companies, workers outside the mailroom may have certain mail-handling responsibilities.

In this chapter, you will learn procedures for processing incoming and outgoing mail in both small and large companies. You also will learn about the equipment available to process mail with maximum efficiency.

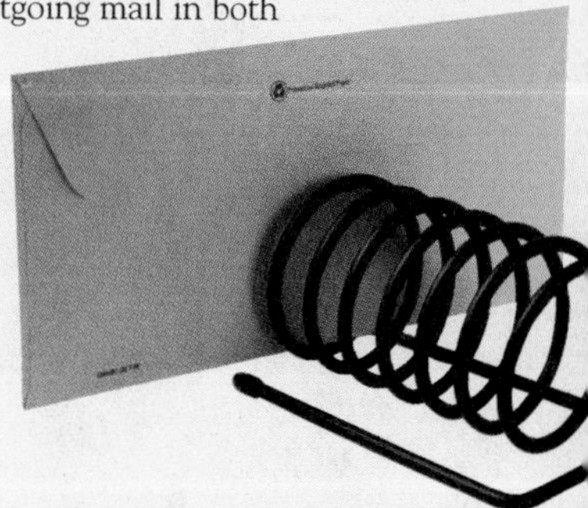

Chapter 12

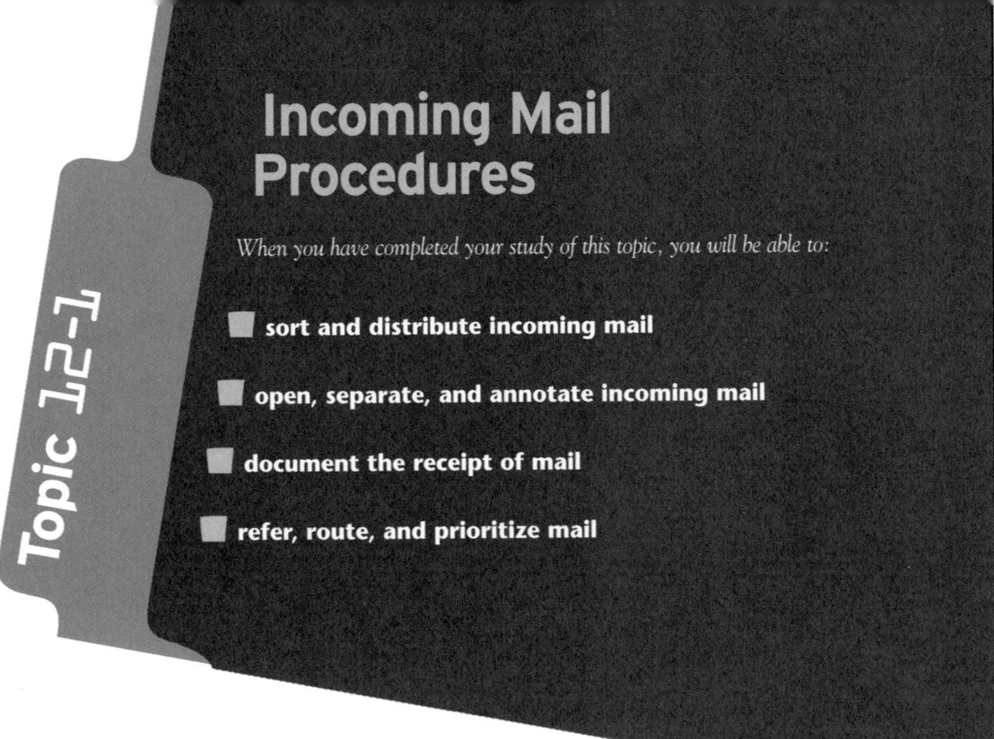

Incoming Mail Procedures

When you have completed your study of this topic, you will be able to:

- **sort and distribute incoming mail**
- **open, separate, and annotate incoming mail**
- **document the receipt of mail**
- **refer, route, and prioritize mail**

Office workers often need to take action promptly in response to items received in the mail. There may be checks to deposit, orders to fill, invoices to pay, literature to read, reports to review, and correspondence to answer. Mail must be accurately sorted and promptly distributed to the appropriate people so necessary actions can be taken without delay. In this chapter, you will learn how to handle incoming mail from outside the company, as well as interoffice mail.

You may be responsible for sorting and distributing incoming mail for the entire company or just for handling your own mail. You may help your supervisors or coworkers process their mail after another worker has distributed it. Your role in processing incoming mail will depend on the size of the company, the volume of incoming mail, and your job duties.

points to emphasize

There is a relationship between the processing of mail and the overall efficiency of the office. Employees depend on timely delivery of mail to complete their work tasks.

teaching tips

Point out to students that procedures for processing incoming mail may vary from one company to another. To help students understand the content of this topic, have them visit the general office or mailroom in your school where they can see how incoming mail and intra-school mail are received and distributed to faculty and administrators.

Also, you may want to ask the worker responsible for sorting and distributing the mail to explain the procedures followed and the equipment used.

1. For what reasons would mail be sent priority, registered, or insured?
2. Why would company procedures state that such mail should be delivered promptly to the addressee?

Sorting and Distributing Mail

Mail for various individuals and departments is all mixed together when it is delivered to an organization. Most companies want all mail sorted quickly so that it can be delivered and handled promptly. Priority letters, express mail, registered mail, and insured mail may be delivered to the addressee immediately upon receipt. In fact, the delivery of such letters usually takes **precedence** over the processing of ordinary mail. The method used for sorting mail will vary depending upon the size of the company and how it is organized.

precedence: priority of importance

IN SMALL COMPANIES

In a small company, you can easily sort the mail at your workstation by making a stack of mail for each employee or department. In a small company, one person may process incoming mail as well as perform other office tasks.

To distribute the mail, you hand-deliver each stack of mail to the appropriate person or department. If you have several stacks or bundles of mail to deliver, you may need to carry them in a pouch, alphabetized expanding folder, lightweight mail basket, or mail cart as you make your rounds through the office. You should arrange the bundles according to the route you will take.

When Ted is finished sorting the mail, he places rubber bands around each stack, creating a separate bundle for each worker. Then he places

1. Why is it important for a mail clerk to sort and deliver the mail with careful attention to detail?
2. Do you think that it is acceptable for employees to receive personal mail at work? Why or why not?

Illustration 12-1:1
The mail clerk delivers mail at regularly scheduled times throughout the workday.

the bundles in a mail cart in the order he will deliver them. Since Angela Duncan's workstation is his first stop, Ted places her mail bundle at the front of the cart. Using this procedure, Ted can distribute the mail quickly.

IN LARGE COMPANIES

Many large companies have mailrooms. A mailroom is a designated area where large volumes of incoming mail are processed. Mailrooms are easily accessible to postal workers who deliver the mail to the company. You are likely to find specialized equipment to aid mailroom workers in opening, sorting, and delivering the mail. Such equipment typically includes electric envelope openers, sorting units, and automated delivery systems.

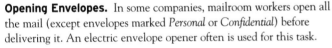

Illustration 12-1:2

This mailroom worker is sorting incoming mail from the post office and from private mail services.

Opening Envelopes. In some companies, mailroom workers open all the mail (except envelopes marked *Personal* or *Confidential*) before delivering it. An electric envelope opener often is used for this task.

An electric envelope opener trims a narrow strip off one edge of each envelope. The amount trimmed off is very small so that there is little risk that the contents of the envelope will be damaged. To reduce the chances of cutting the contents, tap each envelope on the table before placing it in the opener, so the contents will fall away from the edge that you are trimming.

teaching tips

Business and office magazines often have advertisements with photographs of mailroom equipment. You may want to collect samples and have a student committee design a bulletin board display that provides students with an idea of what they might find in the mailroom of a large company.

Sorting Mail. A wide variety of sorting units are used to sort the mail. Each compartment is labeled with the name of an individual or department within the organization. To sort the mail, you place each piece of mail in the appropriate compartment.

Companies with a huge amount of incoming mail have found that they can save time and effort by using a rotary sorting unit. The unit turns easily, and the worker can remain in one place as he or she sorts the mail.

Have students ask family and friends what procedures are used for distributing mail at their places of employment. Are the procedures similar to the examples listed here? If not, how do they differ?

Distributing Mail. Once the mail has been sorted, it is ready for distribution. Procedures for delivering mail within the organization vary from company to company. For example:

- A worker from each department comes to the mailroom to pick up the department's mail.
- A mailroom employee carries the mail in a basket or cart from the mailroom to the departments.
- An **automated** delivery system transports mail to the various departments, as shown in Illustration 12-1:3. This robot-like cart follows a chemical path on the floor and is programmed to stop at certain locations throughout the building. Employees can then pick up incoming mail and deposit outgoing mail.

automated: processed by machine

Have you ever seen an automated mail delivery system, such as this mobile mail cart, in operation? If so, where?

Illustration 12-1:3

Mobile mail carts are used in some large companies to distribute the mail.

Handling Incoming Mail

Some office workers are asked to process the mail before giving it to their supervisors or coworkers. Some employees, however, prefer to process their own mail.

> *Sarah is the receptionist in a small real estate office. For each of her supervisors, she opens the mail, removes the contents, and stamps the date and time on each item.*
>
> *David works in a florist shop where he sorts and distributes the mail along with other duties. His coworkers then process their own mail.*

OPENING MAIL

If the mail is not opened when it reaches you, use a letter opener to open all envelopes. If you are opening mail for a supervisor or coworkers, do not open envelopes marked *Personal* or *Confidential*. If you mistakenly open such an envelope, write on it, "Sorry, opened by mistake," and add your initials. Check the outside of each envelope carefully before you open it to avoid making that error.

As you remove the contents from the envelopes, be sure to verify that all enclosures referred to in the correspondence are actually enclosed. If an enclosure is missing, you should note the **omission** in the margin of the letter. Notify the sender of the missing enclosure right away, especially if it is a check, money order, cash, or stamps.

omission: something left out

Check each letter for the signature and the address of the sender before you discard the envelope. If either is missing on the letter, attach the envelope to the back of the letter, since the envelope usually has a return address on it. Sometimes the envelope is stapled to a document because the mailing date may be important.

Record the current date on each item received. In some cases it may also be helpful to record the time the item was received You can do this with a pen or pencil, a rubber stamp, or a time-stamp machine.

SEPARATING AND ANNOTATING MAIL

As you inspect the mail, put the letters that you will answer or handle yourself in one stack and those that will be handled by a supervisor or coworkers in another stack. You may be able to handle communications

Ask students how they would react in the following situation:

You work in the office of a small company and are responsible for opening and distributing incoming mail. You mistakenly open an envelope marked *Personal* that is addressed to your supervisor. What should you do?

Ask students to describe a situation where the date and time on a piece of correspondence would be critical evidence.

Illustration 12-1:4

Review the contents of incoming mail daily, contrary to Cathy's example

to a supervisor that could be answered by a form letter, circular, or advertisement. Requests for catalogs or price lists also can be handled this way. However, your supervisor may wish to see all **inquiries** that are received.

inquiries: questions

facilitate: speed the process of

annotate: write comments

If your supervisor requests or to **facilitate** answering your own mail, you may underline or **annotate** the correspondence. However, good judgment is necessary here, since too many markings can be annoying.

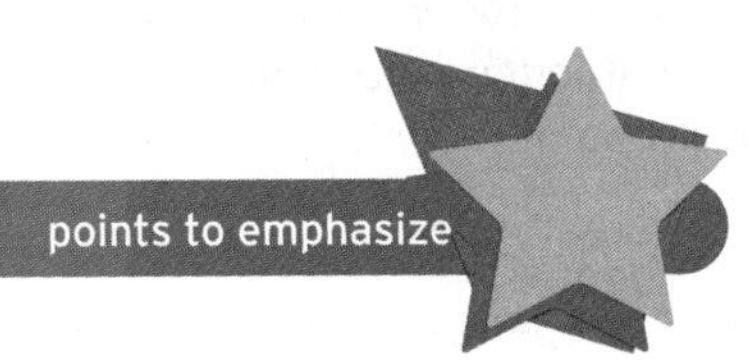

Use good judgment when underlining and annotating correspondence; too many markings can be distracting and confusing.

First, underline the key words and phrases in the correspondence that will aid in understanding the content quickly. Note the key phrases underlined in Illustration 12-1:5. Then determine the answers to questions in the correspondence. Where appropriate, make related comments on the letter. Write the clearly worded answers and/or comments in legible handwriting in the margin, on a note placed on the correspondence, or on a photocopy of the correspondence. Note the annotations on the letter shown in Illustration 12-1:5.

Russell White and Brothers Lumber Company
Route 32
Linwood, KY 40455-0077

December 5, 19-- DEC 8, 19— 11:30 a.m.

Ms. Michele R. Carrell
Ashland Computerland, Inc.
800 Cleveland Avenue
Ashland, KY 44550-0770

Copy sent to Mr. Edwards in Installation Dept.

Dear Ms. Carrell

Our new computer system was installed on November 26, and we were impressed with the efficiency of your installation team. The hardware and software are installed and working well. Feedback from the end-users has been positive.

Ed Jones, your installation team director, advises that we need to add one more workstation to maximize the use of the computer network. Please add another PC2-2020 workstation to our order. Prepared Inv. 22892 12/9

Mr. Jones also reminded us to make plans for our unit director, Mary Ann McCoy, to attend your End-User Workshop on January 6-10. Ms. McCoy is eager to attend, and we know this additional education will improve our utilization of the new computer system. Please send registration forms for the workshop to Ms. McCoy in the Information Services Department. Our address is listed at the top of this letter.

Registration forms sent.

Sincerely

Harold G. White

Harold G. White
Chief Information Officer

de

Illustration 12-1:5

The date-time stamp, underlined words and phrases, and annotations facilitate a quick response.

Copies of previous correspondence, reports, and other related documents may help in responding to the mail. For example, you may attach the file copy of a letter written to Ms. McCoy to the reply you receive from her. Or you might retrieve a folder related to an inquiry from the files and place it with the incoming letter.

DOCUMENTING RECEIPT OF MAIL

You should keep a record of items you expect to receive *under separate cover* (in another envelope or package) to be sure that you receive them. One type of record for separate cover mail is shown in Illustration 12-1:6. Notice that the entry on the first line was made

You may want to duplicate several pieces of correspondence and, after giving students the context in which the correspondence is relevant, ask them to underline and annotate the correspondence.

on August 2 (Date of Entry). The article promised was a report from Reid Brothers. The correspondence indicated that the report was mailed on August 1 (Date Sent) to A. Weir (For Whom). It was received on August 4 (Date Received). Notice on the last line of the record that the tickets mailed on September 25 have not been received yet.

Check the record at least twice a week to see which items have not been received. That way, you can take follow-up action on delayed mail. Workers in the mailroom usually do not keep such records since they do not read the contents of the mail.

Ask students to refer to Illustration 12-1:6 to answer the following:

1. What expected item has not yet been received?
2. On what date was the item sent?
3. To whom and from whom was the item sent?

Illustration 12-1:6

Keep a record of mail you expect to receive in a separate envelope or package.

EXPECTED MAIL

Date of Entry	Article	From Whom	Date Sent	For Whom	Date Received
8-2	Report	Reid Bros.	8-1	A. Weir	8-4
8-5	Micro-cassettes	Foxworth Supply	8-3	J. Tyler	8-10
8-15	Computer Printouts	Lehman & Bennett	8-12	A. Weir	8-18
9-3	Catalog	Cole Mfg. Co.	9-1	H. Rice	9-7
9-25	Benefit Tickets	Jack Hill	9-22	H. Rice	

document: make a written record of

Whether you process incoming mail in a small company or in the mailroom of a large company, you should **document** the receipt of mail sent by special postal services. For example, you should record the receipt of certified, insured, registered, or express mail. You may use a form similar to that shown in Illustration 12-1:7.

REFERRING OR ROUTING MAIL

You or your supervisor may decide to refer certain items to an assistant or associate to handle. To facilitate this process, a *referral slip* is attached to the item. The referral slip shown in Illustration 12-1:8 lists a series of instructions from which to choose. A check mark is used to indicate the specific instruction to be followed.

MAIL REGISTER

Received		From Whom		For Whom	Kind of Mail Received
Date	Time	Name	City/State		
4-5	3:20 p.m.	J.J. McIntosh	St. Louis, MO	B. Rudd	Insured
4-6	9:15 a.m.	Bates Mfg. Co.	Memphis, TN	S. Norwell	Special Delivery
4-9	10:45 a.m.	Ken Stewart	Des Moines IA	J. Jones	Registered
4-12	3:15 p.m.	Haskins & Associates	Erie, PA	W. Yeager	Express Mail

Illustration 12-1:7

Use a mail register to document the receipt of special mail.

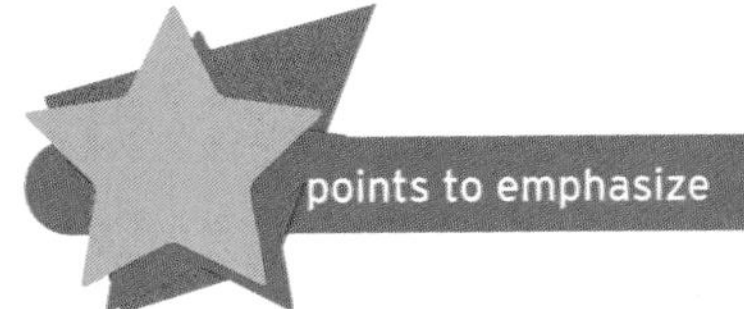

Whether you process incoming mail in a small company or in the mailroom of a large company, you should document the receipt of mail sent by special postal services.

When action is requested of another individual, you should keep a record of the referral. You should note the date the item was referred, the name of the person to whom it was referred, the subject, the action to be taken, and a follow-up date if one is necessary.

REFERRAL SLIP

Date 9/18/--

TO Alice Leary

Refer to the attached material and

- ☐ Please note
- ☐ Please note and file
- ☐ Please note and return to me
- ☐ Please mail to ________
- ☐ Please note and talk with me this a.m. ______ p.m. ______
- ☐ Please answer, sending me a copy
- ☑ Please write a reply for my signature
- ☐ Please handle
- ☐ Please have ___ photocopies made for ________
- ☐ Please sign
- ☐ Please let me have your comments
- ☐ Please RUSH immediate action desired
- ☐ Please make follow-up for ________

REMARKS

Letter should go out no later than 9/25.

Signed Rosa Darlington

Illustration 12-1:8

Mail is frequently forwarded to an associate for action.

Ask students to refer to Illustration 12-1:8 to answer the following:

1. To whom and by whom was the piece of mail forwarded?
2. What action has been requested?
3. Are there any special instructions?

Ask students to refer to Illustration 12-1:9 to answer the following:

1. From whom was the item routed?
2. What action was requested of the individuals receiving the item?
3. Has each appropriate individual read the item?

route:
send on a particular path

There are times when items such as correspondence and important magazine articles should be read by more than one person in the company. You may be asked to make a copy for each person who should read the item, or you may be asked to **route** the item through the office. To do so, attach a *routing slip,* which is similar to a referral slip, to the item. Indicate with check marks the individuals who should read the item.

Illustration 12-1:9
A routing slip is attached to the front of mail to be distributed to others.

ROUTING SLIP

FROM:
Ryan Tolbert
____Information Services Department
DATE: 3/25

TO:	**Date Forwarded**
__Everyone	
__R. Bernardin	
✓R. Carlson	3/25
__M. Carrell	
__J. Fouch	
✓J. Hensen	3/25
__C. Hickman	
__H. Iwuki	
✓S. Lansing	3/26
__M. Lucky	
__C. Tesch	
✓R. Williams	3/27

Please:
__Read and keep in your files
__Read and pass on
__Read and return to me
✓Read, route, and return to me

PRIORITIZING MAIL

prioritized:
put in order of importance

Incoming mail should be **prioritized** for further processing. As a general rule, mail is categorized in the order of its importance. The following arrangement is usually satisfactory, moving from the top to the bottom of the stack:

1. urgent messages, such as documents received by fax, that require prompt attention
2. personal and confidential letters
3. business letters, memos, or other correspondence of special importance
4. letters containing checks or money orders
5. other business letters
6. letters containing orders
7. letters containing bills, invoices, or other requests for payment
8. advertisements
9. newspapers and magazines
10. packages

HANDLING MAIL WHILE AWAY FROM THE OFFICE

Technology makes it possible to receive and forward important mail and messages for immediate action while away from the office. In this way, business matters are not delayed and deadlines are not missed. You will need to decide which mail should be forwarded and which mail should be held for action after returning to the office. The following guidelines may be helpful in keeping track of incoming mail for your supervisors or coworkers who are away from the office:

- Maintain a mail register as described on page 582.
- Communicate with the traveler immediately if important, unexpected action seems required.
- Refer routine mail to others who can respond.
- Answer mail yourself if it is within your area of responsibility.
- Send a synopsis of received mail (or a copy of the mail log) if the traveler is on an extended business trip.
- After the mail has been prioritized, store it in an appropriate place.

Effective processing of the incoming mail helps keep the office running smoothly while the traveler is away and saves time for the traveler upon returning to the office.

Ask students to place the following incoming mail in the proper order by numbering each item:

____ monthly electric bill
____ letter marked *Confidential*
____ local newspaper
____ letter accompanied by a money order
____ advertisement for a seminar
____ letter requesting a copy of the company's latest catalog

Ask students:

1. What mail items should be forwarded to business travelers while away from the office?
2. What mail items might be referred to another person?
3. What mail items might you answer?
4. What mail items would be considered "routine" and could wait to be handled until the supervisor is back in the office?

Reviewing the Topic

1. What is interoffice mail?
2. What three factors affect your role in processing incoming mail?
3. What is a mailroom?
4. What equipment is used in mailrooms to process incoming mail?
5. What should you do if you open a confidential letter by mistake?
6. When you remove the contents from an envelope, what should you verify?
7. How might your annotating a letter save your supervisor time?
8. What is the purpose of keeping a record of expected mail?
9. Give an example of when a routing slip might be used.
10. What is the generally accepted order for prioritizing incoming mail?

INTERACTING WITH OTHERS

You are a records clerk in a small medical clinic. Shelly, the receptionist, is responsible for sorting and distributing all incoming mail. Mail addressed to the three physicians is opened before it is delivered. Mail addressed to the general office staff is to be delivered unopened. Today, however, Shelly delivers a letter addressed to you that has been opened. The letter includes salary information that is both personal and confidential in nature. You are concerned that Shelly may have read the letter.

topic 12-1 review

Should you ask Shelly why the letter was opened? Should you ask her if she read the letter? How would you handle this situation?

What you are to do:

In small groups, discuss the situation and prepare a response to the questions raised. Share your group's response with the rest of the class.

topic 12-1 review

Incoming Mail Procedures

REINFORCING MATH SKILLS

Based on records kept by the mailroom supervisor, about 3,000 pieces of incoming mail are sorted and distributed each month in your company. Additionally, the volume of mail is expected to increase by 6 percent next year.

What you are to do:

1. Calculate the following:
   a. the number of pieces of mail that will be processed this year
   b. the number of pieces of mail expected to be processed next year
   c. how many more pieces of mail will be processed next year than will be processed this year
   d. how many pieces of mail per month the mailroom will handle next year
2. Create a pie chart to illustrate the following distribution of the mail for each month:

   10% express mail packages or letters
   20% advertisements, newspapers, and magazines
   35% interoffice mail
   30% letters, checks, orders
   5% other

APPLICATION ACTIVITIES

ACTIVITY 1 **Expected Mail Log**

Filename: Maillog

You work in the general office of Sperling Enterprises. Because the company receives many items under separate cover, you have been asked to keep a record of these expected items to be sure they are received.

What you are to do:

Use the Expected Mail form in the template file *Maillog*. Complete the form using the information shown in your *Student Activities and Projects* workbook.

See Workbook page 71.

587

ACTIVITY 2 Annotate Correspondence

In this exercise, you will underline and annotate the important information in a letter for your supervisor.

See Workbook page 73.

What you are to do:

Locate the letter to Carmella Huntington in your *Student Activities and Projects* workbook. Annotate the letter underlining key words and phrases that will help your supervisor understand the contents of the letter. Make related comments in the margin of the letter. Use Illustration 12-1:5 on page 581 as a guide.

topic 12-1
review

588

Topic 12-2

Outgoing Mail Procedures

When you have completed your study of this topic, you will be able to:

- **prepare outgoing mail**
- **identify the classes of domestic mail**
- **explain the various services provided by the USPS**
- **arrange for courier service**
- **send materials through an interoffice mail system**

Throughout a working day, many forms of communication are sent to those outside the company. For example, you may be asked to send purchase orders to customers, letters to business organizations, and advertisements to potential customers. It is important that outgoing mail be properly prepared.

You probably have prepared letters for mailing and are acquainted with addressing envelopes, inserting documents, and affixing proper postage. However, you will find that companies have developed specific procedures for completing these tasks in order to handle outgoing mail efficiently.

The way outgoing mail is processed will depend on the size of your company and the procedures designated by the company. If you work in a small office, you probably will be responsible for all the details

teaching tips

Students may be surprised by the variety of ways outgoing mail can be sent. They also may be unaware that so many services are available from the U.S. Postal Service (USPS). To help students understand the content of this topic, you may want them to search the index of the telephone yellow pages to determine the types of mail and shipping companies in your area or obtain brochure/bulletins from the USPS and private companies that explain the range of services provided.

Topic 12-2

involved with processing outgoing mail. However, if you work in the mailroom of a large company, you may weigh and seal mail, apply postage, and mail envelopes that have been prepared and stuffed by workers in other departments.

The United States Postal Service (USPS) processes over half a billion pieces of mail each day! Businesses all across the country use the varied services of the USPS to send such items as letters, financial reports, computer printouts, architectural drawings, invoices, manuscripts, newsletters, and merchandise to their intended destinations. In some cases, the items are destined for delivery in the same city; in other cases, to an individual or an organization in a city halfway around the world.

As a variation of the conventional field trip, have students visit a business or a post office individually or in small groups to learn the range of services provided. Students could then give oral reports in class about their visits.

courier: messenger

Although most outgoing mail is sent through the USPS, there also are local, national, and worldwide **courier** services that deliver envelopes and packages. Most courier services guarantee their delivery times. You also may send mail through an interoffice mail system. As an office worker, you need to be acquainted with the mailing options available to you. This topic will help you learn about procedures for processing outgoing mail efficiently.

Processing Outgoing Mail in a Small Company

In a small organization you may be responsible for processing all the outgoing mail, as well as handling other office tasks.

> *Melynda is the receptionist in a small real estate office. On her workstation is an out basket where all the workers place their outgoing mail. A postal carrier usually picks up and delivers the mail about 10:30 a.m. At 10:00 a.m., Melynda prepares an envelope for each item in the out basket. Then she stuffs the envelopes, seals them, weighs them, and applies the appropriate postage. By 10:30 a.m., the mail is ready to be picked up by the postal carrier.*

drop box: mail box

The USPS picks up and delivers mail to some organizations twice a day. In other organizations, a postal carrier may come to the office in the morning, and an office worker may take outgoing mail to a post office or **drop box** in the afternoon. You need to know the scheduled

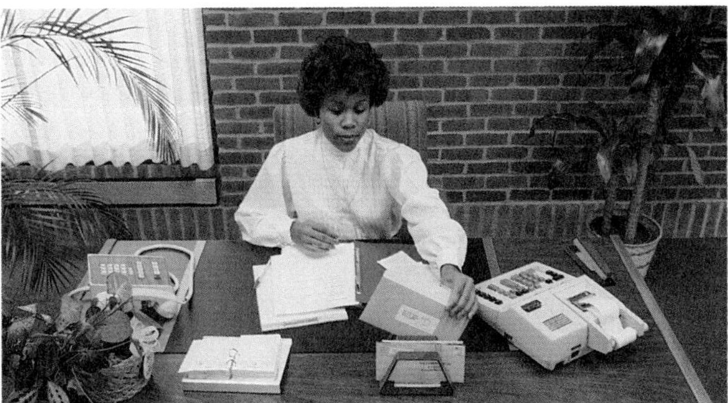

Illustration 12-2:1

This office worker places outgoing mail in a small mail rack on her desk.

times for pickup so you can have the mail ready on time. The USPS recommends mailing as early in the day as possible for the fastest service.

FOLDING AND INSERTING MAIL

Once a document is ready to mail, it is a good idea to give it a final check before inserting it in the envelope. Be sure that:

- copies have been made, if necessary
- letters have been signed
- your initials appear below your supervisor's signature on any letter you have signed for your supervisor
- all enclosures noted at the bottom of a letter are actually enclosed in the envelope
- the address on the envelope agrees with the address on the letter
- the nine-digit ZIP code appears on the last line of both the envelope address and the return address

You usually will insert documents into standard or window envelopes. Folding business documents correctly to fit into envelopes is a simple but important task. You should take care that the creases are straight and neat. A document should be inserted in an envelope so that it will be in a normal reading position when it is removed from the envelope and unfolded.

A document should be inserted in an envelope so that it will be in a normal reading position when it is removed from the envelope and unfolded.

Provide students with $8^1/_2$" x 11" paper and No. 10 envelopes. Then ask students to follow the steps shown in Illustration 12-2:2 to properly fold and insert the paper into the envelope.

The enclosures that accompany a document should be folded with the document and inserted so that they come out of the envelope when the document is removed.

Standard Envelopes. The most common sizes of standard envelopes are $9^1/_2$" × $4^1/_8$" (No. 10) and $6^1/_2$" × $3^5/_8$" (No. $6^3/_4$). Illustration 12-2:2 shows how to fold a letter and insert it into a No. 10 envelope.

Illustration 12-2:2

Follow these steps to fold an $8^1/_2$" × 11" letter to insert into a No. 10 envelope.

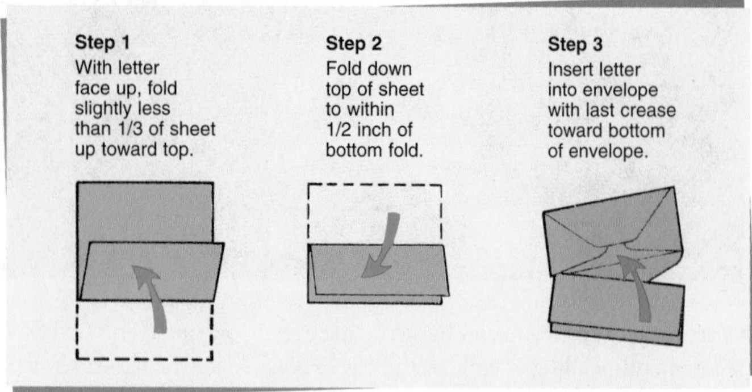

Step 1
With letter face up, fold slightly less than 1/3 of sheet up toward top.
Step 2
Fold down top of sheet to within 1/2 inch of bottom fold.
Step 3
Insert letter into envelope with last crease toward bottom of envelope.

Illustration 12-2:3 shows how to fold a letter and insert it into a No. $6^3/_4$ envelope. The enclosures that accompany a document should be folded with the document or inserted so that they will come out of the envelope when the document is removed.

Illustration 12-2:3

Follow these steps to fold an $8^1/_2$" × 11" letter to insert into a No. $6^3/_4$ envelope.

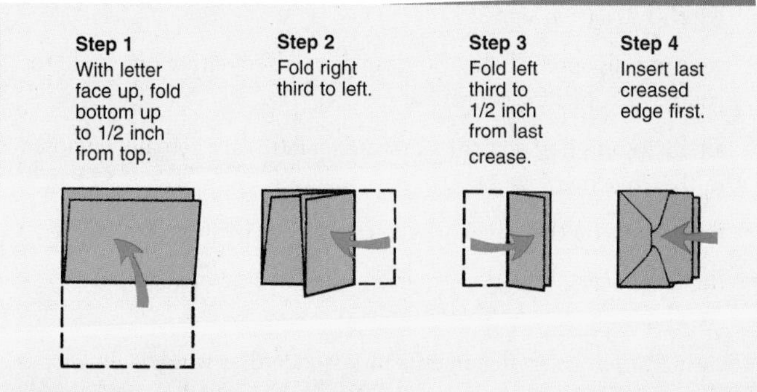

Step 1
With letter face up, fold bottom up to 1/2 inch from top.
Step 2
Fold right third to left.
Step 3
Fold left third to 1/2 inch from last crease.
Step 4
Insert last creased edge first.

Window Envelopes. A window envelope has a see-through panel on the front of the envelope. A window envelope eliminates the need to address a standard envelope since the address on the letter or form is visible through the window. The address on the letter or form must be positioned so that it can be seen through the window after the letter is folded and inserted into the envelope.

Window envelopes are available as No. 10 and No. 6 3/4 envelopes. No. 6 3/4 window envelopes are used mostly for forms or statements that are designed to fit in the envelope with only a single fold. Illustration 12-2:4 shows how to fold an 8 1/2" × 11" page to fit correctly into a No. 10 window envelope.

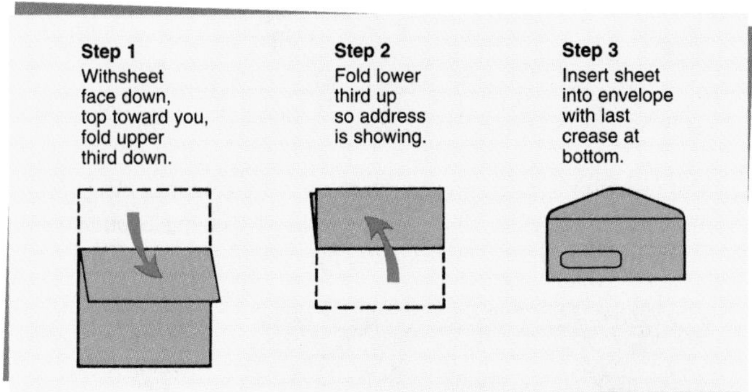

Step 1
Withsheet face down, top toward you, fold upper third down.
Step 2
Fold lower third up so address is showing.
Step 3
Insert sheet into envelope with last crease at bottom.

Illustration 12-2:4

Follow these steps to fold an 8 1/2" × 11" letter to insert into a No. 10 window envelope.

SEALING AND WEIGHING ENVELOPES

Envelopes must be sealed before they are mailed. When you need to seal more than one or two envelopes, you probably will want to use a moist sponge or moistener. To quickly seal many envelopes at once, spread about ten envelopes on a table or desk. Place them address-side down, flap open, one on top of the other, with the gummed edges showing. Note in Illustration 12-2:5 on page 594 how the worker has done this. Brush over the gummed edges with a sponge or moistener. Starting with the top envelope, quickly fold the flaps down one at a time until all the envelopes are sealed.

It is important to weigh each piece of outgoing mail accurately so you can apply the proper amount of postage. Electronic scales are available that automatically calculate the correct amount of postage for each piece of mail. You simply place the item to be mailed on the scale and

Moisteners and electronic postage scales are items designed to help office workers process outgoing mail efficiently. Ask students:

Can you name two additional items that help simplify the process of preparing outgoing mail?

Illustration 12-2:5

A moistener can be used to seal several envelopes at once.

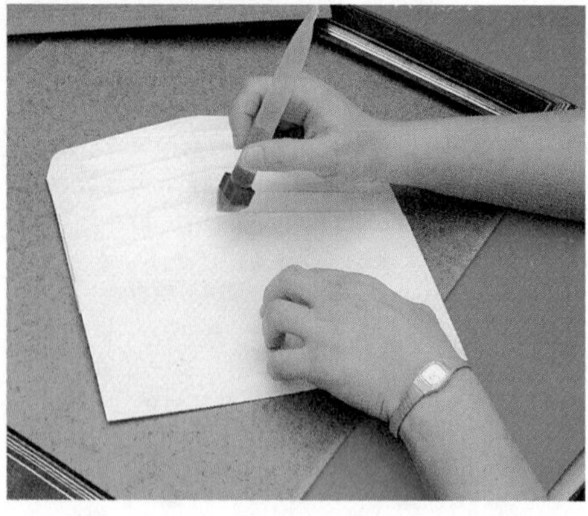

indicate which postal class you wish to use. The amount of the postage is displayed on a small screen. When postal rates change, you update the scale by inserting a new computer memory unit.

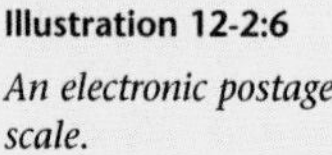

Illustration 12-2:6

An electronic postage scale.

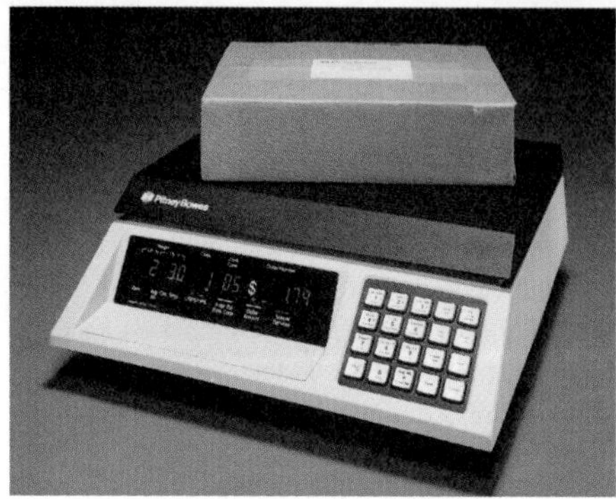

STAMPING/METERING MAIL

Postage must be paid for all mail before it can be delivered. There are various methods of purchasing postage.

Stamps. You may purchase postage stamps in sheet, booklet, or rolled form. Rolled stamps often are used in business because they can be placed quickly on envelopes and packages and they are less likely than individual stamps to be lost or damaged.

The post office sells envelopes and cards that already have the correct postage printed on them. You can buy them one at a time or in quantity **lots.** First-class postcards may be purchased in single or double form. The double form is used when a reply is requested on the attached card.

lots: things considered as a group

Postage Meter. A postage meter is a machine that prints postage in the amount needed. It prints the postage either directly onto the envelope or onto a pre-moistened label that you apply to the envelope or package. You can use the numeric keys on the postage meter to set it to print postage for a letter weighing one ounce and easily reset it to print postage for a letter weighing three ounces. The postage meter prints the date as well as the postage amount. Always be sure the correct date is set on the meter. Some meters also print a business slogan or advertisement next to the postmark. Because metered mail is already dated and postmarked, it can be processed faster than stamped mail.

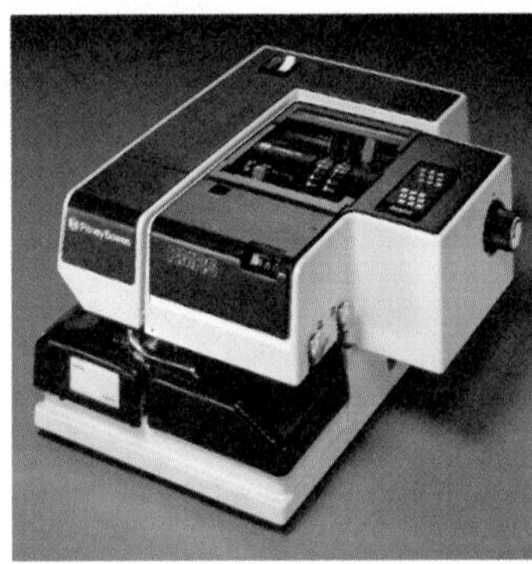

Illustration 12-2:7

An electronic postage meter prints the postmark and the postage.

To buy postage, you take the meter with you to the post office. The postal worker will reset the meter for the amount of postage purchased. As you use the postage meter, the meter setting decreases, showing you how much postage is left. Do not let the postage get too low before buying more. The meter locks when the postage paid for has been used.

thinking critically

Ask students:

1. What is the internal control that is provided by the use of a postage meter rather than rolls of stamps?
2. What is the potential efficiency of using a postage meter instead of rolls of stamps?

Pitney-Bowes, a company specializing in mailroom equipment, has a postage system called *Postage-by-Phone*. To purchase postage, you simply call a toll-free number and use the keys of your touch-tone telephone to enter required information (including an assigned resetting number). You are then assigned a new resetting number, which you enter into the meter. Using Postage-by-Phone, you can reset your meter in less than two minutes.

Illustration 12-2:8

A company that has a Postage-by-Phone system can "buy additional postage" via phone.

Processing Outgoing Mail in a Large Company

You have just learned that in a small company, an office worker may be responsible for all the steps of processing outgoing mail. In a large company, however, these steps may be divided between mailroom workers and workers in other departments.

> *Brenner Industries is a large corporation with many departments. Office workers in each department address the envelopes and insert the correspondence into the envelopes. Each department has a central location for collecting outgoing mail. A mailroom worker picks up the mail and takes it to the company mailroom. The mailroom workers then seal, weigh, and* **affix** *postage to the mail in time for scheduled pickups from the post office.*

affix:
attach, add on

Have students ask their family and friends what the procedures are for processing outgoing mail at their places of employment. Are the procedures similar to those at Brenner Industries? If not, how do they differ?

If you are an office worker in a large company, the extent of your mail-handling duties will be determined by company policy and your specific job.

Handling Volume Mailings

Sending the same items to many people at the same time is a volume mailing. For example, a marketing research company may send a questionnaire to all residents in a city to determine their preferences with regard to particular products, such as televisions or breakfast cereals. Companies doing volume mailings may qualify for reduced postage rates. In order to qualify for reduced postage rates, it is critical for workers in mailrooms to know **current** USPS mailing regulations and standards.

current: up to date

MAILING LISTS

Mailing lists for volume mail may contain addresses for customers, prospective customers, subscribers, or those who live in certain geographic areas. Mailing lists should always be current. That means you should delete, correct, and add addresses as soon as you learn about changes. The post office recommends having the words FORWARDING AND ADDRESS CORRECTION REQUESTED printed on all envelopes. Then the post office will **forward** mail with an old address to the new address. For a small fee, the post office will send you a card giving the new address.

forward: send on

As companies expand their mailing lists, many are choosing to use computer-generated mailing lists. Some of the advantages of using computer-generated mailing lists include the ability to:

- quickly retrieve, change, or delete addresses
- easily avoid duplicate addresses
- select addresses from a master list to create a smaller list for a special mailing
- print letter addresses and salutations on form letters as well as address labels

Ask students to use a computer to compile a database of the names and addresses of all students in the class. Generate a mailing list. Periodically add/delete/update the names and addresses and print a revised list.

PREPARING ADDRESS LABELS

One method of preparing labels is to type all the addresses on paper in a format that will allow you to photocopy the addresses onto sheets of labels. Each time you have a mailing, you simply photocopy the addresses, peel the labels off the backing sheets, and apply them to the envelopes.

Many companies use computers to print address labels. Illustration 12-2:9 on the following page displays a computerized addressing/labeling/folding/inserting system. With such a system, addresses stored on a disk can be printed onto sheets of pressure-sensitive labels. Pressure-sensitive labels can be peeled from backing sheets and affixed to envelopes, using light pressure. Some printers can print as many as 7,000 address labels per hour. You can apply computer-generated address labels to envelopes manually or automatically, using an automatic labeling device.

Transparency master TM 12-2:1 can be used to enhance your discussion of the OCR read zone, the bar code read zone, and the proper address format for envelopes recommended by the USPS.

Address Requirements for Automated Mail Handling

The USPS uses high-speed electronic mail-handling equipment in many of its postal centers in order to speed mail to its destination. This equipment includes optical character readers and bar code sorters. An optical character reader (OCR) is electronic equipment that quickly scans or "reads" the address on an envelope and prints a bar code at the bottom of the envelope.

During the sorting process, the bar codes are "read" by a bar code sorter and the mail is quickly routed to its proper destination. Not all postal centers are equipped with OCR equipment and bar code sorters; therefore, not all mail you receive will have a printed bar code on the envelope.

If the optical character reader is unable to read an address, the envelope is routed to a manual letter-sorting machine. This, of course, increases the processing time. Some of the reasons why an OCR may be unable to read an address are listed here:

- The address is handwritten.
- The address is not printed or typed in the proper format.

You may want to bring to class actual envelopes you have received in the mail. Or ask students to bring envelopes they have received at home. Distribute the envelopes and ask students:

1. Does your envelope have a bar code printed on it?
2. Is the address within the read zone?
3. Does the address format conform to the USPS guidelines? If not, what is incorrect?

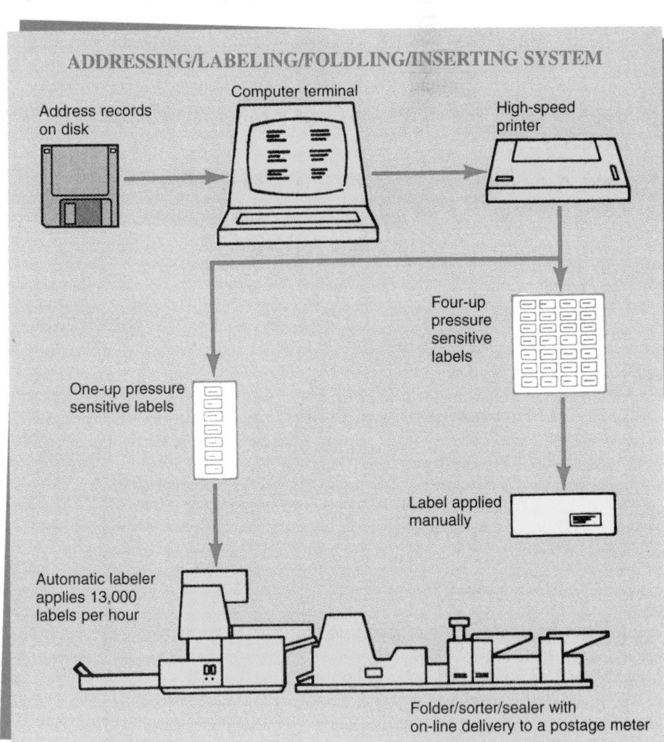

Illustration 12-2:9

Large companies may have an addressing/labeling/folding/inserting system to speed mail processing.

How does a computerized addressing/ labeling/ folding/inserting system speed the process of preparing outgoing mail?

- The envelope is too small or too large for the OCR equipment to handle. (To avoid this problem, use rectangular envelopes no smaller than 3 1/2" × 5" and no larger than 6 1/8" × 11 1/2".)
- The address is not within the OCR read area.
- The complete address is not visible through the panel of a window envelope.

ADDRESS FORMAT

The address should be printed on the envelope or label. It is very important that the characters be dark, even, and clear. The address should be printed according to the following guidelines:

- Use all capital letters.
- Block the left margin of the address.
- Omit all marks of punctuation (except the hyphen in the nine-digit ZIP Code).
- Use the standard two-letter abbreviation for the state (see Reference Section E for a list of these abbreviations).
- Leave one or two spaces between the state abbreviation and the ZIP Code.
- Add the delivery point ZIP + 4 bar code on the envelope, if your software has this capability.

The post office has an approved list of abbreviations for cities and other words commonly used in addresses. You should use these approved abbreviations if the address is too long to fit on a label.

Illustration 12-2:10

Use the proper address format and abbreviations for mailing labels as recommended by USPS.

```
MS EMMA JO BERMAN
132 CANNON GREEN TOWERS APT 6A
SANTA BARBARA CA 93105-2233

MR ARTURO FUENTES
VICE PRESIDENT MARKETING
ROSSLYN WHOLESALE COMPANY
1815 N LYNN STREET
ARLINGTON VA 22209-6183

ATTN THOMAS W THIESEN
BATES MICROWAVE COMPANY
4025 EASTWAY DRIVE
CHARLOTTE NC 28205-2736
```

ZIP CODES

To assure prompt delivery of your mail, always use the nine-digit ZIP Code, if known. ZIP + 4 is the preferred nine-digit ZIP Code system developed by the USPS to facilitate mail delivery.

You are already familiar with the five-digit ZIP Code. The first three digits indicate a major geographic area or post office, while the last two digits designate a local post office. A hyphen and four digits are added to the existing five-digit ZIP Code to help the post office sort the mail more specifically. The first two digits after the hyphen indicate a delivery sector. A sector is several blocks within a city, a group of streets, several office buildings, or another small geographic area. The last two digits represent a delivery segment, which can indicate one side of a street, one floor in an office building, or specific departments in a firm. The Zip + 4 code for 94534-8727 is defined as follows:

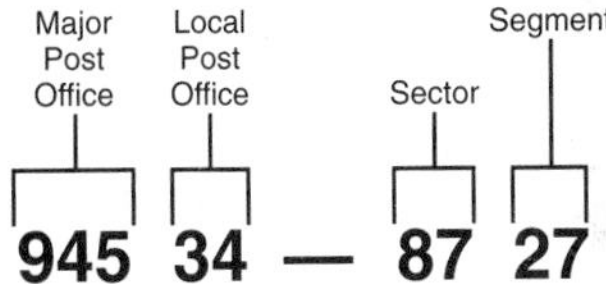

ZIP code directories for both the five-digit and nine-digit codes can be purchased from the post office. If a directory is not available in the office where you work, you can call the post office to obtain a particular ZIP code. You can search for ZIP codes on the USPS website at http://www.usps.gov.

Classes of Domestic Mail

Domestic mail is distributed within the United States and its territories (such as Puerto Rico, the Virgin Islands, and Guam). Domestic mail is divided into various classes, which are described in the following paragraphs.

FIRST-CLASS AND PRIORITY MAIL

The post office will handle and transport first-class mail **expeditiously.** Use first-class mail for the following items:

expeditiously: with maximum efficiency

- personal correspondence
- business correspondence
- bills and statements of account
- postcards (privately purchased mailing cards that require postage) and postal cards (cards sold by the post office with postage imprinted on them)

Ask students to respond to the following situation:

Larry was in such a hurry to mail a letter that he accidentally forgot to key the ZIP + 4 Code on the envelope. (He keyed only the city and state—BOSTON MA.) What do you think will happen to the letter at the post office when the mail is sorted?

Can you name five items that should be sent first class?

Illustration 12-2:11

Various classes of domestic mail are sorted by postal workers each day.

What functions are the postal workers performing in Illustration 12-2:11?

- checks and money orders
- business reply mail

There is a minimum charge for all first-class mail weighing up to one ounce. An additional charge is made for each additional ounce or fraction of an ounce. If you are sending material in an oversized envelope that does not bear a preprinted FIRST CLASS notation, print or stamp FIRST CLASS on the envelope. It is illegal to open first-class mail without a federal search warrant.

1. What is the minimum charge for first-class mail weighing up to one ounce?
2. What is the charge for each additional ounce over one ounce? At what weight does the rate change?
3. Why is it illegal to open first-class mail without a search warrant?

First-class mail that weighs over 11 ounces is referred to as priority mail. The maximum weight for priority mail is 70 pounds. Priority mail is usually delivered within two to three days. The amount of postage for priority mail is based on the weight of the item and its destination. A two-pound flat-rate envelope is also available. Any amount of material that fits in the envelope, regardless of weight, may be mailed for the cost of a two-pound priority mail package.

PERIODICALS

Approved publishers and registered news agents may mail publications such as newspapers and periodicals at the periodicals rates of postage. To do so, you need authorization from the USPS, must pay a special fee, and must mail in bulk lots (volume mailings). Other rates, such as first-class or standard mail, must be used when periodicals are mailed by the general public.

STANDARD MAIL

Standard mail (A) is used primarily to advertise products and services Advertising brochures and catalogs often are sent standard class. Charitable organizations may use nonprofit standard mail rates for their large mailings. Mailings must contain at least 200 pieces or weigh 50 pounds to qualify for standard mail rates. Each item must weigh less than 16 ounces.

Standard mail (B), also known as parcel post, may be used for packages, printed matter such as books, and other mailable items. The rates are based on the weight of the item and the distance it must travel to be delivered. Packages may weigh 1 to 70 pounds and measure up to 108 inches in combined length and girth.

MIXED CLASSES OF MAIL

Sometimes it is better to send two pieces of mail of different classes together as a single mailing to make sure they both arrive at the same time. For example, you may attach a first-class invoice to the outside of a large package sent fourth class, or you may enclose a first-class letter in a large envelope or parcel. When a first-class letter is attached, the postage is affixed to each part separately. When a first-class letter is enclosed, its postage is added to the parcel postage on the outside of the package. You should write or stamp the words FIRST-CLASS MAIL ENCLOSED below the postage and above the mailing address. A piece of mixed mail is not treated as first-class mail. The class of mail that the larger piece falls into determines how the mixed mail is handled.

Special Postal Services

In addition to the regular delivery services, special postal services also are available. You must pay a fee for each of these special services. As a worker who processes outgoing mail, you need to know the different

Ask students how they would respond in the following situation:

You work in the mailroom of a large company. James, a new employee, approaches carrying a large package and says, "I have a few questions about how to mail this package. A first-class letter is enclosed in the package. Does that mean this piece of mixed mail will be treated as first-class mail? How do I identify on the package that first-class mail is enclosed? How is the postage calculated?"

Prepare a response to each of James's questions.

Ask students to determine the following:

1. Which companies in your area offer express mail delivery service within the United States? to Canada? to Europe?
2. What are the guaranteed delivery days and times?
3. Are there any delivery restrictions (for example, deliveries can be made only to cities with airports)?
4. What are the rates for express mail service and what is included with the rate (for example, insurance coverage and/or a receipt)?
5. Are there weight limitations for items (for example, items weighing over 70 pounds) to be sent express mail?

services that are available so you can choose the one best suited to your company's mailing needs.

EXPRESS MAIL

Express mail is the fastest delivery service offered by the USPS. Overnight delivery is available to many locations. Documents or packages to be sent by express mail can be mailed at designated express mail post offices or collection boxes. On-demand pickup is also available in many areas.

You may send any mailable item weighing up to 70 pounds by express mail. Express mail rates are based on the weight of the item and the distance it must travel. A two-pound flat-rate envelope is also available. Any amount of material that fits in the envelope, regardless of weight, may be mailed for the cost of a two-pound priority mail package. The rates include insurance coverage, record of delivery, and a receipt.

Illustration 12-2:12

The United States Postal Service and many private courier services offer express mail services.

SPECIAL DELIVERY AND SPECIAL HANDLING

Special Delivery mail is handled with the same promptness given to first-class mail. In addition, it is given immediate delivery within prescribed hours and distances. The fees charged are in addition to the regular postage and vary according to the weight of the letter or parcel. The mail must be marked SPECIAL DELIVERY. This service is available for all classes of mail.

For a fee in addition to regular postage, packages may receive **special handling service.** Packages marked SPECIAL HANDLING travel with first-class mail between cities. At the post office, special handling packages are processed before standard mail, but after priority mail. They are delivered on regularly scheduled trips.

REGISTERED OR INSURED MAIL

Mail can be registered to give protection to valuable items such as money, checks, jewelry, stock certificates, and bonds, as well as important papers including contracts, bills of sale, leases, mortgages, deeds, wills, and other vital business records. All classes of mail may be registered, but the first-class rate must be paid.

Mail may be registered for any amount. The post office, however, will only pay claims up to $25,000, regardless of the amount for which the package was registered. You will be given a receipt showing that the post office has accepted your registered mail for transmittal and delivery. For an additional fee, you may obtain a *return receipt* to prove that the mail was delivered.

Mail may be insured for up to $500 against loss or damage. A receipt is issued to the sender of insured mail. You should keep the receipt on file until you know that the insured mail has arrived in satisfactory condition. If an insured parcel is lost or damaged, the post office will **reimburse** you for the value of the merchandise or the amount for which it was insured, whichever is smaller.

reimburse: pay back

PROOF OF MAILING OR DELIVERY

An inexpensive way to obtain proof that an item was mailed is to purchase a **Certificate of Mailing.** The certificate is not proof of delivery; it serves only as proof that the item was mailed. If you want proof of mailing and delivery, send the item by **certified mail.** Certified mail provides a receipt for the sender and a record of delivery.

COD MAIL

A company may send merchandise to a buyer and collect payment for the item when it is delivered. Mail sent in this manner is referred to as

Ask students to refer to Illustration 12-2:13 to answer the following:

1. To whom and from whom was the item sent?
2. On what date was the item delivered?
3. Where specifically was the item delivered?

prepaid:
paid in advance

COD—collect on delivery. The seller may obtain COD service by paying a fee in addition to the regular postage. Since fees and postage must be **prepaid** by the seller, the seller often specifies that the total COD charges to be collected from the buyer include the postage and the collect-on-delivery fee. The maximum amount collectible on one package is $500. If the company you work for did not order an item that arrives COD, do not accept the package.

Illustration 12-2:13

Certified mail receipt. To whom was the item sent? Where specifically was the item delivered?

Is your RETURN ADDRESS completed on the reverse side?

SENDER:
- Complete items 1 and/or 2 for additional services.
- Complete items 3, 4a, and 4b.
- Print your name and address on the reverse of this form so that we can return this card to you.
- Attach this form to the front of the mailpiece, or on the back if space does not permit
- Write "Return Receipt Requested" on the mailpiece below the article number
- The Return Receipt will show to whom the article was delivered and the date delivered.

I also wish to receive the following services (for an extra fee):
1. ☒ Addressee's Address
2. ☐ Restricted Delivery

Consult postmaster for fee.

3. Article Addressed to:
MR ROLAND G FREED
FREED-HOLLIS INC
101 WATERFORD PIKE
EVANSVILLE IN 47708-6711

4a. Article Number

4b. Service Type
☐ Registered ☒ Certified
☐ Express Mail ☐ Insured
☐ Return Receipt for Merchandise ☐ COD

7. Date of Delivery
8/22/97

5. Received By: *(Print Name)*
Clyde Faulkner

6. Signature: *(Addressee or Agent)*
X Clyde Faulkner

8. Addressee's Address *(Only if requested and fee is paid)*
Delivered to mailroom at Freed-Hollis, Inc.

PS Form **3811**, December 1994 Domestic Return Receipt

Thank you for using Return Receipt Service.

International Mail

Many companies send mail to other countries. A company may have branch offices or customers in countries throughout the world. Postage for letters and postal cards mailed to Mexico is the same as that for letters and cards mailed within the United States. Rates for mail going to all other countries are higher and the mail weights are limited. Contact your local post office for current rates and weight limitations. Overseas parcel post packages must be packed very carefully to ensure safe delivery. A customs declaration form that accurately and completely describes the contents must be attached to each parcel.

Assign one or more foreign cities to each student. Ask students to research proper address formats for their cities, as well as the appropriate postage for a first-class letter mailed to their cities.

Private Courier/Delivery Service

Many companies use a private courier/delivery service rather than the USPS, especially when a guaranteed delivery time is required. Most cities are served by several companies that deliver both locally and nationwide. Check under Delivery Service in the yellow pages of the telephone directory for a listing of companies in your area. You will want to ask about services and fees in order to identify the courier that best meets your needs.

You must prepare a delivery form to accompany the package that includes information such as:

- your name, address, and phone number
- the recipient's name, address, and phone number
- the class of delivery service
- the weight of the package
- the current date
- the payment method or account number

If you use the courier often, the courier may provide you with forms that are preprinted with your name, address, and account number. Completing the entire delivery form accurately is essential for prompt delivery. Private courier/delivery services do not deliver to a post office box.

Interoffice Mail

In a small company, processing interoffice mail may involve hand-delivering a memo from one worker to another. In a large company, however, interoffice mail is collected from the departments, sorted in the mailroom, and redistributed to the appropriate department or individuals. Interoffice mail envelopes usually differ in color and size from envelopes used for mail going outside the company. That way, interoffice mail will not be sent to the post office accidentally.

In addition to the USPS, many companies also use private courier and delivery services. Ask students to identify the private services that are available in the local community. Ask students to consider what local companies are likely to be the primary users of such services.

You may want to obtain brochures from Western Union that describe the electronic mail services it offers. Circulate the brochures to students as you discuss the variety of electronic mail services available, such as telegrams and mailgrams. Or have students visit the Western Union website at *http://www.wucs.com*

Telegrams and Mailgrams

viable: workable, feasible

Telecommunications technology makes it possible to transmit data electronically from one location to another. As a result, you may work in an office where electronic mail services are used as a **viable** alternative to traditional mail services. Two electronic mail services available through Western Union are described below. Electronic mail will be discussed in detail in Chapter 14.

A **telegram** is a message transmitted by Western Union. The two types of telegrams are voice delivery and physical delivery telegrams. Voice delivery telegrams are delivered by phone within two hours and followed by a printed copy via Mailgram. Physical delivery telegrams are hand-delivered to the recipient the same day if sent by 1:00 p.m. EST. Charges for messages are based on a minimum number of words, with an extra charge for each additional word.

A **mailgram** is a message transmitted by Western Union to the post office that serves the ZIP Code of the addressee. At the post office, the mailgram is printed, inserted in an envelope, and delivered with the regularly scheduled mail. Mailgrams are a speedy and economical way to send longer messages. Charges are based on groups of 50 words. A mailgram is less expensive than a telegram, and delivery is guaranteed by the next day.

Reviewing the Topic

1. How is a window envelope different from a standard envelope?
2. When would a volume mailing be used?
3. What is an optical character reader (OCR)?
4. What address format does the postal service recommend for use on outgoing envelopes?
5. Name the various classes of domestic mail.
6. What is priority mail? What is its weight restriction?
7. What is the difference between special delivery and special handling?
8. Under what circumstances would you use COD mail?
9. Why should interoffice mail be placed in envelopes distinctly different from those used to send mail by the postal service?
10. Describe two electronic mail services available through Western Union.

INTERACTING WITH OTHERS

You work in an office where the mail is picked up by postal workers twice a day, at 10:30 a.m. and 2:45 p.m. Monday afternoon you receive a call from the regional vice president in a branch office. He needs six copies of the company's annual report by Wednesday. If the reports are in the 2:45 p.m. mail today, they will be delivered on Wednesday. You gather the annual reports, place them in a large envelope, and take them to the mailroom. You explain to Glenna, a mailroom worker, that the envelope must go with the 2:45 p.m. mail pickup. Glenna says she understands.

Later in the day, you call Glenna to verify that the annual reports were sent. Glenna sheepishly replies that she was on break at 2:45. When she returned, she noticed that the postal carrier had overlooked the envelope. The annual reports were not mailed.

topic 12-2 review

Outgoing Mail Procedures

609

You are very annoyed. Should you tell Glenna how you feel? If so, what should you tell her? Should you report this incident to Glenna's supervisor? How can you and Glenna work together to solve this problem?

The reports still need to be sent. How would you suggest that Glenna mail the reports so that they reach the vice president by Wednesday?

What you are to do:

In small groups, prepare a response to the questions raised. Share your responses with your class.

REINFORCING MATH SKILLS

An envelope has been prepared for each address on a mailing list of 18,000 names. The mailing machine can feed, seal, meter-stamp, count, and stack 200 envelopes a minute. Of the 18,000 envelopes being processed, 20 percent are being sent to Minnesota, 30 percent to Wyoming, 15 percent to Wisconsin, and 35 percent to Nebraska.

What you are to do:

1. Calculate how long it will take to process all the envelopes using the mailing machine.
2. Calculate how many envelopes will be sent to each state.

topic 12-2 review

APPLICATION ACTIVITIES

ACTIVITY 1 Calculating Postage On Mail

You work in a small office. You need to determine the correct postage for the following items you have been given to mail.

a. A package weighing 4 3/4 pounds to be sent parcel post to Ann Arbor, Michigan
b. A letter weighing three ounces to be sent by express mail (post office to addressee) to Camden, Maine
c. A 12-ounce package containing a printed report to be sent by first-class mail to Santa Barbara, California
d. A two-ounce letter to be sent by first-class certified mail to Denver, Colorado
e. A ten-ounce letter to be sent to a local bank

610

What you are to do:

Figure the amount of postage needed to send each item listed. Use your town as the origination point in figuring the postage. Consult current USPS rate charts, or call your local post office and ask for assistance. Create a document that lists the items to be mailed and the correct postage for each item.

ACTIVITY 2 Folding Mail

You are responsible for inserting outgoing mail into envelopes before delivering them to the mailroom to be sealed and stamped. Today you have mail that must be inserted into No. 6 3/4 envelopes, No. 10 envelopes, and No. 10 window envelopes.

What you are to do:

1. Label a blank sheet of paper No. 10 Standard. Fold the paper properly to fit into a No. 10 standard envelope.
2. Label a blank sheet of paper No. 6 3/4. Fold the paper properly to fit into a No. 6 3/4 envelope.
3. Label a blank sheet of paper No. 10 window. Fold the paper properly to fit into a No. 10 window envelope.

611

12 Chapter Summary

In this chapter, you learned the procedures for processing both incoming and outgoing mail. You should be knowledgeable about the following key points:

- The extent of your mail-related tasks will depend on the size of the company, the volume of mail handled, and your job duties.
- To speed the processing of incoming mail, some companies use electric envelope openers, rotary units to help sort mail, and automated delivery systems.
- Classes of domestic mail include express, first-class, priority, periodicals, and standard. Special postal services are available such as registered mail, insured mail, and certified mail.
- To expedite the processing of outgoing mail, some companies use electronic postage scales, postage meters, computer-generated mailing lists, and automated equipment for addressing, labeling, folding, and inserting mail.
- The USPS uses electronic equipment such as optical character readers and bar code sorters to speed mail to its destination. You can help speed the process by following USPS address format guidelines and by using nine-digit ZIP Codes.
- Telecommunications technology makes it possible to electronically transmit messages from one location to another. Telegrams and mailgrams are examples of electronic mail.

KEY CONCEPTS AND TERMS

annotate
certified mail
express mail
first-class mail
interoffice mail
mailgram
mailroom
optical character reader (OCR)
postage meter
priority mail
registered mail
special delivery
special handling
standard mail
telegram
volume mailing
ZIP code

INTEGRATED CHAPTER ACTIVITY

ACTIVITY Creating a Mailing List

You work as an office assistant at Chaparral Cheese Company. Your supervisor approaches your workstation and says, "Here is a list of this month's new mail-order customers. When you key the names and addresses, please group them by state. Use alphabetic order to arrange the customers within each state. Use the all-caps, no punctuation format recommended by the USPS, the appropriate two-letter state abbreviations, and the ZIP + 4 codes. Spell out the abbreviations I have circled on the list."

What you are to do:

1. Create a mailing list using the customer addresses on page 614. Sort the list as requested by your supervisor. Refer to Reference Section E for a listing of standard two-letter abbreviations and to page 600 in the textbook for an example of the address format recommended by the USPS.
2. Print the mailing list on a sheet of plain paper. If it is possible in your software, print the postal bar codes with each address.

challenge option

Ask students to make the following changes to the customer list:

1. Change Linda Wood's ZIP code to 70112-4686.
2. Change Darryl Brandon's address to 50 Sand Dunes Way.
3. Add Apt. 143 to Kiki Mashusa's address.
4. Delete Ralph Narcissi's name and address and add Mr. Douglas C. Wayland, 1195 Foxmore Drive, Maineville, OH 45039-1140.

See Reference Section E on Workbook page 227.

chapter 12
summary

Mail-Order Customers

Mr. Jerry M. Osterman
1906 N. Market Street
Shreveport, Louisiana
71107-4568

Miss Linda A. Wood
301 Rue Dauphine
New Orleans, Louisiana
70112-4688

Mr. Richard Wiegand
12 Roderick St.
Morgan City, Louisiana
70380-1233

Mrs. Sherri E. Sempf
101 Pinckney Place
Howell, Michigan
48843-2638

Ms. Sandra B. Sholl
301 Centerville Road
Sturgis, Michigan
49091-8244

Mrs. Susan Curlovich
927 Mt. Royal Circle
Apartment 16-G Apt 16-G
Roanoke, Virginia 24014-7634

Dr. Ralph D. Narcissi
95 Staples Mills Road
Richmond, Virginia
23230-4433

Mr. Robert J. Caldwell
373 Pleasant Valley Road
Harrisonburg, Virginia
22801-6624

Ms. Debe M. Behun
61 Jefferson Avenue
Newport News, Virginia
23605-7124

Mr. Darryl M. Brandon
50 Sand Dunes Drive
Monterey, California
93940-4524

Miss Karen S. Bentz
2563 La Paz Road
Laguna Beach, California
92653-4179

Dr. Diane C. Arnold
111 Colorado Ave.
Santa Monica, California
90401-3679

Miss Judi Nalitz
7911 St. Armonds Way
Sarasota, Florida
33577-3912

Ms. Kiki L. Mashusa
555 Sailfish Drive
St. Augustine, Florida
32084-1143

614

Blake Williams
Office Manager

Getting Acquainted with the World of Work

Overwhelmed!

Dear Mr. Williams

Last month I was hired as a mailroom worker by a growing company that had recently created a separate mail department. I want to be an efficient worker, yet I feel overwhelmed by all the postal regulations and services that are available. There is so much to learn so fast! How will I ever learn it all?

Dennis from Tucson

Dear Dennis

I have good news. You do not have to learn it all! Even postal workers must look up answers to questions from time to time.

There are two postal publications that are excellent references: the Post Office Directory *and the* ZIP Code Directory. *You might suggest to your supervisor that the company buy these publications. Those who work in a small company that does not have a mailroom can also benefit from having these publications on hand.*

You and your coworkers can stay current on postal matters by subscribing to the Postal Bulletin *(a weekly publication) or to the* Memo to Mailers *(a monthly publication). There is even a Postal Customer Council your company can join. You also might plan to attend USPS-sponsored seminars that cover such topics as ZIP + 4 and cost-saving ideas for bulk mail.*

You can save your company money by being aware of the full range of postal services. The initiative you show on your job in the mailroom will surely be noticed and rewarded. Take advantage of this opportunity to learn the names of all the workers in your company. Practice your organizational skills. Since your mail department is newly formed, there will be "glitches" in the system that must be worked out. Exercise your problem-solving abilities in dealing with such situations. Both you and the company will benefit. Good luck.

Blake Williams

Office Manager

615

getting started GO

Telecommunication technology is rapidly changing both the way we conduct business and the way we live. We are able to reach all parts of the world instantly to transmit not only our voices, but also pictures, videos, and data. In the past, workers relied mainly on telephones, typewriters, and the post office to exchange ideas and data. Today's workers must be able to use a variety of communications equipment. They must possess strong communications skills to be able to handle the demands of increased interactions with others. Encourage students to observe different ways in which all types of information are being transmitted when they visit their bank, the library, the airport, the mall, and other places. Also, they should ask older adults what changes they have seen in telecommunications in the last 10 or 20 years and how such changes have affected the way tasks are performed at work. Throughout the presentation of this chapter, highlight the importance of the role of the worker in assuring effective use of new technology.

Telephone Systems and Procedures

Today's telephone technologies play a key role in the demand for worldwide communications. Capabilities of telephone systems continue to be enhanced by computerization. Data, text, images, and video as well as voice can be transmitted across the country or around the world with new, state-of-the-art equipment.

As a worker in today's global workplace, you will use a variety of technologies as well as the telephone for your daily communications with others located all over the world. These technologies will continue to evolve as organizations search for ways to increase productivity, efficiency, and the quality of customer service. You must continue to educate yourself and seek out information about changing communications advancements. In this chapter you will become familiar with telephone equipment and services, learn to use effective telephone procedures, and become aware of emerging telephone technology.

Telephone Technology and Services

When you have completed your study of this topic, you will be able to:

- **identify methods of transmitting information (voice, data, text, video, and images) using telephone technology**
- **describe equipment and features of image and voice communication systems**
- **describe effective procedures for using image and voice transmission systems**
- **discuss emerging telephone technologies**

Topic 13-1

Advancements in the way we communicate information have made it easier and faster than ever before to send voice, text, or video messages to others. We can now transmit documents and exchange information with coworkers who are as close as an office across the hall or on another continent 10,000 or more miles away.

Telephone technology is a vital part of today's fast-growing communications industry. A company's communication needs determine what telephone technologies it chooses. As a worker in today's changing workplace, you will benefit from learning about the many features of telephone equipment, telephone services, and the integration of telephone technologies with computers.

Telecommunications is the electronic transfer of information over a distance. All forms of information (voice, video, data, text, and images

1. The Internet provides a wealth of information about telecommunications. Encourage students to visit the websites of major telephone service providers to gather the most up-to-date information about equipment, special features, rates, and emerging telephony technologies.
2. Invite a representative from a telephone equipment retail store to speak to the class about the equipment available for sale to the business as well as the private customer. Many telephone retail store representatives will also present tips for successful telephone techniques and procedures as well as instruction on the use of the equipment.
3. If possible, plan a visit to a company that has a state-of-the-art telecommunications system. Suggestions include: government or military facilities, telemarketing or answering service businesses, the local cable television company and local television station, reservation centers, and international organizations.

such as photographs, drawings, and graphs) can be sent electronically. In today's Information Age, workers depend on their ability to access and transmit up-to-date information quickly and reliably.

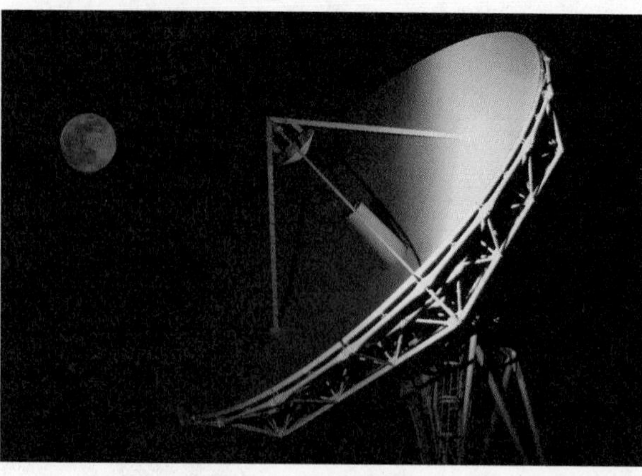

Illustration 13-1:1
Telecommunications technology enables us to communicate globally.

Transmitting Information Using Telephone Technology

Methods of sending information across the country or around the world include telephone lines, communication satellites, microwave towers, and radio signals. Telephone lines and communication satellites will be discussed in this chapter.

TELEPHONE LINES

When you place a telephone call, use a facsimile machine, or transfer information from one computer to another, the information usually travels over telephone lines as either **analog** or **digital** signals. Most companies are replacing older analog lines with digital lines because digital signals can transmit larger quantities of information at faster speeds. This means your electronic message (a letter, a long report, or a chart) is received quickly and reliably. Business computer output is digital rather than analog.

analog: the type of signals that are transmitted over most telephone lines

digital: the way signals are transmitted in a computer

convert: change, make compatible

Some communication systems continue to use only analog signals. They require a device called a modem, which is used to **convert** the

Innovations in transmission of all types of information are continuously increasing the speed and the quality of communicating across distances.

digital output of a computer into analog signals that can be transmitted over telephone lines. A modem can be internal (installed inside the computer case) or external (a separate, attached device outside the computer case).

COMMUNICATION SATELLITES

Satellites play an important part in worldwide communication systems. A communication satellite is a transmitter/receiver relay station that orbits the earth. A satellite dish is a transmitter/receiver relay station that remains stationary, on earth. Satellite dishes receive microwave signals bounced to earth from an orbiting communications satellite. They also send voice, video, and data communications in the form of microwave signals to the space satellite.

> *Jeorge must send a price quote from his office in Miami to a customer in London. Using the company fax machine, he sends the price list to London in minutes via a worldwide satellite communication network.*

Image Communication Systems

Telecommunications technology is used to transmit and receive images in many forms. Text, photographs, video, blueprints, drawings, diagrams, graphs, and statistical information are examples of images that are frequently sent from one location to another. Two common image communication systems, facsimile and videoconferencing, will be explained.

FACSIMILE TECHNOLOGY

Facsimile, often called *fax*, transfers images (text, photographs, drawings) electronically using telephone lines. Fax machines are an easy-to-use, convenient, relatively inexpensive, fast way to transmit and receive information.

Facsimile technology is such an everyday part of communications that fax machines have become a necessity in offices. A company may have one or many facsimile machines. They may have desktop or portable models, which can be used to transmit and receive documents while workers are away from the office. Fax machines are also being purchased

Explain how a modem works. The modem connected to the sending PC converts the digital signals to analog signals so that the information can be sent over the analog telephone lines. When the analog signals reach their destination, a modem at that location converts the telephone line's analog signals to digital signals that the receiving PC can understand.

Communications satellites have contributed greatly to creating a global community. Have students watch a cable news channel (such as *CNN World Headline News*) and list the countries from which live broadcast reports are made.

1. If you have fax software, demonstrate how to send a fax from a PC to a fax machine. Demonstrate use of facsimile transmittal cover sheet templates available in today's word processing software. Browse through the available templates and discuss the elements of each.
2. Take students to the location of a fax machine in your school—perhaps in the library, in the school's administrative offices, or in the reprographics center. After instruction and demonstration, with the cooperation of the staff, allow students to send faxes.

for personal use in homes. You can have a fax installed as an option in your car. Airlines are even upgrading in-flight telephone services to include facsimile.

compatible:
able to work together

As long as the sending and receiving machines are **compatible,** facsimiles can communicate with each other to send and receive images. Scanning technology is combined with telephone technology. The sending facsimile machine scans a page and encodes (electronically "takes a picture of") the information to be sent. The information is transmitted over telephone lines to a receiving facsimile machine. Within seconds, the document is reproduced as an exact copy—or "facsimile."

Fax machine to fax machine is not the only method of transmitting documents as images. An image can also be sent over telephone lines from a computer directly to a fax machine. The computer must have a special fax circuit card and software to control the process. Documents can also be received at the computer from a fax machine.

Illustration 13-1:2
Facsimile machines speed the process of sending and receiving images.

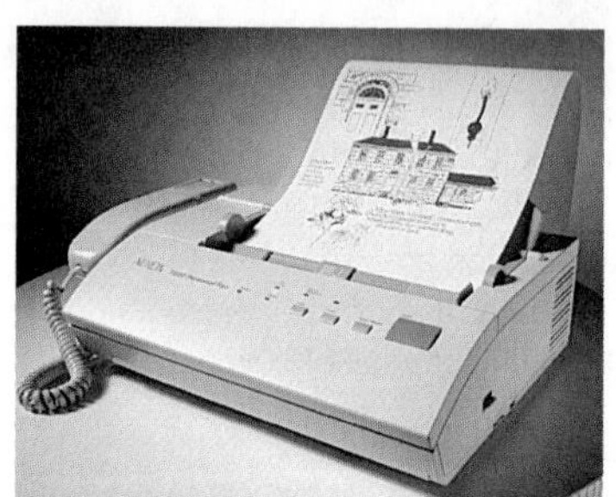

Laticia works for an environmental waste firm in Phoenix that has branch offices in Denver, St. Louis, and Salt Lake City. This morning she receives a typical assignment. An engineer in her office needs to send a copy of project plan changes that are in a word processor document file as soon as possible to a supervisor with a portable fax machine at a customer's waste system construction site outside Denver. Using her computer equipped with a fax card, Laticia is able to send the document within minutes from her computer to the portable fax machine near the Denver office.

Features. Facsimile machines offer many features. Among the more common features are:

- laser or full-color printing
- store-and-forward capability
- automatic dialing and redialing if the receiving number is busy
- automatic answering without a human attendant
- automatic document feed
- activity-reporting of date, time, and number of pages sent and received
- small screens that display messages such as information about transmission and errors or problems with the system
- security features

The automatic answering feature makes fax systems almost self-operating. Most users leave their machines on 24 hours a day, unattended, for receiving messages.

Procedures. Procedures for using facsimile machines vary from office to office and from machine to machine. Many procedures depend upon the sending and receiving equipment to be used. When you are sending information from one fax machine to another, here are some common procedures you may follow for successful transmission:

1. Prepare a facsimile transmission cover sheet or use a word processing template with the following information: current date; total pages being sent including the transmission sheet; name, company name, and address of the recipient of the message; fax number of the recipient; your name, company name, address, telephone number, and fax number; subject of the document or message; and any special remarks you wish to include.
2. Check the accuracy of your count of the number of pages to be sent and the number of pages you recorded on the transmission sheet.
3. Place the pages to be transmitted in the feed tray of the fax machine.

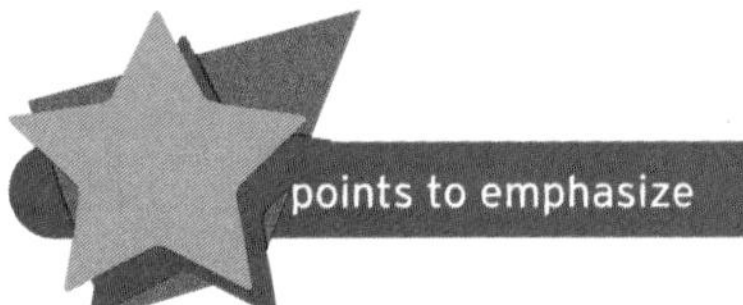

Most fax machines are easy to use; however, features and procedures vary from office to office and machine to machine.

1. Who is sending this fax?
2. Who is receiving the fax?
3. What is the fax number of the recipient of the message?
4. What information is being transmitted?
5. What does the transmission report tell the sender?

Instead of fax transmittal sheets, many fax users include the transmission data in a special header at the top of the document. This is the usual practice when faxing a document from a PC to a fax machine.

Illustration 13-1:3

Fax transmission cover sheet (top) and transmission report (bottom)

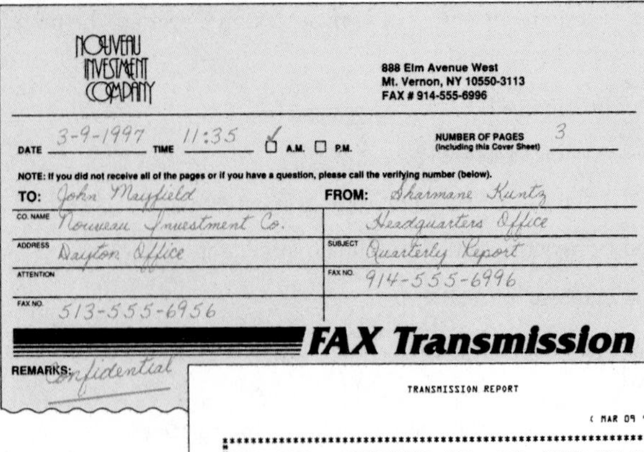

NOUVEAU INVESTMENT COMPANY

888 Elm Avenue West
Mt. Vernon, NY 10550-3113
FAX # 914-555-6996

DATE 3-9-1997 TIME 11:35 ☑ A.M. ☐ P.M. NUMBER OF PAGES (including this Cover Sheet) 3

NOTE: If you did not receive all of the pages or if you have a question, please call the verifying number (below).

TO: John Mayfield	FROM: Sharmane Kuntz
CO. NAME Nouveau Investment Co.	Headquarters Office
ADDRESS Dayton Office	SUBJECT Quarterly Report
ATTENTION	FAX NO. 914-555-6996
FAX NO. 513-555-6956	

FAX Transmission

REMARKS: Confidential

TRANSMISSION REPORT

(MAR 09 '92 11:40)

DATE	START TIME	REMOTE TERMINAL IDENTIFICATION	MODE	TIME	RESULTS	TOTAL PAGES	DEPT. CODE
MAR 09	11:38	513 555 6956	G3ST	02'02"	OK	03	0231

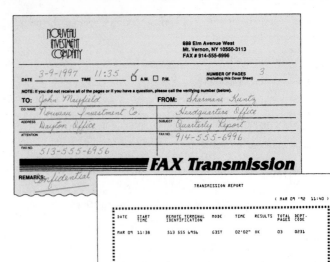

4. Confirm the number and carefully dial the fax number of the recipient.
5. Press the SEND or START button.
6. After all pages have been transmitted, your fax machine will let you know that the transmission has been completed. You may hear a series of beeps or a message may be displayed telling you that your message has been received at the location you dialed.
7. In your office, you may be required to enter your name, department, date, and number of pages transmitted on a fax log sheet.
8. If a report form is printed after each transmission, attach it to the fax cover sheet and return it with the original materials to the sender. In the illustration above, the transmission report includes date, start time of the message, fax number dialed, number of pages sent, and the time used to transmit pages. Note that the results are reported as "OK"—the transmission was successful.

VIDEOCONFERENCING

Videoconferencing is an image communication system that allows people at two or more locations to have two-way voice and video communication. A special conference room equipped with microphones and television cameras and screens is used to conduct meetings in which data, text, voice, and documents may be exchanged.

For example, a group of managers located in Detroit could call a meeting with top management located in the corporate headquarters in San Francisco and a third group of managers located at a branch in Hong Kong. Using videoconferencing technology, they could see and hear each other. Telephone companies are able to provide video services for worldwide conferencing. Fax technology allows the added dimension of document exchange. Videoconferencing is expensive. However, it can be very cost effective when compared to the expense and time required for travel.

Illustration 13-1:4
Videoconferences allow people at different locations to see and hear each other and to exchange information electronically.

Voice Communication Systems

You are very familiar with and have used the most popular voice communication device ever invented—the telephone. Today's telephones are becoming smarter and smarter with each new technological advance. New telephone systems are making voice communication more convenient and are being equipped with features to meet the

points to emphasize

Videoconferencing is expensive. An organization must maintain its own in-house video-conference room equipped with television and telecommunications equipment. Organizations such as hotels or colleges may provide public videoconferencing centers in many locations. It is becoming more and more common for high schools and colleges to have facilities equipped with videoconferencing technology that may be available to the public.

teaching tips

1. If your school system does not have distance learning facilities, chances are a local college or organization does. Visit one of these centers so students can learn how telecommunications is affecting modern educational methods.
2. Have students make a list of advantages and disadvantages of offering courses using distance learning technology.

for discussion

1. What are some special considerations for planning and conducting a videoconference as compared to a regular meeting?
2. What problems might be encountered when conducting a videoconference?

ever-changing variety of user needs in the information age. Some widely used systems and equipment will be discussed here; however, technology is rapidly changing. You must be prepared to constantly become acquainted with new telephone features and equipment as they become available.

Many factors have led to changes in the way companies handle voice communications. Global mergers and the demand for faster, more efficient customer service are two reasons companies have had to consider better methods for handling voice communications. Recent changes in the telephone industry have made telephone service and equipment providers very competitive. This competitiveness has benefited the telephone consumer greatly in better service and lower prices. Companies are able to negotiate for their own **customized** list of equipment and services.

customized: adapted to specific needs

CENTRALIZED SYSTEMS

Centralized telephone systems route calls coming into and going out of an organization. All calls in a centralized system are handled by a single computer or operator switchboard that routes calls to the requested location. Older systems required the assistance of a switchboard operator to answer calls and transfer them to the appropriate department or individual. Many telephone systems in business today are answered by an **automated attendant.** An automated attendant is a computerized system for handling telephone calls.

When an incoming call is answered by an automated attendant, a recorded message is played. Messages vary depending upon company needs. However, the message usually instructs the caller to dial the extension number of the person being sought and may provide the caller with various menu options. Callers make selections using the telephone number keypad. Some systems enable users to select menu options also by speaking the appropriate word or term into the receiver. A computer will identify the spoken command and perform the chosen action. This feature is called **speech recognition.** Additional messages may then instruct and direct the caller.

As you can see, the option of speaking with a switchboard operator is no longer *always* a choice for the caller. Many companies continue to

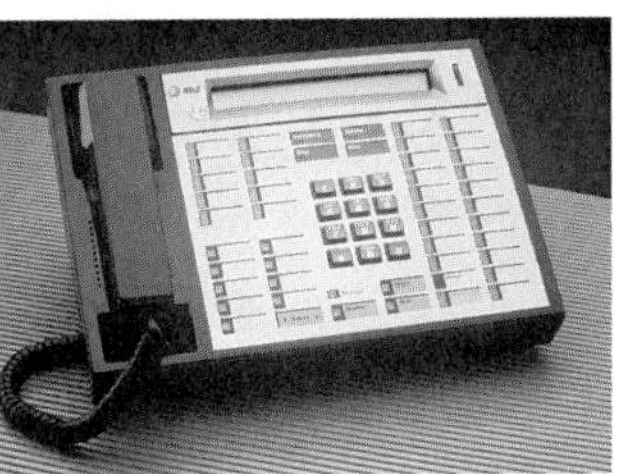

Illustration 13-1:5

Manual switchboards (left) have been replaced by computerized telephone systems (right).

offer an option to speak to a person to provide better service for customers. Some callers prefer to communicate with a person rather than with a computer; others may not have a touch-tone phone, which is usually required for the automated system.

Most callers have adjusted to computerized systems; however, frustration with systems that seem to block human contact is understandable. Businesses must deal with these complaints and do their best to meet callers' needs, thereby preserving good customer relations.

COMMON FEATURES OF TELEPHONE SYSTEMS

Telephone technologies of today are designed to increase your efficiency in handling communication. Many features are available so that you can customize your telephone depending on your duties and responsibilities. The needs of your organization and the size of the system will determine the features available.

A users' manual is generally provided that details procedures for using your telephone keypad to **activate** and **deactivate** all features available. To activate **call forwarding,** for example, you may be instructed to lift the handset, push the * (asterisk, or "star") and 4 keys, listen for a tone, dial the extension number to which you want all incoming calls routed, and hang up. Your incoming calls will then be forwarded and will ring automatically at that extension.

activate:
turn on

deactivate:
turn off

call forwarding:
sending a call automatically to another telephone number

VOICE MAIL SYSTEMS

Voice mail is a messaging system that uses computers and telephones to record, send, store, and retrieve voice messages. Voice messaging systems are popular because they eliminate the problems of time lost

teaching tips

1. Have students visit a local telephone vendor. These are often located in a mall and provide a variety of equipment. Have students collect sales brochures or flyers that show features and prices. Instruct them to make a list of features that are not listed in the illustration and share them with the class.
2. Instruct students to list features of telephones that they or their friends have at home. Most of the features available to businesses are affordable for home use also. Point out that this was not true several years ago.

thinking critically

How do each of these features save the telephone user time? In what way does each feature enhance the effectiveness of a worker's tasks?

1. What is meant by "telephone tag"? How does it interfere with efficiency in an organization?
2. How is voice mail different from simply recording a message on an answering machine?

Illustration 13-1:6

Today's telephone systems provide the business as well as home consumer with many efficient features.

Common Features of Telephone Systems	
Auto redial	Redials automatically the last number dialed by pressing one key.
Call block	Restricts callers from making telephone toll calls or calls for which an extra charge is made.
Call forwarding	Forwards calls automatically to another telephone.
Caller ID	Records or displays the telephone number of the caller.
Call queuing/ Camp on	Reestablishes the connection after a busy signal when both parties are free. The caller does not have to remain on the phone while waiting.
Call return	Redials the number of the last call received for up to half an hour.
Call waiting	Signals (often a beep) an incoming call is waiting while a call is in progress. The first call can be placed on hold while the second call is being answered.
Conferencing	Lets you set up conversations with three or more people at the same time.
Memory	Lets you store and dial numbers at the touch of one button.
Speakerphone	Lets you speak with your hands free.

in playing "telephone tag" or trying to place calls to individuals in different time zones. Most voice mail systems operate 24 hours per day and provide important communication links in an organization.

Each user of a voice messaging system has a voice mailbox. A voice mailbox is a space reserved in a computer to hold recorded voice messages. A caller leaves a voice message that is recorded by the computer and held in storage until the recipient of the message chooses to access it. Unless a message is deleted, it remains in storage and can be accessed later for reference. Because of the ability to store and forward messages, voice mail is sometimes called a store-and-forward voice-messaging system.

Voice Mail Features. Voice mail is not merely an answering machine connected to a telephone. It is a computerized voice-messaging system with many features that can be modified to meet the individual needs of companies. A standard personal computer, a special voice processing card, and voice software are needed. The voice card helps the computer perform many tasks such as understanding and creating touch-tone signals, playing recorded messages, recording sounds, and transfering or retrieving calls. Both the sender and the receiver use the telephone push-buttons to activate and use the features of voice mail. Some of the voice mail features that may be used by companies include:

- long-term incoming message storage capabilities
- message **prioritizing**
- ability to broadcast recorded messages to multiple or all users of the system
- creation of multiple greetings for selection and deselection

prioritizing: ranking in order of importance

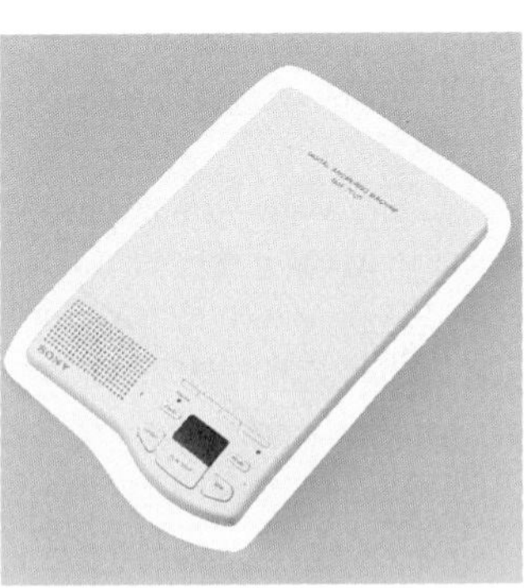

Illustration 13-1:7

Voice mail systems can eliminate the need for answering machines or written messages.

Voice Mail Procedures. Because of the convenience and efficiency of voice mail, its use has become widespread in business. Still, with all its advantages, voice mail does not replace human contact. There are procedures that you can follow to ensure that the negatives of voice mail are reduced and the full benefits are realized.

When Using Your Voice Mail. Follow these procedures to successfully use your voice mail system.

1. Using a tape recorder, have students record appropriate messages for their voice mailboxes. Let them evaluate each other's messages for voice quality, appropriate identification, ample instructions for the caller, and overall professionalism.
2. Invite a representative from a local company that sells voice mail systems to speak to the class about the features of their systems and special training programs they may conduct for new users.
3. Have students practice leaving messages in someone's voice mailbox. Remind them of effective procedures for leaving messages.

What are some advantages and disadvantages of using voice mail? What are the most common abuses of voice mail by users?

- Prepare a message that presents you as a professional and delivers appropriate information and instructions to the caller. Include your name, department, and other necessary information. Give instructions as to how to get immediate assistance if the caller cannot wait for you to return the call.
- Record the message yourself. Speak clearly and distinctly. Pronounce words correctly and use correct grammar.
- If you are going to be out of the office for one or several days, inform callers. Let them know when you will return. Refer them to another worker who can provide help while you are away, if appropriate.
- Check your voice mail several times a day. Return all calls as soon as possible. It is unprofessional to ignore a caller who requests your response or to wait days to return the call.
- Answer your telephone when you are at your desk unless you have visitors in your office or are involved in an important work project. Voice mail can be used for screening purposes. However, do not let voice mail answer your phone for you the majority of the time when you are at your desk. Callers find overuse of voice mail annoying and frustrating.
- Know the features of your voice mail system. Many system vendors provide training and operation manuals for users. If you are aware of your system's features and use them correctly, you can increase the effectiveness of your communications skills used on the job.

When You Are the Caller. There are helpful procedures you can follow when leaving messages for others on their voice mail systems.

- Leave your name, telephone number, company, and a brief reason for your call. Make your message neither too lengthy nor too brief. You want the person you called to have enough information to return your call promptly and efficiently.
- Speak slowly and distinctly. Spell out any difficult names (your name, your company's name).
- Do not communicate bad news or negative statements in the voice message. Wait until you actually speak with the person to convey any negative information.

SPECIALIZED TELEPHONE EQUIPMENT

Telephone technology innovations have resulted in a **diverse** choice of equipment for the consumer. A variety of mobile telephone equipment choices are available to help the traveler stay in touch with the office or home. Whether in an automobile, an airplane, or in a meeting with a client anywhere in the world, there is a telephone product that can provide a communication link. Other specialized equipment are speakerphones, which amplify a caller's voice, and videophones, which provide face-to-face visual contact. Telephone equipment to meet the growing demands and special needs of consumers is making communications easier and more convenient for everyone.

diverse: varied, different

Mobile Telephone Equipment. The nature of business communications today makes it necessary for business workers to have ready access to voice communication systems wherever they are. They may be traveling by car, train, or airplane. They may be visiting customers in locations outside the country. They may have been called away from the company on personal business. There is a method and a product available for them to communicate with their business wherever they are. To enable traveling, out-of-the-office workers to remain productive, in touch, and accessible, wireless services are growing to meet demands. You will learn about three of these products.

Cellular Telephones. Cellular telephones use wireless, radio frequencies to transmit voice across geographic segments called cells. When you dial a mobile telephone number, the radio signal "switches" from

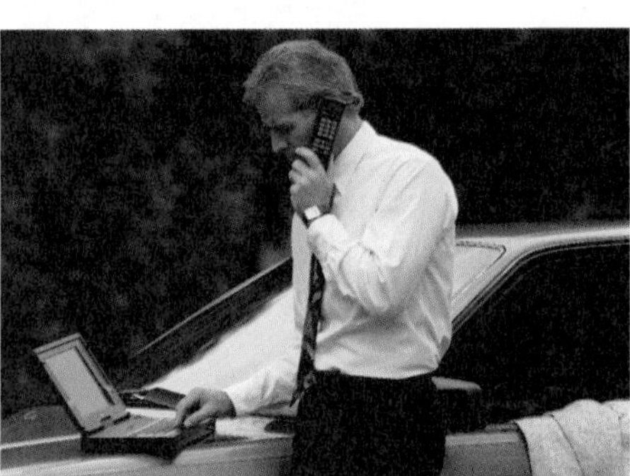

Illustration 13-1:8

Mobile telephones allow workers to keep in touch with the office wherever they are.

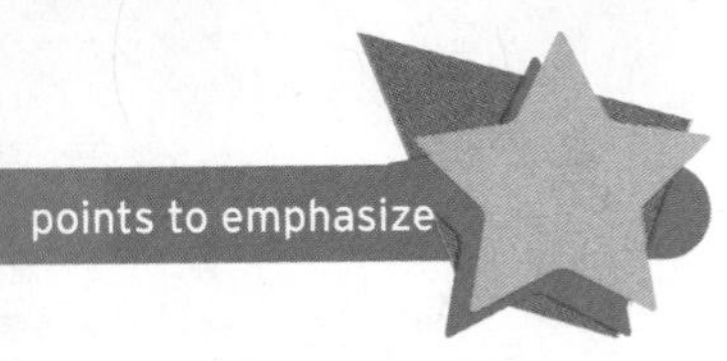

points to emphasize

The popularity of cellular telephones for business use is increasing rapidly. Units have become smaller, more efficient, and less costly.

cell to cell until the right number is reached. Mobile service providers furnish the user with the transmission.

Cellular phones have familiar telephone features such as call forwarding, call waiting, and automatic redial. They are designed to be portable, lightweight, and small. You may use them in your automobile or carry them in your briefcase to use wherever you are.

Pagers. Pagers are very small devices that alert the user of the need to respond by telephone to whomever has sent the "page." Early pagers got the attention of the user with audio beeper signals. They became known as "beepers" because of the sounds they made. Today's pagers use a variety of signals such as vibrations, voice, and digital readout. The recipient of the signal should respond as soon as possible by finding the nearest telephone to call the number on the readout or to call the office.

Illustration 13-1:9

Pagers alert the user that a telephone response is requested to the page.

Airphones. The need for travelers to communicate with their offices or customers even while flying has resulted in airlines accommodating this need. Airplanes are now equipped with telephones that are available for use by passengers for placing calls. Telephones may be positioned at passenger seats or at a location made available by the flight staff. Since these telephones work while in flight, they are called airphones.

Speakerphones and Videophones. Speakerphones may be regular desk telephones or large console models used mainly for conferences.

Illustration 13-1:10
Airphones allow a traveler in flight to communicate with someone on the ground.

Speakerphones amplify voices and allow you to speak without use of the handset. They are used frequently for calls with several participants at either or both ends of the connection.

Videophones, also called **picturephones,** allow participants to actually see each other while they talk. Videophones are used most frequently in conference calls when more than two pople are communicating with each other. Videophones provide an opportunity to see facial expressions and can be an asset in getting to know the caller. Some videophones make use of your computer monitor or television set as a viewing screen.

Illustration 13-1:11
Videophones allow callers to see each other and make communicating by phone more personal.

What are some reasons people may resist videophone use? What would be the advantages of using picturephones for everyday telephone communications?

Features for Impairments. Special telephone equipment and services are available for the visually or hearing impaired. Features that enable the blind, deaf, hard-of-hearing, or speech disabled to communicate on the telephone with others include text telephone (TTY) and the telebraille telephone (TB). With these services a telephone company employee serves as an "interpreter" between the hearing person and the deaf or blind person. The messages are relayed by the telephone assistant by typing the spoken words, which are relayed to the TTY or TB user verbatim. The blind person reads the **Braille;** the deaf person reads the screen.

Braille:
a system that enables the blind to read by feeling a pattern of raised dots

Other features for impaired callers include:

- large-button phones
- headsets or speakerphones for hands-free operation
- speech amplifiers to make voices louder
- loud bells and flashing light indicators

teaching tips

Have students research special telephone features or equipment available for people with impairments to expand the list given here. They may use the Internet or contact the local telephone company. Information about special services may be found in your local telephone directory.

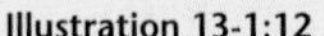

Illustration 13-1:12

Specialized equipment and services are available for telephone users with impairments.

Conference Call Services. At times it may be necessary to place calls that will have three or more participants speaking at different locations with voice-only communication. These are known as conference calls. Decisions may require input from busy individuals who are in different locations. Staff meetings, sales conferences, problem-solving discussions, or any type of information sharing that must take place quickly can be arranged conveniently with a conference call. Conference calls may be handled in several ways: with the user's own equipment, operator-dialed service, or dial-in service.

You may use your own telephone equipment to set up a conference call within a centralized, in-house telephone system. No outside help is needed from a telephone company service provider.

With operator-dialed service, a long-distance operator handles the setup and connections. After you inform the operator of the date, time, time zone, and estimated length of the call, the operator

- informs all participants of the time that the conference call will take place
- makes all the necessary connections at the prescribed time
- calls the roll to make sure all callers are connected
- can provide specialized services such as a recording or written transcript of the conference, or a translator for those who do not understand the main language used.

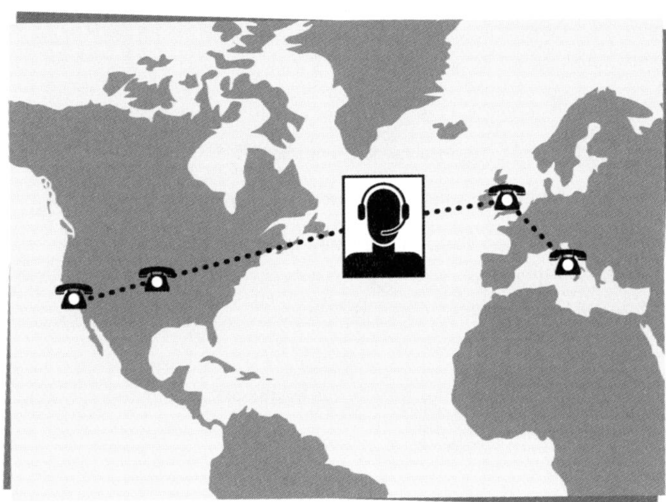

Illustration 13-1:13

An operator can arrange a conference call for several participants in various locations.

Dial-in service allows participants to call a special number at a prearranged time without operator assistance. They may call from any telephone rather than wait for an operator to call them at one specific number.

Successful conference calls require advance planning to ensure that all the necessary information and equipment are at hand. Follow these guidelines in planning a conference call:

- Inform all participants of the date, time, and proposed length of the call.
- Verify everyone's telephone number.
- Send any needed information or items for discussion to all participants in advance.
- Identify the objectives and intended outcomes of the call.
- Call your service provider in advance and give accurate numbers, names, date, time, and expected duration of the call.

Participating in a conference call requires use of your best communication skills. Think of the conference call as a type of meeting where you will both contribute to the conversation and listen to others. Follow these procedures during the call:

- Take roll. Call out names of all participants.
- Lead the call by presenting the agenda and conference guidelines.
- Have participants identify themselves when speaking.
- Speak clearly, spelling out difficult or unusual names and terms. Repeat numbers.
- Avoid interrupting other speakers. Only one person should speak at a time.
- Take notes of important points and comments.
- Apply good listening skills.
- Encourage discussion and participation from everyone.

Telephone Service Providers

Telephone systems may be purchased from many independent vendors who offer a variety of equipment in all price ranges. Many of these providers will customize features, conduct training, and offer product support to purchasers.

Your local telephone company provides services to all users within a specified local area. You can choose your own long-distance carrier for services beyond your local calling area. Long-distance carriers such as MCI, Sprint, AT&T, and Excel are very competitive in their marketing and pricing. They offer many services and features for businesses and other consumers. Carefully compare prices and services before choosing a long-distance service provider.

LONG DISTANCE RATE PERIODS		
Rates	Hours	Days
Weekday full rate	8 a.m. to 5 p.m.	Monday through Friday
Evening discount rate	5 p.m. to 11 p.m.	Monday through Friday and Sunday
Night and weekend discount rate	11 p.m. to 8 a.m.	Every day
	All day	Saturday
	8 a.m. to 5 p.m.	Sunday

Illustration 13-1:14

This chart shows a sample of one long-distance carrier's rate periods for direct-dial calls.

Integration of Telecommunications Technologies

Today's information technologies are integrated. This means that machines that once performed only a single function can now be linked with other machines to expand their capabilities and speed the flow of information. For example, computers can electronically transmit information to printers, to photocopiers, to facsimile machines,

teaching tips

1. Instruct students to locate their latest telephone billing statement and examine it to find the service provider they are using for long-distance calls. Have them divide into small teams and summarize and report their findings about long-distance rates, extended local area rates, special services, and all types of charges.
2. Explain the parts of a telephone billing statement.

and to other computers. They can transmit information to one or all of these almost instantly.

interface: connection

A digital revolution is taking place in the telecommunications industry that integrates previously separate technologies through a standardized, digital network. Integrated Services Digital Network (ISDN) is not an actual network, but rather a set of **interface** standards. These standards enable many types of computer or electronic devices to communicate with other computers and devices.

As telecommunications technology evolves, businesses are acquiring new equipment and implementing new procedures in order to improve communications capabilities. To keep a competitive edge and benefit from increasing productivity, businesses continue to upgrade their telecommunications technology. In an ever-changing workplace, you must be alert to innovations in telecommunications technology that will make your job easier and improve your efficiency.

emerging: coming out, arising

The integration of telephone technology and computers plays an essential role in the development of today's **emerging** communication technologies. The integration of the computer and the telephone is known as CTI (computer telephony integration) or telephony. A new class of technology has been created that provides computer

Illustration 13-1:15

Computer telephony integration provides advanced call center features.

control and access of telephone functions along with telephone control and access of computer functions. New telephony technology equipment offers features such as:

- Simultaneous two-way video, audio, and computer communication that let callers open, view, and edit the same computer files and send notes to each other as they talk.
- Computer software that lets users manage all telephone activity at their personal computer.
- Caller ID service that enables incoming calls to be screened—whether from within or outside the company. When you receive an outside call, you can see the number of the caller. When you receive an internal call, your telephone display screen shows the extension number and name of the person to whom that number is assigned.
- Conference calling that can be initiated by clicking on and dragging together names from within the user's personal computer phone directory.
- Access to banking services that allow the customer to access account balances, transfer funds, pay bills, and print records of all banking transactions.
- Support for accessing the Internet and the World Wide Web.
- Built-in personal information management software that can be connected to other workers' computers.
- Direct shopping from the telephone without having to speak to a **telemarketer.**
- Management of all voice, facsimile, or e-mail messages with either a touch-tone phone or a personal computer.
- **Multimedia** tutorials that help users learn the features and procedures of using advanced voice technologies.

Computer telephony is a fast-growing area of technological innovations. Developments in equipment and user services are rapidly changing the way people communicate through the telephone and computers.

telemarketer: person who sells products or services over the telephone

multimedia: software that combines text with audio and video

teaching tips

1. Ask students to share with the class an article related to new telecommunication technology. The article may be from a magazine, newspaper, or the Internet.
2. Collect advertisements for telephony equipment from professional computer and office information systems magazines.
3. Bring current magazines devoted to telephony (CTI) that you have collected. Often these magazines are subscribed to by local telephone service providers, telephone equipment vendors, or computer stores.

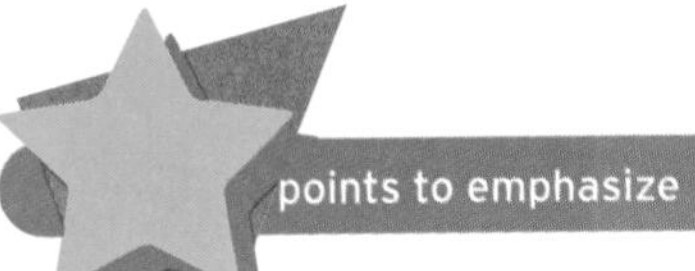

points to emphasize

Computer telephony is a relatively new area of technology that is rapidly growing and innovating. It has come about because of the marriage of the telephone and the computer and promises to continue to change the way we conduct and manage our electronic communications.

Reviewing the Topic

1. Why are most companies replacing older analog telephone lines with digital lines?
2. Explain how facsimile is used to transmit information.
3. List four features that a facsimile machine may offer.
4. What information should be included in a facsimile transmission cover sheet?
5. When an incoming call is answered by an automated attendant, what information does the recorded message that is played usually contain?
6. How is voice mail different from using an answering machine connected to a telephone?
7. What information should you include in the voice mail message you record on your telephone?
8. Describe three types of wireless telephone services available to keep traveling office workers in touch with their businesses.
9. What are three specialized features or equipment available to help those with physical impairments communicate on the telephone?
10. What are five features offered by new telephony equipment?

topic 13-1 review

INTERACTING WITH OTHERS

Your sales team member, Jeremy, is letting voice mail answer his phone the majority of the time, even when he is at his desk. You and Jeremy share sales and service for several accounts. Your clients have complained to you that Jeremy seems never to be at his desk. Also, they complain that he takes several days to answer their voice mail messages. You realize that you are going to have to resolve the situation. What should you do?

- Inform your supervisor about Jeremy's voice mail procedures?
- Apologize to clients for Jeremy's poor voice mail habits?

topic 13-1 review

Telephone Technology and Services

- Tell clients to call you instead of Jeremy?
- Tell Jeremy about the clients' complaints and ask him to handle his voice mail messages following professional procedures?

What is your suggestion for handling this situation?

What you are to do:

Prepare a written response to the suggested actions.

REINFORCING ENGLISH SKILLS

Your knowledge of punctuation rules will be an asset in your written communications on the job. Ten sentences follow that will reinforce your ability to use proper punctuation marks.

What you are to do:

Write or key each sentence, inserting the proper punctuation.

1. She faxed a report from Cheyenne Wyoming to Tucson Arizona
2. Our telephone bill was credited with two months interest
3. Did you place the call to Jeorge my friend from Mexico City
4. On Tuesday January 23 we began using our new computerized telephone system
5. To qualify for a position you must have a years experience using a computer telephony system
6. It was a pleasure showing you our new voice mail system we have a training session planned for all new users
7. We prefer using voice mail for recording messages not an answering machine
8. Conferencing lets you set up conversations with three four or more people at the same time
9. A speakerphone allows hands free speaking capabilities
10. Is the toll free number an 800 or an 888 number

639

APPLICATION ACTIVITY

ACTIVITY **Facsimile Procedures**

You work at the headquarters of Prudent Development Corporation, 8700 Martin Luther King Blvd., Austin, TX 78765-0800. The fax number is 512-555-0139. Your supervisor, Janet Naisbitt, asks you to prepare a well-designed one-page list of common procedures to be followed for a successful facsimile transmission. The procedures list is to be faxed to the office manager at the Denver branch. She also wants you to compose a short memo to include with the list that tells him that this list is to be distributed to all fax users at the Denver location. You are also to ask him to write any additions or comments on the list and return it to you within five days. The fax will be sent to Ed Stoddard, Office Manager, Prudent Development Corporation, Denver, CO. The fax number is 303-555-0102.

What you are to do:

1. Compose a document that lists procedures for successful fax-to-fax transmission, and use good document design and formatting.
2. Prepare a memo using a memo template from your word processing software.
3. Complete a facsimile transmission cover sheet to send the memo and the procedure sheet. Use a facsimile template file from your word processor software.

topic 13-1 review

640

Topic 13-2

Effective Telephone Communications

When you have completed your study of this topic, you will be able to:

- **describe and apply skills required to make a favorable first impression over the telephone**
- **apply telephone techniques and procedures that will enable you to handle incoming calls courteously and efficiently**
- **plan calls efficiently using tools such as published and computerized directories**
- **use proper telephone techniques and procedures to place local and long-distance domestic and international calls**
- **describe techniques for controlling telephone costs**

Students have no doubt had many negative as well as positive experiences when telephoning organizations. Ask them to relate their experiences and discuss what factors made the difference between a good impression and a poor one. Have them list as many factors as possible to be referred to and added to as this topic is studied.

The most universal tool for voice communication is the telephone. Think of the many calls that a company receives and places each day. Workers in the company receive and place calls to others both inside and outside the company to discuss common concerns, to place orders, or to request information. Messages must be taken and recorded either manually or electronically. Telephone calls are often less time-consuming than a memo, a letter, or even e-mail.

Because the telephone is such an important communication tool, all office workers should be able to use proper telephone techniques when answering incoming calls and placing outgoing calls. When you place calls to businesses, your first impression of the organization is often based on how you are treated by the person answering your call. If the person is pleasant, courteous, and interested in helping you, you

1. Arrange for students to "shadow" a switchboard operator or receptionist and report to the class the specific job responsibilities and telephone procedures observed. If this is not possible, invite someone to your class to share the information with students.
2. Invite a telephone industry representative to give a training session on effective telephone techniques and procedures.
3. Invite a telephone equipment sales representative to bring a variety of available telephone products to your class and discuss training in use of the equipment.
4. Arrange a visit to a local telephone facility.
5. If available, obtain a teletrainer to help the students practice effective telephone techniques.

probably form a good impression of the company. If the person is abrupt, rude, or unwilling to help, you probably form a negative impression. When you answer the telephone or place an outgoing call, you will want to give callers a positive impression by what you say and how you say it.

As a consideration in controlling telephone costs, businesses must carefully compare the general services, equipment, and long-distance services available in today's competitive telephone industry. In order to place and receive calls efficiently and economically, you should become aware of the services offered by the telephone companies that provide both local and long-distance service to your office. In this topic, you will learn to create a professional first impression, use directories, and use proper techniques and procedures when placing and receiving telephone calls.

Making a Favorable First Impression

When you handle telephone communications for an organization, you are representing that company. To the individual on the other end of the connection, you *are* the company, you *are* the department. To create a positive image for your organization, it is important that you develop good communication skills. Your voice, pronunciation, grammar, and vocabulary, as well as your attitude, contribute to the impression you make when using the telephone. While technology has changed communication, the need for good speaking skills remains a critical factor in successful telephone interaction.

YOUR VOICE

When you communicate with others in person, you make them feel welcome by smiling and perhaps by shaking hands. You show interest and alertness by maintaining eye contact with them during the conversation. When you communicate by telephone, however, all you have to **convey** interest, alertness, and courtesy is your voice. Elements of your voice that you must pay attention to include tone, pace, and volume.

convey: express

Tone. The tone of your voice refers to the changes in pitch used to emphasize words and to get your meaning across to the listener. You

Illustration 13-2:1

You represent your organization every time you call someone or answer a call.

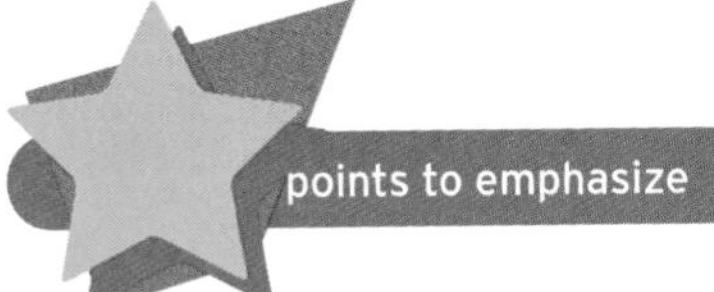

Telecommunications technology is enhanced by employees who are courteous and polite and who create goodwill for the organization over the telephone. In many cases, the telephone is the only contact a customer has with the organization. The caller's impression (positive or negative) of the office worker will last longer than the business conducted and may determine whether the caller does business with the company again.

have, no doubt, listened to speakers who talked in a **monotone.** It is difficult to pay attention when someone is speaking in a monotonous voice. The listener may become bored or may perceive the speaker as indifferent or inattentive. Vary the tone of your voice to express feelings and emphasis of ideas, but avoid using extremes. An **animated** voice reflects interest in the caller and helps you achieve successful communication. Avoid speaking in a very high-pitched voice, a very low-pitched voice, or with an up-and-down, "singsong" manner.

monotone: one tone

animated: lively, spirited

Pace. Pace is the rate of speech. The rate at which you talk to someone on the telephone can affect the ability of the listener to understand your message. If you speak too rapidly, the listener may not hear all the information you are trying to communicate, especially if the information is technical or detailed. On the other hand, if you speak too slowly, the listener may become bored, insulted, or inattentive.

In addition to the nature of the information, you must consider the speech characteristics of the listener. For example, in today's global workplace, you may be speaking with people from different parts of your nation and with people from countries all over the world. You may be conversing with people who, even though they speak the same language as you, have speech patterns and regional dialects that are different from your own. You must learn to adjust your pace to fit the needs of those with whom you are communicating.

Volume. Extremes in volume should be avoided when speaking on the telephone. Do not shout or speak so softly that the listener cannot hear what you are saying. Modulating your voice means controlling the volume so that you are speaking neither too loudly nor too softly. Speak directly into the telephone receiver or mouthpiece.

YOUR SPEAKING SKILLS

project:
send out

Your voice and speaking skills are put to the test when you speak on the telephone. Speaking skills such as word pronunciation, grammar, and vocabulary usage affect the impression you **project** over the phone. While you may have a pleasant tone, good pace, and a well modulated voice, communication is difficult if the person you are speaking with cannot understand your words.

To assist students in developing self-awareness of the quality of their vocal communication skills, tape-record them reading from text of their choice or from literary works such as poetry. Have students critique their own voices for tone, pace, and volume.

Pronunciation. Correct pronunciation of words is essential for understanding. Proper enunciation is also important. Enunciation is how clearly you say a word. It involves trying not to mumble or run words together. For example, you should say "what do you" instead of "whaddaya"; you should say "going to" instead of "gonna." Enunciate word endings such as "ing," "ed," possessives, and plurals.

You will find that most people speak with a regional *accent*. An accent involves a certain rhythm, speed, modulation, and pronunciation of vowels that is native to a particular region. You probably have an accent even though you may not be aware of it. If you find that you must overcome barriers to effective communication as a result of dialects or accents, there are several things that you can do to help you succeed:

- Pronounce words correctly and enunciate clearly.
- Speak slowly, but not so slowly that you insult or appear to be **condescending** to the caller.
- Avoid long words, complicated phrases, or long sentences.
- If you are unsure of any word's pronunciation, look it up in the dictionary.

condescending:
patronizing, smug

Grammar. Just as pronunciation can be a reflection of your professionalism and education, so can your grammar skills. Although some rules of grammar are relaxed for spoken communications, it is still necessary to follow basic standards to project a favorable impression of yourself and your organization. It is permissible to use occasional slang

Illustration 13-2:2
Your voice and speaking skills help you to create a positive impression over the telephone.

or regional or national expressions; however, remember that some expressions may not be widely known or understood, especially if the call is an international one. Other people may use terms that you do not recognize. When you do not understand an expression or phrase, always ask for an explanation.

Vocabulary. You should constantly improve your professional and personal vocabulary. You can learn new terms that relate to your position or your organization and new words that will help you express your feelings, ideas, and needs. Remember that clear and courteous communication is always your goal. Avoid using trendy, slang expressions in formal business communications. State your ideas simply without using highly technical terms or lengthy words.

Many companies deal directly with clients, customers, or suppliers from other countries. Your organization may even be an international

Illustration 13-2:3
Using a few phrases in the language of the person to whom you are speaking can help establish goodwill.

for discussion

Ask students to develop a list of words that are often mispronounced, showing correct and incorrect pronunciation. Examples include *specific, often,* and *height*.

expand the concept

With the increase in international organizations, most workers have to deal with clients from other countries, or perhaps they are working for a company with foreign ownership. Not only will they find it advantageous to learn several common phrases in the language of those with whom they must communicate, but also a knowledge of the customs of that country will increase effectiveness in their business dealings.

one whose owners or headquarters are located outside this country. It is a good idea to learn some simple courtesy phrases to use when speaking with international callers. Your attempts at learning and using some simple, basic phrases will be appreciated by foreign callers and will help you establish a favorable impression. Keep a list of basic phrases along with their translations and pronunciations. Practice them and make sure that you are pronouncing them correctly.

Body language is a major factor when communicating with someone in person. Discuss how body language can still play a role when speaking on the telephone in helping convey a positive, professional impression. Ask students what effect a smile can have on your voice when you are speaking on the phone.

YOUR ATTITUDE

When you speak to someone over the telephone, all you have is your voice to convey information and express your feelings. Even though you may not be seen by the person with whom you are speaking, your attitude is continually being transmitted to that person. Any boredom, anger, or indifference you are feeling is intensified as your message is sent to the person on the line. On the other hand, a smile and an upbeat, caring attitude is also clearly projected to the person with whom you are speaking.

Whether you are the caller or the listener, you must put all your personal feelings aside and take responsibility for responding to the communication with a sincere, positive attitude.

Incoming Telephone Communications

Handling incoming telephone calls requires skill in using proper telephone techniques and effective procedures. When answering the telephone, you usually do not know who is calling or what the caller wants. Your work may be interrupted, or you may have a visitor in your office. It is important for you to know how to handle a variety of situations and take care of caller requests, needs, and problems.

PROPER TELEPHONE TECHNIQUES

You now know that your voice, your speaking skills, and your attitude all affect a caller's impression of you, your department, and your company. It is the goal of every organization to give a positive, professional impression when communicating over the telephone. The following telephone techniques will further strengthen that positive impression.

Answer Promptly. Answer all incoming calls promptly and pleasantly. If possible, you should answer the telephone after the first ring. When you reach for the receiver, also pick up a pen or pencil and a notepad or message form. You must be ready to take notes or a message.

Identify Yourself. Because many companies use automated telephone systems that answer the calls initially and route them to the requested department or person, it may not be necessary to identify your company when you answer a call. However, if you are the person to whom all incoming calls are routed, you should identify first your company, then yourself.

A telephone conversation cannot begin until the caller knows that the correct number, department, or person has been reached. Following are examples of proper and improper telephone answering responses.

Improper: "Hello," or "Yes?" *(These greetings do not give any identification of the person or of the company.)*

Improper: "Hello, hold please." *(This greeting does not give any company identification to the caller. Also, abruptly placing the caller on hold is rude and abrasive.)*

Improper: "Good morning. International Electronics. Our company is number one in the field of international electronics products sales and service. Pat Lopez speaking. May I be of help to you?" *(This greeting is too long and distracting.)*

Proper: "Good morning. International Electronics, Pat Lopez." *(Use this greeting when you are answering an outside call.)*

Proper: "Marketing Department, Leon DiMarco." *(Use this greeting when you are answering an inside or outside call in a company where all calls are routed through a switchboard operator or an automated attendant that has already identified the company.)*

Proper: "Ms. Yamaguchi's office, Lisa Stein." *(Use this greeting when you are answering the telephone for a supervisor or if you are answering someone else's phone.)*

1. Ask students for more examples of improper ways of answering the telephone. They may have encountered other examples when calling organizations.
2. How does the way you answer your telephone at home differ from the procedures you should use at work? Why should the method be different?

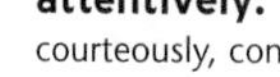

attentively: courteously, considerately

conscientiously: with a sense of duty

Assist the Caller. Your job is to help the caller as efficiently as you can. Never *assume* that you know what the caller wants. Instead, listen **attentively** to the caller's questions and comments. If you know that it will take several minutes to access the information needed for the call, do not keep the caller waiting. Explain the situation to the caller and offer the choice of being placed on hold or hanging up. **Conscientiously** follow through on any promise you make to return a call.

Make sure that you give accurate information to callers. If you do not know the answer to a question, admit it. Either tell the caller that you will obtain the information and call back, or offer to transfer the call to someone who can answer the question. Avoid passing off a caller to someone else if there is any way that you can be of help yourself.

teaching tips

Point out to students the consequences of passing callers off to other workers. Ask students if they have ever experienced this aggravation.

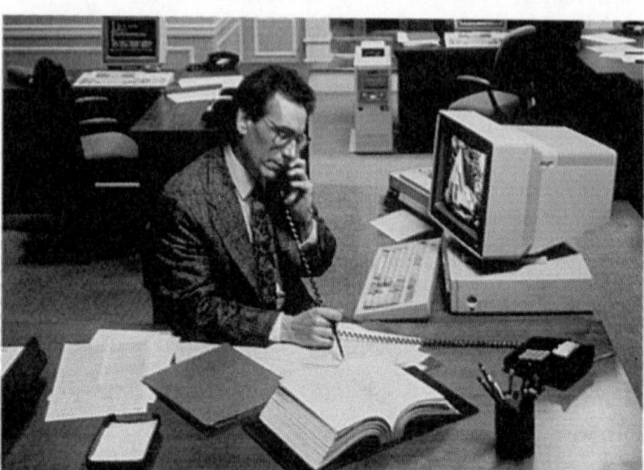

Illustration 13-2:4
Have information and reference materials handy to assist callers.

Conclude the Call. As a general rule, the person who places a call is the one who should end the call and hang up first. If you follow this rule, you avoid making the caller feel as if the conversation has been "cut off" before he or she was ready to hang up.

It is a good habit to use the caller's name as you end the conversation. For example: "Yes, Ms. O'Toole, I will be sure to mail you a copy of our latest catalog today," or, "Thank you for calling, Mr. Haliz. I will be sure to give Ms. Schmidt the information." Such a practice personalizes the conversation.

EFFECTIVE TELEPHONE PROCEDURES

As you answer incoming calls, there will be many tasks that you need to handle efficiently. You may be requested to screen calls, give information, or take messages. It may be necessary for you to place a caller on hold, transfer calls, handle disconnected calls, and deal with difficult callers. Effective procedures for managing each of these situations are presented here.

Screening Calls. In some offices, you may be asked to *screen* the incoming calls. Screening calls is a procedure used to determine who is calling and, at times, the purpose of the call. For example, your supervisor may instruct you to screen calls and take a message from all salespeople who call. You may inform the caller that you will relay the message; however, refrain from committing your supervisor to a return call. Your supervisor may be in an important meeting and ask you not to interrupt except for certain callers. Screening can save you and the caller time because you may be able to help the person yourself or transfer the call immediately to another person.

When screening calls, find out who is calling. Be tactful, yet direct. To learn the caller's name, ask questions such as "May I say who is calling?" or "May I tell Ms. Johnson who is calling?"

Sometimes callers refuse to give their names. If it is the policy of your company to identify each caller by name before transferring the call, you must be courteous, yet firm. Explaining the policy to the caller will usually encourage the caller to give you his or her name. Even if the caller becomes rude or still refuses to tell his or her name, you should at all times be courteous yet remain firm in upholding your supervisor's wishes.

Office Worker:	*"Hannible, Krohe, and Levy. Jerry Timms speaking."*
Caller:	*"I want to speak to Anna Yong."*
Office Worker:	*"May I tell Ms. Yong who is calling?"*
Caller:	*"My name is* **irrelevant.** *Just let me talk to Anna."*
Office Worker:	*"I'm very sorry, sir, but I am unable to transfer a call without first identifying the caller."*
Caller:	*"I understand. I'm Jim Evans, Anna's uncle."*

irrelevant: not important

1. Why would some employers have a policy that no calls are to be screened?
2. Under what circumstances might a caller respond, "No you may *not* place me on hold!"? How would you respond?

Placing a Caller on Hold. There will be times when you must place a caller on *hold* while you answer another call. Ask the first caller if you may place them on hold. Then answer the second call. Ask permission to place the second caller on hold while you complete your conversation with the first caller.

Sometimes you will need to place a caller on hold while you look up information to answer a question. Politely inform the caller that you are placing him or her on hold. If you believe it will take several minutes to find the answer, ask if you should call back or if the caller would prefer to hold. In the latter case, check back frequently to reassure the caller that he or she has not been forgotten.

Transferring Calls. Calls are usually transferred when the caller has reached a wrong extension, wishes to speak with someone else, or has a request that can be handled more effectively by another person or department. The caller may request the transfer, or you may determine that the transfer is necessary. Always tell the caller why the transfer is necessary. For example, you may say:

> *"I'm going to transfer your call to Mr. Rosen. He will be able to provide you with the information you need."*

You may prefer to place the caller on hold while you speak with the person to whom you intend to transfer the call. This will allow you to confirm that this person can help the caller and to introduce the caller for screening purposes.

Handling a Disconnected Call. Occasionally, you will be disconnected while you are talking on the telephone or while you are waiting on hold. In general, the person who placed the call should call back immediately after the disconnection. That person has the telephone number of the party being called and should, therefore, be able to redial the call quickly.

The caller should report a disconnected long-distance call to the telephone company. An adjustment will then be made in the long-distance charge.

Giving Information. There may be times when managers or coworkers are out of the office for several days. In these situations, you must tactfully communicate to the caller that the person is not available and offer to take a message or assist the caller yourself:

Caller:	*"May I please speak with Mr. Lesinski? This is Rosanna Robbins from Advanced Realty."*
Office Worker:	*"I'm sorry, Ms. Robbins, but Mr. Lesinski is out of the office until Thursday. I'm Mr. Lesinski's assistant. Could I help you, or may I ask him to call you when he returns?"*

When coworkers are unavailable to receive calls, give the caller enough information to explain the person's absence without **divulging** unnecessary or sensitive details.

divulging: revealing

Improper

"Ms. Fox has a hair appointment this afternoon."

"Ms. Fox had to pick up her son from school."

"Mr. Chandler is playing golf with a prospective client."

Proper

"Ms. Fox is out of the office until tomorrow morning. May I take a message or ask her to call you?"

"Mr. Chandler is in a meeting this afternoon and won't be available the rest of the day. May I take a message or ask him to return your call?"

Taking Messages. Today's telephone and computer technology have changed many of the procedures for recording telephone messages. Voice mail has reduced the errors caused by incorrect or incomplete written messages. Even with voice mail, it will be necessary for you to record information for yourself such as the caller's name, telephone number, and purpose of the call.

Printed message forms are usually available in offices for recording telephone messages. When you record a message, it is essential that it is accurate and complete. Verify names and telephone numbers by reading back the information to the caller. Ask for accurate spellings of names if you are in doubt. Write the message carefully making sure that your handwriting is legible so you do not waste time rewriting it later or fail to be able to read it. Each message should include the following data:

- date and time of the call
- name of the caller with the caller's company (Check spellings of any names about which you are uncertain.)
- caller's telephone number, including area code if it is a long-distance call (Remember to repeat the number for verification.)
- details of the message
- your name or initials

Illustration 13-2:5

Printed forms are used for taking telephone messages. Record the message legibly and accurately.

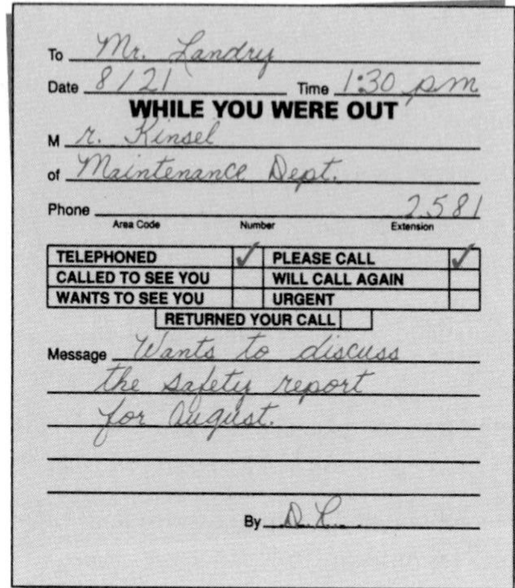

To Mr. Landry
Date 8/21 Time 1:30 pm
WHILE YOU WERE OUT
Mr. Kinsel
of Maintenance Dept.
Phone 2581
Area Code Number Extension

TELEPHONED	✓	PLEASE CALL	✓
CALLED TO SEE YOU		WILL CALL AGAIN	
WANTS TO SEE YOU		URGENT	
RETURNED YOUR CALL			

Message Wants to discuss the safety report for August.

By D.L.

Your office may have software that can be used to complete an onscreen message form rather than a preprinted one to record telephone messages. A typical message screen is shown in Illustration 13-2:6. Using a computer message offers these advantages:

- Less time is needed to key a message than to write it.
- The number of lost messages is reduced since messages can be transferred immediately to the intended receiver.
- Printed message forms are not needed.

1. After examining the printed telephone message form in Illustration 13-2:5, have students design their own telephone message form using their word processing software. Discuss the information that should be included, design factors, and format considerations. What is the advantage of using a form rather than a blank sheet of paper?
2. Have students list the advantages and disadvantages of using a computer to take messages.

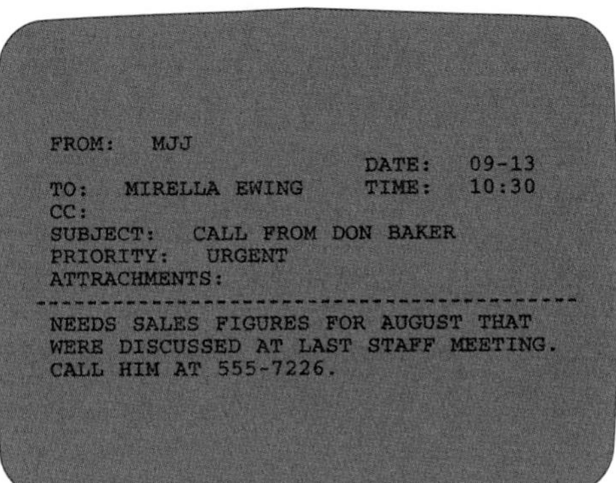

```
FROM:   MJJ
                              DATE:   09-13
TO:   MIRELLA EWING           TIME:   10:30
CC:
SUBJECT:   CALL FROM DON BAKER
PRIORITY:   URGENT
ATTRACHMENTS:
----------------------------------------
NEEDS SALES FIGURES FOR AUGUST THAT
WERE DISCUSSED AT LAST STAFF MEETING.
CALL HIM AT 555-7226.
```

Illustration 13-2:6

This is an urgent message for Mirella Ewing taken by MJJ.

Each computer message you key should include the same basic information as a handwritten message. As you key the message, make sure that is accurate and complete. Verify all names and numbers. The current date and time are usually entered automatically by the system into the onscreen form. The message may be transferred to the receiver's computer screen by keying in the correct extension number. A reminder or some form of electronic notation will appear on the receiver's screen showing that a message is waiting.

Handling Difficult Callers. On occasion you may receive calls from persons who are angry, unreasonable, rude, demanding, or highly emotional. These calls may be few, but they are very stressful. You must control yourself and remain professional when dealing with difficult callers. Your goal is to diffuse the situation without compromising yourself or your company and to maintain **goodwill** with the caller, if possible. Following are a few guidelines for you to follow when dealing with difficult telephone callers.

goodwill: a friendly business relationship

- Try to resolve the matter if possible. Usually the caller just wants the company to solve a problem or rectify a mistake. Do not hesitate to apologize to the caller for any problems or inconveniences that have been experienced.
- Always present a helpful, positive, and sincere attitude even in an adverse situation.

Give students the opportunity to role-play answering incoming calls from difficult callers. You be the difficult caller for the first few calls; then have students portray negative attitudes (hard to please, angry, hostile, rude).

- If the caller is personally abusive to you or uses profanity, end the conversation quickly after identifying the caller and recording relevant information about the call.
- Remain outwardly calm and do not display defensive behavior. Usually, the caller is not upset with you but with the company or its actions. Do not take the situation personally.

With experience and a reliance upon good human relations and communications skills, you will be able to deal with callers who will put those skills to the test.

Handling Personal Telephone Calls. You must understand and follow your company's policy regarding personal telephone calls. Most companies permit a limited number of personal calls; others discourage such calls or ask that a pay phone located on the premises be used. Generally, brief, urgent, or emergency calls are permitted. Long, frequent personal calls are never acceptable in any business. You should learn your company's policy and respect it.

Outgoing Telephone Communications

As with incoming telephone calls, outgoing telephone communications may be made to a person outside or inside the company. Calls may be interoffice, local, or long-distance. It is important that you understand the process and procedures for placing all outgoing calls. Your goal is efficiency and economy.

PLANNING CALLS

Every call you make requires preparation and planning. Most calls may be simple; however, others may require detailed preparatory steps. When preparing for any call, confirm the name and number of the person who you are calling. Identify clearly the main purpose of the call. Outline briefly the points you want to cover during the call. Gather other information or items you need to have available before making the call, such as:

- dates and times of any meetings or planned events that relate to the call
- documents that relate to the topic of your conversation

- questions that you want to ask
- pen and paper or your computer to take notes during the call

Discuss possible consequences of failing to have the items or information listed here for planning a call.

TIME ZONES

Be aware of time zone differences when placing long-distance calls to avoid calling before or after business hours or during lunch. The **continental** United States and parts of Canada are divided into five standard time zones: *Atlantic*, *eastern*, *central*, *mountain*, and *Pacific* (see Illustration 13-2:7). As you move west, each zone is one hour earlier. For example, when it is 1 p.m. in Washington, DC (eastern zone), it is noon in Dallas (central zone), 11 a.m. in Denver (mountain zone), and 10 a.m. in Los Angeles (Pacific zone). If you are in San Diego and need to speak to a coworker in the New York City office, you will need to place the call before 2 p.m. Pacific time. Otherwise, the New York office may be closed because it will be 5 p.m. (eastern time).

continental: mainland, only on the continent

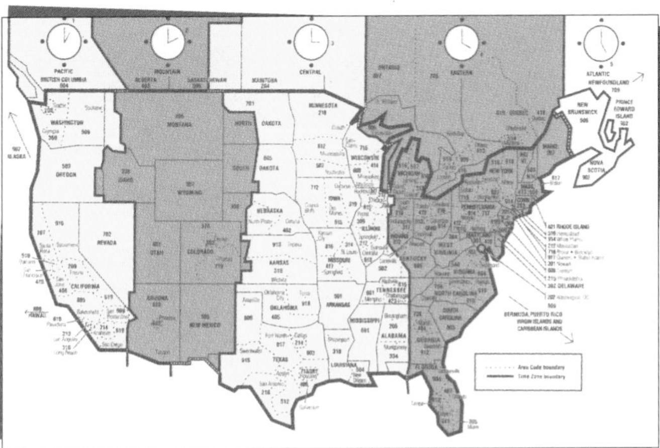

Illustration 13-2:7
This map shows telephone area codes and time zones.

When making international calls, it is especially important to be aware of the differences in time zones and certain customs. For example, in Mexico during the hours of noon to 3 p.m., many offices are closed. Workers return at 3 p.m. and often remain in the office

With the increasing need to place international calls comes the ability to determine the best time to place them. Problems arise when countries are in time zones so far away that in order to reach a client, you must make the call in the middle of the night. Discuss how companies are overcoming this "time barrier" to communications with technology such as e-mail.

1. The continental United States and part of Canada are divided into how many time zones? Name them.
2. Where can you find area codes? What is the area code or codes for Arizona? Texas? New York City? New Brunswick?

until 7 or 8 p.m. If a caller is located in a time zone in which it is impossible for you to call during your regular business hours, you may have to make the call after your normal work time. If you make frequent international calls or calls to distant parts of the country in other time zones, it is a good idea for you to have a copy of a world time zone map such as the one in Illustration 13-2:8.

Illustration 13-2:8

If you frequently place international calls, you should have a copy of a world time zone map for quick reference.

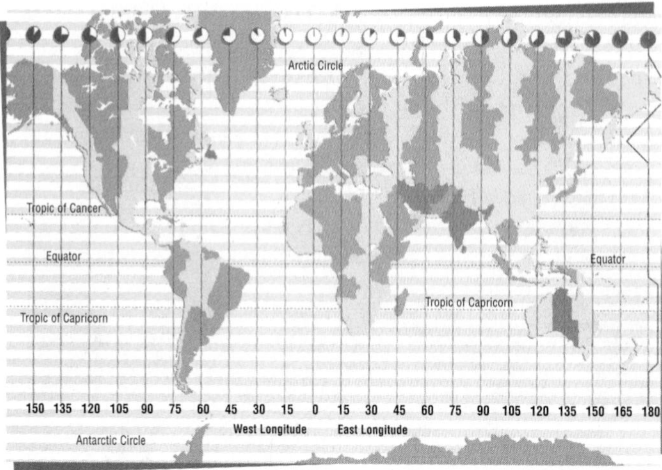

Today's technology makes it easy to place direct calls to over 150 countries all over the world. There are 24 time zones throughout the world. To place a call to London, England, all you have to do to direct-dial is to dial the following sequence of numbers: *011* (international access code) + *44* (country code) + *71* (city code) + *seven-digit phone number*. Consult the *Directory Assistance* section of your local telephone directory or call 1-800-874-4000 for additional information or country codes.

USING DIRECTORIES

There are many resources available for you to use when planning a call. Your local telephone company publishes a yearly directory. Local as well as national organizations publish a variety of business and professional directories. National telephone directories are available on

CD-ROM, and directory information is available over the Internet. You should become familiar with the wide range of information contained in these resources.

Local Directories. Local telephone companies usually provide directories to their customers free of charge. You may want to find the telephone number of a business or individual in your local area. You can usually find the number in the *white pages* of the local directory. If you are searching for a particular service or product rather than a company, you may find the number in the *yellow pages* section of the directory. It is important for you to become familiar with all sections of your local telephone directory. Let's examine their contents.

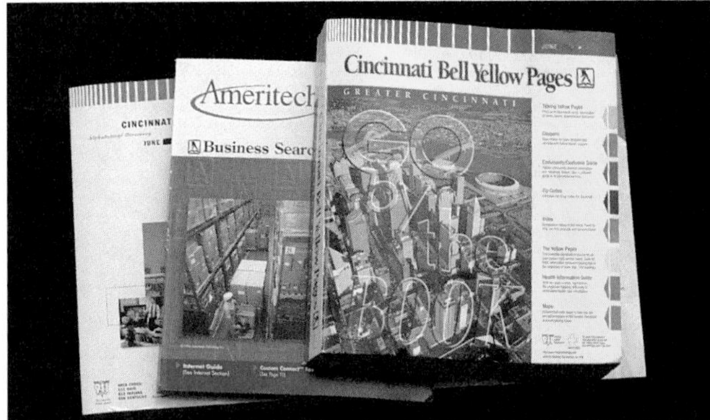

Illustration 13-2:9

Local directories provide a wealth of information besides listings of organizations.

White Pages. The front section of most directories is actually a user's guide for the directory itself and a "how-to" guide for the telephone services consumer. Some of the information you will find here includes types of telephone services provided by the company, local emergency numbers, and directions for making many types of calls. You should read and become very familiar with this section.

The next section of the local telephone directory contains names, addresses, and telephone numbers of businesses, government agencies, and individuals in your city. In some locations, the white pages may be divided into two sections. The first section lists personal names and numbers only, while the second section lists only business names and

1. Have local telephone directories available for each student. Your local telephone company may be willing to provide them free of charge, or you may request that students bring one from home. It would be advantageous for the directories to be the same.
2. Many types of directories are now available. Collect examples of directories to share with the class. Have copies of national directories on a CD-ROM that can be purchased inexpensively.
3. Have students search the Internet for directory information and report their findings.
4. Introduce the local telephone directory to the students by providing an overview of the wealth of information that can be found in it. Many students will be amazed at the variety of information found in a reference that most people use only for listings.

Invite a local yellow pages representative to the class to talk about how this section of the telephone directory is developed and marketed as an important sales tool for local businesses, services, and organizations.

Ask students to assume they have accepted a position as an assistant to the school's top administrator. Have them prepare a listing and format for the personal directory that they believe will be useful in their work. Have them plan the order in which they would list the personal numbers (in order by department then name? by name only? both?). Have them decide whether to use word processing, database, or spreadsheet software. Which software will allow for easy updating, access? Will it be necessary to print a copy? Why? (A discussion of the listings, formats, and software used will help students see the variations in judgments represented in the responses.)

numbers. Sometimes these sections are each contained in separate books. When personal and business numbers are divided, another section called the *Blue Pages* also may be included. The Blue Pages serve as an easy reference for locating telephone numbers of government offices and other helpful numbers such as those of the chamber of commerce, consumer protection agencies, and weather service.

Yellow Pages. The yellow pages contain an alphabetic listing of businesses arranged according to the services they provide or the products they sell. For example, if you want to find names and telephone numbers of businesses in the area that might cater your company's 50th anniversary dinner, you would look under *Caterers* as shown in Illustration 13-2:10.

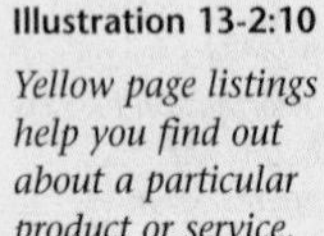

Illustration 13-2:10

Yellow page listings help you find out about a particular product or service.

Personal and Company Directories. You should make a list of all numbers that you call often. Using today's computerized telephone equipment, you may be able to program a limited number of frequently dialed numbers into your telephone. Your company may provide you with a directory of employees working at a particular location. The directory may also include procedures for using features of the telephone system including the management of your voice mailbox. Tips for proper telephone techniques as well as how the company wants you to identify yourself and your department may also be included.

Computerized Directories. Integration of computer and telephone technology is changing how we access all types of data. The types of information contained in the paper directories can also be accessed using a personal computer. National telephone directories can be purchased on CD-ROM. Online computer information services provide access to a variety of data including telephone numbers and services of businesses all over the world.

Listings 1 - 8 | More Listings Modify Search | New Search

Smith, N 2810 Cumberland St NW, Roanoke, VA 24012-7614
Phone: (540) 555-0178

Smith, Nancy 3701 Bear Rd SE, Roanoke, VA 24014-6405
Phone: (540) 555-0156

Smith, Nancy C 4802 Sunnyside Dr, Roanoke, VA 24018-4226
Phone: (540) 555-0198

Smith, Nellie L Rr 6, Roanoke, VA 24014
Phone: (540) 555-0123

Illustration 13-2:11
Access to business and residential phone numbers is available via the Internet.

Directory Assistance. If you are unable to locate a telephone number, call the directory assistance operator for help. Dial *411* for a local directory assistance operator. For long-distance directory assistance, dial *1*, the area code, and *555-1212*.

A directory assistance operator will ask you what city you are calling. Be prepared to supply the operator with as much information as possible about the person or business for which you need the number. Be prepared to give the correct spelling and street address if known. After giving the information, there will be a pause; then you will hear the number repeated twice. Make a note of the number for future reference.

LONG-DISTANCE SERVICE

Long-distance calls are made to numbers outside the service area of your local telephone company. Several factors may determine the cost of long-distance service: time of day the call is placed, type of call, length of call, and type of long-distance call. Long-distance carriers

If you have Internet access in your classroom, have students visit sites that provide telephone numbers and services of business all over the world.

provide a variety of pricing promotions. The consumer chooses a long-distance provider. It is a good idea to shop around and find out about the varied long-distance programs and prices before selecting a carrier. Your local telephone directory usually lists several long-distance carriers (MCI, Sprint, Excel, AT&T, etc.) and their numbers for you to contact. You may also visit these companies' websites to learn of pricing and special promotional offers and regulations. To place calls efficiently and economically, you must become familiar with the various long-distance services available. Long-distance services will be discussed in the following sections.

Direct-Dial Calls. Direct-dial calls are those placed without assistance from an operator. To make a direct-dial call, first dial *1*, which gives you access to a long-distance line. Then dial the area code and the number you are trying to reach. Charges for these calls begin as soon as the telephone is answered. If you make a direct-dial call and the person you need to speak with is unavailable, your company still will be charged for the call.

Specialized Long-Distance Calls. Specialized long-distance calls are more expensive than those you dial direct. Person-to-person, collect, credit card, and conference calls are all types of special long-distance calls.

Person-to-Person Calls. Person-to-person calls are an expensive type of specially assisted calls. To place a person-to-person call, dial *0* (zero), the area code, and the telephone number of the individual or business you are calling. When you have finished dialing, you will be asked what type of call you wish to place, such as person-to-person or collect. You will say "person-to-person" and will then be asked to supply the name of the person you are calling. Pronounce the name clearly and accurately. You may have to spell it for clarity.

Charges for the call begin only after the person you have requested is on the line. If that person is not available, you will not be charged for the call. If you must call repeatedly before reaching the person, or if it takes the person several minutes to get to the phone, this type of call may be less expensive than a direct-dialed call. You do not pay until you begin speaking with the person you have indicated.

Collect Calls. The charges for a collect call are billed to the telephone number being called, not to the number from which the call was placed. To place a collect call, dial 0 (zero), the area code, and the telephone number. You will be asked what type of call you are placing. Speak clearly into the phone, answering "collect." You will then be asked to give your name. Once again, speak very clearly and distinctly into the phone. The call will be completed, and the recipient will be asked whether or not the call and the charges will be accepted.

People who travel for a business may find it necessary to make collect calls to their offices. Customers or clients may be invited to call collect.

Conference Calls. A conference call is placed when it is necessary to talk **simultaneously** with persons at several different locations. With today's telephone systems, you can use special features to arrange these calls yourself. In many cases, conference calls are set up in advance with a *conference operator*. To place a conference call with this type of assistance, dial the number of this specialized service. You can obtain this number from your long-distance service provider or dial the operator and request a conference call. Be prepared to give the names, telephone numbers, and locations (cities and states) of the participants as well as the exact time the call is to be placed. At the designated time, the operator will call you and indicate that the other parties are on the line. Review the tips for planning and carrying out conference calls that were presented in Topic 13-1 in this chapter.

simultaneously: at the same time

Credit Card Calls. For people who travel frequently for business or pleasure, telephone credit cards can be very practical. The user is able to charge telephone calls to the credit card. A special PIN (personal identification number) is issued to the cardholder for security. The PIN number is entered using the telephone keypad. Some telephones, such as those found in airports, are specially equipped to read a magnetic card number when the credit card is slid through a slot.

Prepaid Phone Cards. Another type of phone card that is often used by travelers is a prepaid phone card. This is issued upon receipt of payment for a particular amount. The user receives a single-use PIN number and a *toll-free* access number. The phone system will inform you of

661

In Topic 13-1, students learned about videoconferences. Have students explain how videoconferences and telephone conferences differ. How are they the same?

Illustration 13-2:12

Conference calls make it possible to conduct business without the expense of face-to-face meetings.

Bank vice president in Denver whose bank is financing the Paragon Mall Project.

Advertising executive in San Francisco whose company is planning the major campaign to announce the Paragon Mall Project.

Executive in New York City who is in charge of the Paragon Mall Project and who initiated the conference call.

Today's telephone systems offer special features for arranging conference calls.

the maximum permitted duration of your call. Prepaid phone cards may be purchased in airports, train stations, bus depots, or from your long-distance carrier.

WIDE AREA TELECOMMUNICATION SERVICES (WATS)

A company that makes many long-distance calls may find it economical to lease one or more WATS lines. Instead of charging a regular long-distance rate for each call placed, the telephone company charges a set monthly fee plus a discounted rate for each outgoing call. The geographic service area covered will vary.

Illustration 13-2:13
Prepaid phone cards are convenient for business travelers.

TOLL-FREE SERVICE

As a convenience to customers who call long-distance, a company may subscribe to toll-free service for callers. This discounted service applies to *incoming* calls only, and there is no charge to the caller. For **interstate** or **intrastate** calls, toll-free service with 800 or 888 numbers is available. A company that services customers from Maine to Florida may subscribe to toll-free service that includes all the states along the East Coast. A company with customers in California only may subscribe to the service for that one state only. To determine whether a company in the United States has a toll-free number, dial either *1-800-555-1212* or *1-888-555-1212*.

interstate: between states, nationwide

intrastate: within a state

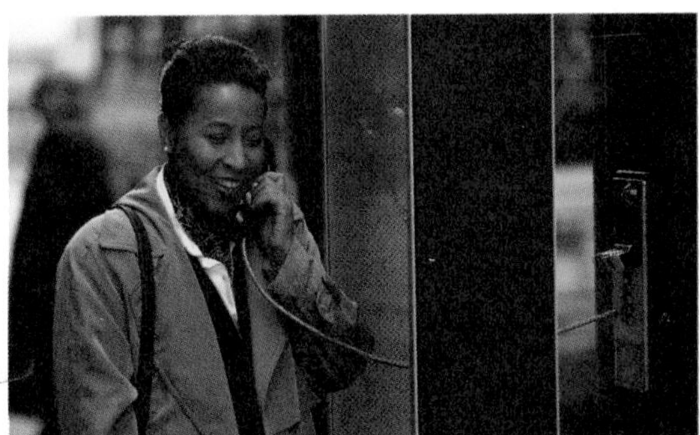

Illustration 13-2:14
Toll-free services help cut costs for your customers.

1. What are the advantages for companies of using WATS lines and toll-free service?
2. Why do you think hotel chains, airlines, and rental car companies offer toll-free numbers to their customers?
3. Toll-free services are now available for home use through some service providers. What are the advantages for the home user?

CONTROLLING TELEPHONE COSTS

As an office worker, you will be expected to help control telephone costs. Some suggestions for telephone efficiency are listed here.

- Use direct-dialing most of the time. Make more specialized, expensive types of calls that require extra assistance only when necessary.
- Plan your calls so the time spent during a long-distance or any other call is used efficiently.
- If possible, call when long-distance rates are least expensive.
- Notify the operator immediately after reaching a wrong number so you can receive credit for the call.
- Be an informed consumer of telephone services. Compare rate plans and promotional offerings.
- Learn how to use the equipment and features of your telephone system.

Reviewing the Topic

1. What factors influence the first impression you make when you respond to a telephone call?
2. Why should you use the caller's name as the conversation ends?
3. What information should you record even when retrieving telephone messages from your voice mailbox?
4. What should you do if you have placed a caller on hold and you feel it will take several minutes for you to locate the requested information?
5. What questions might you ask to learn a caller's name?
6. Give three suggestions for handling difficult telephone callers.
7. Describe information found in the white pages. How are organizations listed in the yellow pages? For what purposes are the blue pages used?
8. Name the five time zones into which the continental United States and parts of Canada are divided.
9. List five examples of information that may be needed before making a call.
10. What are the number segments you should dial for a domestic, long-distance direct-dial call?

THINKING CRITICALLY

You are employed in a growing computer sales and service business, Hooser's Computer Corner. Numerous calls are received daily for the fifteen sales associates, seven service technicians, and four administrative services employees. The owner is considering the purchase of an automated attendant telephone system. Your supervisor is Lin Wong, the office manager. He is confident that the new system would greatly benefit the organization and should be installed as soon as possible; however, he would like to consider your recommendation

topic 13-2 review

Effective Telephone Communications

665

before purchasing the system. You are aware that there are both advantages and disadvantages of using these systems. What do you recommend?

What you are to do:

Make a list of the pros and cons of using an automated attendant at Hooser's Computer Corner. Based upon your list, compose and prepare a memo to Lin Wong presenting your recommendation and your reasons for it.

REINFORCING MATH SKILLS

You work for Carrlson-Greer, Inc., which has offices in Seattle, Houston, and St. Louis. You are responsible for monitoring the costs of the various forms of telecommunications used by the company. As part of your analysis, prepare a table showing the monthly long-distance telephone charges for each regional office for a period of six months. The charges appear on the following page.

What you are to do:

1. Use the information provided to prepare a spreadsheet.
2. Enter a formula to calculate total charges for each regional office for the six-month period.
3. Enter a formula to calculate total charges for each of the six months for all regional offices.
4. Enter a formula to calculate total charges for the six-month period for all regional offices.
5. Enter a formula to calculate average monthly charges for each regional office. Round amounts to the nearest cent.
6. Enter a formula to calculate average monthly costs for all offices. Round to the nearest cent.
7. Format the table so it is attractive and easy to read.
8. Print the table.

topic 13-2 review

666

Long-Distance Charges for Regional Offices

Months	Seattle	Houston	St. Louis	Totals
January	$201.56	$58.67	$250.78	
February	190.45	75.34	277.56	
March	175.66	68.90	265.19	
April	188.34	92.51	281.40	
May	205.22	61.61	275.37	
June	199.29	74.27	259.39	
Total				
Average				

APPLICATION ACTIVITIES

ACTIVITY 1 Company Directory

As a special project, you will create a directory of employees for your office at the Home and Hearth Insurance Agency. The information will be contained in a database that can be accessed and updated easily.

What you are to do:

1. Prepare a database containing the names, titles, departments, and extensions of all the workers at your location using the information provided on the following page.
2. Sort the records in alphabetical order by last name and print the directory showing all fields.
3. Sort the records in alphabetical order first by department and then by last name. Print the directory showing all fields.

667

Name	Title	Department	Extension
Creel, Jenny	Accounting Support	Accounting	234
Hernandez, Jose	Department Head	Information Systems	190
Briggs, Jameel	Programmer	Information Systems	192
Hayes, Zondra	Sales Associate	Sales	300
Cross, Camden	Sales Associate	Sales	304
Brownlee, Bea	Department Head	Sales	308
Zimmer, Brock	PC Support	Information Systems	194
Hayden, Haley	Sales Associate	Sales	310
Parks, Carroll	Department Head	Accounting	230
Hibeeb, Zeah	Accounting Support	Accounting	236
Rhimer, Rock	Department Head	Human Resources	110
Hommler, Sirah	General Manager	Administration	100
Mummert, Eddie	Office Assistant	Administration	120

ACTIVITY 2 Directory Research

See Workbook pages 81–82.

Local telephone directories provide a wealth of information for your use in planning telephone communications and locating people and services. Locate Topic 13-2, Application Activity 2 in your *Student Activities and Projects* workbook. Use your local telephone directory to find the information requested.

ACTIVITY 3 Telephone Techniques

See Workbook pages 83–85.

Role-playing activities will help you develop your telephone skills. Locate Topic 13-2, Application Activity 3 in your *Student Activities and Projects* workbook. Follow the directions provided there to reinforce proper telephone techniques.

668

Chapter Summary

13

Telecommunications in today's Information Age plays a vital role in the way we conduct business as well as in our personal lives. Innovations in the methods we use to transmit voice, text, graphics, and video make it faster and easier to communicate with others all over the world. Living and working in the dynamic global workplace, you should be eager to learn how new, improved techniques and equipment can help you access, use, and share all forms of information. After studying this chapter, you should be knowledgeable about the following key points:

- Telecommunications technology is relied upon by workers in the Information Age to access and transmit information quickly and reliably both locally and globally.
- A variety of image and voice transmission equipment is available, such as facsimile, videoconferencing, centralized telephone systems, voice mail systems, mobile telephone equipment, speakerphones, and videophones.
- Specialized equipment and features available to the telephone consumer include features for individuals with impairments, conference call services, toll-free number service, prepaid long-distance phone cards, Wide Area Telecommunications Services, and telephone credit cards.
- When you answer or place a call for your organization, you immediately make an impression on the other person. Workers should use proper techniques and procedures so that all incoming and outgoing calls are handled professionally and efficiently.
- Workers in an organization should apply efficient procedures when placing outgoing calls. Preliminary planning of outgoing calls will ensure efficiency and economy.
- Many tools are available to help you research information needed to place a call. You should become familiar with information contained in a variety of print and electronic directories.
- You can help control telephone costs by using direct-dial calls, planning outgoing calls, and placing calls when rates are least expensive.

chapter 13 summary

Telephone Systems and Procedures

KEY CONCEPTS AND TERMS

automated attendant
collect calls
computer telephony integration
conference calls
direct-dial calls
facsimile
long-distance calls
person-to-person calls
screening calls
telecommunications
videoconferencing
voice mail

INTEGRATED CHAPTER ACTIVITIES

ACTIVITY 1 Voice Mail Procedures

template activity

Filename: Vmail

Your company, Dee-Lite's Chocolates, Inc., has just installed a voice mail system that is to be used by all workers. Because of your knowledge of voice mail procedures, you have been requested to make a presentation to the company about effective procedures to follow when using voice mail. Your supervisor, Timothy Wolinski, has given you a word processing file containing a rough draft of a partial list of effective voice mail techniques to include. He suggests that you use it, as well as any other resources you may find on the topic, to create a list of guidelines to present to your coworkers.

What you are to do:

1. Open the word processing file *Vmail*. Use this information your supervisor gave you about voice mail, the information you learned in this chapter about voice mail, and other research you may collect to edit and refine the list. Consider the order in which the effective voice mail procedures are presented.
2. Prepare a slide show using your presentation software. Integrate the text you prepared using your word processor. Include appropriate graphics, slide transition and text effects, color, and any other design features effectively to make the presentation interesting and informative.
3. Print the outline and handouts in black and white with several slides per page.
4. Present the slide show to the class.

670

ACTIVITY 2 New Long-Distance Carrier

Filename: Dayrates

Dee-Lite's Chocolates, Inc., is dissatisfied with their current long-distance service provider. Prices have risen dramatically on domestic calls over the last six months. The company remains open 24 hours a day, seven days a week to meet the demands of a growing international market for its gourmet, fat-free chocolates. Long-distance telephone calls are being placed all during the seven-day work period. Timothy has researched several plans. He has downloaded information from the Internet into a spreadsheet that contains information about domestic day rates. All the plans provide about the same international rates. He wants you to compute the average column and then integrate the spreadsheet table into a memo to all administrative staff members. The memo is to be from you. You will request their input as to a recommendation for a new long-distance carrier. Give them one week to respond to the memo.

What you are to do:

1. Compose, key, and edit a memo to all administrative staff members. Request that they examine the rate table and then give you their recommendation for a new long-distance service provider.
2. Open the *Dayrates* spreadsheet file. Enter a formula to average each company's day, evening, and weekend rates. Integrate the table into the memo.
3. Check the document for format and content. Print the integrated document.

671

Getting Acquainted with the World of Work

The Telephone Is Ringing Again!

Dear Ms. Liang

Last month I was hired as an office worker in a health club. My duties include word processing, handling membership fees, ordering supplies, and answering the telephone. I am interrupted often *by the phone. Even though we have voice mail, many of our callers prefer not to leave a message. Their calls are routed to me for answering. Several of the employees for whom I take messages seem to misplace them frequently. Mr. Parra is especially bad about losing messages. More than once he has said something like, "Curt, I can't find that message from Peter Torres. Please look up his number in the phone book for me." So I'm interrupted twice about the same matter! What can I do?*

Curt in Shreveport

Dear Curt

Did you notice the contradiction in your letter? You said that your job includes *answering the telephone, but then you said that you are* interrupted *by the telephone. Remember, answering the telephone contributes to the smooth functioning of your office just as much as the other tasks you perform. The telephone does not keep you from doing your job—it* is *part of your job! When the phone rings, stop what you're doing and give your full attention to the caller. When you have completed the conversation and handled any messages related to the call, return to other tasks.*

You must be helpful when information is requested about a particular telephone message. Consider purchasing a spiral-bound pad of telephone message forms that includes duplicate-copy forms. Each time you record a message, you also record a copy of it. When you remove the original, a copy remains in your spiral pad. If someone loses a message, you can quickly refer to your copy.

An alternative to preparing handwritten messages is recording messages using your computer. It takes less time to key a message than to write it. The message can be printed and delivered to the recipient or sent electronically via e-mail. Your organization may want to consider purchasing special software that includes an onscreen message form. Your electronic message file can easily be printed or transmitted again if someone loses a message.

Mei-yu Liang

Office Supervisor

672

Tele-communication Systems

Communicating over distances is not new. Native Americans used smoke signals to communicate messages. Pony Express riders defied the perils of the wilderness to deliver the mail. The telegraph was an amazing way to send short messages quickly. With today's world-wide communication networks, we can send and receive information rapidly and reliably. We can sit at our computer and send a message down the hall, across town, across the country, or across the world in the time it takes to press a key on our keyboard.

As an office professional, you will no doubt be networked to other workers at your location. Your network may also connect you to coworkers in another city or even in another country. As organizations find more and more reasons to be linked to the Internet and the World Wide Web, you will find it necessary to become network savvy in order to perform your job efficiently and effectively. In this chapter, you will become acquainted with local area networks, wide area networks, and international networks including the Internet and the World Wide Web. You will identify social and ethical issues brought about by rapidly changing network technologies and explore the future of the Internet.

Chapter 14

getting started

Networking has enhanced the use of microcomputers. Organizations have embraced networking because of the improvements in efficiency and cost as a result of the sharing capabilities networks make possible. What started as a simple linking of a few microcomputers to enable the sharing of devices has exploded to become an organization's means of global communication and information sharing.

Chapter 14

Understanding Networks

When you have completed your study of this topic, you will be able to:

- **Describe common features of local area networks, wide area networks, and international networks**
- **Explain the uses of the Internet**
- **Define basic Internet terminology**
- **Explain how to get access to the Internet**

Topic 14-1

Networks are used in organizations to link computers as well as many other types of electronic hardware. Two types of networks, local area networks (LANs) and wide area networks (WANs), help workers complete their daily tasks and share information vital to the operation of the organization. Today's technology, however, does not limit our communications just to internal networking within the organization. Growth and creativity in the ways in which the Internet and the World Wide Web are being used to conduct business are impacting workers in surprising and exciting ways.

imported: brought in from another country or area

exporters: those who sell their goods to people in other countries.

Cal-Giftorama is a national catalog mail-order company specializing in unique, handcrafted items **imported** *from all over the world. A telecommunications network makes it possible for them to place orders to* **exporters** *located in Europe and Asia, as well as to conduct everyday*

business within this country. Their telecommunications system enables them to ship 98 percent of all incoming customer orders within 24 hours of receipt. When a customer places an order over the telephone, a **telemarketer** *is able to determine immediately if the ordered item is available and from which regional distribution center it will be shipped. Within minutes, the order is processed, and a packing list is printed at the distribution center. Soon the order is on its way to the customer. Without the network, it could take five or more days to process the order.*

telemarketer: one who sells products or services over the telephone

Cal-Giftorama has recently developed a home page for their new website on the Internet. The site offers audio files and a live cam in the catalog showroom. Also, visitors to the site will be able to view and order selected items from the **online** *catalog. They feel that if they do not establish a presence on the World Wide Web, they will not be able to maintain their competitive position in the mail-order import business.*

online: connected and communicating with a computer

Telecommunications Networks

A computer network links two or more computers so they can share information. A network used to link computers that are close to each other—usually within several hundred feet—is a local area network (LAN). A network used to link computers that are a long distance apart—miles from each other—is called a wide area network (WAN). Several local area networks may be connected to each other and may be connected to wide area networks. Wide area networks are not limited to this country; they can be worldwide.

Computer networks allow us to extend the power of our computers by enabling us to share data, conduct research, discuss topics with others, and visit places to which we cannot afford to travel. In this topic, you will be introduced to communication networks.

LOCAL AREA NETWORKS

As described earlier, a local area network (LAN) is a communication network that links or connects electronic equipment within a *limited area* such as a single room or building or several rooms or **adjacent**

adjacent: nearby, adjoining

teaching tips

Visit a local business that has a state-of-the-art network. Have the network administrator discuss the hardware, software, peripherals, and topologies used. What types of files do they share? How do they handle file security? What are the advantages and disadvantages of having the network? Is their network connected to the Internet?

Illustration 14-1:1

Networks connect your computer to computers a few feet away, across the continent, and around the globe.

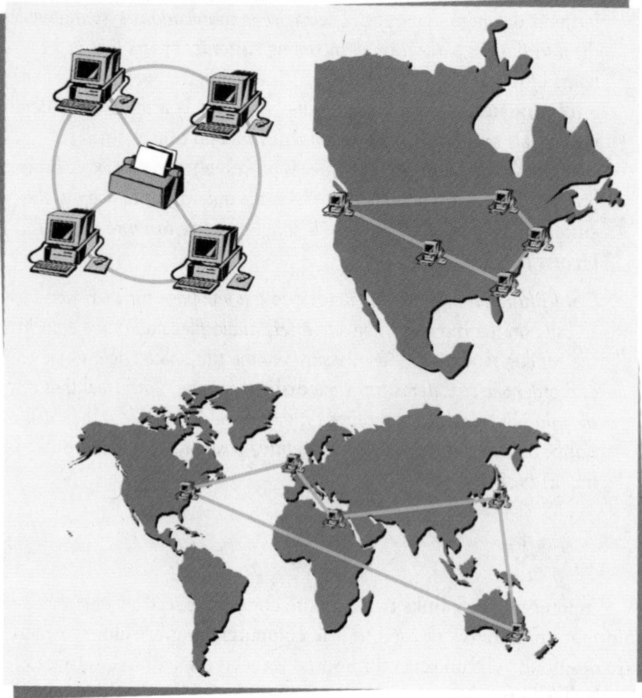

buildings. With a LAN, several computer users can share data files, software, and equipment. LANs allow users to exchange information and access **peripherals** rapidly over specially installed cables. Sharing resources is a major advantage of a LAN. In an organization with a LAN, users can share one costly application software package, exchange spreadsheet and word processing files, access the same customer information, and share an expensive color laser printer. It is easy to see how money as well as time are saved when an organization relies on a network.

peripherals: equipment connected to computers such as printers and scanners

In order to use a network efficiently, workers must first be trained to perform networking tasks such as logging on and off, exchanging files, setting password security, sending and receiving messages, controlling files, and viewing network printer **queues.** To become an informed network user, you should also learn about common network **configurations** and networking hardware and software options.

queues: list of files waiting to be printed

configurations: structures, arrangements

Configurations. You probably have already used a computer that was networked. Perhaps you have two home computers linked to each other or to the Internet. The computers at your school probably are networked—within a classroom, with other classrooms in the building, or with computers in adjacent buildings. What are the characteristics of these short-distance networks? How are the **components** of networks arranged?

components: parts

Characteristics. When you plan a local network, you must first decide where you want your shared files to reside—on each individual's hard drive or on a common hard drive to be shared by all users.

With peer-to-peer networking computers are connected with cables to each other and operate as equals in the networked environment. A computer in this type of network can access software and data stored on the hard drives of all the connected computers. Individual users and the organization determine which data or software files will be

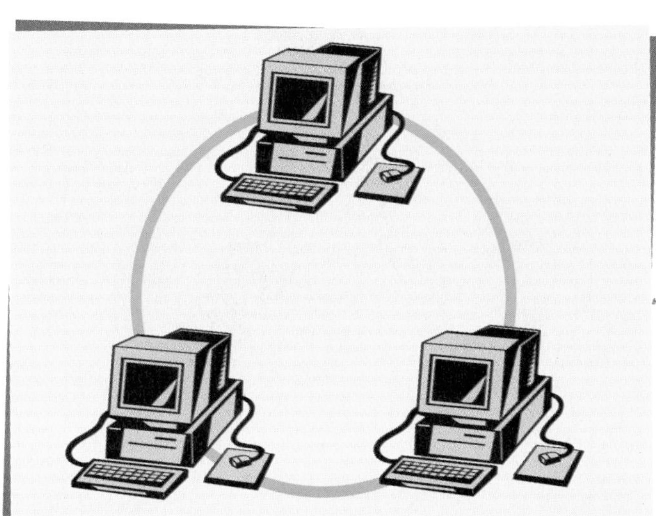

Illustration 14-1:2

In a peer-to-peer network, users make documents and data from their hard drives available to other users.

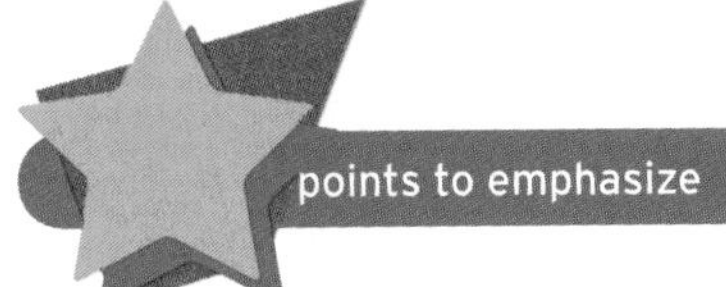

Networks usually have several printers available for users to select. Print queues may be viewed on the screen for checking the order in which documents are being processed. Jobs on the print queues may be deleted, paused, or moved up on the queue to be printed sooner.

Have students identify the type of computer network at your school—peer-to-peer or file-server based.

public
available for sharing, unrestricted

made **public** for other network users to access. All that is needed to set up peer-to-peer networking for most newer computers is cabling and special software. If your PC is older, it may not have built-in networking hardware. You can easily install a network interface card, which is a special card installed inside the computer that allows your computer to "talk" to other computers on the network.

In server-based networking, one computer fills requests for data and program files from network users. The central computer that performs this service is called a file server because of its primary task of supplying or "serving" files to computers on the network. In this type of network, the basic requirements are the same as those for a peer-to-peer network. Every computer to be connected must be cabled, have special software, and have either built-in hardware for networking or a network interface card installed.

Illustration 14-1:3
In server-based networking, users access data and software on the file server.

Topologies. The physical layout of a local area network should ensure a logical flow of electronic information. Physical layout of a network is called topology. Every piece of hardware such as a computer or a printer that is connected to the LAN is called a node. A LAN may have two or three or several hundred nodes. Each one of these nodes has the capability of sharing all the resources on the LAN through their own communication channel or connection, which is referred to as a link. The nodes and links in a network can be arranged in different ways. The three most common physical layouts, or topologies, of networks are *star*, *ring*, and *bus*.

In a star topology, there is a host computer that acts as the manager of the entire network. All computers and other devices are attached to the host. All messages are sent to the host. The host computer is the central processing area for all messages, which are processed and then routed to the requested device on the network. When the host fails, communication between all nodes is stopped. Illustration 14-1:4 shows computers networked using a star topology.

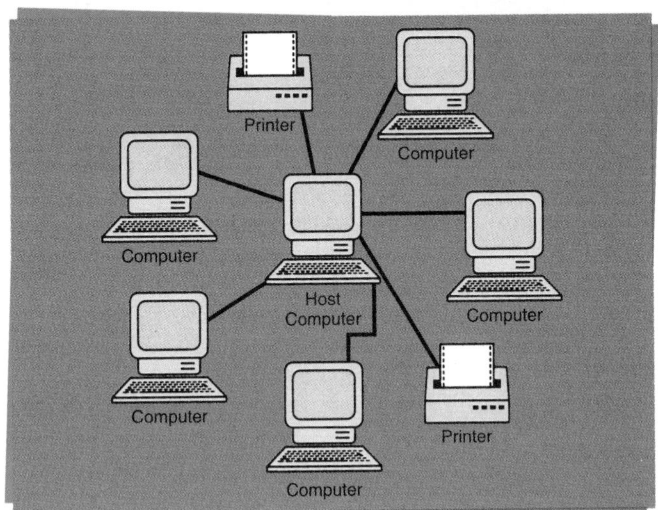

Illustration 14-1:4

In star topology, all computers and peripherals are connected to the host.

When all nodes are attached in a circle without a central host, they are networked using ring topology. Each computer can transmit data to any other computer or device that is connected to the ring.

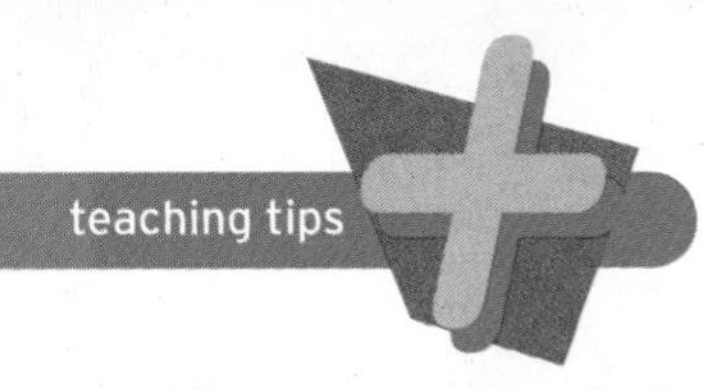

Have students identify the network topology used at your school—star, ring, or bus.

What are the advantages and disadvantages of each of the three network topologies?

Messages simply pass around the ring until they come to the device to which they are sent. If the circle is broken, the message will not arrive at its destination.

Illustration 14-1:5

In ring topology, all nodes are connected in a circle without a host computer.

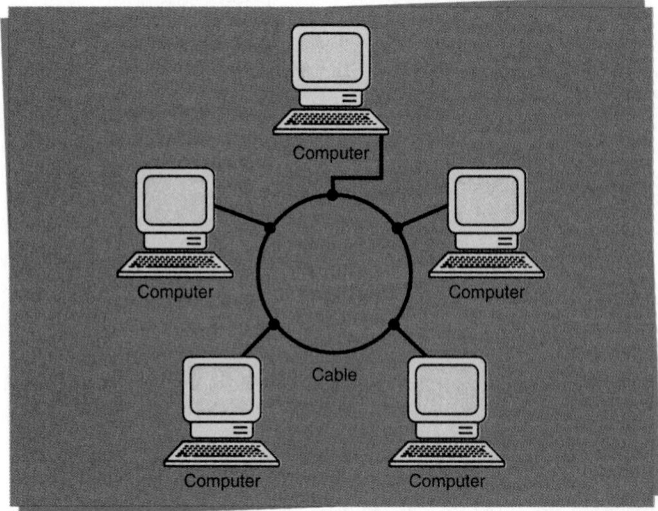

In a bus topology, all computers and other devices are attached to a central communication line (cable). Information travels over the cable line from one computer to another without having to travel through every other node as in ring topology. Bus topology is the most popular LAN topology. If there is a failure of one or two devices on the network, the other devices are not affected. Bus topology is shown in Illustration 14-1:6.

devices: computers or peripherals

Transmission Carriers. The term transmission carrier refers to the cables or other equipment used to link **devices** in a LAN. Three types of cable that are commonly used to link computers and other equipment are *twisted-pair*, *coaxial*, and *fiber-optic* cables.

Twisted-pair cable is composed of two wires twisted around each other. Four pairs of twisted wires are usually wrapped together and encased to form a cable. This type of cabling is similar to widely used,

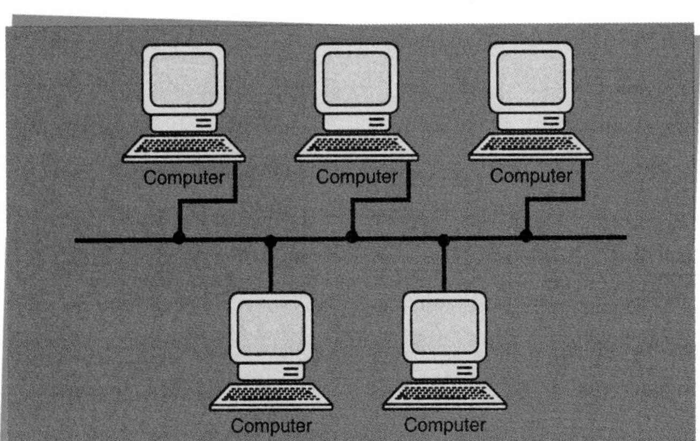

Illustration 14-1:6

PCs in a bus topology are connected to a single communication channel.

older telephone wiring. Twisted-pair cabling is inexpensive. However, data travels slowly using these lines and is susceptible to interference from other electrical devices, especially when it has to travel long distances. When using twisted-pair cabling for a LAN, it is best to keep distances between devices under 250 feet.

You are probably more familiar with *coaxial cable*. This type of cable is widely used by cable television companies. Coaxial cable can transmit a large amount of electronic data more quickly and reliably over longer distances than twisted-pair wire. It is also more expensive. Because of the heavy shielding of its single wire, interference is much less than

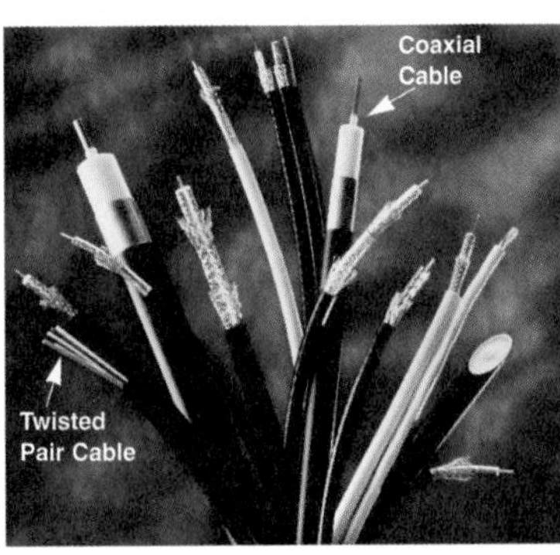

Illustration 14-1:7

Coaxial cable can transmit more data faster and with less interference than twisted-pair cable.

that encountered with twisted-pair cable. Coaxial cabling for networks is preferred by many organizations.

Fiber-optic cables are made from thin glass strands that transmit laser light pulses efficiently at very high speeds over long distances. Each pulse of light represents one piece of data. Fiber-optic cables are unaffected by electrical interference and can transmit massive amounts of data faster than any other type of cable. It is the most expensive; therefore, cost may prohibit its use in many organizations.

Show students the three types of cable: twisted-pair, coaxial, and fiber-optic. You may obtain these from your system administrator or from a local organization such as the telephone or cable company.

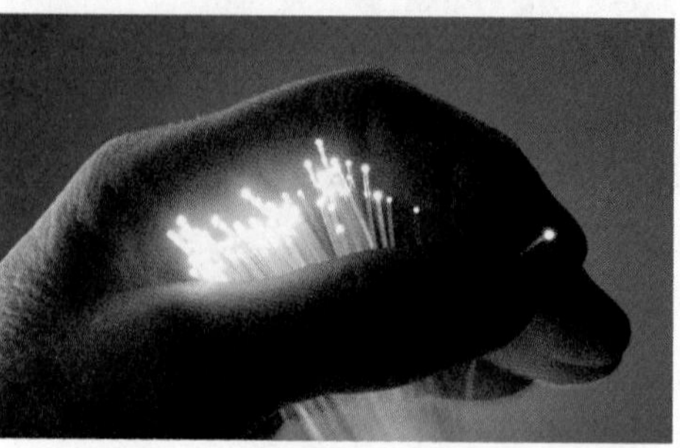

Illustration 14-1:8

Fiber-optic cable is made from tiny strands of glass fibers that send light pulses quickly.

When setting up their networks, many organizations use a variety of transmission carriers to connect devices. They must consider cost, speed, efficiency, reliability, and consequences to the network users when cabling is damaged or destroyed. They may decide to install expensive fiber optics for parts of the network that will have to handle the largest amount of data or link the longest distances. For parts of the network that are physically closer together or will not have heavy data transfer, they may select less expensive twisted-pair or coaxial cabling.

Wireless communication (without cables) for LANs is possible using infrared light waves or radio waves. Infrared light waves transmit information in a straight line and require a clear path between objects for successful transmission of data. Wireless communication via infrared light waves is usually limited to computers, keyboards, monitors, and peripherals that are only a short distance from each other with no obstructions to block the signals. Wireless communication using radio waves is more versatile since the radio waves do not travel in a straight line. Radio waves can be used to transmit data between equipment in a larger area such as several rooms or a whole building.

Illustration 14-1:9
Wireless communication for LANs is limited to very short distances.

Working in a LAN Environment. Computer users in a LAN community should learn how to use the LAN effectively. There are several tasks that new users must quickly learn how to perform—**logging in** and **logging out,** sharing files, accessing files, using e-mail, and using the various devices on the network. New workers may be introduced to the LAN environment in a variety of ways. Some organizations provide hands-on training by support staff; others assign an experienced coworker to train the new user; still others may give the user a network procedures manual to follow.

logging in: gaining access to a computer's hardware or software by identifying yourself, usually with a user ID such as your name and a password

logging out: leaving the computer software following a set procedure

LANs have become a valuable means of managing data communications in organizations. They are cost efficient, reliable, and easy to use. Fewer highly trained personnel are required to manage the network than were needed in the past to maintain large computers and data processing centers. Today, when one or more computers, devices, or even the network itself is down, users can continue to work on their individual computers even though they may not be able to share data or devices. On the other hand, increased loss of privacy and threats to the security of information have become a concern for users in all types of networks.

expand the concept

Network administration is a career in high demand by organizations. The need for knowledgeable, professional managers of computer networks promises to continue to grow as organizations continue to expand their links internally as well as externally.

Network administrators perform a variety of tasks that include troubleshooting, resolution of problems, upgrading, and maintaining all hardware and software that directly affect the network. New users must be added and trained, security must be managed, peripherals must be added and controlled, data must be backed up, and the network must be fine-tuned.

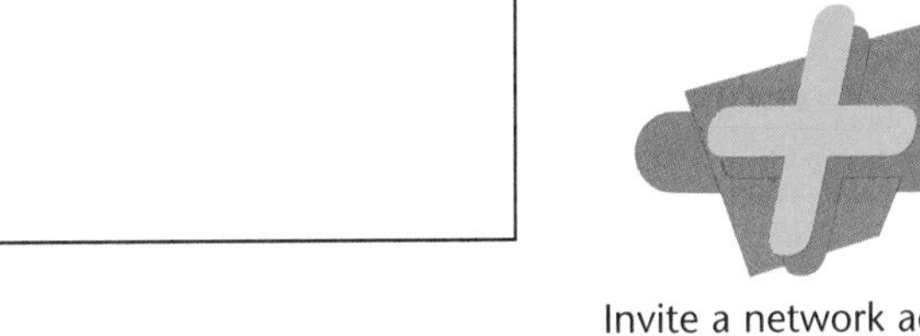

teaching tips

Invite a network administrator to come to the class and discuss network administration as a career including training needed, certifications acquired, job responsibilities, biggest challenges, and rewards of the career.

teaching tips

1. Today's most popular operating systems for file servers are Novell, OS/2, Unix, and Windows NT. Have students research these four systems.
2. Describe and demonstrate your school's networking software if you have a file server-based network. If you do not, visit an organization that uses one of the four operating systems. Have the network administrator demonstrate use of the software such as how users are added and how the print queue is managed.

WIDE AREA NETWORKS

A *wide area network* (WAN) links electronic equipment that is separated by long distances. Wireless microwave and satellite transmissions may be used to send information from one city to another or across continents. A WAN for a small company may cover several cities or states. WANs for a large, multinational company may cover several countries. You may be networked with other schools in your local system, in your state, nationally, and internationally. Your home computer may be connected to your teacher's computer. If you are absent from class, you may be able to get your assignments, complete your homework, and transmit it to your teacher without leaving your house.

Many workers today are taking advantage of wide area networking technology to work at home. They communicate with the office using a computer with a modem and a telephone line to establish a connection and to send and receive information.

Data Transmission. In setting up a wide area network, organizations should choose a telecommunications connection that will best meet their needs. A dedicated line for telecommunications, also called a leased line, remains connected and ready for use at all times. When an organization does not have constant communication needs over long distances, a dial-up line can provide transmission connections only when needed. Both provide a relatively secure, clear transmission from one computer to another. A dial-up line can be more economical, but may be less convenient, than a dedicated line. Since dial-up lines are usually shared with other organizations, at times the line may be busy. Use of telecommunication lines is purchased from a telephone company or other business that specializes in providing these services, such as a satellite communications company.

Microwave transmissions play an important role in data transmission in a WAN. Microwave transmissions are radio waves that can carry data in straight lines from one microwave station to another. Microwave dishes and microwave towers relay signals to each other directly. You have probably seen satellite dishes and noticed the imposing microwave towers on hillsides. The higher the dish or tower, the further the message can be sent. Obstructions between the two relay stations will interfere with the signal. In a WAN, data created on a computer travels by fiber-optic cable or telephone lines to the nearest microwave carrier. The data travels from carrier to carrier until it reaches the one nearest its final destination. From the last microwave carrier, the data is then transmitted over cables to the receiving computer. In international communications, earth-orbiting satellites may play a major role in transmission of the data. Signals are sent from your computer to a satellite relay station. The satellite relay station transmits the signal to an orbiting satellite that will bounce the electronic message to a receiving station on earth. From there, the signal travels over cable to your modem and computer.

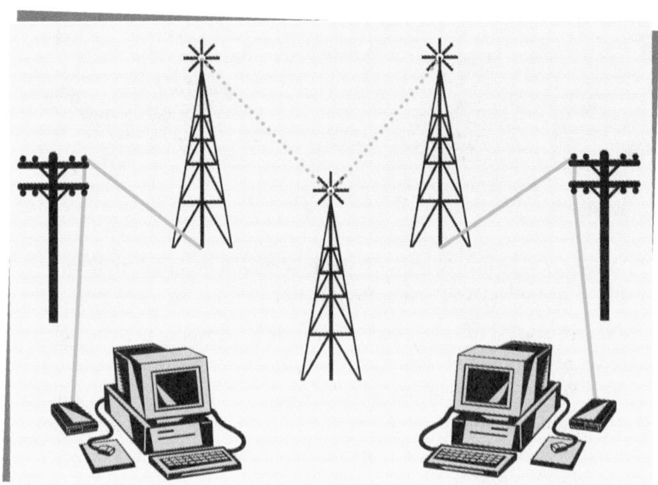

Illustration 14-1:10

WANs may use long-distance fiber optic cables or they may relay messages from one tower to another.

Uses of WANs. Wide area networks, like LANs, are used for file access, data exchange, and e-mail. Electronic data interchange (EDI) allows the exchange of data between different companies that may or may not have compatible computer or network systems. If a clothing manufacturer in Atlanta needs silk fabric from a supplier in Hong Kong, a purchase order can be placed from a computer at the factory in Atlanta to a computer in the warehouse in Hong Kong. The order is filled, the fabric is shipped, and an electronic invoice is sent to the computer at the factory in Atlanta. No paper has been exchanged. It

Microwave towers are spaced miles apart and must be in a straight line of sight of each other. Microwaves do not bend around buildings or other objects and are subject to weather interference. Radio signals, however, are capable of bending around objects and are thus more efficient. More and more microwave towers can be seen dotting the landscape—on top of hillsides and mesas and on top of buildings. Many local landowners and community activist groups are protesting the erection of these towers in their neighborhoods. Find out how your community feels about this issue. What are the concerns? Are there local ordinances prohibiting the towers in certain areas? What regulations are imposed upon their construction, such as distance away from other structures?

Illustration 14-1:11

International data exchange via microwave transmissions.

would take weeks for the order to be received, filled, and invoiced without use of electronic data interchange.

WANs can also be used for distance learning, changing the way schools and colleges conduct classes. *Distance learning* connects students and teachers at different locations, often many miles apart. Video cameras record action and sound as it happens and telephone lines send the information to and from a classroom at a distant location.

> *Mr. Harold Whatley is a master teacher of United States history. His courses are popular and fill quickly with students who have heard of his interesting, exciting classes. Mr. Whatley's classes are limited to 20 students; however, with the school system's new, state-of-the art distance learning facilities, a second class of 14 students is set up in a neighboring school. Both classes meet in specially equipped classrooms, which have computers with wide-screen monitors, video cameras, and telecommunications networking hardware and software.*
>
> *When Mr. Whatley conducts his class, he and the 20 students at his location are able to see and hear the rest of the class at the other location.*

Illustration 14-1:12
Students and teachers may be miles apart, yet see and hear each other.

If possible, visit a local university or community college distance learning facility. What communications technologies are being used to make remote learning possible?

The 14 students at the remote location can also see, hear, speak to, and exchange data with those at the main site. All participants can exchange ideas by talking with each other, seeing each other, and communicating with their computers.

INTERNATIONAL NETWORKS

Wide area networks are not limited to this country; they can be worldwide. There are often difficulties to overcome when establishing connections to computers in foreign lands. Some international standards have been established; however, usage taxes are determined by each individual nation. Because of the demands placed upon countries to be a part of a global economy, many are building communications systems to attract electronic visitors to their lands. Some developing countries see the building of global communications technologies as a vital element of national concern.

The variety of technology available for worldwide, long-distance transmission of all types of data—voice, image, text, and video—has made it a necessity for organizations to evaluate their telecommunications needs and spend their dollars wisely. One thing is certain: the need for global communications links will continue to increase as organizations strive to remain competitive. This hunger for easily accessible international communications has led to the amazing growth of the best-known wide area network of all—the Internet.

The Internet: An Introduction

The Internet is a worldwide network of computers and other smaller networks that allows the exchange of data, commands, and messages. Its beginnings date back to 1969 when the U.S. Department of Defense created an experimental network to allow government and university researchers to communicate with each other, computer to computer. Internet **protocols** were developed to allow data to be exchanged among its users. In order for your computer to communicate on the Internet, it must also understand and use these protocols.

protocols: rules, conventions

In its early days, the Internet was difficult to use and limited to government and university users. When commercially funded networks were added, its use grew quickly. The Internet had arrived. Today, Internet use is expanding rapidly. Thousands of new users access the Internet each day—so many, in fact, that gaining access to particular sites is sometimes difficult. Students, workers, and consumers use the Internet for research, discussion, transferring files, and electronic mail.

Illustration 14-1:13
People all over the world are becoming users of the Internet.

thinking critically

1. What do you think are some of the reasons for the phenomenal growth of the Internet?
2. Since there is no one person or organization in charge of the Internet to manage, police, or guide its growth, how is it able to exist and function?

GETTING CONNECTED TO THE INTERNET

Many government facilities, educational institutions, and organizations have direct Internet access through their local area or wide area networks. Workers can easily gain access to the Internet if their LAN or WAN is connected to it.

Direct access is not the only way to get online. Internet service providers (ISP) can give you entry to the Internet for a charge, usually based on a monthly fee and the number of hours you are online during that month. This kind of access, called dial-up access, requires a computer with a modem, telecommunications software, and a phone line. To gain entry to the Internet, you contact the ISP, which then provides you with a connection to the Internet. A big advantage of dial-up access is that it is inexpensive and easy to set up compared to a direct access line. Most home computers connected to the Internet use an ISP.

When selecting an Internet service provider, evaluate the cost of the service; the company's reliability, security, and overall performance; user satisfaction; restrictions; types of services provided; and quality of customer assistance. Service providers may be local businesses whose customer satisfaction can be researched by contacting your local Better Business Bureau. Often, contacting other local clients will provide you with valuable, firsthand consumer recommendations.

Information services are organizations that provide more than dial-up Internet access. Each one offers its own unique content, organization, services, and software to subscribers. America Online, Prodigy, and CompuServe are all popular information services. When you subscribe to an information service, your Internet activities may be restricted in some manner by that company.

Illustration 14-1:14

Each information service provides its own unique look, features, and offerings.

for discussion

1. What are the advantages of direct access? dial-up access?
2. Which type of access does your school have? If you have Internet access at home, what type of access do you have?

teaching tips

Have students work in teams to research the services and charges of local Internet service providers. After students have shared their findings with each other, data should be analyzed and summarized in a spreadsheet table.

teaching tips

Have students research the content, organization, services, cost, and software offered by information services organizations such as America Online, Prodigy, and CompuServe. They may work in teams and report their findings to the class. Encourage them to use presentation software and provide handouts.

Internet addresses are assigned by the local network manager and may be long and difficult to remember. When giving someone your Internet address, spell it out letter by letter. When writing an Internet address, repeat it to verify that you have written it correctly.

INTERNET ADDRESSES

Before you can send and receive information on the Internet, you must have a unique Internet address. Just as you must have a mailing address composed of name, street, city, state, and ZIP code to receive letters and packages at home, you must have an address composed of specific elements to receive and send information over the Internet. The parts of an Internet address may seem strange until you become familiar with them.

Address Elements. Internet addresses begin with a user id which is a unique identifier such as *dsmith* (for David Smith). The user id is followed by the @ sign, which serves merely as a separator. The part of the name that follows the @ sign is known as the domain. Domains are simply organizational levels separated by periods. To understand a domain name, it is easiest to read from right to left. The highest level of the domain appears at the right and identifies the type of organization. When you read the address *dsmith@eng.unlv.edu*, starting at the right, the *edu* identifies that this address is located at an educational institution. The next section, *unlv*, identifies the specific educational institution, such as University of Nevada, Las Vegas. The *eng* identifies the department, such as English or Engineering, and the last, *dsmith* identifies an individual.

When you pronounce the Internet address Djones@cmu.com, you would say, " d jones at c m u dot com" rather than spell out each letter. Be careful when recording an Internet address. Addresses are usually case sensitive. If you key an address incorrectly, you will not be able to make your connection.

Domains. There are only seven organizational domains at present. They consist of only three letters and are easy to learn. A list of domains is shown below.

Domain	Purpose
.com	Commercial business
.edu	Colleges, universities, and other educational institutions
.gov	Government agencies (nonmilitary)

.int	International organizations
.mil	Military institutions
.net	Network support centers
.org	Miscellaneous, nonprofit organizations

The Internet International Ad Hoc Committee is planning to extend the Internet domain naming system to create 28 independent naming registrars and assign seven top-level generic domain names such as .firm, .store, .web, .arts, .rec, .info, and .nom. When an organization is outside your country, a two-letter country code is used at the end of the address. Every country has its own unique geographic domain code. If there is no geographic code in a name, then the domain is located within your own country. Several country codes are listed below.

Domain	Country	Domain	Country
.au	Australia	.it	Italy
.ca	Canada	.jp	Japan
.de	Germany	.mx	Mexico
.es	Spain	.tr	Turkey
.fr	France	.uk	United Kingdom
.hk	Hong Kong	.us	United States
.il	Israel	.va	Vatican
.in	India		

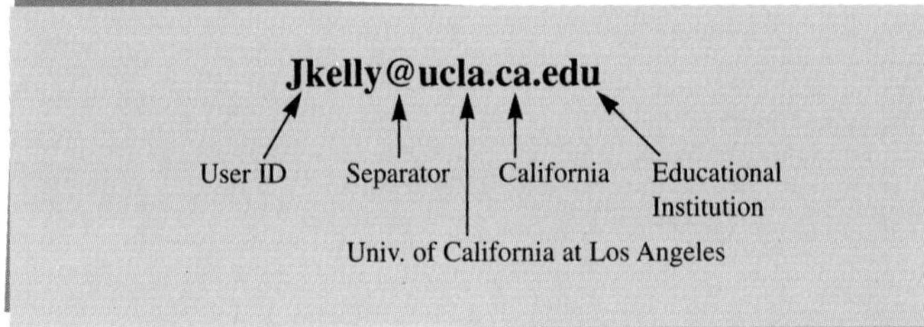

Illustration 14-1:15

Each Internet address must be unique. A user ID is followed by the @ sign to separate it from the domain.

1. What is your Internet address? If you do not have one, what would be an appropriate one for you as a student using your school's network?
2. What might be an appropriate Internet name for:
   - a morning radio talk-show host named Bob Adams who works at WKXX in Canada
   - a student named Johanna Naisbitt at Clayton Community College in Boise, Idaho
   - a home user named Becka Sanchez who uses America Online (AOL) for her Internet service

Many new terms have been created as a result of Internet activity. A vocabulary has developed to describe users and activities of e-mail and newsgroup users. These will be presented in the next topic. Some that students have used or heard include the following:

- the Net—shortened way to say "the Internet"
- surfing the Net—refers to the action of traveling from one Internet site to another
- cyberspace—when you are on the Net, you are in cyberspace
- the Web, WWW, W3—refers to the Worldwide Web, a powerful Internet resource

A few addresses of interesting people, places, and things are identified below. Examine each domain carefully. What or who will you find at these addresses?

- adam@mtv.com
- nightly@nbc.com
- president@whitehouse.gov
- spacelink@msfc.nasa.gov

Now that you understand the basics of the Internet, you are ready to learn about sites and services it offers. Topic 14-2 will introduce you to using the Internet and exploring the issues that keep everyone talking about the Net.

Reviewing the Topic

Understanding Networks

1. What is the primary difference between a local area network and a wide area network?
2. What tasks must network users be trained to perform in order to use the LAN effectively?
3. What tasks does a file server perform in server-based networking?
4. Describe the physical layout of star, ring, and bus topologies.
5. How do networks help organizations manage data communications efficiently when compared to data processing centers of the past?
6. What are the differences between a dedicated line for telecommunications and a dial-up line?
7. Describe how microwave transmission from a wide area network to a receiving computer is accomplished.
8. Briefly describe the Internet.
9. What is needed to get connected to the Internet via an Internet service provider?
10. What are the seven original organizational domains used in Internet addresses? What type of organization uses each domain?

THINKING CRITICALLY

You work for a nonprofit, charitable organization that provides assistance to children with a rare disease. The organization is considering developing a site on the Internet. Your supervisor, Luz Riordan, is not convinced that the organization should do so and has asked you to prepare a list of advantages and disadvantages for setting up the Internet site along with your recommendation.

What you are to do:

Make a list of the pros and cons of the nonprofit organization setting up an Internet site. Write your recommendation in a memo to your supervisor. Include your list of advantages and disadvantages.

topic 14-1 review

topic 14-1 review

Understanding Networks

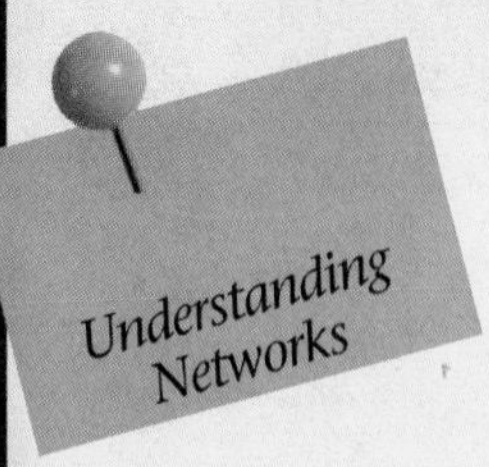

REINFORCING MATH SKILLS

Your employer wants you to get connected to the Internet at home so that you can perform research tasks when working at home. You have been asked to compare service charges for Internet access for home use and make your recommendation. Compare prices using at least four different companies. Use local service providers and information services such as America Online. Prepare a spreadsheet with the following data: name of provider or service, set-up fee, monthly flat rate if available, charge for 50 hours per month, and any other features or services you feel are important for comparison. Provide calculations to find the minimums and averages for columns that contain charges.

What you are to do:

1. Research the requested information. Add other items that you feel should be compared to help make the decision.
2. Prepare a spreadsheet. Enter the data needed to make comparisons. Find the minimum and average amounts for the columns containing charges.
3. At the bottom of the spreadsheet, indicate your choice for the service provider. Briefly state your reasons for your recommendation. Remember, lowest cost may not be the only factor on which to base your decision.

topic 14-1 review

APPLICATION ACTIVITY

ACTIVITY Database of Internet Sites

You work for Dr. Lou Schenk, the head of the Development Department at Bennings College. In your job, you often perform research tasks using the Internet. You have decided to create a directory of frequently visited Internet sites for your own reference using your database software. You have been writing down the addresses on sheets of paper and often have trouble finding them quickly when you need them. You have decided that a printed list, sorted by organization and kept by your computer, would improve your efficiency. As you decide to add addresses, it will be a simple task to update the database.

694

What you are to do:

1. Use your database software to create a database table containing the Internet addresses.
2. Sort the records by organization name.
3. Print a table or list showing all fields in the sorted database.

Disney
bvp.wdp.com/bvpm/

California
www.research.digital.com/src/virtual-tourist/california.html

Boston
www.std.com/ne/boston.html

Computer Games
wcl-rs.bham.ac.uk/gamesdomain

White House
www.whitehouse.gov

Government Information
www.fedworld.gov

NASA Kennedy Space Center
www.ksc.nasa.gov/

Genetics Education Center
www.kumc.edu/instruction/medicine/genetics

Canadian Government Information
www.usask.ca/library/gic/index.html

China Home Page
www.ihep.ac.cn/china.html

Centers for Disease Control
www.cdec.gov

Central Intelligence Agency
www.odci.gov/cia

Decisions of U.S. Supreme Court
www.law.cornell.edu/supct/supct.table.html

695

U.S. Customs Service
www.ustreas.gov/treasury/bureaus/customs/

Parks of Canada
parkscanada.pch.gc.ca/parks/main_e.htm

Mexico Travel
mexico-travel.com/mex_eng.html

U.S. House of Representatives
www.house.gov

Harvard Computer Society
hcs.harvard.edu

Moscow State University
www.rector.msu.su/

Social Work Canada
www.uwindsor.ca/faculty/socsci/socwk/index.html

topic 14-1 review

696

Topic 14-2

Using the Internet

When you have completed your study of this topic, you will be able to:

- **Describe the most common uses of the Internet**
- **Apply proper rules of conduct when using the Internet**
- **Discuss key issues related to Internet use**
- **Discuss future trends in Internet technology and uses**

getting started

Many of your students have Internet access at home and can contribute firsthand experiences to add interest to class discussions. Even those who do not visit cannot help but notice all the attention the burgeoning Internet receives in print, radio, and television media.

While students are studying this topic, have them keep a record of the instances in which the Internet is mentioned in broadcast or newspaper news items. Have them especially note news stories about how communications on the Net help save or improve lives, and news stories about how lives are negatively affected. Encourage discussion of social and ethical issues.

You learned in Topic 14-1 that the Internet is a huge network to which schools, government, organizations, and home users are connected. In this topic you will learn what kinds of information are on the Internet and how to get along with other online users. You may decide to discuss topics with others online, share files, send and receive electronic mail, play games with distant opponents, or promote a business venture. As you explore the Internet, you will meet and interact with many people. Just as you are concerned about communicating effectively at school, home, and work, you will want to learn to communicate effectively via the Internet.

As Internet popularity grows, so do the related issues. What controls can be placed on the information? Should there even be any controls? How can families monitor the information their children access at

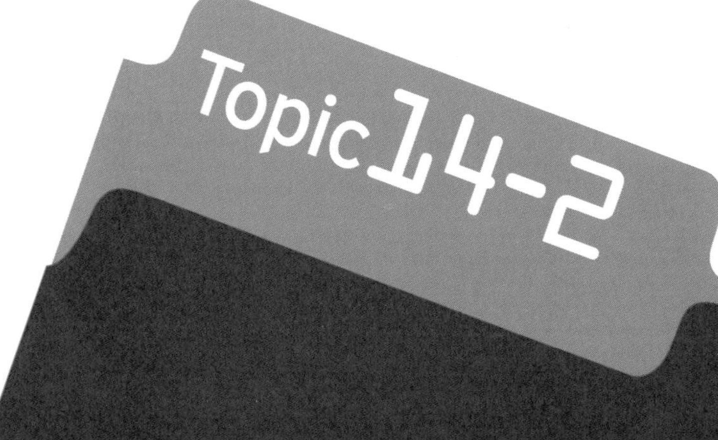

Illustration 14-2:1

The Internet connects users all over the world and delivers information rapidly.

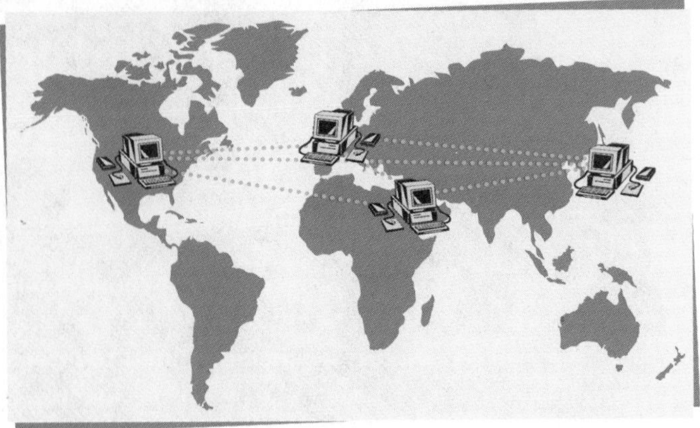

home or at school? What is the economic impact of the Internet? Who will provide Internet service in the future? What are some security measures that can be used to protect information you want to keep private? The Internet holds great promise, but is also creating many challenges. You will want to learn all you can about the Internet and how it may affect you at home, school, or work.

What You Can Do on the Internet

Uses for the Internet seem to be unlimited. As an international network of computers with no central point of control, the Internet offers limitless opportunities for gathering information. The vast resources available allow exploration of topics and discussions with many interesting people. Before the advent of the Internet, if you wanted to obtain information for a report from the library, you had to go there to check out books or other needed publications. If you wanted to compare car prices, check banking interest rates, or visit a museum, you had to travel to do it. If you are connected to the Internet, you can do all these activities online from your computer at home, school, or work. Here are a few other interesting activities you can do on the Internet:

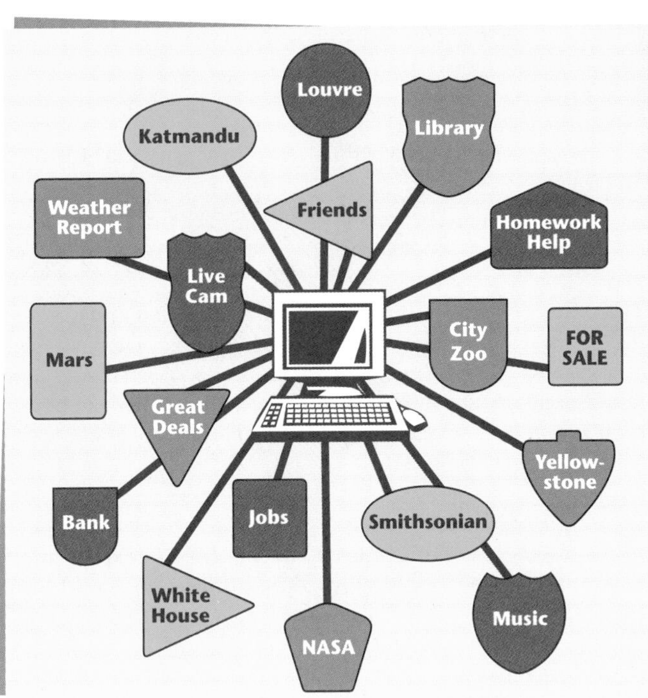

Illustration 14-2:2

Information for work, special concerns, and fun can all be accessed via the Internet.

- **browse** thousands of libraries all over the world
- search for consumer information about products
- sell products and services to consumers all over the world
- shop electronically
- send and receive electronic mail
- discuss topics with others who share your interests
- view live-action camera shots
- visit other countries electronically
- track storms

browse:
look through

For what purposes might a doctor use the Internet? a college professor? a high school teacher? a student? a coin collector? a computer hardware salesperson? a company's personnel manager?

1. Have students divide into teams of two or three. They are to select one topic of interest about the Internet. Articles about the Internet are to be collected from magazines published within the past four months, current newspapers, and the Net. If each student has Internet access, you may want them to conduct their research entirely online. Resources on the Net about the Internet are constantly being changed, updated, and improved. Approve each team's topic to ensure a wide range of research. After collecting the articles, the teams are to summarize the important aspects of the topic and report to the class. Presentation software may be used to enhance each team's report.

- view pictures from the Hubble Space Telescope
- dissect a frog in virtual reality
- visit the Smithsonian Institution

You are, in a sense, a citizen of the electronic world created by the Internet.

Finding Information or Sites on the Internet

The Internet is loaded with information about many topics. Finding the specific information you need among the large amount of data available may be a challenge. There are programs available to help you search for information on the Internet. Specially published directories containing popular or interesting Internet addresses may be purchased as **supplemental** resources.

supplemental: additional, providing that which is lacking

WEB BROWSERS

Web browsers are software programs that enable you to explore the Internet and search for information. There are many browsers available today. You have probably heard of some of them—for example, Mosaic, Netscape, and Microsoft's Internet Explorer. Though the programs vary in appearance and terminology, they offer many of the same capabilities and features, including hypertext.

Illustration 14-2:3

Though web browsers differ in appearance, they all serve the same purpose—to help you explore the Internet.

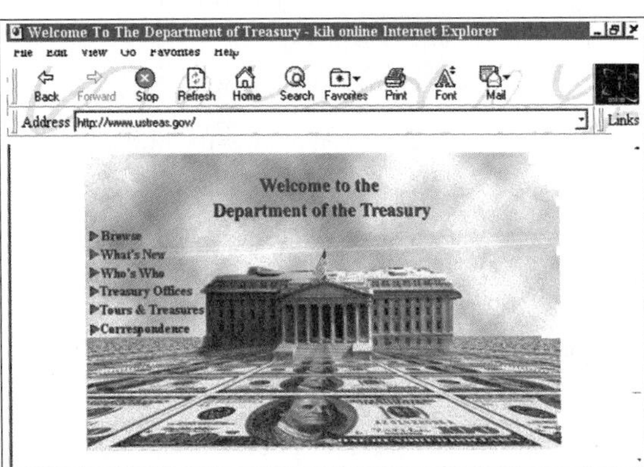

2. Provide hands-on instruction of the Internet for your students. If access is not available for each student in a lab environment in your school, demonstrate to the class from an instructor or media center station.

Hypertext is highlighted, underlined, or contrast-colored words or images that, when clicked with the mouse, take you to another location. Hypertext **links** can quickly take you to another page at the same site or to a different Internet site.

links:
connections, ties

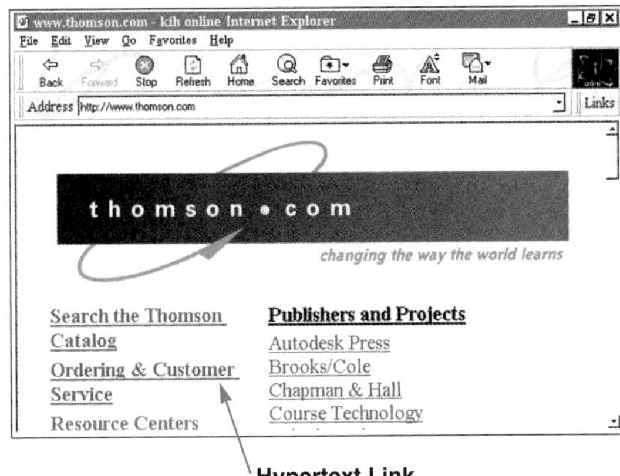

Illustration 14-2:4

When you click a hypertext word or graphic link, you are taken to another page or site.

If you have a favorite website that you visit often, you may want to set your browser to open to that home page. A home page is usually the first screen visitors to a website see. It often contains information about the site, colorful graphics, and links to other pages or related sites.

Illustration 14-2:5

The home page is a visitor's starting point for the site. It provides information and links to other pages or sites.

Provide an introduction to the browser software that you have available. Point out the different parts of a GUI browser: its home page, hypertext and hypertext links, returning home, the Back button, Search.

When moving from one hypertext link to another, your browser tracks your path, allowing you to return to where you started. You can go back one page at a time or return to the page where you started.

1. What is the purpose of a home page?
2. Why is the use of effective design important for an organization's home page?

It is getting increasingly easy to create your own home page. Many home users of the Internet have home pages. Today's software applications have HTML built into them so a user can easily create a home page.

1. Visit other sites. Have students obtain URLs that they would like to visit from magazine ads, television programs, or other sources. It is recommended that you have printed Internet directories in your classroom. Several cities now provide e-mail and Internet listings along with telephone numbers in local telephone directories. When students find sites they would like to share with the class, have them record the following information:
   - URL/Location
   - Home Page Title
   - Description

   A useful Internet directory can be developed as a class project.
2. Caution students about the importance of keying in URLs exactly as they are written. Typos are frequently made, especially with punctuation and case.

URLS

URLs (Uniform Resource Locators) are Internet addresses that can be understood by any web browser as it searches for hypertext documents on computers around the world. You may read a magazine or watch a television program and see an Internet location that offers more information about a particular topic. The location may be at an URL address. You already learned about the parts of Internet addresses in Topic 14-1. URL addresses are somewhat different from regular Internet addresses. They are usually longer and start with http://, which stands for HyperText Transfer Protocol. This is a set of instructions telling computers how to send and receive hypertext data and documents.

Below are some examples of URL addresses. Can you guess the information you might find at these addresses?

- http://www.cdnair.ca (Canadian Airlines International)
- http://www.cs.urich.edu/ (University of Richmond Math and Computer Science)
- http://www.redcross.org (The American Red Cross)

When you want to visit a location on the Internet, you may do so by entering the URL address in a text box on your browser's screen. Pay close attention to spelling, punctuation, symbols, and capitalization when entering the address. URLs are sensitive to the use of upper- and lowercase letters. You may also move to a different location on the Internet by clicking a hypertext link. When you use hypertext links, the associated URLs are often invisible. You merely click on the hypertext entry, and your browser takes you to the Internet address (URL) that has been associated with that hypertext.

Illustration 14-2:6

When you type a URL into your browser's text entry window, key the address exactly *as it has been given to you.*

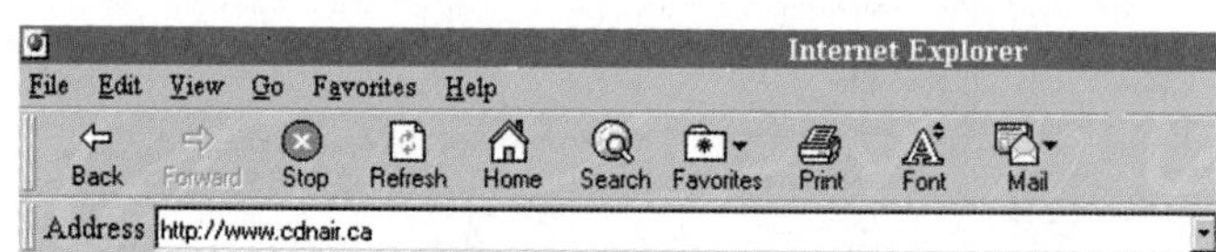

BOOKMARKS

Bookmarks are saved URLs or Internet addresses. When you find an interesting site or one that you want to visit often, you can save the address in a type of electronic catalog called a bookmark list or hotlist. To return to the site later, simply open the bookmark list and click the name of the site. Bookmarks can be set and deleted easily using your web browser.

SEARCH TOOLS

If you are looking for information about job opportunities, doing research for work or hobbies, or planning a trip, you may need help finding Internet sites that relate to these activities. There are many search tools, often referred to as search engines, that can help you locate sites. You may be familiar with some widely used search engines such as AltaVista, InfoSeek, Lycos, WebCrawler, or Yahoo.

To perform a search with most search engines, simply identify and type two or three keywords related to the topic, and then click the *search* button. The search tool will locate sites/documents, called "matches" or "hits," that contain these keywords. Your search may result in no matches, several matches, or thousands of matches. If your search results in a large number of matches, you may want to use more specific keywords to locate the information. On the other hand, if you receive only a few hits, you may have to broaden your search by using more general keywords. You may need to use several search tools to perform a thorough search since not all search tools look at every site that may contain the information you need.

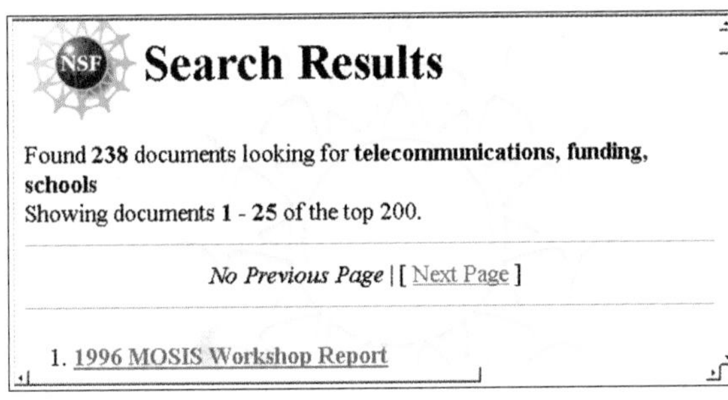

Illustration 14-2:7
Use several search engines for thorough exploration of a topic.

Why should you limit the number of sites in a hotlist?

A user could spend a lifetime surfing the Net and never visit every site. For this reason, it is necessary to use not just one, but several search tools. Also, careful choice of keywords is vital to reduce the number of sites found as a result of searches.

1. Have students use several search tools to search for:
   - travel advisories for foreign travel (countries for which the U.S. State Department has issued travel cautions)
   - information about Yosemite, Glacier, and the Great Smoky Mountains National Parks
   - current weather forecast for the Midwest, the Northeast, Alaska
   - NASA news
   - information about your favorite baseball team, basketball team, football team
   - the population of Taiwan; Sydney, Australia; Egypt; Calcutta, India
   - your local chamber of commerce
   - other topics you or your students suggest
2. As students conduct searches, warn them that they may not gain access to every host they attempt to visit. Some hosts may require passwords, some may not be working, some may not be compatible with their software, and some may require subscriptions.

As you gain experience in searching the Internet, identify search tools that you prefer and learn to use their advanced search features. Read the Help notes available for the search engine to learn what type of sites it searches and what advanced search features it supports. Some search features that can be very helpful in improving your hit list are shown in the following table:

Search Feature	Description
Wild cards	Wild cards are special symbols, such as * or ?, used in keywords to broaden a search. Wildcards allow you to account for plurals, alternate spellings, and alternate forms of words. For example, a search using the key word *Sm?th* would return hits that include *Smith* and *Smyth.*
Logical operators	Logical operators are commands or symbols, such as =, <, and >, that can help you narrow a search. For example, if you want to find information about comets visible in 1997, you might enter the search term *comets year=1997.*
Boolean operators	Boolean operators are words such as *and, or,* and *not* that can be used to describe a relationship between keywords. For example, the search term *red and green* would find all articles that include both "red" and "green." The search term *red* or *green* would find articles that include "red" and "green," just "red," or just "green."
String matches	A search using a string match lists only documents that have all the keywords in the exact order you typed them with no other words in between. For example, a regular search using the keywords *George Washington* would find all documents that contain *either* "George" *or* "Washington" anywhere in the document including articles about George Bush or Washington Carver. If you enter the keywords as a string match using quote marks, *"George Washington,"* you would get only articles about George Washington.

INTERNET DIRECTORIES

Listings of Internet sites and resources can be obtained online or from book publishers. The *Internet Yellow Pages* is an example of a book with comprehensive URL listings by topics and categories. It can be purchased from your local bookstore. Online directories may also be accessed directly on the Internet. It is important to realize that sites are continuously being added and deleted. Consequently, an online directory is updated more frequently than one published as a book. Many search engines and Internet service provider home pages offer regularly updated lists of URLs under links such as *What's New* or *What's Hot*. A search using keywords such as *Internet Directory* or *Web Site Indexes* will produce a list of several directories.

for discussion

1. What is the major disadvantage of using a printed Internet directory rather than an online directory? What are the advantages?
2. How do you access an online Internet directory?

Transferring Files

Millions of files are available on the Internet—research papers and data, software, pictures, sounds, and more. Perhaps a software vendor is offering a free "fix" for a software product problem. The publisher of your textbook may have a site offering student data files or special software **tutorials.** You may have to research a particular topic at work. You search for information about the topic with Yahoo, Gopher, or other search tools. When you find sites with data you would like to use, what do you do? You can transfer or download many of these files from a distant computer to your computer by using something called *File Transfer Protocol.*

tutorials:
instructional activities

thinking critically

List additional situations in which transferring files between computers is needed.

File Transfer Protocol (FTP) is a powerful tool that allows a copy of the file you request from a remote computer to move across the communication lines of the Internet to your computer. There are two types of FTP transfers—*private* and *anonymous*. In a private FTP transfer, you must have permission to access and download files. A private user name or account number and password are needed before you can download files from or upload (send) files to the remote computer. The more widely used type of FTP session is referred to as an anonymous transfer. An anonymous FTP transfer site can be accessed easily without privately issued user names or passwords. There are thousands of anonymous sites open to anyone.

for discussion

What is the difference between a private and an anonymous FTP transfer?

With today's GUI web browsers and search tools, FTP is so easy to use that it may be invisible to you when you use it. In using FTP, you

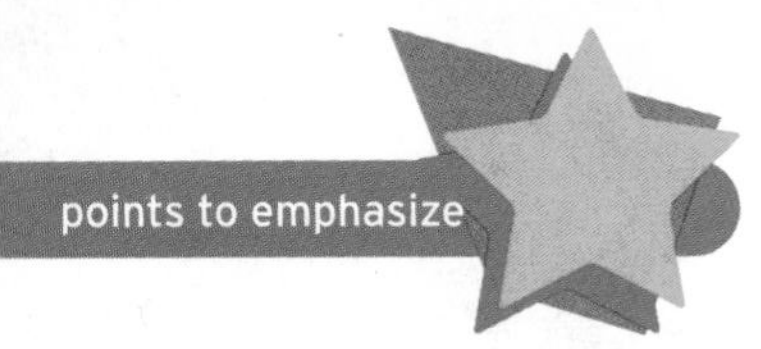

Even with file compression, many files are extremely large. There may not be enough file space on your hard drive or the drive of your network host to download the files.

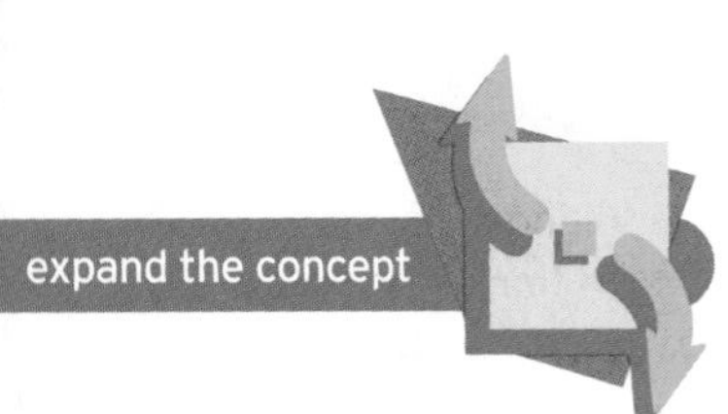

Next to e-mail, people use the Internet most often to share information with each other on a one-to-one basis. Usenet originated as a way for students and professors at the University of North Carolina and Duke University to discuss their research activities online.

modems:
devices that enable computer messages to be sent and received over telephone lines

should monitor the speed of file transfers and the size of files. Program files and multimedia files that contain graphics, sound, and video can be very large. Before downloading, you should make certain that there is ample room on your hard drive to hold the entire file. To boost file transfer rates, faster **modems** and special software that will compress (shrink) files can be used. File compression saves space on the host computer as well as speeding transfer of files across the Internet.

Illustration 14-2:8
Downloading *and* Uploading *occur when files are shared with a remote computer.*

Discussing Topics with Others

Imagine reading the morning newspaper and discussing the articles with their writers! When people want to share ideas and information with others on the Internet, they can do so via Usenet. Usenet, which stands for User's Network, is a collection of topically organized newsgroups. Newsgroups publish articles and messages related to a huge number of topics. Users participate in public discussions about a topic by sending messages that all participants in the newsgroup can read.

Another kind of discussion group is a *mailing list*. Mailing lists are databases containing the addresses of people interested in a particular topic. When you subscribe to a mailing list, your messages are "mailed" to the address of each participant in the mailing list.

Newsgroups. Usenet, the collection of topically organized newsgroups, is not an electronic newspaper. Online newspapers may be subscribed to or accessed through the Internet; however, they differ from Usenet. The articles that appear in newspapers are controlled by their editors. In newsgroups, anyone may contribute or publish an "article," which is referred to as a posting.

Newsgroups allow discussion of topics and may be either *moderated* or *unmoderated*. In moderated newsgroups, one or several people review the postings before they are distributed. Inappropriate or unnecessary articles are eliminated. In unmoderated newsgroups, no one inspects or eliminates postings. In this type of newsgroup, it is necessary for the users to maintain order by following rules of appropriate conduct when they post news items.

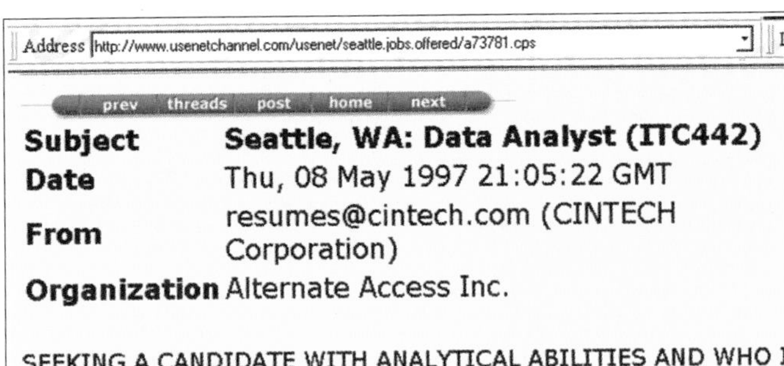

Illustration 14-2:9

This newsgroup posts job openings in the Seattle area.

1. What types of postings might moderators eliminate in a moderated newsgroup?
2. In an unmoderated newsgroup, what are the content responsibilities of the members when posting?
3. What topics might benefit from being moderated? unmoderated?

Newsgroups are available for thousands of topics. Usenet recognizes topics by categories. Some broad newsgroup categories and their focus are shown below.

Newsgroup	Focus
alt	Alternative (miscellaneous) topics
comp	Information about computers
news	Information about news or newsgroups

1. Have students add other newsgroup terms to the list.
2. If students have ever been flamed or spammed over the Internet, have them share their experiences and give examples.
3. Ask students what types of messages are considered spam or flames. Have them give specific examples.

rec	Information about recreation, hobbies, performing arts
sci	Information about science—research and discoveries
talk	Forums on topics that are controversial and debatable
misc	Topics that do not fit anywhere else

New vocabulary terms are coming into use as a result of Internet communications. Users have created terms to refer to people and practices as they communicate on the Internet. Some of these terms may be familiar to you. Can you add any to the following list?

reprimands: scoldings, criticisms

NET Term	Meaning
flame	**Reprimands** sent to people who violate a newsgroup's rules of online conduct
lurker	Person who reads others news postings, but never contributes any articles
newbie	Person who is new to the newsgroup
saint	Person who helps a newbie
spamming	Sending unwanted information to users such as advertising or junk mail
trolling	Posting incorrect information *deliberately* to get correcting responses from others
wizard	An expert on the topic in a newsgroup

Mailing Lists. A mailing list is a directory of Internet user addresses of people who want to have information about a topic delivered regularly to their Internet address. Some mailing lists are maintained by businesses while other lists are private. They must all be subscribed to.

Listserv is a type of automated subscription program. Listserv programs are databases filled with the names and addresses of many discussion groups as well as the Internet addresses of subscribers. Listserv manages subscriptions and the sending and receiving of all postings. The people on the mailing list form a discussion group about a shared topic of interest. In this way mailing lists and newsgroups are similar. The main difference between them is that mailing list messages come in the form of e-mail received in the user's private electronic mailbox. There is no charge for subscribing.

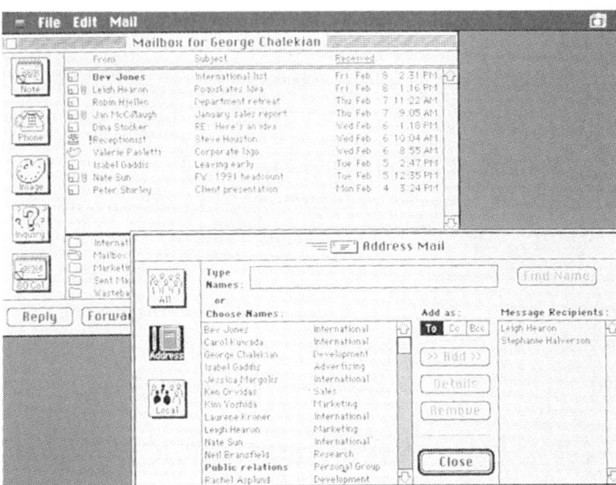

Illustration 14-2:10

Mailing list messages arrive in the e-mailboxes of all the subscribers on the mailing list.

1. Why has e-mail become such a vital business tool?
2. Do you think e-mail will replace the traditional telephone? Why?
3. Do you think e-mail will replace sending documents by the postal service?

E-Mail

One of the most popular, if not the most popular, uses of the Internet is *electronic mail*, or *e-mail*. E-mail is the electronic transfer of messages. LANs and WANs offer e-mail to all computers that are connected, whether they are in the same office or in different countries. Users are limited to sending and receiving messages only to and from those on their network unless their LAN is connected to the Internet. If they are connected to the Internet, they can send and receive messages all over the world. For many workers, e-mail is their main activity on the Internet.

E-mail messages may contain not only text, but also audio and graphics. When an e-mail file is received, it is automatically stored in a user's *electronic mailbox*. An e-mail mailbox is an online computer storage space designated to hold electronic messages. These messages are stored for the owner of the mailbox and may be read, saved for later reference, printed, or deleted.

1. Have students practice writing e-mail messages. Divide them into teams and have them critique each other's messages for use of effective e-mail guidelines.
2. Show students examples of poorly written e-mail messages. You may have them write poor messages and then explain to the class why the message is not effective.

USES OF E-MAIL

Workers in organizations use Internet e-mail for routine communications such as interoffice memos, memos to other organizations, and purchase orders. Longer files containing information such as research findings, corporate financial statements, or client databases may be attached to the e-mail message. E-mail is inexpensive and fast. It can be sent for pennies and received in seconds. It is easy to use and has been embraced by workers at all levels in organizations.

E-mail software varies somewhat in look and feel from one package to another; however, there are certain features that are found in most e-mail packages. E-mail messages contain a heading, body, section for attachments, and signature. E-mail programs allow the user to read mail, check for new messages, compose and reply to messages, delete messages, and send new mail. Some e-mail programs allow you to attach files to be transmitted with the message.

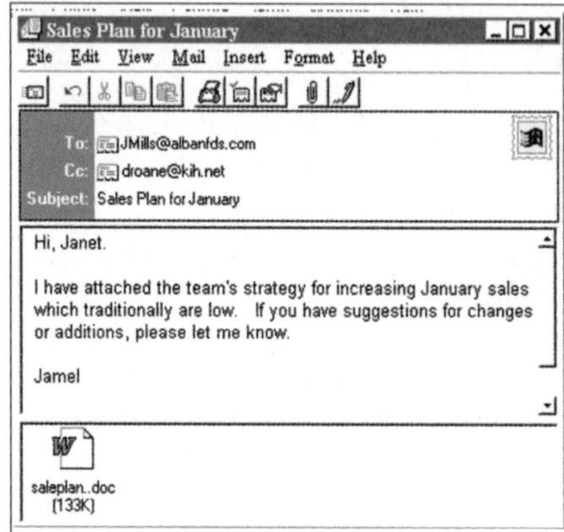

Illustration 14-2:11

Though e-mail software programs vary in appearance, they all offer the same basic features.

E-MAIL ADDRESS BOOK

An e-mail address book is a storage place for the user's most frequently used addresses. Some cities are beginning to include e-mail and Internet addresses in their local telephone directories. However, there are no national or international directory assistance numbers to call to find out the Internet addresses of all those with whom you may want to communicate. E-mail addresses must be given to the user. There are few public directories of personal e-mail addresses of those who are not on a mailing list or in a newsgroup. You will find it handy to have a collection of addresses online in an address book that you can quickly scan when preparing to send a message.

Some city telephone directories now include e-mail addresses along with telephone listings.

IN AND OUT BOXES

The In Box collects incoming messages. A user alert, such as a tone or flashing icon, often accompanies the receipt of new mail. The Out Box holds e-mail messages to be sent to others. It may also hold messages that have already been sent, or these messages may be stored in a separate box or folder. Because these messages are actually stored on your hard drive, you should frequently **purge** your In and Out boxes of unnecessary files. Keeping lots of old files also makes it more difficult and time consuming to locate a message you need.

purge:
empty

PRIORITIZING MESSAGES

Most mail programs will allow you to **prioritize** an e-mail message, that is, to rank it in importance—usually from *urgent* or *highest* to *low*. Be cautious about the use of these priorities. If you send too many *urgent* messages that aren't really especially important, people may not take your frequent priority flags seriously. On the other hand, an *urgent* or *high* message priority may draw needed attention in a crowded mailbox if used sparingly.

prioritize:
rank in importance from highest to lowest

Effective E-Mail Use. E-mail is for quick, informal written correspondence. Remember, however, that your e-mail messages is *recorded*, and may be viewed by people other than the person to whom you wrote. Most e-mail software is managed by the administrator of the host computer who may have access to your messages. Your e-mail may be read by your employer or by coworkers. At work, never write an e-mail message that you would not want other employees or your supervisor to read.

You should follow the same proper writing techniques for e-mail as you do for your other professional communications. As you become experienced with e-mail, you will learn to recognize some of the do's

The e-mail sender reflects his or her personality in many subtle ways. Because an e-mail message is short, each word you use to convey your thoughts as well as the way your message looks should be carefully considered. Overuse of emoticons may make you appear unprofessional or not serious. Even your signature reflects your personality—the way you end your message. Do you end with your full name? a nickname? a smilie? a slogan? your initials? Be careful! You do not want to appear undignified, arrogant, or silly, especially if you are sending e-mail as part of your job.

and don't's of e-mail. To ensure that your use of e-mail is effective and professional, follow the guidelines below.

- Plan your message ahead of time.
- Create single-subject messages using words that are clear and concise.
- Observe proper etiquette and make your message courteous. Avoid sarcasm, which may be misinterpreted.
- Carefully read your message before you send it and make sure it says what you want to say in the tone in which you want to say it. Remember, your message may be made public.
- Use upper- *and* lowercase letters. All-uppercase letters are difficult to read and make your message appear as if you are shouting.
- Limit or avoid the use of smileys or emoticons, which are pictures of faces showing emotions: happy :-) sad :-(. Use of these smileys on the job may make you appear silly or unprofessional.
- Check the e-mail address of the recipient before you send the message.
- Do not send a message that you may regret. Remember that the message is *written*. You probably cannot take it back.
- Check your mailbox regularly for messages. Read the messages and file or delete them.
- Reply to your messages promptly.
- Honor others' rights of privacy. Consider carefully before forwarding messages you receive to others.
- Carefully consider your mailing list subscriptions. Messages can quickly accumulate in your mailbox. If you are not going to read them, do not subscribe to the mailing list.

Promoting Organizations

More and more organizations are going online to perform a variety of tasks that are self-serving. For many organizations, presence on the Internet with a web site is necessary for maintaining a competitive edge in the global workplace. Colleges and universities are maintaining sites with information about their programs. Potential students visit the sites and are able to compare curricula, costs, and other aspects of campus life to help them make a wise choice. What about the colleges that are not on the Internet? They are missing the opportunity to inform many potential students about their programs.

In much the same way, a business must be present on the Internet and visible for potential users of its product or service. Organizations showcase themselves. A well-designed website serves as a powerful marketing tool. Organizations are doing business on the Internet by:

- offering customer support services
- working on projects with employees at other locations or with clients or members of the organization
- performing marketing research activities
- searching for new employees
- posting job openings to solicit applicants
- answering questions and posting to newsgroups
- sending out information about the organization

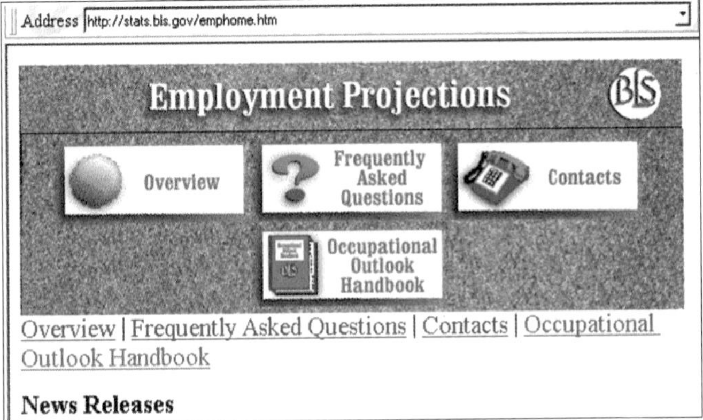

Illustration 14-2:12

A well-designed website can help promote an organization.

Can you think of other ways in which an organization can promote itself over the Internet?

In addition to marketing themselves through Internet activities, many organizations are trying to find ways to make money directly from the

Internet. They may provide a service or a product such as software that the user must pay for before receiving.

Netiquette

The list of netiquette rules is only partial. Have students research other netiquette rules using the Internet or traditional printed materials such as magazines and professional computer journals.

With more and more people crowding the Internet, it has become very important for its users to follow acceptable rules of conduct when exploring sites and responding to other users. Acceptable guidelines for behavior on the Internet have been given the name netiquette. You have been presented with guidelines for e-mail. Many of these guidelines are also considered to be part of netiquette rules. The rules for Internet users were developed for the same reasons that rules exist in any community. They create an environment that is safe, friendly, and productive.

A few commonly agreed-upon netiquette rules include:

- You are responsible for your own behavior on the Internet.
- Do not take other people's words from the Internet and say that they are your own. This is like copying someone else's term paper.
- Do not tie up valuable computer resources by sending junk mail.
- Do not insult or verbally abuse anyone. Use good manners in your interactions with others.
- Download huge files after regular business hours (6 p.m. until 8 a.m.).
- Once you have your downloaded material, log off the remote computer. Do not stay any longer than is necessary for you to complete your business there.

The Future of the Internet

What is the future of the Internet? Many people are trying to predict and imagine just where we are headed with readily available worldwide online communications. Voice and video file delivery promise to open up new uses and attract new users. Easier connection with simplified hardware and software will make the Internet more accessible. Better

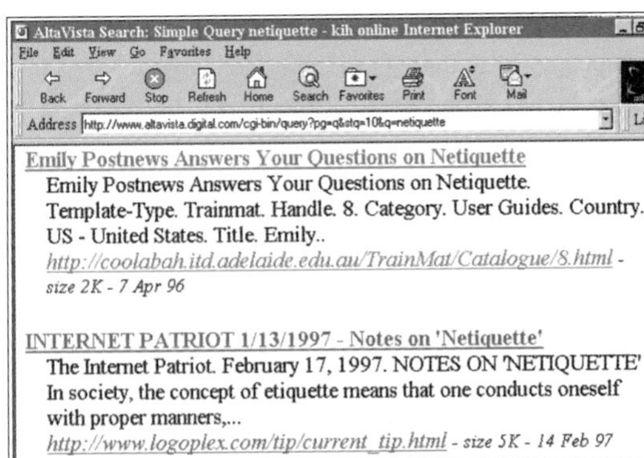

Illustration 14-2:13

Netiquette *is the set of rules for acceptable behavior on the Internet.*

methods of security will safeguard data. Changes are occurring so rapidly that few are willing to predict anything other than the fact that Internet use *will* continue to explode.

With the rapid growth of the Internet have come many concerns. We have learned about some, such as security of information and rules of conduct. However, there are many more issues resulting from the Internet explosion that society must face. Some of these issues will be taken care of with time and technological advancements. Others will be difficult, if not impossible, to resolve.

THE INFORMATION SUPERHIGHWAY

The Internet is not actually the *information superhighway,* though many refer to it as such. The information superhighway is really a future network of networks that is constantly developing to bring information to us faster and easier. As the information superhighway develops and brings us better connections, written e-mail may be almost totally replaced by two-way video and audio mail. The video and audio quality will be far superior to that of today. The need for wires will be almost totally eliminated. Transmission will be accomplished much as it is with today's cellular phones. Your telephone, television, and computer will be combined into one machine.

Web browsers will be even easier to use, customizable, and have many features. It will be commonplace for users to shop and bank

1. There is much controversy surrounding the Internet. Have students make a list of the controversies.
2. From the list of controversies, have students select one on which to conduct research using the Internet itself as well as magazines and newspapers.

from their computer. Major software purchases will be downloaded from software companies' computers directly to the consumer's computer. Software companies will provide better customer support over the Internet. We will have access to features and services that we cannot even imagine today.

1. How will the information superhighway be different from today's Internet?
2. What are some future predictions for the Internet?

Illustration 14-2:14
Written e-mail may soon be replaced by two-way video and audio mail.

INTERNET CONTENT

trivia: unimportant details

Some people question the value of much of the information found on the Internet. Users as well as Internet watchers complain about sites that are devoted to what many judge as unimportant **trivia;** that are poorly planned or managed; or contain inaccurate, pornographic, dangerous, or inappropriate information. Some have predicted that as the Internet evolves, the quality of the content will improve. For example, instead of the short postings that are the norm now in newsgroups; in the future there will be more opportunities for editorial comment and user interaction.

You have probably heard and read about the concerns of society for the protection of children and others who use the Internet. Many people who get on the Internet to exploit or harm others have been caught and punished, but it is not always easy to find and prosecute them. Controversy surrounds the policing of the Internet. Many argue that even if the Internet *could* be controlled, it should not be.

INTERNET ACCESS FOR ALL

As the Internet becomes increasingly important at home, school, and work; how can we be certain that it will be available to everyone? There are widespread misgivings that access to computers and the Internet will be restricted to those who can afford it. Those who are lacking in the knowledge provided by Internet resources may suffer socially and economically. How can society make Internet access available and affordable for everyone? Will there be public places, like our local libraries, where people can go to use the tools of knowledge and information of the future? Just as the printing press, telegraph, telephone, and television changed the world and caused much controversy in their early days, the Internet promises to change our world in ways yet to be imagined.

Illustration 14-2:15

How can society make Internet access available and affordable for eveyone?

Reviewing the Topic

1. List four activities you can perform on the Internet.
2. What are the differences between a web browser and a search tool?
3. What is *hypertext?* How do hypertext links work?
4. What is a newsgroup? Describe the two types of newsgroups.
5. What is a *mailing list?* How are mailing lists different from newsgroups?
6. Why is e-mail such a popular activity on the Internet? What are four features that most e-mail programs contain?
7. What are five tips for effective e-mail composition?
8. How do organizations promote themselves by setting up a website on the Internet?
9. What is *netiquette?* Why is it necessary?
10. Discuss what you feel are three of the most important issues of concern resulting from the rapid expansion of Internet use?

topic 14-2 review

INTERACTING WITH OTHERS

While completing some tasks to meet a deadline, you noticed that a member of your sales team, Jeremy, was using the computer at his workstation to download copyrighted clipart. You observed him pasting the clipart into the department's online newsletter and posting it on the company's website. When you asked Jeremy about his activities, he shrugged and said that no one should mind because the chances of his getting caught were very slim. And besides, he was not really hurting anyone.

What should you do?

- Let the matter drop and ignore his illegal actions.
- Inform your supervisor about Jeremy's use of the Internet.
- Send an e-mail message to Jeremy flaming him for his actions.

topic 14-2 review

Using the Internet

- Talk with Jeremy again and list reasons why you think his behavior is inappropriate.
- Would you handle the situation with other actions?

What you are to do:

Prepare a written response to each of the four suggested actions. If you feel there is a fifth alternative that would be more effective, describe and discuss the action.

REINFORCING ENGLISH SKILLS

You work for Craig-Weston Mansion, a small inn in Novia Scotia, located on a bluff above Pandora's Harbor. A member of your work team has asked you to proofread and edit some copy that is to be added to your organization's Internet website. These statements contain grammar, spelling, word usage, and punctuation errors that will give a very poor impression of the organization. Key a copy of the statements, correcting all errors.

Welcome, to the beautifuly restored Craig-Weston Mansion. Overlooking Pandoras' Harbor in Nova Scotia the mansion becons you to visit. Fourteen well appointed bedrooms with private baths are furnished in antiques. A full hearty breakfast awaits you after a good nights sleep in your own king size feather-bed.

As your day begins chose from walks by the sea or horseback riding on our 5 miles of trails. Enjoy teatime with homemaid treat's galore. Nestle by the fireside, and read your favorite book by it's warm glow. Diner will be prepared by our chef and desert will be served in the parlor. Conversation, and parlor games will make you forget your hurried life back home.

You will I am sure never forget your stay at Craig Weston Mansion.

719

APPLICATION ACTIVITIES

ACTIVITY 1 Composing an E-Mail Message

You are working on a special research project with Larry Moore (whose Internet address is LMoore@hammer.unu.edu). He was supposed to e-mail you a lengthy attachment vital to your completion of the project. He promised to transmit it to you by noon *yesterday*. It is 4:30 p.m., and you still have not heard from Larry. You are becoming very concerned because the deadline for the project is only one week away. You must study Larry's material carefully before you can complete your part of the project. By your estimate, it will take you approximately nine hours to review Larry's data. Compose an e-mail message to Larry.

What you are to do:

1. Compose and key an e-mail message to Larry that is appropriate for the situation described above. Include the proper heading information (To, From, Subject, and Date).
2. Follow proper guidelines (including netiquette) for preparing e-mail communications as you compose your message.

ACTIVITY 2 Internet Addresses

topic 14-2 review

Internet addresses can be very short or very long. They are also case sensitive, which means that the use of upper- and lower-case letters is important when keying in the addresses. When keying an Internet address, often mistakes are made. The mistake may be made when keying or writing the address, or it may be a printed typographical error in a document. In this activity, you will build your proofreading skills using Internet addresses.

See Workbook page 91.

What you are to do:

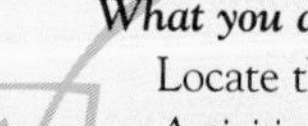

Locate the list of Internet addresses for this activity in your *Student Activities and Projects* workbook. Proofread and mark errors as directed.

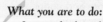

720

Chapter Summary

Worldwide communications have changed not only the way the world conducts business, but also the way people live. People with common interests—personal and professional—access information and send messages to exchange ideas and information. To succeed in today's workplace, it is necessary to take advantage of global communications capabilities. As a worker, you must become proficient in using the tools and speaking the language of communications technologies.

After studying this chapter, you should be knowledgeable about the following key points:

- Local area networks (LANs), wide area networks (WANs), and international networks allow us to perform a wide variety of tasks enabling us to share information and devices.
- Three common LAN topologies are the star, the ring, and the bus. These LANs use transmission carriers such as twisted-pair, coaxial, or fiber-optic cable. Wireless communication for LANs is accomplished via infrared light waves or radio waves.
- Organizations may choose to use a dedicated line or a dial-up line for WAN transmissions depending upon their telecommunication needs. Individuals and organizations may obtain dial-up access to the Internet from Internet service providers.
- To send or receive information on the Internet, you must have a unique Internet address. The parts of this address are called domains.
- The Internet and the World Wide Web are being used increasingly in the workplace and in homes. Software programs such as web browsers, search engines, and e-mail programs, allow users to navigate, find information, and exchange messages via the Internet.

Many social and ethical issues are being raised as rapidly changing network technologies are being embraced worldwide. Growth of the Internet is viewed by many as a double-edged sword. We can face the future with both optimism for its promise and concern for the challenges it has created for the individual and society.

chapter 14 summary

Telecommunication Systems

KEY CONCEPTS AND TERMS

bus topology
domain
downloading
e-mail
FTP (File Transfer Protocol)
home page
HTTP (HyperText Transfer Protocol)
hypertext
LAN
link
Listserv
mailing list
netiquette
newsgroup
node
peer-to-peer
ring topology
search tool
server-based
star topology
transmission carrier
URL (Uniform Resource Locator)
WAN
web browser

INTEGRATED CHAPTER ACTIVITIES

ACTIVITY 1 Internet Search Keywords

When you are conducting research on the Internet at work or for fun, most of the time you will not know the address of sites that may supply you with the information you want. To perform successful Internet searches, it is sometimes necessary for you to try several keywords before finding exactly the right information. It is not uncommon for your search to return hundreds or even thousands of matches! You may have to use alternate keywords to narrow your search.

What you are to do:

chapter 14 summary

1. A list of items for you to find on the Internet is shown below. Make a list of the keywords that you will use to conduct your search for each item.
2. Search for these items. Record the location of the Internet site where you find each one.
   a. job openings in your state or local area
   b. painting of Mona Lisa
   c. calendar of meteor showers

722

d. computer companies that develop and sell word processing software

e. Grammy winners of last year

f. websites that provide live video

g. winter skiing accommodations in Montana

ACTIVITY 2 Designing a Home Page

Your employer is Jam's CD Place, a store in the local shopping mall. The store sells contemporary music that includes rap, country, rock, soul, and jazz recorded on CD. Jam's prides itself on its wide selection of music. "If you can't find it here, you can't find it anywhere!" is the motto of the company.

The owner, Mai DeLuca, is planning a website on the Internet. Mai has asked each team member to conduct research and prepare a draft of a home page design to share with the team. The home page voted as most effectively designed will be presented to a local consultant who will actually create the home page.

What you are to do:

1. Research home page design tips. You may perform your research on the Internet or use printed materials from a library. Key the tips using your word processor. Print a copy.
2. Search the Internet and view home pages of businesses that sell music—CDs, records, tapes. Note which design elements leave a good impression and which leave a poor impression for this type of enterprise. Print copies of two home pages that you feel serve as excellent examples.
3. Plan a home page. If you have software that will create a home page, utilize it. If not, use your word processor or desktop publisher to design the page. Use word art and graphics to add interest. Text, pictures, or icons that will be hypertext links should use blue text or be outlined with blue borders.

723

Blake Williams,
Office Supervisor

Getting Acquainted with the World of Work

Your Résumé—Is It Internet Ready?

Dear Mr. Williams

I will be completing my degree in Administrative Systems Management in two months. One of my instructors suggested that I use the Internet for my job search. So far I have already visited the sites of several companies to investigate their job opportunities and learn something about the organizations. Also, I have explored several online job sites for job seekers. I have selected a service to post my résumé.

I am now ready to develop a résumé to send and post online. I already have a traditional one that I plan to use for regular mailing. Should my electronic résumé be different?

Jon from Jacksonville

Dear Jon

You have chosen a very effective method for your search for a professional position. Many employers are choosing the Internet to help them find new employees. You have already completed the first important steps in a successful online job search: finding out about the organizations for which you would like to work and exploring online job resources. Now you are ready to get your résumé polished for the Internet.

Your online résumé may simply be the file used to print your hard-copy résumé. However, I suggest that you consider several elements to make your electronic version Internet ready.

- Use keywords that are nouns rather than action words. *In your traditional résumé you probably used verbs such as* handled, managed, studied, supervised, *etc. Employers who search for applicants will probably do so by keying in words such as* computer skills, word processing, education, etc. *The more keywords such as these that you use, the higher your chances are of being found.*
- Save your document as an ASCII text file. *When you save your file in your word processor, save it as an ASCII text file. Why? This format can be sent by e-mail and can be understood by all computers.*
- Include an e-mail hyperlink. *In your résumé use an e-mail hyperlink to make it easy and quick for potential employers to contact you at your e-mail address.*
- Be concerned about confidentiality. *Your résumé will be viewed by many people. Find out from the posting service you have selected who will have access to the database. It is best not to include your home mailing address.*

You certainly want to market your experience and education successfully. Use of good design techniques is essential. As more and more people use the Internet for résumé posting, you can be assured that new techniques and multimedia technologies will be used more and more.

Good luck as you use the power of the Internet to market your skills.

Blake Williams

Office Supervisor

724

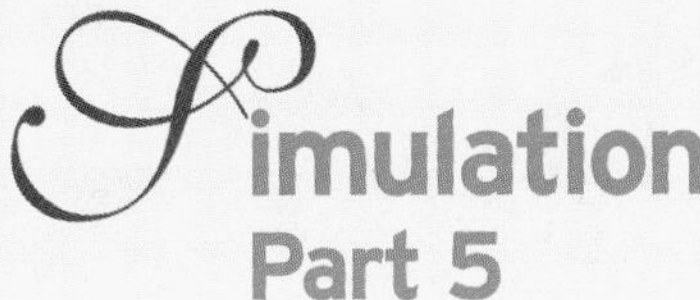

Simulation Part 5

At Work at *Buckhorn Mountain Outfitters*:

Buckhorn Mountain Outfitters is a small camping and hiking equipment business located in the small town of Elk Valley in the Colorado Rockies. In addition to retail sales and rentals, the company organizes and outfits overnight hiking and camping trips into the Elk Valley region.

The business has grown in its first year of operation. An attractive retail sales area, efficient warehouse operation, and modern offices equipped with the latest in computer technology provide a well-designed working environment. The owners, Erik Schmidt and his wife Helga, have just hired you to provide administrative support for Erik and the other personnel. You will be expected to use your computer and communications skills to help the organization achieve its goals. You will be working closely with Erik and Helga, who telecommutes from the couple's home. Other full-time office employees include two accounting clerks and a sales and marketing specialist. You and the other office staff work as a team to solve problems and make decisions that will result in continued success for Buckhorn Mountain Outfitters.

In your new position, you will be expected to:

- manage electronic communications, which, in addition to handling incoming and outgoing telephone calls, include facsimile and e-mail
- use integrated software applications as tools to solve problems and make decisions
- assist Helga in setting up her home office for telecommuting

Your job assignments will be coordinated by Erik Schmidt. You will also be working closely with other members of the office team. Refer to your *Student Activities and Projects* workbook to learn more about your responsibilities and work assignments at Buckhorn Mountain Outfitters.

See Workbook pages 171–195.

725

Personal and Career Development

part 6

Success at work is based on a combination of technical competencies and personal qualities. Both will prove important in finding a job and advancing your career. You will want to understand how to search for a job, how to present your credentials and yourself, and what the expectations are as you begin work. Companies seek employees at all levels who are good team players—cooperative, willing to assume responsibility, focused on meeting organizational goals, and able to work with others effectively. Personal and Career Development focuses on you as a worker and how you interact with others to secure a position and perform satisfactorily. When you complete your study of this part, you will be able to:

- **plan for entry into the workplace and career advancement**
- **describe personal characteristics valuable at work**
- **discuss the basic attitudes that support the goals of organizations**
- **interact effectively with others at work**

getting started GO

The content of this chapter may be studied early in an office procedures course or at the end of the course. With the first option, attention is focused on what work requires and how the course will develop skills and understandings critical for meeting job requirements. With the second option, the focus turns to summarizing what has been learned in the context of considering job opportunities.

teaching tips

This chapter should be taught with realistic job environments in mind. Guest speakers from the major organizations that hire your students, either upon high school graduation or after further study, can add much to the points you want students to understand. Former students now at work in the community are also effective participants in class presentations.

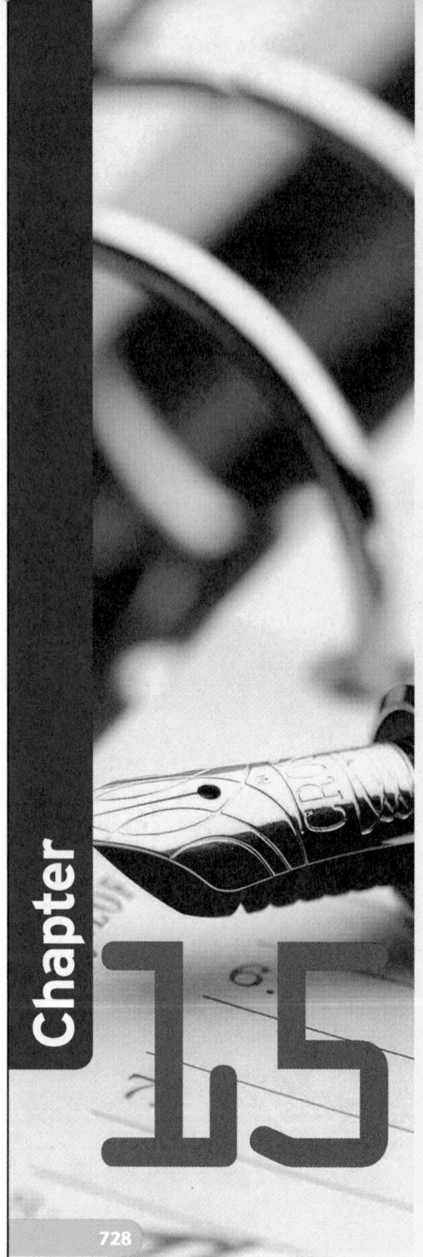

Chapter 15

Planning and Advancing Your Career

You have had many opportunities to consider the types of tasks common to many jobs. You may have made a firm decision about your choice for an initial job or career. On the other hand, you may be planning full-time study for awhile and postponing a decision about your first full-time job.

Regardless of your present plans, you will find it valuable to understand what is generally involved in securing a job. You will become acquainted with various ways of learning about jobs and how to respond to these career opportunities. If you have had part-time or summer work experience, you will undoubtedly have learned about some of the topics of this chapter. Use your study of this material to become aware of your own interests and aspirations. You can feel confident about being successful in your chosen career when you have realistic knowledge about effective job search strategies and job assessment methods.

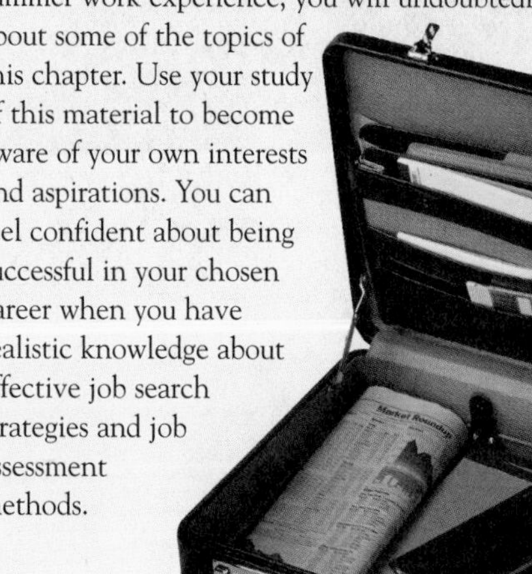

728

Chapter 15

An Effective Job Search

When you have completed your study of this topic, you will be able to:

- **identify the factors to consider when planning a career strategy**
- **discuss the role of a career goal in your planning**
- **describe the steps in planning a job search**
- **prepare a résumé**
- **prepare for an interview**
- **explain what generally is expected of an interviewee**

Topic 15-1

You are introduced to a wide range of activities during your study of this textbook. You have an opportunity to understand better what many jobs require, especially in office-related careers. You can see to what extent positions in today's workplace require information-related competencies. At this point, you may be planning to:

- begin work full time
- begin work full time while pursuing further education on a part-time basis
- begin work part-time and become a full-time student in college
- be a full-time college student with no plans for present full-time employment

A young person has many options in the workplace. Varying levels of education are prerequisite to certain jobs. Students should realize that their interests in jobs or education may change over time.

Increasingly, a high school education is not considered sufficient for many positions in the world of work. Planning for further education, even on a part-time basis, is wise.

You may want to use the educational resources of the community to illustrate how high school graduates combine work and school in their post-high school years.

Discuss specific programs for further study available to high school graduates, including any adult education courses offered in the high school.

Use local employment statistics to help students see what job opportunities are available. Also, use employment statistics in cities to which the youth of your community move in order to have jobs.

Even though an absolute commitment to a career goal may not make sense at this time, considering careers they find appealing can give students clues to where they may want to begin their work life.

Regardless of your present plans, you will find the information provided in this topic generally useful for understanding how to enter the job market.

Thinking Ahead About Careers and Jobs

credentials: evidence of training, education, or experience

career goals: desired achievements related to work such as jobs, education, training, experience, or professional recognition

Prospective employers are not likely to know you. Seldom are they willing to spend extensive time with you to make a judgment about what value you might add to their organizations. This gives you the task of reviewing your **credentials** and presenting your qualifications in a positive manner. This should be viewed as a pleasant challenge since you do indeed have skills and knowledge valuable in many jobs. However, before you think about your credentials, you should consider your present status relative to **career goals.**

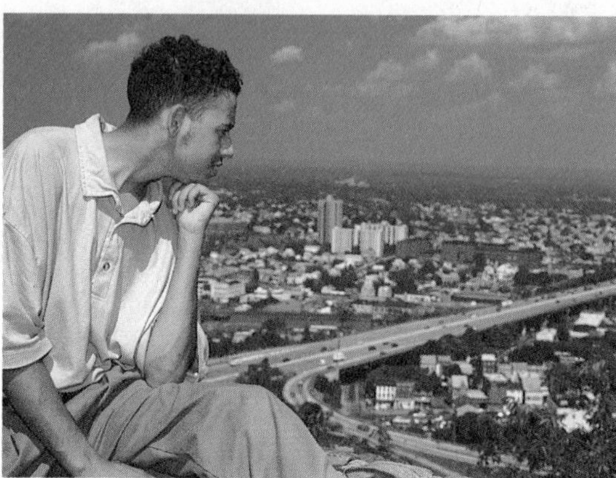

Illustration 15-1:1
This student is seriously considering his career options.

A CAREER STRATEGY

You might wonder why someone who is considering a first job should be thinking beyond that job. Thinking ahead, though, may help you choose a first job that is closely related to long-term interests. Thinking ahead to what you see as a career goal and devising realistic steps to meet that goal is known as a career strategy. With a career goal in mind, you can evaluate beginning job offers in relation to that goal.

Christine worked part-time in a large company in downtown Denver during her senior year in high school. She would like to be a secondary school teacher and plans to work full time for at least two years while she studies education at the local college. Then she plans to become a full-time student. The manager where she worked has suggested that since she wants to be a teacher, she might like to work full time in their human resources department and help the director of their extensive training programs. After an interview in the human resources department, Christine was offered a position. She is looking forward to beginning her new full-time position in late July.

Career planning is not a once-in-a-lifetime task. As you gain experience you will become better acquainted with alternative jobs that match your interests and talents. There are likely to be times when you will want to reconsider career opportunities.

PLANNING WITH A CAREER GOAL ESTABLISHED

As you have learned from talking with other classmates, some of you have clear ideas for your future work goals. If this is true for you, you have undoubtedly thought about what you can do well, what the opportunities are for your chosen field, and in general what will be required to achieve your career goal. With such a goal, you can establish realistic steps in the pursuit of your career. You have given serious thought to a career goal when you can answer the following questions:

- What specific kinds of jobs are available to a person who has chosen the goal I have?
- What job opportunities are projected for the next five to ten years in the field in which I have an interest?
- What are the educational qualifications for entry into the field?
- What educational and/or experience qualifications are needed to advance in the field?

PLANNING WITHOUT A CAREER GOAL

Many students are not sure what careers are most appealing to them. Such students can still enter the workplace and perform successfully.

What are some qualities that Christine likely reflected in her work that led to her being asked to remain with the company as a full-time employee?

Describe the career histories of leaders of the community to illustrate the kinds of career changes that may take place during a lifetime.

Engage the students in thinking about the sources for career goals. Identify factors that led some students to have such goals now and others not to have goals.

Review some of the fastest-growing jobs for the next five years (see *The Occupational Outlook Handbook* or refer to Chapter 2). Have students identify the factors critical in increasing the demand for such jobs.

Is it realistic to believe that employees can be very good workers yet have no career goals?

What can you learn on the job to aid you in deciding on your future work?

Why are some people reluctant to search for jobs?

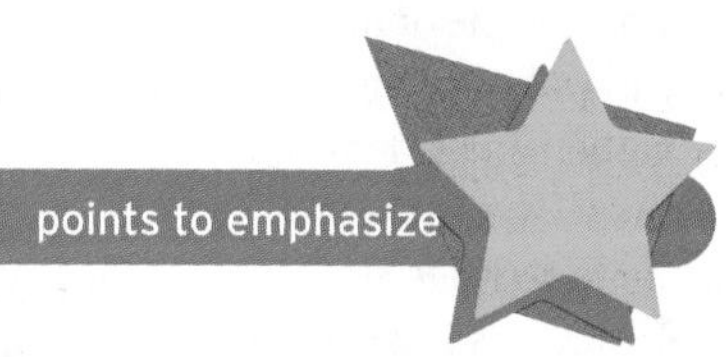

Use local figures of numbers of persons who were employed during the past year.

commitment: firm decision, promise

There are options available to a person who is unsure or has no desire to make an early **commitment** to a particular career. When seeking a job, such a person can highlight a willingness to:

- perform every task assigned according to instructions
- strive always to improve performance
- learn more about the company and make a valuable contribution to its goals

When persons without clear career goals begin working, they encounter a wide variety of positions through their association with other workers. Such knowledge will help them in exploring career options.

Planning a Job Search

Whether you have a career goal or not, you can effectively plan your search for a full-time job. Your success in meeting job requirements need not be related to whether or not you have a career goal. Common steps in a job search include:

1. Become acquainted with the types of jobs you wish to consider.
2. Explore job opportunities related to the types of jobs in which you have an interest.
3. Prepare a résumé.
4. Prepare a letter of application when you have identified a specific job opening appropriate for your education and experience.
5. Forward résumés and letters of application to companies considering candidates for jobs.
6. Accept interviews with companies that wish to talk with you about available jobs.
7. Follow up all job interviews.
8. Accept a job.

EXPLORING JOB OPPORTUNITIES

There are a number of sources available to help you locate specific jobs in which you may be interested and for which you are qualified.

Sources for Learning about Jobs:

- School placement and counseling services
- The World Wide Web
- Newspapers
- Employment agencies
- Government announcements
- Personal inquiry

Illustration 15-1:2

Sources for learning about jobs

Friends, relatives, and former employers often know of good job opportunities for you. Other sources are discussed briefly in the following paragraphs.

School Placement and Counseling Services. You will want to become familiar with the placement and counseling services available in your school. In schools where there is no placement counselor, prospective employers often inform school guidance counselors or business teachers about job opportunities in their organizations.

Illustration 15-1:3

A student is discussing job opportunities with a school counselor.

The World Wide Web. You will want to check a recent Internet directory for World Wide Web sites that have job listings. One such site is CareerWEB, which allows job seekers to search a vast employment

teaching tips

If your school has a placement office, statistics about recent graduates may be useful in giving students an idea of what is actually happening jobwise in the community.

for discussion

What services does the school counseling and placement office provide? To what extent have you used the services?

expand the concept

Identify some sites on the World Wide Web that list positions for beginners in fields of interest to the class. Assign students to find a limited number of jobs of interest.

Use the classified sections of local newspapers to identify positions available. Do the same with newspapers from the closest large cities.

database and post their résumés on the web. Many businesses and other organizations list job openings on their individual websites.

Newspapers. The classified advertisement sections of newspapers list many job openings. Some employers advertise directly, asking you to call or to fax your résumé to them. Other employers use blind advertisements that do not identify the employer and request that applications be sent to a post office box. Magazines, newsletters, and other periodicals related to a particular industry also often have sections listing job openings.

Illustration 15-1:4
Want ad from a newspaper

ADMINISTRATIVE ASSISTANT

To assist financial dept & business affairs. Good math skills. Data entry & various ofc duties. Entry-level position. Send resume w/cover letter to:
P.O. BOX 274, NY, NY 10003

Discuss with students the services provided by local employment agencies.

Employment Agencies. Employers submit job openings to employment agencies, and counselors at the agencies help match applicants' qualifications and goals with jobs available. Private employment agencies charge a fee for their services. Sometimes the person seeking a job pays the fee; at other times, the employer pays the fee, which is usually a percentage of the first year's salary. Government employment agencies provide services to citizens and employers free of charge.

Temporary employment agencies hire individuals to fill temporary jobs that may last anywhere from a single day to many months. Many businesses use temporary workers on a virtually permanent basis. By taking temporary jobs, young workers can gain a variety of experiences and understand better what full-time, permanent jobs will be most appealing to them. In some instances, temporary workers are asked to accept permanent positions.

Discuss the extent to which workers in the local community are employed on a temporary basis.

Government Announcements. Many different types of employees are required in government agencies at the local, county, state, federal, and even international levels. You will be able to get information from your state employment office about state and federal job opportunities.

Candidates for state and federal jobs usually must satisfactorily complete job-related examinations, which are given periodically with the dates announced in advance.

Personal Inquiry. If you have a special interest in working for a particular organization, you may want to write a carefully worded letter inquiring about job possibilities. In your letter you should explain the reason for your interest in being an employee, describe the kind of job you wish, and briefly outline your qualifications. You need not include a résumé with your letter of inquiry, but you may want to state that you will be happy to forward a detailed résumé.

What employment services are available from government agencies in the community?

THE RÉSUMÉ

A résumé, also called a data sheet or vita, is a concise, well-organized presentation of your qualifications for a job. The prospective employer usually will see your résumé before interviewing you. Your résumé should make a positive impression on the reader. It must be accurate in every detail. You may print it on a laser printer or have it photocopied on high-quality paper. Whichever method you use, however, be sure the copies are clean with clear, sharp print.

What should you learn about an organization before you make an inquiry about a job?

A résumé usually has several categories: personal information, job interest, education, work experience, and references (or a statement about availability of references). You may want to include additional categories, such as computer competencies, extracurricular activities, or scholastic honors when appropriate. Since there is no standard résumé form, a prospective employer may consider your résumé to be an example of your ability to organize information in a useful and meaningful form.

You may decide to prepare several variations of your basic résumé, each one highlighting information related to a particular type of job in which you have an interest. As a general rule, list the most important information first. Refer to Illustration 15-1:5 on page 736 as you read about common résumé categories.

Personal information. Information needed to contact you should be listed clearly at the beginning of your résumé. This information should include your name, mailing address, and telephone number. If you have an e-mail address or fax number, list those also. You need not provide information such as age, date of birth, or marital status.

Why do you believe applicants are not required to provide information about their age and marital status?

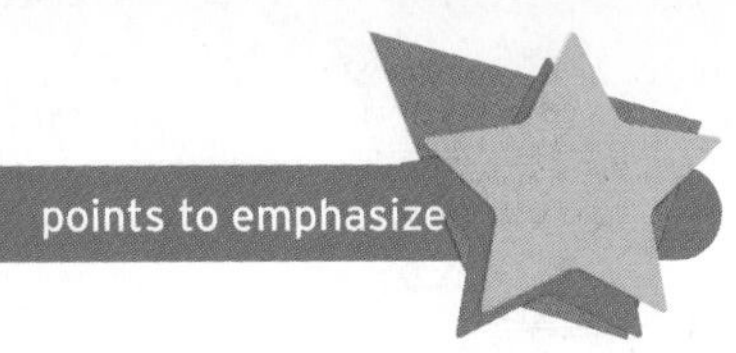

The appearance of your résumé tells a great deal about you. Ask students: Why are applicants not invited for interviews when their résumés contain misspelled words or grammatical errors?

Illustration 15-1:5

A résumé is organized for ease in reviewing an applicant's qualifications.

Valerie Gomez
3467 Mandelin Drive
Albuquerque, NM 87112-0341
(505) 555-0130

Job Interest
An administrative assistant position in an historical museum or college.

Education
Will graduate from Southwest High School, May, 19—
Grade Point Average: 3.57
Class Standing: 34th in class of 329

Related courses:
American History
Keyboarding
Computer Skills
Office Procedures

Special skills:
Keyboarding: 65 words per minute
Good command of Microsoft Office: Word, Excel, Access
Historical research experience in local libraries

School activities:
Vice President of American Historical Club
Member of Student Council

Work Experience
Assistant to the librarian of the historical archives in the Albuquerque Public Library.
(Part-time during school year; full time during the past two summers.)
Student assistant to school librarian during first two years in high school.

References
Provided upon request.

Job Interest. Briefly state the job for which you are applying. A prospective employer will then be able to assess your qualifications in relation to specific job openings in the organization.

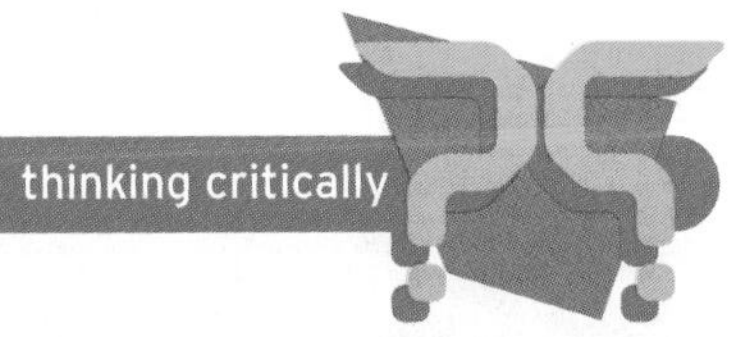

A beginning worker who knew he was a dependable, hardworking person stated under Job Interest, "I'll do anything." Ask students to evaluate that statement on a résumé.

anticipated: planned, expected

Education. List the name and address of your high school and the graduation date or **anticipated** date. List the courses you completed that prepared you for the job market. You may also include any scholastic honors or awards you have earned. You may want to show any extracurricular activities in which you participated, such as membership in special interest clubs.

Work Experience. List in chronological order the jobs you have had, beginning with the most recent one. For each job, include the name and address of the organization, your job title, a brief description of the tasks performed, and the beginning and ending dates of your employment.

At this stage in your career, your job experience is likely to be limited. Therefore, you should include part-time positions as well as any volunteer work you performed. Be sure to indicate clearly the work you did as a volunteer.

References. Employers often want to know what others think of you. References are persons who know your academic ability and/or work skills and habits and are willing to recommend you to prospective employers. It is considered proper to ask permission before using a person as a reference in an application or in an interview with a prospective employer. You may list references in your résumé or you may include a note to the effect that references will be provided upon request. When you list a reference, be sure to include a complete name, job title, address, and telephone number for each one. Generally, three references are considered sufficient.

THE LETTER OF APPLICATION

At this stage in your job search, you have considered your career goals, prepared your résumé, and identified potential job opportunities. Now you must ask prospective employers for an interview. Sometimes at this point, a letter of application is forwarded to prospective employers you have learned are seeking persons with qualifications that you have.

A letter of application introduces you to a prospective employer and requests an interview. While your résumé may be a high-quality photocopy, the letter of application that accompanies your résumé should be an original. The tone of the letter should appeal to the reader, and its content should be concise and informative. Remember, the reader is interested in you only in terms of your qualifications for a job in the company. These guidelines will aid you in composing a letter of application:

What volunteer experiences have you had that you believe should be listed on your résumé?

Ask students to role-play calling someone to ask if the person is willing to serve as reference for a job?

Some classified ads state, "Please do not call; fax or mail a letter." Ask students: Why do you think a company would make such a statement?

Ask students to illustrate the meaning of "tone of the letter"?

- Address the letter to a person, not to a department or position. If you do not have the name of the person to whom your letter should be addressed, call the company to ask for the name and title.
- Explain in the first paragraph the reason for the letter, stating specifically the position in which you are interested.

Illustration 15-1:6

A letter of application clearly identifies the job in which the writer is interested.

3467 Mandelin Drive
Albuquerque, NM 87112-0341
May 10, 19xx

Ms. Gretchen T. Wellington
Director, Hansen Historical Center
356 Front Street
Albuquerque, NM 87102-0356

Dear Ms. Wellington:

Your job opening for a library assistant came to my attention through my school librarian, Ms. Eva Elison. Please consider me as an applicant for the position. I am very interested in working in an organization that is involved in historical research.

I am currently completing my senior year at Southwest High School. I also work about ten hours each week at the Albuquerque Public Library. My work there is in the historical archives under the direction of Ms. Sarah Forman. A copy of my résumé is enclosed to give you more details about my education and experience.

Please consider granting me an interview to discuss employment opportunities with your center. You may telephone me at 555-0130. Since I am at school or work most of the day, please leave a message; I will return your call as soon as possible.

Sincerely,

Valerie Gomez

Valerie Gomez

Enclosure: Résumé

- Briefly indicate why you believe you are qualified for the position. Refer to specific classes, experience, and/or interests you have that you believe are related to the position. Indicate that a résumé is enclosed to provide more details about your qualifications.
- In a final paragraph request an interview.
- Limit your letter to a single page.

The Interview

Most companies interview candidates they believe may meet the qualifications for the positions open. Successful interviewing is a critical step in securing a job that meets your own expectations.

PREPARE FOR AN INTERVIEW

Prepare carefully for each interview you accept. Consider how you will present your qualifications and interests to the interviewer. Anticipate questions and think about how you will respond to them. Learn about the company. What are the company's primary products or services? Are there branch offices? Is the company owned publicly or privately? What do your family and friends know about it? If you prepare well, you will approach the interview with confidence, increasing your chances of making a favorable impression on the interviewer.

MAKE A GOOD FIRST IMPRESSION

At an interview, you are usually approaching a stranger—someone who has had no prior experience with you. What that stranger sees may be highly **influential** as the interview gets underway. Therefore, you must give attention to your appearance. A day or two before the interview, plan what you will wear, considering what is appropriate and at the same time comfortable. Generally, it is wise to choose conservative, businesslike attire, even though you may know that employees in the organization dress casually at most times.

influential: important, significant

ANTICIPATE QUESTIONS

You will be asked a number of questions during the interview. Some are likely to be ones that are commonly asked in such a situation.

If a résumé states the type of job the applicant is interested in and gives the complete background of education and work experience, why is an interview necessary?

Identify a local company known to students. Ask them: What questions would you ask a friend who works at (company name) in order to learn more about the company?

What about a student's typical school attire is likely to be inappropriate for a job interview?

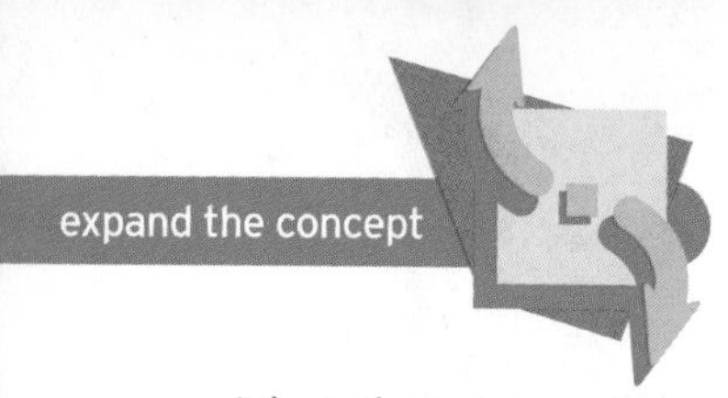

Ask students to provide answers to the common questions. Have them evaluate which of the several answers seem best.

Others may be unique to the interview. Some common questions include these:

- Why does this job interest you?
- What courses did you study that you found most interesting? Why?
- What do you believe are your strongest qualifications for this job?
- What school activities required you to work in groups? on your own?
- How do you evaluate your participation in group activities?
- Why do you think you would enjoy working in our company?
- What are your career goals at this time?

safeguard
protect

Why is equal opportunity in the workplace important?

out of bounds
beyond what is considered legal or appropriate

In the United States, laws have been established to **safeguard** your right to an equal opportunity for employment. Therefore, questions regarding age, marital status, ethnic background, religious beliefs, and physical and emotional disabilities (unless job related) are considered **out of bounds** for questioning. If you encounter questions on these matters, you are not legally required to respond. You may respond simply: "I prefer not to answer that question." You can, of course, answer such a question if you wish.

PREPARE QUESTIONS

What information would you expect the interviewer to provide? Why?

benchmark
a standard by which performance may be measured

Interviewers sometimes ask: "Do you have any questions about the company or the position?" While you are preparing for the interview, you may want to list any questions that come to mind. Some would naturally pertain to the job for which you are applying: "How much orientation is provided for the job?" "How often are employees evaluated?" "Are there promotional opportunities for which employees may apply?" "Has the company established **benchmarks** for the tasks related to the job in which I am interested?" Other questions cover a broad range of subjects, such as the company's mission statement, product lines, and employee benefits.

focal point
something emphasized

You will not want to make salary and benefits the **focal point** of your questions. Doing so may lead an interviewer to conclude that you are far more interested in what you can gain from employment than what you are able to contribute.

What might an interviewer conclude about an applicant who asks only about vacations, sick days allowed, and pay increases?

ARRIVE ON TIME

Arrive at the interview shortly before the scheduled time so that you can be calm and collected when you are called into the interviewer's office. If you are not familiar with the location of the interview, you may want to visit the site in advance, noting how much time you should allow to arrive on schedule. Consider the traffic conditions or possible delays that are likely during the time of day you will be traveling to the interview. Once you arrive, use a visitor parking space in the company parking lot if available. You may need to give your name and the purpose of your visit to a security guard to be admitted to the parking lot or building. Parking lots and garages in downtown or other business areas are often crowded during business hours. Allow ample time to find a parking space and walk to the company location if necessary.

An applicant told the receptionist: "I don't need to fill out this application form; I have prepared a résumé." Was this statement proper?

COMPLETE AN APPLICATION FORM

It is common for a receptionist to greet you and ask you to fill out an employment application form. Complete it carefully in neat, legible handwriting. Glance over the entire application to see what information is requested in each section before you begin writing. Read each question carefully and completely before answering.

Note every item included, and do not leave blanks on an application. You should indicate with a N/A ("not applicable") any item that does not apply to you such as military service, for example. The interviewer then knows that you have read the question. Take a copy of your résumé with you as a source for details as you complete the application. Often the interviewer will read the application form before turning to your résumé.

Engage the class in several instances of introducing an interviewer to an interviewee.

PARTICIPATE ATTENTIVELY

A common procedure is for the receptionist to introduce you to the interviewer. You should extend your hand for a firm handshake and look directly at the interviewer in a friendly, calm manner.

It is natural to be at least a little nervous at a job interview, especially your first one. Instead of dwelling on your **apprehension,** concentrate on what the interviewer asks and tells you. Remember that the

apprehension: dread, sense of uneasiness

Ask students what information they might want to learn during an interview to help make a decision about whether to accept a position, if offered.

interview is a two-way communication process. The interviewer is learning about you and you are learning about the job and the company. Note the do's and don'ts of interviewing in Illustration 15-1:7.

Illustration 15-1:7
Note especially the don'ts of interviewing.

JOB INTERVIEW TIPS

DO	DON'T
• Dress appropriately. • Greet the interviewer with a smile and a firm handshake. • Remain standing until you are asked to have a seat. • Use good posture when standing or sitting. • Listen attentively. • Answer questions honestly and clearly. • Use good grammar. • Exhibit a positive attitude. • Ask questions about the company and its products. • Keep good eye contact with the interviewer.	• Bring a friend or relative to the interview. • Display nervousness by tapping a pencil on the desk, twirling your hair, or any other annoying habit. • Slouch in your chair. • Answer questions with "yeah," "nope," or "uh-huh." • Misrepresent your strengths or accomplishments. • Chew gum, move restlessly, or complain. • Criticize past employers or your teachers. • Ask questions only about the company's benefit package (what the company will do for you). • Stand at the door after the interview is over and continue to talk.

The interviewer will write an evaluation of the interview in which judgments are recorded about key factors such as:

- appearance
- voice and language usage
- knowledge and skills

- effectiveness in working with others
- attitude toward work and learning
- self-confidence
- flexibility
- job interest

Illustration 15-1:8
At the end of an interview, an applicant may need to ask questions to determine the next step.

FOLLOW UP

Review the interview in your mind and jot down notes to yourself about its good points and its weak points. Think of questions that you do not believe you answered well, or that you failed to understand. Review this information later before your next interview.

Write a brief follow-up letter in which you thank the interviewer for talking with you. Indicate again your interest in the job and how you believe your qualifications fit the position. A follow-up letter is perceived favorably as proof of your willingness to follow through after a meeting. If the interviewer does not communicate with you within the time period mentioned at the interview, you should call and express your continued interest in the position.

If you receive a job offer and decide to take the job, you should accept in writing. If you have determined that you are not interested in the

Statistics on employment show that many people drop out of the job market after they fail to find a job in what they believe is a reasonable period of time. Ask the class: What qualities are required to persist in the face of rejection time after time?

Have students discuss the recordkeeping process for documenting a job search.

job, you should write a brief letter stating your decision and expressing thanks for the offer.

Documenting Your Job Search

A job search may be completed in a relatively short time if there are many opportunities in your field of interest in the community where you seek employment. However, job searches sometimes require a considerable amount of time, and you may have to make changes in your strategy and in your job expectations.

Keeping a complete record of what you do and the outcome of each effort is a valuable practice during a job search. Maintain a diary of your activity, indicating clearly the date, time, name of the company, and complete names of all persons with whom you talked. Indicate in your diary the communication you receive after each interaction with someone related to getting a job. This information will be helpful if you are called for a second interview or interview for another job with the same company at a later time.

Reviewing the Topic

1. How might thinking ahead to a career goal help an individual think about a first full-time job?
2. Why is career planning unlikely to be a once-in-a-lifetime task?
3. Identify some questions that a person with a career goal is likely to be able to answer.
4. What are some attitudes employees will find appealing when considering applicants who have not yet established career goals?
5. Where can you learn of job opportunities?
6. What information should an interviewer see on your résumé?
7. What is the purpose of a letter of application?
8. Describe appropriate planning for a job interview.
9. What are some factors that an interviewer will probably evaluate about an interviewee?
10. What content should be included in a letter written as a follow up to an interview?

INTERACTING WITH OTHERS

A large bank that hires many beginning workers asks its employees to participate in evaluating applicants. You are one of the employees invited to have lunch with a potential employee. Consider the criteria you will use for judging the following factors about the applicant:

- appearance
- voice and language usage
- effectiveness in dealing with colleagues
- attitude toward work and learning
- self-confidence
- flexibility
- job interest

topic 15-1 review

topic 15-1 review

An Effective Job Search

745

An Effective Job Search

What you are to do:

In groups of three or four students as assigned by your teacher, discuss the criteria for evaluating each of the identified factors. After a general discussion of each factor, determine what the group as a whole considers the most appropriate evaluation criteria for each factor. Participate in a class discussion with other groups to compare responses.

APPLICATION ACTIVITY

ACTIVITY Job Search

In this activity, you will assume that you are ready to begin full-time employment. You will identify a job for which you are qualified and prepare a résumé and letter of application to use in your job search. You will also consider your responses to typical interview questions.

What you are to do:

1. Identify the type of job you will seek. Choose a job you are qualified for. Describe these factors related to the job:
   - typical titles for this job
   - typical tasks or activities associated with this job
   - typical wages or salary for this job in your area
   - education, skills, and experience required for the job
2. For each factor identified related to education, skills, and experience, explain how your qualifications match this requirement.
3. Prepare written responses for the sample interview questions below:

   a) Tell me about yourself.

   b) What is your greatest strength? weakness?

   c) Where you do want to be in your career five years from now?

   d) What is your greatest accomplishment?

   e) Why should I hire you rather than another applicant with comparable skills?

topic 15-1 review

746

f) How would your current employer or teacher describe your job performance and attitude?

4. Identify at least one organization where there is a position open for the job you have chosen or there is some possibility that such a job might become available.
5. Prepare a letter of application to an organization where the job you seek exists. If a job opening currently exists, apply for that particular job. If not, express your interest in working for the company in the position you have chosen. Ask to be considered when an opening becomes available.
6. Prepare a résumé to include with your letter. You may choose to follow the format shown in Illustration 15-1:5 or a modification of that format.
7. Assume that you have completed an interview for the job. Write a follow-up letter to thank the interviewer and to express your continued interest in the job.
8. Begin documenting your job search. Create a table similar to the one shown below. Record information related to this job in the appropriate spaces.

Job Title:	Order Entry Clerk
Company Name:	MBA Manufacturing
Address:	PO Box 235 Somerset, KY 42501
Phone:	(606) 555- 0127
Contact Person:	Robin McCrae, Office Manager

Date	**Contact**	**Comments**
6/2	Mailed letter and résumé	See attached job ad and copies of letter and résumé
6/15	Phone message from Robin McCrae	
6/16	Returned phone call	Interview scheduled for 6/20 at 9 a.m. at company offices in Governor's Hill Office Park
6/20	Interview	Interview went well. Training provided for order entry system. Flexible hours. Expect to hear from Robin within two weeks.
6/21	Sent follow-up letter	Expressed continued interest. See attached copy of letter.

747

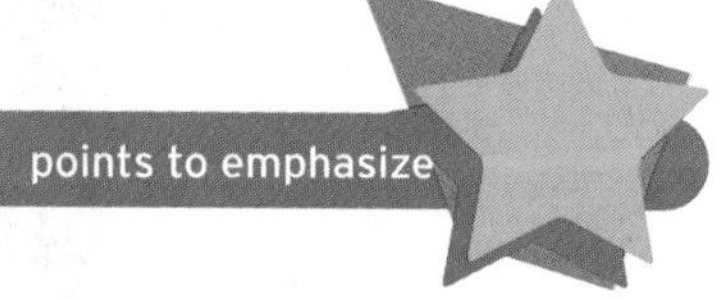

Because a class is likely to have some students who seek jobs after graduation and others who do not, the focus of this topic should be general. The value of understanding how one is introduced to a new job and what is expected can have long-term value to students.

points to emphasize

During an introduction to a new job, you want to gain a sense of the whole organization. Review the company's mission statement, goals, products or services, and structure.

The First Job and Beyond

Topic 15-2

When you have completed your study of this topic, you will be able to:

- **describe typical ways organizations provide orientation for new employees**
- **explain the responsibility for self-evaluation of performance**
- **identify resources for continuous improvement of an employee's knowledge and skills**
- **explain effective ways of facing job changes**

A new job means new learning. As you think ahead about your first full-time job, you may have questions such as the following:

- What will they expect me to be able to do immediately?
- Will I be able to learn everything I should know about this job?
- Will my coworkers be willing to help me?

Introduction to a New Job

Employers expect to provide new employees with an introduction to the company and to new jobs. Company leaders realize that employees who understand their jobs and the total company are likely to enjoy their work and contribute a great deal to the goals established by its

leaders. In some instances, the introduction is provided in a **formal,** organized manner. In other instances, the introduction is done informally by the employee's supervisor or manager.

formal:
done in accordance with an organized plan

ORIENTATION

Initial introduction to a new company and job is called orientation. Orientation programs may be formal or informal. Formal orientation programs are scheduled for a particular time and include a specified series of sessions. Formal orientation programs are common in large organizations, where a number of new employees are beginning their jobs at the same time.

> *A large bank in downtown Charlotte introduced all 25 of the new employees at an all-day orientation scheduled for the first day of employment. At the morning sessions, new employees learned about the company's mission and the activities of the total organization. After lunch, the 25 new employees had small group meetings with managers in the departments where they would be working.*

Informal orientation programs are common in smaller organizations where fewer employees are likely to begin their new jobs at the same time. Generally, an informal program is directed by the new employee's immediate supervisor or by an experienced coworker, who often has a checklist to guide the explanations during the orientation. Some of these topics are likely to be presented:

- goals and policies of the organization
- the company's organization chart and key personnel
- employee benefits provided
- company policies related to ethics, safety, and security
- personnel policies, including performance evaluations
- policies and procedures that guide the new employee's responsibilities

Orientation does not always end with the program offered on the initial day or days of work. Sometimes additional orientation meetings are scheduled after employees have had several weeks of experience in their new positions.

New employees may find it worthwhile to use some of their own time to become better acquainted with their new organizations. Ask students: How would you evaluate a new employee taking home material distributed during orientation sessions?

What kind of notetaking would be appropriate during orientation sessions?

Describe the types of comments that experienced employees might make in an informal orientation program to make a new employee feel welcome.

What value is there in orientation sessions scheduled for several weeks after new employees have been on the job?

LEARNING ON THE JOB

As a new employee, it is helpful to realize that the person to whom you report is aware that you do not know everything that the job may require. Learning on the job is expected and is considered a normal part of your total orientation. Some of the learning is guided by an experienced person, and some is done on your own.

As a new worker, you can expect to be given specific information about the tasks for which you will have responsibility. There may be a clearly stated job description of what you are to do, or you may be in a newly created position. In the latter case, there will be just a general idea of your duties. Because of the rapid changes many organizations are facing, employees' actual work responsibilities may differ from their job description.

What does Vanessa face in an unstructured job? How does what she faces differ from that of a person with a structured job?

> *Vanessa was hired as an assistant to the director of a new laboratory in a growing biotechnology company. Her background in sciences and her work as a lab assistant while in college were considered appropriate background for a person filling a position not yet fully defined. Vanessa likes having an* **unstructured** *job. As she said, "I have to be alert to see where I can be helpful; that's a challenge I'll enjoy."*

unstructured: loose, not determined ahead of time

receptive: open to others, cooperative

Assistance from Coworkers. A new employee will generally find a **receptive** group of coworkers who are generous in helping the new worker understand what is being done. They understand that a knowledgeable coworker is going to be a valuable asset to the unit or department. You will quickly realize which of your coworkers are most likely to respond positively to questions you might have.

Any illustrations of company manuals, even if only tables of content, will aid students in understanding what they can expect.

General Reference Sources. During your orientation, you will become acquainted with basic references available to you. Some of these may be available through your computer, while some may be in print:

- a company manual of policies and procedures
- a complete organization chart
- a calendar of events and a company newsletter
- an annual report, if the company is publicly owned
- a directory of all personnel

Annual reports for local companies that are publicly owned will be of interest to students in getting an overall idea of company missions and goals.

Job-Related Resources. Companies have developed a wide range of materials to aid employees. You will want to learn what company databases are available for your use. If your company has a library or resource center, spend some time, possibly during lunch time, getting acquainted with the range of information that you can access. Your department may subscribe to periodicals, newspapers, or databases that are useful to you in your job.

Evaluation of Your Performance

Companies expect workers to be competent. Most organizations have a plan for evaluating performance and discussing the results with the employee at least once a year. Here are some of the common factors that are considered in such evaluations:

- job knowledge
- quality of performance
- quantity of work completed
- initiative
- cooperation
- flexibility
- adaptability
- judgment
- adherence to schedules and deadlines

New workers are given a period of time for learning their jobs. The trial or probation period may extend over three, six or twelve months. The length of the trial period is determined by the complexity of the job and the level of skills possessed by the employee.

WAYS OF EVALUATING EMPLOYEES

Companies use varying methods for evaluating workers. Evaluation practices may be informal and little, if any, information may be recorded in the personnel file of the employee. On the other hand,

Ask students to describe what they would do initially when visiting an organization's library for the first time.

Use the factors as a basis for discussion of a selected number of jobs in which the students in the class are interested.

Ask students to discuss the factors evaluated, ask them to note the extent to which a factor is important to a variety of jobs.

Ask students to assume they are at work. Have them consider what clues would indicate that they have really learned their new jobs.

Ask students to consider the qualities that they think are most important in a manager who will be evaluating their performance.

Ask students: What personal responsibility does an employee have who was ranked on job knowledge as "inadequate?"

some companies use a clearly stated employee performance appraisal with carefully developed evaluation forms for the various positions in the organization.

Informal Observation. In some companies, the manager is responsible for writing a performance appraisal of each employee at designated times. Generally, the employee signs the appraisal to indicate that it was read. The employee, in such cases, usually has the right to add comments to the appraisal.

Performance Appraisal Forms. In some companies, the human resources department provides an appraisal form to be used for the evaluation of each employee. Note the partial one shown in Illustration 15-2:1.

As you see, there are five statements for each factor evaluated. The judgments listed first after the description of each factor are the most favorable evaluations; those listed last before the comments are the least favorable.

Work Measurement. Some companies have developed standards for specific jobs. Standards based on keystrokes, lines, or pages may be the basis for determining the productivity of an employee doing word processing at a personal computer. Often, standards are specified per hour or per day. Devices that keep track of such factors as keystrokes and lines may allow for detailed **monitoring** of output of many employees, especially those who work in factories and in offices where there are repetitive tasks.

monitoring: observing and noting what happens

In some cases, work measurement is used primarily to determine which employees need additional training and direction to improve their productivity. Work measurement may be valuable to the manager in determining the capability of a total group.

> *A major insurance company interested in increasing productivity of all employees began a study of key tasks. As a phase of this project, the work of employees in the largest departments was measured so that actual performance could be determined. With the standards established, the company introduced training courses to aid employees in achieving the new standards, called* benchmarks.

EMPLOYEE PERFORMANCE EVALUATION

INSTRUCTIONS:
Evaluate the employee's performance on the job now being performed by making an X on the line above each of the following suggested statements that best expresses your judgment about the individual's capabilities. If a pre-printed statement is not an accurate description, a more applicable statement may be entered in the comments section. In order to conduct a more meaningful appraisal you should refer to the employee's job description while evaluating and discussing the employee's job performance.

Employee ______________ **Department/Position** ______________

Supervisor ______________

A. **JOB KNOWLEDGE**
Possession of information and understanding of the work to be performed (how well employee knows the job)
- ☐ Thoroughly familiar with all phases of work.
- ☐ Well-rounded knowledge. Requires minimal assistance.
- ☐ Adequate job knowledge. Requires some guidance and assistance.
- ☐ Limited job knowledge. Requires considerable assistance.
- ☐ Inadequate knowledge. Requires improvement to retain job.

COMMENTS: ______________

B. **QUANTITY OF WORK**
Volume of acceptable work turned out and use of the working time
- ☐ Rapid worker. Usually high output.
- ☐ Better-than-average workflow.
- ☐ Average amount of work turned out, but seldom more.
- ☐ Output of work is frequently less than expected.
- ☐ Very slow worker. Must improve to retain job.

COMMENTS: ______________

C. **QUALITY OF WORK**
Accuracy, neatness, and dependability of results
- ☐ Consistently excellent qualit...

Illustration 15-2:1
An excerpt from a performance evaluation

EVALUATING YOUR OWN PERFORMANCE

To progress in your job, you will want to ask yourself: "How well am I doing my job?" Such an evaluation might be scheduled to be completed approximately a month before the evaluation by your manager. The following steps should be helpful in your evaluation:

1. Determine the competencies that are critical in your position. For this step, a copy of the evaluation appraisal form used or your job description will be useful.
2. List the competencies, one to every other page in a notebook.

Why might employees have difficulty evaluating their own performance?

systematic: following a plan

3. Think about your work behavior on a **systematic** basis, either daily for one week or one day each week for four or five weeks.
4. Record under the relevant competencies any instances of exceptionally effective or disappointing performance, indicating the date of each entry.
5. Assess what you have written at the end of your review period, noting especially instances of disappointing performance.
6. Consider what you might change to improve your performance.
7. Compare your own evaluation with the one given you by your manager or supervisor.
8. Reconsider your own evaluation in relation to that given by your manager or supervisor and make appropriate changes in how you assess yourself.

Celia, who worked in the office of the food editor of a popular home magazine, followed a procedure similar to the one noted above. When she reviewed her competencies, she noted several points under disappointing performance in relation to meeting the schedule. She realized that she set aside jobs far too frequently and did not return to complete them on time. She realized that she must change her pattern of work.

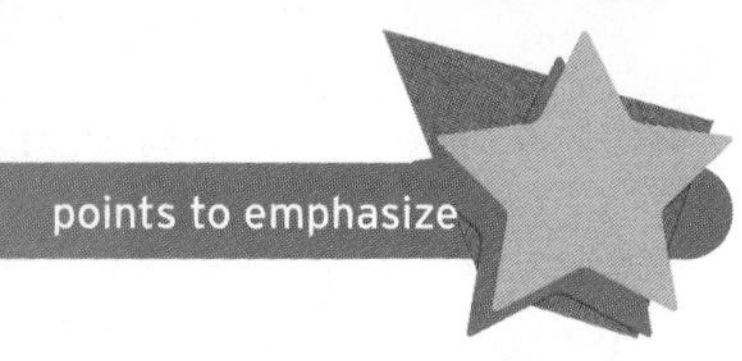

An individual can develop an objective view of his or her own performance.

A new employee who carefully evaluated his own performance was surprised that his evaluation was far more positive than that given him by his manager. What should he do at this point?

What must Celia actually do to overcome what she believes is a poor work habit?

Continuous Improvement

You may realize that a plan for self-evaluation and the performance evaluation made by your manager are closely related to the concept of continuous improvement. The evaluations, if followed up in a thoughtful, realistic manner, should help you be more productive and may lead to promotional opportunities.

CONSIDERING YOUR PRESENT POSITION

Often employees accept how they have always done a task as natural—or as the only way. Yet an employee's critical, objective review of the task often reveals that there is indeed a better way of completing it.

General guidelines for continuous improvement reflect the common issues noted among many types of employees—from professionals to

If you are doing your job well enough to get a satisfactory performance evaluation, why should you even consider continuous improvement efforts?

factory workers. Reviewing your work with these guidelines in mind can help improve your performance.

Guidelines for Continuous Improvement

1. Simplify; eliminate needless steps in accomplishing a task.
2. Build-in organizational procedures as you handle the task itself; do not think of "getting organized" as something that should be done later as a separate activity.
3. Consider the overall life of a new project, making realistic estimates of time required to meet deadlines.
4. Review your judgment about what information is of value. Keep what has value, and discard what does not.
5. Document steps or other information related to the task.
6. Prioritize tasks and complete them in order of importance.

Illustration 15-2:2
Guidelines for continuous improvement

Tonya, an assistant manager in a busy admissions office in a private secondary school, commented after acknowledging that she had finally begun a program of continuous improvement: "Instead of simply performing my normal tasks as I have always done them, I am now carefully observing what I am doing. What a revelation!

For example, I never realized why my clean desk at the beginning of each day became a mess by midday. However, by observing my behavior, I know exactly what I do—which is fail to return material to its proper place when I no longer need it."

CONSIDERING PROMOTIONAL POSSIBILITIES

Although you may be content with your present job, remember to consider the future. While focusing primarily on your current job, also consider what you can do to prepare for future jobs, some of which may be promotions.

Ask students to consider nonvalue-added activity in relation to their learning this year in all their classes.

Why would an organization encourage all employees to undertake continuous improvement in their positions?

What attitudes are important for individuals who would like to be promoted?

Why do people work?

Which of the reasons for working that you have heard reflect unhappiness at work? Which reflect happiness at work?

Illustration 15-2:3
This manager could benefit from continuous improvement exercises.

Within Your Organization. Your knowledge of your organization's structure will help you understand the promotional opportunities available. You will also have interaction with people at varying levels of the company and learn, in informal ways, what qualifications are required. Your observations of what higher-level positions require can help you determine if you wish to strive for such positions.

At Other Organizations. Beginning workers may find limited opportunities to move into jobs at higher levels or with broader responsibilities within their organizations. Such workers need to look elsewhere for promotions. If you find yourself in such a situation, do some investigation of what types of positions relate to your interests and build on the experience you have begun to accumulate. Learn the educational requirements for the specialization in which you are interested.

Resources Outside Your Organization

Your commitment to work requires a decision that only you can make. Some people are personally defined by the work they do. These are individuals who seem to spend all their time involved with their work. There are others whose commitment to work reflects the reality that work is a requirement if one is to earn a living, yet they are responsible and conscientious. Some in this group seek to meet the requirements for promotion, while others do not.

As you think about your own attitudes and what you would like them to be, you will find a serious review of information about fields in which you are interested to be very valuable.

PROFESSIONAL AND TRADE ASSOCIATIONS

People with common work interests often belong to associations that provide programs and activities that may enhance their work skills and knowledge. There are thousands of organizations related to the various kinds of work. Internet resources and local libraries will help you become acquainted with those available. Your company's human resources department may have information about those in your community that you may wish to join.

PROFESSIONAL AND TRADE PERIODICALS

The organization in which you work may subscribe to magazines and newspapers related to the organization's business. Check the resources of your local libraries and become acquainted with what is available either in print or electronic format.

EDUCATIONAL RESOURCES

Think about new skills you would like to acquire to become a more effective worker, such as speaking, handling meetings, or problem solving. You can probably find educational resources to help you develop these skills. Consider local educational programs offered by a local public school system through adult education or by a local college or university. You may also enroll in courses that are provided on the Internet.

Facing Job Changes

As you become more proficient in your job, you may see other appealing opportunities. Also, because of the rapid changes in the structure

The range of interests in the class will determine relevant discussion of professional and trade organizations. Activities of local chapters of professional and trade organizations that are reported in newspapers and on television can be used to introduce students to what is available. Resources on the World Wide Web will also be valuable for extending awareness of what is available.

Copies of periodicals of professional and trade organizations can be used to illustrate the information available for those who want to continue to learn.

Identify a person in the community—possibly relatively young—who has worked his or her way up in a company through a self-designed program of career enhancement.

Discuss with students the motivation required for an individual to set up a program of career enhancement.

Why would individuals consider changing jobs when they are successful in their present jobs?

At this point, what would you have in a job portfolio if you were to prepare one?

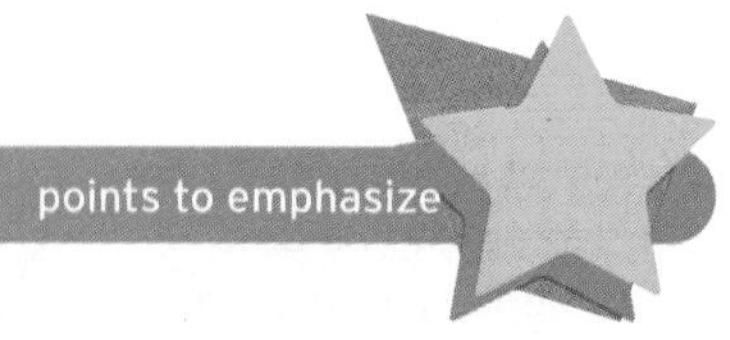

Failure in one job does not mean failure in the next.

and technology in organizations, employees are frequently terminated. Changing jobs may be your choice or it may be imposed upon you. In either case, your response should be realistic and thoughtful.

CONSIDERING OTHER OPPORTUNITIES

To be prepared to consider other jobs when it seems appropriate, you should maintain a *job portfolio* or *career portfolio* file. Among the items you should keep are the following:

- copies of your résumé
- copies of any awards or honors you have received
- letters, notes, and other items related to your work
- programs and newsletters that report your participation in school and community activities
- school transcript of courses completed
- diplomas and certificates of completion of courses
- job descriptions, evaluations, and related information about earlier full-time positions and about your current position

Illustration 15-2:4
Employees should always be aware of alternative job opportunities.

RESPONDING TO JOB TERMINATION

terminated: ended

There is no guarantee that a job will be yours as long as you want it. Your job may be eliminated and your employment **terminated.** In such instances, some companies provide assistance in helping you find another position. At times, companies use outplacement services, which are organizations that provide counseling services to aid displaced employees in finding new jobs. Remember that while one company no longer needs your services, there are likely to be others that do.

Gerri, a copy editor in the advertising department of a large consumer products company, was stunned when the manager told her she was being dismissed. Gerri had been in her job about one year. She knew she had had problems with her assigned project leader, but she thought she was doing the job in a minimally satisfactory manner. After the initial shock, she realized that she should be courageous in assessing the situation. A few days later she faced the fact that she was so **intimidated** *by the project leader that she did indeed fail to even listen to what she should do. Again and again she was* **reprimanded,** *but at such times she didn't stop to think about what was really happening. As she recovered from the blow of the dismissal, she decided that she would try again at another company. She decided that she would not allow another person to undermine her confidence. She would listen, follow instructions, and when necessary, defend what she had done.*

intimidated: made timid, frightened

reprimanded: criticized, condemned

Ask students to consider what a person who was dismissed because of failure to perform satisfactorily ought to do to assure success on the next job.

The Challenge of Work

You live in a **dynamic** world filled with opportunities and multiple paths to learning.

As you begin full-time employment or pursue further education, continue to broaden your awareness of the career possibilities in the amazingly complex business world. Strive to understand your potential as a contributor in the workplace and to face career opportunities with confidence and optimism.

dynamic: changing, active

What are some attitudes that should be developed to help assure a rewarding work life?

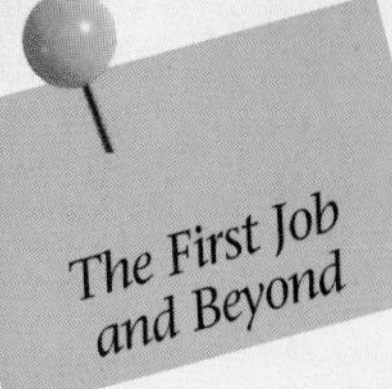

Reviewing the Topic

1. Why is orientation provided for new employees?
2. What general references will aid a new employee in learning about the company?
3. Identify five factors generally considered in an employee evaluation.
4. Describe the steps employees might follow in evaluating their own performance.
5. How can an employee learn about promotional opportunities in the company?
6. What types of information should be collected in a job or career portfolio?
7. What services are provided by out placement firms?

MAKING DECISIONS

Nancy and Ellie both accepted full-time jobs in a local company where they had worked during the summers for the last two years. They received information about when they should report for their first day of work and about the first day's schedule of orientation sessions. Nancy called Ellie and said, "Ellie, did you see the schedule for orientation on Monday, our first day at work? Don't you think we can skip most of the day? I'd say we should plan to arrive at three o'clock when we will learn from our managers what exactly they want us to do on our jobs. Why should we waste our time hearing about things we already know? What do you think?"

What you are to do:

Assume you are Ellie. Prepare a written response to Nancy's suggestion.

APPLICATION ACTIVITY

ACTIVITY Orientation Program

topic 15-2 review

As Human Resources Assistant for the Gainsboro Company, you are responsible for scheduling the orientation program for 11 new

The First Job and Beyond

employees who will begin work three weeks from next Monday. The names and addresses of the new employees appear below. The schedule for the day has been determined. You need to communicate the details to the new employees and those who will participate in the sessions.

Filename: Schedule

Mr. Marvin Hicks
340 N West St.
Tipton, IN 46072

Ms. Gina Agee
332 Taft St.
Tipton, IN 46072

Mr. Jerrold Haufman
520 Armstrong St.
Tipton, IN 46072

Mr. Bill Irby
9508 W Jackson St.
Muncie, IN 47304

Ms. Karmen Keeton
208 N Bayberry Ln.
Muncie, IN 47304

Mr. Ramon Perez
3604 W Alto Rd.
Kokomo, IN 46902

Ms. Fay Thrasher
932 E Sycamore St.
Kokomo, IN 46901

Mr. Kim Yong
16599 Audubon Ct.
Noblesville, IN 46060

Mr. Taylor Sullivan
4011 Mallway Dr.
Indianapolis, IN 46236

Ms. Bonnie Riley
4823 Round Lake Rd.
Indianapolis, IN 46205

Mr. Ray Savage
5217 Melrose Ave.
Indianapolis, IN 46241

What you are to do:

1. Prepare a letter and enclosure for each new employee that will communicate the schedule and location for the sessions. Your rough notes for the schedule are in the file named *Schedule*. Format and arrange your notes into an attractive schedule. Use your name and title, Administrative Assistant, Human Resources, in the signature block of the letter.
2. Send a memo to the seven company executives participating in the orientation program. Mention the name and time of the session in which the executive will participate and attach a complete schedule.

761

15

Chapter Summary

Conducting an effective job search is critical in securing a job that matches your interests and skills. Proper orientation to a new job and continuous efforts to improve your performance can aid in your success and lead to opportunities for promotion. Realistic self-evaluation and planning to secure needed education, training, and experience are important in carrying through your long-term career strategy. The following points related to these concepts were highlighted in the chapter:

- A career strategy is thinking ahead to a career goal and considering your first job in relation to that goal.
- It is possible to choose a job and be successful in meeting its demands without a career goal.
- A carefully prepared résumé and a letter of application will aid in communicating your qualifications for a job.
- An interview is a critical step in getting a job. It is your opportunity to convince the interviewer that you have the education, skills, experience, and attitudes to be successful in the job.
- A follow-up letter should be sent after an interview to thank the interviewer and to express continued interest in the job.
- Organizations plan orientation for new employees to introduce them to the company and to the new jobs.
- Evaluating your own performance is important to your effectiveness on the job.
- Striving for continuous improvement can help you be more productive in your present position and may lead to promotional opportunities.
- Professional and trade associations provide many opportunities for individuals to enhance their work skills and knowledge.
- Job changes, both voluntary and involuntary, are common in today's business world.

chapter 15 summary

Planning and Advancing Your Career

762

KEY CONCEPTS AND TERMS

benchmark
career strategy
continuous improvement
employment agency
follow-up letter
interview
job portfolio
job search
letter of application
orientation
out-placement service
performance evaluation
résumé
self-evaluation

INTEGRATED CHAPTER ACTIVITIES

ACTIVITY 1 Changing Jobs

You can learn a great deal from talking with people about their experiences with a job search and beginning a new job. In this activity, you will interview someone who has changed jobs recently.

What you are to do:

1. Identify someone who began a new job within the past year, preferably in a field in which you are interested. Seek answers to the following questions and prepare a written report.
   - What is the nature of the organization's business?
   - What is your job title?
   - How did you learn about the job?
   - What were the key questions you were asked during your interview for the job?
   - What did you find appealing about the job offer?
   - Has the job turned out to be what you anticipated it would be?
   - How were you introduced to your job responsibilities? Was any type of training provided?
   - What challenges have you faced in adjusting to the new job?

763

ACTIVITY 2 **Role-Playing Interviews**

The interview is a critical step in your job search. In this activity, you will simulate the experiences of being the applicant interviewed and of interviewing someone else.

What you are to do:

1. As a class, select four or five different beginning positions for which students will apply. Choose positions based on the job interests and abilities of the class.
2. In teams of two, identify one person to play the interviewer and the other to play the applicant. For the interview, choose one of the positions identified earlier.
3. As the interviewer, develop a list of questions related to this particular job that will reflect attitudes related to responsibility, initiative, creative thinking, and ethics.
4. As the applicant, develop a résumé to show your qualifications and interests related to this job. Develop a list of questions you plan to ask the interviewer about the job. Anticipate questions that you expect to be asked during the interview and plan your answers.
5. Conduct (role-play) the interview. As the interviewer, complete an evaluation form for the applicant. (The form is found in your *Student Activities and Projects* workbook.) As the applicant, respond to the questions asked as though you were actually participating in a real interview. Review the evaluation completed by the interviewer to learn about areas for improvement.
6. Working in the same team or another as assigned by your teacher, switch roles so that you are now the interviewer if you were the applicant or the applicant if you were the interviewer. Repeat the interview preparation and role playing.

See Workbook page 97.

764

Leslie Norwood
Director of Human Relations

Getting Acquainted with the World of Work

I'm Not Ambitious – Is There a Place for Me in the Workplace?

Dear Ms. Norwood

I'm realistic. I know I will have to earn my living when I graduate. I do what has to be done to pass my courses with decent grades. I don't mind working hard to complete an assignment. I'm the kind of person who does follow through on a promise. Most of my friends are like me—not ambitious. There are some in our group, though, who are ambitious. We tolerate them, but we don't relate to them closely, because the rest of us are turned off about all the discussion of this "what do-you-want-to-be-when-you-grow-up?" idea. Teachers talk about having goals and aspiring to something in your life. I guess it sounds good to many students, but it does not to me.

You see, I believe that you should have an honest interest in what you are doing now; you should do what makes sense to you now. *You shouldn't be scheming to do what will look good for the next step on the so-called upward path to greater achievement.*

Now, as I think ahead to being an employee, I wonder if there is any possibility that I will be chosen to fill a job. What do you think?

Debbie in Toledo

Dear Debbie

You raise a very interesting question. Let me commend you on your independent thinking and your candidness about what you believe. Debbie, your attitude toward being ambitious is understandable. Undoubtedly, you have observed choices being made solely *on the basis of how they will affect some future goal and perhaps centered around material gain. What you have observed is what I would call "distorted ambition." However, there are individuals whose ambition comes from their deep interest in what they are doing now and what further opportunities are available.*

Let me tell you just one brief story: While in high school, a young man worked as a volunteer in a shelter for homeless children. He was stunned by what he saw. He found his participation in the program very meaningful. He decided that he wanted to become a counselor. He became ambitious—he began to think about what he could do when he had completed the education required to be a counselor. Note that his ambition was directly related to something he was doing that he found completely engaging. This is an example of genuine ambition.

Debbie, as I read your letter, I am guessing that you are a responsible, capable young woman. There will be a place for you in the workplace. Perhaps you too will find a career interest that will make you "ambitious." I extend my best wishes to you as you enter the world of work.

Sincerely

Leslie Norwood
Director of Human Relations

765

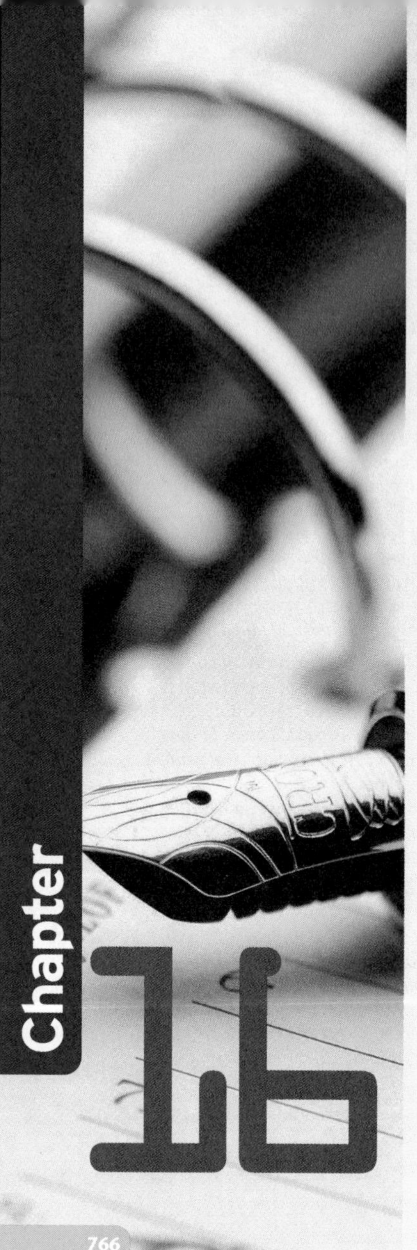

Working with Others

The workplace is different today from what it was even a decade ago because of new technology, organizational structures, and procedures. However, one aspect remains the same—the way people interact. The personal qualities considered essential for work have not changed. They continue to reflect respect for oneself and others. Such qualities are also the foundation from which organizational activity can be launched with confidence and optimism.

In this chapter, you will consider yourself as an individual at work interacting with other workers. You will be introduced to personal qualities critical for success in the workplace. You will learn about common interactions at work and the importance of participating effectively with others.

Chapter 16

766

Topic 16-1

Personal Qualities at Work

When you have completed your study of this topic, you will be able to:

- **describe aspects of personality that are critical for effective performance at work**
- **explain the attitudes that contribute to the success of organizations**
- **describe expectations related to your appearance and manners**

To work is to interact with other people. Even those who work at home interact with others. The character of each person in an interaction influences how effectively the group will work together. In fact, an employee identified as having "good character" is one who has a deep commitment to behaving appropriately.

Four key expectations employers have for workers are reliability, productivity, cooperativeness, and independence in learning. In this chapter, the focus is on underlying personal attitudes and behaviors that support those expectations.

The point of view presented in this chapter is based on two concepts: (1) individuals have personal responsibility for their actions; and (2) individuals respect the rights of others. People are expected to behave in ways that others think are honorable and fair. They strive

You may want to use some of the recent group assignments as a basis for noting how common interactions among employees are.

It may be useful to recall the key points from Chapter 2 that dealt with employer expectations.

Societies develop expectations of various kinds. In the United States, much emphasis is placed on individual responsibility for doing what is considered proper.

Why does an organization care about employees behaving in an honorable and fair way at work?

Topic 16-1

to participate at work, as well as in other activities, in a way that contributes to the quality of human interaction. In the workplace, employees realize that they do influence the nature and quality of their own work environment.

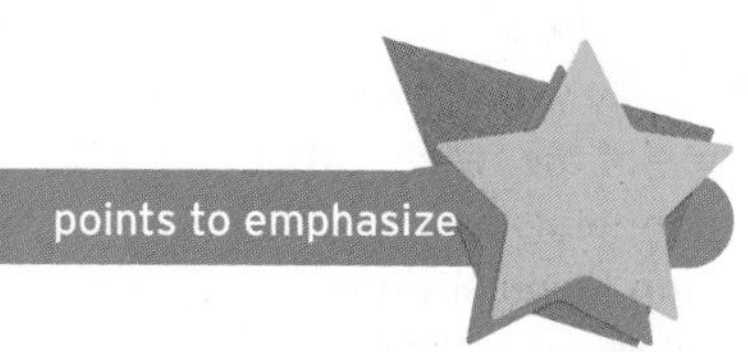

Being candid with oneself is not always easy. While individuals may know the flaws in their personality, they may find it painful to acknowledge them, even to themselves.

Your Personality at Work

distinguishes: sets apart

Each individual is unique. The combination of characteristics that **distinguishes** one person from another is called personality. Your personal characteristics influence how you think, what you say, and how you respond to demands that arise in your daily life. What is remarkable about your personality is that, to a far greater extent than many realize, you have control of who you are and what you believe. This means that you can make changes in your personality.

CHARACTER

The basic values and principles that are reflected in the way you live your life are referred to as character. Your parents, relatives, friends, and teachers have probably made efforts to help you develop your character so that you can live on the highest level of expectations in our society. This discussion, therefore, is not a new topic for you. You may want to use this opportunity, though, to reconsider some basic truths about yourself in a positive, candid fashion.

Why would an executive engage in such a scheme?

Integrity. At the core of your character is what you believe about integrity. Honesty and trustworthiness are synonyms for integrity. Individuals with integrity are valuable at work because they can be trusted to use the resources of the company only for company purposes. Consider what might happen when a person lacks integrity.

The executive's company undoubtedly lacked good internal control. Companies with good internal control review purchases to be certain they are paying standard prices for the quantities and qualities being purchased. What could the company have done to reduce the possibility of embezzlement in this instance?

embezzling: stealing

> *An executive confessed to* **embezzling** *funds in a scheme in which the executive and a vendor agreed to take money from the company. The vendor issued invoices that overbilled the company. Then the vendor shared the amount of the overbilling with the executive. In a period of five years, the two had taken $6 million from the company.*

The executive was sentenced to prison time. Think what would happen in an organization if there were many people acting as this executive did. Such behavior could bankrupt the company in a short time.

Students might be encouraged to read the local papers and note stories on television that describe fraudulent behavior in all types of organizations.

Why is honesty considered the best policy?

Fortunately, most employees are honest and would not **divert** funds that belong to their companies. In its annual report, one major U. S. company described the importance of integrity as follows:

divert:
shift for personal use

> ***Highest Standards of Integrity:*** *We are honest and ethical in all our business dealings, starting with how we treat each other. We keep our promises and admit our mistakes. Our personal conduct ensures that our company's name is always worthy of trust.*

Reliability. Another critical component of character is reliability. Reliability means that what you are expected to do—or what you promise to do—will be done. The responsibilities you accept will not be ignored or dismissed as unimportant. Increasingly, companies cannot watch over employees to see that they perform assigned tasks. Company officials depend on the reliability of their employees.

How has reliability been important to you during your years as a student?

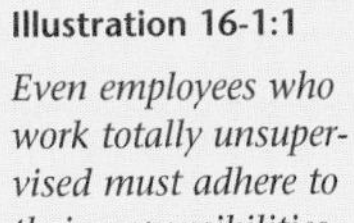

Illustration 16-1:1

Even employees who work totally unsupervised must adhere to their responsibilities.

> *Walt and Rick work from midnight to 8 a.m. in a 24-hour photocopying center. No supervisor ever comes by to check on what they are doing. However, neither would ever think of closing the office for awhile and going off to an all-night diner. As Walt said: "I chose to work this late shift because I love the freedom and independence we have. I would never take my responsibilities lightly. I am willing to earn the rewards of freedom and independence!"*

What do you think Walt should do when a friend comes by at 1 a.m. and asks him to go off to a party for "about an hour"?

SELF-ACCEPTANCE

At the core of your personality is your attitude toward yourself. Experts in the field of mental health stress the value of accepting yourself.

Why do you think some people do not have a realistic view of themselves? What makes the view "realistic"?

What attitudes help a person accept problems while also meeting obligations?

If you think of yourself as worthy, why would you need to note your inadequacies and do something about them?

They have shown that you cannot change your personality without self-acceptance, which requires a candid view of who you are.

To be effective at self-acceptance, you must have a realistic view of yourself. Those who accept themselves have adopted the following basic attitudes:

- Be honest with yourself. This means that you don't deceive yourself about your behavior and beliefs.
- Understand that while you are a unique individual, you also share many of the same wants, needs, and fears of others.
- Believe in your own worthiness, while respecting the uniqueness of others.

Being Honest with Yourself. You cannot be accepting of yourself if you find it difficult or impossible to view yourself honestly. Doing so means admitting your weaknesses and acknowledging your strengths.

Sharing Common Wants, Needs, and Fears. It is easy to believe that you are the only one in the world with wants, needs, and fears. Others may appear not to have the problems you face. Such thoughts, which are usually not grounded in reality, will not solve your problems.

> *Kimberly admired a classmate, Susanne, who seemed carefree, yet earned the top grades in her classes. Kimberly was certain that Susanne did not study, but lived an easy life. One afternoon, Kimberly asked Susanne to join her in a game of tennis during the weekend. Kimberly was stunned when Susanne said to her: "I'd love to join you, but I spend most of my weekend studying. Would you ask me again when school ends?"*

An awareness of how others meet their obligations and how they make choices can help you to understand how much individuals are alike.

Accepting Your Own Worthiness. Regardless of your inadequacies, you are worthy. Every human being is. Self-acceptance means that you are willing to accept your faults, but still be able to live with yourself. Living with yourself means that you can sustain a feeling of confidence and a sense of security. For example, you are not shattered by constructive criticism.

MATURITY

Even though there is potential for growth throughout life, a person in our society is expected to behave in a mature manner by the end of adolescence. Of course, many young people show maturity earlier. To be mature, as the dictionary states, is "to have or express the emotional and mental qualities that are considered normal to a socially adjusted adult human being." To be mature means that you see beyond the moment, that you understand the consequences of your choices, consider the rights of others, and make decisions based on such understanding.

YOU ARE MATURE WHEN YOU ARE WILLING TO

- **Accept criticism**
- **Acknowledge that you do not know or understand**
- **Admit that you made a mistake**
- **Learn from your mistakes**
- **Face your weaknesses and determine how to overcome them**
- **Be considerate of others**
- **Be objective and honest in your relations with others**
- **Relinquish feeling superior to another human being**

Illustration 16-1:2
What Maturity Means

Use Illustration 16-1:2 as a basis for asking students to describe an observation to illustrate each point noted.

Attitudes that Support Quality Performance

The attitudes that support quality performance at work include a strong belief in the work ethic, willingness to participate in achieving the goals of the organization, and a desire to learn. You will want to develop these attitudes to increase your chances for success on the job.

THE WORK ETHIC

As you have learned, high productivity and effective use of resources are common goals of businesses. Productivity depends on the work ethic of employees. Work ethic is a general term that combines a deep belief in the value of work in one's life and a willingness to meet the

What is a reasonable degree of productivity?

Being willing to adjust your own scheduled work to be helpful when an important deadline requires extra assistance is a valuable attitude at work.

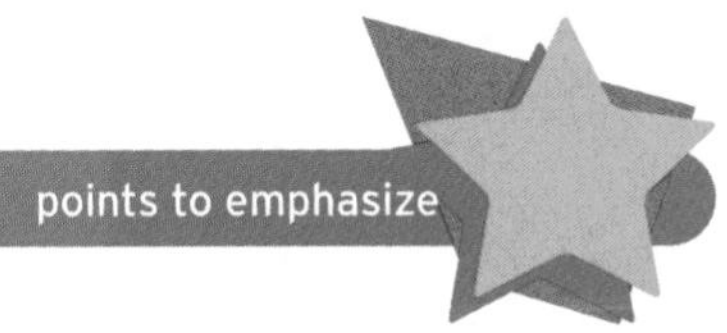

Employees cannot assume that only the specified tasks in a job description are their responsibility. While a job description is helpful in knowing what is generally expected, an employee must remember that employment is related to the total company's goals.

demands of work. Workers in the United States have long been credited with a strong work ethic. Low absenteeism, willingness to work overtime, and low error rates are just some of the factors that reflect a strong work ethic. Companies looking for new locations want to be assured that there is a potential workforce that is willing to work hard to meet company goals.

PARTICIPATION

At the heart of cooperativeness is the willingness to participate in what needs to be done to achieve a goal. You may have heard someone say, "We could never have achieved our deadline if everyone hadn't chipped in and helped."

Well-organized companies develop job descriptions for each position in the organization. However, given the changing nature of business, there are many instances when workers are needed to work outside the job description. A willingness to be helpful is critical at such a time.

> *Sam is a manager in one of the finest jewelry stores in the United States. Managers are not salespersons. Yet Sam is likely to be assisting customers through much of a very busy shopping day. Furthermore, he pays no attention to the typical end of his working day. He stays on the job through the closing time for the store. He realizes that at a busy time, the most important task is assisting customers.*

LEARNING

With the speed of change in modern work life, it is difficult for supervisors or human resources personnel to determine each employee's learning needs. Companies expect workers to be independent learners. This starts with a willingness to learn—a curiosity about what is missing in your understanding or your skills.

Appearances Influence Impressions

perceived: seen, thought of

Your appearance influences how you are **perceived** by others. Impressions at work are important. Judgments are sometimes made on limited evidence such as a first impression. Consider the likely assessment of two new employees whose jobs involve meeting with clients:

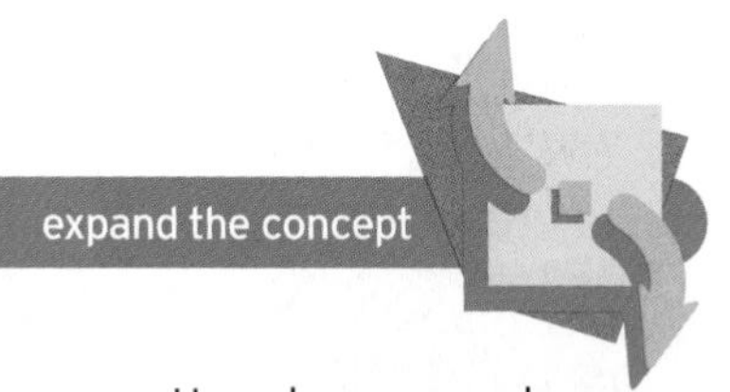

How does an employee know when it is time to learn something more?

Kathy comes to work in messy jeans and running shoes. She believes she is a good employee. Gail comes to work in a business suit and pumps with a low heel. She, too, believes she is a good employee.

What will a new executive meeting each of these two young women think about the value of each one to the company? The executive is likely to question Kathy's effectiveness in interacting with customers.

CLOTHING

If you are dressed appropriately for work, others are likely to think that you are giving proper attention to your job responsibilities. If your appearance is sloppy, others may quickly **conclude** that you are probably not an efficient employee.

conclude: decide, judge

Actually, there is considerable variation in what companies expect in employees' appearances. Some companies are **explicit** about what they consider proper attire for work. Others expect new employees to determine appropriate dress from noting how the majority of workers dress on a regular basis. If you choose to work in an organization that does not state its dress code, the safest course is to dress attractively in a businesslike manner. You want your appearance to convey responsibility, good taste, and wise judgment.

explicit: clear, specific

Illustration 16-1:3
Your appearance should convey responsibility and good taste.

You may want to use photos from current publications, such as full-page advertisements that show individuals in typical work attire. Some photos from leisure magazines might also be shown as a basis for noting attire that is not appropriate for business offices.

To what extent is "casual Friday" allowed in the businesses in our town?

If students are acquainted with a local bank, municipal, or state office, ask them to describe what they believe is appropriate attire for employees in such an organization.

ANNOYING HABITS

Over time some people develop facial expressions that do not express how they feel. For example, an individual may appear to be frowning when frowning has nothing to do with what is being said or how the person feels. Certain facial expressions seem to happen in an automatic fashion—they have become habits.

Other annoying habits, such as throwing back your head to get your hair out of your eyes or drumming your fingers, should be curbed. Take an inventory of your nonverbal behavior and identify what you believe might be annoying to others. Just make a decision to eliminate an annoying habit and follow through with your decision.

VOICE

Workers often must interact within a relatively small area; in fact, many workers may share an open space, with only limited partitions. Conversations can be easily overheard. When you are speaking by telephone or with a coworker, it is important that you speak to that person only. You do not want to speak so loudly that you disrupt others who are continuing their work around you.

Basic Work Manners

You have been learning about manners since you were a child. You may recall a parent saying to you, "Do not eat while you are talking; keep your elbows off the table," or "Shake hands with Mrs. Norris, who has come for a visit." What you know about good manners will be invaluable when you interact with others at work. Only a limited number of points will be discussed here.

INTRODUCTIONS

It is considered gracious to introduce strangers when you know both but they do not know each other. In general, extending your hand to another person is considered a gracious gesture. A handshake should be firm, yet not so strong it causes pain. A limp handshake is often considered a sign that someone does not want to interact with others.

As you interact with others, what "annoying habits" have you noted?

Since annoying habits are often done automatically, how does a person realize they exist?

Have teams of students illustrate talking too loud and too soft for various situations.

How do you modulate your voice so only the person with whom you are talking hears you?

1. Identify several relationships for the practice of introductions.
2. Discuss with students what a proper handshake is like.
3. Have students practice the handshake.

To what extent do you notice handshaking when you are walking at the mall or downtown?

ELECTRONIC ETIQUETTE

New ways of interacting with people require an extension of the rules of good manners. Use of voice mail, cellular phones, speakerphones, fax machines, and conference calls all offer opportunities to improve or detract from your relationship with others through the use of good manners.

Voice Mail. The manners that are considered appropriate when talking with someone in person should be extended to leaving a message by voice mail. The caller should be courteous and remember to leave a complete message:

- Speak slowly.
- Keep the message as brief as possible.
- Include your complete name and telephone number.
- Explain why a return call is essential, if that is the case.

Cellular Phones. Cellular phones enable individuals to be "on the job" at all times. However, you should refrain from using your cellular phone during musical programs, lectures, films, in a crowded restaurant, or other areas where your conversation will disrupt activities or annoy others. If you are using a cellular phone in a supermarket, for example, you should move away from a place where others are conversing in person.

Illustration 16-1:4
Be sure not to disrupt others when using a cellular phone.

Have students role-play calling an office and leaving a message.

Speakerphones. When using a speakerphone, be sure the matter being discussed is not confidential. If you place the call, you should establish that the other person does not mind the speakerphone. When using a speakerphone, give your full attention to the caller and do not attempt to do something else at the same time, even though your hands are free.

Fax Machines. In many offices, several individuals share the same fax machine. It is considered impolite to read another person's incoming messages. When you find a message that has not been distributed, you should read only to the point of identifying the recipient.

Conference Calls. Sensitivity to everyone participating in a conference call is critical for the call to proceed without problems. When you begin to speak, identify yourself. If you must step away from the call, do not put your line on hold if doing so will cause background music to play on the line. Good manners require that you not interrupt someone who is speaking.

GENERAL COURTESIES AT WORK

What courtesies do you regularly include in your interactions with others?

Employees are expected to be aware of the responsibilities of their colleagues. Therefore, conversations should generally be limited to matters of work. Little time should be used for personal talk. Employees often face deadlines, so anyone seeking assistance from a coworker should first inquire if the time is appropriate for an interruption.

monopolize: use or keep to the exclusion of others

Equipment is often shared with coworkers. Employees should not **monopolize** equipment to the point of keeping others from completing tasks. Always be alert to the needs of those around you.

Your Personal Power

What is required before a person is motivated to attempt to change some aspect of his/her personality?

Personal power, in the sense used here, can help you create change in your own life. Giving attention to your own development is important for your future happiness and competency in the workplace. Personal development is as much a function of your own will—your own power—as is the development of technical skills.

Reviewing the Topic

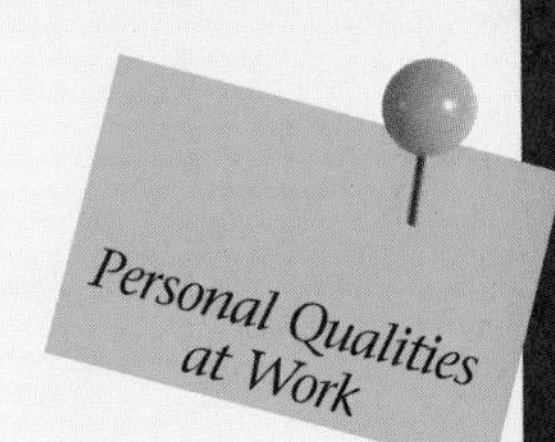

1. What are the two concepts on which this topic is based?
2. How do personal characteristics influence an individual?
3. What is *character?*
4. Why does an organization want employees with integrity?
5. What characteristics indicate that a person is reliable?
6. What are some basic attitudes important to self-acceptance?
7. Describe the person who has a good work ethic.
8. Why should a new employee give attention to his or her appearance?
9. Why should annoying habits be eliminated?
10. Identify some general courtesies at work that do not demand a great deal of time.

INTERACTING WITH OTHERS

Peg, Jeff, and Mark were having lunch when the conversation turned to a fourth coworker, Sally, who was out ill that day. A week earlier, Sally had been told that she would not get the promotion she had anticipated. Sally was stunned by the news. She thought she was competent and handled all assignments she was given. When she revealed the unpleasant news to her three coworkers, she concluded by saying: "How could they do this to me?" "Will you—my friends—tell me the *truth?*" Peg said: "Oh, Sally, don't make this a big deal. In a few months they will call you in to tell you that you have been promoted." Both Jeff and Mark concurred in Peg's comment and the topic shifted.

Now, a week later, the three felt somewhat guilty about sidestepping Sally's question. What they concluded was that Sally was "too loud" for the next level of responsibility. They liked Sally, but she apparently did not realize that she just didn't seem to know when she should talk quietly, when she should just keep silent, and when she should shorten her explanations! It was their conclusion that her personal shortcomings had resulted in her not being promoted.

topic 16-1 review

Personal Qualities at Work

What you are to do:

Work in a team with two other students. Discuss what you should say to Sally, if anything. Prepare your answer in written form. Participate in a class discussion where you note the variations in response among the groups.

REINFORCING MATH SKILLS

Employees in a large department were rated on the following factors:

- positive work ethic
- participation with colleagues
- willingness to learn
- businesslike appearance
- good manners in interpersonal encounters

The ratings were made on a scale from 1 to 5, with 5 being the best. The ratings are shown in the chart below.

Employee	Work Ethic	Participation	Willingness to Learn	Appearance	Manners
Abbot, Roy	2	1	3	1	2
Abrams, Peter	4	4	5	2	2
Bryant, Silvia	1	1	1	3	2
Cooper, Rachel	5	4	4	4	5
Cordero, Ana	2	2	2	1	1
Dones, Carole	4	4	4	4	2
Herbik, Sheri	4	3	2	5	5
Kulpa, Rudy	5	5	4	5	5
Merena, Samina	4	5	5	4	5
Nang, Li	5	5	5	4	3
Ramsey, Nilda	3	2	4	1	2

What you are to do:

1. Compute the average score for each employee.
2. Compute the average score for the total group for each area.
3. Identify the areas where these employees as a group may need some further training.

topic 16-1 review

778

APPLICATION ACTIVITIES

ACTIVITY 1 Personality Inventory

Volumes have been written on the many aspects of personality. In this activity you will describe what you believe reflects your personality.

What you are to do:

Consider each of the factors listed below assuming that you are now a full-time employee and are making an assessment of yourself for your own benefit. For each of the factors listed below, key a brief description that provides a realistic statement of your present status relative to the factor.

- integrity
- reliability
- self-acceptance
- maturity
- work ethic
- willingness to learn
- willingness to participate in achieving goals

ACTIVITY 2 Observations of Positive Attitudes

In this activity, you will study the attitudes of individuals at work in a variety of positions.

What you are to do:

1. Choose whether to observe positive attitudes toward others or toward work itself.
2. For a period of a week, record the following information about people you observe at their work.
   - the place in which you made your observation
   - the job of the person you observed
   - the attitude displayed toward others or toward work
   - exactly what was said or the behavior noted that reflected the attitude you are observing
3. Key a report in which you summarize what kinds of attitudes you discovered through your observations. Include a brief statement of the significance of such attitudes for the individual and for the individual's organization.

779

getting started

In preparation for the initial discussion of this topic, students might be asked to review the teamwork in which they have been involved in this course. Ask them to note especially the value of such experience.

points to emphasize

An interest in people and their behavior in different environments is very important to everyone since social interaction is a universal experience.

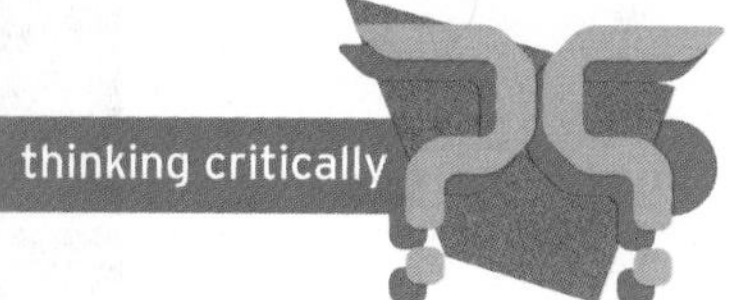

thinking critically

Why is it common practice in organizations to have every individual report to someone?

Human Relations at Work

Topic 16-2

When you have completed your study of this topic, you will be able to:

- **explain what effective interaction with others at work means**
- **describe appropriate responses in handling conflicts at work**
- **assess your ability to work with others**
- **describe some of the basic laws and regulations that apply to the workplace**

Working effectively with others requires an understanding of human behavior. There must also be a willingness to participate with people in a cooperative, business-oriented manner. While you are able to choose your friends, you must accept those with whom you work. Attitudes important in this regard include respect for others, willingness to listen to others, and a commitment to help meet the goals of your organization.

INTERACTING WITH SUPERVISORS

Few people work totally alone or independently. Regardless of the position you hold, you will be reporting to someone. Even key executives report to a board of directors or to owners. The complexity of most organizations requires that there be someone who supervises and guides your work.

Illustration 16-2:1
A supervisor guides the members of her team.

What would you expect a manager to say about a job you have been asked to complete?

WHAT YOU CAN EXPECT FROM YOUR SUPERVISOR

Those who manage others have clear-cut responsibilities. Generally, their tasks include:

- communicating clearly the **mission** of the organization in relation to the work of the department or person
- establishing the priorities of what is to be done
- properly delegating work
- informing each employee of deadlines and quality standards

mission: goal, purpose

Consider both the advantages and disadvantages of managing a department through both careful planning and on an ad hoc basis.

Managers have varying ways of carrying through their tasks. Some managers have staff meetings frequently; others seldom meet, but issue memoranda on a regular basis. Some managers plan carefully and adhere to plans. Some communicate plans to all staff members; others operate on a more **ad hoc** basis, introducing changes as circumstances dictate.

ad hoc: based on what is immediately available

Understand Your Manager's Style. You should be interested in determining how your manager functions. Some managers make explicit their style of management; others expect employees to determine from observations and comments what the style in effect is.

For what reason would a manager describe the work of each person?

There are many factors that **converge** as a manager decides how to function. Some of these factors are dictated by those to whom your

converge: come together, focus

Identify different styles of management for some local organizations that students might know.

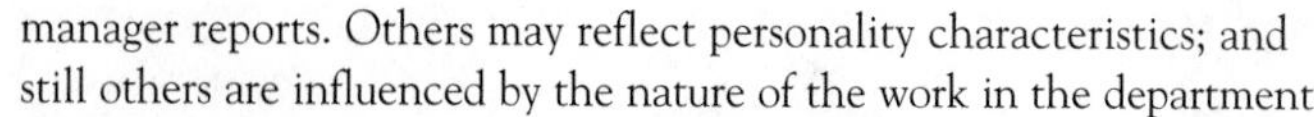

manager reports. Others may reflect personality characteristics; and still others are influenced by the nature of the work in the department.

Your Manager Wants You to Be Successful. Effective managers want employees to accomplish their tasks with success. Everyone wins when employees are skillful and effective. The goals of the company are accomplished. The employee has a sense of well-being because of a job done properly. The manager strives to maintain an environment to nurture such effectiveness.

WHAT YOUR MANAGER EXPECTS FROM YOU

Managers expect employees to adhere to their tasks even though there is no direct, immediate supervision throughout the workday. Furthermore, managers expect employees to keep them informed of unexpected developments about what is being done or about meeting deadlines. Managers expect to have completed work on schedule.

Managers expect employees to evaluate their own work and to meet deadlines. Any additional effort required to have that work meet the established standards should be undertaken without any review by the manager.

Managers expect employees to be willing to meet unplanned situations. At such times regular assignments must be set aside to complete tasks that now have higher priority. Managers depend on the flexibility and willingness of staff to respond to new demands in a busy, fast-changing environment.

Interacting with Coworkers

The extent to which you must work with others will vary. If you are a member of a project team, you may perform many tasks as a group. If you serve as a research assistant, you may spend much time alone following through on the tasks that are your responsibility.

Even though much of your work may be done independently, there will be times when you will need to interact with others. You will interact because you have common needs for information, tasks that overlap, or joint responsibility for some common task.

Describe the manager who wants all employees to be successful in their work.

Connect some of the points discussed in Topic 16-1 to the qualities that are important in a manager. For example, why would staff members appreciate a manager who has integrity?

How would a manager know that particular employees will meet their obligations?

Describe the behavior of a manager who has confidence in the employees under his or her supervision.

Priorities for a department can change quickly because of unexpected developments. Employees need to understand the department's responsibility and respond cooperatively to changes in their work.

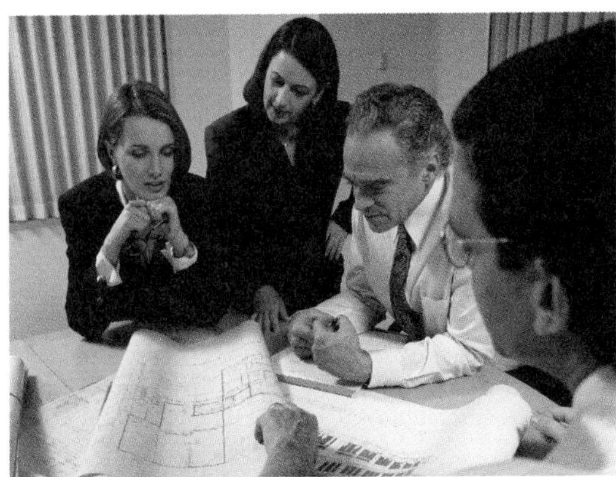

Illustration 16-2:2

A project team performs many tasks as a group.

expand the concept

What attitudes about people in general will be helpful as you work with your colleagues?

COOPERATION

An organization does not make progress with only the efforts of individuals working alone. When a colleague from another department telephones, your natural response should be to want to provide the needed help or information (assuming the information is not confidential).

> *Sandra Hirsh works as a buyer of ingredients for a large candy manufacturing company. She is in constant communication with the company's laboratories where new products are being developed. She calls for information; she sits in meetings to learn reactions to the ingredients being used and desired. She believes much of the pleasure of her work comes from the cooperation from the departments for which she buys ingredients.*

for discussion

A colleague calls for information; you are very busy attempting to meet a deadline that afternoon. The information is needed as soon as possible. What will you say to your colleague?

CONFIDENTIALITY

You will want to be sure you understand what aspects of your work require absolute confidentiality. In some cases, information is confidential only for a period of time. Later, when decisions are firm, there will be wide distribution of information that was earlier restricted.

> *Valerie was a staff assistant to the director of human resources. In her position, she knew all the candidates for key management positions. She reviewed résumés and assisted the director in making decisions. She*

expand the concept

What are some of the reasons individuals do not adhere to their promise to keep information confidential?

Why is Valerie's ability to keep information confidential so important in her job?

knew which candidates were invited to headquarters for interviews. She saw the reports of the executives who interviewed candidates. She understood that all aspects of the recruiting process must be kept in absolute confidence. Valerie made a commitment to herself to never reveal any detail of what was happening. The director was grateful for Valerie's attitude.

AVOIDING GOSSIP

spontaneous: natural, unplanned

Informal communications are common in an organization. This network, called the "grapevine," reflects the **spontaneous** and realistic response to the need to communicate in ways that are not a part of the formal communications system. However, there can be abuse of the "grapevine." This is manifested in the spreading of rumors and gossip, which are incomplete and/or false statements about individuals or situations. Unfortunately, such information is communicated in many places. You should refrain from participating in discussing what you do not know is correct.

Key contributors to the "grapevine" are often popular. Why should an employee resist joining in the dissemination of rumors and risk not being popular among coworkers?

Illustration 16-2:3
Gossiping is not appropriate in the workplace.

ACCEPTING RESPONSIBILITY FOR MISTAKES

People are not perfect. They make errors of fact and judgment. You may have a firm goal to be sure the facts you communicate to others are accurate and to use good judgment in making decisions.

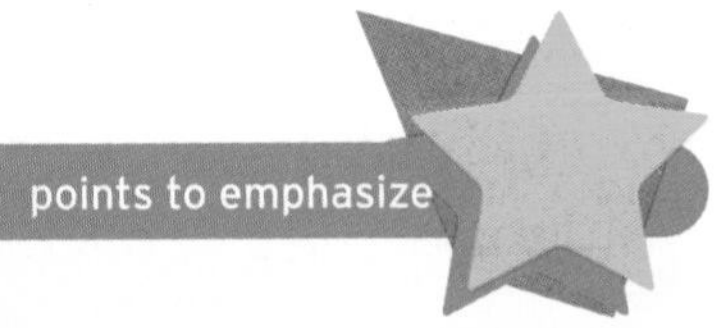

The competent manager, as well as coworkers, should accept the reality that mistakes occur and be tolerant when they happen from time to time.

The assistant **curator** *at the County Historical Society, Debra, realized that she had given a staff member the wrong dates for an exhibition. When the staff member called, Debra was very busy completing a report and failed to check the calendar. She merely gave the dates as she recalled them. Later in the day, she realized that she gave the staff member the wrong dates. She called the staff member and confessed: "Marian, I gave you the wrong dates! I am sorry. I hope it isn't too late to give you the correct information. . . ."*

curator: person in charge of a museum

RESPECTING OTHERS' COMMITMENTS

Some individuals find it easy to put aside their work and engage in friendly, personal chatter during the workday. Brief pauses to talk about nonwork-related matters can be tolerated. However, extended time away from work **undermines** productivity. Most organizations allow brief breaks during the morning and afternoon when employees can meet with friends and associates.

undermines: weakens, threatens

How does an employee who has a little unscheduled time find out if a coworker has time to talk?

Facing Conflicts at Work

A conflict is a disagreement, quarrel, or controversy. Because human beings are not perfect, those with whom you work will have a variety of weaknesses and problems. At times, problems may arise that **impede** good relations among coworkers. Some common areas where conflicts arise are briefly noted here.

impede: hinder, obstruct

CONFLICT WITH YOUR MANAGER

You hope to have what is commonly referred to as a "good working relationship" with the person to whom you report. However, there are times when the relationship may not be good. A misunderstanding about job assignments, insensitivity to seemingly unreasonable demands, and failure to communicate how one feels about performance can lead to conflicts.

Good managers are expected to be aware of what their staff members are doing and to assess the work assigned. However, when there are heavy demands, a manager may fail to think about your work.

Employees are expected to assess their success in meeting job requirements. Managers, too, are expected to assess the quality of work

What attitudes toward others might be missing in a manager who is insensitive to the demands made on employees in the department?

performed by staff members. There are times when an employee may believe that tasks are being done properly, even though there has been no feedback from the manager. Other times the manager may be unhappy with the quality of work completed by the employee who is judging his or her work to be satisfactory. This difference of opinion will be revealed at some point. In the meantime, the employee is left in the dark.

Such a situation is unfair to everyone. The employee may be assuming in good faith that the work is satisfactory based on self-assessment. The manager, with more knowledge and experience, has a standard unknown to the employee for evaluating work. The manager may assume that the employee should be able to figure out what is expected. Such a conclusion by the manager may be unfair. An employee who feels there is some discrepancy between self-evaluation and the evaluation of the manager should ask to discuss the work with the manager.

CONFLICT RELATED TO ETHICAL BEHAVIOR

Sometimes values clash in the workplace. Increasingly, organizations have established codes of conduct for all employees at all levels of the company. Bulletins, training sessions, and self-study materials are used to inform everyone of the rules. These rules are to be honored as employees work with each other as well as with vendors and customers.

Illustration 16-2:4
An employee reviews the company policy related to accepting gifts from vendors.

When do you think the manager is justified in believing that employees should figure out what they are expected to do?

Nothing has been stated about a code of conduct in a company. Where might a new employee inquire about such a code?

You may want to use information from local companies about their own standards of ethical behavior that are sometimes distributed to customers or clients.

You will want to become fully acquainted with the ethical rules that guide the organization in which you work. You want to understand the rules as prescribed. You should not depend on the interpretations of your colleagues.

Companies establish policies and procedures to be sure that their code of ethics is applied. Employees are informed about what to do when they are asked to participate in unethical behavior.

Understanding Relevant Laws and Regulations

Organizations in the United States must adhere to certain laws and regulations of federal, state, and municipal governments. Laws and regulations have been established for a variety of purposes, but basically they all relate to maintaining a fair and safe environment for all citizens.

FAIR LABOR STANDARDS ACT

The Fair Labor Standards Act (FLSA) sets the minimum wages for employees covered by the law. Requirements related to overtime are also specified. An **amendment** makes it unlawful to pay different wages to men and women where jobs are equal in skills required, effort, responsibility, and working conditions. The Equal Pay Act is enforced by the Equal Employment Opportunity Commission (EEOC).

amendment:
change to a rule or law

FREEDOM FROM DISCRIMINATION

Title VII of the 1964 Civil Rights Act makes it illegal to **discriminate** in employment on the basis of a person's race, color, religion, sex, or national origin. This is the principal federal employment discrimination law. Later acts outlaw discrimination against handicapped individuals; against women because of pregnancy, childbirth, or other related medical conditions; or against anyone 40 years or older.

discriminate:
separate, favor

FREEDOM FROM SEXUAL HARASSMENT

An amendment of Title VII of the Civil Rights Act of 1964 makes harassment in the workplace unlawful. Sexual harassment is described as unwelcome sexual advances, requests for sexual favors, and other

The class may want to consider in a general way the conditions that make the work environment pleasant and appealing to workers.

You may want to get brochures from several government agencies for use in class. Students might volunteer to read the brochures and present brief summaries that will augment the discussion in the textbook.

Why does the Federal government in the United States support freedom from discrimination? In what way does such a law aid an individual? In what way does it aid the society in general?

In what ways would a human resources department thwart an executive's efforts to deny a promotion because an employee resists the executive's sexual advances?

Any current cases involving sexual harassment might be used for a brief discussion of the problems that arise in an environment where there is sexual harassment.

You may want to use the classroom as a basis for discussing what a comfortable and safe workstation should include.

Identify the agencies with local offices that provide workplace information. Students might volunteer to visit such offices to collect information to share with the class.

Emphasize the critical role human resources personnel play in monitoring adherence to laws and regulations.

verbal or physical conduct when: (1) submission to such conduct is made a term or condition of employment; (2) submission to or rejection of such conduct is used in making employment decisions; and (3) such conduct has the purpose or effect of unreasonably interfering with an individual's work performance or creating an undesirable working environment.

SAFE AND HEALTHY WORKPLACE

The Occupational Safety and Health Administration (OSHA) is a government agency responsible for ensuring that employers maintain safe working conditions.

UNEMPLOYMENT INSURANCE

Insurance is provided for persons who have been dismissed from their jobs. To be eligible, individuals must have worked for a required time and left their job through no fault of their own. Payments are provided for a stated period of time, depending on the benefits of the particular state where the individuals worked.

SOCIAL SECURITY ACT BENEFITS

The Federal Social Security Act, also known as the Federal Insurance Contribution Act (FICA), provides for the following:

- retirement income
- benefits for spouses of retired or disabled workers
- survivor benefits
- disability benefits
- health insurance

EMPLOYEE RESPONSIBILITY

Your company's Human Resources Department can provide you with employment laws and regulations. If you should have a problem related to a law or a regulation, you will find that generally there is someone in the company to whom you can initially direct your problem. If the violation is not resolved, report it to the closest office of the agency responsible for enforcing the particular law.

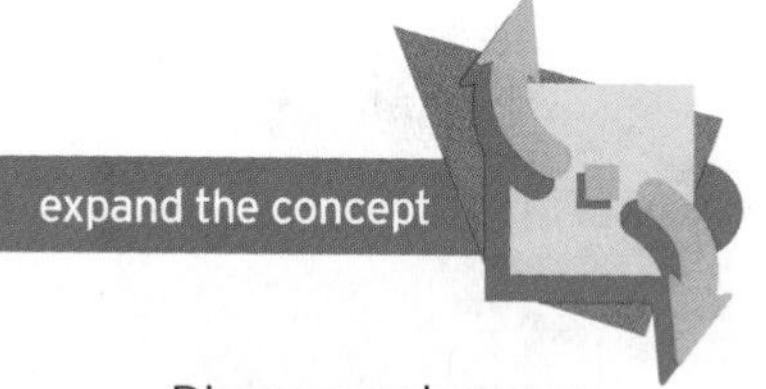

Discuss employment opportunities for persons who specialize in the field of employee benefits.

Reviewing the Topic

Human Relations at Work

1. What is required to work effectively with others?
2. What can employees expect from managers to whom they report?
3. Why does a manager want the employees in the department to be successful?
4. What do managers expect of workers?
5. Explain the meaning of confidentiality.
6. Why should an employee avoid gossiping?
7. Identify one type of conflict that might arise at work.
8. What is the purpose of the Fair Labor Standards Act?
9. Why is freedom from discrimination important in the workplace?
10. What is a worker's responsibility relative to rules and regulations that apply to employment?

INTERACTING WITH OTHERS

Rick's colleague said to him: "Oh, Rick, I just heard something about you . . . I promised not to tell, but I had no idea I would see you so soon after the conversation with your manager. Do you realize that your manager isn't happy with your performance? She told me that you didn't have a cooperative attitude."

What you are to do:

Assume that you are Rick. What would you say to the colleague who revealed confidential information? How would you handle this situation with your manager?

APPLICATION ACTIVITIES

ACTIVITY 1 An Encounter with a Manager

A staff assistant, Ana, had quietly taken on extra responsibilities when another assistant, Kay, was on an extended leave. By working extra hours and through lunch, she is just managing to do her regular work

topic 16-2 review

Human Relations at Work

789

and the absent staff member's work, too. Near the end of Kay's leave, the manager stopped by Ana's desk and said: "Since you are handling both jobs so well, I'm going to recommend that Kay be assigned to another department. We really don't need her." At that point, the manager walked away.

Ana was stunned. Up to this time, she had not commented about what she was doing. She assumed that her manager was aware of the extraordinary efforts she had made to do both jobs. Ana has asked to meet with the manager to discuss the situation.

What you are to do:

Participate with your classmates as assigned by your instructor to role-play the meeting between Ana and her manager or to evaluate and discuss the role-playing situation.

Two members of the class should role-play the situation, one as Ana and one as the manager. The rest of the class should be divided so that some students evaluate Ana's performance and some evaluate the manager's performance. In addition to evaluating the performance, the class should identify the responsibilities of managers in such situations.

topic 16-2 review

ACTIVITY 2 Too Many Interruptions

Kiki is a hard-working assistant manager who is serious about her responsibilities. Her manager seems to have a great deal of free time and often drops by Kiki's office for long talks about personal matters. Unfortunately, Kiki finds these interruptions a hardship. If Kiki receives a telephone call, the manager waits patiently to resume the self-centered discussion.

At the moment, the manager has been in Kiki's office discussing personal matters for half an hour. Kiki needs to call the London office within the next hour before that office closes, and she still has to locate the information they need. Kiki wants to tell the manager that she has work to do to meet a deadline and that these continuing interruptions are a problem. What should Kiki say in discussing these issues with her manager?

790

What you are to do:

Participate with your classmates as assigned by your instructor to role-play the discussion between Kiki and her manager or to discuss the situation.

Two students should play the roles of Kiki and the manager. All others in the class should evaluate the way in which the situation is handled by the two participants. Also, the class should summarize the responsibilities of managers in relation to use of time.

Chapter Summary

16

The personal qualities that individuals bring with them to the workplace and the nature of working with others are the topics of this chapter. Among the key points you should understand from your study are these:

- Character, as reflected in a person's integrity and reliability, is a central component of an individual's personality.
- Self-acceptance is necessary if an individual wants to make personality changes.
- A positive yet realistic attitude toward yourself means that you can assess your own qualities honestly and that you understand that you share common wants, needs, and fears with others.
- Maturing is a long-term process that is critical to full development of a personality.
- Quality performance at work is a common, general goal in many organizations.
- Appearances influence impressions and therefore require attention on the part of individuals at work.
- Individuals are expected to behave in accordance with established business manners that assure pleasant interactions with each other.

chapter 16 summary

Working with Others

791

- Employees need to become acquainted with the expectations and workstyle of their managers.
- Frequent interaction is common in organizations, and ways to ensure fair and honorable association with others need to be understood.
- Conflicts arise at work, but willingness to face them candidly can lead to resolutions.
- Laws and regulations related to work need to be understood by all employees.

KEY CONCEPTS AND TERMS

business manners
character
conflicts at work
cooperation
electronic etiquette
Fair Labor Standards Act
freedom from discrimination
freedom from sexual harassment
handshaking
interaction with coworkers
introductions
maturity
personal power
safe and healthy workplace
self-acceptance
Social Security Act benefits
style of management
unemployment insurance
willing to learn
work ethic

INTEGRATED CHAPTER ACTIVITIES

ACTIVITY 1 Reflections of Yourself

In this activity, you will write an essay of approximately 600 words (2–3 pages) on one of the following topics:

- The attitudes I'll take to work with me
- My perception of my personality
- Key personality characteristics that will be valuable on the job

792

What you are to do:

1. Write an essay on one of the topics listed above.
2. Key the final draft of your essay for submission to your teacher using unbound report style. Use appropriate side headings to identify sections of the report. See Reference Section H for an example of unbound report format.

See Workbook page 236.

ACTIVITY 2 Development as Team Players

In this activity, you and two or three classmates should discuss the following questions:

- What are the critical attitudes necessary to complete a team assignment effectively and on schedule?
- What are your own personal difficulties in being a good team participant?
- What problems may develop in working with others?
- What are some satisfactory ways to resolve problems in working with others?
- What factors make it difficult to resolve problems?
- What is your present assessment of your ability to work as a team member?

What you are to do:

1. Work in a team to have a candid discussion of the questions listed above. The discussion need never identify specific persons. One person should be designated as a recorder of all key points. Occasionally during your discussion, take time to summarize the key points discussed. Key the summary in an attractive format.
2. Participate in a class discussion of the questions, comparing your responses with those of other teams.

793

Leslie Norwood
Director of Human Relations

Getting Acquainted with the World of Work

Is There Anything I Can Do About Being Shy?

Dear Ms. Norwood

We have been studying personality in school once again. I am reminded of a serious problem I have—I am shy! You might wonder how I could have reached this age—17—and not yet have figured out what I can do to overcome this serious problem. Now, as I think of going out to the real world, I am frightened.

As a student, I have been quite clever in not participating in activities where I would be painfully shy. I realized early in school that if you were quiet and didn't volunteer for activities, you could avoid them. Fortunately, there have always been students around me who eagerly volunteer to answer questions or to stand and perform. In the few instances where I have been called on, especially in high school, I have been able to convince the teacher that someone else would love to do the task; and I would defer to the other person. Do you realize that there have been times when my teachers have commended me for my thoughtfulness! I always felt a little dishonest in such situations, but the joy of my classmates overcame my guilt over my ulterior motive!

My shyness ranges from overwhelmingly painful to just tolerable. I think I could be satisfied if I could reduce the incidence of "overwhelmingly painful" situations somewhat. Can you help me?

Trish in New Orleans

Dear Trish

I am sure you realize that you are not alone. There are many shy individuals in the world. There isn't a simple solution to your problem. However, you have the first requirement for overcoming shyness—you see it as a problem and you would like to do something about it.

First, Trish, analyze the circumstances when you were least shy. This will provide clues to what your response ought to be in those situations where you now experience overwhelming shyness.

Second, Trish, in many cases shy people can reduce the pain by shifting the focus of their attention. For example, if the teacher calls on you to comment about the topic being discussed, do you immediately think: "Oh, I am too shy to talk."? Will yourself to think that THAT MUST NOT BE MY FIRST THOUGHT! Your first thought should be directed at the topic—the content under discussion. From that first thought, move to shaping your thoughts coherently to respond in a calm, reasoned manner.

Third, Trish, you must begin to use every opportunity to participate in situations that you earlier avoided. To build your confidence, prepare yourself for the participation. For example, study thoroughly the material that the teacher is going to discuss. Then, think first of the content. You are likely to be in the middle of your response when you realize you are participating—and doing it quite effectively.

Venture forward, Trish. Good luck.

Leslie Norwood
Director of Human Relations

794

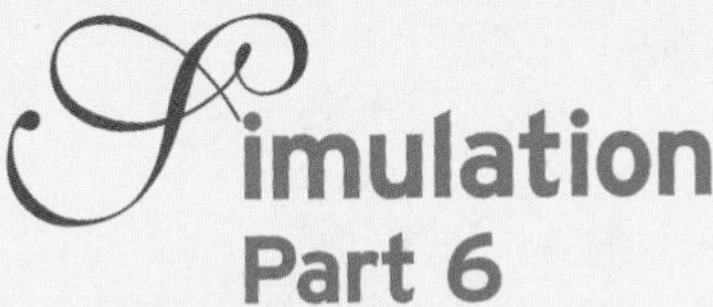

Simulation Part 6

At Work at *Winston Human Resources:*

You are part of the team at Winston Human Resources that provides counseling to help individuals prepare for new careers or find new positions. These people are often employees who have lost their jobs due to company restructuring. The company also provides various human resources services for companies in the Pittsburgh, Pennsylvania, area and does executive recruitment.

The Pittsburgh branch is part of a larger company headquartered in Atlanta, Georgia. Since it was organized five years ago, the company has grown at a very rapid rate. Activities are just getting underway at the new Pittsburgh branch office.

As an administrative assistant to the vice president, Mr. Todd Perenz, and the office manager, Jo Anne Keller, you are expected to work with little direct supervision. As you complete your duties, you will

- demonstrate initiative, independent thinking, and decision-making skills
- research information and make recommendations based on the information
- compose questions for interviews and identify desired qualities for job applicants
- provide information to potential clients
- compose routine correspondence
- compose and create visuals for presentations

Refer to your *Student Activities and Projects* workbook to learn more about your responsibilities and work assignments at Winston Human Resources.

See Workbook pages 197–211.

795

Glossary

A

aperture card: a paper card that holds a piece of microfilm that is visible through an opening in the card (p. 461)
audio-graphic conference: a format for hearing other participants and seeing written information at the same time using a microphone-speaker system, a computer terminal, and an electronic tablet (p. 418)
automated attendant: a computerized system for handling telephone calls with little or no human assistance (p. 624)
Automatic Teller Machine (ATM): electronic machine from which cash deposits and withdrawals can be made (p. 317)

B

bar code: a label, usually self-adhesive, that is preprinted or manually created and is attached to an item to identify it electronically (p. 505)
bookmarks: saved Internet addresses in a type of electronic catalog for quick reference, also called a *hotlist* (p. 703)

C

caller ID service: enables incoming calls to be identified (p. 637)
carpal tunnel syndrome: a repetitive strain injury that occurs when stress is placed on the hands, wrists, or arms while working at the computer keyboard or using the computer input device for prolonged periods of time (p. 382)
CD: compact disc; a laser-written optical media storage form (p. 458)
cells: geographic areas over which voice messages are transmitted wirelessly (p. 629)
cellular telephones: telephones that use wireless radio frequencies to transmit voice across geographic segments called *cells* (p. 629)
centralized telephone system: a telephone system in which all incoming calls are handled by a single computer or operator switchboard that routes calls to requested locations (p. 624)
coaxial cable: cable that can transmit a large amount of electronic data quickly and reliably over long distances (p. 681)
communication satellite: a transmitter/receiver that orbits the earth, providing worldwide communication (p. 619)
compress files: shrink the size of files so they can be transmitted faster and take less storage space (p. 706)
Computer-Assisted Retrieval (CAR): the process of locating records on film by using computer-stored indexes (p. 562)
computer conferencing: a way for participants to have "meetings" by writing messages to each other on their computer terminals (p. 418)
Computer Input Microfilm (CIM): the process of using microfilm or fiche as input for computer files (p. 459)
Computer Output Microfilm (COM): the process of transferring computer files directly to microfilm or fiche (p. 459)

D

data processing: the collecting, organizing, and summarizing of data, generally in numeric form (p. 52)
Database Management System (DBMS): a system that organizes and manipulates large numbers of files in a database (p. 556)
desktop publishing: a term for several software programs that allow users to combine graphics and text in a newsmagazine-type layout (p. 538)
dial-up access: connection to the Internet via a host computer using an Internet service provider (p. 689)
direct Internet access: connection to the Internet with a data line and special software rather than through an Internet service provider (p. 688)
domain: organizational level in an Internet address such as *gov* or *edu* (p. 690)
downloading: transferring files from a distant computer to your computer's hard drive (p. 705)

E

e-mail: electronic transfer of messages that are usually text-based (p. 709)
Electronic Data Interchange (EDI): protocol that allows the exchange of data between companies that may or may not have compatible computer or network systems (p. 685)
Electronic Fund Transfer (EFT): use of a computer and a telecommunications network to transfer funds from one party to another (p. 315)
electronic tablet: an electronic blackboard on which participants in a meeting can record information and receive a printed copy of the information written on the tablet (p. 418)
encodes: electronically "takes a picture" or records information to be sent (p. 620)

796

ergonomics: the study of the effects of the work environment on the health and well-being of employees (p. 380)

facsimile: technology that transfers images electronically using telephone lines; often called fax (p. 619)

fiber-optic cable: cable made from thin glass strands that transmits laser light pulses efficiently at very high speeds over long distances (p. 682)

file: each collection of related information (data) treated as a unit within a computer system or stored on auxiliary media (p. 546)

file server: the central computer in a server-based network that supplies or "serves" files to computers on the network (p. 678)

File Transfer Protocol (FTP): powerful tool that allows the movement of files over the Internet (p. 705)

GUIs (Graphical User Interfaces): the design of programs that use pictures to represent computer commands and files (p. 705)

home page: the main or opening screen for a web location (p. 701)

host computer: the primary computer in a network that acts as the manager of the entire network (p. 679)

HTTP (HyperText Transfer Protocol): a set of instructions telling computers how to send and receive hypertext data and documents (p. 702)

hypertext: highlighted, underlined, or contrast-colored words or images that, when clicked with the mouse, take you to another location (p. 701)

icons: graphics or pictures that represent computer commands or files (p. 723)

image processing system: a system that uses software and special equipment, including scanners and optical disks (CDs), to store an exact reproduction of a document—as well as files, sound, and complex images (p. 556)

imaging: a general term that refers to the process of reproducing the image of a page (p. 537)

imaging: a process for converting all types of documents to digitized electronic data, which can be stored and retrieved immediately (p. 463)

information system: people, information technology and resources, and procedures used to process information (p. 183)

input device: hardware that allows the computer to accept data for processing (p. 174)

Integrated Services Digital Network (ISDN): a set of standards that enables any type of computer or electronic device to communicate with other computers and devices (p. 636)

interactive video: two-way exchange of sound and pictures (p. 418)

Internet: a giant network composed of smaller computer networks that spans the globe (p. 192)

Internet Service Provider (ISP): an organization that provides a dial-up connection to the Internet (p. 689)

intranet: a communication network within an organization (p. 10)

LAN: local area network of computers (p. 552, 675)

link: communication channel or connection (p. 679)

Listserv: a type of automated subscription software program; a database filled with the names and addresses of many discussion groups as well as the Internet addresses of subscribers (p. 708)

microforms: the different forms of micrographics: roll microfilm, aperture cards, and microfiche (p. 460)

micrographics: documents reduced to a fraction of their original size to fit on film or microfiche (see also microimaging systems) (p. 459)

microimaging systems: systems that photographically reduce documents to a fraction of their original size to fit on film or microfiche (see also micrographics) (p. 459)

microwave transmissions: radio waves that can carry data in straight lines from one microwave station to another; wireless transmissions (p. 684)

modem: a device that changes the digital output of a computer into analog signals that can be sent over phone lines (p. 618)

modular workstation: one made up of interchangeable components, such as sound-absorbing wall panels, storage areas, and a desktop surface (p. 375)

multimedia: files or programs containing text, graphics, sound, and video (p. 706)

N

node: in a network, each piece of hardware such as a computer or a printer that is connected to the network and able to share its resources (p. 679)

online: connected to an electronic system (p. 419)

online resources: resources available via the computer (p. 190)

Optical Character Reader (OCR): electronic equipment that quickly scans or "reads" the address on an envelope and prints a bar code at the bottom of the envelope (p. 598)

output device: hardware that prints, displays, or records information (p. 174)

P

pagers: small devices that alert the user of the need to respond by telephone to whomever has sent the "page," which may be in the form of a beep, vibration, voice, or digital readout (p. 630)
peer-to-peer network: a network in which computers are connected with cables to each other and operate as equals, accessing software and data stored on each one's hard drive (p. 677)
personal digital assistant: handheld, limited-capacity computers (p. 191)
personal digital organizers: electronic calendars or schedulers, also known as personal information managers (PIMs), personal data managers, and personal digital assistants (PDAs) (p. 363)
Personal Identification Number (PIN): a special, unique number issued to a cardholder for security purposes (p. 661)
phototypesetting: a photographic process used to set text and art into special columns and widths (p. 538)
posting: to contribute or publish an "article" on the Internet (p. 707)
proximity readers: electronic readers that can sense magnetically coded badges; used in office security systems (p. 392)

R

records management software: the computer software that allows electronic management and control of all of a business's records from receipt or creation, through processing, storage, and retrieval, to disposal (p. 545)
reduction ratio: a term in microfilm photography that is used to describe how small the microimage is compared to the original record (p. 559)
relational databases: tools that allow the user to link data from a number of database files or tables to find information or generate reports (p. 190)
reprographics: the process of making copies of graphic images, such as documents (p. 523)

S

satellite dish: a transmitter/receiver that remains stationary on earth that receives and sends microwave signals (p. 619)
scanners: devices that allow photographs and text to be electronically imaged into computer files (p. 525)
search engines: internet tools that help you locate information and sites (p. 703)
server-based networking: a network in which one computer fills requests for data and program files from network users (p. 678)
speakerphones: telephones that amplify voices and allow speaking without use of the handset (p. 630)
speech recognition: ability of a computer to identify and perform actions from a human's spoken command (p. 624)
state-of-the-art: using the latest technology (p. 7)
surge suppressor: electrical outlet designed to control sharp increases in electricity that may harm appliances or computers (p. 387)

T

telecommunications: the electronic transfer of information over a distance (p. 617)
teleconference: a meeting of people in different locations connected by a telecommunications system (p. 416)
telephony: also called *computer telephone integration (CTI)*; allows computer control and access of telephone functions along with telephone control and access of computer functions (p. 636)
topology: the physical layout of a local area network (p. 678)
transmission carriers: physical media used to link devices to a network; usually cables (p. 680)
twisted-pair cable: cable that is composed of two wires twisted around each other and encased in a protective covering (p. 680)

U

Uniform Resource Locators (URLs): act like a home address to help others locate you on the Internet; URLs are Internet addresses that can be understood by any web browser as it searches for hypertext documents on hosts around the world (p. 702)
uploading: the transfer of files from your hard drive to the hard drive of another computer (p. 706)
Usenet: stands for "User's Network." It is a collection of topically organized Internet newsgroups (p. 706)
user ID: a unique identifier such as *pjones* (for Pat Jones) used when logging on to the computer or a software program (p. 690)

V

videoconferencing: an image communication system allowing people at two or more locations to have two-way voice and video communication (p. 623)
videophones: telephones that allow participants to see each other while they talk. Also called *picturephones* (p. 631)
virtual office: the capability of using the services of an office in a nonconventional way (p. 12)
voice mail: a messaging system that uses computers and telephones to record, send, store, and retrieve voice messages (p. 625)

W

web browsers: software programs that facilitate exploration and use of the Internet (p. 700)
Wide Area Network (WAN): a communication network used to link electronic equipment over long distances (p. 684)
wireless communication: transmission of information over distances without cables via infrared light waves or radio waves (p. 682)
word processing: the preparation of a variety of documents using software programs at personal computers (p. 50)

Index

B

799

R

Acknowledgements

Credit	Page
©1997 PhotoDisc, Inc.	2
©1997 PhotoDisc, Inc.	6
©1996 PhotoDisc, Inc.	9
©Alix Parson	11
©1996 PhotoDisc, Inc.	12
Courtesy of International Business Machines Corporation	13
Courtesy of International Business Machines Corporation	15
©Jeff Greenberg	22
©1996 PhotoDisc, Inc.	23
Courtesy of Apple Computer, Inc.	24
©Mike Wilson	25
Courtesy of International Business Machines Corporation	29
©1997 PhotoDisc, Inc.	30
©1995 PhotoDisc, Inc.	32
©1996 PhotoDisc, Inc.	45
©1997 PhotoDisc, Inc.	49
Courtesy of International Business Machines Corporation	50
©Alix Parson	51
Courtesy of International Business Machines Corporation	53
Courtesy of International Business Machines Corporation	54
Courtesy of International Business Machines Corporation	55
©1997 PhotoDisc, Inc.	56
©1997 PhotoDisc, Inc.	58
©1996 PhotoDisc, Inc.	59
©Amy C. Etra	72
©1997 PhotoDisc, Inc.	73
©1997 PhotoDisc, Inc.	74
Courtesy of International Business Machines Corporation	77
©1995 PhotoDisc, Inc.	87
©1996 PhotoDisc, Inc.	88
©1995 PhotoDisc, Inc.	89
©1995 PhotoDisc, Inc.	92
Courtesy of Digital Equipment Corporation	99
Courtesy of International Business Machines Corporation	100
©1996 PhotoDisc, Inc.	103
©1996 PhotoDisc, Inc.	112
©1996 PhotoDisc, Inc.	114
Courtesy of International Business Machines Corporation	135
©1996 PhotoDisc, Inc.	160
©1997 PhotoDisc, Inc.	161
Courtesy of International Business Machines Corporation	166
©1997 PhotoDisc, Inc.	167
©1997 PhotoDisc, Inc.	171
©1995 PhotoDisc, Inc.	173
Courtesy of Apple Computer, Inc.	173
©1997 PhotoDisc, Inc.	174
Courtesy of Epson	175
©Alix Parson	178
Photography by Alan Brown/Photonics	184
©Jeff Greenberg	188
Photography by Richards-Wilcox	189
Courtesy of Sony Electronics Inc.	192
©1996 PhotoDisc, Inc.	201
Courtesy of International Business Machines Corporation	204
Courtesy of International Business Machines Corporation	207
Courtesy of International Business Machines Corporation	209
Courtesy of Hewlett Packard Company	233
©1996 PhotoDisc, Inc.	261
©Jeff Greenberg	267
Courtesy of International Business Machines Corporation	268
©Alix Parson	269
Photography by Alan Brown/Photonics	276
Courtesy of Honeywell, Inc.	282
©1997 PhotoDisc, Inc.	288
©1996 PhotoDisc, Inc.	290
Courtesy of Merck & Co., Inc.	291
©1995 PhotoDisc, Inc.	301
©1997 PhotoDisc, Inc.	305
©1997 PhotoDisc, Inc.	310
Photography by Alan Brown/Photonics	336
Photography by Alan Brown/Photonics	341
©1997 PhotoDisc, Inc.	351
Courtesy of MAGNA VISUAL, INC.	363
Courtesy of Apple Computer, Inc., ©John Greenleigh	364
©1996 Franklin Quest Company. All rights reserved.	367
©1995 PhotoDisc, Inc.	376
©Alix Parson	379
Courtesy of GlareGuard®	383
©Ron Forth	391
Courtesy of Rusco Electronic Systems, Glendale, CA.	392
Courtesy of New Market Solutions. ©Alix Parson	392
©Jeff Greenberg	394
©1996 PhotoDisc, Inc.	406
Courtesy of Ventana Corporation, Tucson, AZ	409
©1997 PhotoDisc, Inc.	414
©1997 PhotoDisc, Inc.	414
Courtesy of GTE Spacenet Corp.	419
Location courtesy of AAA World Wide Travel, Cincinnati, OH	427
Courtesy of The Hertz Corporation	428
©1997 PhotoDisc, Inc.	433
©1996 PhotoDisc, Inc.	435
©1996 PhotoDisc, Inc.	435
©1997 PhotoDisc, Inc.	436
©Jeff Greenberg	437
Courtesy of International Business Machines Corporation	439
Reproduced by permission of Hayes Microcomputer Products, Inc. © 1989 Hayes Microcomputer Products, Inc.	455
Courtesy of 3M Optical Recording	456
Courtesy of Jeter Systems Corporation	475
Courtesy of Wright Line, Inc., Worcester, MA	478
©Tony Walsh	482
Courtesy of The HON Company	512
Courtesy of Safco Products Company	513
Courtesy of Tab Products Company	514
Courtesy of Tab Products Company	514
Courtesy of Wright Line, Inc., Worcester, MA	516
Courtesy of Fellowes Manufacturing Company	519
Courtesy of Xerox Corporation	525
Courtesy of Eastman Kodak Company	526
Courtesy of Accountor Systems	534
Courtesy of Accountor Systems	535
Courtesy of Xerox Corporation	538
Courtesy of Hewlett Packard Company	539
©Alix Parson	546
Courtesy of International Business Machines Corporation	547
Courtesy of Fellowes Manufacturing Company	554
Courtesy of Curtis Computer Products, Inc.	554
Courtesy of Hewlett Packard Company	555
Courtesy of 3M Optical Recording	557
Courtesy of Eastman Kodak Company	562
©1996 PhotoDisc, Inc.	573
Courtesy of Haworth Inc., Holland, MI	577
Courtesy of Bell & Howell, Automated Systems Division	578
Courtesy of Pitney Bowes	594
Courtesy of Pitney Bowes	595
Courtesy of Pitney Bowes	596
Courtesy of the U.S. Postal Service	602
©1995 PhotoDisc, Inc.	618
Courtesy of Xerox Corporation	620
Courtesy of Sprint	623
Property of AT&T Archives. Reprinted with permission of AT&T.	625
Property of AT&T Archives. Reprinted with permission of AT&T.	625
Courtesy of Sony Electronics Inc.	627
©Mimi Ostendorf	627
©1997 PhotoDisc, Inc.	629
©1996 PhotoDisc, Inc.	630
©1997 PhotoDisc, Inc.	631
Courtesy of Mitsubishi Electric Sales America, Inc.	631
©1996 Telesensory Corporation. Used by permission.	632
Property of AT&T Archives. Reprinted with permission of AT&T.	636
©1997 PhotoDisc, Inc.	643
©1996 PhotoDisc, Inc.	645
Property of AT&T Archives. Reprinted with permission of AT&T.	645
Courtesy of International Business Machines Corporation	648
©Alix Parson	657
© 995 PhotoDisc, Inc.	662
Property of AT&T Archives. Reprinted with permission of AT&T.	662
©1995 PhotoDisc, Inc.	662
Courtesy of Sprint	663
©1997 PhotoDisc, Inc.	663
Courtesy of Times Fiber Communications, Inc.	681
©1997 PhotoDisc, Inc.	682
©1997 PhotoDisc, Inc.	683
Courtesy of International Business Machines Corporation	687
Courtesy of Hewlett Packard Company	688
Courtesy of Microsoft Corporation	709
Courtesy of International Business Machines Corporation	716
Courtesy of International Business Machines Corporation	717
©1997 PhotoDisc, Inc.	727
©Jeff Greenberg	730
©1996 PhotoDisc, Inc.	769
©1997 PhotoDisc, Inc.	775
©1997 PhotoDisc, Inc.	781
©1997 PhotoDisc, Inc.	783
©1997 PhotoDisc, Inc.	784

Strategies for Instructional Planning

Teacher's Edition Preface

The transformation of the office that began approximately a decade ago continues to change the nature of office activity as well as those who participate in the activities. Many workers are required to have a well-grounded knowledge of productive procedures and high-level competency in handling office tasks. Increasingly, practically everyone at work is handling office tasks to some degree. While there continue to be full-time workers who perform office support functions, that segment of the workforce is increasing at a far slower rate than the overall increase in the workforce. This is a marked change from earlier decades, when office support staff employment was increasing at a rate far higher than the average rate for the total workforce.

You, as one of today's office procedures teachers, are a teacher of general education. This may not be a new responsibility for you, because many schools with nonsegregated curricula have students who study office procedures for basic skills they know will be valuable in their future careers, which may not be planned for the field of office occupations.

The responsibility to guide an educational experience that will have long-term relevance requires a serious consideration of skills and knowledge that will be of value to your students as they continue further studies and enter the workforce. The development of this third edition of *The Office: Procedures and Technology* was guided by these assumptions:

- Office education must be presented within a broad framework for understanding the environment in which office functions are performed.
- The categories of office functions need to be identified closely with emerging technologies.
- Basic communication and computational skills continue to be valuable and should be stressed.
- Skills in interpersonal relations from strategies for finding a job to working with coworkers and supervisors must not be overlooked.

Based on these assumptions, the content of the **Third Edition** develops office skills and knowledge that all workers will find valuable regardless of the work they choose to do in a job or a career. Furthermore, the activities provided for students reflect the need to think critically, make decisions independently, organize information, interpret information, and function productively in a consistent fashion.

This section, **Strategies for Instructional Planning,** provides resource information for designing specific classroom experiences for students. The information is subdivided by part, chapter, and topic. Objectives and outlines are included as well as teaching suggestions. Annotations throughout the book present suggestions under the following headings:

- Getting Started
- Expand the Concept
- Challenge Option
- Teaching Tips
- Points to Emphasize
- Thinking Critically
- For Discussion

These teaching suggestions are options to be used at your discretion. They have been designed to facilitate learning, enrich discussion, and expand key concepts presented in the text. These materials, together with the *Teacher's Resource Guide*, will help you develop a course relevant to your students' needs.

The Office in the Business World

1

This part reflects current trends in the workplace. The office practice course is no longer solely for the student who seeks employment as office support staff after graduation. With the extensive introduction of technological innovations, many workers now perform office tasks to some extent. Regardless of their job and career aspirations, students need basic office competencies if they are to carry through their responsibilities with effectiveness and efficiency. Helping students see the significance of the skills presented in this textbook is a worthwhile challenge for today's business teacher.

This part teaches students to:

- describe the relation of the office to the overall organization
- describe typical goals and structures of businesses
- illustrate the types of office competencies workers need
- explain employer expectations and factors critical for developing office competencies

Chapter 1 The Office in a Changing Business World

There are many interesting approaches to the course and the first chapter. In determining your initial strategy, consider information about:

- the career goals of the class
- the nature of organizations in the community
- job opportunities for graduates
- where students go for postsecondary education and the nature of programs they enter

A successful strategy for your class may be to focus on one of the following:

- students' experiences and observations as a basis for gaining an overview of current trends in offices
- the office as information driven, highlighting common competencies needed by many workers
- the ways in which technology has changed the work done in the office

In the initial class session you may want to help students set some general goals for the course, including points such as the following:

- adhering to instructions
- meeting deadlines
- being a responsible team member
- striving to achieve high levels of competencies
- developing a positive commitment to good work habits
- developing an awareness of how to learn in a new environment

Topic 1-1 The Office Today

Topic Objectives

When students have completed their study of this topic, they will be able to:

- describe various types of offices
- describe types of workers who use office skills
- explain how technology is influencing office practices
- describe alternative office forms

TOPIC 1-1 SELECTED OUTLINE

Offices Are Information Driven
Office Functions Are Varied
    Offices Have Varying Responsibilities
    Offices Provide Support Services
Technology in Modern Offices
    Technology Is Changing at a Rapid Rate
    Implications of Technological Innovations
Alternative Offices
    Virtual Office
    Mobile Office
    Home Office
Predictions Are for Further Change

TEACHING SUGGESTIONS

It seems almost inevitable that some students need to be reintroduced to some skill, knowledge, understanding, or attitude that is important in this course. As you plan for classroom instruction, consider student weaknesses that require additional attention. It is reassuring that students given another chance to learn often can overcome barriers that seemingly precluded their earlier learning.

Reteaching Activities

The following are reteaching activities that could be used for any of the topics:

- Guide students through the chapter topics, noting the objectives, the words in the margin, and key words.
- Describe to students how they should pause after reading a specific segment, look back at the headings, and mentally prepare a brief summary of the key points.
- Observe students on a one-to-one basis, helping those who seem to be having difficulty.
- Engage students in a discussion of the key points.

Grouping Students for Instruction

Some group activity can be a part of the first class session. Beginning the course with attention to learning cooperatively and working together sets an appropriate tone for the course.

One effective way of grouping students is to use random assignment, especially during the early class sessions. Groups should not be larger than three or four students. An easy way to assign students to groups is to prepare slips numbered from 1 through the number of students in the class. Shuffle these slips in a small box before each student draws a number.

Then identify who will be in each group by listing the numbers on the board or merely stating that Group 1 is the first three odd numbers, Group 2 the first three even numbers, and so on. For each assignment, a random selection should be made so that each student will have a chance to work with most, if not all, classmates.

Techniques useful in your first class session will depend on how well students know each other. If students are strangers to each other, you can establish small groups for getting acquainted. Students may get acquainted by asking each member to provide a self-introduction including name, courses in business completed, and goals for this course.

You may want to discuss briefly the responsibility each group member must accept to listen carefully to classmates, keep to the subject of the discussion, and thoughtfully consider opinions or ideas that are different from their own. Furthermore, you may want to discuss the etiquette of group activity, including that everyone should have a chance to participate, full attention should be given to the person talking, and two or more persons should not talk at the same time.

Students may be assigned to groups to consider one or more of the following questions after you have given a very preliminary overview of the topic:

1. What office experience have you had?
2. Describe your last encounter with an office worker.
3. In what type of office was the office worker?
4. How effective was the office worker?

In addition to discussing the questions assigned, you may direct the students to take notes and to share with the entire class a summary of the small group discussions.

Topic 1-2 The Office in Relation to the Total Organization

Topic Objectives

When students have completed their study of this topic, they will be able to:

- explain how employees develop understanding of organizations in which they work
- describe common types of organizations
- identify goals for different types of organizations
- explain a common structure for personnel
- describe the role of office employees within an organization

TOPIC 1-2 SELECTED OUTLINE

Understanding the Organization
- Learning from Your Work
- Learning from Resources Available

Types of Organizations
- Businesses
- Not-for-Profit Entities
- Governmental Units

Goals of Organizations
- Goals of Businesses
- Goals of Not-for-Profit Entities
- Goals of Governmental Units

Types of Employees Required
- Board of Directors Determines Policies
- Senior Management Implements Policies
- Division Management Oversees Specific Units
- Middle-Management Supervises
- Technical Personnel Provide Critical Know-How

Structure of Organizations

Office Workers Help Meet Goals

TEACHING SUGGESTIONS

Local organizations can provide a realistic, interesting basis for discussing the content of this topic. Students can be encouraged to read the business section of the local paper. If there are publicly owned companies in your local community, you may want to obtain copies of their most recent annual reports for review in class. If there are no publicly owned companies locally, you may choose to use the annual report of a major company in which your class might have an interest. You will want to consider using resources about organizations that maintain World Wide Web sites that can be accessed without cost.

This may be a good time to remind students of strategies for extending their vocabularies by examining the words identified in the content and defined in the margins. In this initial chapter, you may want to explain how to understand a word in context. Suggest that students read a paragraph, noting the words in bold, italics, or color. Ask them to attempt to define the words based on the content of the paragraph before reading the margin note or using a dictionary to find the definition of the word. For additional reinforcement, ask students to write sentences that reflect understanding of each new word.

For a small group discussion, first select several organizations with which students are likely to be familiar. Then ask students to discuss the following questions for each organization:

1. Is the organization a business, a not-for-profit entity, or a governmental unit?
2. What do you believe are the goals of the organization?
3. What are the types of workers required in the organization?

Chapter 2 Office Competencies

The personal computer has transformed the work of millions of workers. Office competencies are as commonly required now as good handwriting skills were for all types of workers a half-century ago.

There is high probability that every student in a business class will be expected to handle effectively a wide range of what were at one time the skills expected primarily of office support staff.

The office support worker cannot be ignored. The projected rate of increase in the total number of workers in the U.S. Labor Department's category, Administrative Support Services, is a modest 4.3 percent. However, the category will continue to be one of the largest occupational groups in the economy and many replacements will be made. Many workers in this group move to higher-level positions.

Topic 2-1 Office Competencies Needed for Employment

Topic Objectives

When students have completed their study of this topic, they will be able to:

- discuss the need for workers through 2005
- identify office competencies
- explain future prospects for employment where office competencies are valuable

TOPIC 2-1 SELECTED OUTLINE

National Overview of Employment
  Outlook for Employment of Office Workers
  Workers Face Expanded Job Responsibilities
An Overview of Office Competencies
  Word Processing
  Data Processing
  Information Management and Transmission
  General Managing/Communicating with Customers
  Your Future Prospects

TEACHING SUGGESTIONS

The office worker is assumed to be highly committed to efficiency and competency. Throughout this topic, there are references to opportunities for office workers. For students who have no plans to become office support workers, there is value to understanding the role of office support staff. Managers and other office workers can plan work schedules, evaluate performance, and assign tasks in a wiser manner if they have an understanding of what many types of office workers are expected to accomplish and how the work is assessed.

If a copy of the most recent edition of the *Occupational Outlook Handbook* is available, you may want students to read about occupations in which they have an interest. They may choose to read one of the following sections:

Professional specialty and technical occupations
Executives, administrative, and managerial occupations
Sales occupations
Administrative support occupations, including clerical
Precision production, craft, and repair occupations
Machine operators, assemblers, and inspectors
Transportation and material moving occupations
Handlers, equipment cleaners, helpers, and laborers
Service occupations

Topic 2-2 Developing Office Competencies

Topic Objectives

When students have completed their study of this topic, they will be able to:

- describe the goals to which employees are expected to contribute
- explain the general expectations for workers
- prepare a strategy for developing office competencies

TOPIC 2-2 SELECTED OUTLINE

Goals Influence Expectations for all Employees
  Total Quality Management
  Continuous Improvement
  Customer Satisfaction
  Ethical Standards
  Responsible Teamwork
  Global Outreach
  Attention to Diversity
General Expectations for Employees
  Reliability
  Productivity
  Cooperativeness
  Independence in Learning
Strategy for Developing Office Competencies
  Take a Look at Your Key Competencies
  Assess Your Competencies
  Set Goals for Making Progress

TEACHING SUGGESTIONS

Business news is extensively provided in newspapers, business periodicals, television programs, and via the World Wide Web. It is likely that your students are acquainted with some of the material that is provided in this section.

Surveys continue to show that many workers are not functioning at optimum levels due in part to the lack of respect for the work ethic. Respect for work and a commitment to being responsible can be developed in a business class.

Communicating Effectively

2

This part emphasizes the importance of communication skills. These skills are central to much of what is required in a wide range of tasks in the office. Companies assess basic communication skills of both prospective workers and those being considered for promotion. Students will learn to improve their listening, speaking, reading, and writing skills as they study this part.

This part teaches students to:

- describe strategies for effective listening
- practice techniques for improving speaking and reading skills
- describe and apply procedures for writing effective business communications

Chapter 3 Communicating in the Office

Students have studied the communication skills presented in this chapter again and again throughout their school years. However, introducing the skills in the concrete context of what is required in the office should be appealing to students. Many companies provide communication courses for all employees—from beginning workers to top executives—in an ongoing effort to help employees develop the best possible communication skills. You will want to discuss briefly how all students, whether they have poor, average, or good communication skills, can improve their skills using the strategies presented in this chapter.

Topic 3-1 Listening and Speaking

Topic Objectives

When students have completed their study of this topic, they will be able to:

- describe the importance of listening
- explain techniques that aid in active listening
- describe what an effective speaker achieves
- explain the factors considered in speaking

TOPIC 3-1 SELECTED OUTLINE

The Importance of Listening
- What Is Listening?

Effective Listening Strategy
- Be Willing to Learn
- Focus Attention
- Mentally Summarize
- Take Notes
- Ask Questions
- Review What You Heard
- Assessing Your Ability to Listen

Speaking Effectively
- Take an Interest in Communicating
- Speak Clearly
- Use Standard Language
- Express Your Ideas Concisely
- Consider Your Audience
- Be Aware of Nonverbal Communication
- Be Interested in the Listener's Response

Complementary Skills—Listening and Speaking

TEACHING SUGGESTIONS

Using a tape recorder is invaluable for this topic. Ways in which a tape recorder can be used include:

- recording or asking a student to record sections of material from the textbook or from a timely article
- recording of small group discussions. Ask students to evaluate their own and their classmates' skills in listening

- recording of individual presentations before the class as well as group discussions

Recording of discussions of business people who do not speak English as their first language would provide some real-life material for class use. Increasingly, persons for whom English is not their first language interact with those for whom English is their first language. Practice in listening to English spoken with an accent develops confidence in understanding others.

Listening exercises and brief written quizzes can be developed to check students' skills in listening. Then students should check their own level of skill as you give them the answers to a listening quiz.

Topic 3-2 Reading

Topic Objectives

When students have completed their study of this topic, they will be able to:

- explain the attitudes that enhance development of reading skills
- describe the kinds of reading common at work
- identify critical components of reading skills
- explain common techniques for improving reading skills

TOPIC 3-2 SELECTED OUTLINE

Attitude Toward Reading
The Value of Reading Skills
Present Reading Skill
The Reading Process
Improving Reading Skills
  Comprehension
  Vocabulary
  Speed
Reading at Work
  Learning About Your Company
  Understanding Instructions for Equipment
  Following Instructions on Forms
  Responding to Inquiries
  Using Written References/Databases
  Reading as a Single Process

TEACHING SUGGESTIONS

Reading is one of the most powerful skills a student can develop. Inability to read is often concealed. While some do not hesitate to say that they find math difficult, few are willing to concede that reading is difficult for them.

Through the study of prior chapters, you may have diagnosed the reading abilities represented in your class. If most students are good readers, there may be value in meeting privately with the few students who have difficulty. Possibly, in a confidential meeting with you, a weak reader will reveal his or her problem with this activity. There may be services in the school to aid such students. Or you may be able to suggest reading exercises, using the textbook or some simpler books, as sources for help. Among the techniques that might be used with a student to improve reading skills are:

- asking the student to outline a topic in the textbook, highlighting the key points
- asking the student, in a review session, questions about what was read
- giving the student some timed reading
- giving the student an oral vocabulary test to assess word knowledge
- helping a student to see how to determine what a word might mean by noting its use in context

If there is excellent group rapport in the class and students are honest about their deficiencies, groups might be formed for skill development. Good students are often effective teachers. They realize that helping a classmate can help them improve their own skills.

Materials and strategies for developing skill include:

- excerpts from manuals for software, equipment, and other references commonly used at work
- articles about work-related topics that may be in the local newspaper or periodicals that students read
- encouraging students to read periodicals in the library. Identify the ones available in the library that students might read
- encourage students to access sites on the World Wide Web and take notes. Have students compare notes to see if in their reading they identified key points
- use some class time, on occasion, to give students an exercise in scanning or in reading rapidly

Limited small-group instruction may help students be candid about their reading skill. For example, small groups might be formed to discuss the three critical skills of comprehension, vocabulary, and speed.

Topic 3-3 Writing

Topic Objectives

When students have completed their study of this topic, they will be able to:

- describe the nature of writing tasks common at work
- write memoranda and letters that reflect qualities of good business communications
- describe an effective procedure for managing a writing task

TOPIC 3-3 SELECTED OUTLINE

Common Writing Tasks
- Summarizing Written Messages and Meetings
- Preparing Drafts
- Reviewing the Writing of Others
- Composing Messages

Business Writing Is Purpose Driven
- Communicating Policies and Procedures
- Communicating Plans in Progress
- Seeking Specific Information
- Providing Specific Information
- Following Up Oral Discussions
- Sending Messages to Customers

Characteristics of Effective Writing

English Skills for Business Writing

Management of Writing Tasks
- Managing the Task of Writing
- Managing the Schedule for Writing Tasks

Opportunities for Writing

The Interrelationship of Communication Skills

TEACHING SUGGESTIONS

There will be many opportunities throughout the course to develop writing skills. From earlier assignments, you have undoubtedly noted the skill level of students. If the total class is deficient, you may want to devote some time on a regular basis to develop skills. Many assignments that might be handled through oral discussion may be used additionally as written exercises.

Employers are constantly noting that employees do not possess sufficient writing skill to handle their responsibilities competently. Ability to respond quickly, for example, to an e-mail message, adds to productivity. The writing and rewriting that is far too common—and painful to the worker—is wasteful.

Among the activities to be completed in class under the observation of the teacher are the following examples:

1. Write the instructions for driving to the school. Students are to assume that a visitor will be arriving at a local airport, train terminal, or bus terminal, where the visitor will rent a car to drive to your campus. The visitor has never been in your town. The instructions are to guide the visitor to the campus. (The teacher may choose not to give details of what should be included. It is interesting to note how many students give an estimate of time required for the drive to campus.)
2. Write a memorandum asking for the outline for a seminar to be offered on the topic of time management. The students are to assume that they work in a company that distributes memoranda about forthcoming continuing education courses. One recent memorandum invited employees to ask for outlines of courses.
3. Write a memorandum to you, the teacher, describing present writing skills and what the student would like to improve during the course.

3 Managing Information to Enhance Productivity

Timely, accurate information is critical to the success of an organization. Organizations that effectively process information typically grow and prosper. Organizations that do not have information readily available for decision making risk the loss of income and even business failure.

Office workers play an important role in processing information. In this part, students learn concepts and procedures of information processing that they are likely to encounter on the job.

This part teaches students to:

- explain the vital role that information plays in operating a business
- describe common business information systems
- communicate effectively in written form via letters, memoranda, business reports, and related documents
- plan, prepare, and deliver business presentations
- explain the purpose of common financial reports and aid in their preparation
- process financial information—payments, receipts, and bank reconciliations

Chapter 4 Information: A Vital Business Resource

Students must be aware of the critical importance of information to the life of an organization. New and emerging technologies are transforming the way in which office tasks are completed. Office workers need not only an understanding of what information is and why it is so critical to an organization, but also an understanding of the information systems utilized within organizations. Students should also develop an awareness of how technology can enhance the effectiveness of the information system. When students see this relationship, they will have a better framework for gaining insight into the information systems in companies where they accept positions.

Topic 4-1 Information in Business

Topic Objectives

When students have completed their study of this topic, they will be able to:

- define information
- explain how businesses use information
- describe information processing activities
- explain how information technologies enhance information systems

TOPIC 4-1 SELECTED OUTLINE

How Businesses Use Information
Managing Information
  Complexity of Business
  Volume of Transactions
  Current and Accurate Information
  Obstacles to Managing Information Effectively
Information Processing
Information Technologies
  Common Information Technologies
  Computerized Processing
    Hardware
    Software
  Maintenance and Security

TEACHING SUGGESTIONS

You have already emphasized to the students the importance of information to an organization. The following example will enlighten students as to how they benefit from information processing.

Schools process facts about students on a daily basis. Students should understand that the processing of these facts leads to useful information. For example, a homeroom teacher records the names of those students ordering yearbooks and collects student payments. Student names and money collected are of no use until they are processed. As homeroom teachers turn in their lists of student names and the amount of money collected from each, the lists are compiled. From this composite listing, the yearbook advisor knows how many yearbooks to order. When the yearbooks arrive, the advisor knows who should receive copies and distributes them accordingly.

You may wish to use the following questions, or similar questions, as a discussion base to expand this concept:

1. What facts do teachers/school personnel collect on students (attendance, courses taken, grades)?
2. How are these facts processed into useful information (i.e., how are these facts used)?
3. Why is timely information important in this situation?

Topic 4-2 Information Systems and Resources

Topic Objectives

When students have completed their study of this topic, they will be able to:

- identify typical information systems used in business
- describe traditional information resources
- describe electronic information resources

TOPIC 4-2 SELECTED OUTLINE

Typical Information Systems
- Human Resources Information Systems
- Accounting Information Systems
- Marketing Information Systems
- Product Information Systems

Information Resources
- Traditional Resources
  - Marketing Research Firms
  - Trade Publications and Associations
  - Government Agencies
  - Libraries
- Electronic Resources
  - Electronic Databases
  - Personal Digital Assistants
  - The Internet
  - Intranets

TEACHING SUGGESTIONS

After students have studied Chapter 4 they will have a better understanding of the role individual employees play in the overall information processing of a company. To reinforce learning in this chapter, invite several former students who are employed in your community to talk to your class about their job responsibilities and how their jobs fit into their organization's information processing system. If possible, invite someone from a large organization and someone from a small organization. Also consider inviting a recent graduate and someone who has been employed for five or more years.

Prior to the visit, have students work in small groups to develop questions they will ask the guests. Once the students have developed questions in their small groups, discuss the questions with the class as a whole.

Chapter 5 Communicating in Written Form

This chapter introduces students to the various forms of written communication within an office. Students receive instruction on the fundamentals of good writing needed for preparing effective business documents such as letters, memoranda, reports, and tables.

Students are expected to have some previous exposure to keying and formatting the frequently used business documents presented in this chapter. Therefore, the formatting and presentation coverage of document preparation are more of a review than an in-depth study. You may wish to ascertain if students need additional reinforcement on document formats and presentation and supplement these activities as needed.

As you develop this chapter, you may wish to reinforce that much of today's business communication is in written form; preparing written communications is an important task in business organizations. Business letters are typically written to persons outside the organization, whereas memoranda are usually internal communications. Business reports are a source of information for making business decisions. They are basically either analytical or informational in nature and may follow either a formal or an informal format and presentation. Visual aids are commonly used in business reports to make the report more understandable. They not only add interest to the report but may reduce the text needed to explain the information.

Topic 5-1 Business Letters and Memoranda

Topic Objectives

When students have completed their study of this topic, they will be able to:

- identify the characteristics of effective business letters and memoranda
- prepare effective business documents
- explain the function of business letters and memoranda
- identify and use appropriately the parts of business letters and memoranda
- choose appropriate formats for business letters

TOPIC 5-1 SELECTED OUTLINE

Characteristics of Effective Documents
Preparing Effective Documents
  Drafting
  Revising and Editing
  Proofreading
Message Types
  Positive or Neutral Messages
  Negative Messages
  Persuasive Messages
Business Letters
  Presentation of Business Letters
  Letters Parts
  Business Letter Formats
  Repetitive Letters
  Envelopes
Memoranda
  Guidelines for Writing Memoranda
  Memorandum Preparation

TEACHING SUGGESTIONS

To encourage students to write clearly and completely the first time they compose a memo or letter, you may want to give oral instructions only for composing a document. Ask students to take notes as instructions are given. The oral instructions should tell students to compose a memo or letter related to a topic that is meaningful to them. Possible topics are:

- Write a memo to your teacher identifying office equipment and/or software you would like to learn to use.
- Write a letter to a speaker, inviting him/her to speak about a topic of interest to the class.
- Write an e-mail to a classmate suggesting "tips for improving writing skills."

To improve command of basic English skills, you may wish to distribute documents randomly to students and ask them to correct all grammar, punctuation, and spelling errors in the documents.

Topic 5-2 Business Reports and Related Documents

Topic Objectives

When students have completed their study of this topic, they will be able to:

- identify the characteristics of business reports
- prepare reports in formal and informal formats
- create visual aids used in reports
- use software features effectively in creating and editing reports

TOPIC 5-2 SELECTED OUTLINE

Characteristics of Business Reports
Informational Reports
    Gathering Data
    Writing the Report
Analytical Reports
    Gathering Data
    Using Electronic Information Services
    Writing the Report
Business Report Formats
Formal Business Reports
Informal Business Reports
Visual Aids
    Tables
    Graphs
    Spreadsheets
Multi-Page Report Preparation

TEACHING SUGGESTIONS

Ask students to collect samples of the graphs studied in this topic from magazines, newspapers, or other sources and bring them to class. Divide a classroom bulletin board into sections with the graph names and display the graphs. Assign students to work in groups to study the similarities and differences of one of the graph types. Ask students to be alert to features of the graphs that make them more appealing or easier to read than other graphs as well as features that may detract or make the graphs difficult to understand. Have students record their observations. Each group should report its findings to the class as a whole.

Chapter 6 Communicating via Presentations

Although many jobs do not require the employee to give formal presentations, it is common for employees to give informal presentations. Students may encounter several occasions in work-related situations where they will need to present information to others or help supervisors or coworkers prepare presentations. They may even need to be persuasive and motivate or influence others to take a course of action. In some cases, students may be asked to prepare and deliver formal presentations. This chapter focuses on the necessary planning and preparation that must occur for organizing and delivering a successful presentation.

Among the concepts to be developed and reinforced in this chapter are the following:

- planning and organizing the content of a presentation
- designing effective visuals that enhance a communicator's message
- developing the skills and techniques for communicating with listeners effectively

Topic 6-1 Planning and Preparing the Presentation

Topic Objectives

When students have completed their study of this topic, they will be able to:

- profile listeners
- identify the message to provide
- address the interests of listeners
- develop ideas for a message and organize them in a storyboard
- create effective visuals and handouts
- organize team presentations

TOPIC 6-1 SELECTED OUTLINE

Identify the Purpose of The Presentation
- Profile Your Listeners
- Address the Listeners' Interests

Develop the Message
- Organize Your Ideas
- Include Supporting Details
- Consider Listener Advantages and Objections

Choose Visuals and Audio
- Choose the Media
- Create the Visual Elements
- Design Strategies

Create Handouts and Posters

Plan Team Presentations
- Determine Roles of Individuals
- Working as a Team

TEACHING SUGGESTIONS

Give students additional practice in organizing information for a presentation by asking them to summarize the main points from an article in a form appropriate for a presentation. Use an article with few headings so students must read and identify the key points. They might also identify and/or prepare visual aids that would be appropriate for illustrating the key points.

Topic 6-2 Delivering the Presentation

Topic Objectives

When students have completed their study of this topic, they will be able to:

- apply methods for practicing and preparing for a presentation
- describe appropriate appearance for making presentations
- apply proper techniques for communicating with an audience
- use visuals effectively
- conduct question-and-answer sessions

TOPIC 6-2 SELECTED OUTLINE

Practice and Prepare
- Prepare Notes
- Videotape Your Presentation
- Prepare the Meeting Room
- Consider Your Appearance

Present Opening Remarks

Communicate with Your Audience
- Maintain Eye Contact
- Avoid Non-Words
- Show Enthusiasm and Speak Convincingly
- Control Your Posture and Gestures
- Use Good Intonation
- Keep the Audience Focused

Use Visuals Effectively

Answer Questions

Present Closing Remarks

Evaluate Your Presentation

TEACHING SUGGESTIONS

Emphasize to students that improving their skills in organizing and presenting information can be valuable in their current studies as well as in a future career. Consider working with one or more instructors to develop an assignment where students give an oral presentation on content relevant to one of their courses. Students might be asked to give the presentation in both classes. Credit could be given in the office procedures class on clarity, organization, and effectiveness of the presentation; and in the other course for the presentation content.

Chapter 7 Processing and Understanding Financial Information

This chapter introduces students to financial concepts and procedures they may encounter in an office environment. For students who have not studied accounting, the concepts and procedures introduced in this chapter may be their primary source of information regarding financial practices in business.

As you develop the content of this chapter, you may want to emphasize that each employee is responsible for adhering to the established guidelines in completing job tasks. Adhering to established procedures results in higher productivity and fewer errors. In financial matters, the goal is to safeguard assets and achieve error-free output.

Employees can frequently contribute to improving the way in which procedures are carried out in a business. A positive attitude toward learning to do the job well often leads to being able to suggest improvement in procedures. Students should understand that the work of individuals, departments, or other units contributes to the financial goals of the organization.

Topic 7-1 Cash and Banking Procedures

Topic Objectives

When students have completed their study of this topic, they will be able to:

* explain the value of internal control for cash handling
* explain procedures for receiving cash and making cash payments
* prepare a bank account reconciliation
* prepare entries for a petty cash fund

TOPIC 7-1 SELECTED OUTLINE

Safeguarding Cash
- Division of Responsibility
- Internal Audits
- Bonded Employees

Receiving Payments
Making Payments
Electronic Funds Transfer
Reconciling a Bank Account
- Bank Statement and Company Records
- Purposes for Reconciliation
- Steps in Preparing a Reconciliation

Maintaining a Petty Cash Fund
- Establishing the Fund
- Making Payments
- Keeping a Record
- Replenishing the Fund
- Computerized Petty Cash Records

TEACHING SUGGESTIONS

You may wish to reinforce procedures for completing forms, reports, or statements related to safeguarding cash and handling cash receipts with these activities.

1. Provide copies of forms from business; discuss the similarities and differences among the forms illustrated in the text and those collected from businesses.
2. Provide models of completed forms (bank reconciliation statement, deposit slip, petty cash fund report) from an application activity for students to evaluate for correctness, completeness, and application of the appropriate procedures, inserting missing steps or correcting steps out of order. During this discussion, you will be able to determine the areas in which further review may be needed.
3. On an overhead transparency, display a blank form (bank reconciliation statement, deposit slip, petty cash fund report), and complete the form with the class, letting students guide you in filling in the correct information; or ask a student to complete the form.

Topic 7-2 Financial Reports and Payroll

Topic Objectives

When students have completed their study of this topic, they will be able to:

- explain the purpose of a budget, income statement, and balance sheet
- participate in preparing a budget, income statement, and balance sheet
- explain concepts and procedures related to payroll payments

TOPIC 7-2 SELECTED OUTLINE

Financial Reports
- Budgets
- Income Statements
- Balance Sheets
- Formatting Financial Documents

Payments for Wages and Salaries
- Compensation Plans
- Deductions from Earnings
- Records for Payroll
- Payroll Check Distribution

TEACHING SUGGESTIONS

Reinforce student learning related to financial reports with this activity. Obtain several company reports that contain income statements and balance sheets. Have students work in small groups to compare the reports to those illustrated in the text, noting differences and similarities. Ask each group to note information in the reports that they do not understand or have questions about. Have each group report to the class as a whole. Lead a class discussion regarding information each group noted as unfamiliar to them.

Managing Time, Tasks, and Records

4

This part emphasizes the importance of time management; office health, safety, and security; and effective use of records management systems. Reprographics is included as a topic related to records management. Planning for and participating effectively in meetings, and making travel arrangements complete the topics for this part.

This part teaches students to:

- manage more effectively their time, workstation, and office health, safety, and security
- plan and participate in business meetings and make travel arrangements
- manage paper and magnetic records and media

Chapter 8 Time and Workstation Management

The tasks performed by office workers vary according to the nature of the business, the size of the business, and the location of the business. The central themes of this chapter are (1) the importance of learning how to manage time, tasks, and the physical environment; (2) helping students learn the correct procedures for maintaining reminder systems; and (3) introducing office workers to the importance of supporting a healthy, safe, and secure work environment. Technical skills and knowledge must be supplemented with the ability to manage work activities. Without effective management of one's time and tasks, productivity suffers.

Ergonomic factors affect workers' attitudes toward their work and the company; their productivity and job satisfaction; and their long-term health. It is crucial that students learn to recognize physical symptoms resulting from working for prolonged periods of time at a computer terminal.

Topic 8-1 Time Management and Reminder Systems

Topic Objectives

When students have completed their study of this topic, they will be able to:

- identify common time-wasters
- analyze how they spend their time
- plan their work activities
- use common reminder systems
- compare and contrast manual and electronic reminder systems

TOPIC 8-1 SELECTED OUTLINE

Manage Your Time
- Common Time-Wasters
- Time Analysis Procedures

Manage Your Work
- Plan Your Work Activities
- Set Priorities
- Control Large Projects
- Simplify Your Work

Reminder Systems
- Calendars
- Scheduling Appointments
- Tickler Files

TEACHING SUGGESTIONS

Emphasize to students that they should begin now to establish efficient time management procedures. Time-wasters that are common in the office may also be common in students' personal lives. Review with students the discussion on time-wasters found in the text. Then conduct a class discussion and ask students to give examples of how they have wasted time because of unnecessary telephone conversations, excessive socializing, ineffective communication, and disorganization.

Have students keep a time log for a second week after completing Activity 1. Then ask students to analyze their most recent time-log by comparing it with the first time-log they completed. Students should ask themselves: Does my second time-log indicate that I managed my time more efficiently or less efficiently? Have my most and least productive time periods changed in comparison to my first time-log? Did I waste more or less time? Ask students to write a short summary of their findings.

Topic 8-2 Workstation Management and Office Safety

Topic Objectives

When students have completed their study of this topic, they will be able to:

- understand the importance of an organized workstation
- know the meaning of and factors related to ergonomics and its importance to the office worker
- describe significant safety and security procedures for the office

TOPIC 8-2 SELECTED OUTLINE

Workstation Management
- Manage Your Workstation
- Manage Ergonomic Factors
- Manage Your Office Health

Office Safety
- Accident Prevention
- Workstation Safety
- Work Area Safety
- Know Emergency Procedures
- Personal Security on the Job
- Know Building and Office Security

TEACHING SUGGESTIONS

Emphasize to students that the first step toward a safe and secure office environment is accident prevention. Accident prevention depends on responsible office employees who have positive safety attitudes.

Emphasize that employees are largely responsible for their own personal safety also. Tell students to assume they work in an office and are attempting to complete a project before leaving that evening. At five o'clock their coworkers leave for the day and they are alone in the department or building. Conduct a class discussion on what security procedures they should follow while alone in the office and when leaving the building. Ask students who have part-time evening jobs to discuss security precautions taken when they are working or leaving the building late at night.

Chapter 9 Meetings and Travel

The central themes of this chapter involve (1) planning for and arranging various kinds of business meetings, (2) creating documents related to business meetings, (3) planning and following through with business travel arrangements, (4) assisting business travelers in obtaining travel documents, and (5) completing business travel follow-up activities. Handling arrangements for business meetings and travel requires follow-through and attention to detail. Without effective organizational skills, important tasks can be overlooked.

Telecommunications technology is playing an important role in assisting the business traveler to stay in touch with the office while traveling. Technology will continue to increase the ease with which paperwork can be completed while away from the office.

Topic 9-1 Planning and Participating in Meetings

Topic Objectives

When students have completed their study of this topic, they will be able to:

- plan business meetings
- prepare documents related to business meetings
- participate effectively in meetings

TOPIC 9-1 SELECTED OUTLINE

Types of Business Meetings
- Informal and Small Group Meetings
- Formal Business Meetings
- Multinational Meetings

Planning the Meeting
- Before the Meeting
- During the Meeting
- After the Meeting

Participating in Meetings
- Leading
- Brainstorming
- Group Dynamics
- Involving Everyone
- Developing the Action Plan

Teleconferences
- Audio Conferences
- Video Conferences
- Computer Conferences

TEACHING SUGGESTIONS

Students can gain valuable experience and broaden their knowledge about meeting participation by attending meetings of various organizations in the community. Assign students to small groups to visit and report on a meeting of an organization such as the local school board, chamber of commerce, city council, or a civic group. You or a student should make arrangements with the group prior to the visit if it is with a private group. Lead a class discussion on the information students should include in their meeting report.

After all the visits are completed, have each group report to the class as a whole. Discuss procedures or strategies from the meeting that the group found effective or ineffective.

Topic 9-2 Arranging Travel

Topic Objectives

When students have completed their study of this topic, they will be able to:

- use appropriate procedures for planning business travel
- explain procedures for obtaining a passport and visa
- prepare appropriate travel documents, including an itinerary
- describe the factors involved in travel etiquette and travel safety
- complete pertinent follow-up travel activities

TOPIC 9-2 SELECTED OUTLINE

Preparing for Business Travel
- Commercial Air Travel
- Other Forms of Business Travel
- Hotel/Motel Accommodations
- Itinerary and Supporting Materials

Travel Etiquette
- Dress
- Customs
- Documents for Foreign Travel

Travel Safety
Handling Work While Away from the Office
Business Travel Follow-Up Activities
- Expense Reports
- Meeting Reports
- Thank-You Letters

TEACHING SUGGESTIONS

International travel is becoming increasingly common for companies of all sizes. Have students develop a checklist of preparations that must be completed prior to traveling to foreign countries. Several sources of information should be available to you and your students for completing this task (travel agencies, online resources, and businesspeople). The local library may have resources, such as books on traveling abroad. Students who have traveled abroad will have some knowledge of travel regulations and may have documents, such as a passport, to share.

This assignment could be extended by having students prepare simulated travel and accommodation arrangements for a specific time period to a selected city within a foreign country. The students should be responsible for planning all travel and accommodations needed from their homes to the destination city and the return trip.

Chapter 10 Records Management Systems

This chapter impresses upon students the importance of an effective records management system to the smooth operation of an organization. The need for capable information workers who understand and can apply sound records management principles assures a variety of career opportunities in the field. Even if students do not plan to pursue a career in records management, they should understand that their duties in many occupations will involve filing and/or managing records to some degree. All office workers need to understand and apply effective records management principles and procedures.

Topic 10-1 Maintaining Office Records

Topic Objectives

When students have completed their study of this topic, they will be able to:

- explain the purposes of records management
- identify the benefits of records management
- describe types of media on which information is kept
- identify the cost factors involved in a records management system
- describe the phases of the record life cycle
- describe the process for the removal and archiving of records
- describe disaster recovery

TOPIC 10-1 SELECTED OUTLINE

Overview of a Records Management System
- Choosing Appropriate Storage Media
- Providing Proper Storage Equipment and Supplies
- Establishing Procedures for Filing
- Developing an Efficient Retrieval Procedure
- Setting Up a Record Retention and Disposition Policy

Benefits of an Effective Records Management System
Storage Media for Records
- Paper
- Magnetic Media
- Compact Discs (CDs)
- Micrographics
- Imaging Systems

Cost Factors Associated with Records Management
- Equipment, Supplies, and Storage
- Human Resources
- Destruction Costs

Record Life Cycle
Removing Records from Active Storage
Disaster Recovery

TEACHING SUGGESTIONS

To reinforce the concepts presented in this topic, review with students the discussion about storage media for records. Then read the following scenario to them.

Assume you work in the records management department of a large company. The department manager, Jessica Walsh, believes all company employees can benefit from having a basic understanding of records management systems. Ms. Walsh has assigned a question pertaining to records management systems to each employee in the department. The employees will prepare answers to their assigned questions. Then the questions and answers will be compiled into a leaflet entitled "Facts About Records Management Systems" to be distributed to all company employees. The following question has been assigned to you:

Three common types of storage media for records are paper, magnetic media, and microfilm. What are the advantages and disadvantages of each storage medium?

Ask students to compose a response to the question.

Topic 10-2 Paper Records Systems

Topic Objectives

When students have completed their study of this topic, they will be able to:

- identify the components of a paper filing system
- describe four alphabetic filing systems
- explain how a numeric filing system is organized
- explain terminal-digit and middle-digit filing systems
- explain how a chronologic filing system is organized

TOPIC 10-2 SELECTED OUTLINE

Components of a Paper Filing System
- Equipment
- Procedures
- Supplies
- Position of Guides and Folders

Alphabetic Filing Systems
- Filing by Name
- Filing by Subject
- Filing by Geographic Location

Numeric Filing Systems
- Guides
- General Folders
- Individual Folders
- Index Card Control File

Terminal-Digit and Middle-Digit Filing Systems
- Terminal-Digit Filing
- Middle-Digit Filing

Chronologic Filing Systems

TEACHING SUGGESTIONS

To give students practical experience with paper filing systems, you can ask them to establish a filing system for their personal records. Students will gain experience determining appropriate captions and folder positions for their records. Some records that they might consider organizing into a filing system include:

- correspondence from friends and family
- certificates and awards
- information from colleges and universities
- magazine and newspaper articles
- information about a personal hobby, sport, or craft
- documents related to employment, such as tax forms or check stubs

Encourage students to keep their files up-to-date. Starting a records management system now will lay a solid foundation that can be built upon in the future. Some records that students may want to add to their filing system in the future include insurance forms, banking documents, bills such as credit card and telephone, and income tax forms.

Chapter 11 Managing Records

The primary goals of this chapter are to explain more specifically how to manage various forms of records efficiently and how to reproduce hard-copy records. One of the most vital aspects of a reliable records management system is accurate indexing and coding. Related to indexing and coding are three key terms students must understand in order to properly index and code. These three terms are *filing segment*, *indexing units*, and *indexing order*. They are defined for the student in the text. The alphabetic indexing rules presented in Reference Section F found in the *Student Activities and Projects* workbook and on the template disk reflect the guidelines published by the Association of Records Managers and Administrators (ARMA). Students are referred to the ARMA rules while reading the text and completing activities.

Topic 11-1 Managing Paper Records

Topic Objectives

When students have completed their study of this topic, they will be able to:

- explain how to prepare records for filing
- apply efficient filing procedures
- describe the use of requisition cards, out guides, and out folders in charge-out procedures
- describe how inactive files are transferred and stored
- describe storage plans for vital records protection

TOPIC 11-1 SELECTED OUTLINE

Preparing Records for Storage
- Collect Records
- Inspect Records
- Index/Code Records
- Cross-Reference Records
- Sort Records

Filing Records

Storage Equipment
- Vertical File Cabinets
- Lateral File Cabinets
- Horizontal (Flat) Files
- Storage Drawers
- Shelf Files
- Mobile Files
- Card Files
- Printout Storage
- Storage Boxes

Retrieving Records

Removing Records from Active Storage

Vital Records Protection

TEACHING SUGGESTIONS

Emphasize to students that even in companies where magnetic media and microfilm are used, paper is still a major medium for storing records; therefore, students must understand how to maintain paper filing systems. An important step in the process of preparing paper records for storage is indexing/coding. Review the discussion about indexing/coding from this topic. Then give students additional experience by asking them to index/code the names of their classmates or the names of members of a school organization.

Students may refer to the alphabetic indexing rules in Reference Section F, if necessary. After students have indexed/coded each name, ask them to place the names in correct alphabetic order for filing.

Topic 11-2 Reprographic Systems and Procedures

Topic Objectives

When students have completed their study of this topic, they will be able to:

- describe reprographic processes
- explain how office copiers are classified
- identify common copier features and operating procedures
- explain how to control copier supplies and operating procedures
- prepare materials to be copied
- describe phototypesetting/imaging and its uses

TOPIC 11-2 SELECTED OUTLINE

Office Photocopiers
- Electrostatic Copying Process
- Reprographic Technology

Electronic Copier/Printers
Copier Classifications
Copier Features
Controlling Copier Supplies
Controlling Operating Procedures
- Centralized Copying
- Monitoring Devices
- Copy Log
- User Guidelines

Copy Preparation Procedures
- Originals/Masters
- Correction Techniques
- Equipment Checks

Imaging
- Phototypesetting
- Desktop Publishing

TEACHING SUGGESTIONS

Review with students the information about copier features from this topic. Then ask them to name the features that perform the following functions:

1. Copies on both sides of the paper
2. Creates a margin on one or both sides of the paper to allow space for three-hole punching or for binding copies
3. Allows you to copy both pages of an open book onto the front and back of a single sheet of paper
4. Allows you to make a photocopy smaller than the size of the original document
5. Enables the copier to automatically collate the copies

Topic 11-3 Managing Magnetic and Microimaging Media

Topic Objectives

When students have completed their study of this topic, they will be able to:

- explain how to store individual records on magnetic media
- describe supplies used to store and organize magnetic and optical media
- explain why databases are useful in businesses
- describe two ways to produce microfilm files
- explain how computer-assisted retrieval systems are used to speed the record retrieval process

TOPIC 11-3 SELECTED OUTLINE

Records Management Software
Storing Files on Magnetic or Optical Media
- Converting to Electronic Media
- The Importance of Secondary Storage
- Storing Electronic Files
- Identifying Individual Disks and Tapes
- Making Backup Copies
- Controlling File Security

Storing Magnetic Media
- Floppy Disk and CD-ROM Storage
- Reel Tape Storage

Database Management Systems
Image Processing Systems
Creating Microfilm Files
- Photographing Records
- Computer Output Microfilm (COM)
- Computer Input Microfilm (CIM)

Organizing Microforms
Retrieving Records on Microfilm

TEACHING SUGGESTIONS

Arrange to have the class visit the school or local library or a local business or other organization where records are stored on microforms so students can see how the records are stored and accessed. Before the visit, have students work in small groups to develop questions to ask during the visit about how microform records are created, stored, or accessed. Students might also ask how microforms are used in combination with paper, magnetic, or optical disc storage.

5 Mail and Telecommunication Systems

Fast, efficient, and effective communications are critical for the success of most businesses. Whether employees communicate with coworkers and customers around the corner or around the world by mail, telephone, fax, or other electronic means, their ability to handle communications effectively is a valuable skill. This part focuses on developing these communication skills.

This part teaches students to:

- apply procedures for handling incoming and outgoing mail
- respond to incoming calls, and plan and place outgoing calls effectively
- describe the equipment, technology, and procedures for common forms of telecommunications
- communicate and search for information via the Internet

Chapter 12 Processing Mail

Chapter 12 reinforces the idea that systematic procedures are essential for an office to function efficiently. Students need to understand that there is a relationship between the processing of mail and the overall productivity of an office. Efficiently processed mail fosters communication among coworkers and between the public and the company. Thus, understanding how to process mail effectively is crucial to the smooth operation of today's information-intensive organizations.

In the chapter, students will be introduced to the equipment and procedures used to process mail. Therefore, actual demonstrations of the machines (a postage meter, for example) by a manufacturer's representative either in class or during a field trip would help students better understand the interrelationship between equipment and procedures.

Also presented in this chapter are the various mailing services currently available. In addition to the United States Postal Service (USPS), many companies also use courier and delivery services. Students should be encouraged to pay closer attention to the mail and courier service advertisements on television and in magazines. This chapter focuses on the distribution of paper document communications, whereas Chapter 14 focuses on the electronic transmission of information.

Topic 12-1 Incoming Mail Procedures

Topic Objectives

When students have completed their study of this topic, they will be able to:

- sort and distribute incoming mail
- open, separate, and annotate incoming mail
- document the receipt of mail
- refer, route, and prioritize mail

TOPIC 12-1 SELECTED OUTLINE

Sorting and Distributing Mail
- In Small Companies
- In Large Companies

Handling Incoming Mail
- Opening Mail
- Separating and Annotating Mail
- Documenting Receipt of Mail
- Referring or Routing Mail

Prioritizing Mail
Handling Mail While Away from the Office

TEACHING SUGGESTIONS

Emphasize to students that their role in processing incoming mail will depend on the size of the company, the volume of incoming mail, and their job position. Students may be responsible only for their own mail or for that of supervisors or coworkers. A final step in this process is prioritizing or categorizing the mail for further processing. Review with students the discussion about prioritizing mail from this topic. Then ask students to place the following incoming mail in the proper order by numbering each item:

- advertisement for a time management seminar
- letter accompanied by a money order
- magazine about office technology
- letter marked "personal"
- monthly bill from the company's attorney

Topic 12-2 Outgoing Mail Procedures

Topic Objectives

When students have completed their study of this topic, they will be able to:

- prepare outgoing mail
- identify the classes of domestic mail
- explain the various services provided by the USPS
- arrange for courier service
- send materials through an interoffice mail system

TOPIC 12-2 SELECTED OUTLINE

Processing Outgoing Mail in a Small Company
Folding and Inserting Mail
  Sealing and Weighing Envelopes
  Stamping/Metering Mail
Processing Outgoing Mail in a Large Company
Handling Volume Mailings
  Mailing Lists
  Preparing Address Labels
Address Requirements for Automated Mail Handling
  Address Format
  ZIP Codes
Classes of Domestic Mail
Special Postal Services
International Mail
Private Courier/Delivery Service
Interoffice Mail
Telegrams and Mailgrams

TEACHING SUGGESTIONS

Stress to students the importance of using correct address format by reviewing the information on address formats provided in the topic. Ask them to key the following addresses using the proper format on plain paper, envelopes, or labels.

Mrs. Rosalyn Holtzleiter
4290 Wisteria Way
Syracuse, New York 10303-4290

Mr. Akira Higuchi
Higuchi Construction Co.
875 Parkwood Avenue, Suite 20B
Dallas, Texas 75250-8750

Dr. Margaret Fletcher
641 Whisperwood Hills, Apt. 209
Dearborn, Michigan 48127-6410

Attention Paul A. Ramirez
Ramirez Enterprises
1743 Dover Road, Suite 886
New Haven, Connecticut 06512-1743

Chapter 13 Telephone Systems and Procedures

Businesses have been using telecommunications technology for years. Recently, however, the telecommunications industry has been bursting with new technological developments that are resulting in new equipment, new procedures, and the need for new skills. These procedures, skills, and equipment are the focus of this chapter. Prospective office workers must become familiar with equipment and procedures for transmitting data, text, and images as well as voice. Regardless of the new innovations in technology, there are people-related aspects of telecommunications that remain constant. For example, workers with responsibility for answering the telephone must convey a helpful attitude through a pleasant phone personality. All office workers should be able to place outgoing calls and handle incoming calls efficiently and cost-effectively. Using print and electronic directories, handling difficult callers, screening and transferring calls, and controlling costs are additional topics stressed in this chapter.

Topic 13-1 Telephone Technology and Services

Topic Objectives

When students have completed their study of this topic, they will be able to:

- identify methods of transmitting information (voice, data, text, video, and images) using telephone technology
- describe equipment and features of image and voice communication systems
- describe effective procedures for using image and voice transmission systems
- discuss emerging telephone technologies

TOPIC 13-1 SELECTED OUTLINE

Transmitting Information Using Telephone Technology
- Telephone Lines
- Communication Satellites

Image Communication Systems
- Facsimile Technology
- Videoconferencing

Voice Communication Systems
- Centralized Systems
- Common Features of Telephone Systems
- Voice-Mail Systems
- Specialized Telephone Equipment

Telephone Service Providers

Integration of Telecommunications Technologies

TEACHING SUGGESTIONS

A discussion of the procedures that many companies use to expedite callers to the right destination within a company by using the touch-tone buttons on the telephone might focus on the pros and cons of this call-directed technology. Questions to discuss include:

- Is the caller made to feel important when using this system?
- Does this procedure accomplish the purpose of getting the caller's business expedited faster?
- What impression of the company is left with the caller?
- What are the alternatives that a company could use?

Students could be directed to call an organization that uses this technology in order to be ready for the discussion.

Topic 13-2 Effective Telephone Communications

Topic Objectives

When students have completed their study of this topic, they will be able to:

- describe and apply skills required to make a favorable first impression over the telephone
- apply telephone techniques and procedures that will enable them to handle incoming calls courteously and efficiently
- plan calls efficiently using tools such as published and computerized directories

- use proper telephone techniques and procedures to place local and long-distance domestic and international calls
- describe techniques for controlling telephone costs

TOPIC 13-2 SELECTED OUTLINE

Making a Favorable First Impression
  Your Voice
  Your Speaking Skills
  Your Attitude
Incoming Telephone Communications
  Proper Telephone Techniques
  Effective Telephone Procedures
Outgoing Telephone Communications
  Planning Calls
  Time Zones
  Using Directories
  Long-Distance Service
  Wide Area Telecommunication Services (WATS)
  Toll-Free Service
  Controlling Telephone Costs

TEACHING SUGGESTIONS

Divide the students into teams and give each team the local telephone directory for your community. Also, provide any information available from various long-distance providers that serve your area. Ask students to study carefully the material provided and locate specific information (directory assistance, rates, time zones, and so on) that affects the times, costs, and procedures for placing long distance calls. Ask students to write a short comparison of the services and costs offered by the various providers.

Chapter 14 Telecommunication Systems

This chapter focuses on computer networks in general and the Internet. Networking has enhanced the use of microcomputers. Organizations have embraced networking because of the improvements in efficiency and cost brought about as a result of the sharing capabilities networks make possible. What started as simple linking of a few microcomputers to enable sharing of devices has exploded to become an organization's means of global communication and information sharing. Local area networks have connected to wide area networks that may be linked internationally.

The Internet has become an important tool for many workers who use it to perform research, share information, and communicate with others all over the world. Students must be prepared to use the Internet effectively when they enter the workforce. The Internet is in continuous metamorphosis. New websites are being created and Internet resources are improving. With the growth of the Internet have come the expected problems. Heavy traffic, including increased transmission of huge video and audio files, is slowing transmissions and causing problems. Providing security for data continues to challenge users. There are many ethical issues that must be resolved. However, these challenges have not stopped the Internet's growth. People continue to get connected at home and at work in increasing numbers and demand more and better information and technology.

Topic 14-1 Understanding Networks

Topic Objectives

When students have completed their study of this topic, they will be able to:

- describe common features of local area networks, wide area networks, and international networks
- explain the uses of the Internet
- define basic Internet terminology
- explain how to get access to the Internet

TOPIC 14-1 SELECTED OUTLINE

Telecommunications Networks
  Local Area Networks
  Wide Area Networks
  International Networks
The Internet: An Introduction
  Getting Connected to the Internet
  Internet Addresses

TEACHING SUGGESTIONS

Some students may be unable to quickly grasp the new concepts and terminology introduced in this topic. Reinforce student learning with a class discussion of the concepts presented in the topic. Discuss how telecommunications is evident in the home and then discuss how it is used in business. If your school does not have a local area network, schedule a field trip to a company that uses electronic mail, voice mail, and a local or wide area network. Observe and discuss the procedures and skills that employees need to handle communicating electronically.

Topic 14-2 Using the Internet

Topic Objectives

When students have completed their study of this topic, they will be able to:

- describe the most common uses of the Internet
- apply proper rules of conduct when using the Internet
- discuss key issues related to Internet use
- discuss future trends in Internet technology and uses

TOPIC 14-2 SELECTED OUTLINE

What You Can Do on the Internet
Finding Information or Sites on the Internet
    Web Browsers
    URLs
    Bookmarks
    Search Tools
    Internet Directories
Transferring Files
Discussing Topics with Others
    Newsgroups
    Mailing Lists
E-Mail
Promoting Organizations
Netiquette
The Future of the Internet
    The Information Superhighway
    Internet Content
    Internet Access for All

TEACHING SUGGESTIONS

Students may have extensive or limited experience using the Internet. In either case, their experience is probably limited to personal and educational applications. They may have little experience or knowledge regarding how businesses use the Internet. Ask students to research and report on three Internet sites valuable for business applications. They may search online or printed directories and then visit the sites to gain more information. If Internet access is limited or not available, students may find information about Internet sites in magazines and newspapers.

Personal and Career Development

Success at work is based on a combination of technical competencies and personal qualities. Both will prove important in finding a job and advancing your career. Students will want to understand how to search for a job, how to present their credentials and themselves, and what the expectations are as they begin work. Companies seek employees at all levels who are good team players—cooperative, willing to assume responsibility, focused on meeting organizational goals, and able to work with others effectively. This part focuses on the student as a worker and how he or she interacts with others to secure a position and perform satisfactorily.

This part teaches students to:

- plan for entry into the workplace and career advancement
- describe personal characteristics valuable at work
- discuss the basic attitudes that support the goals of organizations
- interact effectively with others at work

Chapter 15 Planning and Advancing Your Career

As students study this chapter, they will learn to prepare for a job search, including developing a résumé and letter of application. Students will also learn how workers are introduced to their new jobs and how to plan for their own advancement. This chapter may be introduced early in a course in office procedures or it might be studied as the ending subject of the course. Placement of the chapter will shift the overall emphasis somewhat. If studied early in the course, particularly if students are participating in a work-study program, you will want to help them prepare realistically for their first association with the organizations where they will work. There could be references to forthcoming topics in the course where students will experience aspects of what is studied.

If this chapter is studied at the end of the course, you may want to ask students to assume that they are seeking a specific type of job, even though their plans are to continue their education full-time in a postsecondary school. Students who have firm career goals may be asked to think ahead to the time when they plan to have completed their basic education for entrance into their career and prepare a résumé and letter of application for their first professional job. If students seek positions in the local community, you may want to invite some speakers who can discuss job opportunities that are available locally.

Topic 15-1 An Effective Job Search

Topic Objectives

When students have completed their study of this topic, they will be able to:

- identify the factors to consider when planning a career strategy
- discuss the role of a career goal in their planning
- describe the steps in planning a job search
- prepare a résumé
- prepare for an interview
- explain what generally is expected of an interviewee

TOPIC 15-1 SELECTED OUTLINE

Thinking Ahead About Careers and Jobs
- A Career Strategy
- Planning with a Career Goal Established
- Planning Without a Career Goal

Planning a Job Search
- Exploring Job Opportunities
- The Résumé
- The Letter of Application

The Interview
- Prepare for an Interview
- Make a Good First Impression
- Anticipate Questions
- Prepare Questions
- Arrive on Time
- Complete an Application Form
- Participate Attentively
- Follow Up

Documenting Your Job Search

TEACHING SUGGESTIONS

You may find that students need a brief refresher about characteristics of good business writing. You may want to reintroduce students to the task of writing a letter of application incorporating the characteristics of effective writing presented in earlier chapters. You may want to discuss the importance of listening closely to all questions and comments made by an interviewer and the importance of standard usage while talking during an interview. Role-playing with the teacher serving as the interviewer and a student serving as the interviewee might be presented before the class to develop an understanding of proper speech. Simple questions such as the following might be used for role-playing:

1. Did you have any problems in locating our office this morning?
2. When will you complete your high school studies?
3. What employment skills have you learned in your high school classes?

Topic 15-2 The First Job and Beyond

Topic Objectives

When students have completed their study of this topic, they will be able to:

- describe typical ways organizations provide orientation for new employees
- explain the responsibility for self-evaluation of performance
- identify resources for continuous improvement of an employee's knowledge and skills
- explain effective ways of facing job changes

TOPIC 15-2 SELECTED OUTLINE

Introduction to a New Job
- Orientation
- Learning on the Job

Evaluation of Your Performance
- Ways of Evaluating Employees
- Evaluating Your Own Performance

Continuous Improvement
- Considering Your Present Position
- Considering Promotional Possibilities

Resources Outside Your Organization
- Professional and Trade Associations
- Professional and Trade Periodicals
- Educational Resources

Facing Job Changes
- Considering Other Opportunities
- Responding to Job Termination

The Challenge of Work

TEACHING SUGGESTIONS

Encourage students to explore possible jobs they might wish to hold over a five-year period as they increase their experience and education. Instruct students to:

1. Identify a job that you would find interesting as your first job and for which you are qualified. Write a brief description of the job and list the general qualifications needed for it.
2. Assume that you are successful in the initial job and that you gain additional education as you gain experience in this job. Identify two related jobs to which you might be promoted after two or more years in the initial job. Do some research in industry periodicals or talk to individuals in your area of interest to determine this information. Write a brief description of the jobs and list the general qualifications needed for each one.

Chapter 16 Working with Others

In this chapter, students will focus on becoming aware of the important personality qualities that are critical for success at work. They will learn about qualities that lead to effectively working with others.

This chapter may be introduced early in a course in office procedures or it might be studied near the end of the course. Placement of the chapter will shift the overall emphasis somewhat. If studied early in the course, you may want to include more references to observations the students have made of individuals at work. There could be references to forthcoming topics in the course where students will experience aspects of what is studied. If studied near the end of the course, you may want to highlight experiences in class that reinforce what is being learned.

The values of the community in which you teach can be related to the content. Messages of inspirational speakers that are reported in the local press may be used to identify the significance and importance of striving to develop good character and to adhere to the values in one's personal life that are respected.

Topic 16-1 Personal Qualities at Work

Topic Objectives

When students have completed their study of this topic, they will be able to:

- describe aspects of personality that are critical for effective performance at work
- explain the attitudes that contribute to the success of organizations
- describe expectations related to their appearance and manners

TOPIC 16-1 SELECTED OUTLINE

Your Personality at Work
  Character
  Self-Acceptance
  Maturity
Attitudes That Support Quality Performance
  The Work Ethic
  Participation
  Learning
Appearances Influence Impressions
  Clothing
  Annoying Habits
  Voice
Basic Work Manners
  Introductions
  Electronic Etiquette
  General Courtesies at Work
Your Personal Power

TEACHING SUGGESTIONS

To reinforce key concepts from this topic, have students complete these activities that focus on personality traits.

1. Ask each student to select one of the personality traits discussed in the topic that is particularly central to the personality of someone that the student knows well. Ask the student to write a brief report that describes the behavior observed that reflects the trait chosen.
2. Ask students to imagine their personalities five years from now. With that in mind, have them write brief statements of how that imagined personality differs from their present personality.

Topic 16-2 Human Relations at Work

Topic Objectives

When students have completed their study of this topic, they will be able to:

- explain what effective interaction with others at work means
- describe appropriate responses in facing conflicts at work
- assess their ability to work with others
- explain some of the basic laws and regulations that apply to the workplace

TOPIC 16-2 SELECTED OUTLINE

Interacting with Supervisors
- What You can Expect from Your Supervisor
- What Your Manager Expects from You

Interacting with Coworkers
- Cooperation
- Confidentiality
- Avoiding Gossip
- Accepting Responsibility for Mistakes
- Respecting Others' Commitments

Facing Conflicts at Work
- Conflict with Your Manager
- Conflict Related to Ethical Behavior

Understanding Relevant Laws and Regulations
- Fair Labor Standards Act
- Freedom from Discrimination
- Freedom from Sexual Harassment
- Safe and Healthy Workplace
- Unemployment Insurance
- Social Security Act Benefits
- Employee Responsibility

TEACHING SUGGESTIONS

In some cases, small group discussions where students talk about their personalities may be more successful than general class discussions because students are likely to be more candid in a small group.

You may want to divide the class into groups of three for discussion of the following questions:

1. What are personality characteristics that we like in those with whom we work?
2. What are the barriers to accepting ourselves as we are?
3. What are the problems we face as we try to assess and improve ourselves?